Sam's Own Words

~**~

Sam's Own Words
From the Diaries of Sam Crippen
1908-1961

A Biography
By Gail Mazourek

Author – Gail Mazourek
Editor – Cynthia Machamer

Special chapter 42, *Finding The Natural,* was written by Holly Timm, genealogist.

Cover design and art is a collage and acrylic painting by Gail Mazourek. The depicted hip roof barn originated in 1944 when the cement floor was poured. The cinder block base was laid and in 1945 the farm owner, Edwin Voorheis, hired the labor to raise the structure. The principal of the biography, Sam Crippen, recorded its progress in the pages of his diaries. The owner of the new dairy barn was his son-in-law.

Printed by CreateSpace, an Amazon.com Company
Also available in Kindle and in other book stores

This biography, "Sam's Own Words," first edition was published in November 2017.

ISBN-13: 978-1977851130
ISBN-10: 1977851134

Library of Congress Control Number: 201791555
CreateSpace Independent Publishing Platform, North Charleston, SC

2 3 4 5 6 7 8 9 10

DEDICATION

A Tribute to Mom,
Lora Babbette Crippen Voorheis
And Dad, Edwin Voorheis,
Also Mom's father and mother,
Samuel and Edith Crippen

None forgotten
Always loved

"O Beautiful, For Spacious Skies, For Amber Waves of Grain..."

Almost the National Anthem, "America the Beautiful"
by Katherine Lee Bates, born August 12, 1859

"America! America! God shed his grace on thee..."

Lineage

Pulaski (Lac) Crippen* and Sophia May Dimon Crippen*
1857 – 1922 / 1856 – 1935

Jonathan Salathiel Crow* and Marilla Leeds Montgomery Crow*
1840 – 1892 / 1842 – 1918

Samuel Paul Crippen* and Edith Crow Haggarty Crippen*
1883 — 1961 / 1878 – 1944

Sam's siblings .... Edith's siblings
(all are deceased)

Lynn Crippen.......................... Chester Crow
Grace Whiting........................ Mary Crow Moore
Claude Dewey Crippen........... Horace Crow
Sadie Madison........................ Arthur Crow
Mary Hess.............................. Lydia Crow
Ralph Crippen........................ Philip Crow
                                              Rollo LeRoy Crow
                                              Erick Mathias Crow

~**~

Samuel Paul Crippen* married Edith Crow Haggarty*
6/19/1913 in Twin Falls, Idaho.

Their children and grandchildren:

Margret Willa Haggarty* married Edward Walker*
    Louise (Lee) Marilla Walker, Harris, Robertson*
        Glen Harris*
        Babbette Marie Flood, Oregon
        Anthony Robertson, Colorado
        Michael Paul Robertson*

Claude Dewey Crippen Jr.*, Colorado
        (Dewey's adopted name—John Stanton Adams*)
        Holly Timm – Florida
        Dory Adams - Pennsylvania
        Carol Adams – Arizona

Christine Jensen*, 1st married Lawall, 2nd Raymond P. Nelson
    2 children, Jack Lawall & Steve Nelson

David Pulaski Crippen*, 1st married Francis Bowden*, 2nd
    Hilda Drake*
    Bonnie Whitman married Al Lodwig*, NYS (Hilda's daughter)

2 children
David Crippen Jr. married Christine Cocchiara, NYS (Francis
    Bowden's son)
        Velma C. Crippen married Harry Zink*, NYS, 3 children,
        Lester Crippen married Emily Watson, NYS, 1 child (Rachel)
        Douglas Crippen *

Lora Babbette (Betty) Crippen * married Edwin E. Voorheis*
    Theodore Paul Herforth (Ted), 1st married Hazel Rightmire*,
        5 children, 2nd Onolea Burdsall, NYS, 2 step-children
    Edwin W. Voorheis* (Bucky) married Jean Chadborne, NYS,
        6 children
    Jean Voorheis*, 1st married Hank Simmons*, 6 children,
        2nd Bob Ames*, 3rd W<u>m</u> Pike*, NYS,
    Gail Voorheis, 1st married Joe Kinard*, 3 children, 2nd Rudolf
        Mazourek Jr.*, 3 children, 3rd Adolf Busse, NYS
    James Voorheis, 1st married Janet Osborne*, 3 children,
        2nd Judy Grover, 2 children, NYS
    Carol Voorheis married (divorced) Fred Osborne, Florida,
        3 children
    Linda Voorheis, 1st married Lauren Rodabaugh*, NYS
        3 children, 2nd Millard Abbott, Florida
    Roland Voorheis married Linda Mosher, NYS, 4 children

Jonathan Ralph Crippen*, 1st married Mary Polovick*, NYS
        2 children, 2nd Lucille Frost*4 stepchildren
    Michlene Crippen, NYS
    Kathlene Crippen, NYS
        stepchildren; Ray, twins-Rex* & Roy*, and Johnny Frost

Steele Dimon Crippen*, 1st married Ruthie Coles*, one child,
        2nd Ruth Latterman Brown*, 5 stepchildren
    Sandra Crippen, 1st married James Brasted, PA,
        2 children, 2nd Roger Rulewich, Mass.
    Steven Crippen, NYS

Shirley Paula Crippen* married Thomas Weber Broadhead*,
        Mississippi

*Deceased

Author Comment

I was privileged to have many resources to use for my grandfather's biography. The story line is authentic, taken from Samuel Paul Crippen's diaries, letters, and numerous artifacts. The history of his day and time are told by his words and my added research. As the author, I have supplied some details for entertainment, which is derived from random fictionalized, fanciful enhancement around facts. This is added to by the personal acquaintance and knowledge of Grandfather Crippen, and the candid memories from several contributing siblings and generous cousins.

Posted letters are used and do contain the original unedited content. An occasional misspelled word has been corrected, but the sincerity of expression by the persons who wrote them is presented. The words chosen from diary pages and attributed to Samuel Paul Crippen from his own words are prefaced for clarity with the lead off, Sam's own words.

Favorite passages from *The Living Bible*, Paraphrased, in the 1972 bible by Tyndale House Publishers sustained my writing. This was the same year that my parents, Edwin and Betty Voorheis, gave their eight grown children this bible as a Christmas present. Mine is shabby from use and marked throughout as I used it over the years. I wish I had started marking it in the first year of use, but years passed before I began the red ink practice of underlining.

Proverbs 16:3 ≈ Commit your work to the Lord, then it will succeed.

Hebrews 12:1–6 ≈ Let us run with perseverance the race that is set before us; looking to Jesus.

Acknowledgements

Without my editor and daughter Cynthia Machamer, to whom I am indebted, this book would not have been finished. Her valuable suggestions and expertise with grammar, punctuation, and sentence construction helped me improve the book for print. Resting in the knowledge that she would catch me wherever needed made it possible to simply write.

The Samuel Crippen diaries, which span 53 years, were obtained with diplomacy and patience at the request of one of his granddaughters, Sandra Crippen Rulewich. It was natural that her late father's wife, Ruth Crippen possessed them. Sandy read the diaries and knew they had to be shared with her cousins, whose lives had intertwined with integral parts of their grandfather's lifespan. Cousin Sandy began a dedicated project of copy and share the diaries with me, Gail Mazourek, while I reproduced the collection for distribution to my seven siblings. The determination to duplicate and disperse all of them took about one year of perseverance.

There are also letters and items that represent years gone by and chronicle a lifetime of love shared with one woman. The materials remain enclosed in a large, flat-top trunk with dark wood lattice, strengthened by metal and leather straps. The brass hinges and lock show rust of 100 years of age. The tall ledgers of listed expenses stored inside support Sam's own words, his written account of his joys and struggles. He collected newspapers from WWI and WWII. He followed the plight of his two sons in the theater of WWII and prayed for peace and their lives.

Contained within the rustic rectangle of memories lay magazines, photos, letters with two- or three-cent stamps, a lady's brand-new size three shoe (left foot) and much more to supply evidence in the account of his life story. Sam's own words are written into records that he kept and stored to leave information behind.

The accumulation is more than most of us leave to define a full life well-lived. Sam's whole life is laid bare and open for inspection. Only then will the unveiled show who he protected and why, to expose his compassion, his kindness, his real character that is not so secret after all.

The treasure trove of Samuel Paul Crippen's trunk and its contents are preserved and revered by his oldest grandson, Theodore Paul Herforth. He shared with me the entire contents of a few hundred items, artifacts, farm journals, also letters for use in writing the Sam Crippen biography. Sam's catch of memories and books are stored upstairs in the family home where Ted and seven siblings grew up. Ted owns and lives there. He served as advisor and preferred reader, providing valuable input to me.

Both Sandy and Ted are acknowledged for their insight, generosity of spirit, and willingness to lend. Most of my siblings have contributed their memories, which have been incorporated. Their names, which include the author, are listed in the genealogical information. Many cousins are also listed.

Two more cousins contributed relevant information. They are Babbette Marie Flood and Holly Timm, genealogist. Both provided answers to questions posed to gain knowledge of several characters included in the story. Babbette sent many writings and poems penned by her prolific mother, Marilla Lee (Louise Marilla Walker). Holly provided her expertise in research and actual records, along with details on how she collected the information. Pieces of facts freely given by Holly are interspersed in the appropriate pages without particular notation as such. Her generosity lends details in some instances that would not have surfaced any other way. I am forever grateful to all parties for contributions.

Table of Contents

Sam's Own Words

From the Diaries of Sam Crippen

1908-1961

A Biography
By Gail Mazourek

Part I

1 – A Regular Pennsyltucky of a Place
Walked 18 Miles, 1908, 1909

It was certain that an ambitious young man who was not attached to a sweetheart was yet to love and be loved. Therefore, the natural current of Sam Crippen's personal radar relinquished his thoughts to another preoccupation of an idea that consumed his waking hours.

Striking out on his own was better taken on by Sam while he was single and had only his own welfare to consider. He summoned the courage to leave the company of a beloved family and reach out for the unknown. At 25 years old, he expected much of himself. His easygoing manner belied the self-assertion he made available in his actions to move forward with his goal. If pushed into a stand against a situation, his stance would surprise any bullyrag character who mistook his quiet demeanor for weakness. Understated blue-gray eyes matched broadcloth pants and shirt that revealed a hint of white undershirt under wraps with his more than six-foot lanky frame.

Sam had read, studied, and been compelled by postings of opportunities, which carried appeals for laborers needed in the western states. The more he read, the more his sensibilities helped him convince his friend, John Long, to go west with him. It pulled on a young man's restless nature and promoted his drive to better himself. At that time, he saw no future of great appeal in his hometown of Galeton, PA. To break the mold, he left familiar farm and lumber work with his father, Pulaski (Lac) Crippen.

Like all Americans, Sam was full of hope. The aspiration was newsworthy in the 1908 *Harpers Weekly*, which asked, "Is it possible that at this very moment we are living in the dawn of the veritable Golden Age?" It set young men up to think of higher hopes and big dreams of opportunities.

Sam had a source of western lore and factual stories in old magazines he had helped to wear out by reading them over and over since his youth. One favored *Century* magazine article of 1888 was "Ranch Life in the Far West." Theodore Roosevelt wrote articles while he spent years in the Dakotas. They were true but grand stories of the untamed west in three major articles, which were illustrated by Frederick Remington. Those writings and pictures drew Sam in while he was a young man.

It was followed by the era when the 14-volume set of books, *The Works of Theodore Roosevelt*, were reprinted as part of the campaign when Teddy ran for the office of vice president of the United States and won in 1897. They were also a winner for the publisher who brought them back to life. Those who couldn't afford them before could now, Sam and his parents among them. He bookmarked passages of further interest to him. An embossed card with a red rose held a spot. It had been scrawled in cursive: *to Sammy Crippen from Nettie Miller*. She was a childhood school chum who had been sweet on him, and was the daughter of the teacher, Mrs. Mary Miller. It was from a time gone by but kept as a fond remembrance.

Sam poured over the Theodore Roosevelt (TR) volumes for the adventures of a man who knew all about the west from his own experience. Roosevelt wrote expert accounts of what the untamed land far away offered. His three ranches in North Dakota were renowned in the news when he became president in 1901. Sam's TR embossed books and the magazines were always at arms' reach in his bookcase. Teddy Roosevelt was in the seventh year of his presidency in 1908. Sam looked back in pride that with his first and only presidential vote so far, he had helped Teddy Roosevelt continue in office. It was now late 1908, and Roosevelt would serve through March 4, 1909, to finish his second term.

This was when Sam and John, each a quarter-century old, made up their minds to travel west by train to see and experience a portion of what Roosevelt had written about. The tracks stretched to infinity ahead of the smoke pouring stack of the iron horse.

Sam recorded his first entry on the white page of a new diary.

Sam's own words...
Wednesday, October 28, 1908 – "Left Galeton, PA, 6:55 a.m. for Oregon."

Sam's stomach fluttered like the fall of autumn leaves as the train whistle announced intention to move. The engine shuddered and vibrated as it strained at the weight of the cars to lurch forward. His eyes were wide as he leaned toward the window to see the green shrubbery start to blur as the speed picked up momentum. His grin next fell on John, his boyhood friend who would share the adventure with him.

At a stop along the railroad route, which reached from east to west across the great vast United States of America, Sam and John sought and took work where they found it. Sam wrote in a singular manner about work but no doubt John was doing the same job. Sam's's diary was a record of only his own experience.

Sam's own words...
Sunday, November 1, 1908 – "Arrived in Libby, Montana 11:42 a.m."
Tuesday, November 3, 1908 – "Worked for Dawson Lumber Co. one-half day at $2.25 a day."

Sam worked for Dawson Lumber from Tuesday through Saturday. The heavy lumber work created moisture to his brow and labor to his back.

It was Sunday, 11:42 a.m., November 8, when he was on his way again. The train whistled its stops in several Oregon cities. He spent overnight in his sleeper seat, which reclined flat for the purpose, from Spokane, WA, to arrive in, Seattle, WA, at 7 a.m. The same aisle position would serve day and night as it did for many fellow travelers. There were those with deeper pockets who spared more funds to pay $1 per berth to secure a private bunk loft behind curtains in the sleeper section. Sam had no desire to spend an extra portion of his hard-earned cash. Overnights were spent in passing through Portland, Eugene, and Roseburg, OR, riding along until he got off and stayed in Marcola, OR. Sam had walked during each daytime stop interval to stretch his long legs while passengers both loaded and exited. He and John traveled and worked for two weeks until arriving in Oregon.

Sam's own words...
Friday, November 13, 1908 – "Worked for S. & P. Co., Marcola, Oregon, one day, three meals."
Monday, November 16, 1908 – "One day for S. & P. Co., three meals."

He changed his board arrangement on Monday, to a boarding house. The regular meals weren't likely to have been part of his pay but were significant enough that he often mentioned them. In the weeks that followed, sunny weather seldom shone, but the coolness prevailed since it was already long into November. All the while, he put in nine- and 10-hour days, but seldom on Sunday.

Sawmill work required a muscled back even though it was not the lumber company from which he drew his paycheck. His lean frame was strong, but long hours took its toll under the repetition to load milled boards for the railroad. He slugged the smooth boards alongside other men in the crew to fill the transport cars of the Southern Pacific Railroad Company (S & P). A few weeks in and those long hours became impossible when he was forced to rest and restore his muscles on a Sunday and two follow-up days in late December.

Sam's own words...
Monday, December 20, 1908 – "Neuralgia, three meals, rainy."

He listed no doctor and no work for the downtime but rested to avoid exacerbation of the nerve pain in his posterior. Sam smoothed back his wavy brown hair and looked out at the mammoth, tall, wooden skele- ton of the flume built to move timber. Logs floated by in the three-mile-long trough down through the Mohawk Valley to Marcola where he recup- erated not far from the mill the railroad served. The Douglas-fir wood cylinders were cut into boards and planed smooth by machine inside the millworks. The heavier wood that took a toll on Sam's back was western larch, which went for rough-hewn railroad crossties and bridge materials. Scrap wood resulted from cuttings for these different purposes and was sent for smelter fuel in mines, of which there were many for gold and copper in the area. Sam worked with the crew that loaded all cuts of lumber on transit cars for the S & P railroad transport line. The team rotated work, so they all had a turn on the lighter weight job to toss loose lumber scraps into the open top railway box of S & P Company.

Sam may have recalled words from Roosevelt who had seen and wrote of the vast primeval forests in rugged areas of the far west. Oregon was as far west as he could go without a dip in the Pacific Ocean. Sam worked nine hours each of the next two days but had the day off thanks to the rain on December 25 with three meals. No mention was made on the diary page that it was Christmas Day. There is no doubt it would have been a different matter had he been home in Galeton, PA, among family. His fond memory likely served him well on how his mother prepared roast chicken and other food for the special day. The pleasant smells from her kitchen probably came to mind. Sam must have smiled as he thought of the delicious fare and the family gathered together. He may have reminded himself that he was a grown man and had left home two months ago for a chance at adventure and his own betterment. The memories were enjoyed, perhaps with a tinge of homesickness.

His mother, Mary Sofia, and three sisters, Grace, Sadie, and Mary, would no doubt bemoan his absence from the table. He pictured, in his mind's eye, his brothers, Ralph, Dewey, and Lynn, nodding their heads in agreement with their father, Lac. Extended family and a few in-laws would be seated. Each one was as hard-working and as poor as the next, but they all contributed to the meal. His state of aloneness, except for the presence of John Long, made it unlike any Christmas before.

Loneliness was a one-day affair on the holiday until he was back to work in the midst of his crew. He worked nine hours on the 26th and made a change the next day.

Sam's own words...
Sunday, December 27, 1908 – "Three meals, changed from the boarding house to bachelor's hall, fair day."

Sam's continued loading of lumber for the railroad finished his six weeks of work on Thursday, December 31, for his short year with a total of 233 hours. Those nine-hour days brought him security well-earned for his livelihood.

~**~

1909

The New Year began with nine hours worked on the first of January 1909. Subsequently, several days contained no work at all, and half days were mixed in. It was the winter's off-season for work here, too, like in Pennsylvania. The whole month of January toil with stormy weather alternated between snow, rain, and sleet.

Sam's own words...
Sunday, January 10, 1909 – "A regular Pennsyltucky of a place, three inches snow."

Pennsyltucky was a reference to back home where he had learned all about that expression. Pennsylvanians and Kentuckians knew well the slang use of the portmanteau where two state names were wrapped up in one word. His Penn state home was in his thoughts, just one of the 46 states like Kentucky and his present Oregon where more than half the population lived in rural areas. How could he not have smiled at his cleverness to remind himself with thoughts of home?

By January 31, the month's total work added up to 142 hours for wages. That was how it went in winter: cold conditions, less work, and less pay.

All the while he knew the work as his constant companion and past time, always present, always necessary. He saw earlier signs of spring for farmers here than in Pennsylvania. Sam's pulse quickened with anticipation as he smiled and wrote his next diary entry.

Sam's own words...
Monday, February 1, 1909 – "Mill One, nine hours, farmers plowing."

Long hours of work heightened the men's hunger when they sat down to eat whatever was on the menu. Sam bit into the stringy venison served up with tangled onions. He planned to make a note of it in his diary,but not before he got his share. It was the first he'd ever had deer meat. The dark brown gravy on the gamey fare provided a flavor that made it go down smoothly. His appetite was as large as John's and the other workers.

Sam loaded lumber from Mill One through the end of the month, every day the same except for Sunday when work ceased. He labored the last of his nine-hour days for February on the 26th and finished with a total of 199.5 hours toil.

Sam's own words…
Tuesday, March 1, 1909 – "Three and one-half hours at the mill, 5.5 hours in Marcola, a dandy day."

He turned 26 years old on March 3.

Dandy did not continue indefinitely. Neuralgia visited again on Sunday, March 7, and into the next day. Sam was back to gainful employment for a few days, but the next Monday he had a short day and smaller pay.

Sam's own words…
Monday, March 15, 1909 – "Five hours work, walked 18 miles to the woods and back."

Just a leisurely stroll for a young man in his prime! There was no excess of fat on his 170-pound frame to slow down his size nine feet. His lean body was well muscled from weight borne during his weeks, months, and years of constant movement. His mind wandered back east again where his rural life had been surrounded by trees like it was here. He leaned against a rough tree trunk and breathed in the smell of spring on the breeze. No park benches sat around to offer a seat to a guy who had walked nine miles to get there. Imagine a climb up to a sturdy limb to watch the wind sway the budding branches overhead while he thought of home. Three months' absence lent a nostalgic fondness for the life he had always known. He had renewed reason to appreciate it now in these spare hours of downtime. Tree sitting clarified his thoughts and cemented the decision for his next step.

In the morning he and John walked to Donna, OR, and hired out to Mohawk Lumber Co. for two hours and had only one meal for the day. Sam slept in a barn for the next three nights while 10-hour days kept him more than a little busy. It had its merits with three meals a day. It was an easy change to sleep the night in bachelor's hall on Saturday, March 20, after a long workday.

Sam's own words...
Sunday, March 21, 1909 – "Fair day at Marcola, stayed with Baines family, walked back to Donna, OR."
Monday, March 22, 1909 – "Ten hours, three meals at 20¢ a meal, slept in bunkhouse, divided bedding with Jonathan and nearly froze."

For a third day, he and John worked and shared quarters and friendship in the same job, same conditions. They commiserated with each other and may have talked on the subject of too-few bed covers and chilly nights. The next entry, which Sam underlined, makes that more than likely.

Sam's own words...
Wednesday, March 24, 1909 – "Quit our job, one meal, walked back to Marcola..."

Apparently, they ate breakfast before they departed. Walking was a way of life, nothing new about that to get from place to place.

On Thursday, March 25, they worked nine hours for the Southern Pacific Railroad Company at Mill One, juggling railroad ties. "Juggling" was Sam's good-natured term for loading them on the rail cars. They had been milled into the particular type of product before they were handled by the S & P crew with which Sam worked. The sameness of days continued.

Sam's own words...
Sunday, March 28, 1909 – "Some rain, Ralph's birthday, a lonesome day, Jonathan writing to Idaho."

His friend John's correspondence was not his foremost thought as memories of his youngest brother, Ralph's playful comradery surfaced. He turned 12 years old back home with the folks in Galeton, and Sam's remembrance brought on his most sentimental thoughts. Ralph was about half of Sam's age and no doubt looked up to his big brother who had gone west. A younger brother could easily hang on every word in letters read by the family when Sam wrote home. Ralph might have yearned to see his older brother and even more so if he had known he was on Sam's mind. Possibly a smile played at the corners of Sam's mouth along with his thoughts of Ralph and the family.

Sam was aware that being the oldest of seven children put pressure on success as those who kept track of his progress wanted to hear of the great adventure. Nevertheless, without half thinking about it in those terms, they had a stake in it. Sam had never ventured too far from Galeton, PA, and now he was all the way on the other side of the country. If he wilted in the face of a difficult situation, he might as well give up. Did he have what it took to forge ahead? He'd already decided which direction as he squared his shoulders.

The last three days of March with its nine-hour days ended their stint with S & P Co. Sam's hours totaled only 159 for the month. On April Fools day, he and John settled up with the railroad and went to Springfield, OR, with their friends, the Baineses. It was cold, windy, and rainy four days straight.

Sam's own words...
Monday, April 5, 1909 – "Rainy, went to Goshen, looked for a wood job, walked 14 miles."

It became evident that Sam had located a position when he drew all of his money from the bank at Eugene, OR. He settled up with the Baineses, head of the work crew. On Wednesday, Sam and John boarded the 11:55 a.m. train for Idaho. It chugged out of Portland by 6 pm, and rolled all night. On Thursday, they looked out on snow and ate dinner in Huntington, ID, at 11 a.m. Arrival in Minidoka was at 11 p.m. where the night was spent in yet another unfamiliar city Sam had learned the name of only on the itinerary. The train departed with its stiff passengers at 11 a.m. for Buhl, ID, where it arrived at 3 p.m. Another five hours and Sam felt glad to acquire the pre-arranged lodging at Southworth's ranch where they built their bunks on a cold and windy Saturday.

Sam's own words...
Monday, April 12, 1909 – "Went to work for Denny Bros., dragged 22 acres, four horses, one day."

He had begun farm labor, which he was familiar with, but on a smaller scale from his Pennsylvania youth. His second day was fair and windy while he rode a plow sulky behind four horses. The solid iron seat was a molded contour with holes, and it fit his behind but did not cushion it. On the third day, he wrenched his knee and was lame but continued work. On Friday, he bought gloves at $1.25 to use when he held the reigns of the horses for plowing, and also to use for picking up stones. Sam remembered his father's words: "Any farmer knows that a good crop of stones can be counted on for harvest." He had removed many a rock in his younger days, and it was second nature to do it now. If the biggest ones were not withdrawn from the fields, they could break plow points and machinery.

Sunday was a welcome day of relaxation after a week of hard work. A walk over to Salmon River took him to do his wash and back to the ranch to hang them up to dry. He must have liked it there and went back in the evening to climb up out of the canyon. The twists and turns in the trails and sights from the heights were a grand way to spend time for a few hours recreation if not rest.

On Monday, Sam raked and dragged sagebrush. He felt involuntary tears sting the reddened corners of his eyes. The sustained wind was responsible for his sore orbs. Even though it was April 21, 1.5 inches of snow fell and was tossed by the robust wind. Of course, both are excellent conditions for picking stones from out of a field and digging a ditch. He drove a team of horses and dragged earth all day for several days through the rain and wind. Best of weather for that, too.

Another familiar job became less favored by him. The constant motion of wrists to grub sagebrush roots out of the ground caused sore joints that followed him through the end of April. May was a succession of work where he used a drag, a rake, a leveler, and a crude stone barge to throw stones onto. He guided the horses to the hedgerow as the closest and easiest location to get rid of rocks. He threw them off, out of the way.

Sam's own words...
Saturday, May 8, 1909 – "Picked stone...one pound Star Tobacco 50¢."

He had no time on Sunday to relax and enjoy his new acquisition of smoking. Sam grubbed brush for three days in cold, windy conditions.

Sam's own words...
Tuesday, May 11, 1909 – "Received a letter from home, the first in two months."

A smile spread across Sam's face as he read the page his mother had written. He savored the moment while he held the paper against his chest. At last, he had news from his folks. No doubt he read it over again while he planned a reply.

Sam's own words...
Sunday, May 16, 1909 – "Cold and windy, wrote a letter home, went to the P.O."

In the post office lobby, there was a slot to push the envelope through for mailing on the Sabbath. He'd have no time for it on a weekday since those were taken up by his responsibility to labor for Denny Brothers. The weather was more often warm now, and the wind remained. Sam had some diversity of work to run a fanning mill, to make a dike, and to help dig ditches.

Sam's own words...
Monday, May 24, 1909 – "Irrigated...one # G-Union Leader, 50¢ tobacco."

He continued his acquired enjoyment of smoking, a pleasure for any time he could kick back and rest his backside. This was a different brand, same price.
They built a fence, also a dike to store water up, and erected a flume for irrigation. The work and water needs went forth day after day.

Sam's own words...
Wednesday, June 2, 1909 – "Irrigated, prepared garden for planting."
Friday, June 4, 1909 – "Irrigated, made garden, pair overalls 80¢, tobacco 50¢."

The garden must have the continuous water and would amount to little without it. Sam operated a corrugator, which was equipment to dig long, parallel furrows down the rows of new plants to allow water flow 10 days in succession. The wind kept pace.

Sam's own words...
Monday, June 14, 1909 – "Irrigated, a little rain, wind, one # Star tobacco 50¢."

The weather always matters to a farmer.
A choice was made to go back to the Star brand of tobacco. Sam continued daily to send water down the furrows in a rush to wet and vitalize the plants.

Sam's own words...
Sunday, June 20, 1909 – "Irrigated, went down to Castleford in p.m. and fished awhile."

Recreation! But there was no mention that he caught any fish. Still, it was a good day to be alive even if he had started out with work. He planned ahead for the purchase of specific items he needed. They would be bought after work on his next weekday.

Sam's own words...
Monday, June 21, 1909 – "Irrigated, one # cut 50¢, writing material 30¢."
Tuesday, June 22, 1909 – "Irrigated, fair, received a letter from home..."

Receiving and answering correspondence was of high importance to Sam. Letters needed to go both ways to keep the home connection.
He cut and raked hay, made a bridge, mowed and raked more, just what you'd expect from a farmer in late June, day after day. As usual, he was not idle. Sam always had a purpose under heaven.

2 - Flathead
Moving, 1909

Sam's mind was busy all the while he worked. There is no doubt that he read all he could for information and gathered more from talks with those who labored for the same employer, Denny Brother's Company, while they boarded with Southworth. The conversations at every work lull and during evenings in the bunkhouse concerned the ideas some of them had about the Flathead Indian Reservation in Montana. They all knew that part of the vast reservation parcel had passed out of Native American ownership to the United States government. Sam read with interest about the Indian Chief, Sitting Bull, a colorful savage who fought to stay on Flathead. He refused relegation to a life spent living only on the portion that the U.S. government allotted to the Indians for settlement. Sitting Bull and his tribal warriors had escaped over Montana's border into Canada after a battle. They'd had a mighty clash with the U.S. government. The 4,000 Indian fighters had been chased out of range.

Not everyone had saved money like Sam, but he wisely may not have mentioned it to any of them. He and others wanted to get in on parcels that would be available for pioneers and homesteaders settlement. If he didn't somebody else would. He couldn't change anything for the Indians, but maybe he could for himself with a little money, hard work, and perseverance. It stayed in his mind.

Sam's own words...
Monday, June 28, 1909 – "Raked hay, fair day, wrote inquiry for information on how to register for land on the Flathead."

He did more than talk about it with the crew of men and in his quiet way, made the scribbled leap to ask for information. He wanted to determine if it was a chance where he might better his own situation. It had been in his mind daily to follow through with fact-finding steps to see if he could develop the idea. His calm way of follow through served him well.

On the remaining hot June days he raked hay, cocked hay, and pitched hay. The coarse animal food was his lot for work in one way or another, days without end. He probably spit dry grass, too, when he slept on it at Ed Denny's during the July 4 weekend.

Sam's own words...
Monday, July 5, 1909 – "Went to Twin Falls (Idaho), rained hard in p.m. Stayed in rooming house, $5."

Twin Falls and the Buhl countryside ranch where he worked were within a few miles distance from each other. He could benefit from a change of scenery, but perhaps what he had spent time on in Twin Falls was to find an address to which he'd send his letter to the Flathead vicinity. While there, the usual tobacco was bought. On Tuesday, he ate dinner in Buhl but came back to Denny's ranch, a fair-weather day. Then Sam pitched hay for six days straight, 22 loads one day and 30 the next. Irrigation was kept up 13 days in a row on all of the planted crops.

He went for a swim on Sunday, July 25, the first time for the year, and it was a dandy way to come clean. It preempted a trip northward that he had planned and was about to follow through. The trip would take him on the elevated rail tracks through passes between hills, into valleys and out again. Idaho and its northern neighbor, Montana, had identical terrain.

Sam's own words...
Monday, July 26, 1909 – "Left for Montana from Twin Falls 7 p.m. Stayed in Pocatello all night. Depart 8 a.m. for Missoula."

Wednesday, July 27, 1909 – "Arrive Missoula, Montana 2:35 pm, registered right away, depart for Butte, Mt. 6 p.m., arrive Butte 11:00 night."
Thursday, July 29, 1909 – "Depart Butte, 1:45 p.m., arrive Buhl 11:25 p.m."

The train had him back just before midnight from his purposeful trip. He was up the next morning to help Southworth's with wheat on the last hot day of July.

August was a busy time with the harvesting of wheat, hay, and clover. Sam and his fellow workers used every appropriate machine available for the gathering of these crops. They irrigated, mowed, and threshed as well as drove horses to pull hay and grain wagons. Sam's friend, John, took his pay and left for Galeton near the end of the month. He had lasted 10 months. Sam would miss him a lot.

Sam's own words...
Sunday, August 29, 1909 – "Stayed over Saturday night at Denny's. Slept with crew Sunday night."
Thursday, September 2, 1909 – "Too wet to thresh, another thunder-storm, sick with Cholera Morpheus at night."

September began with a regular Pennsylvania-like storm. He thought of the scene as familiar when he likened the onslaught of rain to home. The next night he self-diagnosed with Cholera Morpheus, no mention of a doctor. He knew his diarrhea and vomiting through the dark hours was generally called this. He had no way to know yet that the last cholera outbreaks would occur from 1910-1911 in the United States. It was a regrettable presence in his world now with open discussion by those who survived it. Many had died from the intestinal infection, but he threw it off quicker than most and went back to work with no further mention of assault to his body from the dread disease.

Sam threshed all through September but made quick trips to Buhl when a machine broke or weather intervened. He was interested in the purported opening available of the west-end land. Since Jonathan had gone, he'd made a new friend, Andy Gardell, with whom he met up (away from the crew) in Buhl to talk over possibilities. The acres encompassed lush grasses and fertile ground around the town of Buhl. Along with a moderate climate, the area was ideal in which to raise animals and crops. Annual rainfall was about 10 inches, but in the sagebrush desert, the irrigation project for the soil in Southern Idaho was sorely needed. Sam and Andy had studied and anticipated the introduction of large-scale irrigation to the Magic Valley area that encompassed the west-end tracts. It all came together when the privately owned Twin Falls Land and Water Company was reorganized in 1909 as the shareholder-owned Twin Falls Canal Company. Twin Falls and Buhl became a major regional economic center to serve the agriculture industry when the valve was opened to reroute the Snake River into the new canal. The land at an elevation of 3,660 feet has more than 300 days of sunny skies, excellent for farming.

Sam's own words...
Sunday, September 26, 1909 – "Stayed Saturday night and Sunday in Buhl, back to camp in p.m."
Tuesday, September 28, 1909 – "Rainy, west-end land opening, made a bargain for 40 acres of land."
Wednesday, September 29, 1909 – "Rode 25 miles on horseback, finished arrangements on land."

The acres were looked over from the back of a horse. Neither Sam nor Andy could swing a deal on their own, but if they pooled their money and efforts, they decided they could pull it off. They looked at each other with satisfied smiles as they leaned forward on the saddles and nodded their approval. They galloped back to the livery stable. September ended along with spent money for a good cause.

Sam had enhanced his ability to succeed with the joint ownership of a ranch. It would require work to which he was no stranger, and he believed they would make a go of it. If his partner was as honest as himself and planned to work as hard, how could they go wrong? October had its own allotment of labor right where he was when the weather cooperated.

Sam's own words...
Sunday, October 3, 1909 – "Cool wind, lying around cook shack thinking, reading, rain."

He was not immune to a common cold, a stomach ache, or general discomfort. Monday caught him like that, but he worked anyway even though he was bothered with his neuralgia again. October moved forward with full work every day.

Sam's own words...
Sunday, October 17, 1909 – "Fair day...papers from home."

The Galeton newspapers were enough to quicken his pulse at the pleasure of reading all about the vicinity of his hometown. How he must have poured over them, hungry for news of familiar people and businesses.

Sam and Andy had worked around to the time when they could move to their west-end ranch. They had high hopes with realistic expectations of hard work.

Sam's own words...
Sunday, October 24, 1909 – "Went over to our ranch, smokes 10¢."

He and Andy put in morning work hours for Denny's while they used the remainder of each day to move their belongings to their ranch. The last Saturday of October, Sam drew his check for $40 and went to Buhl for items he needed.

Both men continued work for Denny's and finished threshing. Southworths hired them a couple of days to pitch clover and alfalfa.

The weather turned foul for farming. It either rained or snowed and did not dry out. Southworths boarded both men even though there'd been no work for two weeks. Sam's method of worry was to write on his diary page about the wet conditions that prevented work. It continued that way.

Sam's own words...
Sunday, November 20, 1909 – "Continued rainy, small pay weather."

A continuum of the rain and wind kept on. Sam wrote a letter home on Thursday, exasperated with "continued, continued, continued" written day after day in his diary. "We all done the same on Friday," he wrote. And that meant not one iota of work while they waited for alfalfa to dry and the weather to settle. Thanksgiving arrived.

Sam's own words...
Sunday, November 28, 1909 – "Ate turkey with Denny boys, down to canyon in p.m."
Monday, November 29, 1909 – "Bought a team of horses, fair day, alfalfa drying up, at last, $80," (for the horses).
Tuesday, November 30, 1909 – "Raining again, making ready to go to ranch, settled up with Denny, walked to Buhl."

December was determined to be cold and windy. It was minus two degrees on December 2. Without work, expenses mounted. Sam and Andy moved to their ranch on December 3. By December 6, Sam had listed costs as they paid for items: supply of spuds $48.95, wagon $35, lumber $16.30, groceries, etc. $2.80. It continued to be wintry, and three inches of snow fell. More snow arrived as they built a barn on December 7.

Sam's own words...
Wednesday, December 8, 1909 – "Put tar paper on shack, door, eight inches of snow."
Thursday, December 9, 1009 – "Andy sick-abed, cut sagebrush, and tinkered around."

Andy lingered in his bunk four more days before he started to get better. Sam carried on with the necessary work. He dug brush, grubbed brush, and burned brush. Their cook stove was the source of heat. Sam went to get a load of hay for their horses. He fed men and beast while he counted on Andy's recovery.
"Such is life in the west," Sam wrote on December 12 while it snowed. He did more work on the barn and added additional tar paper to the shack to stop the wind coming through the cracks. During the week, he wrote a letter to Galeton Bank Company to apply for a loan.

Sam's own words...
Sunday, December 19, 1909 – "The life of a recluse is at times dull, read everything I could get my hands on."

He had always saved letters and newspapers from home and went over them all again. Andy had much less to read, but Sam was in no position to be fussy. He received a letter from Fred Southworth on December

21 and wrote to him four days later. Believably, Sam had to ask for hay on credit if he hadn't already on the last load. No doubt Southworth wondered how the men had gotten along. He also kept a connection with skilled workers he counted on for later. This was the same day their canal went dry. They commenced carrying water since the easier access no longer flowed close by to serve the needs of men and horses.

Sam drew a load of straw for the equine creators of manure. The ochre base of straw bedded their horses down warmer and manure shoveled best with the fodder underneath.

Sam's own words...
Wednesday, December 29, 1909 – "Went to Buhl, received letter and cards from home, also a letter from Galeton Bank."

A small loan was in the offing and could barely keep them going until the weather favored their part of the world. Sam grubbed plentiful brush to burn. Trees were not in optimum supply here as in Oregon.

~**~

1910

Sam received a 1910 calendar from home, a possible belated Christmas present. It pictured Mark Twain who stood in a pose on the combination January/February page. There he was with his chalky shock of hair and mustache, complete with a white suit and matching shoes. The small 4" x 8" calendar with six pages contained witty quips taken from some of the famous novellas and novels written by Mark Twain. *Roughing It* is a book of semi-autobiographical travel literature written by the American humorist, and it is reasonable to believe that Sam may have read it. He knew all about Twain, who had headed west to Nevada earlier in his life and learned from it that he was more suited to writing. Anyone from back east, as Sam was, would have known of Twain and Samuel Clemens as being one in the same. Mark Twain was from Elmira, NY, not all that far north of Galeton, PA, just 60 miles apart. It was the perfect calendar for Sam.

He could not know that the famous 65-year-old writer of the novels *Tom Sawyer* and *Huckleberry Finn* would die the next year in April 1910 and would be laid to rest in the Elmira Cemetery.

December 1909 ended with a chill of sleet and snow.

3 - Winter's Grip
Efforts, 1910 - 1911

January 1, 1910, was no improvement with its eight inches of snow. It was a dull day followed by more snow that night. He pulled on his Arctic boots, glad of the purchase made earlier when he'd had the money. He clenched each buckle closed with a snap and stood up to put his weather resisters to good use against the deep snow he was forced to trudge through from the shack to the barn.

Sam's own words...
Sunday, January 2, 1910 – "Drew a load of hay, done washing, supposed it was Monday."
Monday, January 3, 1910 – "Done chores, one foot of snow..."

Winter's grip hung on tightly while frozen precipitation fell and deepened. They went out in whatever weather the day offered, bent forward against the onslaught of freezing wind to get to the barn for the chores that waited. It was necessary to hang on tightly to the barn door lest the wind gusts fling it off. He and Andy talked about just making it through the rest of the winter. Worry shadowed their faces.

Sam's own words...
Thursday, January 6, 1910 – "Went to Buhl, received a letter from Grace telling of the burning of home, wrote home, wrote to Galeton Bank Company, 12 degrees below zero."

Sam's lips pursed into flat lines as he read the bad news from home. His breath let loose in a deflated sigh. He shook his head that he could not send one bit of help. The news was a blow as if he had been punched blindside. Nobody had escaped troubles. His letter home was all he had to offer. He considered it mighty weak.

Sam wrote a special note to his sister and didn't forget to wish Grace a happy birthday for January 10, just ahead. His letter to Galeton Bank no doubt included signed papers to return to them to finalize and secure the loan.

The cold month of January wore on with more of the same cold wind, chores, and lack of money. Sam had another letter from home as he worried about his folk's problems to find a different place to live. Even then they had to have a house furnished. He wrote again and commiserated with them. He answered Grace's letter. When she wrote, it was on behalf of the entire family. She made sure to catch him up on all news.

Grace was two years younger than Sam, the closest to his age out of his six siblings and closest in friendship with a strong bond between them. All of them were younger than Sam. He liked to hear of each one when Grace had anything to relate.

As he finished the last correspondence, a thought struck: he tipped his head back for a moment and closed his eyes in gratitude that he had left his Teddy Roosevelt books with Grace. They had not been deposited with his folks and therefore had not burned. He and Grace enjoyed similar taste in reading, making it the obvious choice to leave them with her. He took a pained breath, struck with remorse that he showed too little caring in his glad escape of the loss in front of their greater one. He closed his eyes.

The last time he had made a deposit in his Buhl bank account was back in December. He had depleted it weeks ago. Sam borrowed $10 from Denny and went to Buhl after potatoes and oil. The deep snow had been thawing, but of course, it snowed again as he grubbed brush to burn for heat and cook their food. For two days, his teeth were sore. He was conscious of cold air and kept his mouth closed tightly to prevent the wind from entering. There didn't need to be one more reason to set his mouth in an austere straight line. Trouble seemed to linger in one of its new favorite hangouts. It was not quite enough to be out of work and broke. Sam started February with a sore jaw.

Sam's own words...
Thursday, February 17, 1910 – "Went to Buhl, groceries and $1.50 meat, snow."
Saturday, February 19, 1910 – "A terror of a day, high wind and snow."

Sam wrote a letter home.

Now it was back into the extreme weather to haul hay and grub brush. He braced himself against the wind to load and bring sagebrush in close for stove use. The cook stove was in constant use but did not give off much heat. Snow drifted into swirled devils and piled against the barn and shack during two days of high wind. At least the animals ate it as a substitute for water.

Sam's own words...
Tuesday, February 22, 1910 – "More snow, went to Buhl, groceries on credit."

They needed the food, but it hadn't been easy to ask for credit. Sam waited until customers left before he'd lifted his head, stopped averting his eyes, and made the request. Was it his imagination that the proprietor could see right through his clothes and see his legs shake? The worry that ate at Sam left him with less of an appetite. How would they continue? Yet, he was not ready to give in to his first winter on his own land.

On the last day of the shortest month, February, snow began to thaw. The drifts and high banks melted fast, and the canal contained water. On March 1, Sam went to Buhl again. He recorded in his diary, "Creeks overflowing, hard to ford them."

A week later the creek was all but dry and water scarce. His worry did not stand still. It walked along with him quite well while he carried water, grubbed brush, and fixed a wagon. The situation had no immediate improvement. Sam made a reluctant choice and wrote what had to have been an unthinkable letter to his father.

~**~

Buhl, Idaho
March 7, 1910

Dear Father,

On account of so much snow and bad weather, we have not been able to do any work that we could get money for and so we are unable to buy the seeds for our garden.

We owe for some hay and groceries and if it is so you can spare it would like to borrow $100 dollars until next fall but think we can pay you before.

We are having fine weather now, and the snow is all gone and expect to go to work right away, but we cannot get the money quick enough that way as it would be too late for a good garden.

I hated to ask you for this, and maybe you think I am making a big mistake, but I believe we will make a lot of money.

Do not send a check as I might have trouble getting it cashed. A registered letter would be the best. I miss you all very much but if I live I will try and come home next fall. This is a new country, and pretty hard for a poor man to start and in time I think I will not be sorry I came.

I will close hoping to receive a reply from you soon.

From Sam

My partner did not have much money, but I think he is perfectly honest, at least I will see that he does not beat me very bad. He claims to have had lots of experience in the garden business as he worked for his uncle in Nevada who had a big garden. We would have had enough money, but we could not work as long as we expected last fall.

Do not say anything about this letter for you know how some people will say, "I told you so."   Sam

~**~

Sam's own words...
Monday, March 14, 1910 – "Went to Buhl, some wind, received a letter from home."

Grace wrote and also sent along a message that their father, Lac, had received from his friend who knew Sam.

~**~

Clifton Sta., Va., R#1
February 3, 1910

Mr. Lac Crippen, Dear Friend,

I just received your letter and was glad to hear from you but sorry to hear about your bad luck in losing your house. I hope you are doing well with your job.

You did not say whether Sam had come home yet from the west. I was looking over the Galeton papers regularly and never saw it mentioned...

Please let me hear from you soon.

Yours, F. M. Hagman Jr.

~**~

Sam did not seriously consider leaving for home but stayed to try to make the ranch turn a profit. To give up meant acceptance of defeat. It would be too hard to lose all they had put into a success. He owed it to himself and his partner, Andy, to continue the fight. He couldn't see it any other way. The usual letters from home were like a lifeline, but this one had unsettled him to read that his father's friend expected that he had gone back to Galeton. It set his determination harder.

Some of Sam's trips to Buhl had included contacts made in efforts to get work. His letter to Father had stated the truth about expectations of work. He didn't need the reminder on the Mark Twain calendar, "When in doubt, tell the truth."

Sam's own words...
Tuesday, March 15, 1910 – "Worked for water company, Andy went for work, fair and warm, doing my own cooking."
Saturday, March 19, 1910 – "Worked for the water company...still alone, Quaker Oats, 50¢."

The early years of a healthy start with oatmeal for breakfast stayed with him by choice. It wasn't called the comfort food for nothing. Sam preferred human company over being alone. His expressionless face lacked any sign of a smile as he went about his chores.

Sam worked eight days for the water company with Sunday off in between each of the four days. On his free day, he drew a load of hay and one of sage brambles, fuel for the horses, and fuel for the stove. He planted two hills of potatoes for what he called an "experiment." Sam was anxious for the growth season to begin. He was still alone but glad there was water in the canal again.

Other contacts Sam had made brought sporadic work as the temporary employment for the water company ended. He threshed seven hours for Mr. Bing and two hours for Mr. Runnels.

Andy came home on March 24. Sam relaxed while Andy could not repress his grin. Spring had arrived and with it, renewed hope.

Sam received the loan from his father and also his wages. He went to Buhl bank and paid off a $50 loan. He mailed the order for seeds he and Andy had made out.

Back at the home ranch in the morning, Sam plowed. He went to the Burns ranch to remove brush and to plow but had to give it up when the land was too wet. The next day he plowed and got a load of hay for himself.

Sam's own words...

Sunday, March 27, 1910 – "Hired out to Mr. Brazeau for $45 a month."
Monday, March 28, 1910 – "Borrowed $25 from Buhl Bank for three months."

Sam was hopeful again. He was thankful that with a little time and hard work, the juggle of money and steady work on their garden business would pay off. It also required the juggling of jobs for wages.

His work for Brazeau began Monday on a windy day as he turned dirt over and then harrowed the same soil. He continued six days through Saturday. It was convenient that the wind, rain, and hail held off until the last evening.

Sunday was Sam's own day, he supposed, but first he butchered a hog before he went home. He received the pleasure of postcards from sisters Sadie and Grace but it was back to Brazeau's in the evening.

It was a busy job, never an idle moment as he plowed the garden, ran a No. 2 Fresno and harrowed. The horse-drawn Fresno was a scraper with huge wheels. The newer models with steam engine tractors to pull them were the latest innovation but were not affordable for Brazeau and other small employers. It didn't stop conversations among workers who described large crews of canal diggers who used the newer 1910 version. No doubt, Sam, and all the rest of the hands, were just as interested as the next guy but had no delusions they'd ever get to use one.

Work continued six days a week, and on Saturday evening he purchased his tobacco for 75¢. It had been non-existent for Sam since the previous October. It was out of reach for the winter when money was tight. He looked forward to the enjoyment of it now. He kept the same pattern, home on Sunday to plant more in his garden. This time, it was peas. He always went back to Brazeau's by evening. Between helping run the old Fresno and plant trees to establish an orchard, he served them well.

Sam's own words...
Wednesday, April 20, 1910 – "Made ditches and shoveled them out. The wind is howling for fare."

Sam harrowed and leveled, then hauled his dirt away. There was a fence to be built. After finishing the enclosure, he went home Saturday night. By the time he left his ranch Sunday evening, he had planted his onion sets. Each week was steady repetitive work. April ended.

Sam got his water company paycheck of $18.75 and paid it to G. Williams for hay. Satisfied with his juggle of money with one more necessity taken care of by what he earned, he purchased 25¢ worth of tobacco, which was a luxury.

Sam's own words...
Sunday, May 8, 1910 – "Quit Brazeau's. Settled up in full, check $20.30."

The weather was hot, the season for Sam and Andy to put all of their labor into their garden business. Sam irrigated, and they both hoed the peas that were up. They worked as hard for themselves as they had for wages. Sam enjoyed his tobacco again. Andy left once each week to wend his way to Buhl again for their necessities. He picked up another 50¢ worth of tobacco for Sam and brought him a letter from Galeton. Sam worked.

They drew manure, plowed and harrowed, and hoed potatoes.

Never a dull moment as the week went by. Andy went to town again and Sam repeated his order for 50¢ worth of tobacco. He enjoyed it when he could relax in the rare moments of downtime.

June was warm while they planted corn and irrigated. The brush was burned, and they set out the cauliflower. Looking out over it brought satisfaction to them. It had become quite a garden as they maintained it.

Sam's own words...
Tuesday, June 7, 1910 – "Plowed in a.m., worked for water company in p.m....windy."
Friday, June 10, 1910 – "Corrugated garden, picked peas...windy."

Fresh peas were a treat for supper. Andy went to Buhl again and came back with 50¢ worth of tobacco for Sam while he stayed back and hoed cabbage. The next four days they set out more cabbage, irrigated spuds, and planted additional corn. They staggered what they planted to ensure that output would become ripe at different times.

It was Buhl again for Andy, but he was not expected to return until he finished his job. Sam labored enough for two people.

Sam's own words...
Saturday, June 18, 1910 – "Irrigated and hoed cauliflower, fair, warm, and alone."

On Monday, Sam wrote again of being alone and added that Andy was haying for Brazeaus. He came home on Tuesday evening after five days of work. That night Sam went to Buhl and bought a pair of shoes that cost him $3.50. On Thursday he went to Denny's ranch and hired on at Southworth's to mow ditches, for a start. He hired himself out every day until Sunday, July 3, when he came home and irrigated potatoes. Sam did the same water "trick" again on Monday and also did his wash. In mid-July, he had paid off an earlier $25 loan from Buhl Bank.

Sam worked 25 days straight between Denny's and Southworth's, using his team of horses. He had good business sense and charged extra for them. By July's end, he had spent $1.10 in four increments for his tobacco enjoyment. Sam and Andy continued work to divide time between Denny's, Southworth's, and their home ranch to make a go of it. Water rights had not come free in a land where canals furnished irrigation. At the start of August, they had borrowed $134.40, thanks to Sam's well-established credit with Buhl bank. The three-month loan had paid only for water.

August was a mixture of warm and cool weather as they worked on alternate days for the two employers. They harvested hay and oats. Sam pitched, threshed, and bundled it.

Sam's own words...
Sunday, August 7, 1910 – "Honored the Sabbath once again, warm, wrote letter home."

His correspondence to and from his Galeton home was fewer during long, hot, summer days of intensive work on two ranches and their own. They were aware of obligations to be paid off and intended to do so. They worked right through September to bale, bundle, and cock hay.

Sam's own words...
Sunday, October 2, 1910 – "Wrote letter home...cool and windy."
Tuesday, October 4, 1910 – Went to Buhl and back to our ranch...hay wet, settled with Southworth."

They paid the Buhl bank in full for the water rights loan. Work continued on for Denny's day after day, and at times they used their team of horses.

Sam's own words...
Monday, October 17, 1910 – "At our ranch, plowed out spuds, cool...rain."
Friday, October 28, 1910 – "Drew hay on shares for one-half, warm, fair."

The men dug potatoes four days straight, which took them into November. On the second day of the month, they went to Buhl and sold four sacks of spuds and also lumber. They bailed hay for Denny's. Several days were half for wages and half for their own ranch. At times, they brought a load of hay home as pay. They had become good partners and worked hard for their livelihood for the common cause of their homestead. They both worked to grub brush for various outfits.

Sam's own words...
Monday, October 28, 1910 – "Went to Buhl after groceries and grub hoe, arctics and socks $4.50, warm."

Sam referred to the weather with his *warm* comment, but it applied to his intent with the purchase of Arctic buckle-type rubber boots and socks for his feet just as well. They owed for the grub hoe, and they would use it to real advantage and make it worth the $42.50 due in December. Mr. Pitts and Mr. Runnels hired them for grub hoe work. Sam and Andy grubbed brush every day of December, work they had lined up ahead of time. Andy went to Buhl three times and Sam to Twin Falls once in December. The machine debt was paid in early December due to all of their efforts.

The cold wind hastened Sam's steps to get chores finished and return to Mr. Russum's. The smell of the cook shack held supper's promise and tantalized the hungry ranch hands. Roast pork dinner was a fine meal on a Sunday. It was the first day of the New Year, 1911. By Thursday, the job ended, and Sam moved to his home ranch again.

The next Sunday he helped Mr. Pitt move a dog house and paid a visit to Mr. Brazeau. He always scared up work whether it was for now or later. Four days of snow put a stop to such plans when it fell all day, every day, at times six and eight inches.

Sam's own words...
Sunday, January 15, 1911 – "Done chores, read nearly everything. Lonesome. Cold..."
Monday, January 16, 1911 – "...done only chores and read. Eight inches snow."

He enjoyed news of what was going on in Galeton and the rest of the world. Sam wouldn't have missed reading the November 1910 news just past, headlines about the Wright Brothers first commercial flight and would've marveled at the news that Henry Ford had sold 10,000 automobiles last year. An auto was a novelty to him and others. The Galeton and Buhl newspapers chronicled the stories that astonished along with local reports for each area.

Some of the reports intrigued but also furnished an education while Sam made a reasonable effort to stay current with events.

Andy came home on January 18 and brought the horses with him. Sam had worked for Mr. Pitt for two days before January ended and again in February as well as a sparse eight hours for Mr. Russum. Work lessened while harsh weather reigned.

During two cold months, Andy went to Buhl seven times. Sam had made only a couple of trips after mail and sent a letter home. A postcard came from his sister, Sadie. March held more promise as Sam worked for Russum on his sagebrush. Griswald came after spuds, a coveted sale. They finished the brush contract on March 17. Around this time, Sam and Andy went to Buhl now that they had both money and plans.

4 –Plans
The Trip–1911

Over the winter, Andy and Sam had discussed a plan they both wanted to carry out. It was hashed out in every detail as they met their obligations. Now it was put in writing as one got out from under and the other took on the entire risk of the Forty. But risk was not how Sam saw it.

Sam's own words...
Sunday, March 19, 1911 – "Mr. Eldredge accepted our contract."
Tuesday, March 21, 1911 – "Clear...cool, gave A. Gardell warranty deed and took over mortgage on our 40 acres. Hired out to Mr. Pitt."

The mortgage was to run four years at six percent interest and end in 1915. Andy had sold his half of the Forty to Sam, who had no problem to secure the loan for the ranch. His history of paid off loans with Buhl bank stood well where he had built up substantial credit. In some part, the gentle countenance radiated from his tall frame produced a reliance on him as an honest man to do business with. Nothing nefarious came to mind in his character.

Sam and Andy had work lined up and a deal made between them. The men now had separate abodes but kept a firm agreement for work to benefit them both. It was a natural turn of events for two people who worked hard for what they wanted.

Sam shoveled ditches, plowed, and planted spuds. Stones had to be picked off fields before he could harrow or run leveler for employers and himself.

Sam's own words...
Tuesday, April 18, 1911 – "Warm and fair until 4 p.m. then one of the worst wind, dust, rain, and snowstorms I've seen."
Wednesday, April 19, 1911 – "Stormed and blew until noon, a terror. Done chores and cut spuds."
Monday, April 22, 1911 – "Paid off $25.25 to Buhl Bank, which carried 25¢ interest."

Sam listed a necessity: Formaldehyde for treating grain and seed potatoes for smut and scab. His directions required a mix of one pint of formaldehyde with 35 to 40 gallons of water. Let potatoes soak for one to two hours.

Sam made more trips to Buhl, at times staying overnight when his loneliness got the better of him. As he worked for himself and Mr. Pitt, his work made use of a float, a grader, and a corrugator. Work was the most prevalent and mandatory of what drove Sam. The occasional word from home was most needed. He welcomed a postcard from his sister, Grace, and a letter from Ma.

The work took him right on into all the usual momentum as the season opened. An incubator was set up on Sunday. At the end of April and again in mid-May, Sam visited Andy. He continued full-time work for Mr. Pitt, irrigated crops every day, and ran a whole gamut of machines.

Sam's own words...
Tuesday, June 6, 1911 – "Went to Buhl after chairs, etc., and irrigated, helped blacksmith, cloudy, warm."
Wednesday, June 7, 1911 – "Irrigated and hoed weeds, Attended wedding in p.m...."

Mr. Pitt's marriage came at the beginning of hay harvest. Sam went right on with work. Irrigation of oats continued as haying began. He mow -ed and ran a Bull rake with a team of horses. The mares were hooked to each side of the contraption, which had several long wooden teeth that moved underneath the coarse forage. He hauled timothy hay. It was neces-sary to get around to visit Twin Falls for groceries and Buhl bank. At the end of July, he dragged off a dead horse and settled up with Mr. Pitt.

Sam's own words...
Tuesday, July 4, 1911 – "At Buhl: Came out to Castleford, arrived 3:30 a.m."

On Wednesday, July 5, Sam started with the new employer where he mowed and ran a Bull rake on long, warm days. On Sundays, he'd do his own work but go back and operate the rake without a day of rest. July brought on more heat while his work changed to wheat stacker, hauler, and bundle wagon operator. He worked the team of horses as hard as himself. Another employer, Mr. Schooler, was added. Sam was in demand. The same jobs continued through July and into August. Then he added on a job for Dr. Stewart, who needed a thresher and so did Mr. Jackson for the same reason. It was not in the offing for him to drop dead like a horse.

Sam finally had a free Sunday on September 3 and did his wash. He worked seven days straight for Schooler.

Sam's own words...
Wednesday, September 13, 1911 – "Came to Buhl...seen Andy."

Now he worked 15 days straight for Singleton. He paid a visit to Twin Falls and Buhl again for groceries and tobacco, a pair of pants at $1.25 and a 25¢ pair of socks. When Sam ran into Andy on Sunday, October 15, in Buhl, it had been a month since their last chance encounter, and they no doubt enjoyed it.

Sam's own words...
Tuesday, October 17, 1911 – "Went over to Dr. Stewarts to work."

He mowed, raked, and hauled hay for five days. Work for Singleton ended, and he continued labor for Dr. Stewart in Twin Falls.

This was the city where Dr. Lydia Crow, osteopathic physician, lived with her brother, Phillip Crow. Lydia had never married. She may have been acquainted with Dr. Stewart as an associate or patient or both. She was a dreadfully ill patient of H. J. Billington, O.D. Lydia died of tuberculosis on

October 25, 1911, at the age of 37. Philip and the ophthalmologist, both signed her death certificate. She was about two years older than her sister, Edith Crow Haggarty. It is likely that through the connection of working for Dr. Stewart that Sam met Edith. He wouldn't forget her.

Sam continued work for Dr. Stewart who made house calls, which required horses, a wagon, barn, fences, and granary, also crops of hay and grain to feed the equines. Sam dug a cistern in seven days time in between all kinds of chores and also hauled oats and manure. He managed to build a granary. November was half gone as he started work on the Stewart house and constructed a fence and threshed oats for the doctor.

December arrived. He settled up with Schooler, Dr. Stewart, and Singleton. Sam went to Buhl with Singleton and saw Andy. He stayed overnight there, and they talked about old times and the future. No doubt it included the trip that Sam was on the verge of taking. Back from his visit with Andy, Sam arranged some maintenance help on his property while he was away.

He paid $4 road tax and land tax of $18.50 for his 40-acre ranch even though it was not due until December 31. Money was drawn out of his Buhl bank funds, $100 on December 6, and another $106 on the 12th.

Sam went to Twin Falls and stayed all night. He may have called on Edith again, more likely than not, and departed Twin Falls the next morning just after 7. His travels took him through all of the states he had seen before on his trip west. Gladness pulled the corners of his mouth upward as he left Buffalo, NY, for the last leg to Galeton. It had taken five days by rail to arrive, and he wrote on the page for the day "home again." It was with satisfaction that he walked down a country road to home. It was a different house than before because of the fire, but home was where his folks were.

Sam's heartbeat quickened as Pa stepped out from the barn door. His worn barn coat and beaten felt fedora evoked Sam's fond memories. The ready smile beneath was Sam's welcome home.

His parents, Lac and Sophia, were glad to have him for however long it might be, but they would have to share him with all of his siblings and their spouses. Ralph, now age 16, and Dewey at 14, were the only ones who remained at home with Mother and Father. Imagine their grins that likely spread far enough to make their ears protrude as they set eyes on Sam.

Sam's own words...
Tuesday, December 12, 1911 – "Went to Galeton, bought suit of clothes."
Wednesday, December 13, 1911 – "Went to town, bought work clothes, went up to see new road, rainy."

Sam's new clothes for Sunday-go-to-meeting cost him $19, and the labor grade gabardine of blue-gray worsted cotton was $19.35. He was ready for social opportunities and work. It curved up the corners of his mouth slightly to cut a fine figure and make his folks proud. People always had their comments while they stood in small groups. If they put his visit in the paper, as they were prone to do, why he would make a good showing. He hadn't forgotten the mention of such things in his father's friend's letter. Most likely he'd read a report on Sam now. The newspaper was fond of dropping names just like people did.

The new road was the topic discussed among all of the men who held neighborhood conversations. It looked good now with its smooth rolled gravel but wait until winter ravished it with pock-marks. It would still lead to and from destinations, mud, and all.

He lent a hand at home to dig a hole. A closet had to be moved, no problem. It was an outhouse closet to be moved over a new pit. The pile of dirt left over was used to fill in the old cavity.

Sam went to help Mr. Lockwood butcher, another job he was good at. No harm in making a few bucks where he could. He went to town a few times and enjoyed the hometown experience awhile. Likely, someone was always discovering him and shaking hands before plying him with questions about the west and his experiences.

Sam's own words...
Sunday, December 17, 1911 – "Clouds...went to Sunday School..."

The congregation prayed for Lockwood's baby. Sam bowed his head. It was all that could be done now for their situation.

The woods lured Sam for old time's sake. He had grown up here helping his father farm and cut lumber. Now his two youngest brothers were

Father's apprentices. Sam may have hummed with contentment in the woods, a hymn, *Tell Me the Old, Old Story* or *Blessed Assurance*. The familiar songs of the morning church session comforted Sam who had heard them in church for all of his young years at home.

Lockwood's baby died on Wednesday, December 20. Sam helped where he could and saved Mr. Lockwood some steps he was not up to taking. Sam walked up West Branch and hired De Groat, the grave digger, for $40. Sam was sorry it would be a sad Christmas for the Lockwood family.

Cold temperatures encroached and turned rain to snow. More fell each day.

Sam went over to see Uncle Dock on Christmas Eve and his sister, Mary, the next day. Mary was 21 years old, eight years younger than Sam. Her husband was Frank Hess who Sam liked really well. He and Frank went here and there together while he stayed with them at Whitesville for four days before Sam returned home.

Sam gave some thought to his own life of bachelorhood, in part from the witness of the happiness between Mary and Frank. His thoughts of a woman he had met back in Twin Falls, ID, hadn't been left behind. But right now reason had him follow through on another action to be taken. It was one of the reasons he had brought a good sum of money home with him.

~**~

1912

His teeth had caused him pain for a long time, and he was determined to remedy the situation. He had made an appointment on one trip to town, and on January 3, he had 15 teeth pulled. His mouth was disagreeably sore for a couple of days, but he decided that it had been mild after all, now that he had caught a cold in his jaw. It was a terror like the weather ahead.

Sam's own words...
Tuesday, January 9, 1912 – "Cold and windy, a terror, 20 degrees below zero."

In a couple of days, he was in excellent shape along with the weather. His younger brothers were glad when Sam could help do chores again.

Sam went to town for entertainment one evening. It could have been live music, maybe a ragtime band at a dance, or a storyteller at the church. It was too cold for the outdoor sport of horseshoes. If he'd opted for home entertainment, it would most likely have been Chinese marbles or checkers. His younger brothers were good as player or referee. They could tease without mercy if given the chance.

Sam enjoyed the *Leader Dispatch* newspaper every day and decided to have a subscription sent to Buhl for himself. It could help ward off loneliness.

Sam's own words...
Friday, January 12, 1912 – "...30 degrees below zero, called on the dentist."
Tuesday, January 16, 1912 – "Cut Hemlock skids...wind, 28 degrees below zero."

Maybe he needed to satisfy the doctor that all was well inside his mouth, and anyway, the after-care calls were built into the price. He had more healing to do and hoped the weather had warming to do.

While the weather remained frigid, the temperature did not dip quite so frigid again, as he had so far recorded. A couple of moderate days were welcome as he helped with chores and shoveled snow.

Sam's own words...
Saturday, January 20, 1912 – "Shoveled snow, went to town in the evening, colder, letter from Andy."

It was a welcome correspondence that put his mind at ease about Buhl concerns and also reinforced his and Andy's solid friendship.

By January 26 Sam had shoveled snow eight days in a row. Rain and snow had made it slippery and was a factor for foot injury while he loaded logs. It put a damper on the help given his father while Sam was home. He was unable to step on it the next day. A lame foot was no way to start February, and he thought he'd exercise it right out of existence. Why not walk to town and back? And so he did. He was lame for two more weeks. It didn't stop him from attending Sunday school and doing a few chores, but he stayed around home a lot. In a private conversation on one occasion, he may have talked with Pa about a particular woman still on his mind.

The last call to the dentist was scheduled in mid-February and concluded the whole episode of his teeth.

Sam's own words...
Wednesday, February 24, 1912 – "At home, snow and rain, went to party in the evening."

He was an eligible bachelor with an aura of hero about him. After all, he had moved out west and had come back home with money in his pockets. There must have been some young ladies in Galeton who wished he would remain.

A second party a week later was a sort of farewell to neighbors, family, and friends. No one wanted to see him leave.

Sam's own words...
Monday, February 26, 1912 – "Snow, rain, went to town, bought watch charm 75¢."
Thursday, February 29, 1912 – "Went to town, packed my clothes, ate supper at Grace and Roy's."

Galeton could not hold him. The dangling do-dad of a charm was not for his wristwatch. Its addition on a feminine timepiece in Twin Falls was what he had in mind.

His sister, Grace, was just two years younger than he. They talked often and easy with one another and valued each other's opinion. She and Roy lived near Ma and Pa and made it convenient to spend time together.

Sam had caught a cold and his mother, Sophia, made cough syrup to send with him on the trip back. Sam smiled as she tucked the recipe into his shirt pocket in case he needed it later. The concentrated essence of 2.5 ounces of Mentho-Laxine cost $1.80. It was mixed in syrup that was made of a half pint of sugar and boiled water.

Sam had been home just under two months when he packed what belonged to him and boarded the Galeton train for Chicago. Once there, he took the Rock Island line to Colorado Springs. There was a switch to the Midland Railroad to Grand Junction, Colorado where they had to lay over due to a wreck. He was back in Buhl by the afternoon of March 6 and went to Singleton's ranch to a hoop hoop and hooray welcome.

Sam was back to the familiar farm environment and chores on his first morning back. Singleton and George were all too glad to leave the work to him and went to Buhl. George returned, but his employer stayed away as had been his pattern. Sam was trustworthy, a person to leave the work with and it would get done without the need of a monitor.

Sam initiated himself with the heavier work to dig post holes. It did not negate the need to do the chores and cook.

Sam's own words...
Sunday, March 10, 1912 – "Done cooking and chores, mule kicked me in the face..."
Sunday, March 17, 1912 – "Done chores and washing, got supper, wrote letter home..."

Now he would work with a sore face as he dug more post holes and worked timothy ground. The cold wind never stopped. He had plowed Singleton's land and commenced with three days of the same for Mr. Waters. Sam harrowed to smooth out the long rows of clumps. His life of farm work and food preparation continued right on into April as he roughed up the land, this time for clover fields. It was cloudy, cold, and windy. Just to prove what April could resort to, it snowed and not just a little. Sam reported a terrible blizzard with the wind that stopped ground work for a couple of days. He worked on the fence and took the black mare and then the tan one to Campbell's for service. The colts were put to pasture.

Sam's own words...
Thursday, April 25, 1912 – "Plowed with walking plow, cool and windy,(1 day)."

Sam habitually wrote "1 day" to indicate how many days he could look back on, marked for wages due him. He spent the whole day following the walk-behind plow, and it was no easy task. He may have preferred a sulky plow where a man sits on a seat and bounces down the rows while he directs the horses that pull it. The animals worked hard for hay to chew and a ration of oats in their feed bunk, but it was not any tougher than what the men put themselves through. In the course of a day's work, Sam did it all, plowed, drilled grain, and drew hay. The month of May blew up a chilled snow squall early on just because it could. The farm labor went on with the layout of ditches. Sam put in a sluice.

Sam's own words...
Sunday, May 12, 1912 – "Got dinner, done washing, wrote to Grace."

Sunday seemed like a picnic against other days. It was downtime earned when he could get the work far enough ahead to have one day off. He reminisced about his family again, but he was making a life here. He had another plan to follow through on, one he had started before.

5 – Future
Happiest Day 1912, 1913

Now the time might be right to pick up again on a long-range idea Sam had held onto. It was another week before he had the time to act. His active mind worked overtime, and over time his mind created an active plan. He wrote this letter.

~**~

> Buhl, Idaho
> May 21, 1912
>
> Government Land Office
> Missoula, Montana
>
> Gentlemen:
>
> I am looking for a homestead and am interested in the land on the Flathead Indian Reservation.
> Please advise me as to whether there is any land open to entry on or near the reservation.
>
> > Yours Truly,
> > Samuel Crippen

~**~

The month of May was when farmers went into full swing with crop establishment. Sam drew hay inside and put in a ditch. He plowed, and V'd a ditch and repeated it three days in a row, not just one little old ditch and done with it. There were fences to fix, irrigation to send through the deepened ditches and help needed from him to start a gang plow.

How many jobs can a man do? Sam is the expert here, and his words record what was accomplished. He, like all successful farmers, had to have an ambitious work ethic, unique type of men who put up with all kinds of weather.

That was one week's worth of jobs. It also took that long before Sam received an important letter, one for which he had awaited. It came on official letterhead.

~**~

Department of the Interior
United States Land Office

Samuel Crippen   Missoula, Montana
Buhl, Idaho   May 24, 1912

Sir:

Your letter of the 21st instant received.

There is considerable land on Flathead Indian Reservation, which is still vacant and subject to homestead entry. All the land on this reservation which is subject to homestead entry is appraised at from *(sic)* $1.25 to $9 per acre, and the entry man is required to pay the appraised value one-third at time of making filing and the balance in five equal annual payments thereafter, beginning one year from date of filing.

This office is not informed as to the character of the quality of land that is vacant. For this information you are referred to Alex R. Rhone, Camas; H. J. Burleigh, Plains; G. E. Whitman, Dixon; Coker F. Rathbone, Ronan, Montana, any of whom would undoubtedly be glad to give you what information they have concerning the vacant land in their vicinity.

Very Respectfully
Register, *(sic)* Jonah Schult

~**~

The report gave Sam more insight from the facts presented. He hadn't seen the real difficulty inherent to the task of taking more steps. It became apparent that he would have to go there to look at the land. He did not rule it out but left it to ponder for another time.

After he had picked rocks from fields, plowed, drilled, and irrigated, Sam was the cook half the time for the Singleton outfit in the evening. He was an expert in hard work and the machines operated, all learned on the job. After these duties, he managed to plant and work in a garden. Is there any wonder how much enjoyment it was to sit down in the evening to the leisure of a smoke and read the newspaper?

The black block letters of the April 15, 1912, headline announced terrible news that a massive ship on its maiden voyage had struck an iceberg and sunk, killing 1,500 people. The ship was the RMS Titanic. He'd have comprehended such news with brevity and shook his head over the sad loss of life. Pictures intruded upon the minds of those who imagined passengers in cold water and no seats left in the lifeboats, according to the story. Sam was a man of compassion and would've shuddered and turned the page to study market reports.

Half the year was gone.

Sam's own words...
Sunday, June 2, 1912 – "Done washing, went over to Andy's in the evening."
Sunday, June 9, 1912 – "Irrigated, cool and partly cloudy, wrote letters..."

Maybe Sam wanted to talk with his friend about the detailed letter in which he had received information of the Flathead Reservation and see what his thoughts were on it. Sam may also have mentioned his thoughts on matrimony to Andy. His letter to Oregon was written the next Sunday.

The letter to Edith Crow Haggarty went to the home of her sister, Mary. Their mother, Marilla, was also on an extended visit with Mary, one of Edith's eight siblings. Marilla Crow lived in the family homestead near Mary but visited in the homes of each of her children at various times. Marilla's husband, Jonathan, had died years ago in a horrible railroad accident. Edith was 15 years old when it happened. She had mentioned it to Sam as part of her family history. Sam listened with compassion that resonated with Edith.

Irrigation was done every day without exception as Sam waited for July, the month which had been the subject of his most recent letter to

Oregon. It was how he and Edith had arranged her visit to Twin Falls for the middle of the month.

Sam's own words...
Friday, July 12, 1912 – "Went to Buhl in a.m., Twin Falls in p.m., stayed at night..."
Saturday, July 13, 1912 – "In Twin Falls, warm, stayed at night."
Sunday, July 14, 1912 – "Came back to Buhl in evening, stayed all night, chilly day."

Sam was back to work, but with a happy heart that put a spring in his step. He didn't know when Edith would be able to come back to Twin Falls again, nor did she. She went back to Oregon. While in Twin Falls, Edith had sent $1 back there for her six months membership for Hall of Mizpah, Grand Chapter of The Eastern Star. She would have explained to Sam that the Order of Eastern Star was an organization upholding the belief that we are all part of the brotherhood of man, sisterhood of women, under a Fatherhood of God. Members try to live by a high moral principle and gather in chapters in a spirit of charity, truth and loving kindness. He was in full agreement with that, and it informed him of Edith's character. She and her sister, Lydia, had opened Daughters of the American Revolution memberships in September 1903. She may not have found any active chapter near Mary's home, a prompt to also join Mizpah.

Sam went back to irrigation work.

Sam's own words...
Tuesday, July 30, 1912 – "Irrigated, helped put binder together, went and voted."

Sam considered it essential to use his voice. It may have been a local vote of some kind that he attended to. It was a well-known fact that Idaho had already elected to enfranchise women to vote in 1911 as many states in the west had. The western areas of the nation were first to embrace it, except for Oregon, which followed a year later. Sam did not malinger after contribution of his civic duty.

The hay needed irrigation. Sam was the man to do it each and every day onward through August. Timothy and alfalfa were ready for harvest, and he was the man for that, too. Sam mowed and raked hay, shocked wheat, and completed chores. September arrived while he was still the man for all jobs on Singleton's ranch. Andy came over to see him in mid-September, no doubt to discuss crop results and enjoy their friendship.

Sam wrote letters on the last Sunday of September. October moved right along just like the work, no stoppage. For several days he hauled timothy, alfalfa, and manure. Dung had piled up as a result of his cleaning the barn. He jigged sacks through the middle of the month. That led to the need for sediment-free seed to put in the bags. One job always led to another on its back, Sam's back. October required mittens and tobacco. They cost him 35¢ each. Only the price was the same since one item was necessary and the other, maybe not. Sam enjoyed his smokes in the limited time he had for it.

He took a mare to Campbell's again, this one for its third stud visit.

November signaled a change on the horizon but not immediate.

Sam's own words...
Monday, November 4, 1912 – "Came back from Singleton Ranch, made an agreement with Andy."

Sam had gone for a visit to Andy's one day earlier and told him of future plans, which included Edith. Sam gave no indication that she was aware of that yet. The deal between he and Andy was a first step, which would be carried out early next year as Sam's plans took shape.

Singleton and George Swan were both gone from the ranch from Saturday through Wednesday. It left the work, all of it, in Sam's capable hands. Each day he marked down another day's pay and lamented that he was alone. He gave himself a break on Sunday. After chores, he went to eat dinner with a friend. A lonesome span, followed by a letter from Grace, heightened his appreciation of her thoughts. He purchased 25¢ worth of tobacco.

Sam's own words...
Sunday, November 17, 1912 – "Done (*sic*) chores and cooking, half sick with a cold."

Singleton and George had been back three days before Singleton made another exit. Sam's cold hung on all the while he kept up his work. He hacked and coughed and turned red with the strain. His mother's cough syrup helped. It took until the next Sunday to beat the virus. Andy visited him on the same day, and Sam prepared their meal.

November ended with snow.

Sam was used to cook's duty nearly every day while the chores and a variety of small works depended on him, too. In this winter month with fewer jobs to do, he would see more of Andy. He paid his friend a visit and then visited Mr. Schooler. Sam kept up contacts with an eye to work in the next year where good relations were desired.

Sam's own words...
Sunday, December 27, 1912 – "Done chores, wrote letter to Oregon, three inches snow."

He started the year with Edith on his mind and ended it the same.

~**~

1913

Winter farming lacked crop work, and wages were not available for everyone at the usual fee. Sam was an exception as he remained at Singletons and other men were free to go here and there for days at a time while Sam continued the daily chores that held the place together. He drew pay while others played. Singleton counted on him to haul hay, build a fence, and fix a windbreak. The wind and expectations of snow required the breaker. He got a load of straw and then went to Southworth's to cut a stove pipe hole. He walked to the post office and found a letter from Grace that provided a reason to smile as he returned to the ranch.

Four inches of snow made an appearance, more or less expected.

Sam's own words...
Monday, January 13, 1913 – "Done chores, hauled hay, went to Stewarts after reach..."

The reach was for the underside of a wagon with the repair job to follow. Schooler's cistern needed to be cleaned. No doubt it was a concrete, box type reservoir in-ground to collect drinking water. After he left Schoolers, he went to Miller's for oats and got a wagon. When he returned to the ranch, Singleton left, and George came back. They had no reason to worry about any of the work.

Sam's own words...
Friday, January 24, 1913 – "Came to Buhl in p.m., stayed all night, moderate."
Saturday, January 25, 1913 – "In Buhl all day, Twin Falls in evening, stayed all night."
Sunday, January 26, 1913 – "In Twin Falls, a regular spring day, came back to Buhl in evening, stayed all night."

Most likely, he visited someone special, Edith Crow Haggarty in Twin Falls.

He was not much in demand for labor, and a change of scenery brought enjoyment before a business transaction culminated on Monday. It was another good reason to stay in town. He got the abstract and secured the deed of S.E. Y4-N.W.1/4 Sec. 19. Tw. 9. Range 14 E.B.M., Buhl. It was the previous agreement that he and Andy had made on the piece of land he would call the Forty. He wrote a check for $15 to Andy on January 1, to cover a transaction incidental.

February had its cold wind, but it began a moderation of weather as he hauled hay, lumber, manure, and rock. Chores were his everyday activity.

Sam helped work on a new house for Singleton during the next two weeks as he kept up the chores and cook's duties. The new abode was ready for Kalsomine by the middle of February. He mixed the slaked lime with water and applied it to the outside of the building and maybe to the inside walls, too, since he was at it for two days. Sam knew the old saying: "Too proud to whitewash and too poor to paint." Whitewash was a cheap imitation for paint. Sam would have known about the incident of Tom Sawyer whitewashing a fence as punishment in a memorable image in American literature. It appears in *The Adventures of Tom Sawyer* written in 1876 by Mark Twain. There was nobody here that Sam could trick into doing the job for him, not that he would have.

George Swan went to Buhl after a cook since Sam let it be known that his own plans were about to be carried out. For the remainder of his time at

Singletons, Sam was as busy as ever. He butchered two hogs, worked on a bridge, and hauled hay, dirt, manure, and rocks. They were all jobs as familiar to him as Edith's face. He oiled more than one horse harness, sowed timothy seed, and sacked wheat and oats, which he hauled.

It was March now, with work in full swing, and they would require his continuous work until their right-hand man removed himself as planned. He plowed and ran a disk harrow while he kept an eye out for Singleton's property.

Sam's own words...
Sunday, March 30, 1913 – "Done chores...George on the look-out for horse thieves."

They had been made aware of horse thieves in the area after animals had vanished. They all knew that horse thieves liked to add to their own job description by robbing banks, trains, and citizens, maybe even check forgery. Singleton had gone to ranchers' meetings on the issue and had reported to Sam and George that there was no talk of lynnch activity as had been so in the recent past. The formation of Anti-Horse Thief Associations in almost all counties had been active to send convicted outlaws to the penitentiary.

The *Leader-Dispatch* of Galeton and Buhl newspapers had informed them all that the 16th amendment to the U.S. Constitution had been ratified and authorized the federal government to impose and collect income taxes. It could have been more of a worry to Sam than were the horse thieves.

On March 21, he paid $19.95 taxes on his land.

Sam continued work for Singleton.

Sam's own words...
Tuesday, April 1, 1913 – "Run disk harrow, five horses, wind, snow, and rain, earned my money."

There was no doubt that he was worth his money. The current weather conditions were the cause for more of a struggle while he pushed on for six more days to harrow, pick stones, and drag fields. He concluded his work for Singleton.

Sam's own words...
Tuesday, April 8, 1913 – "Settled up in full, $161, left Singletons."
Wednesday, April 9, 1913 – "Hired horse and rode out to my Forty..."

There was no problem since his place was just as he had left it.

He stayed three nights in Twin Falls and Buhl. He was sure to have spent time with Edith and her little girl, Willa. His thoughts of Edith played foremost in his mind as the brightest pleasure while he went back to his usual work, but closer to Twin Falls.

Sam had visited Mr. Anderson for whom he would perform work. To start off, he brought him a load of coal and commenced with other jobs for a busy week. He plowed, did chores, and milked seven cows for the duration.

Apparently, word traveled about Sam's excellent workmanship. Mr. Burns hired him on. He cleaned the barn and hauled straw to start each day. In spite of the afternoon rain, Sam plowed until it was time to milk eleven cows each evening.

Sam's own words...
Sunday, April 20, 1913 – "Done chores, The most happy day of my life. (Mine too, Edith), fair and cool."

Edith was still in Twin Falls at the home of her 36-year-old brother, Philip Crow. Sam's happy heart must have brought a smile to him while he wrote his euphoric statement. They were both elated with plans to marry.

He had asked. Edith had answered. "Yes!"

Monday he was right back to work as hard as ever. He plowed, harrowed, and performed chores.

Sam's own words...
Sunday, April 27, 1913 – "Done chores and made a five horse evenor, Edith, Willa, and I went down to the canyon."

Snake River Canyon was beautiful with its shrub lined paths, rocks, and alcoves to explore. The ribbon of river rippled far below and surely sparkled and sang of happiness for the trio who picked their way along a footpath. Sam and Edith could have floated as if they had gliders on their feet, as light as their hearts that beckoned an eagerness to lives that would soon be entwined. The mood was easy for 11-year-old Willa to catch as she floated along with them, fairly dancing as a child is prone to do when happiness is contagious. The petite pixie of a girl had dark tresses like her mother.

Sam and Edith were united in their gladness, each to love and be loved. Sam had someone to care for, to work for, and to bestow his affection upon. It would be different, but also a pleasure to adjust to someone whom he knew appreciated what he did.

He had only Sunday off, but his happy thoughts accompanied him all week while he did mundane chores and the larger jobs for farm crops.

Sam's own words...
Sunday, May 4, 1913 – "Done chores and went to church and store, windy."

Sam attended church with Edith.

On Monday, the same jobs continued all over again, just what he was used to. He also drilled in peas, cleaned irrigation ditches to prepare for later, and treated wheat.

Sam's own words...
Sunday, May 18, 1913 – "Done chores, went down to Ford in p.m., rainy..."
Monday, May 19, 1913 – "Drilled peas, fair, Edith and Willa went to Twin Falls, letter from Ma."

Sam boarded with his employer since he had to be on hand and ready to work. He saw Edith and Willa on Sunday. While Sam was at the ranch to work, they were in Twin Falls at Philips. Sam's smile must have broadened when he saw that a letter had come from Mother. She had received one in Galeton from Sam about his impending marriage. It contained her answer.

~**~

Galeton
May 14, 1913

Dear Sam,
I received your letter a week ago and have just got around to answer it, having been very busy house cleaning.

I was surprised that you are thinking of getting married, and so were we all. Grace said, "I don't want Sam to get married out west for I am afraid he will never come home again." But I think you will want to come and see us just the same, and if you don't sell your land and have to stay there, it will be so much better for you not to be alone. I shall feel that you have a home and someone to care for you and that is better than working for strangers who care nothing for you.

If she is all you say she is, and I think your judgment is pretty good, I am sure she must be a good woman. I sincerely hope that you will be happy and we will all love her because you do. Hope you can both come and see us this fall, but if you can't come home, we'll come to see you sometime in your new home.

Your Pa doesn't say anything much, only laughs and says you are old enough to know what you want.

He is busy making garden. Dewey is helping at home, and Will Eaves is plowing on the Gates farm. We have rented it for this year. Frank (Hess) has been papering it. We have rented the house to an operator.

Mrs. Bruce has come back here to live. Her name is Metcalf now, and she says no place suits her like this or seems like home. I told her your house was for sale. She said maybe they would buy it. I will talk to her some more about it or have your Pa for he is better at making a deal than I. If they don't buy it, will try someone else and will do the best we can for you.

Ralph is working at the car shop and comes home awful black but says the work is not hard.

Sadie is with us yet. She does sewing for the neighbors. Well, I must close. It is 5 o'clock, and I must get supper.

From Mother

~**~

Sam's heart was full as he tipped his head back for a moment and closed his eyes. Ma's approval was what he had needed. It sustained him to have news from home. His siblings' activities were of interest to read about. Best of all, though, was to know of his parents' total acceptance of Edith just because he loved her. His mother's words were enough to call up sentimental tears. Mother's words would be a source of pleasure again and again . How glad he would be to share them with Edith when Sunday came round again.

His work on Anderson's ranch kept him from Edith, who remained at Philip's in Twin Falls. She wanted to see him whenever he could make it happen. Their minds were in sync like their hearts. Sam went to Buhl and Twin Falls on Saturday evening to be in her company and her in his. He intended to stay in town all night but could find no bed.

Sam's own words...
Sunday, May 25, 1913 – "Came back to Buhl and ranch with Edith and Willa, warm."

He was glad to show Edith and Willa where he lived and worked. No doubt he beamed with pride to introduce them as his soon-to-be wife and daughter.

Six days of work remained in May. Anderson deposited $75 in the Buhl Bank account for Sam.

June 1st was upon them. He and his intended with her little girl spent Sunday afternoon down in scenic Snake Canyon and had an enchanted picnic in a bye spot. It was a happy interval before he put in another work week.

Sam's own words...
Saturday, June 7, 1913 – "Edith and Willa in Buhl. Lonesome, warm."
Sunday, June 8, 1913 - "Irrigated, chores. Still lonely, shower in p.m."
Monday, June 9, 1913 – "Settled up in full with Anderson $10.50, came to Buhl."

On Tuesday, Sam went out to his Forty and back, probably on a rented horse. It was just to check on it. He stayed in Buhl at night. On Wednesday, he and Edith billed out their goods for the need of a list of their requirements and what the cost would be.

Sam was in Buhl all day Thursday with Edith and Willa. They finished the list and billing task before going to Edith's brother, Philip, in Twin Falls.

6 – Elation
No Paying Proposition, 1913, 1914

It was so like Sam to groom a garden. He could not allow weeds to take over vegetables or flowers. Philip and his wife, Lenore, got to see that side of their soon-to-be brother-in-law during four days when Sam made himself useful with all manner of odd jobs. Could Edith have failed to be proud of Sam? It didn't hurt at all that Willa was used to him and had all the little telltale signs that she liked him, too. She looked up from her play or a book at times when quiet conversations were in progress. Edith would have been well aware of any smile from Willa if it went in Sam's direction. Her quiet self-entertainment in child's play garnered her lots of information about plans for after the wedding. She didn't mind at all that she would go with her grandmother, Marilla Crow. She had been in Oregon many times with Grandmother and Aunt Mary and Uncle Jack Moore. Her two cousins, Maude and Mabel, were a little older than she.

Sam's own words...
Sunday, June 15, 1913 – "At Philips, ate dinner with Dr. Sawyer, fair."
Monday, June 16, 1913 – "Bought entire outfit, at Philips all day long...warm."
Tuesday, June 17, 1913 – "At Philips, helped pack and worked in garden, fair."

Sam bought a fedora for travel and a suit to be married in at a cost of $34.50.

The fancy, bordered marriage certificate was fitting as the Christian minister signed his name, W. E. Harman. Next, the Recorder, E. J. Finch, signed it and then the Deputy Recorder, Philip H. Crow. The two witnesses who signed it were Lenore and Philip Crow. The Idaho state stamp was pressed into the gold seal to emboss the certificate and proclaim it official. Sam and Edith were joyous. The document would be mailed to them in Crabtree, Oregon after the entry was written into the county record.

Sam's next diary entry communicated his elation.

Sam's own words...
Thursday, June 19, 1913 – "My wedding day. Life seems bright for both of us. Left for Oregon 5:55 p.m., a dandy day."

They arrived in Portland the next day and put up at the Imperial. Edith wore a white dress, an ankle length straight frock with thin vertical stripes. It was her wedding dress, which she had made to use for more than one special day. Rain fell almost unnoticed by the jubilant pair, unable to dampen their moods. The next evening Edith's mother took Willa and journeyed to Lebanon, OR.

The newlyweds spent two more nights at the Imperial. The slim duo's delight with each other showed on their faces. Their palpable happiness at the close proximity of each other was perceptible to anyone who gazed in their direction.

The enamored couple had a small window of indulgence before them. There were no significant choices to make, save those for enjoyment, to watch what was presented in the theater. As Sam and Edith gazed at the plush atmosphere of the opulent cavern, it became as much a part of the show as the silent movie reel they had paid 25¢ to view. The silent films in vogue were making their slow crawl across the country from New York City to the meager number of theater stops. This was as close to the Oregon west coast as the 1912 films would travel. When the piano chords faded, the lights dimmed and went out as the curtain opened on the bright screen. Their fingers may have laced together in the hushed darkness for the 20-minute reel, *The Ghost of Sulphur Mountain*. They were enthralled the next evening, perhaps by *Daddy Long Legs,* a Sherlock Holmes production by Arthur

Pulaski (Lac) Crippen-father   /   Sam Crippen age 30

Sam and Edith Crippen wedding picture
Snake River Canyon backdrop

Edith Haggarty
Crippen age 35

Edith and daughter, Willa at age six (window), 1908 photo post card sent to Edith's sister, Dr. Lydia Crow, Osteopath, in Kirksville, MO. "Hello Sister — We are glad to see you. Willa and I stayed last night with friends who are camping near the lake. Will be with them tonight also. Will write soon.
Edith   (sent from Ashtabula, Ohio)

Willa Haggarty age 11

Conan Doyle. It is safe to say that they probably did not see the alternative choices, *Tarzan of the Apes* or *Robin Hood.*

The connubial couple boarded the train for a slow journey toward Albany, OR. They stayed overnight at beautiful Newport and then Albany before arrival at Jack and Mary's home. Willa may have fairly danced in her exuberance upon her mother and step-father's return. Edith, much the same as Willa, was elated to see her daughter and mother as well as Mary and Jack. She might naturally have been pleased to introduce Sam to her brother-in-law. The house was familiar to her, and she felt at home. Edith had spent her time between visits with them more often than she had stayed with Philip and Lenore, but Sam was the newcomer. His outlook was his usual calm approach with plans to start a job search and find a place to live. He must do both, soon. They were made very welcome and able to relax while Sam found his footing to take care of his new family.

Sam and Jack went to Lebanon after their freight and the next day to look at a farm. He and Jack made a loop around to stop in Crabtree to see if the mail had followed Sam and Edith yet. Sam had a bill from the Leader Dispatch Company in Galeton, Pa. He would not renew the newspaper until he knew what his new address was to be. The $1.50 for the half-year subscription was always worthwhile.

Sam is especially happy to see a letter forwarded from Buhl where Grace had sent it. He recognized Grace's neat handwritten envelope before he saw her name, which made him smile. Jack noticed the pleasure on his face. Sam good-naturedly confessed to a letter from his sister. Jack was in as good a mood as he told Sam to go ahead and take the time to read it. Jack walked over to the blacksmith's to talk in the open barn entrance.

Sam began to read.

~**~

Galeton, Pa.
June 9, 1913

Dear Brother Sam,

I have been thinking about you all day and will write a few lines to ease my mind.

The girls are both in bed, and Roy is working on the night yard engine, so I haven't anything to distract me.

It is very cold here, we had a white frost last night, and

59

nearly everything was frozen, and it is just as cold to-night. We won't have any fruit around here and not much of anything else unless we have better weather.

Pa and Miles Conable are in Buffalo after horses. Pa is looking for a driving horse, and if he finds one, he is going to get a new wagon.

Ralph works in the shops now. He is boiler-markers helper, and he seems to like it. Dewey is driving one of the teams trucking logs.

Sadie and Annabel went to Westfield, PA, today to Archie's brothers for a visit. Archie is out of a job again as usual....

Well, Sam, your wedding day is pretty close at hand, and it makes me sad to think about it, but I don't suppose it does you. I hate to think of your going still farther away from home. I would like to see you and have a good talk with you once more. After you get to Oregon, be sure and write to me. I would like to send you some kind of a wedding present but will wait until you get settled, but you know you have my best wishes for a happy, prosperous life and I will think of you on June 19.

I was washing one of Roy's woolen shirts today, and I said to him, "You won't wear this shirt again this summer will you?" He said, "No, it is too small, you can send it to Sam for a wedding present as he will probably need it after he gets married."

Uncle Doc had a letter from Myrtie the other day, and she says Gary is getting weaker all the time. He can only walk from his bed to the next room now, and he can't eat much of anything except fruit. I am afraid he won't never (sic) get better, and Myrtie is terribly worried. Gary wants me to come down, and I am going the last of June.

Well, Sam, I must close and go to bed, and I suppose this is the last letter I will ever write to you while you are in Idaho. Be sure and write soon when you get to Oregon.

With love and best wishes. From Grace.

P.S. Geo Swan is in Oregon. His address is Bune, OR. His horse fell on him and broke his leg not long ago. He wrote and wanted to know your address.

~**~

Sam appreciated all of the family news Grace wrote about but had not expected reluctant reaction to his marriage. She could wish him the best all she wanted, but she had first expressed enough disapproval to cause him concern. He cared about what she thought. His close relationship with her gave him compassion for her dismay with him. He hadn't supposed she would think of his marriage as any loss to her, certainly not an end to their closeness. He wanted Grace to feel better about his chosen circumstance and have no misgivings on his wedlock. His matrimony was not subject to change. How could he keep this letter private from Edith and give it time so that no hard feeling developed between them, sight unseen, two people whom he loved?

He had no wish to keep anything from Edith, and he would not start a marriage that way. He would have to gently talk with Edith and frame it as Grace's sisterly love along with her usual up-front opinions.

Sam remembered back to a postcard Grace had sent him in 1907, a card he still had from Jersey City, PA. It was the year that she and Roy had lived in that locality. She missed Sam then, too. Grace had written, "Come down, and I will help you find a wife." She wanted her esteemed big brother near her. He had been 24 years old at the time, and now he was 30 and Edith was 35. Grace was 28. It made him all the more grateful for Mother's ready acceptance. He hoped she would have a real influence on Grace's attitude over time. He had no choice but to leave it at that. He hoped Grace would understand in time and that she may have gotten it out of her system just by writing about it.

He would not mention the contents of the letter on his diary page.

On two successive days, the Crippen and Moore families all went together to pick cherries and blackberries.

The weekend had no paying proposition, but Sam helped with chores and hoed corn in Jack's garden. He was true to his industrious nature, with the contribution to the Moore household while he, Edith, and Willa remained there.

Sam received a letter, which had been forwarded from Buhl, Idaho to Lebanon, Oregon. His mother had answered his letter but had learned that he and Edith had already moved to Oregon. She wrote again, and Sam received both letters at once. She liked abbreviations. Sam was used to them and had some of his own.

~**~

Galeton, PA
June 18, 1913

Dear Sam,

In answer to your letter, would say we are all well and happy.

You seem fond of surprising us lately. I wish I could be there and go to Oregon with you. Has Edith ever been there and has she always lived in the west?

I am all alone today. Sadie and Annabel are visiting at Westfield, PA, at Archie's brothers. I just heard that Archie has skipped a $35 board bill downtown and don't know where he is. But they have a warrant for him, and I hope they find him.

Your father is at Buffalo after horses with Will Conable. He is going to get a driving horse for us...

Mr. Metcalf thinks of buying the house where Newmans live. If he does, your Pa says he will take yours. Metcalf wants to raise chickens. There could be more room for them to walk around down there.

Dewey says tell you to bring your wife home. He wants to see her.

Your Pa is back, and Dewey just took our horse up to the barn. It is a dark gray four-year-old. Dewey says she is quite a nice one.

Ralph went to town last night and joined the union.

I would send your rent money but would like to send the money for the house and that together. Write and tell me if you need money bad. I will send it at once. I hope we can send the money for the house soon...

Now be sure and write and tell me all about everything.

There is an excursion Sunday to Niagara Falls (NY), and we talk of going to it, come back the same night.

Love to all, Mother

~**~

Galeton, PA
6/18/1913

Dear Sam,

I suppose you are looking for a letter. I received yours last week. Am glad you like it in Oregon and hope you will do well there.

I wish I could have some of them strawberries that are plentiful there. This is a very poor season for all kinds of fruit and strawberries have not been less than 15¢ a basket. The late frost killed all the apples and pears.

The boys got the cards you sent them, today, and Dewey said he would like to be out there and get some of them apples to eat.

It has been very warm this summer. How is it there?...If you stay there, I am coming to visit you maybe next spring. I can come alone if it is necessary for I don't think anybody else will come.

Grace is nearly well again. She was in bed two weeks with tonsillitis. Dr. Steele said it was the worst case he saw. It was as near diphtheria as it could be and not be that. You know how the girls go in the water and she went in one day when the water was cold. Mary was with her, but it did not hurt her. I think Grace will be more careful in the future. Her general health is better. She hasn't had the trouble with her side since a year ago. Roy did not go to Gettysburg or Grace to Jersey Shore.

Grace and I are going to Jersey Shore the first of August if nothing happens.

Sadie has been home since last November. She has found out that there is no use trying to live with Archie. There are letters and pictures in her possession that the lawyer tells her is evidence enough. She has started proceedings of divorce. We are helping her.

I will tell you all about it some other time, how she got the letters and what he had been doing.

We have a new surrey and went riding yesterday for the first time with the new horse.

You say you have the best wife in the world. I know she has a good husband, one that will appreciate her. I would like to see both her and the little girl. I am sure she is nice.

We have just heard that Gary is worse and that he is a hopeless case. It's a shame.

I had my teeth out on the third of July. He used something to numb the gums, and I did not feel any pain, and my mouth has not been a bit sore. I was not a bit sick and went right ahead with my work as usual....

I will close for this time. Write and tell me if you get the farm and all about it.

From Mother

Thank you and Edith for the shopping bag. It is very nice and just what I needed.

~**~

Sam tucked the letters in his shirt pockets as Jack stepped up. They walked to the house together.

Jack knew Sam had a job to start on Monday.

Sam's own words...
Monday, July 7, 1913 – "Ran mower for the company, (1 day)."

It was warm every day as he continued with work and family life. There was a heat wave across the nation and the newspapers exclaimed about the high temperatures recorded. On July 10, Death Valley, California, hit 134 degrees Fahrenheit (56.7 C), the highest temperature recorded in the world. If Sam were alive, today he would know that it remains an unbroken record.

In mid-July, Andy Gardell, wrote in answer to Sam's letter.

~**~

Buhl, Idaho
7/16/1913

Mr. Sam Crippen
     Crabtree
Dear friend,

I received your letter a few days ago and was glad to hear from you. How do you like that part of Oregon?...

How are the crops there? It is warm here now every day and things look fine, but water is getting low in the later- als, as usual, this time of year. Had a fine first crop of hay and will have a good second if water holds out for a while yet and third is too far off to tell about. My oats are certainly fine waist high, and one more watering will ripen them, and there is a fine stand of clover all over what was sowed.

Miss Kelly and her husband, Mr. Mc Gram, were here about two weeks ago and they said I could have their place another year. So I will take your place too if we can agree on a price this fall as I want to do my plowing this fall if it is possible.

Was sorry that I could not come to Buhl to see you before you left but I was haying at Reynolds and it would of *(sic)* laid two or three of us off if I came to Buhl. So could not come. Wrote you a postal telling you that I could not come but I guess you did not get it. We are going to haying again at Reynolds Monday the 21st of July. I will be busy from now on again for a while.

Southworth sold his lambs in Chicago (Illinois) the other day and realized $6 per head. Gave him $5 clear of expenses. That's the only thing to make money out of.

Well goodbye. Good regard to all and write soon.

From Andy

~**~

Sam thought about Andy's crops as he recorded similar work to mow, shock, or hay it. They filled weekends with picking berries, cherries, and Logan berries. He did chores each day for a company he did not name, but it was temporary work. He helped to put up fruit, never standing back from work that needed to be done. He shoveled gravel for the township during the last three warm days of July.

Sam made his usual best efforts to earn a wage, but the newlyweds had no place of their own yet. When he got the letter from Andy about all of the familiar crops for work on a ranch where they had both worked, he may have wished he was back there. But he wasn't, and he would try harder to make a go of it here since it would please Edith to have her mother and Mary's family nearby. Their 70 years old mother, Marilla, lived in the old family home on a hill a few miles from Jack and Mary. She was no longer young.

Sam had farm work to start in August. On the first of the month, after chores were done, he looked at a farm that he wanted to lease. In a few days, between chores and hauled oats, they looked at a place for rent in town but did not take it. He pitched hay for a new temporary source, did chores, and cut wood. In successive days, he hunted for a cow, cut corn, and went after plums and oats. He would not take unfair advantage of extended hospitality. Sam pulled his weight.

He thought with fondness of his folks and Galeton when he wrote a letter home.

Sam's own words...
Tuesday, August 19, 1913 – "Went to Crabtree, OR, and looked at a farm, warm."
Friday, August 22, 1913 – "Rented farm near Crabtree $150, Went to Albany and back."

The one-year agreement for the lease of the 50-acre fruit tree farm between Sam and Mr. R. V. Waddle was drawn up by attorney L. M. Curl. All crops harvested by Sam would belong half to Sam and half to Waddle. There was a kitchen range on the premises, which Sam purchased for $15 cash.

Sam was again in charge of his own abode, in charge of plenty of work and in charge of trying to make a go of it. He and Edith and Willa needed supplies to set up housekeeping. Edith wrote the staples on a crowded list that held 52 items and the expected price after each one. They included spices 10¢, salt 75¢, yeast 5¢, soap 25¢, matches 25¢, and clothes pins 25¢, among the many necessities. They went to the T. C. Turner Co. of Lebanon, OR, the same day to collect their goods.

They were carefree again with self-sufficiency, and it gave Edith and Willa the means to keep house, cook, and do laundry. At 11 years old, Willa could be useful with skills she learned from her mother. Edith required her help to put items away in the pantry.

Sam had one more job to thresh for B. Renley, which he did in 14 hours. Now he could get to work on his orchards.

A bright spot was a hurried letter from Grace. It had been a while since she had written because she had been sick. Sam smiled at the sight of the recognizable hand-written envelope.

~**~

Galeton, PA
Aug. 18, 1913

Dear Sam,

I will write you a few lines this morning in a great hurry so that you will know that Pa has made arrangements to get the $600 for you from Mr. Long by the 8th of September. He could get it sooner, but Mr. Long would lose his interest if he draws it out of the bank before that time. Also, Pa said that he might be able to send it himself before that time, and he would have had it, but we had such a poor winter for him to get his logs in last winter.

I am in a great hurry, so I am writing this before breakfast.

We are all well, and Mother and I expect to go to Jersey Shore to see Gary next Saturday. Will write to you after I get back home.

With love, From Grace

~**~

Sam cut wood all morning long. Jack came out in the afternoon to see the farm and haul a load of logs for him.

Sam's own words...
Thursday, August 28, 1913 – "Mowed out pear orchard, went to depot after pear boxes, cut wood and helped clean house."
Friday, August 29, 1913 – "Bought cow from Jack and brought her home ...warm."

Sam sawed the logs into chunks. The cow ran away, and he brought her back and fixed the fence. September had predictable cold and cloudy weather. It took him the first five days of the month to pick pears, for which he had a buyer. He shipped the pears.

During this time, Sam wrote on a diary page that Willa was sick. The fact that he included it in his diary was a sign of his care and concern for Edith's daughter. His hard work neither prevented a tender heart nor caused him to lose sight of what was important.

He cleaned the chicken house, sawed more wood, and picked plums. There must be more to keep a man busy. Sam weighed the wheat and oats he'd bought, pitched bundles, and jigged sacks. He was efficient and hired himself out to jig bags for three people. He put in 26 hours for F. Wisner, 5.5 hours for Mr. Holiday, and five hours for J. T. Richards.

Gary died September 14, 1913. His only daughter, Myrtie, would mourn the hardest and Sam supposed he was the sorriest for her. It was another good thing that Mother and Grace had compassion and had gone to see him. He mused that Gary was a step-second cousin but had figured more prominently in both their boyhoods than now. Still, it was sad.

Sam had work to do.

Edith was sick. Sam could see that she felt ill and was in bed. He did the wash, went after hogs, and got groceries.

Sam's own words...
Thursday, September 18, 1913 – "Cut a little wood and arranged things in the house, warm. Jack brought Mother out."

Mother Crow was happy to see their surroundings on her short visit. Edith was ill five days, and Willa stayed inside to watch her and give her water to drink. Sam worked hard all the time, right on through all his concern. He didn't have a wage-earner job, but he had plenty of his own tasks at hand. He did chores, picked plums, and performed the housework. Then there were more pears to pick. Some of them were out of reach and had him balanced on a ladder to grasp them. He expected those neglected branches would need a trim before another season. Jack brought Russell when he came out. The three of them took plums to the dryer to process into prunes. He worked for himself but was glad to work for Turnidge a few days for wages.

Sam was happy with Edith but not with his half profits on fruit produce. It had also become apparent that enough payable jobs to supplement their needs as had been available in the countryside of Buhl and Twin Falls were not available here. Sam and Edith had discussed it before and were now able to conclude that it caused too much struggle for him to make a go here no matter how hard he worked. There would be less work in winter, either place, and he could stand that better on his Forty while getting settled in and getting ready for spring.

His September 29 letter gave notice in writing to R. V. Waddle that they would leave by October 25 and would not return. He got some work with Turnidge and a Mr. Boag and some of his own jobs needed attention. He and Edith both had severe colds. Sam made cough syrup to relieve their throats.

They knew a particular bit of information by now, and "a bun in the oven" came to bear on their discussions. Edith was in agreement with the letter that Sam wrote. It was some relief to cut his losses and sell what he could before they vacated the situation. He most likely sold the stove, cow and hogs, all items they wouldn't want to send by freight to Buhl. The transportable part of their household was packed and ready when Jack and Mary visited them. The two men took the wrapped burden to the depot.

Sam must have smiled with pleasure when he opened an unexpected short letter, which contained small pictures from his brother, Dewey. It was close up on five years since Sam left Galeton to travel west but still a wonder to see how much his brother had grown. The wool Gatsby cap cocked on Dewey's head may have played the corners of Sam's mouth upward into a smile. The shortness of the message no doubt added to his pleasant reaction. He figured the passage of time to come up with 15 years as Dewey's age and shook his head. It was no harm at all, he supposed, for Dewey to set himself apart with the dapper flat top. Real life and work would bring him down to earth soon enough, wouldn't it? After all, Sam had set himself apart by coming west.

~**~

Galeton, PA
Sept. 30, 1913

Dear Brother,
I will send you my picture to show you how I look. I am going to get it taken again on a postcard and then I will send you another one.

Goodbye, Dewey

~**~

Sam's own words...
Monday, October 6, 1913 – "Rainy, came to Lebanon, paid F. C. Turner Co. grocery bill $22.10, Spear order $15."

Sam's money was on the way to him from Father, and he was fully prepared to provide care and comfort for his growing family. He and Edith had poured over the Pennsylvania Spear & Co. catalog for home furnishings. No doubt Willa had some interest in their selections. Part of the discussions would have included how they could renovate the shack into a warmer and comfortable home.

They ordered six cane chairs and a breakfast table, three rockers, a Victor Victrola, a white iron bed, springs, mattress and two pillows, kitchen base cabinet, couch bed, linoleum, desk, and two plain chiffonier bureaus. The pack-slip showed that these were tall chest of drawers without mirrors. The order, which totaled $100.43, would be paid off by the month.

Sam and his little family stayed at Jack and Mary's for another week before departing to follow their cargo to Buhl. He kept busy, true to character and made himself useful at Jack's. He ran the clothes washer, dug potatoes, and cut wood. They left from Albany, OR, on October 25.

It took two days and nights of train travel to return to Buhl, where they arrived on Monday, October 27. The next day they went out to Sam's Forty and cleaned the shack. Groceries and hardware were needed, and they secured them the same evening but stayed that night in Buhl.

Sam's own words...
Wednesday, October 29, 1913 – "Went out to Forty in p.m. with my wife and daughter and it is really home now."

Sam put a coat of Alabastine on the shack's outer walls. The thick stucco would help to keep the cold out. Weeds for fuel also offered heat.

They went after their freight goods on the last day of October.

November blew in with wind and rain. Sam fumigated and banked the shack base around the outside walls. The foul weather called for inside work, which needed to be done in preparation for the expected arrival of the new furniture. Sam applied all-purpose Alabastine to the inside walls as another barrier against the cold and to provide better walls. The furniture had not arrived yet, but his usual industriousness took shape in grubbed sage brush to burn for heat. He started on the excavation of a dug cellar, which was not an overnight project.

Andy needed a hand, and Sam was glad to hire himself out for 29 hours during the course of several days. It didn't end there since Andy wanted help to thresh in two sessions for another nine hours.

A letter from Grace arrived on November 11.

~**~

Galeton, PA
Nov. 5, 1913

Dear Brother,

I will try and answer your letter tonight to ease my conscience as it has been troubling me for several days. I have just put the girls to bed, and Roy isn't home yet so I can write without being bothered.

I suppose you are awfully busy and back home again by this time. Your house must be larger than it was when you and Andy kept "Bach" isn't it? Did you buy new furniture or did Edith have some?

Pa sold the gray team today for $600. We hated to see them go but he needs other things worse, and he has another team left.

We had the picture of our house taken last week, and I am going to send you one so you can see how our shanty looks since we have got it fixed up.

Have you and Edith read the book *The Trail of the Lonesome Pine*? If you haven't, I am going to send it to you. There is a song and also a play written after this book. I like it and think that you would. Would you like the *Grit* novels to read? There is a good serial in it now called *Dukane,* and it's a dandy. If you would like to read it, (?) I will send them for you to read on the long winter evenings.

I am cleaning house, and as you are married, I suppose you know what that means or will someday.
Alice, Ruth, and Annabel all go to school and are learning fast. Ralph asked Annabel if she learned anything to *(sic)* school and she said, "Yes," that she could spell cat and dog. He asked her how and she said, "art rat and god dog." So you see she certainly is learning. Does your little girl go to school or can't she where you live?

Ma says that she and Dewey are coming to see you in the spring...

Pa had some nice dandy pigs, and he said that he wished that you lived nearer so he could send you a couple of them. And he wants to know how much a good cow is worth there. Be sure and answer this question and you may get a Christmas present. He is going to send you more money in a few days.

Cretia Crippen's husband, Franklin, died last Tuesday. Her girls are young ladies now and write to Ralph and Dewey and send their pictures. I don't think there is any more news, so I will close with love to you all.

From Grace

~**~

Sam remained fully apprised of what took place back in Galeton when he finished a letter from Grace. She seemed to be over her bent feelings about Sam having married out west. He would answer all of her questions and would thank her for the generosity of the offered books they would be glad to have from her. Edith was happy at the prospect, too. She had brought some reading material with her, and Sam had found some articles to enjoy. There were several volumes, 1896 and 1897 *Munsey* magazines. They had fashions that Edith and Willa sometimes poured over. One particular piece that held Sam's interest was *How Buildings Are Moved*. He'd have time later to read from *North American Review*, an article titled, *A Chat About Gardens*, from 1890.

Several more magazines from 1899 waited for cold winter nights when he could find time for them. Sam knew there were newer publications from 1902 and 1908 also. They all had a price of $1 per year for subscriptions. *The Delineator* caught his eye, a 9" x 12" that was a bit bigger than *Munsey* magazine. It had fashions for boys, girls, and women, as well as stories about cooking and love. But it also had an article, *Gardening for Profit,* and he looked forward to reading it.

Sam met Andy in Buhl and used his own sound credit to cosign with him for a $25 loan. Andy was buying a used Studebaker farm wagon on the strength of Sam's signature along with his own. It was to be paid in one year at 10 percent interest.

Sam's own words...
Saturday, November 15, 1913 – "Finished cellar in a.m., went to Buhl after coal, lumber, and groceries in p.m..."

The basement, which had taken seven days of digging, was hollow-ed out, but he had work to do inside of the cave before he could store potatoes and beans in it. He applied more Alabastine on the exterior of the shack and banked more along the basement room. The work in the cellar slowed while Edith was sick again and Sam kept house and cooked. Willa did small jobs to help him.

Sam may have read aloud to Edith as she lay back to listen to newspaper news with a special message from the president.

"Righteousness exalteth a nation' and 'peace on earth, good will towards men' furnish the only foundation upon which can be built the lasting achievements of the human spirit...Now, Therefore, I, Woodrow Wilson, President of the United States of America, do hereby designate...a day of thanksgiving and prayer, and invite the people throughout the land to cease from their wonted occupations and in their several homes and places of worship render thanks to Almighty God." Woodrow Wilson concluded: "In Witness Whereof, I have hereunto set my hand and caused the seal of the United States to be affixed. Done at the City of Washington this 23rd day of October, in the year of our Lord one thousand nine hundred and thirteen."

Sam's own words...
Saturday, November 22, 1913 – "Worked on cellar in a.m., went to Buhl in p.m. after furniture and groceries, cold wind."

On Sunday, he unpacked the partial shipment and set up furniture. Like most children, Willa would have tried a cane chair pulled up to the table as soon as it was ready for use.

Sam made a cellar door, cleaned beans and did the wash. Together, he and Edith prepared Thanksgiving dinner of parsnips, baked potatoes, and beans. Earlier Edith had made pie crust even though she was still not at her best. Sam split, seeded, and peeled pumpkin to cook into the pulp she needed for pie.

At the turn of the century, 1900, the Libby Company had expanded their canning operation of corned beef and added on vegetables and fruit. Libby grew pumpkins in the mid-western states for the canneries. Edith may not have been able to afford canned pumpkin, but she more than likely knew of its existence and would have embraced the idea.

Willa had written a story about the first Thanksgiving in her scrawled cursive. Sam kept it in his valuable records, and that must have pleased the child. It is likely that Sam's attitude promoted a healthy relationship. The essay was preserved in the trunk along with many artifacts, letters, newspapers, and the couple's marriage license.

Why stop now when jobs waited, and he could finish November up right? Sam moved fruit to the cellar, cleaned the cistern, and completed housework.

Edith remained ill. There were days she was a little better but not yet well. A tender touch between them said more than words. Sam sympathized and was supportive. She appreciated a husband who took care of her daughter, too.

Edith was five months along in her delicate condition. Sam was no doubt enamored with the telling plumpness beneath her apron and the idea of his first child.

He had put their shack in good condition, a home comfortable to live in with his wife and daughter. Yet, he continued to call it a shack and had smiled that Grace had called her improved house a shanty, much in the same humble terminology.

Money dwindled as winter closed in. It was necessary to be frugal.

Sam's own words...
Wednesday, December 3, 1913 – "Laid flooring, cut stovepipe hole, moored stove..."
Thursday, December 4, 1913 – "Made cupboards, painted floor, Edith feeling bad..."

Of course, he was worried about his dear wife, but as usual, he could worry while he worked close by and inside. He kept an eye on her and was pleasant to Willa, who responded with smiles. Dark hair fell toward her face while she leaned over the table to read a book her mother had put before her. Edith had been a school teacher in Wyoming and had brought books with her. Willa knew the 1887 book, *Samantha at Saratoga* by Marietta Holley, had been kept for her. Holley writings were favorably compared to that of Mark Twain. The book had been a Christmas gift to Edith from 1898. The writing inside the front cover conveyed when and from where it came. Many years in the future, Willa would pencil inside it, her own married name, *Willa Walker*.

There was another book on the shelf titled *Gods and Heroes* by Francillon (1894). It was from Aunt Lydia. The penciled writing inside the front of it said *Lydia E. Crow, May 4, 1901, Ord, Nebraska*. Before Aunt Lydia died, she had given it to Willa.

Sam applied Kalsomine to the bedroom walls again and then applied the Alabastine stucco over it. He laid flooring and finished odd jobs. Cellar steps were made with the two by fours cut for his planned addition on the barn. He took one day to build the extra space on the side of the animal enclosure. The next day Sam and Andy went after hogs.

Sam's own words...
Saturday, December 13, 1913 – "Brought furniture from Buhl, borrowed $50 from Mr. Tillery, made two payments on furniture, $30."
Sunday, December 14, 1913 – "Unpacked furniture, cleaned floor and laid linoleum."

The desk and both tall chiffoniers were the last of the furniture to arrive. The desk was to be important to them to write letters and store the paper, envelopes, and stamps. Sam used it right away to write a letter to Jack and thank him for a box sent to them. Mother Crow had sent them $50. It was appreciated and also required a written thank you note in response.

They had important papers that would have priority drawer space and many cubbyholes for various uses.

Halfway through December, Sam sent a small 3" x 6" booklet home to Galeton with Christmas sentiments. The title of it was *Forbearance,* printed in 1910 by the Hayes Lithograph Company of Buffalo, NY. Each page contained a poignant phrase surrounded with flowery motifs. One that would have appealed to Sam and his father, Lac, was this: *The tendency to persevere, to persist in spite of hindrances...it is this that distinguishes the strong soul from the weak.* The small book was inside the trunk with a handwritten salutation in front, which said:

> *Dear Father - My sincere wishes for a Happy*
> *Christmas and New Year. Love from all, Sam*

Sam grubbed brush to burn in the stove every day because money was too scarce to spend it on coal. Nobody had hired him, and he had hunkered down for the winter. The mood was bleak even though it was almost Christmas. They spent what they must on groceries of $5.05 to go with potatoes, vegetables, and fruit that they relied on from the dugout room below.

Sam's own words...
Monday, December 22, 1913 – "Quite a blizzard in a.m. Our shack some cold with sage brush for fuel."

It was necessary that they wear extra clothes inside to try to keep warm. Sam grubbed and cut brush to burn and carried it on his back.
Nineteen thirteen ended a little dreary. What would next year bring?

7 – Grub and Scrub
David, 1914

Sam's 1914 diary had the usual face page information. He listed repetitive self-statistics and his new location as the Forty, six miles southwest of Buhl. His age was 30 years, and he was light complexioned. In the case of emergency or severe illness his wife and Mr. Lac Crippen of Galeton, PA, were to be notified. Each year's diary started with an update.

Finances to start January were nonexistent, but Sam had a letter with $50 sent as a loan from Jack and $75 borrowed from Mr. Anderson. Without much work available, he needed the loans, and thanks to his good name and credit he got them.

Sam bought coal to heat against the January cold. It worked better than sagebrush to provide comfort for his wife, who was ill. Two days in a row Edith felt worse. While Sam worried, he continued to grub brush for use and stretch the coal. Taxes were due, and $18.31 was paid on January 6, also $5 to the dentist, and $9 to Andy for shared freight costs.

Sam's own words...
Saturday, January 10, 1914 – "Went to Buhl, sent for sewing machine and bought washing outfit, cold and clear."

Sam mopped the kitchen floor, blackened the stove, and did the wash.

The washer apparatus made it easier for him and Edith, according to which one of them was able to do that chore. It was what he thought of as a necessity for a "woman-with-child," and there would be many baby items to wash as soon as the baby arrived. Edith was eager to receive and use the sewing machine that was on order for $16.69. She lay propped up in bed and had crocheted several pieces of border trim in different widths to add onto little gowns and coverlet edges.

Sam went to see Mr. Morris, and the next day they went together to get groceries. He had short work to help Mr. Morris load hogs in moderate but cloudy weather. Snow made an appearance every few days.

Mr. Loveless needed chores done for a whole week. Sam was glad to take the job.

On January 31, the sewing machine arrived in Buhl, and Sam brought it home to Edith. Willa must have been interested to watch her mother use it and learn how it worked. She knew how to sew by hand and could use tiny stitches to attach lace to little nightgowns. It had been learned from the necessity to darn socks. Willa knew the obvious that she would soon have a sibling.

February blew in cold and windy, no change from January. Sam walked to Mr. Anderson's, 2.25 miles away. A little work was found here and there, from Mr. Morris and Mr. Pitt. He put up ice and butchered and grubbed brush. At home, there was housework and his chores.

Sam was glad to hear from Grace and sat down at his desk to write a letter home. The sewing machine that was in daily use now needed adjustment. Edith felt an urgency to complete a layette for their new baby's needs.

In Buhl, Sam inquired at the bank for a farm loan. He helped Mr. Morris again, and Mr. Loveless asked him to perform four more days of chores. Whatever job could be gotten, he took, but it was not enough, not equivalent to full-time pay.

Sam, Edith, and Willa went into Buhl so both adults could sign papers for operation money. He was much relieved, and his jaw not set quite so tightly. But a smile didn't surface; after all, his going deeper into debt allowed no comfort. There'd be no digging himself out until the weather signaled work into full swing in the spring season. The weather turned milder but was not without a snow squall on March 1.

He gathered brush to have ready for use and did the wash. In a good natured way, it was written down as grub and scrub.

The loan allowed Sam to buy a cow for $62.70 and to put a lock on the shack door. He hauled a jag of hay for the cow. Work lined up as he built a hog pen, filled the water cistern, and worked on the outhouse. The frigid wind had come through cracks in the privy walls, too swift for comfort.

Sam purchased a wagon from Mr. Newhart for $15 and paid $225 for a team of horses from Mr. Roessier. He was anxious to start the work just ahead. He helped Mr. Morris draw loads of hay and brought himself one load. The horses and one cow would devour it. Each day required grubbed brush, but Sam had many jobs. He brought chickens home, did the wash, and built a bookshelf. Mr. Russum hired him, and he welcomed the chance for paid labor.

The work began. He plowed, harrowed, and raked brush. There never seemed to be a shortage of brush in Idaho. What if all of it, the work and Sam, came to an end? His consideration was serious because of his young family. He decided that they needed protection if the worst should happen. A life insurance policy with W. J. Hamilton from Prudential Insurance Company had cost him $10 for six months. The $19.44 to pay a whole year had been a little steep for his pocket in late February, but he planned to pay it by the March 26 deadline to keep the policy in force. Edith was, of course, the beneficiary and no doubt appreciated it along with peace of mind for both of them.

More work trickled in but not fast enough to meet obligations and support his family well. Sam didn't lack worries nor jobs to do even when they were on his home ranch. Sam did them all, pay or no pay. Money was required for the impending birth as Edith's time was drawing near.

Sam's own words...
Friday, March 27, 1914 – "Plowed and harrowed in a.m. Took Edith and Willa to Buhl in afternoon"
Saturday, March 28, 1914 – "Plowed and harrowed, done cooking, Lonesome."

Willa was home by Monday. She had turned 12 years old on her March 19 birthday. She could go to school and come home to be alone in the shack and make herself useful while Sam farmed. They both waited for Edith to announce the birth.

Sam's own words...
Wednesday, April 1, 1914 – "Drilled in wheat and clover seed, received message telling of the birth of 'our boy' at 7:45 am., Tuesday, 31st."

Baby boy, David Crippen, was a robust newborn weighing 11¾ pounds. Edith wrote to Sam several times while she was confined in Buhl for recuperation. Sam answered Edith's letter, foremost, but he wrote a letter home to Galeton just days after his son's birth. Willa was back with her mother again and got acquainted with little brother. The letters continued back and forth between the new parents until Edith wrote that she could return home.

Sam's own words...
Sunday, April 12, 1914 – "Broke the Sabbath, but I just drew a load of hay, cleaned shack and planted a few onions, peas, lettuce, cabbage, corn, and beans."
Monday, April 13, 1914 – "Went to Buhl after Edith and boy but Mrs. Denton decided to bring them out, and they had a runaway and were hurt."
Tuesday, April 14, 1914 – "Went after Edith and Willa. Edith badly shaken...Glad to have my folks home."

Sam's emotions are all there between the lines. A runaway horse could have had much worse consequences.

The bills for Dr. Sawyer, $25, and Miss Electra Nesbit, $37 for hospital fees, had arrived. Sam was prompt to pay them with money he borrowed for the purpose. The payments to the bank followed. He had bought coal to keep his family warm and also a generous supply of groceries at $7.05. It eased his mind to provide comfort for his wife and children. He'd had steady work while they were gone and it would continue.

He had spent $9.20 for wheat at the same time Andy ordered barley. They combined their freight to economize, and Sam's share was $4. Cooperation was fully extended between one another wherever they could see the benefit.

Sam plowed, harrowed and planted. It was done in between house-work and a large wash while Edith slowly improved. Now he knew firsthand how useful the washer had become. Too much time was consumed to hang clothes on the line. One job led to another.

He planted a huge garden with spuds, beets, radishes, tomatoes, and onion seed. The clover required irrigation. Sam helped Mr. Morris three-fourths of a day to clean ditches.

He and Edith welcomed congratulations from Galeton on their baby boy.

In early May, Sam took the cow over to Young's and paid $2 for bull service. He irrigated strawberries and clover and butchered a hog, which he hung up. Within a few days, it was cut up, packed in a barrel in the cellar, and salt brine poured in. Edith was still weak, and he may have helped with the task of cooking and reducing fat to remove impurities. Pig fat rendered, yielded lard needed for cooking and baking.

Sam's crop and garden labor were constant. He bought a screen door and lumber to make boxes.

The relished $120 payment on his Galeton house arrived.

He went to Morris's and bought little chicks. Imagine three reactions. Willa thought they were so cute, but Edith said they wouldn't be little for long. Sam just smiled. He had paid $16 for timothy seed and a talking record for Edith to play on the Victrola. It was a small pleasure they would all enjoy in the evenings.

Sam's own words...
Saturday, June 6, 1914 – "Turned water on alfalfa and went to Buhl after Mother and groceries. Frost... made land payment with interest."

Snow the day before and now the frost had Sam concerned for tender shoots that appeared in his garden. A little time abated his angst.

He pushed himself and his team of horses at home and also hired out to Andy and Mr. Reid with relentless hours kept into July. He charged for use of his labor and the equine pair but found time to work on his own ranch with them. Only a little time had been spent with Edith's mother and his wife and children in the evening before he was compelled to sleep. He had noticed that his boy was growing and was well cared for and that Willa was sweet on her baby brother. Sam likely managed a smile for her and was glad for her help to her mother since he must work.

Sam's own words...
Saturday, July 4, 1914 – "Irrigated: Ate picnic dinner in Mr. Bockman's grove, partly cloudy and a little rain."

It is no surprise that he took time for the Fourth of July! He made it a family day. Mother Crow enjoyed the outing before she went back to Philip and Lenore Crow's home on Sam's next trip to Buhl and Twin Falls.

The next day on Sunday he tended the water and tried to rest. For the remainder of July, Sam worked non-stop for himself, Andy, Reid, Mr. Loveless, and Mr. Russum. August arrived with dog-day temperatures. His pace did not slacken as he shocked hay and hauled wheat while irrigation continued. If all the work meant money, he ought to have been rolling in dough soon.

Sam's own words...
Sunday, August 2, 1914 – "Irrigated, hot, Edith sick with headache."

As busy and as he was, he worried about Edith. He'd give anything to erase her pain.

Sam hired out to run the slip scraper in ditches for Andy, the bundle wagon for Reynolds, and the thresher for Mr. Morris. He used his own horses.

Edith's head hadn't gotten better until she had a tooth treated two weeks later on August 17. While they were in Buhl, they had pictures taken of baby David posed with his lace-trimmed gown and blanket on the photographer's staging divan.

Mr. Andrews and Mr. Prince required Sam's help to thresh. Mr. Russum needed him eight hours to stack peas.

Sam's own words...
Sunday, August 23, 1914 – "Edith and I went to Buhl to meet Mary, ate dinner with the Dentons."

It was a well-earned interval for Sam and a relished time away to see Edith's sister down from Oregon for a visit. Forty-Five-year-old Mary came home with them. In a few days, she and Edith enjoyed a trip to Buhl.

Edith had been very pleased to show her sister the new furnishings and the shack improved with stucco. They appeared to be prospering. A lot of work had transpired, and as long as Mary stayed on, she helped Edith with the garden and preserves. The cellar received produce into storage for the winter. They juggled work along with Mary's enjoyment of her new nephew and her sweet niece, Willa.

Sam worked for Mr. Andrews and Mr. Loveless to thresh, irrigate, and corrugate. The money came in but was spent as he paid a $70 note at the bank. He drew on his banked supply of money for him and Edith for necessities. There was a $1 shoe repair, a 78 rpm record for $1, and peaches for $2. Their hard work and sweet life had its perks. Mary enjoyed the music with them, perhaps the song sung by Bill Murray, *I Wonder Who's Kissing Her Now?* Bruce Young wrote and released it in 1909.

Sam got a supply of $8 worth of coal as signs of the cooler weather appeared. They had their first frost on the early morning of September 12.

Sam's own words...
Tuesday, September 15, 1914 – "Very stormy, cold a.m., worked on a cow shed in p.m."
Thursday, September 17, 1914 – "Went to Buhl after coal. Edith, Mary, and children went on a visit to Twin Falls."

Their brother, Philip, wanted to see both of his sisters, and a visit was ideal while Mary was still with them. They planned to stay over because Philip's wife, Lenore, was a gracious hostess and they anticipated that she could hardly let them go. They would have smiled as they told Sam it would be longer than a day visit.

Sam's own words...
Sunday, September 20, 1914 – "Went to Buhl to meet train. Edith and son came home, but Willa had to stay because of an operation, Wind."

Four days later they were glad to go to Buhl after Willa and groceries. Sam was forever stacking clover and neglectful to explain further if Willa's procedure was for the remedy of an injury, ailment, or dysfunction in her body. Speculation reasons that her tonsils and possibly adenoids had given trouble every time she had a cold, which was often. They may have been removed.

Sam had a letter from Grace and answered it a week later.

He worked in the cellar to make room for 20 sacks of wheat that he hauled from the field. It was a crop he could sell.

Russum needed Sam's help to make hay. Sam would work with him when others would not but was not too impressed with the ill-tempered man at times.

Sam's own words...
Monday, September 28, 1914 – "Helped Mr. Russum make hay. I like him today..."

He allowed Mr. Loveless use of his team, which may have been a favor to be returned if needed. When Sam had his horses back, he brought watermelon from the field, another crop to sell. Barley was drawn in next.

A box of apples arrived from Galeton. The delight brought smiles all around.

Sam worked for Andy, Mr. Reid, and Anderson on different days, mostly with hay. He sandwiched his farm work in between them. Andy hired him for several 10-hour days to run a slip on eroded ditches where sides had caved inward. As the thick iron bottom was pulled, it moved over the dirt and gouged into the soil to smooth it back into the former compacted V'd ditch shape.

Sam's own words...
Sunday, October 18, 1914 – "Cool, about half sick with a cold. Edith not very well."

While Edith was under the weather Sam's neuralgic back plagued him for several days. A headache added to the fun before Sam felt better, but he did his chores. Sunday seemed like the right time to write a letter home.

The weekdays were not so laid back. Sam filled them with plow, pitch or haul of one thing or another right into evening in time for chores. They sat down to supper as soon as he had finished. He went into Buhl Saturday night for groceries and coal. On Sunday, only the necessary chores were done, and a letter written to Edith's mother. On Monday, Sam dug a portion of his potatoes and threshed for Mr. Ring. Tuesday morning, he and Edith went to vote.

Sam dug spuds at every chance to add to a pit for storage. Other-wise, he threshed for Mr. Ring and Mr. Reynolds. Andy bought 4,066 pounds of potatoes from him. Andy and Russum helped with the job. When they were all removed from the field, Sam harrowed over the land. There were more to dig, but they'd wait on other things, which took priority.

Sam was able to settle up with the Buhl Bank & Trust and Swanner Mercantile Company where he had bought groceries and hardware on credit.

Mr. Russum had him dig potatoes eight hours and thresh peas. He was ready to thresh clover for himself, Andy, and Morrison. Afterward, Sam got back to more of his own spuds and dragged them to the pit. He also transported peas to town for Russum and brought back the man's coal. Russum soon had more work for Sam.

Sam's own words…
Thursday, November 12, 1914 – "Mr. Russum fooled me all of the a.m., so I did nothing. I forgive him. Hauled clover seed to Buhl."

Sam's mild manner came through in how he treated Russum well when it was not how the man addressed him. He had shown up there to work. Russum changed his mind but had him hang around and wait with the implied expectation of labor. The man was an irregular person, and most others wanted no dealings with him. Sam took more of Russum's peas to town on Saturday. While he was in Buhl, he sent a postal money order of $33.43 as the payoff to the Spears Company in Pennsylvania. The furniture was paid in full. He must have smiled as the sealed envelope slipped into the postal slot with the payment inside.

He sold 1,043 pounds of clover for $130.60.

It was easy to relax on Sunday, and Sam went to see Mr. Loveless in the evening.

Andy needed help to load hay, and Russum had potatoes to dig. They looked for help from the best worker they had. Sam's bean harvest was next on the agenda. He pulled them and threshed them before a trip to Mr. Pitt's sale and bought a harness for $20. He took a note to pay it off in a year's time. Mr. Loveless and Andy had more work for Sam. Sam never said no or that he was too busy. Sunday, November 22, dirt was pushed over one potato pit, and then Sam hauled brush and barley.

Sam's own words...
Wednesday, November 25, 1914 – "Burned brush...horses left home."

He hunted the animals a half day with no luck. The deserters were not ready to be found. It was enough to lose sleep over, but when a hard-worker is exhausted and lies his head down, slumber follows. The next day was a repeat. He shook his head when he told Edith about the ordeal. He needed those horses. On the third day, he spent all day searching for them and found them eight miles from home. He was upset over time lost and ready to work them hard. Hay was hauled, dry manure put on potato pits, and a load of brush drawn.

They went to the school house in the evening. No doubt Willa felt valued. She was proud to have parents that took interest on how she had performed in school.

Some of the same jobs were repeats and brush was always in that category. Sam didn't clean a chicken coop all that often but it was time for it on December 4. When finished, he fumigated it for lice. At an earlier time, Sam plainly impressed on Willa that she must not be careless if she gathered a few eggs for her mother. If she touched her head on any surface, she could become infested. She was careful.

Mr. Morris helped him four hours to clean clover seed. Sam helped him take a cow to Scully Ranch and back to be bred. The cold eastern gale hindered the fanner operation. Sam cleaned Mr. Morris's clover seed for 6.5 hours. The wind changed direction and blew dust from the exercise into his face.

Sam went to Buhl for groceries and coal while he also took two sacks of clover seed to sell to B. P. & G. Co. He banked up the chicken coop to protect his chickens from the chill of the constant blowing wind.

It was December 8, and he mailed Edith's envelope with $2 for 18 months renewal of her Mizpah membership.

They all had colds, but Edith's and David's were the worst.

Sam grubbed brush as often as he ate. Andy went with him to Buhl after groceries. He drew hay for two days and helped Edith wash clothes two days in a row to get caught up.

Willa and Edith were ecstatic with the company they expected. Sam was amiable and pleasant that Mary was coming down from Oregon.

Sam's own words...
Thursday, December 24, 1914 – "Went to Buhl after Mary; brought out coal and groceries, went to schoolhouse in evening."

It was a joyous Christmas Eve, and Willa quite likely was complimented on her part in the Christmas play. A shy smile spread across her face showing how she felt about the praise.

After Sam had done the chores on December 25, he put up some shelves. He was bothered with a toothache the next day, and it was not so easy to be pleasant now, but he would not act otherwise.

On Sunday, Mr. Russum came to call. He may not have known that Sam was a man with a Christian upbringing, but he desired to have him as a friend. Mr. Russum hadn't always acted as if he cared, but Sam's own private forgiveness and forthright kindness may have found the better part of the man's nature. Could it be that Mr. Russum recognized that Sam was authentic and the Christmas spirit had been present for months because of this uncommonly decent man? The season didn't bring it out for just one day with Sam.

In the evening, the family visited Morris's.

Sam settled up with Andy in full, and it had a good feel for the end of the year. He would have liked to be able to pay everyone he owed and become debt-free. He thought of Mr. Anderson to whom he still owed $70 out of $75 from a loan back at the end of January. It would soon be a year, and it bothered him. He had to let the thought go and intended to pay it as soon as he could. His family came first.

Mr. Schaffner wanted the same good result, and he settled up with Sam for threshing.

The incessant snow and wind blew.

Andy accompanied Sam to go after groceries.

Sam's own words...
Thursday, December 31, 1914 – "Edith and I took Mary to the train..."

8 – Thunder and Lightning
A Pal - 1915

When weather turned moderate during the first month of the year, it was a gift, which didn't happen often. Cold and windy was typical, but when Sam found the canal dry on January 2, it was trouble if that were to become the norm. It stayed that way for several days through a careful watch. He had no sweep of a wand to fill it with water, the magic like Houdini used to perform a straightjacket escape. The newspaper's regular news had had a recent supplement about the attention-getter of such extraordinary feats that regaled readers.

Sam was bothered by his sensitive teeth again (those he still had) but work waited. Hay had to be drawn and brush grubbed. He coaxed the loose roots up and out of the ground. Sam tinkered with odd jobs, helped around the house, and wrote a letter home.

He started work for Mr. Helsley to herd his sheep, feed them, and build a fence. The job was to last right through the end of January. During this time, Andy needed help in spurts, and Morris's had him milk cows. Sam also kept up with his own ranch efforts. Snow fell a few times and produced a big blizzard on January 12.

A letter, which had arrived from Grace, needed to be answered when he wrote home. She kept up on news, too. Sam had read that the United States House of Representatives rejected a proposal to give women the right to vote. Grace may have wanted his idea on it, perhaps skewed toward allowance for them to vote. All of the women Sam knew, like his mother, Grace, and Edith certainly had views and would be worthwhile voters.

For most of January's last week, Sam had a neuralgia episode in his back but did his chores and any job he needed to do around home.

Edith received her shoes that they had sent for at a cost of $3.40.

Helsley's sheep still kept Sam busy every day. He went to Buhl on the night of January 30 and had three teeth pulled. His jaw bothered him all the next day.

He did a few hours work for Mr. McLeod now and then.

Grace burst with news in another letter February 1. This time he hadn't heard yet of the significant tidbit she was excited about. Did Sam know about the first long distance coast-to-coast phone call? He must've smiled as he read her excited run-on sentences about Alexander Graham Bell, who talked to his former assistant, Thomas A. Watson, while he was in San Francisco, California. It was news all right, but it didn't mean that it was available for the common man yet or that such a person could afford it. Sam knew his having a family left him out. He wouldn't waste time for want of a convenience so modern that no one else had it yet.

Wind, hail and sunshine all within a short span of time didn't seem to bother the sheep and horses much. They continued to munch hay as Sam drew the usual four loads for their benefit. He was the one on notice of his neuralgia the last four days.

Mr. Loveless sent him an $8 check. It was followed by the first fine day in some time, according to Sam. He hadn't meant only the weather as he showed the check to Edith. They needed the money.

Edith and Willa went to a party the evening of Saturday, February 6. It could have been a Mizpah get-together, or just neighborhood women gathered from miles around. Maybe they wanted to talk about the fact that the House of Representatives nixed women's right to vote.

Mr. Anderson came out for a visit on Sunday, February 7. He conversed with inordinate friendliness while he made some points that Sam said he would think over.

Sam tried to coax water to come down his ditch. It would make chores a lot easier and quicker if he didn't have added work to carry water for animals. Anderson had made his point about that. Other places in other states had no water problem.

Their cow had a calf on February 9.

Sam's own words...
Thursday, February 11, 1915 – "Hauled four loads of hay to sheep, Stormy, Edith feeling bad."

She was sick for a second day, and he was concerned.

Sam heaped the four loads of the habitual daily hay in front of the sheep. Melted snow followed by rain made for soggy mud roads that were undesirable for horse and wagon. The cold and moisture was the same culprit that worked against Sam's backside.

Mr. McLeod paid $24 in full payment for work Sam had done, and how he needed it.

Sam's own words...
Wednesday, February 17, 1915 – "Got water to house, cleaned chicken coop and fixed our road, moderate."
Thursday, February 18, 1915 – "Cleaned and filled cistern, got potatoes out of pit. Mr. Downs and family came out."

He drew hay and manure one day then went after coal, groceries, and milk pans the next. Chores and all kinds of odd jobs waited in Sam's lineup of work. On Tuesday, February 23, he paid a visit to Anderson toward evening. A plan formed with this man as they both discussed possible changes and a future relocation.

Sam harrowed in the last week of February. He was about sick with a cold. He wrote a letter home while the sniffles had him under the weather.

Mr. McLeod had Sam get him four loads of straw. Sam still had his own work regardless of the hours for wages added on.

Sam's own words...
Saturday, February 27, 1915 – "Went over to Morris's after beans, etc. in a.m., harrowed in p.m. and went to Literary."

The Literary lecture was almost certainly about Griffith's newest writing titled *Birth of a Nation,* which had been made into the longest film ever recorded. It was one-hour long and had been seen by millions, a landmark event in the history of silent films. The book discussion in Buhl would be well-attended. To see and be seen by neighbors, doctors, and creditors was valuable if only for that aspect. It was not wrong for Edith to appreciate that point along with her and Sam's love of reading.

That night they heard about innovations made in movies for the book's film debut on February 8, in Los Angeles, California. They might have marveled to hear about close-ups of facial expressions, flashbacks, and unheard of rehearsals to make the film better. The talk preceded the eventual partake of the movie that Sam and Edith hoped for when they'd have a better financial position and location. The possibility reminded them both of fond marital memories of less than three years earlier when they had last seen two films.

Sam and Edith could not yet know of the short span of Hollywood's first movie stars, Lillian and Dorothy Gish, Mary Pickford, and Lionel Barrymore. They would all become famous in 1919 with the more animated and sophisticated silent films.

They might have had a discussion on the way home to agree on their next decision driven by what Sam had talked to Anderson about. It would bring a change of direction that required them to move. Edith was all for moving to Wyoming, closer to her friend, Lora Nichols.

Sam's own words...
Sunday, February 28, 1915 – "I put our house for sale, cold east wind."

His decision may have been driven in part by shared information with Anderson that he had gathered about the Montana Flathead Reservation land. Anderson had started the conversations about Wyoming, just over the shared border between those two states. He wanted to leave the current hard work area for what he thought would be greener pastures, but he did not want to go alone. It may have been a surprise to Sam when his decisive friend had first broached the subject. Sam had believed that Anderson's work was so fruitful and involved with farm life that to move would be his last thought. But Sam had listened and then talk had come around to the subject of Flathead.

Sam continued to harrow the next day of March 1 and helped Morris butcher three hogs. Several pursuits kept him busy. He did chores, doctored a mare on Monday morning, and harrowed and corrugated in the latter half of the day. Anderson came out that night, glad to further the conversations they had had. He couldn't have been more genial. Edith overheard the conversation at the kitchen table.

Sam's own words...
Thursday, March 4, 1915 – "Corrugated in a.m. Mr. Methwin came to look at Forty."
Friday, March 5, 1915 – "Hauled hay for McLeod, very strong wind, Edith sick."
Saturday, March 6, 1915 – "Hauled load of hay and manure in a.m. Went over to Andersons in p.m., paid $60 interest on mortgage."

Sam paid $32 to Twin Falls Canal Company, and receipts show $18.35 paid for Twin Falls County tax. It is a pretty good indication of why he borrowed $100 from Buhl Bank & Trust with the note signed on February 20. The three items added up to $110.35. It would drive a man to want to find a more profitable way to make money. Hope drives many an honest man in hard times. These times qualified.

His bill for taxes was printed on thin pink paper, and the white receipt attached by a 1.75-inch common pin, uncommonly long. The substantial pins were an item of dual uses in the household, whereas Gem paper clips that had been available since the 1890s were not as versatile with the loop and torsion only able to hold papers. Sam had plucked the pin from Edith's pin cushion. The standard pins date back to the middle ages of Europe when they were in use. If Sam couldn't afford paper clips, then there is doubt that Edith could afford a China doll with the entire satin skirt stuffed solid for a fashionable pin cushion. She may have had the traditional use, felt cloth red tomato type with a strawberry that dangled from the braided thread.

Sam and Anderson went to Castleford and back while they continued talk of their plans. Sam stayed on at Anderson's Sunday and was on hand to sell his mares to M. J. Shiffler on Monday before he went home. It was a good piece of money.

Sam's own words...
Wednesday, March 10, 1915 – "Hauled manure in a.m., sorted and sacked potatoes, Anderson came out, and we decided to go to Wyoming."

Now it was definite. It must have uplifted Sam to have a buddy join in total support of a dream idea that he had held for a long time. He would not be alone to claim Flathead Reservation land south of Canada's border as soon as they made money to do so. He would be closer to the location to take a look at the parcels available. This was a chance, shared by a friend, to pull up stakes and move. Both men had been fed up with the sparse water situation.

Anderson needed help, too, far more than Sam knew.

On Thursday, Sam took his wheat over to Andersons and also drew hay over there for the man's stock. His friend needed the loan of the commodities. The amount Sam still owed Anderson would soon be paid off at this rate.

Sam showed the Forty again. He dug and sacked potatoes for two days to sell them. The cow and her calf were taken to the state veterinary to be sold.

Anderson and Sam had paid for the rental of two train cars while they were in Castleford. They loaded their goods into them for the trip. Sam continued to help Anderson. During this time, Edith, baby David, and Willa were in Twin Falls at the home of Lenore's niece, Marjorie, who had several children. Edith was needed for a temporary span to take care of them since their Great Aunt Lenore was away and Marjorie must work.

Sam was shocked by what happened next.

Sam's own words...
Tuesday, March 22, 1915 – "Took cattle to stockyards: Our cars were attached, came to Twin Falls in evening."
Wednesday, March 23, 1915 – "Came back to Buhl and paid attachments on cars, $19.05, wind."
Thursday, March 24, 1915 – "Hired goods taken out to Forty and took livestock out. Stayed all night with Andy."

Sam was in turmoil over sour events and thwarted plans when they were stopped, grounded by legal papers. His Flathead venture would not happen, not now, not next month, not ever. He told Andy about it, and they discussed details of the attachment. The legal papers made it clear as to why it had happened. Two partners who owned Buhl Hardware Company had the sheriff of Twin Falls County serve on Anderson, the defendant. Sam's writ of attachment was a safeguard to make sure he did not have any property of Anderson's in his possession with intentions to remove it. Any items owned by the named person were to be turned over to the sheriff. It was all in pursuit of a small fortune, $211.84 owed by Anderson to the business owners. They would not allow sellable items to be railroaded away to parts unknown.

This harsh episode may have brought on the origin of Sam's substitute words used versus cuss words. He would not utter speech that took the Lord's name in vain. His string of exasperation syllables were:

Thunder and lightning and seven hands around!

Sam wrote to Edith at Marjorie's in Twin Falls. He may have sat longer than usual to consider the right words to use and shook his head. What a disagreeable state of affairs and no fun to have to write about the reversal of plans. Would she understand? Would it make him look as bad as he felt? He decided to come right out and tell her all of the details of what had taken place. Through no fault of his own, the Wyoming and eventual Montana move was out of the question, dead once and for all.

Sam had one mare left, or so he thought. The hole to bury her was dug March 27. Andy loaned him a team of mules to get him over the hump. Sam was thankful for an end of the miles walked to try to find a team to buy. He had written to Edith about that, too. Sam needed her home and was beside himself with disgust over the Anderson debacle and necessity to resettle back on the Forty.

To top it all off, Anderson had the nerve to be sore at Sam because he had not elected to take his last money to pay the $211.84 bill. It was Anderson's to pay, none of Sam's affair. He'd have had to put himself in deep debt to continue the move but finally saw how it really was. Anderson had figured Sam as the guy to bail them out without heed of Sam's worry over past debts owed and his intentions to pay. Now he wondered if the businessmen were right, that Anderson was skipping out on his obligations. Sam's new doubts had him wondering how much more there was to know about the man.

He heaved a sigh of relief when he received a letter from Edith.

~**~

Twin Falls, Idaho
March 27, 1915

Dear Pal,

I've been waiting to hear from Lenore so I could be sure about coming home. I have not heard yet but know I can come home by Thursday noon. I'll be glad to get settled again.

I'm sorry that we had such a mess. But glad that I am not in Mrs. Anderson's place.

David is feeling some better, but I think he has lost four or five pounds. He is so cross.

The four children have minded very well since their mother has been gone.

There has been some trouble about some money being taken out of the house. I can't find out where it went and try as I might. It was $1.25 Lenore's money, but it worries me a great deal. However, I can't help it, so there is no use fretting.

Willa has been pretty good. She doesn't get sleep enough, so it's hard for her to stay good-natured. I must stop now and get breakfast. Hope you have heard from home.

Lovingly, Edith.

~**~

It eased Sam's mind to hear from Edith. She had taken his news in stride and appeared unruffled by it. He worked on ditches and moved goods back into his shack. He went to Buhl to seek out another team.

Sam's own words...
Sunday, March 28, 1915 – "Cooking and widower."
Monday, March 29, 1915 – "Went to Buhl, bought team from A. W. Bryant bought harness $39.25."

Wednesday, March 31, 1915 – "Worked on ditch, still a widower, fair."

It was apparent that he missed Edith terribly and needed her support. It came in the form of another letter from her.

~**~

Buhl, Idaho
March 29, 1915

Dearest,

Lenore wrote to Marjorie that she won't be home until Wednesday of this week. I think I had better stay until Saturday as there is *(sic)* several things that I want here and if I come Thursday, I won't be able to get them. I mean here at the house. Maybe Lenore won't want to let me have them anyway, but I am going to try. It keeps me pretty busy and pretty close at home with five children to look after. If they were mine, it would be different but as it is I'm afraid to go anywhere and leave them even a short time.

Should have washed today but had neuralgia so badly that I had to put it off. Marjorie has a sore throat again today so is at home.

Willa hasn't had sleep enough so is a bit cranky at times but straightens out when I go after her.

I am anxious to get home. Don't you try to do anything with the house until I get there. I know it is very hard for you not to have us at home when there is so much to do but I can't plan to leave until I am sure that Lenore will be here. Of course, she doesn't know that I am going back to Buhl and so doesn't know that she is keeping me.

I must get busy and make David some rompers.

Just heaps of love, Honey. Everything will be alright *(sic)*. I do hope that you have a team by now.

David just pulled Phyllis's hair and you ought to have seen the scrap.

Goodbye Dear, Edith

~**~

April Fools Day held no more unforeseen tricks or lessons on Sam. All was well, and he had only two more days before he would go to Buhl to get his love back.

Meanwhile, it was work as usual. Sam widened ditches, ran the Fresno and burnt brush. He raked thistles and added them to the burn pile before he harrowed. He resowed the thin spots in the clover.

When he went to Buhl after Edith and David, he brought coal out home, too. Willa stayed behind a while longer.

A brown newspaper clipping was saved 100 years ago from Sam's reading material, a small but poignant piece of prose, which signifies how Sam and Edith thought of their love and relationship.

~**~

A Pal
by George Matthews Adams

A Pal is a diamond, pearl, ruby class – very rare and very precious. But different in this way – fine and scarce as a real Pal is, intrinsic value does not enter into his possession.

A Pal comes – somehow – then he stays and sticks and gives.

A Pal loves, forgives, sympathizes, understands – above all, understands. You don't have to explain or excuse to the one who is your Pal.

A Pal always comes to you when you need him most, and he isn't scared away a bit if the world deserts you. He is there to stay because, don't you see, he is your Pal, and you want him, and he wants you. And that explains everything.

There is something infinitely wonderful about one's Pal that you can't often express or explain.

A Pal doesn't keep things back. A Pal is honest, above-board, open and expressive. A Pal can make mistakes, and they are just mistakes, but if he isn't your Pal, then they are blunders instead, and you may resent and be unhappy and sadly sorry – but somehow with a Pal, you love right through everything and are the stronger bound for the very weaknesses that sometimes hide strong feeling unexpressed.

A Pal is always around – in spirit and in feeling. He does not understand the fair-weather quality. If it rains, he is still your Pal. If it cyclones, he is just the same as when the sun is brightest and warmest. A Pal hovers above.

My Pal is always around when I am most in need, and I am inspired and spurred ahead.

I shall win all things worthwhile because I have a Pal and there will be no secrets except for that utter freedom and frankness of expression between us, back and forth, which in itself becomes a double secret to the world but no secret at all as far as we are concerned.

If you have a Pal, you have the world – and nobody can take it from you.

~**~

The week was filled with the work to make corrugated furrows for irrigation of the new clover growth. Potatoes were cut for seed and planted. Sam had talked with Russum and Morris when he drew a jag of hay. No doubt, they spoke of labor needs coming up.

Sam's own words...
Saturday, April 10, 1915 – "Went to Buhl after Edith, got baby walker and tools at Depot, groceries $2.70, eggs $2.32 on credit."
Monday, April 12, 1915 – "Went to Buhl after lumber for porch and ditch bridge, bed spring, etc. $7.75."

He used the wood for the precise purpose he had needed. Now he crossed the bridge over his ditch and watered any garden row. It made his work easier. He had storage intentions for his porch.

They received a letter from Grace, and it took Sam a whole week to find time to answer it, on April 21. Edith mailed it for him on Saturday in Buhl since she went there every weekend. She visited kinfolks and secured groceries the first of May while Sam planted a crop of popcorn, irrigated alfalfa and clover, and set out strawberry plants in what would become a sprawled garden. He itemized page after page when Thompson commenced to plow for him on May 4. Andy worked for him, too, as Sam alternated the swap of work through what he called some awful weather. They planted crops of corn and wheat. Sam planted his own spuds, solo.

Sam's own words...
Saturday, May 22, 1915 – "Planted beans and irrigated wheat, a hail storm in p.m. Great weather."

Was Sam capable of 'great' sarcasm?

He drilled in barley and other grains with a borrowed drill and then corrugated. Carrot seeds were done by hand. The 700 pounds of barley grain had been paid for from a Buhl Bank and Trust loan. He brought back a 150-pound purchase of coal. He worked on chickens for Morris and also advanced his garden work. Sam found no reason why he shouldn't put up hay for Thompson 8.5 hours on a windy June 5.

Edith continued her weekly trip to Buhl. Willa was a big help with baby brother David, who was already just over a year old in March. His big sister adored him. Willa had turned into a 13-year-old teen the same month. She stretched taller and remained thin but healthy. They collected a letter from Grace again while in Buhl.

Sam found it a necessity to work seven days a week. It allowed him to include work for Thompson, with irrigation of wheat and barley, along with haying and hauling it for use. Sam did not feel well on Sunday, June 13, but his grain needed water, and he elected to do it.

Sam's own words...
Monday, June 14, 1915 – "Irrigated barley and wheat with Edith's help, feeling bad."

On Tuesday, he felt a little better but still needed Edith's help. Willa was in school and not available to watch David. He napped, and Edith kept a watch on him. Sam's Pal helped him one more day, and then he was back to normal again.

Sam hoed his garden as no others did theirs. He worked nine or 10-hour days for Andy to cut, rake, shock, and also haul hay. Thompson needed the same kind of help. Part of the work was reciprocated with swapped hours, but all of it was entered into Sam's ledger. If money was owed to one or the other, it showed up in Sam's meticulous records.

He added work for Reid and shocked hay a few hours.

Edith made the usual Monday trip to Buhl for their needs.

There was no day off, no day of rest when threshing began the first week of July. To determine which job was bigger was hard since Sam weeded his carrots by hand after his hoe work on them.

He had last written to his mother on July 11 and did so again on the evening of July 28. He told her he had spent his day to plow weeds, haul brush, and tend water, all on a warm day.

Mr. Ring was in need of help to thresh. The work trade-off for Andy and Mr. Thompson carried into August with no let-up in the three men's work. It was Sam and Andy who did the most trade, but money was owed to Sam. He added eight hours on to help Mr. Elliott with brush and hay. He somehow managed to build the porch, put in screen windows, and clean the cellar. Both storage areas needed finishing. The porch would serve as summer respite for the short term and space for grain later until he sold it.

Sam's own words...
Thursday, August 26, 1915 – "Cut clover and weeds, cleaned house, helped Willa wash and tended water, Edith feeling bad, warm."
Friday, August 27, 1915 – "Helped wash, tended water and cut wheat along ditches, Edith sick..."

Work was non-stop regardless of concern over Edith. It was not within reason for Sam to entertain stoppage of the continuous cooperation of work with Reynolds, Andy, and Morris. They had added Galloway in the threshing operations along with Reid and Mr. Elliott. They performed as a human-machine network, a meshing together of seven men who worked long hours.

Edith was better but hadn't felt her best for several days. Sam had to take a break for a quick trip to Buhl to get his mother who was supposed to arrive on the train. She did not appear on September 5 as scheduled.

Sam's own words...
Monday, September 6, 1915 – "Went over to Morris's after cot, and to Buhl after Mother, warm."

Sam had to go again. There was no choice but to find time to deal with it the next day. He was relieved to find her there on the second trip. She had finally been able to travel west to experience Sam's life as several of her letters had wistfully spoken of over time. He could see that the journey had exhausted her. It did not dull her happiness to see him even when her baggage had not arrived with her. Edith and Willa warmly welcomed Ma, as Sam called her. Sophia was glad to see how they looked and approved in full measure of them and baby David.

Sam doctored a sick horse. The work on wheat and barley continued for him and his crew. It had cost him $2 for eight meals for the masculine machine. He recorded it in his ledger on the expenses side. His mare was so lame on September 15 that she could not work and he got Andy's horse to haul straw for hogs.

Sam's own words...
Thursday, September 16, 1915 – "Hauled barley straw to stock. Had doctor for Edith."
Friday, September 17, 1915 – "Took load of wheat to Farmer Union: 2,100 pounds - $25.45: Had doctor for Mother."
Saturday, September 18, 1915 – "Sold W. J. Thompson 1,940 pounds of barley, sacked and weighed it."

He was relieved to raise the money to take care of his women folk, both precious to him. He had to mow. Morris waited for the mower next.

When Sam took 1,995 pounds of wheat to Buhl and sold it for $24.95, he spent $6.50 on groceries, $3 on shoes, and $2 for peaches.

Without question, Mother had a fine time loving on David. She no doubt approved of Sam's family and saw how sweet Willa was with her little brother. She had intended before arrival to treat Willa as her own granddaughter. It was easy.

Sam took Ma over to Morris's. A break for a new experience and also that he was proud to introduce her to their friends, which would do her good. She enjoyed them quite as much as her own family. He noticed the undesirable condition of the road and had to fix it for the huller machine to travel over it to reach his bean fields. Sam pulled beans and grubbed brush to get ready for its arrival.

In late September, loans came due along with bills to be paid.

Sam's own words...
Saturday, October 2, 1915 – "Grubbed brush in a.m., went to Buhl in p.m., paid C.W. & M. Co., Buhl Trust Co., and Swammer $50."

The first payment to C.W. & M. Co. was $40.90 for his wagon as the receipt showed. The second one paid off a small loan from the bank. The

Swammer bill for his $50 worth of groceries and dry goods gotten on credit was last. He and Andy worked together on Sam's crops to mow, thresh, rake, shock and haul until October 9 when he worked alone on his own alfalfa and hauled a slip load to his barn. Sam threshed a few beans. He had good reason not to stray far from home for Edith's time was near.

Sam's own words...
Sunday, October 10, 1915 – "Prepared for the coming of our baby girl: Lora born 11:30 p.m., very cold high wind."

He had spent the day not far from Edith for their infant was on the way. It is likely that he wrote about the Sunday birth after the fact because he mentioned a baby girl on the way. They named her Lora Babbette. Sam wrote Betty on a slant across the diary page, apparent that he had decided what he planned to call her and it stuck. Edith had named her new daughter after her friend Lora Nichols in Wyoming. No matter how far apart the two women were, they would remain friends with fond memories of when they taught school lessons to the children of homesteaders and miners. Willa remembered *Aunt* Lora with affection and approved of her new baby sister's name.

Grandma Sophia helped with David, but he was an active toddler. Sam thought it was too much to have Ma's vacation become just a work routine to cook and keep house. He spent the next morning trying to find a hired girl but didn't have much luck. But he had put the word out, and a person could turn up.

In the afternoon, Sam raked hay and went to get Thompson to hay it. In the next three days, he ran the slip 24.5 hours for Andy. Each of those days he wrote that Edith and baby had gotten along fine. Ma managed with Willa's help.

When Sam went to Buhl on Saturday for groceries and coal, he paid $2.50 for road tax. He had tried again to find a hired girl, then came back and worked 7.5 hours to hay for Thompson. Sunday, Sam went after Mrs. Gates and brought her out to the ranch to perform housework. He finished out the day to shock a half acre of alfalfa and thresh a few beans.

Sam's own words...
Monday, October 18, 1915 – "Waited on Edith and hauled hay to barn in a.m., run slip for W. Reynolds in p.m., fair. (1/2 day)."

He was glad to spend what little time he could carve out to wait on his wife. Edith was a lovely sight in his eyes and a good mother. He also wanted to console her because they had a letter from Monmouth, OR. It had been mailed on October 15, but with Sunday in between, they had just received it. It was hard on Edith while he read her niece's letter to her. The news about her sister, Mary, devastated Edith. Excerpts from the long letter follow.

~**~

Monmouth, OR
October 14, 1915

Dear Ones,
We were so glad to hear of little sister's safe arrival. Mama has been so anxious every mail.
I brought mama home today. She stood the trip home nicely but dreadfully tired, resting well tonight. We have an excellent nurse...
I wanted to think there was some mistake, but the doctors who operated are decisive. They say three months will be the longest possible time she has left but probably only a few weeks. They could not get the entire tumor out and said the surrounding organs have the same spots. She is cheerful and hopeful. Maud is coming Saturday, and I think Ethel, too.
We would all be just bushels of glad if you came out.

Lots of Love to you all, Mabel

~**~

Edith was bereft at first. She was close to her stricken sister, Mary. It was personal. Her heart was bruised, and she worried on behalf of her brother-in-law, Jack Moore, and their girls, Maude and Mabel.

Of course, they could not go to Oregon. Edith was not well enough to consider it after baby Babbette's birth just a week ago. They also could not leave when Ma was there, and Sam could not leave his crops. He would write a heartfelt letter of condolence and also communicate that Edith remained ill. She was, in fact, delicate as if an unknown entity caused her to recover slower than others might. But neither of them considered it in that light for more than a moment since they had no comparison close at hand.

Sam ran hay slip for Reynolds 8.5 hours for two days on October 19 and 20. He also kept up his own chores, took care of his squash and beans, and arranged for a huller. While he waited for his turn to use the machine, he helped Elliott hull clover eight hours. He worked for King to thresh and process his grain.

Sam's own words...
Thursday, October 28, 1915 –"Helped King hull clover three and one-half hours. Went over to Elliott's after 89 pounds of potatoes. Ma and Edith went along."

Sam was altogether pleased to have Ma and Edith along with him to visit their good friends, the Elliotts. It would help to pull Edith out of the doldrums over the recent news about Mary. The fresh air invigorated her now at two weeks since she had given birth.

Sam sold 15 sacks of red clover seed, which amounted to 1,670 pounds and bought coal. The next day he sold 13 bags of clover seed weighing 1,470 pounds, to Buhl Grain & Produce Company for $20 cash. He bought dry goods and meat and hired a girl for $20.

Sam was never idle. He took Andy's wagon home, returned a borrowed slip, and pulled and topped his onions before going to fetch a fanning mill. On November 1 he harvested more onions and beets and burned brush. They went to the Morris's for dinner the same day. Ma enjoyed their friends immensely, too. There wasn't much over which she bothered to have an adverse thought. Life was too short. Sam may have had a similar attitude gained from his formative years growing up in her household.

He settled up for hay gotten on credit and paid a threshing crew.

Sam's own words...
Sunday, November 7, 1915 – "Visited with Mother and took her over to Morris's for a last visit, borrowed their wagon."

Monday, November 8, 1915 – "Got up at 1 a.m. and took them to Buhl, burned brush and done housework, letter telling of Edith's sister's death."

Edith missed her mother-in-law's companionship. Sophia loved and affirmed her acceptance as Sam's wife. It was worse yet to learn of Mary's death from cancer at only 47 years old. It had been barely three weeks since the bad news arrived that she was terminal. Sam spent a quiet time with Edith over the sad news to try to console her. He counted on Willa to stick close to her mother because he had to get back to work. Edith knew that he must, but she was certain to appreciate that he had taken valuable time with her. Mary's death had an effect on him, too, but duties waited.

9 – Trouble
Ralph Only 20, 1915 - 1916

Sam picked up potatoes 8.5 hours for Elliott and then did his farm chores. He put in four more hours for Elliott the next day and finished out the afternoon plus the next two days for 20 hours on tubers for Reid. The cold wintry days took their toll on him. He was not worth much on Saturday and Sunday. Sam was ill.

On Monday, he went to Buhl in need of groceries for which he spent $4.80. Bills were due. Sam paid $107.40 to Buhl Bank and $111.42 to Swammer Mercantile. With receipts stowed in his ledger, he couldn't help but think it was work, bills, worries, the usual. He may as well be sick, too.

Sam was still under the weather Tuesday when he fixed up windows for winter. He sent H. H. Parker $9.28 for 106 pounds of pork he had gotten. His illness held on for a week through work on chores and garden. Sam pulled beets, cut corn, and hauled hay. Mr. Russum sold him a horse.

Sam's own words...
Tuesday, November 23, 1915 – "Went to Buhl, took baby to doctor. Windy, stormy evening."

He and Edith both worried. Baby Lora Babbette, his Betty, was six weeks old and was a sick little girl. Sam wrote a letter home to wish them a Happy Thanksgiving and let them know that Betty was ill. Childhood resilience had her recovered before the message reached Galeton.

There was a morning snowstorm on November 25, but they went for their Thanksgiving with the Elliotts. Their own squash from the cellar added to the meal along with pumpkin pies that complemented the feast. For this day, the work would wait. They were all grateful for God's bounty.

Friday brought the same merry-go-round of work. Sam hauled hay and straw. It was frigid Saturday for a trip to Buhl. He came back with money and settled up with Morrises, the whole $45.50 owed. The shaking of hands and good will all around cemented their trust.

The colder it became, the more the wind found entry to cracks and crevices. Sam banked up the shack and hauled hay and straw in the midst of stormy weather. Andy needed Sam's help to butcher a hog just as November ended.

December 1915 debuted with the cold east wind. When Sam finished sorting spuds for Mr. Reid, he worked for Elliott to sack potatoes and transported them to Buhl for him. He helped Andy butcher again and took a load of his own potatoes to Buhl to sell. His wheat was sacked and stored in the screen porch. He hauled a jag of hay and barley and then plowed for three days.

It was time to help Andy butcher again because Andy sold meat.

He couldn't turn over frozen ground on December 10, so he went to get a mill with which he fanned seed to clean it. The seeds were heaviest, and the unwanted debris would blow out away from it.

After supper in the evenings, he and Edith caught up on reading. Recent news reported that the one millionth Ford auto had rolled off the assembly line in Detroit, Michigan. Best of all was the letter from Grace.

~**~

Galeton, PA
December 6, 1915

Dear Brother and Family,

I have intended to answer your letter for a week, but have been having one of my sick spells again and haven't felt well enough and don't know as I shall finish now without taking a rest.

Ma seems to be just about the same as usual, better one day and worse the next. She can't do any work or sit up very long at a time. She has worried over Ralph's condition. He is lots better and able to walk around some. He did not have a full run of pneumonia. I don't think the Dr. knew just what did ail him, but he was terribly afraid of tuberculosis. And so were we all for a couple of weeks. But the doctor sent some of his spit to the State Department of Health and had it analyzed, and he received a report a couple of days ago. They said there were no consumption germs but his lungs were full of poison.

He is giving him a treatment and wants him to get lots of fresh air. He is awfully poor but has a good appetite and is gaining in strength...

I have partly made up my mind to have an operation myself. Both doctors seem to agree that it is my appendix causing all the trouble. The sooner it is removed, the better for me. I certainly can't stand it much longer. Every spell I have leaves me so weak and nervous. I can't eat anything that I want, and I have a healthy appetite.

We were all very sorry to hear that you needed the money so bad to use, but Pa says he can't possibly raise any money now and you know he sold your house on a contract. Mr. Metcalf is to pay $60 and interest on the whole amount ($300) once a year, and it comes due as soon as June 10. Pa thot (sic) that would be about the time of the year that your payment comes due, and so had it put in the contract to be paid when it would help you most.

It cost Pa all of $700 cash from the time he sent Ma to Idaho until he got her home again. And now Ralph sick and he not being able to help you a little. He has talked to me about it by the hour, and we have devised all kinds of schemes, but I can't write them. If only you were here to talk it over with.

If you have to sell your land there, you had better decide to come back east again for a while at least.

If you could sell your land there and get back here with from $1200 to $1500, you could buy a good farm here with tools, stock, and everything to start right in with and have an income right from the start. I don't mean right here but somewhere in a good farming section. A farmer that has 12 good cows and raises ensilage to feed them can make a good living off them for 12 months of the year.

Besides, we have so much better market here. Hay is

worth here from $15 to $25 per ton. Potatoes $1 a bu., Wheat $1.25 bu., Oats 60¢ bu. We don't raise as large crops as there, but you see that we get better prices for what we do raise. It doesn't cost as much to harvest a crop either. After you had tried the east, if you wasn't *(sic)* satisfied you surely could go west again. Think it over.

Lynn shipped some of his chickens to Atlantic City and got 22¢ a pound live weight. They raised about 150 in their incubator.

I have been all day writing this and think I have written a long letter for a sick woman. I have a hired girl.

Frank and Dewey have given up going to Emporium, Pennsylvania to work.

Tell Edith to write when she gets time.

Pa cut out some farm advertisements and wanted me to send them to you. There is a farm of 30 acres below Williamsport, PA, that he is talking of buying for himself someday.

He is coming after this letter to mail now. Write soon and let us know what you have decided to do.

With Love, From Grace

~**~

Grace's letter took a lot to digest. He could feel her words pull on him as much for Pa as for herself and all of the family to try to entice him to come back east. He was not immune to their plea, but he had so much going on where he was that it was out of the question right now. There was pressure from every direction. Maybe later he could think it over like Grace said, but he had to raise money here somehow for his obligations. He would answer Grace with honesty by telling her that. It would disappoint her, but he was in no position to do otherwise.

He was hopeful again about his brother, Ralph, and believed he would regain his health. At least that was a relief. Sam answered Grace's letter a couple of days later. He would have mentioned Grace's health and ask to know if she went through with the appendix removal and how it turned out.

Sam helped Mr. King to butcher, drew his own hay and went after groceries so they could feed hungry threshers. Each ranch where the crew labored was obligated to supply food for them as part of the bargain.

Edith went to Buhl with him to sign a chattel mortgage for a cow he bought at Bartlett's sale. The cow would freshen and produce milk after the birth of her calf to be born next July.

Sam's own words...
Saturday, December 24, 1915 – "Hauled jag of hay and barley and straw. Helped Edith and went for Xmas tree."

Sam most likely helped with food preparation. Pumpkins are not easy to cut, seed, and peel to make them ready to cook into pulp for pies. They liked mincemeat pie just as well and worked on that, too.

Sam's own words...
Sunday, December 25, 1915 – "Took dinner with Morris's. Letter and Christmas gifts from home."

The farmers with their families bowed their heads at the Morris table, thankful for the ability to do hard work but take rare times like these for neighborly fellowship and shared food.

Chore work resumed with a noticeable west wind as cold as from the east. A betting man could always bet it was present from some direction. Sam butchered one of his hogs. Edith needed the lard from it, too, another bounty for which to be thankful. She would have known about Crisco, a brand of vegetable shortening produced by the J. M. Smucker Company of Procter & Gamble. It was introduced in June 1911 and had become popular with those who could afford it. That left Edith out.

He helped Andy to butcher again for the market.

In Buhl, Sam bought lumber for a shed and posts to continue a fence. He unloaded it back at his ranch and hauled hay and barley while the cold blasts of wind hindered his operations.

On December 31, 1915, Sam recorded 12 degrees below zero. Winter had made its harsh announcement.

~**~
1916

January 1 seemed like a good day for Sam and his entire family to visit the

Reids. To be in the company of good friends on New Years Day was a swell start to the wintry month in front of them. It lived up to its billing and presented no easy task for Sam to harness up the horses and wagon with straw to transport his family in a warm enough manner to travel the few miles to the neighbors. The babies needed to be bundled up. Willa helped.

For two weeks, Sam didn't write one word in his diary, but he wrote home and also to Grace. It took five days for his letters to arrive in Galeton. All the while, Sam was busy with troubles because of the worse-than-usual weather. He read in his newspaper that the West suffered unusually cold temperatures. In Browning, Montana, it dropped from 44 degrees Fahrenheit to minus 56 degrees F in one day, the greatest change ever on record for a 24-hour period. (Still is.)

Sam's own words...
Sunday, January 16, 1916 – "Very cold and windy, canal overflowed and ice all around buildings."

Sam worked on the water and ice the next few days through the wind and the blizzard of a snowstorm. No matter what the conditions, he hauled hay for animals and brush to burn. Twelve posts were forced into position in the frozen ground. Sunday came around again, and after evening chores they visited the Morrises.

Sam set another dozen fence posts regardless of rain and blizzard conditions. It became so disagreeable and icy that a trip to Buhl was not possible. The muddy ruts had frozen with thick ice that made it impassable. He had fought his way with horses and wagon as far as Thompson's and settled up with him. That had been enough of a sample for adverse conditions. Sam went back home.

His letter from Grace was more agreeable than the atmosphere outside that had turned against him.

~**~

Galeton, PA
January 22, 1916

Dear Brother and All,
We received your very welcome letter and will answer now and let you know about the big fire that we had here in

Galeton last Wednesday morning. I have enclosed a sketch from the Williamsport paper that describes it better than I can.

I haven't heard yet whether they intend to rebuild or not. The *Leader Dispatch* building burned up, so you won't get the paper for a while.

Am glad that you are all well. This part of the country is having an epidemic of Grip on account of the open winter. You said that it had been so cold there, but it hasn't here. It is just like spring, and we didn't need any fires yesterday to keep warm and had the doors open besides. So many of the mill men are sick that they had to shut down all but the big mill and take men off the docks to run that. Roy is working in the hardwood mill now. They wouldn't allow the engineers to be firemen anymore since business has picked up because there is running for them in other places. Roy didn't want to go away from home to work so he got a job in the mill awhile until he can have a job running out of Galeton.

Frank (Hess) came home from Emporium Thursday, from a sprained back and couldn't work. He intends to go back as soon as he gets better, and I wouldn't be surprised if Dewey went back with him. Dewey is still working in the mill but don't like it very well. When he got his check last pay day, he gave it all to Pa except a few dollars that he owed downtown.

Ralph doesn't seem to get any better. He looks so bad and still has night sweats. He isn't taking much of anything, only Native Herb pills and a little cough medicine once in a while, and he has a terrible cough. The least exertion makes him cough so hard. Poor boy. I feel so sorry for him, but he won't take any advice kindly. If Ma tells him to take his medicine, he gets so cross and says it isn't anyone's business whether he takes it or not. But don't write anything in your letter about what I have told you because he always wants to read them and he would know that I have written about him and wouldn't like it.

Ma is gaining but still real nervous, but she worries so much about Ralph. She gets out lots more than she did and can work quite a bit some days. Of course, she has days when she doesn't feel as well, but she sleeps good nearly every night. She is so slim and has lost lots of flesh.

Pa and Dewey have colds, but otherwise, Pa is well.

We were glad to hear that you have decided to come back east and hope that you will win out. What eastern farm catalog did you send for? Pa thinks that you would do well to come east and get a good truck garden near Philadelphia or some large city. He is studying farm ads all his spare time.

Yes, I read the book that I sent you but in such a hurry that I skipped some of it. It pleased Ma to think that David remembers her. She tells us lots of his tricks, and it makes us want to see him worse than ever. When she first came home, she talked so much about the baby that I thot *(sic)* Ma liked her the best, but she thinks that David is so smart for a child of his age and that he will make his mark in the world.

My girls are getting up, and I will have to get them some breakfast and go over home and find out what Pa wants me to write.

Well, Pa couldn't think of anything...to write and is waiting for me to finish this letter so he can take it down and mail it.

Goodbye and write soon. With Love, Grace.

~**~

Sam might have remarked to Edith that it was a lot of news in one letter. His face usually registered his worry over his younger brother, Ralph. He may have been frustrated that he couldn't even mention much about him in a letter. Grace had been right to warn against it. Sam wouldn't want to cause him any hurt feelings.

Sam would miss the *Leader Dispatch* and figured they would not be back in print soon. He had to smile when he read how glad his family was that they planned on a move back east as soon as it could be managed. But right now Sam had to get back to post setting. Plans would not change right away because there was a lot to do before he could undertake such a move. He went to work on posts, but no doubt smiled with the thought of Pa seated at the family table with his head and shoulders bent forward to study farm ad catalogs. Pa had put a lot of hope on his oldest son's return. It would bother Sam to disappoint him or anyone back home. He and

Edith were committed and intended to make it happen.

It was Sunday again, happened every week! He went down to Mr. Elliott's and paid $5.36 to settle up with him. He had squared up with Thompson and Morris the week before. On Monday, he went to Buhl accompanied by a cold wind. They needed groceries for sure now, regardless of severe weather, so he couldn't turn around again and intended to brave it.

Sam's own words...
Wednesday, February 2, 1916 – "Hauled jag of hay and straw, the largest snowstorm in seven years."

It thawed for several days and turned snow to water. Sam took the time to write a letter home, careful not to mention that he was sorry that Ralph was so ill. But he was sorry, and it caused him to worry about his folks. It would be the best option if he could get home and see Ralph and everybody, but it was not possible now.

He had a variety of jobs every day, straw, hay, fence, and chores. Andy needed help to load hogs and a beef cow. Sam butchered a pig for himself. That would help with meals for a while. It would also supply lard that was in short supply again. After Edith had cooked it down, she was sure, on successive days, to use it to make flaky pie crust.

With all the melted ice and snow, the roads became a muddy mess. The long wet sinkholes sucked at the horse's hooves and the wagon wheels. Regardless, Sam made another trip for groceries, went to Morrises and to Mr. Downs after spuds. While he was in Buhl, he bought coal at $3.90 and paid $2, leaving $1.90 as a balance owed. Money was in short supply.

Edith was sick. Sam worried every time she was in a weakened condition.

Posts went in easier than they had in frozen ground. Sam intended to finish the fence. After a few more pointed stakes were pounded into the soggy soil, cattle roamed in the lot on Sunday. Sam went down to C. Marlott's sheep camp to see how the operation was run. He repaired his bridge, hauled two loads of hay for Morris, and bought hay for $2.75.

Sam's own words...

Thursday, February 24, 1916 – "Went to Buhl to see about some money, borrowed $150 from Citizens Bank."

His bank book was a small brown one (100 years old at this writing) and the receipt for the paid off note of November 1, 1916, was tucked inside. The $150 was put to good use paying $16.64 on delinquent land tax. It included a late fee of 93¢ even though he was only a week late. He sent a money order of $10.11 to Prudential Insurance Company for his life policy.

Back to work. Sam hauled hay and manure and repaired the barn. On Saturday, he went to Buhl and paid a dry goods account for $8 and made a splurge purchase on tobacco that should provide at least a month of enjoyment.

Sam appreciated his sale of threshed clover to Mr. Wire.

On the last day of February, he went out of his way to make a condolence visit to Mr. and Mrs. Wassum because they had lost their baby.

More snow fell in March. He got hay from Brewer's and brought the corrugator home with him from Morris's. It was time to pay $60 on his mortgage in Buhl and get groceries. He took Mr. Morris's calves to Buhl and helped him load some goods. On another trip to Buhl, he had Edith's eyeglasses repaired and saw Mr. Hammel from whom he borrowed $9. It was due back June 1 with an interest of 10¢.

Bright spots sometimes appeared, and the one in front of Sam right now was a letter from Grace. It temporarily took his mind off how he had had to borrow from one source to pay another.

~**~

Galeton, Pennsylvania
February 27, 1916

Dear Sam and Family:-

My family is all tucked in bed for the night, and I will try and answer your letter as I know that you must be anxious to hear from home.

We are having snow and wind and cold weather now for a few days. The storm has blown so all day that I could not see across the road sometimes. I read in the paper last week about the cold weather you are having all through the west.

Pa is hauling some logs since the snow came. He let some of his logs out to other men and is helping to get them in. Pa only works until about noon and comes home as he has all the chores to do alone. He hasn't been feeling quite well for a couple of weeks. I am worried he lifts too hard.

Ralph isn't any better and never will be I am afraid. He and Ma were over here awhile this afternoon. He is real weak and has no appetite lately. We have had three different doctors for him. Dr. Hurd expects a specialist in lung diseases here any day, and we are going to have him examine Ralph. His window is open for sleep, and he takes medicine better than before. He read your letter and Edith's and said that he already knew all that you wrote about tuberculosis, and that is all he had to say about it. We try to take him out every day when it is not too stormy for a ride so that he will get the air. He and Ruth and I went yesterday, and Pa and I drove him down to Lynn's Thursday.

They have all been sick again except Lynn. Helen nearly had pneumonia, and when she got a little better, Marguerite had the same thing. Iva got worn out taking care of them and got sick and was in bed two or three days. Lynn worked right along, and she stayed alone nights with the children. He is in debt some for Jean's sickness and funeral expenses, and they have all been sick so much and run up a big doctor bill, and he thinks he can't lay off.

I have escaped the "Grip" so far and haven't had a cold this winter, and am feeling lots better in all ways. Also, am not taking any medicine into my stomach anymore and am eating Bran, common wheat bran like we feed to cattle. Perhaps you have read what good food it is for the bowels and stomach. My doctor told me about it, and it has helped me so much that Ma has begun to eat it also and it is helping her. She doesn't have to take so much physic and is getting stronger. Aunt Lizzie Crippen is taking it also, and it is doing wonders for her. She also sees this doctor I have. He prescribed it for nearly all of his patients, he told me. I make bread with it, and we all eat it.

Well, I didn't get my letter finished last night and will write more now.

Mary and Frank went to Emporium a week ago last Saturday to stay a couple of weeks until Frank is ready to come home and begin papering and painting. He is there doing carpenter work at 40¢ an hour.

Did I write and tell you about Claude Dimon? He has been sick all winter and had to give up his position in Philadelphia and come home. He and his wife and two little girls are staying at his Uncle Clints. He has Brights Disease and is in bed, and they are afraid that he won't never be well again.

Ma just came over, and she said tell you all that she would like to see you and will write as soon as she feels well enough and to kiss the babies for her. What is Babbette's weight, and did your gray horse's foot ever get well?

Lynn weighs 205 pounds now. You will have to come east and get fleshy like all the rest of us.

Ma wants to know how Mrs. Elliott is and did she go to the hospital? And how is Mrs. Reid's little girl?

Roy has had three trips running on the railroad this week and is out today, but it is in some other engineer's place, who is off sick.

We would all be overjoyed to have you come east and settle here on a good farm. You say it doesn't seem as if you had been there seven years, but it does to me. There has *(sic)* been a lot of changes in seven years you have been gone, and I hope it won't be seven more years before I can see you all.

I am afraid that Babbette will be grown up before I get one of her pictures and I would like to hear David talk.

It will soon be your birthday, won't it? I never forget it and always think of you.

Gladys died five years ago the 2nd of March.

Ma seems to be slowly gaining. Once in a while, she has one of her sleepless nights, but when she does, it doesn't make her feel as bad the next day, as it did a few weeks ago. Her nerves are really bad some days. She worries about Ralph so much because she isn't able to wait on him, and she thinks he don't get as good care as he should. Sadie is rather selfish and always thinks of herself before anyone else, and don't fix anything that he can eat. Of course, she has quite a lot of work to do, but she is so well and strong that it seems as if she might do more for him. Her and Dewey went to

Sunderlinville the 22nd to a masquerade ball, and she made them both a suit. I help her all I am able to and fix something for Ralph to eat whenever I go over home.

I had a letter from Maud Osgood (Mary and Jack's daughter) today, and she just recovered from a serious operation. She is nursing on Long Island for an insane woman and has been there three years.

I have written a long letter and not much of anything either.

Well, answer soon and don't change your minds about coming back home to live when you decide to make a change.

Tell us all the news and how you are getting along.

Goodbye from Grace

~**~

Sam ruminated through the main facts of the letter and hoped that both Ralph and Pa would both be better when Grace wrote again. He didn't think it sounded too good at all for Ralph and was sorry he was not near enough to contribute to his care. Sam appreciated every effort that each of them made to get Ralph out for fresh air and prepare healthy food for him. He made a mental note to remember to tell Grace and shook his head to imagine the condition of his sick brother.

So many of his siblings and their spouses were sick back east. It was good that Grace was so well now and he'd tell her so when he wrote. He had to smile at her admonition to him not to change his mind to come back home. She was candid that she wanted her big brother back with his family in tow.

It was Sunday, but chores didn't stop for the Sabbath. Old Bob was sick, and Sam tried to work on him and help him out.

Sam's own words...
Monday, March 6, 1916 – "Doctored Bob, worked on ditch, the horse died about noon, buried him, an awful wind."
Tuesday, March 7, 1916 – "Set fence posts, Andy brought home his bride. Had a big Shivaree in evening."

The Shivaree was fun for people from miles around as they gathered outside Andy's place. They threw up a disruption for the newlyweds, which

119

was to be taken in stride by the couple as a rite of passage. After the event was over, they could settle into married life with their peace and quiet unmolested by neighbors out to have a little fun.

Sam set posts for three days and on the fourth day, set braces on the fence. He went all over the country to look for hay. Mr. Campbell let him get a ton for $7.50. He was a little short on cash and had a balance of $2.26 yet to pay. He started to haul it Monday and got the remainder on Tuesday. A letter was received from Grace.

~**~

Galeton, Pennsylvania
March 9, 1916

Dear Sam and Family,

I received your letter, and we were very glad to hear from you and hear that you are all well.

You are having bad luck but can be thankful it isn't any worse.

Pa has been urging me every day, as usual, to write to you again. He seems to be feeling real well and strong and works every day. His gall bladder operation appears to have helped him wonderfully.

Mother is lots better and has been down to the hospital to visit Ralph twice and stayed all afternoon. She does as much work as Sadie now with no rest and no medicine needed at present.

Mary is unable to be on her feet and can't do anything but is getting better.

Ralph is still in the hospital. It was four weeks from last night since he went there and he is terrible homesick. His birthday is later in March, and the nurses made him a cake and put six candles on it and tried to cheer him up. His cough is better, and the Dr. thinks it is acid poison all through his system that keeps his fever up. Every afternoon it comes up to about 100. Some days it is almost normal then it comes back again. They don't give him anything to eat only eggs and milk, and he is getting so thin but looks better than when he went there. His eyes are brighter, and he has good color. But the Dr. doesn't want him to come home until he gets the fever down. We go to see him nearly every day, and he had rather have us women come than any of the men. He never complained and still doesn't now, and has been a good deal sicker than any of us have realized, just because he didn't complain. He is only 20, and I hope he will soon get better so he can come home again. Ma was nearly wild when he first went. She missed him so much after having him there all the time to look after.

That hair of David's and Babette's was too cute for anything. David's is lighter and more like yours. Ma says Babette's is lots lighter than when she was there. Oh! How I wish I could see their little heads.

Roy has been gone four weeks and won't be home before the 25th of April. It is lonesome with him away so long. Two weeks is the longest he was ever away before. He is looking for furnished rooms so we can go over awhile to live.

The ground is white with snow. It began yesterday morning and continued all day and night. The farmers haven't any of their spring work done. Dewey plowed a little last week but can't do anymore until this snow goes off.

Galeton is surely going to have a creamery soon. Pa had a special invitation to a meeting yesterday afternoon to discuss creamery business.

Write soon and about your crops. We are always anxious to hear how your fields are growing and all about your farming.

Do you get the *Leader Dispatch*?

Will close with love to you all.   From Grace

~**~

Sam was relieved that Ma and Pa were so much better, but Ralph was a different concern. Even though he was better, he was still hospitalized, and his condition was worrisome. Sam wished again to just once set eyes on him and talk to him. As the team was harnessed up, he thought about Ralph and Ma's worry over him.

Sam was apprehensive about another letter from Grace. He'd been so busy with his work that more than a week had slipped by while he meant to answer the last one but hadn't gotten to it. He'd read all of the news, good or bad, whatever it had to be.

This time Grace was the most worried of all because Sam hadn't had time to write. She didn't know the half of what work and responsibility he had before him. He did know the half of what he and his sister thought of each other, part of the reason they were the two prolific family communicators.

~**~

March 18, 1916

Dear Sam,

We all thought about it and settled on the idea that Babbette is sick and you hadn't written so as not to worry us. Well, it concerns us more if we don't hear.

We all feel encouraged about Ralph. He is still in the hospital but is in much better health than when he first went in. His rheumatism is gone but not the cough even though it was less. He remains in bed all the time and still has to eat milk and eggs. Dr. Farwell gave him a skin test and sent his spit out every day or so for tests to catch any germs if there are any. Ralph has the best of care, and it only costs $15 per week besides the doctor fee. Ralph's improved state has
made Ma better also, and she has gotten stronger. She goes out more, and I've seen her walk up to Mary's in deep snow. Frank and Mary came home a couple of weeks ago.

We have cold weather and lots of snow. It was 20 below zero last Friday night, the coldest it has been this winter. Roy is working at Emporium since March 11 on the powder line where there is danger but gets good wages.

Sadie has a beau. Anyone being as healthy as Sadie has little to complain about. She imagines she has troubles.

Dewey works at the mill but plans to quit and help Pa after the first of April if the snow goes away.

Tell Willa that Roy said he didn't get that box of candy that she was to send him for Christmas.

We are all worried over Babbette.

Will close with love to you all.   From Grace

~**~

Sam may have smiled about the sister sibling snipe that Grace dropped about Sadie. The letter also showed him how valued he was to them as if he didn't know. They were just as valued. He wanted to move back home as soon as he could manage.

Sam knew he could not delay a letter. He'd get Willa to write, too, after she read Grace's letter with the message for her.

Just past the halfway point of March, Sam began to plow, harrow, and corrugate. It consumed several days that were dedicated only to his home ranch. He burned brush, arranged things in the cellar, and made a plow harness. The manure was hauled, and 32 hills of spuds were established before he plowed and harrowed for Mr. Hammel. He was hired by Mrs. Morris to take chickens, ducks, and turkeys to Buhl. He bought a Majestic range for $60 while he was there.

Sam's own words...
Sunday, March 26, 1916 – "Set up range and a big improvement over the little stove, partly cloudy."

The acres of work on fitting out his fields with plow, harrow, and corrugation took most of his time unless he had a paid job to help another neighbor or rancher.

He butchered three hogs at 120 pounds each and helped Andy ring 14 pigs to inhibit rooting behavior. Andy had enough hogs to do damage with their noses to burrow into the ground to expose material of interest only to them, an instinctive response for pigs. Andy naturally didn't like it because they upturned soil and destroyed their confines as far as they could roam. Destruction was reduced with the rings in use.

They cut up swine flesh, packed the meat in a barrel, and added the salt brine. The sausage preparation ensued. Sam anticipated how good the spiced meat would taste with eggs and pancakes.

Sam's efforts for crops were never done for long but were interspersed with various duties, like a trip to have a heifer bred, build a fence, or go to Buhl after fence stays and groceries. When he could consolidate and accomplish more than one purpose on a trip, he did so.

On April 7, Mrs. Sawyer came out to see Edith. On the 12th, Edith went to Buhl with Dr. Bula, a chance ride to get there. Dr. Bula lived in Twin Falls near where Philip and Lenore lived. Willa and Babbette went with their mother, but David stayed with Sam. Five days later Sam and David rode to Buhl after Edith.

Life was full. Work was always in front of Sam or was Sam always in front of work? The circle of jobs revolved time and again, no complaint from him. He cleaned ditches, irrigated clover, and made a trip to Buhl for coal, groceries, feed, and hardware. He worked on his fence and helped Andy load hogs. He plowed a field then cleaned and filled his cistern. It was the usual for several days of work.

What happened next was not mundane and was downright worrisome.

10 – Willa/Billo
Edith Irrational, 1916

Edith's somber face told Sam that Willa was still gravely ill. They monitored her lethargic condition, and now she was worse and unable to eat. Why didn't she improve? Worried glances shared between both parents telegraphed concern. David sensed the mood of worry that had taken over. He fussed and whined.

Sam's own words...
Friday, April 21, 1916 – "Willa sick, tended water and fixed fence."
Saturday, April 22, 1916 – "Sorted potatoes in a.m. and harrowed in p.m. Willa worse."
Sunday, April 23, 1916 – "Willa very sick. Dr. Sawyer came out and took her to hospital. I took Edith to train in p.m."

Sam was anxious, and he needed to take the time to go and borrow $35 from Citizens Bank for 60 days to help Edith and Willa. He was minus his wife and two daughters and had David to watch out for while he waited for news about Willa. He took David to Mrs. Andy Gardell for care so he could get some work done. He expected word from Edith that did not come and wrote on his diary page, "No word on Willa." Then he was relieved to have a condensed message on a one-cent postcard from Edith. She sent a letter two days later.

~**~

Twin Falls, ID
April 28, 1916

Dear Pal, Willa's temperature was down to 102 degrees again this morning, but I suppose it is up again now. This morning Dr. Coughlin said he thot *(sic)* she was holding her own. She had a very good night. It will most likely be a week or more before I can come home. This has to run its course before I dare leave. If she holds out as well as she is doing now, she will have vitality enough to bring her thru *(sic)*.

I hope you and David are not too lonely. Write to me. Dr. Harry had to go to Connecticut last night. He thinks his mother very ill but it may be his Aunt Ada.

Love to both of you – Edith

~**~

Sam's own words...
Sunday, April 30, 1916 – "Irrigated, cleaned ditch, did housework. Lonesome and worried about Willa."

He couldn't take David out much with high winds. By Tuesday, May 2, he took his son over to the Elliotts, and Sam went to Buhl to see about the wheat seed. He had hoped to get his wife and girls on this trip, but he could not get Edith because Willa was not at all well yet and still in the hospital. Sam wrote to Edith.

~**~

Buhl, Idaho
Wednesday Evening, May 3

My Dear Girl,

Was glad to get your letter today, and didn't know but what you had decided not to write to your lonesome boy. Lonesome is the word for I left David boy with Mrs. Elliott yesterday and haven't seen him since.

I was in Buhl yesterday, trying to get some seed wheat and give a crop mortgage, but without success, although I didn't ask anyone but Failer.

Phoned to Dr. Sawyer's four different times in p.m., but there seemed to be no one there, and when I got home – no David or no letter from you. It turned a little bluer than common blue.

I saw Mrs. Elliott when I came from town, and she said David seemed quite happy and didn't cry much or long after I left him in the a.m.

Goodbye Dearest as it is getting late and I must get some rest. Kiss my precious girls for me and come home and kiss me for yourself as soon as you can.

Good Night Dear Heart

P.S. I certainly miss David when bed time comes.

~**~

A letter arrived from Grace with $50 in it from Pennsylvania. It was like an oasis in the desert, but a letter from Edith brought more worry. Willa was worse. Sam mulled over the bad news of Willa's fever that kept her in danger. He wondered if it would require a change in Edith's intention to come home Wednesday while she balanced on the jagged edge of worry. Willa had been ill for three weeks and still fought to overcome what was likely caused by the measles outbreak. Sam and Edith were aware of the seriousness of the epidemic that swept the nation.

Measles killed nearly 12,000 people in the United States in 1916, 75% of them younger than five years old. Willa may have been in the 30 percentile of rubella patients who suffered severe complications from the disease, such as pneumonia and encephalitis. If the Crippens could have looked ahead to 1963, they would have seen that the incidence of measles decreased by more than 98%, following licensure of the preventive vaccine. Epidemic cycles no longer occurred. Sam and Edith knew of no safety net of this kind for their children.

In the next three days, Sam managed a lot of work before he went after his son.

Sam's own words...
Wednesday, May 10, 1916 – "David and I went to Buhl after Edith, but Willa was worse, and she couldn't come. Windy."

Not only was he disappointed that Edith couldn't come home, but the toll that the worry took on him and Edith over Willa's severe illness wore on both of them.

On Thursday, he took a 225-pound hog to Buhl and sold it for 6.25¢

a pound. ($14.06.). He purchased wheat seed for $5.05. The best outcome of the trip was to find that in one day's time, Willa was a little better.

Friday he took care of David, who had a cold. His work was limited and he could not plow and did almost no irrigation.

By Saturday, it was a relief that Willa was no worse. Sam washed diapers and did housework. Then he wrote a heartfelt letter to Edith and his girls.

~**~

Buhl, Idaho
May 14, 1916

To my Dears,

Was very thankful to hear that Willa is holding her own against such odds.

If you can come home as you have planned, Dear, I don't know as we would gain much by taking David down there. Of course, I can't accomplish any farm work and look after him, but it would be quite a job to get him ready and would lose about as much as I would gain.

You ought to have seen the little fellow when I read his letter and explained it to him. His eyes just shone, and he said, "Happy, happy." He certainly misses all of you but asks about Billo the most I think: That's because he saw her taken away in a car and he knows there's something the matter with her.

No, I haven't any hens set because they have all set out. Andy borrowed one of them.

Your dishes didn't arrive yet.

It is after nine o'clock, and I am too dumb to write a letter like I ought to write to the girl that counts with me more than my own self.

David had a nail in his shoe, and it has made his foot sore, and he didn't sleep much last night. I have been putting fat pork on it, and it is much better tonight, and he doesn't complain much now.

Good night lover girl, and I pray it will not be long until you can come home to your boys, knowing that Billy will be safe.

Good Bye Dear Heart

Sam's own words...
Thursday, May 18, 1916 – "Rainy. Couldn't do much, but housework and take care of Son. Lonesome."

He missed his wife and two girls and wished for them to come back in the house with him and David. Sam tended water. David watched, and Sam did his wash along with housework. He wrote Edith again and went out of his way to send her a letter that had arrived at home, one he knew would cheer her. His own letter was short.

~**~

Buhl, Idaho
May 16, 1916
Dear Edith,
Am sending you a letter from Maud, otherwise, there wouldn't be much use, as there isn't much to write. Son and I are getting along as well as we can expect to without Mama, Billo, and little sister.
I hope Willa improves every day, and that all of you can soon be home.
David's foot will be well in a day, or so, I think.
Goodbye for this time and lots of love to all my dear ones.   Sam

~**~

Maud had written about her father, Jack, doing all right after Mary's death, but she missed her favorite Aunt Edith. She was very sympathetic about her little cousin Willa and wished for good health to return to her.

Sam's own words...
Saturday, May 20, 1916 – "Tended water and went to Buhl after Edith in p.m. Happy to get my love back again."

Edith had been gone from home 28 days. Willa was still ill and remained in the hospital, slow to come back to good health again. It was expected to take additional time.

Sam made an all-out effort to catch up on his work now. He plowed in wash-outs, went after $21.30 in seed wheat, and took a heifer to bull service. On a trip to Buhl for coal and groceries, Sam treated wheat, harrowed and tended water. It didn't take imagination to find a job to fill every hour of every day. It was rainy, so he went after the drill and would have to wait to use it when dry conditions returned.

Grace would expect a letter from him to alleviate their worry over Willa. They would be more than glad to read that she would recover. To send a letter was also his insurance to get a message back. Edith had just learned of plans for continued care for Willa, and they would be glad to know about the details.

Sam's own words...

Friday, May 26, 1916 – "Edith went to Twin Falls to move Willa from hospital. A little rain in a.m."
Saturday, May 27, 1916 – "Drilled in wheat. Willa was moved to Simmons. Edith came home. A nice day."

Willa needed daily nurse care, which would be private care near the hospital and doctors. Mrs. Simmons was paid $55 and later $25 more that Sam recorded for the additional weeks that Willa lay ill, attended by the private nurse. Sam signed notes at 8% interest to pay the doctor and hospital off on time payments.

Farm work was in full swing. He must plow, harrow, corrugate, drill, and irrigate, whatever it took to promote his enterprise.

The work and bills had ganged up on Sam. A letter from Buhl Department Store, Sinclair & Shank, where they had credit for groceries, asked him to pay his $8.16 bill in full. They had sold the store and wanted to square the books. He had all kinds of debts to worry his mind and planned to pay them, but not all could be paid right now.

Grace wrote, but Sam was too busy. Edith wrote back. She kept track of Willa's progress and also the two little ones at home.

Sam was caught up in work with other farmers. They all worked on the farms of their neighbors to cooperate with whatever crop was in season to be harvested. The efficiency of a man-machine six strong on fields could do far more than one man alone. Sam kept meticulous records of his and the other men's hours for where they worked and for whom. Some ranches were larger, and they would owe wages at the end since it could not turn out an even number of hours spent for work-in-kind. He, Andy, and Reid farmed together day after day on each other's crop management and irrigation.

Sam's extensive garden kept him busy with irrigation of the rows where he hoed and weeded as June played on. He didn't allow weeds to get a foot hold and take precious water. Planting was incomplete because the staggered start of corn and potatoes was to ensure that they ripen in several stages instead of all at once. He juggled problems, crops, and money.

At the end of May, Sam went into debt for $36.25 on a mower that he would pay off the next year at the same time. His receipt for the loan shows the purchase as one Big Dix McCormick Mower.

Sam's own words...
Friday, June 16, 1916 – "Irrigated wheat and planted potatoes, warm, received payment on house, $76."
Saturday, June 17, 1916 – "Irrigated wheat. Took white heifer to bull. Went to Buhl after groceries."

He had counted on the $76 arriving in June. It was needed before it came. Sunday was spent at home but was not free of work.

Longer weekdays of nine or ten hours labor came with hay harvest. Sam worked his three horses to run a slip for Andy and kept careful records.

They saw the Elliotts and other neighbors when it was possible. Sam did only his own work by mid-July. He worked on alfalfa and clover, his water works, and the garden. When he went to Buhl for necessities, he stopped in to see Mr. Hammel in both June and July to make regular payments of $10 on his note.

Sam's own words...
Saturday, July 29, 1916 – "Irrigated. Went to Buhl in p.m. Edith went to Twin Falls."
Sunday, July 30, 1916 – "Went to Buhl after Willa and Edith! Warm."

Willa was sure to receive ample attention from a family glad to have her home after eight weeks absence from them. David would have been excited to see his Billo. It is certain that Willa loved on him a bit extra the next day when he had an accident and ran a fork in his back during playful exuberance. He was treated with concern, but the doctor said he was in no danger. Baby Babbette needed attention, too, and Sam recorded that she was not well, but it was not a serious matter.

August began as one of Grace's letters arrived. After all of the strained nerves through Willa's illness, Sam and Edith must have exchanged a pleased glance between them, as they sat down to read his sister's missive. Sam counted on her for most of the news from home even when it brought sad news about Ralph, but this one was benign.

Sam plowed up potatoes to make them loose in the dirt and easier to dig out for pick up. Irrigation of all other standing crops persisted. Hay was mowed, raked, shocked, and hauled. The co-op man-machine used each other's labor again for strong man bull-work.

Sam's Jersey cow found her calf. He built a pen and shut the juvenile inside so it could not run off again. Andy's hay stacks were finished for now, and Sam worked on his own for two days. Andy had more roughage feed ready for Sam's labor, which he worked on through August 15. Now it was Schaefer's turn, and Sam worked for him. He ran hay slip and horses for 10 days to almost finish August, all the while keeping up his chores and gardens. There was no day off, but they went to visit Elliott's on Sunday evening.

Sam's own words...
Sunday, August 27, 1916 – "Tended water. Mr. R. P. Flueger came out to look at Forty. Warm."
Monday, August 28, 1916 – "Tended water. Dug sack of potatoes, hunted binder and man to cut my wheat."

Sam had no luck in finding a man to do the job, not yet. In Buhl, he paid another $10 to Hammel and talked to P. Flueger again. He helped Jim Carey thresh, worked with Andy in his granary, and repaired his pasture fence. It was a good thing for Sunday so he could relax, well...almost. It might have been a foreign word to him. They took an evening visit to the Elliott's.

On Monday, he arranged for Guy Winters to run binder while Sam shocked wheat. They double-teamed the next four days to reap Sam's wheat. Then Sam helped Brazeau thresh, harrowed for Andy, and grubbed and hauled his own brush. Mr. Bates saw the use of such support and hired Sam to help him thresh.

Sam's own words...
Saturday, September 16, 1916 – "Went to Buhl after groceries, coal, sacks, etc. Contracted wheat. David sick."

His mind was on David even when he was beyond busy with his duties, which was his method to love and support his family. Andy had him work seven days straight to plow, corrugate ditches, irrigate, and shovel out ditches.

Sunday was an excellent day, on which Sam sold 30 tons of hay at $8 per ton to J. T. Skillern. There was definite need for his well-earned money. He received $50 toward the $240 total.

September was prime time for farm work, in particular, to drill, irrigate, and make a pond for Andy, right after they stacked his wheat.

Sam went to Reid's on Sunday, October 1, to get the mower that he needed for clover. All that he cut down became beaten by a rain and hail storm. The next day he cut more clover and raked all of it. Wind and rain pummeled it in the evening hours, the kind of weather devastating to a hay crop. It denigrates the quality of the nutrients for livestock. How could it not bring forth that original phrase of Sam's?

Thunder and lightning and seven hands around!

October meant he needed to pay another $10 to Hammel. He took care of it on a Wednesday grocery trip. Duty on his mind pulled him back to the ranch where he and Reid carted and stacked wheat.

Sam fixed his bridge and threshed for Andy and himself.

Sam's own words...
Saturday, October 7, 1916 – "Took 46 sacks of wheat to town: 805 pounds, Reid took in 30 sacks. Brought out coal. Rainy."

It may have been that Reid had a bigger wagon for 30 bags of wheat while Sam delivered the other 16 bags to Buhl. He paid Reid $4 and had him return with a load of coal. Sam had other business in Buhl. He took out a loan from Miller & Viele Co. for $210, with which he paid the Twin Falls Water company and relinquished $60 to Aldrich Mtg., the interest on his mortgage.

When he transported almost his last wheat of 1,900 pounds to Buhl, he also went to see Mr. Fleuger. He did not waste the return trip and he, too, brought a load of coal home. Next day he was right back to work and helped Andy move a derrick and work on his granary for six hours. He shocked clover for himself two afternoons.

Sam's own words...
Saturday, October 14, 1916 – "Bred Jersey, walked to Buhl, went down to school entertainment in evening. Paid Bartlett note on Jersey."

The walk to Buhl, no doubt, was to tug the Jersey along to service. He finished his wheat on Sunday and let Reid get half a sack of the grain.

A school event was an enjoyed connection to keep and to value Willa. It introduced her younger sibling, David, in a natural way to what school was in his future. It promoted the worthy opinion that David already had of his Billo. He was happy to go into the world of big sister.

Sam's own words...
Tuesday, October 17, 1916 – "Went to Buhl and sold Forty to J. J. Rugg, received payment to bind bargain. Reid shocked two hours."

Sam and Andy mowed, shocked, and raked for several days. Galloway worked half a day for him. Sam went to Buhl on Saturday, October 21, to draw up a new deed. He sold Martha and a heifer for $95. It was a good enough name for a cow, rather gentle. Naming a farm animal as a pet can reduce willingness to sell them, but sold she was.

For the next two weeks, Sam worked for Andy on alfalfa since he would not plant crops for himself after the Forty sold. They must have talked a good deal about what Sam wanted to accomplish. Sam took Edith with him so they could look for a place near Gooding, Idaho, not that far north of Twin Falls and closer to Andy.

Sam's own words...
Saturday, October 28, 1916 – "Went to Buhl, finished land deal, notes and Interest from J. J. Rugg $192.20, taxes $20, abstract $19, check number 568, $500."
Monday, October 20, 1916 – "Bargained for forty acres of land four miles north of Gooding. Came home in p.m."

The deal with Rugg was finished up. Sam had found a property that held promise. He was out from under the Forty and into another, but he still had his alfalfa and potatoes to harvest on the original Forty.

Sam had jumped back into another fry pan and hoped to make a better profit to have more money to move east when he could manage it. He would have little to show for a grubstake if he went home now. He needed to get ahead on money if he could find a way to do better than just break even.

Work continued with Andy and Reid. Sam got their help to thresh hay and dig potatoes. Andy bought 1,200 pounds of spuds from him at 60¢ a hundred pounds, amounting to $7.20.

A significant letter came from home, a long message passed on from his mother that she had received from Grace. Roy and Grace had moved and lived in Corning, NY, now, which was a longer distance to travel by horse and wagon or even the train to the folks in Galeton, PA.

~**~

Corning, NY
November 3, 1916

Dear Mother and All,

Well, Roy went to see Ralph yesterday. He stayed with him about two hours and got back home about 10 o'clock.

He says Ralph is awful weak and thin and it tires him to talk much. And said just talking to him made him sweat. It was so hard for him.

Ralph told Roy to have me write to you for him and tell you how he was because he is too weak to write.

He wants Dewey to come and see him. Roy said tell Dewey to come Saturday, and he would go with him on Sunday. Tell Dewey to be sure and go for Roy thinks Ralph is pretty bad.

There is a hole in his lung, and the pus runs from it all

the time, and it hurts him when he coughs. Roy says he coughs hard. Ralph gets up though and walks to the toilet and back and sits on the edge of his bed.

Roy told him all the news and Ralph tried to talk, but he coughed so hard from the exertion, that Roy told him not to talk.

My piles are worse again, and I had neuralgia all night and have it yet this morning. Was going to have my teeth out but can't until the piles get better.

Oh! I saw President Wilson, and so did the girls.

A flying machine went over our house this morning about 7 o'clock, the first one I ever saw.

I haven't got my breakfast dishes washed, and Roy is waiting to mail this letter, so I will cut it short.

Ralph wants some fruit. If Roy can find any good peaches and plums, I am going to send him some.

How is Frank? I hope he is better. Write all the news and tell Mary to write. Now write soon and tell Dewey to try to go see him.   Love Grace

~**~

Sam no doubt shook his head with set lips and no smile in sight after he read the disparaging news about Ralph. His poor brother was in terrible shape, and Sam could no more pay a visit to his brother than squeeze money out of an empty pocket. His solemn thoughts went with him. There was never a time that he lacked for work to do.

Monday, November 6,ʼ advanced with a snow squall. He paid $66.15 to Gem State Lumber Company in Buhl and used the trip to town to have a wheel repaired. A green cardboard with verses meant to encourage was given out by Gem Lumber, and Sam tucked it in his shirt pocket. He, Edith, and Willa appreciated the sentiment of the four stanza poem, compliments of the manager, E. B. Jonathan. Sam likely referred to it when he sat at his desk and stuck it into a wooden slot.

~**~

The man who wins is an average man,
Not built on any peculiar plan;
Not blessed with any peculiar luck-
Just steady and earnest and full of pluck.

When asked a question he does not guess;
He knows, and answers 'No' or 'Yes';
When set a task that the rest can't do
He buckles down till he's put it through.
So he works and waits till one fine day,
There's a better job with bigger pay;
And the men who shirked whenever they could
Are bossed by the man whose work made good.

For the man who wins is the man who works,
Who neither labor nor trouble shirks;
Who uses his hands, his head, his eyes-
The man who wins is the man who tries.

~**~

Sam's own words...
Tuesday, November 7, 1916 – "Helped Andy butcher. Edith and I went to vote, wind."

In this United States presidential election, Woodrow Wilson gave narrow defeat to Republican Charles E. Hughes. Sam did not disclose his choice.

He was back to dig his spuds alone on Wednesday and kept at it. Andy and Reid dug with him on Thursday, but only Reid stuck with him Friday. Sam helped Andy finish stacking his alfalfa seed on Saturday. It remained cold.

He had more than a week of frustration trying to get threshers to come to harvest his clover. They eluded him and worked anywhere but for him. When he got a machine, it could not be started. By the time he worked on the nemesis machine and got it to run, it was Galloway's turn, and Sam helped him thresh. Then he assisted Andy to conquer alfalfa for a day and a half. It had taken three weeks to get his turn for his clover.

Sam's own words...
Monday, November 27, 1916 – "Went to Buhl, took in 932 pounds of clover seeds. Cloudy and some rain."
Thursday, November 28, 1916 – "Went to sale, bought light wagon, tried to rent a place in p.m. Cool."

He'd raised a few dollars when he sold his seed but found no rental. The date was coming closer when they had to leave the Forty to the new owner, J. J. Rugg. Edith went to Twin Falls on Friday, December 1, to see Rugg about renting the house. She stayed on for a while at Lenore's.

Sam went to his brother-in-law, Philip's home, to get Edith on Sunday. He had a letter from Mother.

~**~

Galeton

Dec. 4, 1916

Dear Sam,

Well, Thanksgiving is over, and I am alone again. Grace and Roy and children came home, and Lynn was up to dinner. Iva and the kids went to Wellsville to visit her sister and brother. Mary and Frank took a trip to Ceres to visit his brothers and are not back yet.

We had roasted chickens and homemade mince pie. Turkey is 40¢ a pound here. I dressed four of our old hens and sent them to camp for the men's dinner. They all worked that day. I go up about two days every week and help Sadie.

Mary and I sent a box of fruit and cake to Ralph and Grace sent some things from Corning. Dewey was out there two weeks ago. Your father wants to go at Christmas time. I don't think there is much change either for better or worse. I would like to go and see him but it is a hard trip, and I am afraid to try it.

We all think you might better come home and not buy more land there, but perhaps you know best. I hope you will get a good place to live this winter. If you were here, you could live in Grace's house. Roy wants us to move over. Some of their things are there, the piano and all the heaviest things are there, and they would like someone in there as it is too damp for the piano.

It is cloudy and looks like rain. Have you had any rain out there? How are the Elliott's and do they live in the same place?

Well, I must close and get Annabelle some dinner. Our family is small.

One of the teamsters is off with a sore throat, and Lac is taking his place and will stay at the camp nights, and we are alone.

Write soon.   Love to all from Mother

~**~

Well, it was clear that Ralph was about the same and had received fruit and other treats, thanks to Ma and two of his sisters. Sam would have been as glad about those comforts as he was to know what everybody at home and lumber camp were doing. In some ways, he saw the logic Ma and everyone had with their wish that he would just come back now. But Sam wanted to prepare himself better for success when he got there. It was still a question of the money he would need. It would take more than pocket change just to travel there with his wife and children, and he had debts to settle up. He put big expectations on himself.

He and Edith were still not settled and needed to know where they would live. He went to Buhl after her on Sunday, December 3. Rugg had told her they could rent the house on the Forty.

Through the week, Sam drew hay and straw and put a thatch roof on the barn. He went to Buhl to see Rugg about the financial agreement to live on the Forty. Cold and stormy weather prevailed. He saw Brazeau about a place and went over to Gooding to check on the supposed land deal. It was stalled, and his check for $100 was in limbo, not to be cashed. Did the title search reveal a problem? It would come to light if that were the case.

He helped Andy butcher, mowed hay and clover, and did odd jobs. There was a trip for coal and groceries another day.

Sam paid Willa $9.26 for her lambs. She had learned a lot doing the work to raise them with his help. Like any girl of 15, she was happy to receive the money.

It was already December 9.

Edith had to go to the dentist on the 12th. Sam helped her do the wash on Thursday, December 14. The next day he went to town and paid his debt of $98 to Bryant and borrowed $100 from Fleuger. It was a necessary ploy to push the debt further out without becoming delinquent.

Sam's own words...
Sunday, December 17, 1916 – "Took Edith over to Elliott's. Went over to Brazeau's, banked up shack."

It was an opportunity for Edith to see friends, a chance she knew she would not have again for a while, but longer than either of them could have ever guessed.

Sam butchered a hog for their use and carried hay to his animals in the chilled wind and snow. It required lard rendering, too, and kept Edith busy.

It was Saturday, December 23, when he had gone to Buhl and arrived home at 6:30 p.m. and found Edith ill.

Baby Jonathan was born at 11:45 p.m. Edith had convulsions and Sam was alone with her and Willa. He called the doctor who came early the next morning. Mother and child were attended. The grave look on the doctor's face was mirrored by Sam's ashen countenance when Doc told him that the infant would not live. He had done what he could and pronounced his educated opinion.

Sam's wife and child lay ill, silent–their infirmity silencing. He leaned toward Willa to pat her arm–shore her up–the shoring never needed more surely than now, the now elusive shore.

Earlier, Sam had cleaned their baby up and wrapped him for warmth. Imagine when the doctor had gone; Sam bent his face to the small head and rested cheek on cheek to love him. If he could give his boy the will to live, he would. He breathed the delicate baby scent in before the tender placement of his fragile son back with Edith. Come what may, the child would be warm and perhaps nursed, but only a chance. Edith was irrational all day. The next day she rested quietly, and the weak baby had the instinct to suckle. Sam knew Edith had to eat and drink if she and the baby were to thrive. Perhaps squash was prepared. The soft orange mush was the easiest thing he could have gotten her to take. Oatmeal was another soft choice to digest. If he thought to do it, he washed her hands and face. If he could have willed her back from delirium to better health, he would.

At 7 p.m. Edith became irrational. Sam called the doctor again, and he came out about 1 a.m. He may also have expected to make out a report and death certificate for the infant but noted that the boy still lived.

Tuesday, the day after Christmas, Edith improved somewhat in the morning but was irrational again by evening. No doctor showed up. He came early on Wednesday and said Edith would get well. Quite likely he knew that Sam and Willa wondered if she would recover and needed the reassurance because of her desperate situation. The infant, Jonathan Ralph, survived still, occasionally nursed, a natural occurrence for Edith with her offspring. Habits do remain in place, and this one survived through illness as if it were muscle memory.

Sam learned that David and Betty had been exposed to measles when they were with Edith at the Elliott's 10 days before. He hoped exposure would be all, no development of rash and fever. He had enough to handle and more than sufficient troubles to worry about.

Sam's own words...
Friday, December 29, 1916 – "Edith a little better, doctor came in evening, cold east wind. It is hard to be so poor."
Saturday. December 30, 1916 – "Edith gaining some, quite irrational part of day...wind, shack cold, no doctor."
Sunday, December 31, 1916 – "Edith seems to be alright again. Doctor W. called. Dr. Sawyer's wife made a visit. Mrs. Elliott took the children to her house. Edith still improving. I certainly miss the children."
Monday, January 1, 1917 – "Edith rational for first time since baby Jonathan Ralph came. Am very much relieved."
Tuesday, January 2, 1917 – "Edith still getting along alright. I still miss my babies."

Baby Jonathan stayed with his mother to nurse, his only chance at life. He had already lived 10 days longer than the doctor believed he would when he gave him up at birth. Sam made no more diary entries for nearly a week with his heart and hands full. His mind struggled in overload.

Then it changed.

11 – Telepathic, One Sweet Time
Brazeau, 1917

The worry over Edith was as near too overwhelming as Sam had ever experienced. He couldn't help but wonder if his world would ever be the same again. Small relief was felt but not with a surety that his world would right itself to its former better state. It had all the help he knew how to give. His slumped shoulders and grim face spoke more than he could begin to say aloud. A letter from his mother was a welcome lifeline.

~**~

Galeton
Jan. 3, 1917

Dear Sam,

I received the letter telling about Edith's sickness, and I do hope that before this reaches you, she will be better. Be sure and write every day for I am so anxious about her, but I have learned to trust in God and don't worry as I once did.

I hate to add to your troubles, but Ralph is very low. Lynn has been out there and is going back Friday. We are looking for the worst to happen at any time.

It is too bad the children are exposed to measles, but I don't think the little baby will have them. If he does, it will be very slight.

I am all alone today. The others are all at the lumber

camp. We have sleighing here, and they are hauling logs.

I will close and write to Grace.

Love and Best wishes, From Mother

~**~

Sam's own words...
Sunday, January 7, 1917 – "My Dear Brother, Ralph, died after suffering over a year. Had a telepathic message from him and felt that the poor boy was about to leave this world."
Wednesday, January 10, 1917 – "Grace's birthday and poor Ralph's burial. Edith still very sick. I feel so worried."

~**~

Galeton, Pennsylvania
January 10, 1917

Dear Sam:

My Birthday: And I have to write and tell you that Ralph is dead; died Sunday the 7th at 9 o'clock at night and is to be buried today at 2 o'clock.

Lynn was with him and brought him home on the train last night, the same that we came on from Corning. He don't *(sic)* look very natural. It is six months since I saw him last and he has changed terribly.

I hate to write and tell you this when I know you have so much to bear already. It was bad for poor Ralph but would have been so much worse if it had been Edith to leave all those babies that need her so much.

I can't write much this morning but will write all later.

Lynn was nearly done out when he got home. It was a lot to go through all alone among strangers, and we haven't had time to talk to him very much yet.

I do hope Edith is lots better by this time.

Write me. I expect to be home the rest of the week anyway.   Goodbye from Grace

Ma takes it well, better than we expected. Uncle George came last night. Pa just came in and said tell you to come home when Edith gets well.

~**~

Sam's own words...
Friday, January 12, 1917 – "Received a letter from Grace telling of Ralph's death. Am very sad and disheartened. God help my Dear folks."

And God help me, too, he may have beseeched as he looked toward heaven. Worry permeated every area of his life at present. There was hardly anything left to go wrong. Logic would have it improve.

He may have started to doubt the validity of selling his Forty since the Gooding deal had fallen through. Most likely there was no way to get a clear title. His check was back in his possession, the $100 still in his bank account. With his wife ill and his brother passed on, it was about all he needed to be downcast. The worry lines between his brows seemed knit together into near permanency. Time crawled as he took care of Edith and baby Jonathan Ralph.

Grace's letter held no surprises and was a comfort in shared details of his family's trials back home. They were all in this life together, and the distance in miles heightened the need for connection in a troubled time.

~**~

Corning, NY
Jan. 15, 1917

Dear Sam and Edith,

I am back in Corning again. Came back Saturday afternoon and I promised Pa that I would write to you. He wants you to come home as soon as Edith is well enough to stand the trip. If you haven't the money, then he will send it to you. We need you, and you need us. He is certain that you can do better here than there. Think it over and come.

I hope that Edith is much better by this time. I was so worried when I heard of it. Ma sent me your letters. If only we could have come to help you with the babies. Roy and I were ready to take them all, in case it was necessary.

You may think it is bad to have them so close together, and it is in one sense, hard on Edith. But think what a comfort they are and well worth all you go through to get them. Alice was 15 months old when Ruth was born, and Ruth 13 months old when Gladys came. I thought it was awful then but think differently now. Would go thru it all again...

What have you named the baby? I want to see you all, but the babies worst of all.

Iva and her children came as far as here with Lynn when he went back to White Haven Hospital the last time.

They came Friday night and Lynn went on to W. Haven Saturday morning. They went home on Sunday afternoon. Their baby is just dandy. He is so big that you would think he was a year old.

Lynn got back to W. Haven on Saturday and stayed with Ralph until his death at 9 o'clock Sunday night, January 7th. He was awfully glad to see Lynn and talked to him about different things. He asked about the little horse that Pa bought for him and Ma to drive before he went there. Lynn left the hospital about 6 o'clock to go to the hotel for his supper. He asked Ralph if he wanted anything for his breakfast. A piece of jelly cake and a bottle of pop was what he'd like. Lynn told him he should have them in the morning. While Lynn was eating his supper, a messenger came after him, that Ralph was worse. Lynn took an automobile right back, and when he got there, Ralph knew him but couldn't talk anymore. He was conscious until the last but was so weak that he couldn't move in bed alone and just moved his hands for two weeks before he died. He is better off, but we miss him so much. Pa seemed to take it hard. He isn't very well this winter.

Ma kept her nerves under control pretty well. She wouldn't look at him after he was brought home: she knew that she couldn't stand it. The P.O.S. of A. buried him. He was insured for $250 in that lodge and had a $1,000 policy in Pacific Mutual. Dewey paid his insurance after he was taken sick and Ralph spoke of what a good brother Dewey was to him. Said there wasn't many brothers that would be as good. Mother had a paid-up policy in Metropolitan on both boys, but the policies and both receipts burned up and she don't know as she can get it without them.

Dewey is Pa's right-hand man. He drives one of the teams every day in the woods and Sadie keeps the camp. She is so fleshy that she won't tell what her weight is anymore. Mary is fleshy this winter, weighs 196 pounds. I am still the smallest one, getting thinner every day since I came here to live. I am on the sick list now: just manage to get around the house. Roy helps me. He is awfully good. Every day I appreciate him more. I have been laid up so much with piles. I get so nervous that it takes the flesh off me.

I get homesick here. I would never like city life. The

country suits me. I went last fall and gathered autumn leaves to send to Edith, but have felt so miserable that I have never sent them. I enjoyed the trip on the mountain after them and thot *(sic)* of you and Edith and wished that she could have been here to go with me.

I have a girl border who worked in the glass factory, and it keeps me tied down. I wouldn't have taken her only she is a girl from Wharton that used to work for me there. She didn't know anyone else here, so I really had to take her.

Did you get the Christmas packages alright *(sic)*? We didn't send anything for the baby but will send his later. Do David and Betty wear rompers to play in? Ma and I thot *(sic)* that we would make them some. What do you need for the little baby?

My girls are getting so large, and it won't be long before they are young ladies. I hate to see them grow up.

It was awfully kind of Mrs. Elliott to take David and Betty. Is Willa as well and strong as ever?

Write and let us know what you think about coming home. We want you. We surely believe that you can do better here.

I must close and get dinner. My girls are home.

Love from Grace

~**~

Sam anticipated that they would be glad to hear from him that baby Jonathan Ralph Crippen would forever be a namesake for their dear Ralph. He had to write and let Mother and Grace know. His jaw and his mind were set from the effort to try to think of the right way to say that he would not consider coming home now. Deep in thought, Sam shook his head. It was awe-inspiring to be so wanted, and he missed them as much but demanded more of himself than to take Pa's money and go home on the effort not earned by himself. Sam pulled his tall frame up and squared his shoulders. He had better expectations of himself.

Sam's own words...
Monday, January 22, 1917 – "Went over to see Brazeau. We went to Buhl after groceries, cold enough, Edith hasn't set *(sic)* up yet. Doctor came out."

Tuesday, January 23, 1917 – "Did housework and took care of Edith! She sat up about 15 minutes, the first time since December 23. Very windy and cold."

Sam went to Brazeau's for a load of straw and to continue a significant conversation on a deal that he and Brazeau had signed for Sam to lease Brazeau's property close to Twin Falls. The agreement was to take effect on February 1, 1917; all spelled out in mimeographed blue typeface. Sam was to perform all labor and furnish the seed, pay threshing bills, and deliver all crops of seed and grain to Buhl. Hay was to be sold in the stack on the land and proceeds for both types of harvests to be split in half as profit for himself and Brazeau. Sam was the party of the second part, buying a half interest in the livestock. He was required to feed and care for said stock. Any increase, calving and such, would be equally shared along with the cost of the feed for all animals.

To offset Sam's labor, Brazeau was to provide all machinery for use that was on the farm and expected to keep it in good repair. Sam bought full interest in the poultry and would receive all proceeds that he could make from them. He paid 50¢ each for the 125 hens and entered it in his ledger as an expense of $62.50. Brazeau retained full ownership of his bee hives, but Sam would receive one-quarter of the honey for hiving the bees and doing necessary apiary work. Brazeau furnished all bee hive supplies.

For the next three days, Sam was encouraged that Edith sat up 15 minutes daily. He might smile yet, but he still had apprehension over her weakness. Her hair was undone from a knot behind, too uncomfortable to lie back on. Her dark hair fanned out on her pillow to frame her delicate face that was as white as the porcelain face of a Dresden doll. By the end of January, she was worse from an ulcerated tooth. Sam's grim mouth refused to turn up at the corners. He hung around close, taking care of her and doing housework. They talked about Jonathan Ralph starting to look healthier, and both touched his pink cheeks. Sam told her of the Brazeau deal and that her part was to get well and he would take care of the moving and work details.

They took comfort in reading the newspaper with good news and bad. The report was that the United States had severed diplomatic relations with Germany. On a personal note, they discussed changes coming for themselves now and later. Edith was exhausted but happy to know that Sam planned for her to go to Oregon when she was well enough, a last trip home for her before the proposed removal to Sam's Pennsyltucky home at the conclusion of the Brazeau episode.

Weather moderated in the last days of January. It was a bit of hope with snow going fast, but then more powder fell.

Sam's own words...
Tuesday, January 30, 1917 – "Done washing, hauled a jag of hay, an awful day, a blizzard. Edith not feeling so well."
Thursday, February 1, 1917 – "Edith about the same. Done housework, took care of Edith. Am busy from 6 a.m. till 11 p.m., 16 below zero."

Edith remained in the same ill condition. Occasionally she sat up but was unable to get out of bed. Sam pushed himself at the current pace and was exhausted at day's end. It was no wonder that he had a pain in his side. The weather and Edith's condition had held up the plans for himself and Brazeau.

On Sunday, February 4, Brazeau visited to discuss his move off the farm before Sam and his family could move there. It would take a while, and Edith was unable to assist. Sam hired Mrs. Olson to begin the pack up of the household. He had Andy deliver 500 pounds of coal to Brazeau's for Sam's use as soon as he could move his family in. Sam and Reid helped Brazeau pack two days in a row. Sam bought Brazeau's old kitchen range for $60.

It was February 8 when Sam moved his household to Brazeau's farm. Edith was not on her feet. Sam was careful in her transport to the new residence where she was tucked in bed. They were both relieved that the arduous wagon ride was over. It had been worrisome for Sam and uncomfortable for Edith with baby Jonathan. Sam accomplished it as part of another long day of work.

Sam's own words...
Friday, February 9, 1917 – "Done chores and tried to arrange things. Brought cow and calf over. Sold my three old horses, 700 # potatoes, chain and harness and stack of alfalfa straw to Andy Gardell for $150. Holstein

cow and heifer were bred."
Saturday, February 10, 1917 – "Sold A. Gardell 4,775 (4¾) tons of hay at $10 per ton, total $47.75."

When Sam took the bovine for service, he got himself 10¢ worth of tobacco and wrote it in the ledger. He set up their household and made it a home as well as he could. He had many items, animals, and more hay to sell. Andy was a willing buyer but hadn't enough cash. He added $75.75 on his tab of credit with Sam and promised to pay the new total of $300.75 by November 10. Sam needed the money but hated to disappoint his friend.

Reid and his wife, Laura, went to work for Sam. It meant the children could come home from Elliott's. No doubt David and Betty were happy to be home with their parents. Willa was home but in school.

Reid was hired for farm work at $45 a month and Laura at $25 for care of the household and children. Edith languished in her sick bed. Among anyone there, she probably was the least happy with her situation. Sam was always concerned and overworked.

Sam's own words...
Sunday, February 11, 1917 – "Done chores, hauled straw for bedding in p.m. Gardells came down in evening. Edith stronger."

Having friends as favored company to come for a visit and Edith's improvement made Sam's day of rest complete. There was no rest from the everyday chores of the livestock care. The next day he went back to the Forty to sort his spuds, and he sold Andy 734 pounds more at 2.5¢ a pound ($18.35). Sam bought pork from Reid, 30 pounds at .11¢ a pound ($3.30).

Sam's own words...
Friday, February 16, 1917 - "Hauled load of alfalfa and stacked it by hand. A disagreeable day. Edith gaining very slow. She can walk a little by hanging on walls."
Sunday, February 17, 1917 – "Cisterns dry, canal dry. Have to depend on thaw, ice, or Deep Creek. Having one sweet time."

Sam watched his wife's struggle to regain her health each day.

The extra work and the time it took was the opposite of "one sweet time." Sam hauled water and five loads of manure and weighed up 863 pounds of oats.

Sweet time turned into snow, and it blew all day Tuesday and early Wednesday. By Thursday Sam believed Edith was stronger and would benefit from fresh air. He helped her climb up on the wagon to be seated and enjoyed her company while he took a ram home to its owner. They stopped in at Andy's. The shared trip brought hope and pleasure to both of them. Sam was as pleased as Edith that she stood the trip all right and she continued on that path, stronger each day.

Sweet time was still in force on Sunday, February 25, with the wind so strong that it blew the chicken coop over and raised H in particular. Three hens and a rooster were lost. By Monday, it had calmed down enough to set-up the chicken coops again. More snow fell on the whole scene, just a sugar dusting on top, of course.

Sam's own words...
Tuesday, February 27, 1917 – "Took Edith to the train. Hauled load of clover in a.m."

It was reasonable that Edith go to Oregon and finish her recuperation there with her mother while help was in place at home to care for children and the household. Baby Jonathan was nursing and went with his mother. It would be the first opportunity for Marilla to see her newest grandchild. Willa continued in school.

Sam got a workout. He went after coal and had luck when he was able to bring back 1,080 pounds. Another day he took Brazeau's four fatted hogs to Buhl. They weighed in at 880 pounds at 11¢ a pound for $96.80. He brought a load of straw to use, and he rented his bull to Hoover, who took the animal home with him. It was Friday, March 2, when he took the cream to Buhl to sell. On the same trip, he had the rake repaired for $1.50, sold 120 pounds of corn for $2.50, and paid 50¢ for his dinner.

Sam's own words...
Sunday, March 4, 1917 – "More snow, wondering how Edith is and why she or someone didn't write. I guess I'm doing the most worrying."

Monday, March 5, 1917 – "Snow and strong cold wind all day. A letter from Edith and Mother, for which I am thankful. News of Frank Dimon's death."

Now that Sam became apprised of Edith's safe arrival at her mother's home, he could go about his work free of worry. Tuesday he went to Buhl after feed and groceries. On Wednesday, Sam hauled eight loads of clover and went to his Forty and brought his mowing machine over to Brazeau's. Thursday, Sam went to Warner's for 3,200 pounds of seed wheat. He experienced more snowfall in the last half of the day. The next day was awful with a blizzard on bad roads when wheat was taken to Buhl for cleaning. On Saturday, it snowed all morning, and he had no mail.

Sunday, March 11, he heard from Edith that she would come home on Wednesday. He sold cream for $4.12 in Buhl on Monday and made a visit to Brazeau. The two men made their agreement on the price of every item Sam had bought from his landlord.

Sam had thought over the situation for when Edith would again be home and just strong enough to take on the household. He advised Reid that his pay would soon stop until spring opened up. It went hand-in-hand that Laura would also leave.

Sam's own words...
Wednesday, March 14, 1917 – "Edith came home, for which I am very thankful. Cold and windy. Cliff Reid's feeding another lamb now."

Edith had been gone 15 days in all and Sam was pleased to have his wife home. It had been just short of three months since Jonathan Ralph was born when life became precarious and unbalanced for the whole family due to Edith's illness. Relief was embraced as spring's renewal and near normalcy set in.

Edith was still weak and easy to tire.

Lambing started. Cold weather had no influence to slow the process. On occasion, one of the ewes would disown her newborn lamb, and bottle feeding became necessary. Triple births could mean the mother lacked enough milk for the extra demand. Opportunities presented openings again for Willa to inherit ownership of more than one lamb and the care of them.

On Friday, Sam had to take the stock down to Deep Creek to drink. He also went over to Hoovers after his bull. He tried to get coal in Buhl, but none was in supply. The frigid wind sent the chill through cracks and crevices to make it uncomfortable inside. The icy air was in play when they went to Mr. Wassums and then the school house Sunday evening.

The weather moderated but still lacked warmth on Monday, March 19, when Sam rode to Buhl for coal, groceries, and hog feed. Tuesday was like a spring day with all its promise of rejuvenation. Sam hauled straw and manure before he cleaned up his granary.

The harsh wind came as a cold blast on Wednesday. Sam did not feel well but performed his mandatory chores in spite of it. He cleaned up the grounds around the house.

Thursday, in Buhl, Sam and Brazeau signed the papers on the final figure of what Sam owed his landlord and partner. The note held a total of $896 for two years. The venture was equally valuable to both men and the same 50/50 at stake.

Sam's own words...
Friday, March 23, 1917 – "Cliff and Laura went home. Lee Hoover came over, and we dehorned seven head of stock. Cold wind. David not well. Edith improving slowly."
Saturday, March 24, 1917 – "Done chores and chopped and hauled two barrels of ice. Cut and salted down 70 pounds of beef."

David was well again on Monday and beamed as Sam placed him high up on the seat to ride between him and Edith into Buhl. He was nearly three years old and delighted to ride to town with his parents. When they returned home, they had a card from Roy telling of Uncle Ross's death.

Sam made a trip to town on Tuesday for coal but found none. He bought rubber boots at 50¢ and tobacco for 10¢. This was the day Sill Chick started work for Sam. He hauled manure.

On Wednesday, March 28, Sam was able to get 1,165 pounds of coal and brought it to the farm in deep ruts of sub-standard roads. The roads were no help to Sam's frame of mind. He rode along with sad thoughts of Ralph and later wrote in his diary that it was his brother's birthday.

Edith was less well on Thursday. After Sam had cleaned the yard, he did the wash and mopped floors. His generous help gave her comfort, but she would have chosen good health over her poor state if she'd had such a choice.

To finish out the month of March, Sam hauled manure two days in a row and pulled the wrecked chicken coop roof out of the garden. He tried to fill and stop up a hole under the head gate.

Sunday, April 1, started stormy and disagreeable. By Tuesday, the weather improved enough for a trip after groceries. Reid had paid $42.50 to settle his account of debt owed to Sam. It came handy for Sam to pay Runyon Bros. in full for past credit on groceries. He had oats ground and splurged 60¢ on tobacco and matches. After Sam had finessed the temperamental water, there was time in the afternoon to do the wash. Clothes were not in extra supply, and the children needed diapers, clean rompers, and blouses.

With work finished, there was time to pour over the newspaper together. In the Boise, ID, evening news that Sam and Edith subscribed to, they read that President Woodrow Wilson had asked Congress to declare war on Germany. Days later they would learn that Brazil had severed diplomatic relations with Germany as well. Sam kept a sober eye on such war news with its increased escalation. An army of 500,000 men was to be raised at once. Madison University of Wisconsin was reported to say that any students enlisting would be given college credits for military service.

Sam and Edith could easily have laughed when they read that 1,000 students marched and sang *We'll Hang the Kaiser in a Sour Apple Tree.* They both found items of interest in the *Evening Capitol News.* Sam no doubt paid attention to local grain and livestock market prices along with potatoes, hay, and clover prices.

Wednesday evening he cared for the younger children while Edith and Willa went visiting. They may have enjoyed the Elliott's or Lenore and Philip close by in Twin Falls.

The Brazeau farm was a bigger operation than the Forty Sam had owned. Sill Chick was kept busy to plow, harrow and corrugate. He paid the man $45 a month and worked himself just as hard. Sam hauled 1,700 pounds of alfalfa from the field and pitched and carried manure out from the barn. While Sill Chick handled his assigned work, Sam went to Buhl after seed wheat. It took two trips, one on the next day to bring it home. In Buhl, he had paid Brazeau $12.77, his due for half share from the cream skimmed off milk for two months. He left 631 pounds of alfalfa and clover seed at the farmer's union to be sold. Of course, water problems plagued him several days with the effort to try to get water flow. He and Chick plowed and harrowed in tandem.

Sill Chick rode into Buhl and brought 1,615 pounds of coal out from town while Sam plowed and harrowed. He was stopped in the field at 3:30 p.m. with a wind and snow storm, beautiful April weather.

Sam worked on the water all day on Sunday, April 15, trying to get at least a dribble into the house cistern.

Sam's own words...
Monday, April 16, 1917 – "Edith, David and I went to Buhl after groceries, feed, plowshare, etc. Took in cream and eggs, cold wind."

The plow's wrought-iron moldboard had a steel share that was easy to replace when a repair was needed. By Tuesday, another snow storm dropped white powder, but by afternoon Sill Chick started to plow. Sam succeeded in getting water into the cistern again. Edith had his help with laundry. He continued work on water, this time for the livestock reservoir.

Sam wrote a letter home on Wednesday during snow squalls. At least snow had a use since cattle ate it.

By Thursday, he had water flow, and Sam plowed for three days, and each evening Brazeau made a visit. They discussed trees on the property and made a decision on what to do with them. Plowing continued day in and day out, and the water effort hung on, too. The on again, off again canal took too much time and effort to water the stock. The sky opened up again Saturday morning while Sam studied it, trying to guess what the development of storm clouds would bring. Sam welcomed rain had worried for nothing that it was another snow storm coming.

On Sunday, he went to Warner's after his boar. He and Edith cleaned the house.

He might have wondered if the canal systems here worked less well than other irrigation projects located in the west. He knew his revered Teddy Roosevelt was famous for making headway with the nation's infra- structure after the instigation of 21 irrigation projects. Regardless, there were days when he was not enchanted with the water system.

Sam's 1917 ledger from the middle of April supplied entries of a business that had been set up by Sam, Edith, and Willa. The shop notes were handwritten by Edith and Willa. After her 15th birthday on March 23, Willa was hired to work at $20 a month. Sam and Edith's farm was close in near Twin Falls, not far from their beauty shop. The rental place expense was $15 paid in August. On Edith's supply list and customer services, she wrote that $2 was paid for the chair rental and $7.50 on the hair dryer. Sam kept the financial record for Willa's wages and listed them in his ledger and check stubs when he wrote a check to pay her. He was too thorough to neglect recording an expense that existed. Edith listed the necessities, and the shop's charges to patrons, and expenses. Her record keeping was minuscule compared to Sam's.

Expenses:

Hair creme, shampoo, scissors - each 50¢
Hair nets and polish – each 45¢
Hair pins - 25¢
Emory boards - 25¢
Second payment on dryer $5
Express Delivery $11.50
Repair on hair dryer - $1, later repair - 75¢

Edith and Willa kept pages of customer's names along with the service performed for each and the price paid.

Shampoo and cut 65¢ and 85¢
Cut or shampoo alone 50¢ each
Manicure 50¢
Hair dyed or scalp treatment $1 each
Bleached $1.50
Scalp massages 50¢ and $1
Bridal hairdressing $3

It went on week after week. Dr. Bula had a scalp treatment and massage. Dr. and Mrs. Sawyer had massages. Dr. Harry T. had bleach applied, scalp treatments, and creme treatments. Many wives, daughters, and single women had hair dressed after a shampoo and cut. The enterprise continued.

There was no further mention of Willa's attendance at school, not unusual for a girl who was to be 16 years of age the next spring. Sam's ledger showed that she was listed as Willa Crippen. It supported the pride of considering her to be his little daughter as he had written years earlier. It hints that she had most likely been known by the name in school.

Sam's own words...
Tuesday, May 1, 1917 – "Helped wash: Worked on fence: did not get work done until 9 o'clock because of dry canal. Chick pulled four rows of trees."

The days blended into each other as repetitious work never ended. Sam's chores took six or seven hours, and the garden needed plowing. The work day lengthened. Sill Chick turned over dirt and ran the float after Sam planted seeds. The float pulled the dirt over the seed and smoothed the soil.

Sam had enough odd jobs to keep him busy but also assisted Sill Chick in the fields on crops. Chick ran float for two days while Sam harrowed, treated wheat, and tended an old sow. Sam drilled in wheat while Chick harrowed and drew hay.

The cistern for cattle was dry again Thursday, May 10. The two men worked until 9:30 p.m. to water the stock by taking them to Deep Creek. They managed to get a small amount of water in the cistern by 10:30 p.m.

On Friday, Sam drilled in more wheat while Chick had a chance to succeed in the garden and chores. Sam kept a close eye on one animal kept in the barn. His mare, Fanny, was restless and stepping around in her stall. Sam read the signs correctly. Fanny's Colt chose this day to be born.

Sam's own words...
Saturday, May 12, 1917 – "Drilled in wheat. Chick tried to repair fence and make garden but fell down on both. Betty got stung by bees and scared all of us."

Betty's screech at the full capacity of her lungs brought everyone to her rescue. She had wandered too close to the beehives and encountered the hot little seats on worker drones that rallied defense against the one-and-a-half-year-old toddler. She meant no harm at all and had no notion of the danger she had bumped into. Edith soothed her, dried her tears, and carried her inside for a nap

The bee attack certainly furnished a topic of conversation on Sunday when company came to visit. Edith's brother, Philip, the Wilcocks', and Brazeaus came out. Another subject discussed may have been the ca- nal that was dry often enough to be a problem. The price each of them paid the Twin Falls Canal Company was part and portion of the dissatisfaction voiced. The Snake River was not being diverted efficiently enough to the channel. They all hauled water from Deep Creek Hamlet, named aptly for a deep creek there. The time it took drained away the time they needed to do farm work.

Monday was another day added to water woes made worse with the high wind. It prevented corrugation on the second day of the same conditions and discouraged Sam He cleaned out the cellar and managed to plant two rows of potatoes. By Wednesday, May 16, Sam finally corrugated, and he quickened his pace a little, glad to make headway on his work again. There was water in the canal, and he had to repair the pump since it had lost its prime. The month of May wore on as Sam cleaned ditches. He expressed his exasperation with the frugal water. "Chased ten inches of water," he wrote.

It was a pitiful amount, and without a doubt, it occurred to Sam that they had never faced a short water supply in Pennsylvania and had not needed to pay for it either.

Sill Chick used the spring tooth harrow on dead alfalfa while Sam worked in his garden. He butchered a hog on Saturday. Brazeaus paid them a friendly visit on Sunday, but such visits also served for the owner to keep a check on his farm and gauge progress and proper care. They wanted the Crippen family to prosper and easily pay half proceeds to them. They all kept up with the news from the paper and discussed it. There had been recent front-page headlines that on May 1, the Selective Service Act had passed in Congress, giving President Wilson the power of conscription. The draft had been instated. The trouble with Germany had not abated. The draft would be put into practice on June 5, 1917. Canada was not far behind the United States in its same purpose. Sam, like all the men of his time, followed it with interest.

Monday, May 21, was the perfect time to set out tomato plants. Sam cleaned ditches out of need, but the timing was not perfect. Tuesday he cut up pork, packed it in a barrel, and poured brine on it. The sausage was made next. The only job left was rendering fat to lard. Edith would be busy cooking it down and canning it. She counted on Willa to continue with beauty shop clients. A shower was welcomed on Wednesday morning before Sam went to Buhl after garden seeds, oats, and groceries.

Sam's own words...
Thursday, May 24, 1917 – "Tended 25 inches of water, grubbed apple trees, sowed two acres of oats, part cloudy and a little rain."

Irrigation was closer to effortless with that much water, coupled with corrugated rows to let the water ripple where it was needed. The pulled trees had stray roots that had to be dug out, grubbed over, and the cavity filled in, on which Sam and Sill both labored. Those trees pulled out had been older and less productive with roots that reached deep. On Friday, Sam hauled trees away and what he couldn't finish was left for Saturday. Sill Chick harrowed, planted oats, and corrugated to allow water flow through the rows. The planting was ready for Sam to irrigate on Sunday. He also cut seed potatoes into pieces that would have an eye to sprout and grow from every piece.

Sunday had its allotment of visitors and Edith no doubt had a confection made with honey to offer them. She and Sam enjoyed friends after a work week brought them all around to Sunday again. This week it was Sawyers, Crows, and Brazeaus who paid visits. Philip and Lenore were pleased that their son, Don Crow, would start work for Sam on June 8, a week away. Sill Chick had given his notice.

Sam was back to his spud production on Monday. He planted them when he was finished with his water coax for crops and garden. On Tuesday, he went to Buhl for 1,040 pounds of coal, which cost him $4.10.

159

The water works for Alsike clover and alfalfa was his priority on Wednesday. It carried over into Thursday, and he brought hay to the livestock.

Sam had weighty business on his mind and attended to it on Thursday, May 17, when he made a trip out to Gooding to see Andy. He found him home, but Andy offered no money, only promises. He had made no plan to start payment of the money he owed. Sam rode homeward with thoughts that it was odd, unexpected that no portion of the money was paid to him. He needed it, but he had work to do.

He had Sill Chick plow six days right on through the next Thursday, and it included the former section of apple orchard they had flattened. He kept Chick well occupied on Friday and Saturday to run float over the vacated tree section. Saturday, June 2, ended Chick's last workday at noon.

Brazeaus made their Sunday visit.

The month of June required corrugated rows followed by almost daily irrigation. Sam had a few days of solo work. He did chores, hauled hay, and drilled wheat and oats. Mr. Feucher came and sheared their sheep on Wednesday, June 6.

Sam's own words...
Thursday, June 7, 1917 – "Irrigated wheat. Edith and David went to Circus."
Friday, June 8, 1917 – "Irrigated wheat. Planted potatoes. Don's first day."
Saturday, June 9, 1917 – "Irrigated wheat and potatoes and alfalfa. Edith went to Buhl, took 52 chickens – 229 pounds (wool 20 lbs.), an awful windstorm. Edith was beaten out of 78 pounds in weight on her chickens, at least, by Mutual Creamery Co."

David was an excited circus goer. He was old enough to enjoy a new activity and learn new information. He was a tired boy when they returned from Boise, Idaho. The quilt in the wagon bottom furnished his comfort for a nap when Edith drove home after attending the A. G. Barnes Big 4 Ring Wild Animal Circus. It was billed as "The Show That's Different." Different was true for three-year-old David, who had just been to his first circus. He would tell Daddy, Betty, and Billo all about it in the evening.

Necessary irrigation took place nearly every day, and Sam had Edith's nephew, Don, help. It cut down on work for Sam as the only one chained to that job. Don was on the payroll at $35 a month since he was under 20 years old and Sam expected to teach him duties. Sam would need patience because he was accustomed to experienced hires who could do independent work.

Sam found it hard to believe what was on the weight slip for the chickens. He questioned Edith about who weighed them at Mutual Creamery. There was no blame put on her for it and Sam was sorry for her distress when she was forced to accept what they gave her. It was unexpected that they would cheat a woman out of her hard-earned money. Sam knew there was no recourse for the fraud committed since it could not be redone. It was sure to be a topic of discussion with their Sunday visitors who needed to be warned about the creamery's dishonesty.

The 20 pounds of wool netted $5.

June had so far been cold, windy, and disagreeable. It was also unpleasant when everyone in the family was sick to their stomachs. Sam irrigated wheat each day regardless of his discomfort. Don did not work for 2.5 days, but Sam mowed hay for livestock a couple of times. Friday, June 15, was warm and he planted tomatoes. He and Edith were glad to feel better.

A night out was a rarity for them when they went to Chautauqua on Saturday evening. The excitement of the anticipated entertainment event had been talked about for weeks by friends and all of the people in surrounding communities. A circuit Chautauqua had sent out promotional brochures weeks ahead to all the villages and towns within the circle of Buhl, Twin Falls, Pocatello, and Gooding. In the two days before show time, word circulated that the traveling show business crew had set up a huge tent near Twin Falls. It preceded the entertainers and speakers soon to arrive.

The program would be presented for several successive evenings before they moved on to follow the agenda for their touring season.

Sam and Edith expected to hear some ministry, but the programs were rumored to include more entertainment than in years past. They had evolved into added topics of current events, travel, and stories. They often had a comic twist. The reputation of their most prolific public speaker, Russell Conwell, appealed to Sam. Mr. Conwell would be delivering his famous *Acres of Diamonds* speech. He was close to his five thousandth delivery of it. The theme was *Get Rich Young Man, for money is power and power ought to be in the hands of good people. "I say you have no right to be poor."*

Music was billed as, *The Old Country Fiddler,* who played violin, sang, and was a ventriloquist and comedian. He told tales about life in rural New England, and that alone would have interested Sam. Edith was curious since they would be moving to the area.

The popularity of the Chautauqua movement was attributed, in part, to the social and geographic isolation of American farm and ranch communities. People like Sam and Edith and their neighbors would have a natural hunger for education, culture, and entertainment. They would remember it and talk about it for an extended time.

When Sam finished with the mild flood he'd set loose on the wheat: he alternated the stream to Alsike clover. On the 18th, Edith took Don to the train to go home because he was sick. Sam went on a separate trip to Buhl after coal and repairs. He made a payment that was due on a bank loan.

Sam's own words...
Wednesday, June 20, 1917 – "Irrigated wheat and oats. Mr. Bailey took four head of yearlings and calves, $80. Hauled load of hay."

Sam kept his written record of irrigation because the success of his abundant crops and garden depended on the rotation of it. Without a paid farm hand, he was overworked.

When Dolly had her foal, a filly, it delighted Willa to watch the wobbly-legged offspring. She may have brought David close enough to see it. He would go anywhere with his Billo.

Sam planted corn and had hired Joe Bailey to shock hay by hand. Joe used his own team to mow and worked both jobs back and forth. After eight days absence, Don returned to work on Tuesday, June 26. Sam needed him. So many jobs begged attention that wore him out. He hired Paul Baily to help Joe, who stacked hay while Paul ran the bull rake that Sam had repaired the day before. Don was kept busy through Saturday before he went home to spend the day with his family on Sunday.

On the Sabbath, Sam tended water and hauled hay for animals. In the evening, they went to Gardell's. Don was back that night and ready to do work on Monday, July 2. Sam had him irrigate since he could do that without an overseer. Sam mowed foxtail and weeds in the orchard. It was extra warm.

They ate dinner with Baileys on Wednesday. Garden work, irrigation, and mowing continued with Sam's lone efforts since Don did not work on Thursday.

Sam's own words...
Friday, July 6, 1917 – "Irrigated and mowed alfalfa. Don pretended to work. Edith took butter to Runyons."

Edith would not let the extra butter go rancid. She knew how much she needed for her family and could sell the rest to make pin money for her effort. Willa handled more of the hairdresser tasks. Edith needed time for all of the domestic chores.

In five days time, Sam had put Don down for only two-and-a-half days of wages. He broke it down to $1.33 a day since the young man was slow and reluctant with his work. Don regularly malingered. It made it hard for Sam to manage because he was Philip and Lenore's son. Don was not ready to be a full-time man yet. He went home mid-day on Saturday but was back Sunday evening.

The Sawyers visited the Crippens on Sunday.

The veterinarian came out on Monday to doctor animals. It may have been an examination for calving since no problem with livestock was mentioned.

The two Baileys, Joe and Paul, continued hay harvest for Sam with their team of horses. Sam was busy with his barn chores, bee hives, and gardens. He had a job to keep Don productive, but he was steady enough as the water tenderer. It was easier on Sam to keep him at that and never mind other jobs. He marked Don down for three days of work during the week that led up to July 11, the end of his employment with Sam. He had more or less earned the accrued check that Sam wrote him for $22.63.

Sam's own words...
Friday, July 13, 1917 – "Tended water, mowed around in orchard and worked in garden. Warm. A letter from Grace."

He would have to make time to write to Grace and Ma both. It was natural that they wondered when the plans to come home would materialize. They did understand that the harvest had to be completed before such a move.

On Sunday, Sam handled the irrigation before he went to see Gates about cutting his grain. It was set to be a large scale production from many acres that would be ready in August. The wheat would require forced moisture flow until harvest.

Sam started the quest to have the mares bred and took them on their first trip to stud service on Monday, July 16.

A smile played around the corners of Sam's mouth as he finally wrote home. His letter would put an end to anyone's anxiety over thoughts that he had changed his mind about the move. They needn't worry even if he wrote less during busy harvest just ahead.

Tuesday, July 17, he manipulated water through the corrugated runs, hoed corn in the garden, and plowed potatoes. He had a good deal of garden work.

Saturday, July 21, he went to Buhl after repairs for Brazeau's binder and mower. While there, he sent off payment of $39.45 for Edith's life insurance.

Monday, July 23, started off with chores and water works. They had to be done ahead of the trip to take mares, Dolly and Fanny, over to Hoovers to be bred. It took a lot of time and pushed other jobs aside until later. It was 11 p.m. before Sam got to bed.

Tuesday came too soon, and it started all over again with the water rotation. He repaired the smoke house and put the swather on the mower machine. Joe Bailey worked for him three hours on Wednesday to cut Alsike clover. He had the Campbell boy cooperate with him three more days on

Alsike. Sam was busy with all manner of jobs but fell back to gar- den care when possible. He pulled weeds and picked up potatoes and carried both out of the rows.

Saturday, August 4, he bought 125 pounds of binder twine at 18¢ a pound ($22.50). He was prepared for Mr. Gates's arrival to thresh his grain as planned. Plans gone astray were not welcome.

12 – Three Trunks
Unmentionables, 1917, 1918

Sunday, Sam tended water and knew it would be the last day off he would enjoy for a couple of weeks. He didn't read tea leaves. He knew all about threshing. It was all inclusive: to thresh, mow, rake, shock, load, and haul.

Sam's own words...
Monday, August 6, 1917 – "Tended water, cut and pulled weeds, shocked clover until 3:30 in the morning."

He was off to a grueling start to get work done that he would not have time for when Gates and the threshers arrived. Tuesday he tended water and fixed up slips to haul clover seed. Sam cut more weeds. Brazeau came out in the evening, eager to follow details of the crop plans. On Wednesday, Sam went to town to find a suitable material with which to cover the slips.

Sam's own words...
Thursday, August 9, 1917 – "Helped Mr. Gates thresh three-quarters of the day and threshed for myself."

They had begun but suddenly it became so windy on Friday that they could not thresh at all. But they did not stand idle. Sam and Gates worked on the binder all day and made sure it was in top shape.

On Saturday morning two grim faces waited for all of the threshing crew to arrive. Sam shocked wheat for Gates in the afternoon while Gates used old Bill, Sam's horse. Sunday was no day of rest. Sam cut and shocked wheat while Gates and his team threshed for seven hours. Reid worked by hand six hours. Monday saw the finish of that process. Gates and Smith ran binder while Sam, Reid, and Joe Bailey walked the fields all afternoon and shocked up wheat.

Tuesday wasn't quite a repeat of the day before. Smith tried to cut Bailey's grain, but it was too wet. Sam took his mares to stud again at $2 each. It was not down time for him as long as he kept himself productive.

Mr. Bailey shocked wheat for Sam six-and-a-half hours while Sam hauled hay, shocked wheat, and cleared ground sections.

Edith went to Buhl on Wednesday, August 15, to check on Willa at the beauty shop. They most likely needed to talk about tapering off customers' appointments and selling off hair products at discount.

Sam was involved with the harvest. On Thursday, he went to see someone about cutting the remainder of his ripe wheat. He mowed alfalfa. The other men mowed, raked, and bunched hay, also loaded and hauled it.

Sunday again; it was August 19, and Sam tended water. They went to Olson's after supper. They discussed the general news, a mutual conversation to which they all looked forward. As farmers, they probably had an interest in the story of "The Green Corn Rebellion." It was a central Oklahoma reluctance against the WWI draft. The Working Class Union reacted to the imposition of military conscription. It was an ill-fated but heroic armed resistance to the United States entry into World War I. A few of the Idaho farmers wondered if they needed to worry about the draft themselves. Sam was not so worried, and he may have considered it a remote possibility.

The crew of men commenced work Monday on the wheat that Smith had cut. They worked on grain, hay, and straw. Sam used Fanny and Roxy with the rake. Friday, they worked through 9 p.m. and Saturday, until five o'clock.

There was no downtime on Sunday. Sam was inspired to work on the hog pasture fence, sharpen the mower sections, and tend water in his not-so-free time.

Sam's own words...
Monday, August 27, 1917 – "Mr. Bailey and I mowed hay until 4 o'clock: tended water and went until 9 o'clock as usual."

The cut hay had to be raked, loaded and hauled to add to stacks. Alfalfa was ready for a stacker run. August 30 marked the finish on the stacking of the second cutting. On the last day of August, Sam took 1,016 pounds of Alsike seed for cleaning. It was valuable seed. He figured it was also the last day that Sadie was unmarried as she was set to wed Bob Madison on September 1, as learned from Grace.

August also marked the end of the hairdresser enterprise. The beauty shop had been in operation five months. Scarce water in Twin Falls may have urged the close of business. Willa's recorded wages totaled $101.25.

On Sunday, September 2, the only work Sam did was tend water and feed animals. His full work never failed to resume on Monday. He stacked wheat and noted that a registered heifer had a calf. Tuesday he took the mares to stud service once again. The third time was carried out to ensure that it was successful.

Sam may have grown tired of tending water, but there would be no use to continue farming without it in this section of the country. He called on his patience.

Sam's own words...
Wednesday, September 5, 1917 – "Stacked wheat and tended water. Olson's came over in evening. Betty and David sick."

Mr. Olson knew Sam would be on top of the news and may have mentioned that he had read that the Canadian government was to follow the United States' lead. Its House of Commons passed a law to instate the draft. The men nodded.

Betty was already sick ahead of David. Both children improved by Thursday

Sam had stacked wheat seven-and-a-half hours, a whole day, for Joe Bailey, and returned to tend to his water works. The next two days he stacked his own wheat and fixed fence. The fix didn't go far enough. Cows got out on Sunday, and he found his reason for more fence repair.

Sam stacked wheat four days straight. He cleaned and repaired a grain bin and sold the Jersey calf to Schaefer for $10.

Friday he went to Buhl after coal for the threshing machine. The machine's 25 hp engine was manufactured by the Illinois Thresher Co. in Sycamore in 1917. Steam only lasted about 40 years, but it was good, efficient power. It might take over an hour to stoke the power, but once the steam was up, those engines didn't let a farmer down.

While Sam was in Buhl, he sold 773 pounds of Alsike seed at 21¢ a pound. He recorded the $162.33 and kept the receipt to square up with Brazeau. Saturday, September 15, he was back to stacking wheat. In the evening, they went to Olson's.

He contracted with Smith to have his oats cut. Monday he went to pay a $50 note at Buhl Bank, due every month.

David was sick again, and as hard as Sam worked, he still kept his children in mind.

Tuesday he worked to get set for threshers to come on Wednesday, September 19. The crew threshed 632 bushels of wheat. Sam believed the 28 acres should have produced 1,500 bushels, but what he got was what he took. It was added to the burgeoning granary.

The farmers practiced fair play and assisted with each others' crops as usual. Sam helped Mr. Elliott thresh six hours on Thursday. He also unloaded his own wheat and took Mr. Bachman's wagon home.

Sam's own words...
Saturday, September 22, 1917 – "Took 3,875 pounds of wheat to B. M. & E. Co. Rainy in p.m."

The Buhl Milling & Elevator Company was a buyer of farmer's grain and feed crops. They also made flour and sold sacks. It was just the start of Sam's treks to sell his crops.

Sunday came right on queue along with Smith to cut oats. Sam moved the swather over to the cutter and attached the mechanism. Its purpose was to narrow the feed of grain to a smaller path.

Sam picked up the windfall of peaches in the orchard. Bruises would cause more waste if the fruit were left lay too long. If his memory served him well, it brought a smile at the thought of peach pie or cobbler. Edith would not disappoint him. They visited Olson's after supper and may have taken a peach confection with them to share.

Monday, September 24, was designated for odd jobs. Sam hauled jags of hay and straw, covered tomato vines with straw mulch, and sharpened his sickles. He sold hay to Campbell.

Tuesday had a purpose further than its own end. Sam fixed up a wagon box and loaded it full of wheat. It was ready for a trip to Buhl another day. He shocked oats and repaired fence. Could he have warmed to the idea that there was more peach dessert waiting?

On Wednesday, he transported his 3,615 pounds of wheat to Buhl Milling & Elevator Company.

Thursday, Sam had oats to haul and stack. Another job loomed, which was not relished, but necessary. There may have been some squeals heard while he tended to the castration of the male piglets. Sam knew some of them were up to 10 days old. If he'd waited much longer to clip testicles, the little porkers would be too robust for one man to hang onto. He remembered helping Andy with his when they were just over three weeks old and knew he didn't want to make that mistake. Andy's had bled more, too, because of their age. Andy could be quite a talker on occasion. While they had been in the middle of the piglet task, Andy implied that his pork for the market had to be sweet. It should not have a boar odor when it cooks. If they weren't taken care of through castration, that taint would be the result. Sam had kept a firm hold on each wiggler and nodded his head while Andy did his part, which was snipping.

Sam's own words...
Saturday, September 29, 1917 – "Took 3,615 pounds of wheat to Buhl Milling & Elevator Co."

He tucked the weight ticket receipt into the front of his 1917 diary along with one that he had placed there a few days earlier.

September ended on a Sunday with only odd jobs on Sam's agenda. Monday he needed to take a trip to Buhl to settle up with Brazeau on hay, wool, and 10,883 pounds of wheat. Half-share was $419.10. Sam was a man of his word, and Brazeau had known that when he signed the contract agreement with him. Brazeau may have thought it a shame that Sam was to leave and go back east. Maybe he imagined a second-year contract with a hard worker and honest man like Sam Crippen.

Sam tended water early Tuesday, brought his bull home, and carried hay to the barn. Olsons came over in the evening.

October held plenty of work. Sam cut sweet clover, did odd jobs, and mowed alfalfa along the road and yard. The alfalfa had served to discourage the growth of tough Canada thistle. If it had been allowed to take hold, it would be hard to get rid of. He hauled a load of hay and raked more of it. Then he picked peaches. Olsons came over after fruit jars.

Saturday, October 6, Sam went to Buhl after 100 pounds of sugar, which cost him $9. The peaches would be Edith's added work until canned.

Laid-back Sunday meant Sam could relax with only chores and odds-and-end jobs on the agenda for once. Gardells came over for a visit and bought 75¢ worth of peaches before they went home. It was not in Sam's character to ask on the Sabbath for the outstanding money owed him. Andy would have known that.

Sam had Monday planned. He loaded a wagon box with 3,550 pounds of wheat and delivered it to Buhl Seed & Grain Company. A jag of hay was hauled Tuesday, and the head ditch cleaned out to be used to make water flow into corrugated rows. He pulled a few beans and mowed weeds in the potato patch. He needed another jag of hay Wednesday and mowed the orchard by the house and near the hog pen. Olsons came for a visit in the evening.

Thursday, Sam went to help Joe Bailey with his cistern then borrowed and brought Bailey's wagon home so that he'd have two on hand. Loading them was his work for the rest of the day, and he put his back into the job.

Sam's own words...
Friday, October 12, 1917 – "Mr. Bailey and I took wheat to Buhl Mill Co., 3,620 #, and 3,505 #. I raked hay in the evening."

Saturday, October 13, 1917 – "Hauled a little hay, loaded 3,500 # wheat and took it to Buhl Seed & Grain Co."

Sam used the Buhl Feed & Grain Company instead of the Milling & Elevator Company. He and Brazeau had discussed fairness in use of both companies, and possibly it served to keep them in good stead with both.

Sunday was not taken for leisure. Sam shocked and hauled hay, and loaded wheat in two wagons. Mr. Rugg from Sam's former Forty brought a Jersey cow to leave in the pasture with Sam's bull. It was understood that a fee to include stud service and feed would be charged.

Sam and Joe Bailey drove the wagonloads of wheat to Buhl. Bailey took 3,465 pounds to B.M. & E. Co. while Sam delivered 3,590 pounds to B.S. & G. Co. Sam secured the weight stubs.

Tuesday, October 16, was spent in return labor to help Joe Bailey again to complete his new cistern. The strong cold wind made any job unpleasant.

Edith had three teeth pulled. She had held the side of her face and suffered from the pain too long. Her work was caught up, and she was forced to attend to her needs.

Wednesday Sam found it necessary to bring hay to the livestock. He had hauled it to them from the stack often, and now he had to mow. Sam sharpened sections of mower blades and started laying it low. It was a fight with the cold wind. For the next three days, Sam and Mr. Bailey harvested alfalfa for half of each day. Sam filled the other part of the half days hauling hay and gathering squash. On Saturday the two men went to Buhl in the late afternoon.

There was never any doubt that Sunday was work filled. Sam and Mr. Bailey both mowed in the morning. Sam raked and hauled hay in the afternoon. Water was absent from the lateral ditch, and Sam hoped it was not of long duration to cause extra work.

While Joe Bailey raked hay for eight hours on Monday, Sam and Edith made a pond. They must have used their horses to pull loads of dirt up and out. They accomplished it with willpower and might. Sam helped Elliott thresh a quarter of the day.

Sam and Edith bought a war bond for $50. It was their first introduction to the idea of financial securities, like many of their neighbors. The U.S. Treasury issued securities termed *Liberty Bonds* to help finance the war effort and build patriotism. The Crippens were not new to patriotism. Subscribing to the bonds became a symbol of patriotic duty in the United States.

Sam and Mr. Bailey raked alfalfa until 3 o'clock Tuesday when Joe Bailey left to gather his own hay. Water appeared back in the ditch and the parallel lateral by evening, and Sam considered it his good fortune. Wednesday had the opposite effect when winds were so high that they could not stack hay. But Sam hauled a load of it before they gave it up and went to Buhl. Thursday was met with success to run the stacker. By afternoon, he and Joe dug and picked up some of Sam's spuds. On Friday and Saturday, they worked on Bailey's potatoes. They contended with wild wind conditions all three days.

Sunday was just another day if described by the work done. Sam picked up potatoes six hours for Joe Bailey. It was windy and cold as usual. Olsons came for an evening visit.

Joe Bailey helped stack hay on Sam's farm Tuesday, Wednesday, and Thursday to the finish. They moved the stacker to Bailey's farm where Joe's son, Paul, would help him. Sam hurried to accomplish some of his other work. He hauled hay, fixed the corral, and hired Mr. Steele to work for him. Steele moved over to stay at the farm. Sam ran the bull rake.

Mr. Campbell had come out to measure hay but refused to do so for three days. His theory could have been to let it settle longer and hope it measured less to get the price lower. Maybe he wanted rain on it to weight it down. Only Campbell knew why.

Sam worked for Joe Bailey on Friday and Saturday. He raked three hours and collected potatoes 10.5 hours. He drew hay for himself Friday, November 1.

Sunday was meant for breathing deeper when allowed, a more relaxed day. Sam did the minimum to haul hay and cleaned the cellar. They enjoyed a visit to Olson's in the evening.

Monday's occupation for Sam was to dig his spuds all day long. He finished them Tuesday and took part of them to the cellar. The rest of the day he brought in hay to his livestock and did odd jobs. Joe Bailey threshed beans for him.

Sam took the potato digger home to Bailey's on Wednesday, November 17. Olsons came after a cow Sam had sold them. Sam threshed beans, hauled hay, and harrowed his potato ground. He wasted no time, not that anyone could have noticed.

The digger was put to proper use at Bailey's on Thursday. Sam picked up potatoes for him 8.5 hours. On Friday, he was home where he did chores and shocked hay. Saturday he went to Buhl after groceries and coal, but the latter was not in supply. It had become too popular an item with the advance of November's usual chill.

On Sunday, all he did was haul a jag of hay and minimal water management since crops were harvested. Animals still needed water.

Sam's own words...
Monday, November 12, 1917 – "Hauled two loads of hay and dug carrots, etc. Went over to Olson's for a party in evening and stayed till 3 o'clock in morning."

Maybe getting two loads of hay in for animals was a smart plan for the next day when he would be short on sleep and energy. He never neglected his cows and horses.

Tuesday was rainy. Sam figured out the number of tons in his haystacks. Schaefer turned his sheep out on the field stubble. Sheep eat closer to the ground than any other farm animal. For the first few weeks after harvest, stubbles present a mixture of feeds like straw, fallen grain, and green feed. It is necessary nutrition for the ruminant mammals. Sam knew how sheep herds were managed in conjunction with methods approved by Boise River Wildlife Management of Idaho Fish and Game. He and Schaefer may have discussed that before the season. Officials say they like the sheep to graze on white top, a noxious weed. Ewes also eat skeleton weed early in the season. They really like it and the same with cheatgrass. Grazers help reduce fire danger in the foothills. Sam was on board with taking a lot of the fuel load away by this method.

Wednesday, he was back to potatoes, which he sorted and sacked. He delivered 1,300 pounds of spuds that he'd sold to Runyon. Thursday he took four loads of hay to the barn. He and Campbell measured haystacks in the late hours of the afternoon. Sam was aware of the measurements already and needed no more shenanigan delay tactics from Campbell.

Sam's own words...
Friday, November 16, 1917 – "Went to Buhl and settled up with Campbell, 90T, plus 239 foot of hay at $15 per T. $856.90."

Sam was satisfied with the hay sale that he would be splitting with Brazeau. On Saturday, he sold their mailbox, a sure sign of the pending move, but early in the process. When he had a definite buyer, it was an opportune time to make the sale. The bull-rake was brought into the barn, its season over and done. Sam noticed that the ewes had commenced breeding, a sign that things would remain the same here on this farm that Brazeau would resume management of early next year.

He did as little as possible on Sunday. He was thankful to his creator that plans moved ahead with reasonable success and the money to carry them out had been earned by constant effort. The Olsons came over, both families aware that opportunities for visits would dwindle. Edith and Sam enjoyed them immensely, and the two families would have to adjust to the relocation of the Crippens across the country.

Sam's own words...
Monday, November 19, 1917 – "Took my mixed alfalfa and clover seed to Buhl. Sold for 10¢ per pound, 628 pounds at $62.80. Bought trunk and dry goods."

The trunk signaled the need to pack. The dry goods from Buhl Department Store mentioned in the checkbook stub on that date was $1.55, which purchased three pair of socks for Willa with 45¢ left over for her.

It was already November 20, a Tuesday, on which Sam repaired the fence and went to Warner's sale in the afternoon. He did not make a purchase but would have enjoyed chats with neighbors near and far, all farmers like him. On Wednesday afternoon he dug post holes and bought 15 pounds of beef at 13¢ per pound, $1.95.

Sam's own words...
Thursday, November 22, 1917 – "Worked on haystack and fence in a.m., Took Willa to train in p.m. Willa cash $5.50."

Willa's turn had arrived, a last chance to travel to Wyoming to see her Haggarty relatives. She had not seen her father in a long time, and this was her opportunity before relocation to Pennsylvania. Willa was most likely the bearer of one jar of honey for Lora Nichols, her mother's friend, where she would stay overnight. Her father was to come down from his copper mine and meet her there to take her up to the cabin she had known years earlier as a younger child.

Willa had earned money working on hair and farm chores. She was in an excellent position to enjoy her reunion journey. She hugged her family goodbye. David most likely clung to her and did not want his Billo to leave. Willa loved her young siblings, and when she hugged them goodbye, she would have promised to return.

Sam had more fence posts to install all day Friday. It was rainy on Saturday, and he performed chores even though he was sick all day. Olsons came out about noon.

Sam's own words...
Tuesday, November 27, 1917 – "Helped Steele in a.m. Went to Buhl in p.m. after Willa."

There was some excitement associated with the prospect of Willa's return home after five days absence. She was no doubt just as happy to be back with her family.

While they were in Buhl, they bought a 13-pound turkey at 15¢ a pound for $1.95.

Edith no doubt got up early on Wednesday to stuff and roast the bird. Willa had time in the kitchen over food preparations to tell her mother about a drawn-out visit with Lora Nichols. Edith planned to write to Lora once she had a new address to give her in Pennsylvania. They went over to Olson's to celebrate Mrs. Olson's birthday and share Thanksgiving, too.

It was rainy all day Thursday, but Sam made a fence around his one last haystack. It may have been to keep the ruffage off limits from cattle.

He had already made a deal with Campbell and told Brazeau about it. The measurements were figured and had to stay the same.

Sam's own words...

Friday, November 30, 1917 – "Hauled jag of hay and straw. Went over to Andy's but he had gone. Sold stove, churn, and rooster for $55. Sold two breechings and collars, $5."

The dedicated trip to see Andy was not productive. Sam had hoped his friend would now have set aside the money he owed him since the note was past due. He needed it paid before they departed to go east, and what a help it would have been.

The breeching is the harness's braking system and has a broad strap that lays across the horse's hindquarters and smaller straps that lay across the rump. Hold back straps attach to rings on the shaft of the cart or wagon. The breeching has a stuffed crupper that goes underneath the horse's tail and may fasten complete with flank and rump straps. Sam and all the farmers and ranchers used them to distribute the load more widely over the workhorse body.

On Saturday, he and Steele sacked and weighed 4,000 pounds of wheat that Steele was buying from Sam

Sam's cow, Alice, had a heifer calf. It would also be sold.

Sunday was spent at home. He hauled two loads of straw and put it on a shed roof. The cows required the usual jag of hay as it turned cold.

On Monday, December 3, Sam went to Buhl after coal, groceries, and their $85 dry goods order that had been patiently awaited. There may have been new clothes for the family's planned relocation. An excellent first impression was to be made. He bought three suits of underwear at a cost of $10.17 and gloves for $1. It may be a good bet they were items for Sam since ladies lingerie was unmentionable.

The cooling trend prevailed with the snow it dropped on Tuesday evening after all day fence building. In the evening, Sam wrote Willa a $14 check for labor. The hair business had ended at the onset of September, and this was for farm work. She cared for chickens, calves, and sheep. Sam and Edith knew that a young woman needed money for her own use, personal and what not.

Sam went to Buhl on Wednesday to start talks on the settlement with Brazeau. On Thursday, he saw Hagedorn so they could compare hours and pay even up with labor not matched by equal time worked. Another trip was made to see Andy and no money was available. Andy, however, knew that Sam's two colts were up for sale and made a deal to buy them for $70, which he added to his already past due bill.

Friday, December 7, was colder yet because of the wind. Sam sacked wheat, hauled hay, and fixed fence. On Saturday, he went to see his landlord again to further their talks. Sunday and Monday, he figured and refigured what he still owed Brazeau.

Sam took his family to visit Olson's on Monday evening. Their friendship would keep them connected until it was no longer possible. Tuesday was cold and windy, an excellent day to take a load of wheat to Buhl. Wednesday he hauled hay and straw and fixed fence. Thursday, he and Brazeau agreed on their final settlement. Friday was odd jobs day and regular chores.

Sam's own words...
Saturday, December 15, 1917 – "Hauled load of hay and straw. Went over and found out Andy had come and taken his colts, etc. to Gooding."

Well, Andy got the colts and other items, but they were not purchased yet because he hadn't paid anything. He still owed a few hundred dollars to Sam.

On Sunday, Sam did chores, and they went to Olson's. The close relationship would make the parting hard.

In Buhl on Monday, Sam went to see Mr. Hammel about a sale. He paid $10 interest on his Fleuger note at the bank and picked up a letter from Grace at the Twin Falls post office. While he was in Twin Falls, he got Mother Crow's dome top trunk from Lenore. It revealed feminine decor when Lenore opened the top to retrieve a few items stored inside. The under lid was decorated with a bordered wallpaper print and a small picture of a lady in a large brimmed hat looking out from the center. A compartment built in beneath the left side of the dome was meant to contain lady's unmentionables to keep them private. Edith would put it to proper use. Willa had her own trunk.

Sam's own words...
Wednesday, December 19, 1917 – "Hauled load of hay, done chores and made book box."

The book box was constructed of solid lumber to protect their valuable reading materials and volumes in transit. They had often read aloud from Edith's 1899 book of poems, *Departmental Ditties*, by Rudyard Kipling. There was the thick black volume, *The Achievements of Stanley and Other Explorers,* by Hon. J. J. Headley, the 1878 edition. Edith was fond of her gilt-edged pages of Homer's *Iliad* in small print. She might have recited to Sam straight from one of its pages of introduction that the amazing rhyming poetry may never be equaled. He valued them all on parity to her ardor, even the 1880 *Complete Poetical Works* of Jonathan Greenleaf Whittier from the moment Edith had shared them.

Willa owned *The Poetical Works* by Lord Byron. She might have acquired it from a former school friend for Christmas. It was inscribed inside, *To Willa from Paul 1917*.

Sam, Edith, and Willa's relaxation at home in the evenings had always been made more special by their mutual fondness for poetry.

On Thursday, Sam fastidiously packed the numerous books and magazines. After careful measurement, he had built the shipment box so they could send the entire collection east ahead of them.

Friday, Sam worked with the water, the laundry wash, and the chores. Saturday, he went to Buhl and made arrangements for a sale. Sunday required only a few chores be done, and he brought hay into the barn.

Sam's own words...
Monday, December 24, 1917 – "Went to Buhl for Xmas for the children."

He got $10 from the bank and spent another $2.75 by check at People's Drug Store on gifts. Back on December 13, he had given Willa a check for $6, which he noted on the stub to be for Edith's travel hat and the rest for Willa. It had to be a pleasure for Sam to give them all a better

Christmas than he was able to the year before.

On Christmas day, Sam did the chores and spent the day with the family. They went to Olson's in the late afternoon, a happy occasion for both families.

With the holiday past, he distributed his sale bills in Buhl to advertise the bulk of what would be auctioned the next week on the first Friday in January 1918.

Sam stopped at the post office for mail since they had no mailbox to receive letters. He had an envelope from Andy and saw that the date it was sent was December 21, four days after Sam's last call at Andy's place.

Would the hoped-for check be found inside? Sam peeled a thin strip off the end of the envelope and pulled out the lined paper. He began to read.

~**~

Gooding, Idaho
Dec. 19, 1917

Mr. S. Crippen,

Dear friend, received your note when I was over but could not get over to see you. It was 8 o'clock when I got there, and the next week I started to load and worked until 10 o'clock. The next day it was 11 o'clock when I started for Hagerman, so was late getting there as it's a long way.

Will say that I do not know how I can pay the note right now. Will try to go to work on road over here and make what I can of it. If the weather is good, I can get on the 5th of next month. Will do so. As soon as I can fix to go, I was going to sell my team but could not of (sic) got moved over. It is a very bad pull over here.

I had to mortgage all of my things to make payment on the land, so I am out of money for awhile. But hope you do not think that I do not want to pay you, by not coming over to see you.

Andy Gardell
Gooding Rt. no. 3

~**~

Sam's lips pursed tight to suit his somber mood now that none of his money was forthcoming anytime soon. Then what were his chances after the trip east? He didn't want to doubt Andy's sincerity, but this was the last kick to finish it. It hadn't been a consideration that it would be this hard to get owed money from Andy. Sam couldn't have believed it earlier, but now he must. It left him no recourse for his thoughts, thoughts that he mulled over many times in the busy days ahead. Had he been duped on purpose while he had blind trust in their friendship? It was a soured relationship because Andy now seemed dishonest. How many times would Sam shake his head over it? He tackled work while his disbelief refused to let go and circled back around with the same thoughts like a record on a talking machine.

Thursday, Sam went non-stop all day as he drew hay and started to get ready for the sale. A letter from home provided a pleasant break to read that they all counted the few weeks until Sam and his family could be embraced. They did not desire it more than Sam at this point.

On Friday, he went after coal and had barley ground for hogs.
Saturday was the day of odd jobs and sorted potatoes.

Sunday was known to all as visit thy neighbor day. The complement of visitors who came out included the Downs family, Lenore Crow, Mrs. Sawyer, and Mrs. Campbell. Their visits were all the more cherished because they would soon end altogether.

Monday marked the last day of December, and Sam drove his horses and wagon to the depot with two heavy boxes of books and the flat trunk he had bought and packed. The valuable tomes cost $8.94 freight and a box of household goods was $8.84 to Pennsylvania. The large roll of bedding shipped at $3.89 with 50¢ R.R. charge and 65¢ excess baggage charge. Freight of $2.26 was recorded on a check stub for Sam's trunk case. They were all sent on the Oregon Short Line Rail Road owned by the Union Pacific Rail Road. He bought Gem razor blades for 50¢.

The two feminine ladies' trunks would go later.

The first two days of January were spent taking goods and small tools over to Hagadorn's Auction Service. It was the busiest time imaginable with the immediate decisions of the auction. Sam did not have a new diary, but he used a small lined note tablet until late in the month. He was too busy until he was on the home stretch.

He wrote his check stubs to show the purchase of buns and meat, etc. at $11.50 from G. S. Peck Company and another for meat at $4.10 was probably to grind hamburger. It could have been food to be sold at the auction because they were residents of Brazeau Farm but for a few more days.

Friday, January 4, the date of the sale, was upon them. The total sale brought $265.80. On Saturday, he paid Hagadorn and his clerk of the auction $17.74 for the service performed.

January 5 was spent as the last day the Crippens and Olsons would have together. They stayed all day. Their friends took them to Twin Falls in the evening. They spent the remainder of their time in Idaho with Philip and Lenore. They had shopping to do in Buhl and Twin Falls. Willa's and

David's shoes cost $6.85 combined, Edith's $7. Her gloves were $2.50 and Sam's pants $2.80. Tobacco added $1. David's suit cost $8.75. Sam's bath, haircut, and shampoo came to $1.35, and the children's haircuts were 70¢.

Edith's and Willa's trunks were shipped to Pennsylvania on January 10. Sam neglected to list the price. Perhaps his mind was busy, stunned by friendship abandoned. Details of his and Andy's past friendship had continued to surface with the struggle to realize that Andy had put him at a disadvantage to recover or resolve the matter. Andy had been clear enough on how the lack of money was playing out past the departure date for the east. It seemed on purpose now that Sam had turned it over in his mind enough. He'd been slow to realize the impossible odds to get his money.

Andy was like January, frozen over with no thaw in sight. Sam went to see the lawyer, Mr. Taylor, about the debt.

Sam would have kept up with the news as usual regardless of the lax diary. He and Philip were a great pair to discuss whatever they learned of by word of mouth or news print. Anyone who read a newspaper knew about the Spanish influenza and that the flu pandemic was rampant. It was first observed in Haskell County, Kansas, and was followed by a nervous nation wondering how many more deaths must be tolerated.

Sam's own words...
Saturday, January 26, 1918 – "Helped around house. Anxious to get home."

He helped Edith and Lenore in the house for three days, with all the details necessary to get children and baggage ready to leave. On Monday, Mrs. Sawyer took the whole family downtown to Twin Falls for dinner. It was a gesture of friendship and farewell meant to spare Edith from the preparation of a meal. She and Sam appreciated the generous gift.

Tuesday was full of hustle and bustle. Sam went to town to purchase family medicines at a cost of $17 in preparation for their needs during travel. He paid a last visit to see Dr. Sawyer and then to the depot where he bought railway tickets for the entire family. It was a final step, and he may have held his breath to pay out $179.40 for his family of six.

Another $9.90 was added for a sleeper to Chicago, which he and Edith had discussed as necessary to manage children.

Sam bought a watch for the trip at a cost of $3.80.

Sam's own words...
Wednesday, January 30, 1918 – "Very busy all day getting ready to take train on the morrow."

Regardless of restless sleep the night before, the morning would have been an excited daybreak for children and grownups alike. Willa had experienced train rides often enough with and without her mother. She could help settle the little ones down in her caring way. Her position within the family had never suffered as new siblings arrived. Love from her mother and stepfather was solid and left no reason for rivalry.

Sam's own words...
Thursday, January 31, 1918 – "Left Twin Falls 7 a.m. Zero weather."

They were in snowy Omaha, NE, by 10:30 p.m. Friday after two full days of travel. A second night with the use of the sleeper and a third day's travel on the rails brought them to Chicago, IL, at 2 p.m. on Saturday. The fourth day, Sunday, brought them into Wellsville, NY, at 9:45 p.m. where they stayed the night in a hotel.

Monday morning was spent on baths and putting on new clothes. Sam was in agreement with Edith, who insisted that they and the children would be presented in as good a condition as they could manage after their grueling cross-country train ride. They had agreed on it before departure from Twin

Falls. Sam and Willa helped with the younger ones, and all of them were ready to have breakfast.

The overnight accommodations, food, and the train from Wellsville, NY, to Galeton, PA, cost an additional $28.15. Sam's totals for the trip added up to $217.45. They left Wellsville, NY, at 1:30 p.m. and arrived in Galeton, PA, at 6:30 p.m.

Sam's own words...
Tuesday, February 5, 1918 – "At home and mighty glad of it."
Wednesday, February 6, 1918 – "Visiting with my folks and old friends."
Thursday, February 7, 1918 – "Grace, Ruth and Alice came out."

Sam's Own Words
From the Diaries of Sam Crippen
1908-1961

Part II

A Biography
By Gail T. Mazourek

David Crippen 4

♡

Willa Haggarty 16   Betty Crippen 2.5

John Crippen 14 mos.

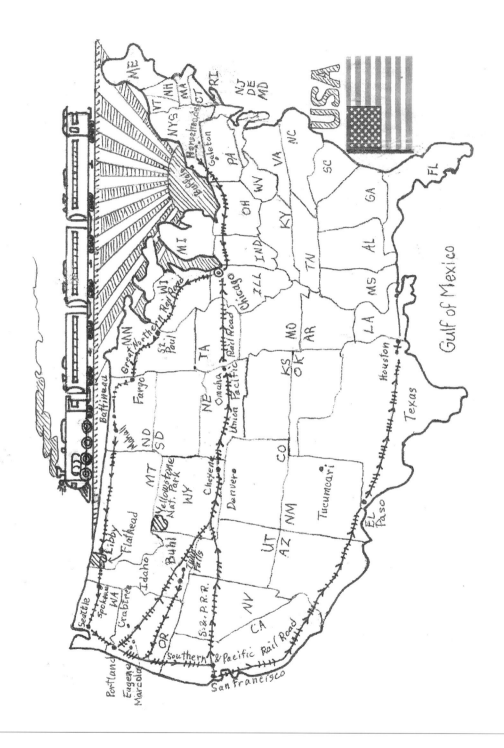

13 – Home
Lawyer, Horseheads, 1918

Sam and Edith enjoyed two-and-a-half weeks with their children in the heart of the Crippen family home in Galeton, PA. No family member was left waiting to meet Sam's family. Visits were non-stop with his siblings and their families to become reacquainted after Sam's 10-year absence. They adored Edith and the children as much as Ma—Sophia had told them she did since her visit out west. Willa was embraced as their own and was teased to prove it. She was admired for her beautiful dark hair from her mother but most of all for gentle treatment of her siblings. She was quite a girl in their estimation, and she fit right in. They enjoyed how David called her Billo, and they all tacked on their own adaptation of the nickname and called her Billy.

All good times were enjoyed, but a dose of reality was discussed behind the scenes between Sam and his father, Lac. Responsibility was always on their minds, and they discussed the idea of the farm they wanted to have together. Lac had researched enough for 10 people and had determined that the area around Elmira, NY, held the most promise for a farm. He was a happy man to have his oldest son home again to talk over tentative plans.

Maybe the dream Lac had not let go of could become reality now that his son had returned.

Sam's own words...
Tuesday, February 26, 1918 – "Father and I went to Elmira, stayed all night with Grace and Roy."

Grace was beyond happy to have them, and Roy was in full agreement. Their home at 103 West Henry Street was bursting with hospitality. Grace's girls, Ruth and Alice, were delighted to have Grandpa Lac and Uncle Sam there.

On Wednesday, the men looked at a farm for sale near Elmira. Thursday was spent getting in touch with several acreage holders' listings through real estate companies. Friday and Saturday were spent looking at all of the properties. They were ready for show and hoped to sell.

Sam's own words...
Sunday, March 3, 1918 - "At party put on by Grace, made me a birthday cake and the girls whipped me."
Monday, March 4, 1918 – "Went over and saw the Jeffreys' and Mrs. Maukly's 336-acre farm."

The two nieces, Ruth age 10 and Alice age eight, gave Sam 35 licks, one for each year, and had a great time doing it. They may also have shown their Uncle Sam that they enjoyed his book, Robinson's Shorter Course, First Book in Arithmetic, Oral and Written, which had resided on Grace's shelves from the time Sam had gone west. His name, Sammy Crippen, was written inside with the date December 9, 1892. He'd have been nine years old when it was bought for him at E. E. Hyer, Druggist & Apothecary in Galeton, PA. Ruth and Alice were the perfect ages now to use it in fourth and fifth grades but would have new ones for a comparison.

The search for a farm went forward as they spent Tuesday, Wednesday, and Thursday looking at farms in Horseheads, NY. Sam wrote a letter to Edith and the children who were staying with his mother, Sophia, in Galeton. She was glad to have them, and both women waited on word from their spouses.

With 10 days gone since leaving Galeton, Sam wrote to Edith.

~**~

Elmira, NY
March 7, 1918

My Dear Edith and Kiddies,

Maybe you think I have forgotten you, but never any such thing like that. I am just crazy to see you, but we haven't found the right farm yet.

We have looked at several farms around Elmira, but none of them were just what we would want except one that we got a line on this morning. The one we liked is only three miles from the city, and contains ninety-seven acres; all river bottom land and street car line and macadam road goes thru (sic) the place. It has great big barns, two silos, and a big dandy house with radiator heat, acetylene lights, water, etc. and the price is $10,000. – What?

Yes $10,000, but it is worth every cent of it, and Pa says we will buy it providing we can get the right kind of terms. It looks as tho' (sic) we might. The owner is in a bad health and wanted a day or two to talk it over with his wife. I know you would be wild about it, Dear.

We are just as busy as we can be looking at farms every day and will have to find one this week, as Pa says he has got to come home Saturday to look after affairs.

We ought to find some desirable ones in that time and pick out the one that appeals to us the most in every way.

I hope Dewey is getting well, and he must be, or someone would let Grace know.

We have taken in two shows, and I certainly enjoyed them but would have enjoyed them more if you could have been with us.

It seems as though we haven't had a home for ages, but just imagine how happy we will be when we do get one again.

Do the children miss me much? I certainly miss them and tell Willa she isn't left out in the missing either.

Well, I must close and get some rest tonight so.
I can be on my job tomorrow, as NY real estate agents are just as foxy as those of Idaho.

Good night dear ones and heaps of love,

From Daddy

~**~

Sam's letter described the situation for the farm hunt accurately and carried reassurance to Edith and the family, which was his intention. He truly desired to have Edith at the shows with him. Sam and Lac most likely laughed as loud as any of the theater goers who viewed Charlie Chaplin's version of a tramp in the short film, The Immigrant. The American comedy was lively with piano and actions of the mustached, top-hatted comedian for 22.5 minutes.

The second film was of greatest interest to Sam. He likely told Lac that Sioux Chief Sitting Bull had a big reputation in the western states with notoriety that had enlarged since his death in 1890. It was an opportunity for Sam to see the whole life story of the colorful renegade. Lac probably knew something about the renowned Indian, notably the pictures of him in the feathered headdress from the Buffalo Bill Cody show. They'd both have been in agreement to see the show. Imagine a drum beat added to the music to accompany the show's atmosphere inside the theater.

Sam's own words...
Friday, March 8, 1918 – "Found 106 acres two miles north of Horseheads that looked good."
Saturday, March 9, 1918 – "Decided to take Horseheads farm and we made payment of $500 on same. Started for home."

They no doubt were glad to find the farm for the startup of their new life and reserve it with a down payment. Lac made it home to attend to his weekend affairs.

Business also needed to be conducted with a Galeton banker to secure the Horseheads farm as soon as Sam and Lac could correlate the time to do business. Both men had a trusted relationship with Galeton Bank & Trust company.

Sam had his mind set on a private matter that had followed and festered in his memory. He had decided to commence action and soon. On Tuesday, March 12, he went to see a lawyer to talk about the Gardell situation. Let-linger would not solve it. It was up to him to move on it or take the loss. He'd had neither word nor money from Gardell, only silence. Silence was the message of no payment. Sam was advised that it required a lawyer to handle it in Idaho. Edith sent a letter to the lawyer in Buhl, Mr.

Taylor, to get the action started.

Sam and Lac went to several different lawyers on Wednesday in their search for the right council at a fair price to handle their land transaction. They had the loan, and now securing an attorney was in the works.

Sam had a short period of time to spend with Edith. They went to a show on the evening of Saturday, March 16. A favored film making its de-but into theaters in late 1917 and early in 1918 was *The Spreading Dawn* from Goldwyn Pictures of New York City. The silent drama of 30 minutes duration was a story of love gone wrong, but with a happy ending. It likely was a sweet stolen time of holding hands for Sam and Edith.

The business affairs took time. Meanwhile, Lac had Sam's help with his chores and lumber in Galeton. They had plenty to talk over. Sam made visits to John Long and Mr. Quick. He was gratified to talk with old friends. No doubt they would hate to see him move away again.

Willa's 16th birthday was on March 19. A sepia picture of her and her three young siblings was made in Galeton. The image was put on a postcard, a standard practice of the times. Several were sent to Sam's parents' address in Galeton. It showed two-and-a-half-year-old Betty with a large bow on her head. David was about four years old, and baby John was 14 months in the oval photograph.

Willa's birthday was also the day that U.S. President Wilson signed daylight saving time zones into law.

Sam's own words...
Thursday, March 21, 1918 – "Borrowed $200 from Galeton Banking Company for one month."
Saturday, March 23, 1918 – "Went up and looked at farm again in a.m. and made another payment of one-thousand dollars on same."

On Sunday, Sam woke up at Grace and Roy's. He couldn't go to Horseheads without also stopping in Elmira to spend the day to see Grace. No doubt they touched on the news of daylight saving time that was now law and was set to go into effect on March 31. Sam went back to Galeton in the evening.

In Galeton on a busy Monday, Sam went to the hospital to see Dewey.

Most likely he had the flu like so many during the 1918 influenza outbreak. On Tuesday, Sam mixed cow feed and went to town in the afternoon. Wednesday saw him in Galeton to arrange a railroad car, which cost him $38.96. Back at Pa's, he hauled wood late in the day. Thursday, he lost no time in carrying house goods and a load of lumber to the boxcar.

Sam's own words...
Friday, March 29, 1918 – "Took another load of goods and stock to car and shipped them to Horseheads."
Saturday, March 30, 1918 – "We left for Horseheads and Elmira. I arrived at our car about 3 p.m. Brought stock and load of goods home."

The railroad transport was roomy with the lumber making a partition between livestock and household items. Sam had driven Lac's second team and wagon to bring his family up from Galeton to their new home. The rig was also put to good use to take their belongings to the farm.

On Sunday, Mr. Scott, from whom the farm was bought, helped Sam bring the last of the stuffs from the box car. Mr. Scott was altogether helpful with his own team and wagon. It was quite enough work for one day. At last he and Edith and children were moved into the farm house.

Mr. Scott was back to work all day on Monday, to help Sam. The household was arranged, and Edith was all set to take care of her family. Sam paid the man $6, a generous day's wage and worth every penny to Sam because the other wagon and team had made shorter work all around. He was not finished yet and went to the depot after the second trunk for Edith.

Sam was intent on chores for Tuesday, all day work. He removed two loads of manure and did several different jobs, which made what he called a fine day. Wednesday was not quite so fine with rain and snow, but nothing new to him, no complaint. The loads of dung were spread on tobacco ground. Thursday was spent on chores and odd jobs before he went to town after feed for the seven cows and four horses. Two each, cows and horses, bought from Mr. Scott with the farm, were there already.

Sam purchased a pocket knife for 75¢ and returned with Edith's list of groceries to bring the tab to $16.50.

Friday and Saturday were about identical with chores, cleaning the barn after animals, and feeding them. He hauled corn in from a field. The chores and a pump repair were finished by the time Grace and her girls came out for a visit to look around. Sam enjoyed showing the place while he, too, looked over the farm again. Grace's happiness to have her brother so close could be relied upon.

Lac arrived from Galeton on Sunday evening, and Sam was glad no problems had held him back. He mentioned to Pa that one cow sustained damage in the journey and the compensation claim had been made already. Sam had called veterinarian Dr. A. Battin, of 452 E. First Street, Horseheads. It cost $6. For the next two days he and Pa accomplished their plan to cut wood, do chores, and also went to Elmira twice to work with the lawyer. Concentration was on the finish of the contract with Mr. Charles in charge of the loan from Montour National Bank.

Pa went home to Galeton.

It snowed for a couple of days. The $1.15 worth of coal was needed as much as $1.39 for groceries. Sam caught a cold but nevertheless, cleaned out the barn. He went to Horseheads for feed and grass seed on Saturday. He was still sick on Sunday when he finished chores and mixed cow feed. It was April 15, and Pa would be back in a couple of days. Sam wanted to show progress and clean stables. In spite of his illness, he sowed orchard grass, bluegrass, redtop, and timothy on the hill. Sam spent $2 to have a heifer bred, one they'd bought from Mr. Scott. He went after groceries and coal and added $1.10 worth of tobacco. By Wednesday, he'd removed five loads of manure to have the barn clean when Pa arrived toward sundown. The animals were ripe for three more loads of manure on Thursday.

Edith needed to pay unexpected carfare with Totem Taxi Company of Horseheads to get to a phone connection in town. The ride and a long-distance phone charge totaled $1. Marilla, Edith's mother, was quite ill and not expected to last much longer from an unnamed illness. Sam was concerned as usual, but work continued.

He and Lac repaired the disk harrow and went to town after needed items. Necessary purchases were Metholatum at 25¢ and Pa's mattress, which cost $5.50. Sam plowed all day Friday and into Saturday while Pa did all manner of odd jobs. Sam added his help on the end of Pa's work so they could go to town in late afternoon for groceries, a stove pipe, and a plowshare, each for 85¢.

The necessary chores were finished on Sunday, gotten out of the way in time for enjoyment of company. Dykens and Whitings came out. Grace's and Roy's girls had an instant love for their little cousins, David, Betty, and John, as soon as they had arrived in Horseheads. They played well together while both older girls doted on the younger children.

The grown-ups discussed the crops and headlines of the day. It was sensational news that a German, The Red Baron, WWI's most successful fighter pilot, had died in combat on April 21, 1918, near Amiens, Germany, by the Somme River. He was considered the top ace of the war, being officially credited with 80 air combat victories against the United States. His feats were much admired regardless that he was German.

Sam plowed six days straight. Pa and Dewey cut wood, cleaned ditch, and removed manure from animal quarters. There was no shortage of odd jobs along with milking and other barn chores. Ma and Dewey went to Grace's on Friday when it was finally warmer.

The children all had colds, and Sam was on the brink of another one himself. The 25¢ for Mentholatum bought earlier came in handy now. Sam welcomed Sunday rest.

He was back to horse and plow on Monday and Tuesday.

Sam bought $7.70 worth of groceries on credit. The pantry staples such as flour and yeast had dwindled.

Sam's own words...
Tuesday, April 30, 1918 – "Plowed nine hours, not feeling well, a letter from J. W. Taylor."

It was eight days before Sam was well again, and all of the children were ill. David had an ear ache severe enough to make them all sorry for him. Sam worked regardless of how bad he felt.

The blue mimeograph typed page from lawyer J. W. Taylor was inked with his signature. The page contained an in-depth explanation about the Gardell situation.

~**~

J. W. Taylor
Attorney at Law
Buhl, Idaho

Mrs. S. P. Crippen
Horseheads, NY   April 26, 1918

Dear Madam,
  Replying to your letter about Gardell's note, beg to say on receipt of Mr. Crippen's letter I decided to take what Gardell offered rather than run up a large bill of expense for suit. When I wrote Gardell, he again began to hedge and said all he could pay right now was $125, and that he would pay now and give a note for the balance, due October 1, 1918.
  I immediately started to sue him, but on examining the note found that it does not say where the money is to be paid. Under the law of Idaho, I could not bring an action here in this precinct but would have to sue in district court. As the district court is almost a year behind in its calendar, I could not very well begin suit there. I, therefore, sent word that I would accept the $125 and the note in addition for the balance, but have not yet heard from Gardell. If he backs out again, I will be compelled to sue in district court or else go into justice court in Gooding County. Probably the latter would be less expensive, and I would do better there.
  Mr. Crippen made a grave mistake in not consulting a lawyer when he took this note. It might have cost him $1 to have matters done right, and he would have had his money some time ago. Gardell will try to beat him if possible but had better leave nothing around loose while trying, for I will get it if he does. I will let you know as soon as he answers.
  Trusting that you will like your new location and that Crippen will consult a lawyer next time he takes a note, I am

Yours Truly,
J. W. Taylor

~**~

Sam's own words...
Tuesday, May 7, 1918 – "Plowed eight hours. Children and I feeling better. Willa went to drug store to work."

Willa's job at Horseheads Drug Company in Hanover Square was her exciting step out to gain independence. She so lovingly helped Edith with her younger siblings that the toddlers were apt to miss her most of all. They had to settle for less of her time as she took steps to make her way further into adulthood.

It was likely that Willa traveled at eight miles an hour in the horse and buggy to go to work. Every house and building had a horse block and hitching post in front. Lac and Sophia owned the conveyance that she may have started out using. Later, Sam recorded carfare for Willa at 50¢ and other times at $1.10 and $1.25 for several trips. No doubt she paid.

A carfare of $10 was in the record a few times for Lac's travels to Galeton and back. There were ends to tie up as he continued to have business affairs through the end of 1918 and beyond, in his former longtime location.

When you plow as many days as Sam had, more long days are needed again to harrow the same fields. He got started on it, but he also had to cut wood for the stove, bring in well water, and do chores. There was no end of work to shovel and spread manure.

Edith had written a grocery list to be filled on the next trip to town. Their two-and-one-half-year-old toddler, Betty, needed shoes, which cost $1.65. Edith had the helpful habit of writing the price of each item after it so she would know the total. Her list included:

8 bars Lenox soap 48¢	2 bread 30¢
1 # crackers 22¢	2 # 2 wicks 4¢
10 # sugar 95¢	1 salt 10¢
2 peas 36¢	2 corn 40¢
2 tomatoes 36¢	2 jars dry beef 50¢
2 salmon 60¢,	1 macaroni 18¢
2 raisin 30¢	2 # rice 24¢
1 yeast form 5¢	oranges 40¢
1 gilt edger 30¢	1 Borax soap 7¢
1 (baking) soda 24¢	

These groceries cost a total of $6.44, and all of it needed.

Sam's own words...
Tuesday, May 14, 1918 – "Drew manure in a.m. Harrowed p.m. Dewey came."

Dewey was a welcome sight, and Sam warmed to his brother's arrival accompanied with his lopsided grin. Twenty-year-old Dewey had all the earmarks of successful manhood around the corner, but the boy in him was still present. Sam was closer to Dewey than to his brother, Lynn, simply because Claude Dewey was single yet and lived with Ma and Pa. Lynn was 31 years old, closer in age to Sam's 35 years. He was also married and, like Sam, had responsibilities.

Dewey would make the work go easier and maybe faster for Sam and Pa.

There was no maybe about the need to plant a large garden and field crops. Early vegetables could be planted in the middle of May. Sam planted 4.5 acres of peas, radishes, and lettuce. He ran the float to cover the seeds. It was a start on the garden that would feed them all.

Animals needed food, too, and it pushed the need for crops. Sam drilled in oats on Thursday and went to Elmira on Friday and paid Fidelity Fire Insurance $12.95. He got a haircut for 85¢. There was still time to harrow ground the latter part of the day. On Saturday he went after feed and seeds and paid the grocery bill at the Ann Page Company. Sam preferred his obligations be paid up, but it was a struggle. He needed a shirt and shoes, which cost him $5. They would be made to last as long as possible. Money was tight, and the economy was not getting any better as WWI continued.

Sunday was a reprieve from tug-of-war with crops. He had chores to do but then he could spend time on his ledger. He added notes, prices, and lists that had been put in the back of his diary waiting for time to catch up. It brought the accounting ledger up to date so Sam could keep it that way. He had run out of room in the back of the diary. All expenditures and income were entered with his attention to detail. Lac was no doubt pleased with Sam's extensive records. They would know from whence money came and where it went. Mostly went.

It was Monday, May 20, and they signed a note for $100 to cover interest on the land contract. Mr. Charles, loan officer of Montour National Bank, finessed the transaction. The first payment would come due four months later in September.

They harrowed corn and bean ground. The seeds were on the way, arriving by freight. Nine bushels of beans cost $63 and five bushels of corn, $19.75. They brought the shipment home on the 21st and drilled in field corn. By the end of the next day, Sam had planted eight acres of ensilage corn and another half-acre of peas. The evening rain fell at the perfect time. That was enough to make a tired farmer smile.

Sam sowed grass seed then plowed the garden and a flat field. Pa planted the sweet corn. Together, Sam and Pa put in 10 rows of potatoes and covered them.

Sunday came but not gently. Edith took the Totem Taxi again and made a long-distance phone call to her brother, Horace, in Grand Island, Nebraska. She learned of her mother's death, which had happened a few days earlier, two weeks short of Marilla's 75th birthday. The news was expected but landed hard.

Later, Edith would be grateful to consider her mother's Dome-top trunk as a keepsake from which she would not part.

The last week of May was full, begun on Sunday with a cow chase and fence repair. On Monday, they hauled wood and manure and planted sweet corn. Sam helped Edith do the wash. It was a chance to spend time with her and to comfort her.

Cow Pattie heaven required manure carted out of the stables every day and spread over ground to fertilize it. Sam wrote a formula in his diary, how to make good manure better: spread 1.5 pounds each of lime and ground rock phosphate to droppings of each cow every day. Tobacco acres benefitted from the scatter for the week.

Before the week was out, they went to look at Ward's land, planted more corn, and took in sales at a couple of farms. The horses were shod, the barn cleaned, and more tobacco land turned over, incorporating the manure spread earlier. A visit to Grace's one evening was an enjoyable end to the hard work day.

Saturday, June 1, brought a welcome missive from J. W. Taylor, the Buhl lawyer, with a check for $100. It was needed and informed Sam and Edith's reason to smile. Sam believed that Gardell had calculated well on the additional $200-plus that he owed but withheld. The balance could not be counted upon and might never be paid. Sam turned his mind from the whole affair. He had work to do.

Sunday was a day made special by a visit from Sam's second cousin, 42-year-old Lucretia Crippen Barrett, who came up from the old Crippen homestead, located in West Branch Township in Galeton. She was seven years older than Sam. Lac's father, Erastus, was the original builder of the house, but his son, Edward owned it. Edward was Cretia's dad. The Crippen cemetery lay in a field behind the house and barns but was not yet Edward Crippen's final resting place. Many of the Crippens visited the cemetery for upkeep and sentimental loyalty over time and would for years to come.

On Tuesday, June 4, Sam bought a washing machine for $16 and a tub and boiler at $4.

Roy and Grace were pleased to bring Cretia to the farm that Grace had told her all about in letters. Cretia's curiosity about the west was satis- fied as Sam answered all of her questions. No doubt her natural curiosity about Sam's wife, whom he'd married in Idaho and brought back with him was also satisfied.

Oscar Birch from Galeton visited them on Monday and was invited to bring his family next time.

Another active week of fitting out tobacco and bean ground advanced. Bean soil required disk work, which was parceled out in portions over three days between other jobs. Sam used a road grader to make a ditch. He took a load of goods up on the hill for Mr. Charles. Sam shod horses Friday and had time for more disk work on bean ground.

Roy Whiting needed a little help on Sunday to take down a windmill. Oscar Birch brought his family for an overnight, and they went back home on Monday.

The work week started all over again. Farmers don't get bored. They get busy.

Midday Monday, Sam made a trip to town to purchase plants. The tomato and cabbage seedlings were set out. Cleaning out the creek supplied a little more recreation for Sam. He was satisfied with another job finished.

Tuesday was the scene of corn cultivation and money expenditure. He and Pa bought one cow, two heifers, and a calf from the T. H. Ward farm for $290. The newcomers names were Speck, a cow, and heifers Bess and June.

Lucille, the calf, tagged along, and the name shortened to Lucy. It brought their milk cow number to eight head. Milk was sold to A. Voight Company at 6¢ a quart. The month of May was a few cents short of $90 listed in the ledger for milk income. Other May income was $8 paid to them for a bull calf they sold to Mr. Charles.

Milk was poured into tall metal cans, which required tags. They bought a small supply of the labelers, a quantity of 40 at $4.40 that had constant need of replacement.

The cow, horse, and pig feeds were each a different mixture ground separately at Kinley's custom grinding in Horseheads. Sam had a habit of buying 100 pounds of middlings at $2.75, an inferior grade of split grain scraps to mix with pig feed. It stretched and lessened the cost of swine upkeep. He would have one batch of feed ground, buy the milk tags from the mill, and stop at the A & P Company for groceries. He'd cultivate corn in the afternoon. Time was not wasted.

Sadie came up from Galeton for the first time on Thursday, June 13, and Grace had the pleasure of bringing her out to the farm. Grace was no doubt all smiles on both counts, to see their sister and show her the farm. Sam might well have smiled as he spring toothed the bean ground, cleaned beans, and fixed fence. It was good that his sisters enjoyed their time together. By Saturday it turned off rainy and cool as he planted the beans.

June was half over on Sunday, June 16, and the year reached its halfway point. It was a day for visitors. Dykens and Whitings came out. They might all have discussed lighthearted topics, but not to the neglect of serious WWI news headlines. Days earlier the reports were about the first airplane bomb raid by an American unit in France. That talk would have led around to discussion of the draft. Uncle Sam's big government hinted at the need for required registry of men in their middle 30s.

Could the younger Dewey have resisted making a statement to Sam? "You're too old. They won't want you." His banter would not have had a serious note, nor would it have been taken wrong. But laughter? Yes.

More conversation would be sure to include that the epidemic Spanish Flu outbreak had worsened. They could not yet know that 30 million more people would die from it in the last six months of 1918.

Sam was back in work mode for Monday and ready to toil in the soil with use of one implement or another. When he and Lac purchased the farm, they bought essentials, which Sam listed. These necessities were already on the property and retained with cash. The first of items were obtained for $350. They were a couple of wagons and a wagon box, a rake, two plows, two drags, one mower, chains, ropes, and tools. A separator and milk cans were thrown in. Another $300 bought horses and harnesses, two cows for $100, two calves at $40, and a sow with her eight piglets for $100. The last item was 75 chickens at $60. The total was $950.

Sam worked over corn, bean, and tobacco ground then planted a few spuds. His initial foray to buy tobacco plants was unsuccessful, and he came home empty handed. While he was out, a land payment of $40 was paid to Mr. Charles at Montour Bank, a remuneration that would come due every month through 1924 on the six-year note of $3,200 total.

Sam's own words...
Wednesday, June 26, 1918 – "Plowed on hill, mowed alfalfa. Willa, Edith, and David went to show."

Slapstick comedy appealed to them as they enjoyed taking David for his first show, which heightened their fun. They might have seen the 12-minute silent flick *The City Slicker* and also an 18-minute reel, the short comedy western *Two Gun Gussie*. The echoed laughter of the audience was sure to have caught on with four-year-old David as he sat between his mother and Billo.

Sam finished plowing on the hill. His activity covered a lot of territory as he disked, harrowed, and marked potato ground. He drew a jag of hay to the animals. This time tobacco plants were available. He set them in the ground on Friday and got more on Saturday. He was rained off on Saturday afternoon and forced to set tobacco plants Sunday morning. June ended.

The first warm week of July was all about planting potatoes, corn, and buckwheat. On a trip to town, he bought two bunches of shingles at $2.70 for the barn. There was another week of field work before the roof was touched. Pa had hired himself out to Russell twice, and it amounted to 7.5 hours wage. Sam cultivated tobacco, put up a hay fork with a rope, and drew hay to the barn.

Sam's own words...
Sunday, July 14, 1918 – "Dewey, Grace, Roy, and girls came out. Roy couldn't work on windmill, too windy."

Dewey fit in well where he lived in the household of his sister, Grace. His young nieces, Ruth and Alice, no doubt laughed a lot over his playfulness.

The windmill had been taken down for repair weeks ago, but Roy had no luck with the weather. The wind was the reason it broke and the reason it stayed dismantled.

Sam spent part of each day on hay to get it in the barn. He hired out to Russell three hours, fixed the cultivator, and used it on beans.

Edith's brother, Philip, arrived by rail on Monday, July 22, from Twin Falls, Idaho. No doubt Edith and Sam had known he was coming and the house sparkled from preparation and anticipation.

Pa arrived from Galeton where he had gone the Friday before. He started in on hay and left Sam free to cultivate beans. Dewey came over on Tuesday. Tobacco was hoed three days and the week was spent. By the time August rolled around the binder broke twice on rye that was wet and tough. They repaired the machine and continued to cut, bind, and haul crops. The rye was finished and would cause no more problems.

Sam bought himself overalls for $1.65 and David's at 95¢.

Philip fit in with busy farm life while he visited with Sam and Edith. He became acquainted with members of Sam's family and was heartened that his sister, Edith, was immersed in a life with caring in-laws. He hadn't had any doubt, but now he had a solid picture to inform his mind when he was far away again. Lenore would want to hear all about it. Philip's two-week visit ended when they took him to the train on Monday, August 5. Love and best regards were sent back to Lenore.

The hay detail went on in various operations for two more weeks while other jobs and crops were handled. The rye cereal grass was harvested mainly for its seed. Wood was hauled, tobacco hoed, and weeds pulled. On Friday, August 9, Sam was still at it as he filled the whole day to clean the cow barn, cultivate tobacco, and go to town after feed. While he was there, he paid Edith's Western States Life Insurance, $38.29.

Saturday, Sam cultivated more tobacco and potatoes. It turned off rainy, and he worked on the cow stables.

Sunday's welcome interval brought visitors: Roy, Grace and Alice, Cretia and her daughter, Hulda. Mr. Taber came out from nearby Mecklenburg. The visiting relatives felt like a reward after the week's work.

Five days repetition of the previous week's jobs began. The days were interspersed with need to repair a wagon tongue and the binder. Sam put Bordeaux mixture on spuds to control disease and paid for a Liberty Bond.

Sunday, August 18, was a great pleasure when Grace and her children brought their brother, Lynn, and his wife, Iva, out to the farm for the afternoon.

Lac hired himself out to help Hilton thresh for 1.5 days.

Work on oats and straw had started. Sam also hauled water and wood. It was hot and dry while fences needed repair.

Sunday came around, and Sam drove around. He, David, and Lac went to repay a visit to Mr. Taber in Mecklenburg. While they were out, they swung around to see Mr. Charles and pay the $40 bank payment.

On Monday, Lac shod a horse and mowed alfalfa. Sam pulled weeds from potato rows and mowed hay by the railroad tracks.

Tuesday evening was a big production for a trip to Elmira after four pair of shoes for the family. It cost Sam $10. Edith's corset and hosiery, etc., were another $3.50.

Sam read a war-related article in the Elmira Star-Gazette every day. The only skirmish of World War I on United States soil was heady, unsettling news. It brought the Germans and Mexicans into conflict with Americans in Nogales, Arizona. The urgency created a close look at the U.S. draft again, and Sam had to give it a second thought. He might be forced to register since the age had been pushed to 35. Would they need men so badly that family men of his age would be required to enlist? Of course, he would do his duty, but he had a duty here for his family, too.

Frank and Mary came out to the farm with Roy, Grace, and children on Thursday. Sam had just finished picking plums.

On Friday, Sam went to Tompkins Corners to start a search for another cow purchase. He also topped off tobacco plants. The frothy cream colored fronds atop the tall foliage were bent low by his action. Broad-leafed green plants all received the toppled top message to decline further growth.

August ended with more weeds pulled, a log hauled for wood splitting, and more tobacco work commenced.

When Frank and Mary came back from Interlaken, NY, they stopped for another visit at the farm before returning to Pennsylvania. Family was always welcome. They knew it and enjoyed any chance for a visit.

September had harvests just ahead. Sam pulled peas and continued with tobacco. He looked at another cow and came on back to shoe horses. Pa was just as busy. They went after a cow from Berkitt's farm, cut burdocks, and worked on preparations for cement in the stable. On Friday, they bought five sacks of cement and four pounds of nails in Horseheads and brought it back on the wagon. On Saturday, Sam drew a load of sand as they continued improvements in the barn. Pa went to Roy's in the evening.

Fall plowing had been started for wheat. It kept up competition for several days with need to cut wood and hang tobacco. Hard frost dropped in on September 10, early.

A distasteful duty preyed on Sam's mind.

14 – Draft, Outhouse
Tobacco Crop, Steele, 1918, 1919

S am jostled along with his wagon and team, past Horseheads into Elmira proper. It was two miles over and two miles back, a further drain on his time. He would get this duty over. The half hour added to go to Elmira and back to comply with the draft notice would be put behind him. He had taken the time demanded to force his compliance. Now his druthers took over and got him back to Horseheads to buy five pounds of twine at $1.28 and a file, 15¢. The steady clip-clop, clip-clop and jingle of harnesses brought him back to the farm where they had "many irons in the fire." Sam had smiled at the tired old cliché with no more appropriate use than the truth before him.

Sam's own words...
Thursday, September 12, 1918 – "Registered for selective draft, hauled manure. Pa worked one hour for Russell. Rainy."

Sam's newly acquired, light green card signified his compliance with his legal duty to register and would heed the call to duty if his name was pulled in the lottery. It wouldn't have been his favorite choice to go fight. He dreaded it, but the nation needed to persist with its allies against Germany. He wasn't alone. Lynn and Dewey and all men from age 18 to 35 were likewise compelled. They all consulted constant war news, which was considered reliable information printed in the Elmira Star-Gazette.

Regular duties brought him to happier thoughts. Sam and Pa with the team of horses worked on buckwheat for Russell. They managed their chores as they put in a few hours Friday and Saturday for their neighbor on September 14 and 15.

Sam's own words...
Tuesday, September 24, 1918 – "Finished hanging tobacco and drew manure. Carl Crippen made us a visit."

Sam was satisfied with huge leaves hung to cure in a room under the barn roof. It opened up time for Sam and Lac to do other work that was never really finished. In addition to their own driven tasks, they put in hours for Longwell, Swager, Russell, and Burris on corn. They cut, hauled, and filled silo with the maize. They and their team of horses were in demand.

On Friday, September 27, Sam went to get Edith's new lens, which cost $3. She needed the stronger set to serve her weakened vision.

His second cousin, Carl Crippen, age 26, was soon to graduate from seminary with the title of reverend. His first charge would be a Methodist Episcopal church in Horseheads. He had come to see it and take the opportunity to visit relatives. He was the son of Carl Clinton Crippen, a brother to Erastus, who was Sam and Carl's grandfather. The younger Carl's brother, Erastus L. Crippen, was named after their grandfather who had died in 1889 when Sam was a small boy of six years old. It was harder to make time for his cousin since it was not a Sunday visit. But Sam was glad to extend a welcome to his seldom-seen relative.

Sam's own words...
Monday, September 30, 1918 – "Harrowed and drilled in wheat. Went to town, borrowed $47 from bank."

Sam was short on money, and when he borrowed it was not for his pocket. He paid the October bill of $20.75 for fire insurance and his life policy of $10.11 to Prudential. The $25 to Dean for threshing 61 bushels of rye and 139 bushels of oats took the balance plus a few dollars added.

Sam's own words...
Sunday, October 6, 1918 – "Cleaned oats, done chores. Pa feeling bad."

Sam was glad it was the Sabbath so Pa could rest without guilt. He had zero persuasion to convince his 61-year-old father to shoulder less of the workload.

On Monday, Sam repaired the fence, went after groceries, and had 561 pounds of oats ground. For three days, he plowed on field number one. He pulled peas at the end of two of those days. Lac worked 7.5 hours with Hilton to bale hay. On Saturday, Sam helped Russell clip cows for three hours. The horns were off, and a few bled more than others. He went to town after milk can tickets.

The weather could turn disagreeable in mid-October, and cold days had begun to hang on. Five tons of oat and rye straw was pressed, and beans pulled and piled. Wood was cut and apples picked. A vision of an apple pie could have occurred to Sam. All of the activity was sandwiched between chores and milking cows, morning and night. No doubt, Edith's big supper awaited them.

Sam and Pa enjoyed each other and cooperation with the shared farm. The last week of October held sweat work to dig 22 bushels of potatoes. Sam cleaned the cellar and picked more apples to put in it. They sold five ton of straw at $14 a ton ($70). Pa mended the wagon, and Sam hauled the loose animal bedding to Horseheads. He bought a hot water bottle and tobacco that totaled $2.50, nails and mouse traps at 70¢, and came back to the farm with feed.

Pa went after a load of apple pulp on Thursday. It was $1 each load for the pigs' benefit.

November came on strong with a chill. It pushed picking more apples, pulling beans, and putting up a stove. Sam went to Russells on Sunday, November 3, and borrowed a stove. He cleaned a milk can and swept the house to help his wife. Edith's late-term pregnancy had made work harder for her.

Monday started out rainy. Sam unloaded beans he had drawn into the barn the evening before. He figured he may as well clean the barn. The rain quit, and Mrs. Hilton did the wash. Sam intended to keep hired help for Edith when needed until after the birth.

With so much work to do, parts of it were duplication. A barn with animals inside often needed to be cleaned. Colder weather in the air meant beans and potatoes had to be finished. They pulled beans, piled them, and picked up spuds. Thirty bushels of them were collected and more waited under the sod.

A trip to Horseheads for feed and groceries was necessary. Lac made a separate run for pulp to feed pigs and stretch the ground pig feed. Every frugal step saved a portion of the more expensive grain.

November 9, 1918, headlines in the Elmira *Star-Gazette* fairly jumped off the newsprint:

KAISER ABDICATES THRONE

The smaller print went on to explain a revelation told by German prisoners to the American Army. "What is the use of staying out there to be killed on the last day?" It was the comment of scores of prisoners brought in the day before by Americans.

The paragraph related that the captured Germans were a more discouraged lot than usual. Most of them declared that since their government was quitting, and they appear to be convinced that it was so, it was absurd for them to neglect the opportunity to surrender.

Sam's own words...
Monday, November 11, 1918 – "Dug potatoes and hauled manure. Peace at last for this world."

The November 11, 1918, headline in seductive, red block letters announced peace, and underneath followed black, block type, only a bit smaller.

GREAT WAR IS OVER! PEACE! PEACE! IS HERE.
GERMANY HAS ACCEPTED ALLIED ARMISTICE TERMS.

November 12 was the last work detail on spuds. Sam went after feed, a washboard for 75¢ and nails, 20¢. He ordered Edith's magazine, Woman's World, a five-year subscription at $1.65. How could they have passed up that bargain?

It was onward to autumn with a chill suitable to butcher and hang up a hog. Potato ground was not left waiting but was harrowed over. Sam hauled in the peas and picked apples. Three days of harrowing included rye acres. He threshed the peas, drilled in grain seed, and did his chores.

On Saturday, November 16, after the evening chores, Lac went to Galeton for the week. Even though it was Sunday, Sam drilled in more rye, unloaded pulp for pigs, and cleaned the barn. On Monday, the pork was cut up, placed in a barrel, and filled with salt brine. He sorted and sacked potatoes and went after a couple of calves they had bought at $5 each.

Sam filled each day with all manner of jobs. He transferred spuds from the barn to the basement of the house. He gathered turnips, beets, and cabbage to store there, too. A stone crock came into use. The cruciferous cousin to kohlrabi would be transformed into sauerkraut with salt and patience.

Sam's newspaper clipping lay in his ledger with the explicit instructions to cut 40 pounds of cabbage into thin strips. He compacted and pressed it down with generous salt added every few inches of depth. In three or four weeks, after a stone held the top plate down, the pound of salt and 15 heads of cabbage would reduce to kraut. Further along at the end of the process, the resulting liquid would be poured out and an inch or more of the top removed from the fermented kraut. Sam may have imagined it would be delicious cooked with smoked ham hocks.

After Sam had put peas through the fanning mill, he sacked oats and cleaned the stables. Thursday required a trip to town after feed and groceries. He was good at filling Edith's list. Back home, feed was mixed and chores completed.

Sam stepped up his efforts again on Friday. He cleaned out the barn, put more cabbage in the cellar, and cut wood. It was time to milk, but first he chased cows. Saturday morning chores were postponed while bovine wanderers were trailed again. It dictated fence repair. He'd probably have been glad to have Pa's help again.

Lac arrived in the late evening.

It was Sunday, November 24, as Sam and Lac brought the yearlings home that they had purchased. Roy and Grace brought Ma to the farm. Together, Edith and the two women planned the meal they would have at the farm on Thursday. Ma and Grace would prepare food to bring. Monday's first order of business was overdue fence repair. Later, Sam helped Donovan and Mr. Treat thresh to finish the day and did it a- gain on Tuesday. Pa went to a sale after chores. On Wednesday, he went after a load of pulp, a job he owned. Sam traveled to Horseheads for a drug store item, aspirin for 20¢, and tobacco. He picked up trash and cut wood. They sawed wood together on Thursday, then cleaned the barn and shed. They knew it was November 28 when Ma and Roy's family would soon arrive for Thanksgiving. Chicken was served with potatoes, gravy, rolls, and many prepared dishes. Everyone counted on the dessert.

Sam harrowed and drilled an acre of rye on Friday before going after feed and groceries. He filled Edith's dry goods order listed out at $15 for her needs to prepare for the expected baby arrival. She would make proper use of the items to sew baby clothes.

Sam's own words...
Saturday, November 30, 1918 – "Went to Elmira and attended Farm Bureau meeting, Pa and me. Cold."

New York Farm Bureau of 1918, a few months old, was new for Chemung County. Sam and Lac paid their membership dues of $2 for the year. They knew what other farmers knew, that food was in short supply. War indirectly facilitated leaders' efforts to fully organize Farm Bureau. It was a social time for like-minded men, but more importantly, it disseminated information about farm methods and best practices. New York dairy industry and milk producers of all size enterprises benefitted from it, sometimes through legislation. They still do.

Stanchion repair took place on Sunday after Sam's breakfast. He mixed cow feed and performed chores. On December 2, he made the time for his haircut and shave for 70¢. That trip to town was sure to have the purpose of bringing back feed and groceries; otherwise, he'd consider the return trip wasted.

The first week of December had all of the regular work, but they worked on stables every day. Sam hauled stone, gravel, and sand for the improvements that were under construction. The concrete and the need for a stove of his own for heat occupied Sam's thoughts. He found a stove to buy on December 10, and they finished the stable floor December 11. Meanwhile, they'd purchased a cow from John Caines for $40 and a pork barrel for $2. Manure was hauled and the water pump repaired.

It was rainy and icy, and then it snowed. Sam cut wood, helped

McDonald load hay, and went for feed and groceries. Edith was adamant that he should bring back sewing machine needles for 10¢. She wanted to finish sewing the layette.

On December 14, Sam plowed for three hours. Pa went to a sale. He bought a set of four horseshoes, size six, for $1.79. It was Sunday, December 16, by the time Sam had time to cover the floor with a piece of roofing material. He required it before the setup of the stove. He most likely was gratified to have it done and to know it was appreciated by Edith. Now, the borrowed stove could be returned to Mr. Russell.

After morning chores on Monday, Lac took a wagon and team for a load of pulp. They'd use it as long as the scrap apple leavings of fall were available. Tuesday morphed into Saturday while all kinds of odd jobs were finished. It was in addition to work on the barn, manure, and barnyard. Nothing strange there, just the same old thing. A hog was butchered between a trip to town and manure detail.

Sam's own words...
Saturday, December 21, 1918 – "...Dairy Inspector came. Warm in evening."

No warning of inspection was given, but they knew the clean dairy conditions expected and lived by it, always ready. Any dairy in operation would follow sanitary practices if they wanted to send their milk to market. Sam and Lac had no problem with compliance. It was their livelihood in a limited local consumer situation.

The urban milk market of the early twentieth century was a rough-and-tumble world of fluctuating farm supplies, weak consumer demand, and cutthroat competition. Although national firms processed and sold other food products, milk distribution remained a local concern until the late 1920s. In the days before bottling plants and refrigerated milk trucks, entry into the market was easy, and hundreds of milk dealers and farmers fought for a share of that market. Fierce competition among the many suppliers meant that cutting prices became more important than improving milk quality. Yet no development in the first two decades of the twentieth century had a greater impact on this multitude of dealers and the structure of the industry itself than the public pressure for pure milk.

They wanted formulation of municipal health regulations dealing with milk. The elimination of city cow stables, the pasteurization requirement, the establishment of bacteria standards, and public education about milk quality raised the costs of selling milk, forcing hundreds of dealers out of business.

The remaining dealers increased their market shares, taking advantage of the heightened consumer demand for high-quality milk. The most significant advances on the farm, the use of milking machines, and the use of trucks to transport milk to the city came during and after World War I. Pure milk regulations and the public pressure for their enforcement became the first engines for change in the structure of the urban dairy industry in which Sam and Lac engaged.

If Sam could go ahead in time and look back at the wisdom of this view, would it have changed his direction? But nobody could do that. It was still December of 1918, and like all years past, now, and future, they had to work to survive.

Chores, plowing, and manure management continued. The manure boat sailed daily with Sam and his pitchfork to load and spread the animal excrement mixed with bedding straw. That vessel saw a lot of action. It was a muscle-builder. Horses built their appetite while pulling a boat that did not float.

Stormy described the weather.

Sam's own words...
Tuesday, December 24, 1918 – "Went to town after groceries and Xmas. Dragged home some wood."

Sam guided the horses in another drag-exercise to fetch the log close to home.

He included his meager necessities in the Christmas list filled. Purchase of two pairs of canvas gloves cost 40¢. His new 1919 diary, along with tissue paper, was 52¢. The thin paper was likely to wrap a gift for each child and maybe gloves for Lac.

Christmas was a quiet day. It snowed the next three days while Sam plowed, went after feed and groceries, and banked the house with straw.

He drained the water system since the colder temps threatened to freeze and burst pipes.

Sam's own words...
Sunday, December 29, 1918 – "A big baby boy came to our house about 8:15 a.m. Mrs. Hilton came out. Named Steele Dimon Crippen."

Relief flooded into Sam's thoughts. Perhaps deep in his mind resided gratitude that there'd been no repeat of the desperation that attended John's birth. He hired Mrs. Hilton to attend Edith and his boy for two more days.

In 1900, less than five percent of women gave birth in hospitals. Midwifery was prevalent in 1918, a year in which records show that the United States stood 17th out of 20 nations in infant mortality rates. Maternal mortality reached a plateau with a high of 600 to 700 deaths per 100,000 births between 1900 and 1930. Such deaths were more common in poor families than in elite ones.

New York City's first maternity clinic to serve women's prenatal health needs was founded three years earlier in 1915. The Women's City Club was an organization of about 200 women formed for the purpose of enabling women with civic interest to work together for the sake of a community. The Club's membership consisted primarily of middle- and upper-middle-class women. Most were married and did not work. Club work offered them an opportunity to participate meaningfully in the process of social change. They created and developed a maternity center between 1917 and 1920 to work in close collaboration with the City Board of Health. Twelve thousand babies under one year of age died in New York City in 1917, and about 75,000 pregnant women were without medical or nursing care, so the need for these services was great. That year 17 cities in the United States and Canada sent 24 nurses and visitors to learn about the center's pioneer work.

Was fashion more important when the Lane Bryant clothing company became the first to introduce maternity clothes in 1904? Edith never had maternity clothes; she wore everyday housedress'.

Pa made sausage while Sam did chores on Monday. They went to Horseheads together in the afternoon and were back for chores.

Tuesday, the last day of December saw wood cut and dragged home.

~**~

1919

Had Sam given himself and Edith a Christmas present, an installed phone? His entry after his name and address in the front of his pristine new diary listed their first ever home telephone as number 4-T-23.

The pork was ready for brine on the first day of January. They sold two cows for $90 and $35, respectively, the same day. Lac went to Galeton in the evening.

Sam worked alone on January 2 and 3. It involved the usual chores and milking, manure detail, and a trip after feed. He finished banking up the house against weather that was turning colder. Pa returned Friday evening.

Sam's own words...
Saturday, January 4, 1919 – "Done chores. Pa went to sale, quite cold, five inches snow."
Sunday, January 5, 1919 – "Four degrees below zero. Grace came out. Edith and baby doing well."

It was fortunate to have the house already banked against the white fluff that fell and better yet that Sam's wife and new son were in good health.

While Sam spent a little time with Edith, he made out four orders. The farm enterprise would pay for three magazines: *Country Gentlemen* for one year - $1, *Successful Farming* for three years - $1 per year, and *The Stockman* for one year - $1.25. For good measure and a loving gesture to Edith, Sam ordered a music record at a cost of 60¢. Which one might they have chosen from 1918? *A Good Man Is Hard to Find* with Eddie Green or *K-K-K-Katy*, a World War I-era song written by Geoffrey O'Hara, or *Oh! How I Hate to Get Up in the Morning* by Irving Berlin?

Sam's upbeat position plummeted momentarily when he read the unexpected news of the death of former United States President Theodore Roosevelt. The 26th president had died on January 6, 1919, in his sleep at the age of 60. He was buried two days later near his home, Sagamore Hill, in historic Young's Memorial Cemetery in Oyster Bay, NY. Sam read the newspaper to follow details. They had even mentioned Roosevelt's White Stanley Steamer ridden in while he was president. One of Sam's favorites of all time was gone.

Sam couldn't dwell on it for long in the middle of a recession. Life on the farm went right on, especially since they'd been unable to sell. Mrs. Chaffee had sold them a heifer for $83, and they took her to Russell's to be bred. He helped Russell bring a cow and calf from off the hill. He cut down a tree and dragged it homeward. Sam did chores, threshed and cleaned beans. There had to have been time for supper in the mix.

On January 7, Sam paid $13.23 school tax to Mrs. Ira Wilcox, tax collector.

Sam's own words...
Friday, January 10, 1919 – "Went to Elmira to see dairy and milk show."
Saturday, January 11, 1919 – "Banked up water tank, hauled manure boat, cut log, went after groceries. Lynn, Grace, and Alice came out."

While in Elmira, he bought himself overshoes for $1.80.

Sam hadn't seen his brother, Lynn, in quite a while and it must have brought smiles to both of them. Grace and 13-year-old Alice wore their usual smiles when they came to the farm. After a look at the new baby, Steele, Sam most likely showed Lynn the new concrete in the barn.

Sunday was a strange time to have a Dairymen's League meeting. But go they would. Perhaps the Sabbath gathering after evening chores was for the convenience of farmers. The object of subscription was to furnish funds with which to organize, pay the organization expenses, promote better prices for milk, push for beneficial legislation or defeat hostile legislation. Local management encouraged the welfare of dairy interests in the territory of its operation.

All farmers and milk dealers were interested and made up the well-attended meetings. More milk was sent to New York City, but Farm Bureau was not involved in the demand for higher milk prices. Farmers often got the short end of the deal and Dairymen's League worked toward a better situation.

Sam threshed his beans all week. The task intertwined with chores, feed, and grocery trips, and cleaning beans. On January 13, he took the top off ensilage. The upper layer dried and rotted to form a protective crust, which preserved the corn underneath to feed the cows

Sam's own words...
Friday, January 17, 1919 – "Went to Montour Falls, paid Charles $40 on land contract and $50 on note – balance $42 for four months."
Saturday, January 18, 1919 – "Drew water to wash, went after coal and groceries, a regular spring day."

He lacked part of the money due on the note but did the best he could with a promise to raise the balance. Poor...it stalked him still, as it had in Idaho.

Sam filled Edith's list to bring home a $2 tea kettle, a 15¢ pancake turner, and a 90¢ house broom.

Lac helped with chores and manure before he went to Galeton on Sunday evening. He stated his intention to be gone until Thursday afternoon.

Sam spent the typical week on chores and manure every day. He brought wash water inside for Edith. The mild and windy day was just right to hang clothes on the line. He threshed more beans and finished cleaning them all by Wednesday when it turned colder, windy, and stormy. He had already cut and hauled wood two days before. The feed and grocery trip was made when he took beans into town to sell.

Sam's own words...
Thursday, January 30, 1919 – "Cleaned beans, 2,671 pounds from eight acres at 10¢ per pound."
Friday, January 31, 1919 – "I had to take less than 8¢ a pound (about $223.58). Paid for Liberty Bond, $15.37."
Monday, February 3, 1919 – "...Hauled water, cut wood, fixed tobacco shed doors."

Pa had returned Thursday evening as expected.

It was quite cold, and more wood was on Sam's agenda. He cut a log, dragged it home, and chopped it into manageable chunks, and it was only February.

The tobacco leaves were no longer green. The aged brown leaves clattered against their counterparts hung close together on wires from wall to wall. The stiff breeze from the open door hit them and rustled the dry forms. Sam finished the repair on the doors and left the product to dry further.

He worked all the jobs he could lay his hands on. Sam started a smoldering fire in the floor of the smokehouse with hickory chunks that he had cut a few days before. The pork was removed from brine and hung inside the small enclosed wooden shelter. It was a place in which a fire would be kept smoldering for a few weeks, which would slowly release its smoke, and in which the smoked meat could hang safely from vermin and thieves. The saltiness of the brine had served to remove moisture from the pork. Smoke would finish the job to preserve the meat.

Pa had gone after pulp. Between chores morning and night, they managed to cut wood two days in a row and make a trip to town. They enjoyed each other's company when a trip to the city could be taken together. Sam left his shoes for repair in the new Personius's shoe repair store opened on the Southside of Elmira. They went to Kinley's for feed and Gold Medal flour. The flour and 25 pounds of cornmeal cost Sam $4.50. Back on the farm, he and Lac sold F. Weink two ton of hay for $20 a ton in the barn versus delivered (net $40). It was easiest if the new owner had to come after it and load it on their own wagon to draw it home.

Sam sold a calf for $5.

Saturday, February 8, 1919, was the first effort Sam made to try a new milk buyer, W. Houck. He would later switch to this vendor. He and other dairymen paid freight to send their cans of milk. Twenty milk can tickets cost $2.70. They had paid a total of $20.91 for November, December, and January alone. The necessary expense was sure to go higher as they added a cow or two for milk production and profit.

Sunday was as pleasant a day as Sam could ask for. Maybe he thought so partly because they had a visit from Grace and her girls.

Water had to be carried into the house for cooking, bathing, and washing clothes on Monday, laundry day. After Sam finished hauling water for Mrs. Hilton for the wash at $2.75 for the day, he cut wood. His cousin, Marguerite Crippen Taber's husband, Mr. Taber, came out from Mecklenburg, NY. They rode along to Horseheads together and enjoyed the visit. Sam bought a wash pan for 65¢. On Wednesday, after chores, Sam hauled manure. The two men conversed while they went to town after Sam's feed and groceries. Mr. Taber went home in the afternoon.

An obligation came due. Sam paid $180 to J. Howe, the interest on the mortgage.

Sam's own words...
Thursday, March 13, 1919 – "Mr. Kane came over, and we took tobacco down."

It marked the start of the process to get the tobaq ready for market. The leathery leaves had hung limp to shrivel for six months on the wire clothesline. Each dry upright leaf required care as they were removed one at a time and stacked on the floor. It required more than a single operation to finish it.

On Friday, Sam drew manure, burnt brush, and got a load of wood. It was all in addition to the barn chores and milking duty. He had been kicked by a cow that caused him to spill a pail of milk while he sat on a three-legged stool to milk.

When he and Mr. Kane took down more tobacco on Saturday, they carried enough to the house to begin work on it in a warmer situation. The dedicated back room would be comfortable for the men during the next phase of the process.

Sam's own words...
Tuesday, February 18, 1919 – "Stripped tobacco, went to town for feed and groceries."

The raw Nicotiana was pulled loose from the center artery of each dry leaf. It was a substantial stalk in appearance. They accumulated in a pile as if they were short branches of wood. While Sam was in town, he purchased pipe tobacco for 96¢. It was a supply that should last three or four weeks.

On Thursday, February 20, Lac went to Galeton for five days that would have him absent through Tuesday. Sam's duties continued with chores, manure, and wood. A portion of each day was used to pull down more mummified leaves, strip them, and clean the room of brown crumbs too small to pick up. The new broom came in handy.

Before Pa had gone, they'd bought a Holstein heifer from Mr. Charles. Sam took the young black and white bovine to be bred. He used Monday in a productive manner to doctor a cow, unload coal, and go after feed. Mr. Charles was paid $40 on the land contract. Back at the farm, he mixed feed and hauled manure out of the barn. There was never a shortage of animal waste.

Sam's own words...
Tuesday, February 25, 1919 – "Took load of tobacco stalks to field, doctored cow. Pa came home."
Wednesday, February 26, 1919 – "Brought tobacco from shed to house and stripped it. Cold and windy."

Pa was back and shared the concern over the affected cow that was under Sam's care. Help with chores was welcome and needed especially while tobacco work required a few hours a day.

The daily Star-Gazette, which cost $1.50 for three months, reported all the local news, but also news outside the area when it was deemed of interest to most readers. Sam and Edith may have taken special notice that a state familiar to them, Oregon, had become the first state to place a 26¢ levy on a gallon of gasoline. It didn't affect them much, yet, but a taxi ride would see a modest increase. Pa often went to Galeton by carfare since it was swift transport. A less noticed news paragraph with a small caption announced: "Act of United States Congress establishes most of the Grand Canyon, Arizona, as a United States National Park."

Sam took Thursday and Friday, February 28 and 29, off from tobaq stripping. He had other work for those days. He transported seven bushels of Rosen rye to the Erie Depot for W. H. Meeker. Manure had to be hauled and spread. He went to Elmira to pay $180 to C. J. Howe on the mortgage. It seemed like yesterday that he had just paid, but it was six weeks ago. While he was in town, he bought pen and ink for 75¢. Sam finished the windy day hauling wood.

Tobacco work went on all day Saturday.

Sam's own words...
Sunday, March 2, 1919 – "Willa and Edward came out. Done chores...Grace and girls visited."

Grace was dying to meet Edward.

Willa would soon be 17. No doubt she was eager to introduce her intended to the folks. Most likely, Edith invited them to come together and sit down to a meal.

Tuesday concluded the strip work on the nicotine crop. It had taken 2.5 weeks. Sam carried the stripped leaf skeletons to the field to burn. On Thursday, Roy and Grace visited and found Sam sick. He could not do much on Friday but was better by day's end. He went to town for coal and groceries on Saturday.

Finally, he had to have the vet for the sick cow. It set him back $6 that he could not afford. Mr. Weink bought 1,720 pounds of hay from Sam. No doubt he let it be known that he had hay for sale at $25 a ton because he needed the money.

Sunday's lighter load left chores, housework, and a cow in need of doctoring.

Monday revolved around barn work. Sam phoned O'Hanlon about beans he wanted to sell. The price of $8.40 cwt. (per hundred weight) must have suited him when he sold 2,514 pounds delivered for $210. That meant some work to load it, but they were used to it. That was settled, and he went out on a run after feed and groceries. On Tuesday, he took Bess to service, a heifer they'd paid $75 for a few months earlier. She would be age two by the time she carried a calf for nine months. Pa went to a sale.

"Dollar Day" in Elmira was a significant event, a day awaited each year by everyone to be able to afford necessary family footwear. Sam went after shoes for the family on Wednesday, March 12. He came back to mundane chores, manure, and wood, accompanied by the wind.

On Friday, Sam put a rack on the Houck truck and loaded it with hay. Houck bought 2,518 pounds of hay at $25 per ton, delivered. He loathed dealing with Voight to whom they sold milk.

He switched to Houck at the same 8¢ a quart and was satisfied.

Bushels of potatoes had been sold off each week from December through February. They had sold at the usual price of $1.50 a bushel, and they needed to keep what they had left for their own use. By the middle of March, Sam plowed whenever chores were done. He had to stop to cut wood before chore time again. Either job put him square in the cold wind.

Pa went to Galeton on Thursday evening, March 20. He planned to be away from the farm for a solid week.

Sam carried on like before with every job he encountered. He sold a red bull calf for $5 and a heifer calf for $6. Hay was loaded for Mr. Weink, an old bay mare bought from Albert Roughman, and chores finished. On Saturday, Sam hauled manure, drew wash water, and paid carfare of about 36¢ to go after groceries. Evidently Lac had taken the wagon and team for his lumber work. It required leaving Sam short of horsepower. There was no complaint.

Sam's own words...
Sunday, March 23, 1919 – "Done chores. Grace, Roy, and girls came. Mr. Scott stopped in. Willa came home sick."

Mr. Scott was a friend from the time when he had sold Sam and Lac the farm.

Willa needed a good day with her mother. She could recuperate better with Edith's mothering. Willa was not afflicted with a serious illness. Besides, she and Edith had lots to talk over, plans for the future.

The weather turned terribly cold and windy. It stayed that way for the rest of the week while Sam faithfully did chores and pulled a foul boat of manure with the help of the old bay horse he'd bought.

On Thursday, March 26, Sam paid $40 on the land contract. Pa returned with a load of his goods as planned. Ma and her granddaughter, Ruth, trotted along in Sophia's horse and carriage as they came over from Grace's soon after.

The weather continued fresh and windy into Saturday night.

Sunday calmed. Grace and Cretia came for a visit.

On the last day of March, Sam hired out to help Mr. Kane cut wood. Pa helped Donovan load and haul hay.

Sam's own words...
Tuesday, April 1, 1919 – "Went to Elmira and paid G. J. Howe $200 on mortgage. Saw lawyer about contract."
Thursday, April 3, 1919 – "Borrowed $98 from Montour National Bank for four months. Bought cow from L. M. C. for $85 on a four-month note."

What were Sam and Lac considering? It would be revealed but not today. The fact was that money was short. A money juggle was a clue, but a sign of trouble? Nevertheless, they had work to do.

Sam sowed grass seed, wheat, and three acres of barley. Saturday he went after groceries, plowed, and brought his sows home from Thomas's in the afternoon. Sunday was placid with a visit enjoyed from Grace and the girls.

On Monday, Pa plowed. Sam took three bushels of spuds to town to sell. He went to Elmira in the evening to see Mr. Van about a farm loan.

Tuesday required a trip to the train station to move the balance of Pa's goods to the farm. Sam had time to plow before chores. On Wednesday, he went to the A. & P. Co. after groceries and to the Kinley Mill after feed. Back on the farm, he went up the hill after the spring tooth harrow.

Sam's own words...
Thursday, April 10, 1919 – "Hauled out manure. Man came to look at our farm."

It is no longer a mystery that they had decided to sell the farm if they could. No doubt they hoped for a profit because of the improved barn with concrete floors.

A possible conversation between Sam and Lac from a couple of weeks back probably took hard facts into consideration. "Pa, with four children and a wife to feed, I cannot survive the downslide of milk prices."

Lac may have answered, "Hard to say how low the market will go and for how long. What do you say we try to sell and get out from under?"

"Yes, but we may take a licking either way."

"Now Sam, we may take a bigger loss if we stay. No decision is still a decision."

Perhaps Sam sighed. "That settles it then. Maybe a buyer will choose to get in while our selling price is lower than we'd ask if milk prices soared."

"If we don't make a profit, maybe we can break even," Lac may have offered.

Sam needed a few dollars. He took five bushels of potatoes to town to sell. It would give him $7.50 for groceries. Back home, he cleaned out the pantry and arranged the shelves with the new items. He repaired the tobacco shed. It rained. The dampness matched his gloom.

On Saturday, Sam made quick work to spread manure, went after a young bull at Thomas's, and plowed. He thought about their situation through all of his activities. They needed more income and not just for Sam's part. Pa had agreed.

Only six cows were online to be milked. The milk went at the low price of 6½¢ a quart. Their average for a week was 343 quarts. It was clear that the approximate $95 to $100 for a week was a losing proposition when split between them. Debts and animal feed obligations had to be paid as urgently as family needs.

Monday's agenda held the intention to groom the place for its best appearance wherever possible. Sam pulled and hauled brush on the line along the garden. He repaired a harness, which was a good job to do while he wanted to think on his situation. Manure disposal was next to spread a boatload of it on the vegetable patch. Limbs were drawn away before he went after tags for milk cans.

Of course snow showed up on Tuesday. It didn't last. On Wednesday, it rained hard and kept them inside after Sam and Pa finished the chores. Sam helped arrange things in the house. Finally, they were able to cut wood and load hay. They were anxious to get back to work. On Thursday, they hauled manure and rubbish before a trip to town for feed and phosphate. The crops needed more than manure for fertilizer. Plants use phosphorus from the ground, and it has to be replaced for the next plants to thrive.

They ignored light rain and continued to work.

Sam supposed his own work could wait while he helped Ray Douglas. Together they loaded 2,225 pounds of hay that Ray had to deliver to his buyer. Sam sorted potatoes and cleaned the cellar until chore time. On Saturday, April 19, Sam plowed in field number one, hauled manure, and filled dirt into a hotbed. During plowing, he planned what to plant in the protected frame for seedlings. After a six-week start, they'd be moved to the garden. They must grow their food.

Sunday was a return to happy times. Roy and the family came out.

Grace and her girls stayed all night. Sam's mind was still on his garden plans as he wondered aloud in the well-known company, how long before his seeds would arrive? He had poured over a nursery catalog and sent for them awhile back.

Sam's own words...
Monday, April 21, 1919 – "Done chores, went after coal, seed at depot, groceries, etc., plowed, cold."

Sam plowed for three days, in between the chores that were on both ends of each day. He made a trip to town for feed and noticed how much colder the air felt. There was a reason for that since it proceeded to snow for two days. Boats of manure slid on the ground easier while Sam made the slick snow work in his favor. He and Pa cut wood. More rain and snow didn't help the cold Pa had along with everyone else in the family.

Sam took out a load of manure on Sunday. He hauled wash water to get ahead of Monday when he usually brought it inside for Edith. He had Monday planned, or so he thought. Roy and Grace were of the same mind. Roy had most likely rented or borrowed the truck, which was in his possession, to move their belongings. Sam was ready and willing to help them. The vehicle broke down right off the bat and dashed plans. It may as well pour down rain, too, and it did.

Besides chores on Tuesday, Sam plowed, harrowed, and sowed grass seed on the hill. A need for feed and groceries required a trip to Horseheads and back. Fences were repaired on Thursday and Friday. More rain fell.

Sam bought flour from Kinley's Mill. G. H. Goodyear was paid $67.39 in full. Sunday allowed time for more fence repair. A couple of rambunctious heifers would find any flaws left to chance, their chance.

The weekdays were taken over with the preparation of the ground for planting. Manure spread previously was turned under with the plow. Mid-week, Sam went to Erie Depot for spuds and turned Grace's garden.

Sam's own word...
Sunday, May 11, 1919 – "Cloudy, damp, dreary."

Monday, May 12, 1919 – "Went to town for feed and groceries. Went to Big Flats to sell tobacco. Borrowed $4.37 from Grace."
Wednesday, May 14, 1919 – "Harrowed, and Ray Hilton drilled in oats. Mr. Kane came after tobacco, 26 bundles."

The loan from Grace may have covered the price paid to Mr. Kane to use his larger, heavy-duty wagon to deliver the 1,000 pounds of nicotine bales to the buyer in Big Flats. Sam had sold it at 5¢ a pound to gain $50. The tobaq chapter closed when the money was in his hand.

Barley was drilled, also five bushels of seed corn that had cost $19.95. On Saturday, Sam sowed alfalfa on what had been tobacco ground.

Five-month-old Steele was sick for the day.

It was due time that Sam prepared the soil in his garden. He plowed and harrowed it on Monday, before the trip to Montour Falls Bank to make a $50 mortgage payment.

It rained four days, the last one on Saturday. Sam still managed to work around it or in it to load hay for Denny Donovan, clean the stables, and draw manure. He took the borrowed boar home on Friday. It was the day picked for the start of a two-day shovel job to dig the new pit for the outhouse.

Sunday, May 25, Sam did chores and housework and topped it off with a heifer chase. He'd have to walk the fence line and find the new flaw in the old fence.

Back to outhouse duty, he hauled stone for the privy vacuity wall. He lined the cavity with the rocks and moved the two-seater closet over the pristine void. The pile of dirt was shoveled into the old hole immediately. It took the best part of a day between early and late chores.

No doubt, Lac had his own job or helped Sam with his. The garden installation commenced, and six rows of potatoes were planted. Together they prepared fields and drilled in peas and corn. By the end of Tuesday, May 27, they had made progress on the crops to a point where Pa took a needed five-day trip to Galeton.

On the Sunday of Lac's return, a day of rest, they may have read of Einstein's Theory of Relativity without giving it any deep thought. According to the theory, stars with light rays that passed near the sun would appear to have been slightly shifted because their light beams had been curved by its gravitational field. This effect is noticeable only during an eclipse because the sun's brightness obscures the affected stars. Well, they had their work to do, and Einstein had his.

The original expedition led by Sir Arthur Eddington to prove or disprove 40-year-old Einstein's theory was one of the key discoveries of the twentieth century. The common man, such as farmers, could believe that it was a great discovery even without understanding its significance to their lives. Learned physicists had even put aside the fact that the theory had come from a German. The world was not too happy about Germans just now after the end of WWI so fresh in their minds.

Sam considered his maker to be in charge of the universe and himself in charge of his farming. It was enough deep thought for him with serious work of his own. He may have been sure that he received divine help with that at times as long as he did his part.

Pa had to leave Monday evening, again.

Sam didn't miss a beat as he drilled in 12 rows of sweet corn for their own food. He plowed, harrowed, and planted a field of maize for the silo, too. A trip was made to go after feed, groceries, and hardware. He turned earth until the plow broke and was in need of a plowshare. Pa returned to the farm on Monday to partner up with five days of turning dirt. It rained on three of those days, but work continued. Sam harrowed for R. Hilton part of one day. They put a lot of work behind them before Lac went to Galeton again. He had to attend court Monday, probably jury duty, and take care of business. Dewey would expect him.

June 14, 1919, was reason for a discussion between Sam, Edith, Grace, and Ma. Women's rights had taken a leap into history and was noted by everyone, even Willa. The United States Congress had approved the 19th amendment to the United States Constitution, which guaranteed suffrage to women. It was sent to each of the states for ratification. The milestone did not pass unnoticed by the Crippens. Most likely every state would ratify it to make it unanimous.

Sam harrowed corn ground and found it to be quite wet. He let it rest on Tuesday and hoped it would dry out. The time was needed on Tuesday to fix up an $80 note to give to Mr. Ward at Chemung Canal Trust Company for a needed loan. He had hired Conklin for field work, and the man must be paid. Sam cleaned out the barn, hauled manure, and did the chores.

Pa came home Sunday, June 15. Conklin quit. Work did not falter under the team of Sam and Lac once again to plow, drag, and cultivate.

There was that one event to attend on a Monday evening for Sam and Edith.

15 – Walker
Depression, 1919

The day started out normal, first the chores, and then Sam cultivated corn. A switch to harrow another field was followed by a change of machines to snap drag on the flat over the seeds he had broadcast by hand. Sam pressed himself to get it done and start chores early.

Pa may have said, "I'll milk the last one, Sam. Go ahead and get cleaned up."

Sam was to accompany Edith to an event of importance. Most likely, Ma was there to watch the children for the short time their parents were out.

Willa M. Haggarty of Horseheads, NY and Edward M. Walker of Elmira Heights, NY were married Monday evening, June 16, 1919.

The 5" x 7" ivory hued remembrance cover flourished in fancy gold letters, *Our Wedding Souvenir*. C. E. Christian, pastor of the Baptist church, signed it. Witnesses who signed the certificate were Edith Crippen and the reverend's wife, Mary L. M. Christian.

The newlyweds would live in Edward's Elmira Heights apartment.

> What, therefore, God hath joined together,
> Let no man put asunder. Mark 10: 7 – 9

Tuesday began day one of married life for the young couple.

Sam was back at work in the fields. He plowed, harrowed, and snap dragged on the flat. Corn was drilled in portions for two days. Potatoes were planted and took all of the men's time on Thursday, Friday, and Saturday. Pa was smack in the middle of all the teamwork, just how Sam preferred it. There was more to do.

Sam's own words...
Saturday, June 21, 1919 – "Planted potatoes, plowed and cultivated corn, paid J. O. Shea $10.60 for Rawleigh products."

W.T. Rawleigh was a worldwide distributor of household and pharmaceutical products. The line represented lucrative medicinal items, nutrition, gourmet foods, cleaning products, personal hygiene, and perfumery. Skin, hair, and body care were included. They even had animal products. Rawleigh introduced their first product in this range in 1895 called Stock Tonic Supplement, which was researched, developed, and evaluated on their own farm. A lucrative market for all of the products existed for direct sellers door to door. People like Sam and Edith wanted the quality items.

Generations of Americans grew up waiting for The Rawleigh Man to arrive at their front door with his sample case of goodies to add spice to their life and to heal their ailments. The Crippens ordered quite a bit as did many of their neighbors. Their order could have been salve, vanilla, pepper, lemon and orange oils, herbs, menthol for making cold medicine, and scissors.

Sunday was a day of rest other than the non-negotiable chores, or a day of travel. Pa went to Galeton.

Monday kicked into high gear as planting continued and hay was cut and hauled to the cows for immediate consumption. It rained two days, but Sam worked around it and in it. Not only corn but peas and pumpkins were planted as the week wore on.

Sadie arrived Friday. There may have been a lull at the lumber camp in Galeton. She and Dewey kept the operation underproduction for Pa. She was the cook for the whole crew, and Dewey was the foreman of the lumber operation. Sadie's appearance at the farm was a bright spot for Sam. She likely rode to the depot with him after the ditcher that he and Pa had bought. The portable machine cost them $65 plus $3.42 freight. The trench digger was a credit purchase from the Owensboro Ditcher & Grader Company of Kentucky.

Sam set up a heat stove on Sunday. Pa came home in the evening after one week's absence. No doubt, Sam was glad that Pa was there to help shoulder the load again. Potatoes were harrowed, corn cultivated, and hay mowed.

The nation's news that came out on Monday, June 30, 1919, announced that The Treaty of Versailles was signed. It marked the formal end of World War I. The recession immediately after the war was said to have been brief, lasting only seven months from August 1918 to March 1919. It didn't feel like it was over, not to Sam. But he and everyone he knew felt glad that it could soon improve as they hoped and prayed.

Sam went to Mr. Johnson's and paid $75 for a cow. He went to town for groceries and butter that cost him $5.75. The hay by the railroad tracks was cut and drawn to the barn. It went to direct use of the cows and horses.

Their friend, Mr. Scott, the farm's previous owner, came out on Sunday. Sam helped a bit in the house.

On Monday, he harrowed in millet and put in potatoes. Two loads of hay were raked and hauled. A cow was hurt Tuesday evening, a possible slip on concrete in the barn. Wednesday morning Sam hurried to go after $1 worth of medicine to treat the injured animal. He could not wait for a Rawleigh remedy to be ordered.

Field and garden work continued all week. By Thursday, he had time to repair the hay rack and helped Pa shoe horses. The $4.70 for iron horseshoes, square nails, and hardware were charged at Hibbard Hardware in Hanover Square, Horseheads. The run-up tab was $38.79 and would be paid in full when fall crops were sold. As busy as they were, the July 7 news in print was worth a second look and had to have captured Sam's attention. He was well aware that the country could be crossed by railroad travel as he had done. He'd have pictured its contours as he thought of what the United States Army convoy would encounter. They started out from Washington, DC, on an expedition across the continental United States to assess the possible and problematic crossing of North America by highway. Sam and

Pa and anyone within earshot speculated that the Army over-land traverse required several months to complete. There was none, but local roads and cow paths across the wilderness. A highway system did not exist.

There were those who would ask why it was needed. Did the ordinary man even believe it was possible? Sam no doubt was well traveled enough to think in the affirmative. Henry Ford certainly would have been for it.

The wounded cow was doctored again on Friday. Sam spent the first half of Saturday to help Russell with his hay.

Sam's own words...
Sunday, July 13, 1919 "Went to Dr. Sharpe's after cow." $42 for the milking animal was paid with high hope to build her up for more milk production."

They began to cut both wheat and rye. The binder required repair. Sam tinkered with it on and off for two days, among other jobs and the hindrance of rain. They cultivated corn, and Pa mowed over across the creek. The chores, barn cleaning, and manure haul occurred daily. Sam stole time to get groceries when he made necessary trips for feed or hardware. He managed to purchase his tobacco and the children's candy at such times. David, Betty, and John must have been excited when 10¢ worth of candy was brought home to them.

News intruded upon the natural world again with front page headlines on Monday, July 21. The Wingfoot Air Express crashed. The dirigible (airship) caught fire over downtown Chicago. Two passengers, one air crewman, and 10 people on the ground were killed. Two people parachuted to safety. Sam, Edith, and Lac read about it with interest and concern before they started their full work day. Sam glanced over a blurb about the Chicago race riots.

His fields in Horseheads had his attention. He pulled weeds and went to town for feed and groceries. The rest of his work week was consumed with hay and grain.

The ditcher was put to use alongside the canal to dig an open trench. It was created to handle the overflow of canal water and direct it to wetlands further away from farm fields. He couldn't let it encroach and denigrate his fields.

More wheat and rye were processed. The granary was put to its practical use. Potatoes were cultivated to keep weeds down to a minimum.

Sam's own words...
Sunday, July 27, 1919 – "Took Willa's trunk to Elmira Heights."

No doubt, it was a family trip as Edith and the children rode along on the wagon. David would have been excited to see his Billo. The newlyweds of six weeks may have been excited and proud to have the family visit.

Mow, rake, and chop. Several crops filled the days of the father and son duo. The barn did not stay clean nor the fence repaired. It was a steady effort to stay ahead of the work. Even the weeds reappeared to beg mowing.

Sam inspected the canal as August began. He worked on the repair of the pig pen, sowed sweet clover, and helped thresh. The thresher required fuel oil to run it, and he bought five gallons at a cost of 95¢. The straw was put in the shed. They continued the hay harvest. The second week of August was spent on barley and oats.

Sam took the time to make picnic tables on August 20. Family life was important to him and Edith. Imagine the approval when David and Betty tried out the seats. John, at 2.5 years may have followed right behind them. Wouldn't the children have scrambled with glee when Sam tossed penny candy onto the red and white checkered oil cloth with which Edith had covered one table? He'd have given her the balance of the paper bag of sweets to dole out later.

Sam's own words...
Thursday, August 21, 1919 – "Went to town after ice cream for the reunion."

The creamy treat came in small round containers with a little tab to pull the lid off. The cost of the lot was 90¢. Sam neither named where the reunion was held nor who and how many attended. Imagine, though, that it took place in Horseheads on Sam and Lac's farm. Maybe the new wall-paper bought on August 4, which cost $3.15, suggests that the farm house was spruced up for such an occasion. Grace and Ma would have helped Edith apply it. The Galeton Crippens knew how to find the farm as many of them had demonstrated already.

They moved machinery under cover. Hay harvest went forward, and more corn chopping for cow feed continued. It was the constant thrust on through August. Plowing started.

Sam's own words...
Saturday, August 30, 1919 – "Took load of hay to J. Collins, 2,600#. Pa and Ma went home. Rainy in p.m."

The hay sold at $20 per ton.

Lac and Sophia were in Galeton four days, through Tuesday. Imagination is not needed to know that Sophia had many friends and relatives in Pennsylvania who were glad to see her. She hadn't been back for six months, unlike Lac, and had seen only those family members who had been able to make the trip to Horseheads. Sam and Edith had benefitted from Pa and Ma being in Horseheads since everyone came to see them, too. More than likely, Lac enjoyed taking Sophia along with him now on what was a pleasure and business trip. The carfare was $5.25.

Sam bought Edith's list of grocery items. The onions, celery, and mustard seed were $1.16. She intended to make bread-and-butter pickles since cucumbers were ready in the garden.

Meanwhile, Sam maintained chores, cleaned stables, and drew manure. The horses would pull the boat a few feet and stop at Sam's behest so he could pitchfork the contents off to fertilize a field.

Ma and Pa were back by Tuesday afternoon.

On Wednesday, Sam went to Montour Falls and paid Mr. Charles $50 and another $25 plus interest to the bank on a $100 side note.

Plowing and corn harvest continued. Cows were fed corn fodder. The coarsely chopped stalks and leaves were juicy sustenance that would promote milk production. Turning up furrows took place every day except Sunday. Regular chores went non-stop.

The newspaper report held Sam's interest on September 7. The

United States Army expedition that had started a convoy across America on July 7 ended in San Francisco. It had taken them two months. No results were known and would not be speculated on by the government. The information gathered had to be analyzed.

Sam's own words...
Wednesday, September 10, 1919 – "Plowed and done chores in a.m. went to Elmira in p.m. and paid $30 on Ward note."

There was always a note due, an installment on a loan that had helped them keep their farm enterprise in operation.

Sam was sick with a cold, but he went into Horseheads for feed and groceries. He carried corn to the animals, mixed feed, and fixed fence. He had time to do odds and ends jobs until chore time.

On Sunday, Mr. Kane, who had sold him the cow, Jane, for $65, came for a visit.

For several days they plowed, harrowed, and drilled in wheat.

Sam paid $10 to Mr. Charles on the land contract.

Longwell hired Sam and Lac with their team to help fill his silo. Mr. Treat had the same idea, and Sam kept track of hours spent there. They kept up with their own chores and barn cleaning. It would not do to let manure pile up. Silo work continued.

Sam's own words...
Saturday, September 27, 1919 – "Filled silo. E. W. & L. Railroad Co. paid $40 damages for injury to cow."
Sunday, September 28, 1919 – "Took De Kohl La Polka Lima up to Russell and clipped her and then to fairgrounds."

It had been a long time coming, the 40 bucks, since February when they bought the farm 8.5 months ago. Finally, compensation arrived for the damage to their cow referred to as Red Skin.

The registered De Kohl heifer was on display at Chemung County fairgrounds. Maybe she would bring a ribbon, but if not, at least she was reason for fair going later.

Ensilage was chopped and put in the silo Monday.

Small debts could be pesky but had given real help at the time of the

Gail Mazourek

loans. Sam paid back Mr. Miller and Mr. Welty $2.50 each and $2.92 in full to Donovans. He drew corn on Tuesday and went to town after coal and groceries. Wednesday, he was back to the corn, and he brought fodder to the cows.

Sam's own words...
Thursday, October 2, 1919 – "Put three loads of corn in silo, went to Fair in p.m."

Sam spent $1 at the fair. He may have bought "Fairy Floss" for his children. It was first introduced to a wide audience at the 1904 World's Fair with great success, selling 68,655 boxes at 25¢ per box (equivalent to $6 per box today.) Today the sweet confection is known as "cotton candy."

Pa went to the fair on Friday. Sam and Lac went together to the registered Holstein sale at the fairgrounds on Saturday. Information on prices could be gained and would serve them well when their heifer would freshen and bring them more money.

The newspaper of October 2, 1919, carried a headline to shock everyone. President Woodrow Wilson had suffered a severe stroke. It was not known on that day that he had been rendered an invalid for the remainder of his life. His left side was impaired, but his mind was intact. He died in 1924. Sam and Lac, along with their neighbors, may have discussed high hopes for Vice President Thomas R. Marshall, who could step into the role temporarily until President Wilson was rehabilitated.

Sam took an engine up to Russell's on Monday to fill a silo. He went on into town for feed and groceries. On Tuesday, he was back at Russell's to help with ensilage.

Sam's own words...
Wednesday, October 8, 1919 – "Plowed in a.m. Airplane went by. Rainy in p.m., made out application for F. loan (sic)."
Thursday, October 9, 1919 – "Helped Russell fill silo, we had a birthday supper for Betty, four years old."

It was an unexpected sight, Sam's first ever, to see an airplane fly overhead as he plowed. Most folks in Horseheads would have been surprised. Those who saw it would have talked about the phenomenon. He knew Grace would believe him and may have wondered if Edith saw it. He

240

went on with work. The newspaper later told about the sighting of the 1918 Thomas-Morse S4-B Scout. The plane called Tommy had a noisy engine.

It is sure as can be that Sam's four-year-old girl smiled as the cake was placed on the table in front of her. Betty's face would have been lighted by the glow of candles as the family sang, "Happy birthday to Betty. Happy birthday to you."

Sunday, October 12, was frosty.

For three half days, Sam followed the team behind a plow.

He went to Elmira one morning with the completed application for the farm loan. Thursday and Friday he helped McFail fill silo in the cold wind. On Saturday he dug six rows of potatoes, went for feed and groceries, and drew manure.

Sunday came again so soon but was welcome before the onset of another work week.

Sam helped Mr. Russell drill his wheat. He opened ensilage to start as feed for cows. The stables were cleaned, a fence made, and a field plowed. A trip to town changed his scenery. On Wednesday he helped Burris dig potatoes. Thursday he took a 2,355-pound load of hay to C. L. Judson for $20 a ton, which amounted to $23.55. J. B. Beck was the weight master in Horseheads, with the use of Jones U.S. Standard scales.

Sam dug more of his spuds Friday and Saturday.

Sam's own words...
Friday, October 24, 1919 – "...Took out insurance on David, Betty, and John."
Saturday, October 25, 1919 – "...Went after seed rye and groceries. Lynn and Iva came."

Sam paid his fire insurance of $20.75 to Hay & Bradley. E. E. Sturdevant had sold him life insurance on the children, which cost him $2.60 on all three.

He had ordered seven bushels of Rosen seed rye on September 15 from J. H. Forell in Sears, Michigan, at $2.25 a bushel for a total of $15.75. Sam tucked the money order receipt in the ledger. When he picked up his rye order at the Millport Depot on Saturday, the freight was $1.47.

It was a pleasure to see his brother, Lynn, again. They were closer than old friends. No doubt it was the same for Ma, Pa, and Grace. Edith was glad to host company who pitched right in to get dinner on the table. Their fine company departed on Sunday.

On Monday, Sam put the picnic tables away, made a hog shelter, and cleaned stables. Tuesday he did housework in the morning and went after coal and groceries in the afternoon. Chores took up both ends of his day.

Of course, the rye seed meant he would start to harrow all of the earth he'd plowed up earlier. He dug four rows of potatoes before evening chores.

On Thursday he helped Edith with housework again after the morning's stable duty. He and Pa threshed seven hours for Russell before evening chores. It would tend to give a man an appetite. Sam was thin regardless of what he ate because he worked it off.

Friday was a day for feed and groceries. He also took racks off a wagon and put a box on. It was rainy on Saturday, November 1, as he went after a load of pulp. He husked corn and did odd jobs.

The news came through from October 28, to become a headline, although it had no effect on the Crippens' lives. Prohibition was authorized in the United States. Congress passed the Volstead Act over Woodrow Wilson's veto. The ban was set to go into effect on January 17, 1920, under the provision of the 18th amendment to the United States Constitution. It would make it illegal to consume or possess alcohol. It inadvertently started the gangster era with the infamous Al Capone in the lead. Men of his ilk became wealthy by opening illegal bars called speakeasies.

Sam noted that the coal strike had begun by the United Mine Workers. That could affect all of them if coal became scarce. There was no time to twiddle thumbs wondering how that would turn out. He had work to do.

Sam dug potatoes four days out of the week and mixed in a dozen other jobs. He harrowed through the wind, snow, and rain on November 7. On Saturday he loaded coal for Grace. He hadn't seen Grace alone in quite a while. It was a short opportunity to talk. She might have mentioned how Dewey had filled out and bulked up. Being a lumberjack was a muscle maker and Sadie's culinary skills at the camp could lay half blame on her if it suited.

Dewey was a tall, handsome man, no longer a boy.

Sunday was laid back. Sam could sit down and ruminate, enjoy his family, and smoke his pipe.

Monday changed the pace back to hectic, exactly what Sam was used to. He drew manure, dug potatoes, and drilled rye. Tuesday Sam loaded hay for Collins. Wednesday he packed 1,855 pounds of hay that he took to H.W. Kinley for $20 per ton, net $18.55.

Eleven-month-old Steele was quite sick on Wednesday evening. Sam and Edith were worried still on Thursday night. Sam harrowed potato ground and picked up spuds with his mind on his youngest son. They called in the doctor.

The weather kept a chill in the Friday air while Sam plowed, hauled manure, and burned weeds. The bonfire job was not hard to take in the cold air. Little Steele was better but still under the weather through Monday. Sam cut wood and did other jobs.

Sam's own words...
Tuesday, November 18, 1919 – "Farm was appraised..."

The appraisal was required before a farm loan could be approved. It would soon be known if they were to have the needed revenue.

Sam made a ditch on the flat. He tried to plow but the machinery broke down. He had to put it off and went to cut wood on the hill. He and Pa repaired the plow on Thursday before Lac went to Galeton.

McFail came over on Thursday to help Sam thresh. On Saturday Sam thrashed six hours to help Donovan. He had an extra amount of work to do with Pa absent, and he worked on the Sabbath. Lac was gone four days and returned Monday evening.

Sam's own words...
Tuesday, November 25, 1919 – "Butchered hog, plowed some on flat, drew out boat manure. Stormy."
Wednesday, November 26, 1919 – "Done chores and went to Elmira, renewed heifer note at Second National Bank, $110."
Thursday, November 27, 1919 – "Done chores, drew manure, ate Thanksgiving dinner with Roy and Grace."

Cold weather meant they could hang the pork for a few days before it was cut up for the brine barrel.

The heifer note was for the registered De Kohl La Polka Lima for which they owed $110. Sam paid $8.54 on the note before he renewed it. They'd had no choice but to refinance. The recession had continued its grip on the economy since August.

Thanksgiving was a renewal, a reminder of the blessings they had, not for what they may have wished for. Their good health and shared food with those they loved were appreciated. With heads bowed, every family member knew gratitude uttered in the words, "And bless this food to our use, Amen." Times like these held them fast, a family knit together by love and faith.

On Friday, November 28, Sam banked up the house and went to town for coal and feed. He stopped at Erks's and the nearby tea store to spend a minimum on needed items. It was 87¢.

Sunday allowed a day of rest to close out November.

A $50 note on the land contract was due and paid on Monday to Mr. Charles at the Montour Falls Bank. Sam bought feed and groceries, this time from Kinley's since he got flour and butter there, too. They sold plenty of "etcetera" if you had the money for it.

After he had drawn out the manure on Tuesday, Sam went to the depot for calf club heifers. They weren't there until Wednesday when he went back. They had paid $67 and $112 for winning stock raised by a 4H Club. This effort after the war had been a way to get youth involved in worthwhile projects and clubs to learn something about dairy.

Cold weather deepened and so would the manure if it was not drawn out of the barn each day. Chores were never at an end as long as cows and horses inhabited the barn. Sam built a pulp bin in the end of the building for the apple scraps they would be hauling. When the box was ready, Pa got a load of pulp. They could dole it out from there, and the wagon box was empty and ready for another trip before they were completely out. Meanwhile, they could use the wagon box for other jobs.

Pa worked a couple of 6.5 hour days with Mr. Treat while Sam did the work on their own farm.

Sunday's earned rest was welcomed.

Lac helped Mr. Treat seven hours each on Monday and Tuesday. On Wednesday, Sam butchered the Kane cow, Jane, that had been bought for $65 in May. She had milked well and paid for herself until they dried her up. It might have been done if she had mastitis and was treated with antibiotics. It would have been done if her milk production was low or if she was more than four or five years old and at the end of her usefulness for dairy. Sam was not explicit about the reason.

Sam's own words...
Thursday, December 11, 1919 – "Took cow hide to town. Went to Elmira to see Chemung Canal Trust Co. about note, paid $25 and interest."
Friday, December 12, 1919 – "Took orders for beef and delivered sold meat in p.m."

The 60-pound cowhide sold for $17. Sam may have sold meat door to door, not uncommon for him. He sold 290 pounds at 17¢ and 18¢ a pound to total $50.48. He couldn't have been disappointed with the total, $67.28. Another 110 pounds were kept, but a portion of that was given away. Grace may have received some since Ma lived with her and Roy.

Slow Sunday slipped by too fast.

Feed dwindled, and Sam went to grind grain and get groceries on Monday. Back at the farm, he and Pa shod horses, which took considerable time. They filled in with odd jobs that lasted until evening milking time.

On Tuesday, Sam took a load of hay that weighed 1,855 pounds to Judson at $25 a ton, to net him $23. When didn't they need the money?

Real cold air set in to stay. Sam banked up the water tank for the barn with straw. Grace needed a load of coal. She could count on Sam to use the wagon box to get it for her. He didn't mind working it in between the full load of everyday work.

They butchered a hog on Saturday, December 20. The $50 land contract payment was paid to Mr. Charles on Monday. Sam went to Elmira Heights Tuesday to sell pork. Willa lived in the Heights. Edith may have had him stop in to invite her and Edward over for Thursday.

An appraiser came to the farm again on Tuesday.

A horse was shod Wednesday along with all the regular chores. Sam went to town on the afternoon of December 24, regardless of snow and wind.

He spent $1.25 on gifts for Edith and the children.

Sam's own words...
Thursday, December 25, 1919 – "Willa and Edward came out and had Xmas dinner with us. Fair and cold."

Willa was with child. Her young siblings no doubt liked having her there. Smiles abounded as she was called Billo or Billy. A cut of pork from the recent butchering may have been a parting gift, a most welcome one.

December 26 was back to the everyday and manure was hauled. Sam went to Hibbard's after two pounds of nails for 50¢ and welding compound, 25¢. Evening chores waited. Lac went to get pulp on Saturday after chores and manure duties were behind them. These things never changed.

Sam's own words...
Monday, December 29, 1919 – "Took 10 bushels potatoes to Erk, brought back feed and groceries."

The spuds that sold to the grocer for $1.50 per bushel returned $15 to Sam. He spent $7.49 for groceries and 10¢ on sewing machine needles for Edith. It must have been with satisfaction that he sold food he'd grown, and the proceeds bought other provisions they needed.

Pa got pulp again, and Sam unloaded it the next morning. Another load was brought home on Wednesday, December 31.

Prosperity was not just over the horizon as 1919 ended and the depression deepened.

16 – Silo
Below Zero, 1920

On Thursday, January 1, it was 10 degrees below zero. The chores were the first accomplishment of the day. The warm bodies of the cows, heifers, and horses provided the only heat inside the barn. Sam's job to draw the manure out was done in a frenzy of movement as he pitchforked it out of the boat. His exercise warmed arm muscles but neither his face nor his feet. He might have hurried inside to a warm kitchen where the tea kettle was kept hot on the range. Tea was a staple and needed replenishment.

On Saturday, January 3, Sam went to town in a car for which he paid 25¢. He spent $1.20 on groceries that could have included loose tea steeped in boiled water from the spouted kettle. No record of a tobacco purchase had been entered since back in October. January 4 warmed all the way up to four degrees below zero.

On Monday, Sam wrangled the usual dung and went after sustenance for animals and humans. He spent $3.92 with the Ann Page Grocer and elsewhere bought two pair of socks and shoestrings. Tired of cold feet, possibly he planned to wear two pair of hosiery at once in his work boots.

Sam's own words...
Wednesday, January 6, 1920 – "Drew out manure, went to Elmira and saw Farm Bureau man, C. J. Howe, also Atty. C. A. Phillips."

Mr. Howe was the man who handled the second mortgage note on the farm. He may have advised Sam to seek Phillips's council. Attorney Phillips was the man from whom Sam inquired about the procedure to apply for a Federal Reserve loan.

The popular belief was that the market economy had zealously overextended itself with mortgage loans into 1920. The Federal Reserve has broad supervisory and regulatory authority over state-chartered banks and bank holding companies, as well as foreign banks operating in the United States. It is also involved in maintaining the credit rights of consumers. Sam and Lac might find relief if they could refinance at a much lower interest rate. Farmers far and wide were in the grip of the depression, and the Feds had to do something to turn it around.

Edith's new housedress arrived. It had cost $2.45. With all the work of running a farm household and caring for children, she may have longed to have a store-bought dress. She was aware of a new trend. The pressure to buy ready-made clothing rather than homemade had set in. Sam's work clothes did not change from his understated blue-gray broadcloth pants and shirt that revealed a hint of white undershirt at his neck.

The harsh cold hung on, and a storm dropped snow on Friday, January 9. Sam cleared snow away to make paths. School taxes were due and payable to Mrs. Ira Wilcox for the sum of $13.23. Sam and Lac scraped it together and paid up. They were well aware that money did not stretch far with inflated prices that strangled power to buy.

One look outside and Sam was sure that more snow had to be shoveled on Saturday. The cold snap had a grip on the weather, wind, and worry. He went for a load of ensilage to feed cows. When he came back for Edith's list, he rode after feed, coal and groceries. She had a separate list of drugs. The A. & P. Co. tab was $5.02, the milk of magnesia and aspirin $2.80, and six ounces of saltpeter, 20¢. Also known as sodium or potassium nitrate, saltpeter had many uses. As a strong oxidizing agent, it was used for fireworks, explosives, matches, sensitive toothpaste, food curing, and fertilizers to make soil more fertile. With the small amount that Sam purchased, it was most likely ham preservation that he had in mind since he never mentioned any fun with fireworks in January.

The function of food curing with saltpeter could cause harm or even death. It could easily be mistaken for table salt. The transparent, colorless, white crystals of potassium nitrate were not edible on their own and contained salt, sodium nitrate, and glycerin with FD#3 used to color it bright pink to prevent the cure from being mistaken for regular salt. Saltpeter is commonly used to make bacon, hams, corned pork and corned beef. It produced the characteristic pink color to the products.

Sam might have thought he was a spendthrift because of the $8.02 total expenditure, but no tobacco was purchased. It wasn't that he hadn't thought about it, but then he thought he wouldn't.

Sam's own words...
Wednesday, January 14, 1920 – "Drew two loads of manure. Saw T. W. Van, strong cold wind."

Sam paid $2 in Farm Bureau dues to Mr. Van. It was no time to let membership lapse when the organization was like a lifeline to farmers, advising them and advocating with the Feds on their behalf. The 84¢ carfare there and back hit hard but was necessary.

Thursday the paths had blown full of snow again, and Sam cleaned them. A letter arrived Friday from Mr. Charles. The mortgage note was due. No money jumped out to pay for it.

Come Saturday, David was speckled red with measles. He was feverish, and his eyes hurt all day. It was the same on Sunday. Of course, Edith tried to keep a wet cloth on his forehead, but he tossed and turned. Her worry about him could make her lose patience.

On Monday before manure hauling, Sam went to Horseheads for feed and limited groceries. He came back a hero with 35¢ spent on ice cream for David. Sam caved in and bought tobacco, also cough drops and Vaseline for 52¢ total. It snowed all day.

Tuesday, January 27, was windy and piled the same snow in drifts. Lac went to Galeton for two days. Sam splurged for 60¢ worth of tobacco and $1.43 in drugs. Did he deem it not worthwhile to be without his tobacco all the while worry was his companion?

Snow with wind drift continued through Saturday. All of the children were sick by the approach of the evening hour. None improved until

Gail Mazourek

Tuesday. Sam may have swallowed hard when he could not bring more ice cream. He was ill on Wednesday just as all of the children were well. Pa got the silage down from the silo three days in a row. Sam dragged through chores but was good for nothing more.

Sam's own words...
Saturday, January 31, 1920 – "...Went after coal, very cold, 14 below zero."

Sam had survived, and it was a good thing because Pa was sick by Monday. Chores, manure, and silage were all Sam's now. On Wednesday, Edith was ill, and Pa was no better. He played at being better on Thursday, but it didn't last. Would the cold, the snow, and their illness ever let go of its grip on them?

More snow covered the area. What was this? Manna from heaven? Suppose not since he couldn't eat it, and this was not the desert. Sam guessed there'd be a shovel in his near future. It blew around and piled up. The roads drifted full. Chores were kept up and manure removed while the rest of his time was spent on snow shovel duty.

Sam's own words...
Monday, February 9, 1920 – "Done chores, three loads manure, Pa walked around a little."

Relief was in sight now that Pa could get out of bed again. The improvement was as welcome to Sam as it was to Pa. The man whose square jaw line was in evidence on Sam's own chin would rally and remain his partner. Sam's steps were lighter.

Tuesday brought milder temperatures. After six weeks, extreme cold was broken. A god-fearing man like Sam could almost hear the high note from the "Hallelujah" chorus.

Sam hired Russell to take a load of hay to Kinley's for him. The 1,670 pounds at $25 per ton netted $20.87. Sam later purchased cough drops for 6¢ and tobacco was 15¢. He worked solo on the operation of the farm while he waited for Pa's complete recovery.

More snow fell Friday. Sam finished chores and worked in the house. He monitored Pa's health and strength, which was slow to return and in fact had not improved.

Saturday's chores, an ensilage trip, and the manure caper were completed. Sam had the doctor in for Pa. The $5 for Dr. Bowman was necessary. Sam was still a lone worker. That was not what worried him.

The week ensued the same as the days just past while Wednesday skies dropped more snow. Sam learned that Grace was ill. He hadn't left the place in a few days but was forced to it on Saturday for the need of feed and groceries. He spent $4.18 at Erks.

Sam had finished the chores on Sunday when Mr. Grant Taber stopped in. Later in the day, Sam wrote a letter to the Federal Reserve Bank. This farmer was still a fact finder, no rash moves.

Snow was too familiar of a sight again on Monday.

Tuesday, February 24, he went to the Second National Bank in Elmira and paid $25 plus interest on the De Kohl registered heifer note. He spent $1.10 at the tea store and brought back feed and groceries. Wednesday he went for coal and groceries. Coffee, matches, and baking powder cost him 93¢ at Erks. Montour Falls was Thursday's destination, and on the return trip, he spent 87¢ at Ann Page Company. Friday found him in Horseheads for feed at Kinley's where he bought 25 pounds of flour at $1.79. He and Edith knew the prices at every store. She wrote her list to group individual items for that purpose. Sam shopped around to spend as little as he could. He would soon be forced to pay out what had been saved for obligations. Sam was sure of the necessity for frugality.

Another week of two men's work had been done by one.

February ended on Sunday.

Monday, March 1, Pa had recovered enough to go to Galeton to watch operations there. He could not work on farm or lumber yet, but most likely he was restless. The farm was in capable hands with Sam. Lac could neither doubt that nor let his Pennsylvania lumber business go unchecked any longer.

Tuesday, after chores, Sam went to Elmira and paid $370 on the mortgage note. He had the barn to clean, manure to draw, and wood to chop. The snow melted fast during a couple of mild days. Friday turned it on its head. Pa returned in a snow blizzard. The wind stayed for Saturday.

Sam's own words...
Tuesday, March 9, 1920 – "Done chores, went to Elmira after shoes for Pa, self and children."

He and Pa's size nine work shoes with eight eyelet holes, which laced to just above the ankle, were $3.98 each. The children's shoes (four pair) were $1.40 each. Betty and David's buckle artics were a combined $4. The carfare of 60¢ made the total $18.16.

The newspaper had recent reports on the rise of illegal alcohol in use. Crime increased since the prohibition law went into effect in January. The problems so far were in the hills and mountains of southern states where dense forest offered hidden territory for operations. Warm weather was attractive in which to run whiskey still locations. Sam and Lac may have wondered if it would become a northern problem for that aspect when warm weather broke. They may have mused, what's to keep determined bootleggers from setting up operations in a basement? Al Capone's bootleggers already delivered the brew to their illegal bars and speakeasies.

On Thursday, March 11, after morning chores, Sam went to Elmira and paid Chemung Canal Trust Company $25 plus interest on the Ward note. He had paid a hired man, Conklin, with the borrowed money. The balance was whittled down to $50.

Friday's melt off had reduced snow and ice to water that had spread over the flats. Saturday joined forces and snowed all day.

Spring hadn't announced its presence with mild weather yet, but the Swiss and the black heifers came in. Their two calves were soon sold for $9. That same day, Sam moved a load of goods to Millport for Mr. Russell to earn $4.

Mr. L. M. Charles from Montour Falls Bank visited them on the next two mornings, Wednesday and Thursday. They had talks about the Federal Reserve Bank.

Sam's own words...
Friday, March 19, 1920 – "Done chores. Edith went to hospital to see Willa. I went to Elmira to see attorney, Phillips."

Willa was the proud mother of her and Edward's baby daughter, Louise Marilla Walker. Louise had been born on Willa's 18th birthday, March 19, a date that mother and daughter would always share. The Walkers had been married nine months. Edith was a grandmother at age 42 and Sam a grandfather at age 37. All of them shared March as their birth month.

Not one of them thought of the birth regarding one more added to the 107,823,000 United States population at the time. What would they have thought of that number tripled to 325,805,147 by the year 2015?

Sam's talks with attorney Phillips were on the details that would enable him to borrow from the Feds to pay off Mr. Charles at Montour Falls Bank for the mortgage. He'd have questioned how it could put them in a better position.

Saturday was a stormy, snow-filled day. Sam and Lac dug into odd jobs. Of course, it was sandwiched between chores on each day's end and manure duty in between. Sunday was relegated to barn chores only.

Monday they were in a hurry to get past morning chores.

Water was hauled to the house for the wash before manure was hauled. With that finished, Pa was free to go to a sale. Sam went after coal, feed, and groceries. Clothes hung on the lines and flapped in the breeze when he returned.

Tuesday required Sam's trip to Montour Falls to pay a $155 note. Pa drew a load of apple pulp in the warm sunshine. On Wednesday he went to another sale. He thoroughly enjoyed the atmosphere of cattle, horse, and farm machinery auctions.

The money that was paid out for the recent notes left them short.

On Thursday, March 25, Sam authorized Attorney C. A. Phillips to start a title search of the farm property to work toward a federal loan. He had talked with Mr. Charles, the federal bank officer, and the Farm Bureau representative and had all the information he needed to move forward. They were all on board.

Sam must have smiled as Pa went to his third cattle market of the week. He liked to see him enjoy himself even if he never made a purchase.

Sam took a 1,300-pound load of straw to Mr. Wethune and brought back coal. He drew manure out of the barn.

Saturday was the day that the two heifers, Black Mulley and Red Skin had their calves. That made two more fresh cows.

Sam's own words...
Sunday, March 28, 1920 – "Susan came fresh. Very busy doing chores and taking care of fresh cows, etc."

Susan was on the same timetable as the other freshened cows. Sam had planned for it. He and Lac were occupied to take care of four more milkers and the last two new calves. That was in addition to chores, the usual stuff. These cows added work. They milked each of them and fed the two weaned calves in the pen. The milk production went out to the market. Money was the object.

Monday milk marked the first shipment from the Crippen farm to D. S. Phips, a new vendor. Sam commenced plowing on Tuesday. He broke up the day to take Mully to service. Lac went to Elmira and paid T. J. Wintermute $52.14, the land tax that was due.

Sam plowed to end March and begin April. He was behind the plow day after day. It was no job for 63-year-old Pa who would not shirk from such duty. Sam preferred to keep on it and have Pa do other important jobs.

Sam harrowed and broadcast seed in the snow and rain of April 5. His tall, solitary figure walked at a constant pace across the field to spread seed with the sweep of his arm repeated time and again.

On Thursday he went to town in search of a churn. Hand-powered crank butter churns with glass jar bases were used to make butter for home use. Some were as small as one quart to make small batches of butter churned with a wooden paddle. Butter was sweet for only a couple of days without refrigeration and would turn rancid. The small Daisy glass churn was a popular production.

Sam's own words...
Wednesday, April 7, 1920 – "Plowed, very cold winds and snow. Ma came in the evening."
Thursday, April 8, 1920 – "Drew out manure. Lois W. De Kohl heifer came fresh, went after coal and groceries, cold wind."

Ma stayed at Grace's. She no doubt informed them of a move coming up for Grace's household. Help would be needed from the men. Sophia also wanted to arrange a ride for herself to the railroad depot the next Wednesday for her trip to Galeton.

The Lois W. De Kohl heifer added the fifth calf born. Sam started the move for Whitings on Thursday, by the transfer of Grace's coal to her new abode. On Friday the manure boat sailed. Sam also sorted potatoes while Pa went after apple mush in a cold wind. The next Monday Sam sold 381 pounds of spuds at 5¢ a pound to net $19.05. Tuesday, April 13, he moved Roy's goods to the new address. The wagon was fully loaded. He took Ma to the depot on Wednesday. Their cow, June, was taken for service on Thursday. Pa went to a sale on Friday. He bought a horse, which was what he had looked for all along.

Sam went on errands. He stopped at the post office, which pleased Edith. She had received a small book from Lora Nichols. Lora dated it 4-10-20 and signed it, To Edith With Love. It was titled *In The Desert of Waiting, The Legend of Camelback Mountain* by Annie Fellows Johnson.

Sam was constant with either the plow or harrow and was the same faithful worker with manure. On a rainy Wednesday, he sold June's calf for $5. On Thursday, April 22, he mailed a letter to Dewey. Ma could have delivered it in person if Sam had made it ready in time. Pa went after more apple grunt on Friday. Sam planted garden in the frigid wind on Saturday. For two days, he worked on the windmill pump. No doubt it included the use of oil to squelch a squeal.

Sam's own words...
Wednesday, April 28, 1920 – "Plowed. Pa went after coal Grace needed. Lima De Kohl freshened. Rain."

Lois and Lima, registered cows, were both fresh. Milk had been increased for the market. Their calves would be recorded.

Plow and manure jobs abounded. Pa hauled cow waste on Friday when Sam marked off Grace's garden for potatoes. She counted on Sam's help as her brother and friend who never thought to say no.

Sam went to Montour Falls on Saturday. Mr. Charles received the regular $50, and another $40 went to Montour Bank on a side note. Sam brought back feed and groceries along with a post office package for Edith. Her new dishes had arrived.

Pa went to a sale on Monday. It was just as well since there was a cold wind. Sam experienced it when he drew out the manure. It was the same Tuesday for plowing. He went to town after grass seed and groceries.

Back at the farm, hay was loaded and delivered to C. L. Judson. Wednesday, Sam bought seed oats at $1 per bushel and drilled them in.

The flats were too wet to disk on Friday. He harrowed his garden on Saturday and measured it off for fruit trees. Apples, plums, and peaches would be a good fit. He went to town for coal on rainy Saturday, for Grace. When the flat finally dried off later on Sunday, Sam broadcast seed and spring toothed it into the soil.

Holes were dug for seedling trees on Monday. Sam plowed and went after feed. Together, he and Pa repaired fence and set in 12 fruit trees.

Tuesday turned rainy but posed no problem for Pa to pursue pulp. Sam spread barn waste. On Wednesday, he went after coal, seed, and groceries. They continued to plow, harrow, and plant barley and alfalfa. It remained cold and windy. Sunday was welcome when they did naught but the barn chores.

On Monday, Red Skin was taken to service. Sam went after feed. Work went on and on for fields, garden, and barn.

Ma and Uncle George Dimon arrived. He was a valued brother-in-law to Lac and a favorite with the entire family.

A hog yard was petitioned off on Wednesday. Corn and oats were drilled Thursday while the threat of rain held off until Sam finished. He drew hay on Friday for horses, loaded hay for Wethune, and harrowed. A lot of visiting had gone on with the pleasure of Uncle George's company and may have pushed fence building off until Sunday to catch up.

Sam's own words...
Monday, May 24, 1920 – "Plowed, went to Horseheads and Elmira, $25 on De Kohl note, renewed it for $60."

The whole bill had come due, but the money to pay was not in hand.

It got extended for next payment to keep it from being in arrears. The bank continued to add interest for which it was entitled.

Sam kept himself busy. He plowed, harrowed, and planted corn ground for three days. If he had any thought of boredom with the repetition of the work, it never surfaced. The diversity was in the weather, animal health, and break down of machinery and fences. Just call it work.

Thursday he planted rows of potatoes. On Monday Sam went after groceries. Other than chores and manure runs, another week was spent on corn.

May was over, and June was on. On the third and fourth days, Sam put the ditcher to work on the flat. The shallow trenches were ready before Saturday's rainfall. Pa and Uncle George were right there to give input and watch the operation. No doubt, Sam enjoyed his demonstration of the machine while they looked on.

Sam went after coal and tea and did odd jobs.

Sam's own words...
Monday, June 7, 1920 – "Letter from Federal Land Bank."
Thursday, June 10, 1920 – "Paid $25 on Ward note. Saw attorney, Phillips. Worked on bridge across creek."

Maybe things were about to align. Nice to contemplate while Sam continued field and garden work. He marked out more potato rows. Pa sorted, cut, and planted potatoes. Sam drilled in beans.

Sam's own words...
Monday, June 14, 1920 – "Went after feed and groceries. Mr. Charles and all of us went to the city to fix up loan."
Thursday, June 17, 1920 – "Took first degree I.O.O.F."

Maybe all parties were on board now as they headed to Elmira. At least they would all be in the same room, and no party would be left in the dark to iron out details of a federal loan.

Sam had corn to cultivate. The weeds could get a deeper hold in the soil if he were not on his game but it didn't hurt to enjoy a friend if the chance came. Will Thomas showed for a visit.

Sam was not against enjoyment, especially if it went along with his kind nature. The mission of the Independent Order of Odd Fellows was and still is: to visit the sick, relieve stress, bury the dead, and educate the orphan. There were lodges in every state. Dues were $1 a year. Burial expenses were not paid by any other fund in these Non-Social Security, Non-Medicare days.

I.O.O.F. members advanced by degrees, which were conferred by ritual and pageantry into a higher rank. Sam could see the greater purpose of it because of the examples around him. Pa already struggled with diminished workability and higher expenses if he saw a doctor at all. Sam wanted to figure a way to help himself and society solve the way to prepare for senior years.

Pa went to Galeton on Friday, June 18.

Sam's own words...
Saturday, June 19, 1920 – "Cultivated corn. Seventh anniversary of our marriage."

Sam had a reason for his good mood and the milestone with his Pal was at the top of his list. Work was carried on. He never minded a wagon ride after feed and groceries, which he went after on Monday. Orchard grass was mowed and potatoes harrowed on Tuesday and Pa came home in the evening after four days absence.

More potato ground was marked on Wednesday. Sam spread chicken manure on it. Thursday, he went after coal, raked hay, and dropped spuds.

Sam's own words...
Thursday, June 24, 1920 – "Took second degree in I.O.O.F."

He had a good feel about membership in the Odd Fellows organization. More than likely, he enjoyed like-minded men who set themselves toward altruistic motives. It may have reminded him of something he knew; that Edith enjoyed Mizpah and DAR for the same reasons. He and his Pal understood each other and were drawn together.

There was always a fence leaned on too hard by animals who reached for a choice blade of grass just out of range on the wrong side of the wire.

They worked on fence repair, drew a load of hay, and rigged a rope and fork to the hay loft.

Sam recorded Uncle George's first day of paid work. He had proved his worth from all of his past experience of farm operations of his own. He was not there for a full-time job, but he would work with them during a busy time. Sam may have seen that Uncle George picked up where Pa slowed.

Sam's own words...
Saturday, June 26, 1920 – "Went to Elmira to see C. A. Phillips. Drew in load of alfalfa, cultivated corn."

Attorney Phillips may have explained how slow the wheels of deals move. That explanation could not cure what Sam had on his mind. Monday was a day set to drain more money from the pockets. He went to Montour Falls and paid $20 plus interest on a $370 note to keep it at bay. It was all he could manage.

He cultivated corn and planted more of it. Other corn was harrowed. Sam had a rotation of work going on to create a ladder effect with all processes involved.

On Tuesday, he went to Horseheads on errands and telephoned Attorney Phillips in Elmira about the federal loan. What was the holdup?

Pa mowed hay and cultivated corn. They cleaned out cow stables. Uncle George gave a hand at least an hour per day, and Sam recorded it on a small tablet for future payment. The last day of June was Wednesday, and Uncle George drew a pay of $10. It was based on 4.5 days' pay at $2.22 per day for skilled farm labor. Uncle George cultivated corn in the afternoon.

Thursday hay was hauled and a corn field worked on. Sam went to the Odd Fellows lodge in the evening.

Sam's own words...
Friday, July 2, 1920 – "Drew load of hay. Went up to Mr. L. M. Charles and Elmira to concluded loan with Federal Loan Bank."

Sam must have been gratified after Friday's piece of business while he mowed hay, cleaned the barn, and spread manure on Saturday.

The mortgage of $4,500 had transferred to the Federal Loan Bank of Springfield, MA, at 5.5% interest. The terms would be easier on them and prevent losing the farm. A payment of $146.25 would be due June 1st and December 1st of every year. The initial payment was made at the signing. They still had all of their other notes to pay, but this relief made it easier to manage.

The same chores needed to be done, but all jobs seemed lighter now with less pressure on the ability to pay obligations. Sam raked, shocked and hauled hay. Potatoes were cultivated. It was all done again during the week in addition to fence repair and a hog pen made. Pa mowed a backfield. On Friday the Farm Bureau man, Mr. Holman, came out. Sam went after groceries, drew hay, and fixed fence on Saturday. Pa traveled to Galeton Sunday morning.

The cattle found a weak link in the fence and Sam was off to chase them. Hilton cut wheat for him Monday while he fixed a fence. Tuesday he shocked wheat and rye. Uncle George helped with chores.

Pa came home Monday night to do what he could.

On Wednesday Sam cut, raked, and shocked hay. The week was spent on alfalfa, corn, and hay harvest. Sam also drilled in 2.25 acres of buckwheat. He took one ton of hay to Kinley's at $25 ton. He hoed squash.

A ferocious thunderstorm brought torrents of rain Thursday. Nothing escaped the drenching. On Friday Sam went after coal, shingles, and feed. He repaired the barn door, cut weeds, and dug potatoes. It took him into Saturday when he and Pa did many odd jobs.

Fence repair occurred in portions within each of the next four days. Finally, the shingles were all attached on the barn roof. Sam went after groceries Saturday. He pulled weeds and chased cows, probably with exasperation. The weather was cold when August came in as if it were already September.

Uncle George had worked 23 days and was paid $51.06 for his valuable work.

Sam went to Montour Falls on Monday to pay $10 plus interest on a $74 note. He came back with coal and groceries. On Wednesday, Pa cultivated corn and Sam made two loads of hay. Thursday he got three loads of hay and Pa cut barley. Work slowed because of rain on Saturday

Sunday was their earned respite with tea served to suit their leisure time out. The news mentioned among them was that new-fangled tea bags had become available in the local tea store. They decided they'd all like to try them out.

Those first tea bags were hand-sewn fabric bags; tea bag patents date as early as 1903. First appearing commercially around 1904, tea bags were successfully marketed by the tea and coffee shop merchant Thomas Sullivan from New York, who shipped them around the world. The loose but pre-measured tea was intended to be removed from the sample bags by customers, but they found it easier to brew the tea with the tea still enclosed in the porous bags.

The second week of August was unremarkable. The days went along as full of work as they had always been. Sam went to town on Monday for feed and groceries. He paid Mr. Charles $26.29. The modest amount due was remarkable when he thought about it. The barley harvest commenced, and rye ground was plowed. Sam moved Mr. Brown on a hot day. He was paid $10 rent for his wagon and team and $5 for his labor.

Uncle George helped Edith. He may have wanted to show appreciation for the meals eaten at her table. Did he clean the floors, hang clothes on the line, or cut up pumpkins? Sam didn't explain in his diary, but he noticed the gesture by the fact that he recorded it. The whole family accepted Uncle George's presence and treated him as though he belonged, and he did. They saw the relationship that cemented Lac and George as brothers-in-law. Sam could easily smile when he saw the two of them converse several times a day. He was not immune to good fellowship.

Sam's own words...
Friday, August 20, 1920 – "Tried to plow but Harry Perry came and I visited with him, fixed fence, turned oats."

The two farmers may have discussed the new phenomenon reported in the news: the radio had been invented. The first commercial radio station transmitted on August 20 in the United States from Detroit, Michigan. Neither Sam nor Harry had seen or heard one yet. They did not know how many pieces of apparatus it took to hook up and listen to the radio in its early debut. It would not become prevalent in homes yet. The radio equipment involved in a communication system included a transmitter and a receiver. Each had an antenna and appropriate terminal equipment such as a microphone at the transmitter and a loudspeaker at the receiver in the case of a voice communication system to send signals.

It was also news that the Ford Model T continued to sell well.

Sam supposed he could make up for the time he stood talking to a neighbor. He shod horses and went after feed, coal, and groceries.

Lac went to Galeton on Sunday

Uncle George was still there and helped Sam when Grace and Ma let him be. Sam plowed three days while his uncle harrowed.

Pa came home Saturday.

Sam was confident of Dewey watching out for Pa's safety in the woods of Galeton. Grace and Ma, no doubt, fretted to each other about Pa. It was their way to worry out loud. He could no longer work all day like his sons. Lac's boys may have had a pact between them to look out for him. Lynn had carried the folks through the rough times when they all lost Ralph. Now Sam and Dewey had stepped up to shield Pa.

Dewey lived in their folks' last house in Galeton when he wasn't at camp, typically August. He had paid $25 for rent in 1918 $20 each in 1919 and 1920. Sam missed Dewey when he thought about him. The two of them would do right by Pa.

Uncle George had worked 14.5 hours in August and received $32.20 in pay.

Sam sold two baby piglets to Mr. Fowler for $5 each. Maybe the rest would stay in the pen now. He was always in fix mode for either the pig sty or the pasture fences.

He made a trip to town Monday, September 6, for feed and groceries. The trip was all for nothing. He hadn't considered that it was Labor Day and stores were closed. He plowed all day Tuesday while Pa and Uncle George chuckled through their shared jobs.

Sam threshed on Wednesday, which used some of his coal supply for the machine. Pa helped Westlake thresh on Thursday. It was the same day that Edith, Grace, and Uncle George went to the Watkins fair. Most likely the children went, too.

Pa went to Pennsylvania on Friday.

Sam borrowed Mr. Sopher's corn harvester for the week ahead.

Pa returned Tuesday evening. Lac was welcome to help with chores. Sam put straw under cover and cleaned silo and the barn. He cut corn on Saturday and was ready to fill silo. Sunday was to be enjoyed as a respite before the labor of more silo filling on Monday.

Sam's own words...
Monday, September 20, 1920 – "Went after feed and groceries. Pa fell from silo."

17 – Emergency
Sold Shores, 1920

Sam returned from a trip to grind feed. He drove his team and loaded wagon next to the house. Before he unloaded feed bags at the barn, he'd hand the groceries off to Edith through the door at the rear of the house. It was handy that the door opened to a short hallway access to the pantry and kitchen.

Where was she? He supposed she had to attend one of the children or was it bread in the oven? Maybe both. Had he ought to set the box of items inside? He tossed the reins over a hitching post as he jumped down to the ground. He had counted on Edith's usual smile for him. The box balanced on his left hip with his long arm over the top to grip the bottom. He reached for the door just as six-year-old David burst through.

"Pa! Grandpa fell off the silo." David swallowed hard to catch his breath.

Sam's imagination had started to work overtime. It was enough to raise the hair on the back of his neck as he followed David inside. He sat the groceries on the table as he hurried past.

"Grandpa couldn't breathe or walk, Pa. Mama screamed for Uncle George to come out of the barn!" David ran out of breath.

Sam stood at the foot of Lac's bed to look him over. Lac's eyes were closed. The color had drained from his face. Sam stood with elbows out and knuckles pressed into fists on each side of his body below his belt. He shook his head in denial of what had happened. It was clear that Pa was battered and skinned up. Edith took Sam's elbow and pulled him toward the door.

"Uncle George has gone after Ma but first to call a doctor," she said. "We think Pa has broken ribs, but the doctor is the one who will know for sure."

Sam remained glum. Now he was the one who was short of breathe. They could only wait while time crawled. Sam couldn't sit down. He stood in the doorway of Pa's room and winced whenever he heard a groan that signaled that his father was still alive.

Ma and Uncle George drove in with the horse and carriage.

Sophia went into Lac's room while the rest of them gave her space to see the old man. She started clucking right away. "Now don't move, Lac. Stay still, and the doctor will be here as soon as he can," she said.

Sam supposed Ma would feel better if she could fuss over Pa. He shook Uncle George's hand. Their unspoken worry was sure to include an opinion that Lac would be laid up for a while.

Dr. Bowman arrived and walked in with a beaten leather satchel, ready to help his emergency patient. Sam watched him listen to Pa's chest and feel of his ribs. Pa groaned.

"You've wrenched your back, cracked a few ribs, and will have extensive bruises, Mr. Crippen," Dr. Bowman said.

"You help Doc bind up his ribs, Sam. I'll start the milking without you," Uncle George said as he went out to start chores.

Sam nodded his head toward Ma when the doctor gave Pa a shot for pain.

"The pain will remind him not to move around a lot right away. Cracked ribs will stir some pain even to breathe," Doc said to all of them gathered around.

They would rely on aspirin for him after the heavier medication wore off.

Sam had to get himself out to the barn and help Uncle George milk the cows. He supposed Pa would sleep now after the drug took hold and the trauma of all he had gone through lessened.

Later that evening, Sam took a turn on nurse watch before he opted for a few hours of sleep. The restless night of checking on Pa turned into daylight. He had several days of work ahead to fill silo. It would take longer because Pa was out of commission. It was Tuesday, September 21, and Uncle George worked with Sam for an hour each evening through Friday. Help offered at the end of the day pleased Sam when he was tired.

Sam's own words...
Saturday, September 25, 1920 – "Finished filling silo at noon. Went after drugs, etc."
Sunday, September 26, 1920 – "Pa a little better. Repaired pump and wagon, etc."
Monday, September 27, 1920 – "Frank, Mary, Sadie, and Dewey came..."

No doubt, it was a relief to Sam to finish the filling up of the 30-foot tall wooden cylinder and leave corn harvesting behind. He needed supplies that he went after for the cattle and the household. Pa required more aspirin. He was several shades of black and blue.

The Galeton contingent had arrived because they wanted to see Pa for themselves. Love and support was in full supply from all of them. Edith, Ma, and Grace were sure to have put together a delectable meal. Uncle George stayed after he helped Sam with chores. A week had passed since Pa's accident, and Uncle George agreed with Sam that Lac had improved. It didn't mean he was moving much.

Tuesday, September 28, 1920, Sam went to Elmira and paid $60.30 to the Second National Bank on the De Kohl note. Back on the farm, he picked up corn out of the field and fixed fence. There was no waste of fallen corn. Pigs would benefit from the gleaned maize. He put it under shelter Wednesday and cut buckwheat. The manure boat sailed just before chore time. Uncle George arrived for milking. He wouldn't be around to help Sam on Thursday. Thursday was stormy with high wind. Sam walked Wykoph De Kohl to Inglehart for service on Friday. The wagon box was repaired before chore time.

Sam's own words...
Saturday, October 2, 1920 – "Plowed, done chores. Pa quite a lot better."

The entire family was glad to see Lac recover, although he was not expected to be fit for work anytime soon.

Colder air had moved in as Sam spent the week at work with Westlake to fill his silo. He'd gone to Horseheads for feed and groceries. Sam paid A. R. Hooke the $18 owed him for feed corn bought before harvest. He helped McFail fill his silo on Friday.

Sam and Ma no doubt talked about Lac's recovery progress. Pa was restless. Ma was traveling to Galeton with him and intended to make sure Dewey would prevent any exertion from his father. The three would have been in agreement that Pa could observe only. There was to be no hands-on to set back his healing.

Lac and Sophia departed for Pennsylvania on Sunday, October 10. They missed out on the birthday cake for five-year-old Betty.

Sam made a necessary trip to Horseheads for all the current needs. He helped fill McFail's silo on Tuesday. Sam picked apples. Mr. Brown took 10 bushels of apples to town for Sam Tuesday. He returned him two loads of pulp Wednesday. Uncle George helped Sam one hour each on Wednesday and Thursday. Other than buckwheat that Sam drew on Thursday, he plowed and harrowed right on through Saturday.

Lac came home Sunday. Sophia stayed in Pennsylvania.

Sam likely was glad to see Pa and have his company. There wouldn't have been any illusion that his father could work, but his ideas and their discussions were popular with Sam.

Sam harrowed, drilled wheat, and went after pulp. He fixed a wagon, drilled in rye, and shod Madge. Another week was over and done.

Sam was efficient and always busy with farm chores, crops, and repairs. Pa was on the fringe, unable to add his labor in Galeton or Horseheads. No doubt he was glad that Sam, Dewey, and Sadie were competent, but he was restless when Sam went for the pulp that he used to get. Sam dug potatoes. Lac couldn't help there either. Sam kept at the work day in and day out. He shod Old Goonie without assistance. He slowly filled the cellar with apples, potatoes, and squash.

Sam received a letter.

~**~
Second National Bank
Elmira, NY
October 28, 1920

Mr. S. P. Crippen
Horseheads, NY

Dear Sir:-

The committee has audited the bills for the recent Calf Club Sale and find the expense of each animal was $5.20. This included the care and tuberculin test.

The total amount of your indebtedness on the animal will be $130.65. Will you please arrange to take care of this at your earliest convenience?

Very Truly Yours,
Clerk: P. C. Salmon

Second National Bank
Holstein Calf Club

~**~

The second letter was identical except for the price. Calf number two was $82.90.

Sam went and paid $63.55 and signed a note for the balance of $150 that was to be paid in three months. He wrote it on the outside of the envelope so he'd remember the details and dates on his heifers.

On Sunday, October 30, Lac went back to Galeton to watch lumber operations for the week. Uncle George went down on Monday, November 1. Most likely they both had it in mind to vote where they were registered.

On Tuesday, Sam watched the children so Edith could take a car ride to register her vote.

Sam carried on with his operations through November as weather chilled. Chores, manure, and potatoes were his current occupation.

On November 8, he paid a Federal Land Bank note of $107.25. He cut and skidded wood and pulled beans.

Sam's own words...
Tuesday, November 16, 1920 – "Helped Edith in house, cut wood and done chores. Pa went for a load of pulp."

There can be no doubt that Sam was as glad as Pa when he could take over his old pulp job. Most likely Sam was receptive to his help with chores also since it was not a hefty job. Sam went after coal for Grace, which was a difficult job of shoveling it into the wagon box. Pa was still prevented and protected from such exertion.

Of course, money had to be raised by selling farm products or animals. On Sunday, November 21, Sam caught chickens and sold 214 pounds live for $32.48 to Mr. Swain. It helped pay the $63.55 due at Second National Bank in Elmira. Sam possibly stopped in the Heights to invite Willa and her family for Thursday. Feed and groceries were attended to on the way back.

A hog was butchered and hung up a couple of days before Thanksgiving.

Sam's own words...
Wednesday, November 24, 1920 – "Drew load of pulp. I met Erie train in evening. Lynn, Iva, and Sadie came."
Thursday, November 25, 1920 – "Drew out boat of manure. Willa and Edward ate dinner with us."

They were all as thankful for family members as for the food they had grown and raised. David had his Billo for a part of the afternoon. It is easy to imagine that she good-naturedly vied with him to pull on a chicken breast wishbone for the longest half. She may have let him win. Willa had to care for her eight-month-old baby, Louise (Lee).

Work was picked right up again on Friday with manure always a factor in the lineup. Sam cut up part of the pork. Fifty-three pounds went to Grace. Sam took De Kohl cow for service.

Sadie and her husband, Bob Madison, came for a visit.

Sam's own words...
Friday, December 3, 1920 – "Drew wood, did housework. Edith had her teeth pulled."

No complications developed for Edith. Sam was back to his outside work. He banked up the house against the cold and wind. Several odd jobs took his attention.

In the next two weeks, he loaded and sold 3.5 tons of straw at $15 per ton. He raised $ 52.52, knowing he had a place for it.

Pa was sick Friday, December 14. Sam was no doubt relieved when he was quite a bit better by the end of the next day. He went and paid the school tax of $27.84. On Saturday, he loaded a ton of hay for $25 and delivered it to Fred N. Peck on the much-colder day. He looked for snow to fall soon.

It is sure that Lac helped where he could but was not full steam yet. Would he ever be? They butchered a sow for themselves and a smaller pig for Grace. It was all processed, and hers was delivered December 22.

Lac went to Galeton on December 23 where Sophia had remained.

In his diary Sam mentioned nary a word about Christmas, a tree, or any gifts this year, maybe an oversight. It did not snow until the evening of December 26. Sam ended December with pump repair, skidded wood, and a stink boat hauled.

~**~

1921

January 1, 1921, dawned clear, cold, and calm. No circumstance loomed as large as to be untenable. The farm chores and manure were so ordinary an operation that they were predictable, and like old friends, comfortable.

Edith had not attained comfort yet. She required yet another tooth pulled on Monday, January 3.

Sam cut up pork in a cold back room for three days out of the week when he got a chance after farm chores. The cuts were finished, and he rubbed salt into the longest pieces.

Apple pulp was still available, and Sam went after seven loads in two weeks' time. The manure boat sailed in competition with and no doubt caused by pulp consumption.

During that second week of January, on the 11th, Sam butchered the 348-pound white heifer. He took cuts of it to D. H. Schabacker for $1 per pound, net $42.50. It was prime meat, tender because it was a young animal.

With less farm assistance, Sam cut a few corners for ledger records that were left sparse or non-existent to start 1921. He resorted to sporadic entry in a small lined tablet.

On Thursday, January 13, Sam paid dog tax of $4.25 to the clerk, E.

A. Burgess as listed on his tablet. Sam never mentioned a dog in his diary. Could it have been a Border Collie or a Hound or a mix of the two? A lesser mutt would have been suitable for a farm dog. The price of the license could have suggested two dogs, but he wrote in the singular, "dog license."

Sam's own words...
Sunday, January 16, 1921 – "Edith went up to Mrs. La Forge's."

Sam watched the children so that Edith could visit her friend for feminine company. It was good to get away from cares of the day and to make plans to have an evening out.

The rest of Sam's week was steady work. On Wednesday, he paid $16.10 school tax to Mrs. Ira Wilcox. Thursday, he went to visit with Mr. La Forge. From there he went after coal for Grace. He delivered it to her Friday.

Sam's own words...
Saturday, January 22, 1921 – "Went to show in evening."

Mrs. La Forge may have babysat while Sam and Edith went by car to Elmira's Regent Theater on East Water Street. Hal Roach of Elmira made famous his "Lonesome Luke" comedies there. In 1919, Roach had formed Hal Roach Studios in Culver City, California. It would not be a surprise if Grace and Roy went, too, since the title of the movie was similar to book subjects she had read. It was exciting for people to see a film made famous by a local young man.

In the last week of January, Sam threshed beans, buckwheat, and rye. It never ruled out a trip for pulp, the spread of manure, and skidded wood. On a trip for feed and groceries, Sam borrowed a churn from Mr. Treat, a wooden one of large capacity, most likely. He might have had it in mind to make a lot of butter to sell to local stores since they had trouble selling their milk for a high enough price. Sam was in pursuit of another buyer. He had an outlet for 490 pounds of beans at an approximate $14 that he took to the depot. The spoiled top layer of ensilage in the silo was broken to uncover the preserved corn underneath. The moldy silage was spread out along with manure on a field.

On Wednesday, Lac went to a funeral in Galeton and returned Thursday.

Sam's own words...
Saturday, February 5, 1921 – "Went to Elmira to try and sell milk. Warm."

He found no new buyer for the milk. That called for more butter to be made from cream. Sour milk was cooked into cottage cheese. Stores may have taken limited amounts of that to sell, also. It was a good thing the Crippens liked buttermilk to drink.

The warm weather trend stayed with them.

Sam cleaned buckwheat, drew straw for horses, and went after feed and groceries. After morning chores on Wednesday, February 9, Sam went to Elmira again to see about selling milk. He found no new handler and continued begrudgingly to send it to A. Voight.

Sam's own words...
Thursday, February 10, 1921 – "Drew out two loads manure. Dewey came. Sold Brown Swiss heifer, $42."
Friday, February 11, 1921 – "Done chores, took 10 bushels of wheat to mill at $1.70 bushel ($17). One foot of snow."

Sam hadn't had the pleasure of seeing Dewey for a while, not since Pa's fall from the silo. The two of them were capable of silly grins just to lay eyes on each other.

One foot of snow did not stop Sam's trip to Horseheads on Saturday. Neither did it deter a visit from Frank and Mary out of Pennsylvania. He enjoyed them all for a while but work loomed.

Stormy weather didn't excuse the need to clean stables and scatter waste every day. Sam took a necessary trip to Horseheads on Tuesday with a side trip to deliver a mattress to Grace's, most likely for Dewey's use.

It had turned quite cold, typical of late February. The snow helped Sam to skid wood easier as logs slid along the ground.

Sam's own words...

Friday, February 23, 1921 – "...cut wood, went to Montour Falls and paid $25 and interest on $300 note."

Wednesday, February 24, 1921 – "Went to Elmira, paid Second National Bank $25 and $2.25 interest on $150 note. Brought heifer from Wilcoxes, drew manure."

With wood chopped and bills paid, Sam was in good shape. Mr. Charles took a heifer for $65. Cold wind continued as regular as manure distribution. Sam tried to find a male hog from neighbors farms to hire for sire. No luck. They all preferred that he bring his sows to their pig pen. It meant more work for Sam, none for them, same fee.

Pa went to a sale.

Sam went after feed and did odd jobs to end February. March marched on with disagreeable weather.

The Elmira Star-Gazette carried news that Warren G. Harding was inaugurated as the 29th president of the United States.

Sam put up a bushel of potatoes for La Forge. He cleaned cellar, hauled pulp, and manure boated. It was no highlight, just his daily due. Visits with Campbell and Thomas were enjoyed. Sam took coal to Grace. He went to Elmira on Friday, March 11, to again see about selling milk. Perhaps his stop at the Farm Bureau was more than paying dues. He may have inquired about names of more milk vendors to try.

The everyday chores, pulp runs, and manure haul continued. On March 14, Sam loaded and moved Westlake's goods to Millport and earned $4. On March 17, he loaded and sold hay to Mr. C. A. Gilkey. As March advanced, spuds were sorted, spoiled ensilage drawn out, and wood skidded. He'd done them all before and would do them again. Obligation to sell milk to A. Voight without 100% satisfaction continued since they must sell it.

Pa went to Galeton on Tuesday, March 22. Uncle George returned the next day.

Sam paid his life insurance, $8.89, to agent A. D. Kipp with 10¢ postage.

In spite of cold wind and storms in the last three days of March, Sam plowed the garden. He delivered coal to Grace and took two loads of goods to

Horseheads for her. April 2 brought a Montour Falls Bank note of $39 due. Sam paid the interest on it.

Sam's own words...
Sunday, April 3, 1921 – "House caught fire."

Sam did not elaborate on the circumstances or area put he swiftly put the fire out.. A spark could have set the banked up straw ablaze near the chimney. He went to see Joseph C. Creighton in Elmira, most likely to apply for an insurance claim on the damage.

Meanwhile, he had plenty to do. The yard was cleaned up, brush drawn away, and coal taken to Grace. He shod a horse, plowed, and brought out manure. His black heifer freshened.

Sam's own words...
Thursday, April 7, 1921 – "Plowed, showed farm to Mr. Frank Folts. Went to spiritual meeting. Got word Uncle Clint very low."
Friday, April 8, 1921 – " Went to Horseheads to phone to Sunderlinville to Dr. Sharp."
Saturday, April 9, 1921 – "Done chores, cut and skidded wood, repaired house. Uncle George went to Uncle Clints."

Pa came back from Pennsylvania the evening of April 10. No doubt he confirmed for Ma and Sam about Uncle Clint. Sam's call for information from the doctor had been the catalyst to send Uncle George to be at his brother's side.

On Monday, Sam went after a separator to divide cream from milk. He took the sewing machine to Horseheads on Tuesday, likely for adjustments and maybe repair. Sam may have left it while other errands were done and then picked it up on the way back. It was the same day he butchered a "reacting" heifer, his term for it. He could as easily have called the young cow a bad actor. In the evening of April 12, he took three chickens to Roy for which he may have gotten $3 plus. Wednesday he went to town and sold beef. He plowed for the next three days.

Sam's own words...
Sunday, April 17, 1921 – "Cold. Old Goonie kicked John over right eye. Drew out manure."
Monday, April 18, 1921 – "Plowed, went to town after feed and took John to Doctor, Stormy."

Five-year-old John was jolted, and his forehead may have developed a worrisome knot and bruise overnight. Sam kept up with his work, but he and Edith both felt better to have Dr. Bowman see John. No other action was needed and no lasting effect lingered.

Sam plowed Thursday. Before evening chores, he took sows up to Ralph Davis' farm. It might be that all of the boar owners made a pact to keep sires on the home farms. They all required the sow owners to do 100% of the work to transport females to and fro. They made out okay without lifting a finger.

Regardless of intermittent rain, Sam plowed for three days. Otherwise, he did chores, shod a horse, and skidded wood. It took strength to do the work of a farmer.

Sam's own words...
Sunday, April 24, 1921 – "Willa and Edward came out. Mr. La Forge paid us a visit."

Sunday's friendly visits were a boon to all. Little Louise (Lee) was two years old and Willa no doubt smiled with pride as she showed her off again to her family. Willa's siblings, David (7), Betty (6), John (5), and Steele (3), were young aunts and uncles to Louise. They could join hands and dance in a circle around their little prodigy. The importance of their status over little niece Louise was not lost on them. Their delight in her was evident and reflected in the clap of her chubby baby hands. Might they have taught her the Pat-a-cake ritual as a toddler?

> Pat- a-cake, pat-a-cake,
> A baker's man.
> Roll it up and throw it up
> And fry it in a pan.

Lime, grass seed, roofing, and groceries were brought back from Horseheads on Monday. Sam harrowed on both Tuesday and Wednesday. He returned a sow back to its home farm Wednesday. On Thursday, he cleaned grain and drilled in barley and alfalfa. On Friday he went after seed oats, dry goods, and machine oil, etc. In the afternoon, he drilled peas, barley, and oats while managing to plant potatoes and pull the slop boat three days of the week.

Sam's own words...
Wednesday, May 4, 1921 – "Went to Elmira and paid taxes, plowed and harrowed, cold and cloudy."
Friday, May 6, 1921 – "Plowed cow lot by barn, cleaned cow stable, helped Pa on roof. Fair."
Sunday, May 8, 1921 – "Had motorcycle contest on pasture hill."

The property taxes of $54.20 were paid to the Chemung County Treasurer. Sam may have supposed that Pa would be extra careful not to fall off the roof.

There was no disclosure of the amount of rent charged for the hill field for one day. The roars from the gunned motors reverberated on the ideal uphill course as the riders vied for the win at the top. It was sure to have been anything but a dull day on the Crippen farm.

The calm contrast came with two weeks of plow, harrow, and drill. Alfalfa, peas, oats, and sweet corn were planted. Manure piled up as only four loads were sailed in the two-week span. Sam helped Pa build fence.

Billy Thomas came for a Sunday visit.

Sam sold one ton of hay to E. Sopher for $20.

A quick grocery trip was an opportunity to pay $6.70 for the month on fire insurance. Sam couldn't pay the price for the whole year.

The news was noted on May 19 as it slipped past. The Emergency Quota Act was passed by the United States Congress to establish national quotas on immigration. It tried to answer the high unemployment that followed World War I. How many jobs could they hope to save for American citizens?

Sam's own words...
Saturday, May 21, 1921 – "Went after Mr. Beasley's manure spreader, drew out two loads to backfield, done chores. Pa went to Galeton."

In the four days that Sam had the borrowed or rented the spreader, he distributed three loads of waste per day to the back fields and what he called the flats. When Pa returned Monday afternoon he would have noticed the clean stables at chore time. It was back to the old boat, their beleaguered method of waste scatter.

Sam renewed the note of $125 at Second National Bank for another three months. A few days advanced him to the $146.25 with $22.50 interest on the principle balance at the Federal Land Bank.

Manure was pulled and spread day by day just to keep even. Saturday required four loads labored over in the rain. Cows and horses are prolific poopers. Sunday coasted, but five boats floated on Monday, Memorial Day. Sam plowed to end the month and start the next. He harrowed the same fields and planted more corn and potatoes.

He made note on his tablet that he had been shorted $1.35 by Voight for milk. He could have steamed and probably boiled over with his release: "Thunder and lightning and seven hands around!"

Sam's own words...
Saturday, June 4, 1921 – "Plowed on flat in a.m. Dewey harrowed on flat in p.m. Pa went to Galeton. Uncle Clint Dimon had a stroke."
Sunday, June 5, 1921 – "Done chores. Took bed, etc., down to Willa in the Heights."

Pa's brother-in-law, Clint, was his foremost concern. He would lend support to the family members and see his condition for himself and Sophia. Dewey filled in labor that Pa had been set to do.

The bed for Willa most likely was a child's bed for Lee, who may have outgrown her crib. Sam's etcetera may have alluded to twin-size bed sheets.

When Sam was not on barn duty or field work, he mowed the lawn, went for groceries, and mended a fence.

There was good reason that Dewey remained present with the family in Horseheads. When Pa returned, they all talked over details of a deal that had been brewing. It took time and discussions to satisfy each player.

Sam's own words...
Sunday, June 12, 1921 – "We are to get $1,000, and they are to assume our share of farm debts."
Monday, June 13, 1921 – "Went to Elmira and legally turned our share of interest in the farm over to Roy, Grace, and Dewey."

Sam and Lac divided their profit, for that was the way it went with all debts turned over. The lumber business in Galeton had finished. Pa and Ma would live at the farm with the new owners. Lac would draw a few   wages now and then for valuable work and expertise. He would not be marginalized.

The deal would not have been attractive to nary a buyer nor relative if not for the Federal Land Bank, which lowered previous large payments and saved many a farm in the troubled times.

Sam began a hunt for a farm for his sole ownership. The real estate man, Mr. Bowan, started him out to look at a property in Elmira. Sam was not impressed.

Saturday, June 18, was a happy day for the Crippen children when Sam bought them all new shoes. He paid $5.61.

His farm quest quadrupled on weekdays as Sam viewed more than a dozen properties located in Elmira, Horseheads, Pine Valley, Alpine, and Millport. He had no desire to leave the vicinity of his family, his business contacts, or his farm friends.

He continued chores and prepared for hay season. He attached a rope and hook on a pulley at the top of the barn to hoist hay high to the loft opening.

The Slater farm in Millport remained in Sam's mind, and he went for a second look. The house needed closer scrutiny to figure on its viability for the family. It required too much makeover. No deal.

Pa went to the post-mortem Oscar Birch farm sale on Saturday, June 25.

Sam repaired fence and went to Elmira to see A. Voight to talk about the milk price that was too low. The last two days of June he dropped spuds and phosphate, cultivated corn, and covered potatoes. He started Grace's transfer to the farm. He loaded the goods and moved them with his wagon and team.

July 1 he made hay, buried a calf, and sailed stink boat.
Sam and Pa wanted to dicker a deal and continue work together. They talked about it off and on, and it had a bearing on what type of land Sam looked for.

July moved ahead while Sam heaved hay, cultivated corn, and fixed fence. An occasional shower sufficed.

July 4 news was welcome to anyone with any sense, Sam supposed. United States President Warren Harding had signed a joint congressional resolution that declared an official end to America's state of war with Germany, Austria, and Hungary.

Sam's own words...
Monday, July 11, 1921 – "Cultivated corn. Went to Johnson Hollow and bought Leon Forrest farm. Paid $650 down."

This deal started a new chapter for Sam with a few new contacts as a result. On a trip into town, he stopped to see A. Voight again on the milk situation. He came away dissatisfied with no positive change. Sam had resolved that he would make a new decision and leave the milk situation in good stead for Dewey and Roy. Pa would notice, too, even though he was not an owner.

He made hay, cut wheat, and shocked grain. Chores and manure never let up and neither did Sam.

Sam's own words...
Sunday, July 17, 1921 – "Went up to our farm: Grace, Willa, Edward, and children went along, and we had a time."
Monday, July 18, 1921 – "Commenced sending milk to D. H. Main."

The three families enjoyed their adventure to acquaint themselves with the soon-to-be new location of Sam, Edith, and the children. Big hearts and camaraderie abounded.

Sam had great satisfaction in his switch to the new milk vendor to leave the best price in place for Dewey and Roy. It was a fraction, only half a cent per quart more, but a raise nonetheless. He would also leave the work in current status as he cut weeds full of burdocks, drew in hay and wheat, and harvested barley and rye.

The Western State Life Insurance Company for Edith's policy helped them out with a loan of $114. They kept the payments current and would try to pay it back. Otherwise, the payout would be worth less at the end.

July 18 held more promising news from the field of science. The entire Crippen family must have taken notice. The first Bacillus Calmette–Guérin (BCG) vaccination against tuberculosis was given. Sam thought of his dear brother, Ralph, and Edith thought of her beloved sister, Lydia.

Would any of the Crippens have to fear the dread disease again? They did not yet suspect what was ahead.

In Great Britain, however, there continued to be considerable skepticism, and the statistics of Calmette and Guerin, who discovered the vaccine were sharply criticized later in 1928 by a Professor M. Greenwood. Moreover, in the United States, Petroff and his colleagues at Trudeau Sanatorium reported in 1929 that in a specimen of BCG supplied by Calmette they had isolated virulent tubercle bacilli, casting grave doubt on Calmette's assertion that BCG was a "virus fix." Despite these disturbing reports, Calmette and Guerin remained confident that BCG was safe, until "the Lübeck disaster" happened.

In 1930, the tragic failure in Lübeck shattered confidence in BCG. In this northern German city, a scheme to vaccinate newborn babies was undertaken by Professor Deycke, director of the Lübeck General Hospital, and Dr. Alstädt, chief medical officer of the Lübeck Health Department.

BCG was supplied from the Pasteur Institute, Paris, but prepared for administration in the tuberculosis laboratory in Lübeck and the oral route was used. After four to six weeks, a large number of the infants developed the disease. Of 250 vaccinated, there were 73 deaths in the first year, and another 135 were infected but recovered. The German they attributed to negligent contamination of the vaccine by virulent tubercle bacilli in the Lübeck laboratories. Two of the doctors concerned received sentences of imprisonment.

By the late 1940s, several studies had appeared providing evidence for the utility of BCG in protection against tuberculosis. In the 1950s, major trials were set up by the Public Health Service in the United States. Although the efficacy of the BCG vaccine continues to be controversial, live attenuated BCG is still the only vaccine in use for the prevention of TB in humans. It is effective against the severe forms of TB, and its use prevents a large number of deaths that would otherwise be caused by TB every year.

But it was still 1921, and none of that was known yet.

On Sunday, July 24, Sam and his family went to Willa's. David had become old enough to pronounce her name well, but he may have preferred to call her Billo. No doubt the affection between big sister and little brother was intact. Sam went to the Heights again Monday, this time to see D. H. Main, the new milk buyer. Most likely he let Mr. Main know that the milk would continue but under his brother, Dewey. A check for the milk should no longer be made out to Sam.

News reached the Crippens from the front page of the newspaper on July 27. DISCOVERY of INSULIN it proclaimed. Researcher Frederick Banting at the University of Toronto announced the discovered hormone, insulin. It was touted to be the probable answer in the treatment of diabetes, about which little was known. The Crippens did not know how it would eventually help humanity. It hardly applied to them, did it?

Sam finished making hay on July 28.

Sam's own words...
Friday, July 29, 1921 – "Went to our farm and cleaned out house."
Sunday, July 31, 1921 – "Went to our farm, cleaned out pantry."
Tuesday, August 2, 1921 – "Edith sick. Rainy, done housework."

Sam had split up wood and taken it to the new place for a good start. No food could be cooked without wood to burn in the kitchen range. He also went to Montour Falls to pay a $39 note. While out that way, he looked at several horses. In the course of the next three days, he did house-work, packed dishes, and washed clothes. He had a lot of experience with every task.

On Friday, Dewey took a load of goods to Sam's farm for him. Sam drew in oats and alfalfa on Saturday. He was back to housework. Sam packed more of the household articles and the children's things. Edith was still sick on Sunday, and by Monday, so was Sam. He could not let that stop him from work that must be done. Tuesday he built chicken coops on the new farm. On Wednesday, he and Dewey moved more of their goods up to the new abode. It was August 10. Sam and his family stayed at the farm from that evening on. Thursday he brought up his cow and calf. The cook stove was put up on the rainy night. He concentrated Friday and Saturday for installation of a water reservoir on the stove, built a pig pen, and cleaned the barn. He was glad of the work done for a good impression when Mr. Miller and his son came over. He cleaned the existing chicken coop on Sunday. Roy and Pa came for a visit later that afternoon.

Sam cut weeds and did many odd jobs Monday. He went after his hogs and a portion of his chickens and finally made it to bed by 11:30 p.m. The next day Dewey brought out more chickens and the remainder of their goods. Sam and Edith were both sick for a couple of days.

On Friday, Sam went to Horseheads for a crosscut saw, which cost $2.75. Groceries included 20¢ worth of tobacco. He bought $7.18 worth of screen to bug proof screens for windows and doors. He repaired a rocking chair. Monday he had more chickens to bring from his old farm. Otherwise, he cut wood and did odd jobs. Tuesday he worked all forenoon on a harness and went after feed and groceries in the afternoon.

He had lumber to stack and dry goods to pick up in Elmira. While there, he got a haircut for 75¢. There were weeds and briars to cut. He carried beds upstairs and put them together.

By Friday, August 26, when Grace and her daughter, Ruth, came up, Sam and Edith were far from well. Edith was sick Saturday. Sam did housework, put tin over rat holes, and put up five window shades he had bought. He hung four curtains.

Sam's own words...
Sunday, August 28, 1921 – "Father came out, and we went up to Millport to see Mr. Rhinehart about skidding."
Monday, August 29, 1921 – "Went to Horseheads after log chain and singletree. Sold four and one-half dozen eggs at 37¢ ($1.66)."
Tuesday, August 30, 1921 – "Put hooks on heavy harness and brought two loads of wood from hill. Warm."

The timber had been the attraction to buy the hill farm. Now Sam would start to sell trees under contract. They broke away from lumberjack work on Wednesday. Sam went to Horseheads to salesmen's training association. He spent $3 on groceries. Afterward, Sam stopped down home, concerned that Grace was quite sick and Edith was still unwell. He skidded wood Thursday and Friday.

On Saturday he went down to see Father to talk over lumber progress. Was he worried about Pa? The outward sign of it was to call him Father in his diary.

Later Willa and Edward came for a stay. Willa helped Sam clean house in the afternoon. She saw that her mother was not well.

On Monday Sam brought more wood down off the hill. Grace was better and came out with Lynn's folks and Dewey. Willa and Edward went home.

School started September 6. Sam walked a ways with David and Betty to school. He put up a mailbox and skidded wood. Later, he took the cow to be bred to Mr. Pease's bull. On Wednesday more lumber was felled and pulled off the hill. Mr. Smith came to have a look at the place. Sam finished the day to mend fences.

He made 21 fence posts and took them to Father at 10¢ each. Friday he cut down dead chestnut trees and skidded them downhill. He made a few posts and repaired the screen door. Saturday, he made 26 posts and took them to Father. Uncle George came back up home with Sam.

Monday was washday and Sam assisted all morning. He got Mr.

Miller to cut buckwheat and alfalfa. It left Sam free to cut and skid timber all week long. Uncle George helped on Friday, but it was a job for a young-er man like 38-year-old Sam. The wood was dragged down the hill and would be split into posts for Father. But not on Sunday. Mr. Whitney paid Sam a visit.

Posts were made and delivered to Father on Monday. Sam stayed to cut corn for 2.5 hours. Dewey was not ready with a cleaned out silo yet, so Sam helped Mr. Rawley fill silo. Rain on Wednesday did not keep Sam from cutting corn on his old farm. They paid him $3 per day, and he was well worth it.

Sam's own words...
Thursday, September 22, 1921 – "Helped Father fill silo."

Neither Sam nor Dewey wanted Father to climb the silo. They'd never been sure of the reason for the fall. Had Pa failed to run the blower to disperse gas before he went up and looked in? Could he have been dizzy as a result when he got a whiff in his face? Father did not know much after he had been knocked senseless. They had not been feeding cows from the silo at that time. Corn was fed straight from the fields yet. The brothers decid- ed that Father may have gone up to run the bucket around at the end of the funnel to distribute the top layer of silage flat instead of leaving it in a cone pile that was pointed up in the middle. Father had never been sure afterward of just how he had done himself in. What Lac was sure of now was this one thing: he had no desire to climb the silo. If he tried it, his boys would not allow it. They need not fret.

Sam paid carfare of $5.55 to go after groceries and tobacco.

He repaired the roof on his house, did odd jobs and gathered chestnuts. Mr. Miller worked a few days with him to finish harvest of his buckwheat and alfalfa. He was glad to be done with jobs that required horses. Old Madge was lame.

He continued to cut posts from all the lumber he had piled up. On the weekend, he and the children gathered 30 quarts of chestnuts.

Sam went to Horseheads on Monday for groceries and to sell chestnuts. More of them were sold Tuesday in Elmira. A bushel made a gain of $8 or $9, which was about 30 quarts. He neglected to record an exact price in his diary. His lack of precise records at the time is most likely because he was not in a partnership that required ledgers now. The freedom may have felt good for the time being, but his old habit would return.

Wednesday, Sam spent $1.63 for mineral oil and milk of magnesia.

Thursday he cut down more poles to skid down the hill. Old Madge had rested and recovered. He went to Horseheads to see Uncle Ed Dimon. His uncle repaid the visit on Friday.

An envelope postmarked October 4 arrived for Sam. It was from Leon Forrest, from whom he had bought the farm. He found a friendly letter Inside but one that also had a request.

~**~

Elmira Heights, NY
October 3, 1921

Mr. Samuel Crippen

Dear Sir,

As I haven't heard anything from you, I thought I would drop you a few lines.

I suppose by this time you are busy up in Johnson Hollow. Hope you are all well and doing fine. I suppose you are gathering chestnuts by this time.

Did you get many huckleberries? And how did Miller's crop turn out? Will you have any potatoes to sell? Have you got any apples? They are rather expensive this fall. I suppose you had some tomatoes. I hope you did. We had lots of them.

Have you got any wood saved and could you get down a big load right away? If you haven't any saved could you bring me a load of pole wood? Will you please write right back by return mail and let me know and tell me what the price is?

There was a lot of places I could get it, but I would rather patronize you. I am all out of wood entirely and have got to have some right away.

I hope Mrs. Crippen is well and also the children...
Be sure and let me know about the wood right away.
Yours in haste.

Leon A. Forrest
262 W. 8th Street
Elmira Hts, NY

~**~

Did Mr. Forrest regret selling the property? Did he still feel entitled to the fruit of the land? Had he sold it because he could not meet his payments? Well, no matter.

The man was in need. Sam could extend credit as long as he secured a signed contract. Everyone Sam knew or became acquainted with faced the same hard times. To remain benevolent was Sam's nature, but to take care of business was to provide for his family. Sam would have to see what he could do, and he'd answer all the other questions when he took wood to Mr. Forrest.

The Millers dug 36 bushels of potatoes for Sam. He may have paid them for their part in spuds? Saturday, Mr. Knickerbocker came out to look at the place. Sam picked more chestnuts in the afternoon and sold them to stores on two more trips to town for groceries and other items. They sold four quarts for a dollar. When he sold to an individual, he charged 30¢ a quart. Grace and Uncle George came and cleaned up the last of them. She would have known how to slit an X in each one and fire-roast them or put them in an oven for 15 minutes. Sam got 50¢ or 55¢ a dozen for his eggs.

Sam's own words...
Wednesday, October 12, 1921 – "Went down home in p.m. Cold and windy. First frost."

He cut more poles and took Edith over to Midway for groceries and "etcetera."

Sam dug a row of potatoes. Frank, Mary, and Mother came out. He

287

had departed from calling his parents Ma and Pa to Mother and Father.

A weak link can cause a problem. Sam mended a wagon thill. It would not do to have the long shaft snap while in use where it slipped through the harness on a horse pulling a wagon. He worked over posts the rest of the week.

Sam and Edith continued the much enjoyed habit of reading together. He'd had literature since the salesman training he completed a month ago. The two of them studied and discussed it.

Sam's own words...
Monday, October 17, 1921 –"...Went to Horseheads after feed, sent agreement to Shores-Mueller Co."

It had taken awhile to prepare the contract because Sam had to get signatures of three co-signers. They were Lac Crippen - farmer, LeRoy H. Whiting – mechanic, and Carl D. Crippen – farmer, all from Horseheads. They were attesting that "The salesman was honest, reliable, and industrious." Not one of them declined to sign for Sam.

Sam would be able to buy at wholesale from Shores-Mueller Company and sell retail. A weekly report and remittance would accompany each order. He was eager to order his samples to show to potential customers and make sales.

Now, he waited to be accepted.

18 – Shores Line and Timber
Willa Girl, 1921, 1922

Sam would not be idle while he waited. Work was his preferred mode of wait. He cut and skidded poles. Wood whittled down became posts that he sold for 10¢ each. The wood lot on the hill was his money maker on the property. On October 21, he went to Elmira and to the Heights where he paid bank clerk Frank B. Eaton $150 plus interest on the mortgage.

Sam had helped Edith wash, bought groceries, and tugged timber. He went to Montour Falls with Father on Monday. The attention that each paid to the other provided equal enjoyment of good company and conversation between them. Sam would have mentioned that his Shores-Mueller contract had been accepted after a nine-day wait. On Tuesday, October 25, he sent the company an order for the samples he needed.

Another day he went down home for 2.5 bushels of seed rye at $3.38 and 100 pounds of wheat for his chickens at a $2 expense. Wednesday was spent harrowing the rye on former potato ground. He cut wood, caught chickens, and bought groceries.

Sunday involved no extra work but to milk the cow and feed horses. Grace and Mother came out. Sam smiled and talked with them as much as Edith and the children did.

On Monday, the last day of October, Sam went to see W. H. Dykens to sell chickens. On the rainy day of November 1, he threshed buckwheat inside the dry barn.

Sam's own words...
Wednesday, November 2, 1921 – "Marketed 11 roosters, 51 lbs. at 22¢ per lb., net $11.22. Cold and rainy."

The rain fell four days in a row. Sam cut wood each day in addition to doing several odd jobs. He took grist to Pine Valley and went up to Mr. Straits where he filled a bed tick with straw. Sam had a sore back due to his long-lived neuralgia. He went to see Mr. Jimmer about wood with more of it to sell. He worked on building a stone boat and finished it on Friday. It snowed on Saturday amidst cold wind.

He went to Elmira Sunday and saw Mr. Forrest about letting the man cut wood. On Monday he saw William La Baron for the same reason. He signed a contract with both men to sell them timber on which they would furnish the labor to cut and haul away. In the back of his mind, he remembered sound reason to do business with a contract, not a handshake. A gentleman's agreement would not suffice under the law. Not all men were gentlemen.

He cut wood on Tuesday, and went to vote.

Sam had begun to wonder about his samples order from a couple of weeks back. He wrote an inquiry letter to Shores-Mueller Company. When would the expected goods arrive? With the letter written, he banked up the house to keep the wind out and heat in. It was stormy all day.

Thursday, November 10, Sam traveled down home for a visit and went on after groceries in spite of the continued storm. The next day he cut and skidded wood. Mr. La Baron did also for eight hours. Disagreeable weather held off until evening. On Saturday he went to Millport after groceries. When he returned, he cut up wood into useable chunks.

Sam was pleased on Sunday when Father came out and ate dinner with them.

Manure on Monday amounted to fertilizer when he spread it around orchard trees. He finished that day and three more to cut, skid, and chop wood.

Sam's own words...
Thursday, November 17, 1921 – "Helped Mr. Strait butcher. Went down to Campbells to borrow kettle and barrel. Cut wood."
Friday, November 18, 1921 – "Butchered Hog. Took grist to Pine Valley. Rain p.m."

His plans were laid for the near future, but it was Sunday. Sam cleaned the house and relaxed. Downtime would have some life in it with four children to consider.

David and Betty were in school on Monday. Sam went to Horseheads for ingredients to process pork. Salt for brine and sausage spices were purchased. The barrel was filled with swine flesh and brine by the time he returned the kettle to Campbell's on Wednesday. He'd caught 16 roosters, which he transported to Horseheads and sold for 22¢ a pound. He had fed them well, and the profit satisfied him. They netted him $17.72 for his pocket, a temporary repository.

Sam's own words...
Thursday, November 24, 1921 – "Thanksgiving Day. Made sausage. Father ate dinner with us. Cut stove wood."

Sam may have been as thankful to have his father with him as to have food, family, and a future. He was on the brink of his next phase, if only the Shores products would arrive. Saturday's nasty weather in the form of rain and snow settled in. Sam went to Horseheads for a 75¢ haircut, an expensive necessity. A trim with scissors would extend a haircut just so long in between stints in the barber chair.

On Sunday, November 27, he cut stove wood and trimmed fat. It was kept chilled in an unheated back room, ready to render into lard. The rainy day carried over into Monday. Sam took the children to school and went to the mill to grind grist. Tuesday, he put up another stove and cut enough wood to make do. Wednesday brought on a group effort to buzz his wood. Pa, Dewey, Uncle George, and Grace helped him for almost five hours. His abundant supply was stacked and ready for winter. He would use what he needed and sell the rest by the cord.

Sam's own words...
Thursday, December 1, 1921 – "Went to Millport depot after Shores-Mueller goods and to Pine Valley for feed and groceries."
Friday, December 2, 1921 – "Swept rooms, cleaned out closet to make room for Shores products. Went down home."

He had news to share that his merchandise had arrived. No doubt he would have been pleased to report to his folks and extended family on what he would soon start to sell. They planned on purchases from him. On Saturday, he did chores and helped Edith reduce and preserve lard. He tried to arrange Shores products. It consumed time to inspect items. He learned about each one in such a way as to know what he would say to customers about his offers. The process was not a bad job to have while a cold wind blew outside.

His enterprise of cut wood was dependent on the chill in the air. Dewey bought 4.25 cords at $2.50 a cord ($10.63). Sam delivered 12 cords to a buyer at the same price per cord ($30 total). He sold a couple of stacks to Mr. Jimmer and took one cord to the school house. Wouldn't it be nice if Mr. Forrest paid for his cut timber?

Sam went to Horseheads to buy lumber for a wagon box. The Shores product samples needed to travel with him in a display. His neighbor, Charles Strait, was hired to start on the project. Mr. Strait examined the products to determine how he would build the box. He planned to become a customer, too. Sam, meanwhile, caught chickens and sold $12 worth. He brought Uncle George home with him. Three days later on a Monday, the retail show box was ready. He had a few things to get done before he could start.

Sam took a load of hay to Millport for $20 on December 7. He sold 100 posts for the standard price of 10¢ each to gain $10. He bought mittens for Father and Dewey, perhaps for Christmas gifts. It cost him $1.50. Did he make them wait or did he know that they needed them now?

Sam's own words...
Tuesday, December 13, 1921 – "Done chores. Went to Elmira after Revenue stamps."

The tax sticker may have been applied to some of the products Sam was to sell. Vanilla could have been one of the items since it had a small.

amount of alcohol in it. The Revenue stamps were a tax appropriated by the government to pay federal revenue expenses. Marking goods in some way to indicate that the government had collected its due was another way to help keep both sides honest. Even the postage stamp could be thought of as a form of revenue stamp. Postage stamps show that a letter or package has been paid for. (It was how the government collected taxes in Sam's day.)

When Sam wrote a check to Montour Falls Bank for $41.90, he affixed two stamps to the back of the check. They were 1¢ each. His check of $435 to the Second National Bank of Elmira received 10¢ revenue stuck on the reverse. The small squares were then canceled by use of an ink stamp to stop further use and prove that the required tax had been paid.

Sam could not have known that this would remain the federal tax method into 1967. He and all citizens paid for World War I expenses this way. He could not yet know about World War II costs.

His line of goods included household items and products to help farmers. Some of the elements survived in Sam's trunk, but most are listed in his Shores-Mueller ledger or sales flyers in the envelope with his contract.

Barn Use:

Miracle Mite Eliminator
Louse powder
Fly powder and gun 60¢
Fly Chaser – 1 gal. $1.20
Worm powder 50¢
Heave remedy 50¢
Horse liniment $1
Stable salve 50¢
Machine oil 25¢
10 # axle grease $1.15
Tire patches 70¢

Household:

Spices –½ lb. Cinnamon 30¢,
    ginger, nutmeg, cloves, pepper
Poultry seasoning, sage
Flavoring – vanilla 60¢, maple,

peppermint, lemon,
Baking powder 35¢
Soap, 10¢Wash tablets 30¢
Shampoo 35¢
Dental Cream 25¢
Talcum, Face Powder, Face Cream,
   Face Lotion – each 25¢
Family salve 50¢
Corn remedy 25¢
Kidney remedy tablets $1
Camphor Liniment $1
Anti-Pain Oil 75¢
Aspirin 60¢
Laxative Syrup $1, Lax tabs 50¢
Cough Syrup $1, Cough tabs 50¢
Sarsaparilla $1

Sarsaparilla and root beer are made from the roots of native North American plants. Both originated as similar tasting tonics and were highly prized for their medicinal value.

Sam's own words...
Wednesday, December 14, 1921 – "First day selling Shores-Mueller: $8.40 worth."

Sam's life as a retail salesman on the road had begun well in cold weather.

Saturday he banked up more of the house exterior and did chores and odd jobs. A trip to Millport to sell, also to get feed and groceries, finished the day. On Sunday, he arranged the front room and rearranged his Shores goods for his start on Monday.

Sam's own words...
Wednesday, December 21, 1921 – "Made out order for Shores line. Sent them $8.58. Went to Elmira after Xmas goods."

It was a determination on Sam's part that had him out December 22 to sell shores goods. He also did chores, skidded wood, and banked up the barn.

He went to the school house Friday evening for the children's Christmas program. Edith was not well enough to attend. Saturday stormed into inclement weather. Father made it to their door Christmas Eve to enjoy time with them.

David and Betty had no school on Monday, and he took them down home with him to get chicken feed and buggy thills. On Tuesday and Wednesday, he sold the Shores line.

Blustery and stormy weather clouded the last three days of the year, through Saturday, December 31.

~**~

1922

The start of January was so cold that Sam had to lay off his efforts to sell Shores for a while. He found plenty of other things to do. Sam went to Mr. George's and Mr. Personius's to get paid for his wood. In Millport, he talked to the railroad agent, no doubt to notify him of his expected order and future regular deliveries from Shores-Mueller Company. Contact from them to tell him when his wares arrived could have been arranged. Another check for $5.22 on sold items was sent to the company. His own profit was kept back, no doubt already spent. The company got 60% to his 40%.

Sam performed his chores and then did his best to help Edith every day while she was limited.

Sam's Own words...
Friday, January 6, 1922 – "Pa came out. David went home with him. Went to Millport and paid life insurance of $41.90."
Saturday, January 7, 1922 - "Done housework, chores and went to Millport after Shores shipment."
Sunday, January 8, 1922 – "Edith feeling bad."

David was age 7.5 years and happy to go with Grandpa. Of course, nobody down home would spoil him.

Sam worked on chores, housework, and wood each day while he consistently wrote that Edith was ill. On Wednesday, he went after David and chicken feed for the usual $2. It was a terribly stormy day, and Edith was worse by evening. She seemed better by Thursday for which Sam was grateful as he shoveled snow. He was relieved when she was "some stronger" on Friday as he again did chores, housework and cared for children.

He managed to complete his report for the Shores-Mueller Company.

Father and Mother came on Sunday. They could see that Sam had his hands full with work, four children, and a sick wife. David went home with them. Possibly his Aunt Grace had requested to have him again for she had only girls.

The situation continued. Sam walked to Millport two days in a row to find oysters for Edith. He paid 65¢ for one quart. He had the doctor in for her on Wednesday. Grace and Pa came and took three-year-old Steele home with them. Edith was a bit better when Pa delivered wheat for chicken feed on Thursday. Sam would not take a step off the place right now.

Sam's own words...
Friday, January 20, 1922 – "Shirley came to us about 10:30 o'clock. Edith very weak."

Shirley Paula Crippen was born and named after her father. Their shared middle names were a sign that would hold them each in the center of the other's affection as she was on her way to become Daddy's little girl.

Sam shouldered the brunt of all household and outside responsibilities as Edith convalesced back to better health as if on a slow motion train that was unable to climb the hill. He may well have reminded himself that they had come through worse in Idaho. It was a long time ago, wasn't it? They would get past this. He was sure of it, given time.

Sam met his duties head on day after day. He went to Millport once each week when he needed groceries. His retail sales would not be conducted until Edith regained ability to manage the household again.

Three weeks passed before she was able.

Sam's own words...
Thursday, February 9, 1922 – "Sold Shores goods. Stormy."

Friday was a replica of the day before, and Sam was at last able to branch out his sales route. He intended to catch up on the news and snatched a header from the papers now and then, hungry to know and see beyond his own farm. Had it been a whole month since the first successful treatment of diabetes had been made in Toronto? What kind of a pie needed a patent? An Eskimo pie? Just days ago the first Readers Digest had been published. It sounded interesting for him and Edith, but it was not within his reach now, no more than was a radio. President Harding had installed the first one ever in the White House. Sam had dawdled enough on the printed word. He had to get caught up with his work.

On the weekend he bought his growing boy, David, a pair of shoes for $2.50, and did housework, cut wood, and skidded it home.

Edith had improved. Together, a new anxiety concerned them. They worried aloud about Edward and Willa because his health had deteriorated further. It was a throwback on Edward from his Army days when he had come back ill with tuberculosis. It had gone into remission then. He had been one of the lucky ones. And now?

Sam's own words...
Tuesday, February 14, 1922 – "Done chores and housework, sold Shores goods in p.m. Edward much worse."
Wednesday, February 15, 1922 – "Went to Horseheads after feed and delivered 30# poultry powder to H. O. Rodabaugh."
Thursday, February 16, 1922 – "Cut and skidded wood. Cold and stormy. Wrote letter to Willa."

The letter, no doubt, was written to encourage their dear daughter. If they could have banished the problem from the young couple, they would have. On Sunday, Father and Mother came for a visit in the afternoon.

Sam did chores, housework, and sold Shores every afternoon for five days. He sent the company $5.37 with orders but retained his profit.

Sunday appeared again, and the wash was taken to Mrs. Strait. It would cost him $2. He went after groceries Monday and canvassed, too. It was too cold to do so again for the next three days. Sam caught up on the wood, housework, and prepared three meals on one day. Friday and Saturday saw him on the road again to sell.

It was March already. It had slipped in without warning, right past February.

His days had not swayed from chores, housework, and sales. Sam as glad to load and sell hay to Mr. Brink. He was in need of wood, too.

Sam's own words...
Wednesday, March 8, 1922 – "Went to see Dr. Pettit with Father. Listed farm."

Uncle George went to Horseheads in Lac's stead since Lac was sick. Several people in the neighborhood were ill. Mrs. Kent had died and been buried. Mr. and Mrs. Strait were ill. Sam did the chores for them on Sunday. Girt Straight could not take on Edith's laundry.

The next day Sam was back to his own schedule but worried about Edith, Father, and two-month-old baby Shirley, who had a worrisome cold. He sold his wares every other day regardless of also not feeling well. He wrote three letters but not in his spare time since that did not exist. Most likely the heartfelt missives went to Lenore in Twin Falls, possibly Jack in Oregon, and relatives in Galeton. Lynn, Mary, and Sadie would share news and worries over Father. Had he ever made a full recovery from the silo fall? They would want the latest information firsthand from Sam. It likely included Willa and Edward's situation. He went to Horseheads to send it express.

Sam was sick for a week but managed the barn and house, which required a run for feed and groceries. On Monday he sold Old Madge to J. J. Spargo for $125. He paid an installment of $12.32 for his own life insurance to agent, G. D. Kipp.

Sam's own words...
Sunday, March 26, 1922 – "Cleaned house. Mr. Northrup came out to look at farm."
Monday, March 27, 1922 – "Went to Elmira to look at cars and see Mr. Northrup."

It appeared that Sam had an honest to goodness buyer and he would not dither. He planned on a profit over what he had paid. A car was in his plans as Sam looked at models in Horseheads and Elmira over the course of several days on the way for feed and groceries. He skidded wood down the hill and thought of the attributes and prices of cars he had seen.

Mr. Strait's team was used for one-and-a-half hours on Thursday, March 30. There was soon a pile of poles on hand to work over for posts and firewood. Sam supposed he'd better go and pay his taxes of $19.93. On the way back, he purchased groceries and chicken feed in Millport.

Father came out on Sunday. There was never a time when he wasn't welcome. Edith's youngest brother, Erick, and his family arrived from Idaho. He was 38, the same age as Sam. Hard times brought him east with the hope of better job prospects.

April was busy with wood, a horse purchase, and hen setting. Several fowl had turned broody with the inclination to hatch their own eggs. Sam would be rewarded with a healthy, self-sustaining flock. Some of them would set on eggs out in the yard, which was not the safest place at night if predators came around. Sam would relocate them to his inside nests and let them brood over as many eggs as their bodies could cover and keep warm. No more eggs would be laid by them until their chicks hatched in about three weeks. All he had to do was keep water and feed close. Not all of the hens would turn broody. Sam could still count on eggs to use.

Sam sold Shores goods several afternoons and did housework just as often. On one of his trips to Elmira, he saw Mr. McCorkle to get the final figure he would owe to pay off his mortgage when his farm sale was finished. He sold it for $3,400 on April 26 to Laura and Frank Toby.

Sam had looked at a 60-acre farm near Wellsburg earlier. He went to Elmira on Friday, April 28, and closed on the transaction with McCorkle. He also had the satisfaction to buy his first car, a Model 90 Locomobile with an internal combustion engine.

Mr. Toby hired him to split up posts on his farm. Sam supposed it was easy enough to do for a couple of days since he hadn't moved yet.

The first week of May was mostly spent packing. John and Steele were taken to their grandparents Friday night. On Saturday, Sam concentrated on packing all day. On Sunday, May 7, they were invited to eat with the Straits. Monday they moved all they owned to their land bank farm near Wellsburg. Sam put up a stove right away. He cleaned part of the house before they went to Father and Mother's to stay Tuesday night. Erick and his family had found a place to rent near Wellsburg close to Sam and Edith.

Wednesday was the day Sam designated to go after his auto. He saw Mr. Howland, who took them out to the farm in the car. Mr. Warner came in another vehicle to transport Mr. Howland back to Elmira. Sam had paid $25 down on the car and $6.21 for the license on it. The minimum qualifying age was set at 17. The certification gave its holder 'freedom of the road' with a maximum 20 mph (32 km/h) speed limit on dirt roads, the most common kind of road at the time.

Neither a test on how to drive was required, nor was a driver's license needed. Europe introduced the driver license requirement but not until 1934, with the passing of the Road Traffic Act when many more cars were on the roads.

Sam later wrote checks in various amounts for a total of $146.35 for the car. It was not a new car, or it would have cost $600 to $800 for a 1922 machine.

In the first decade of the 20th century, there were no stop signs, warning signs, traffic lights, traffic cops, driver's education, lane lines, street lights, brake lights, or posted speed limits. The second decade just past for Sam held slight improvements since cars had become popular. Our current method of making a left turn was not known, and drinking-and-driving was not considered a serious crime.

There was little understanding of speed. A driver training bulletin called "Sportsmanlike Driving" explained velocity and centrifugal force and why when drivers took corners at high speed their cars skidded or sometimes "turned turtle" (flipped over). It does not appear that Sam had such a pamphlet. None was found in his trunk with the canceled checks, which show what he paid for the car.

Sam's car would sit there now. He had not driven yet, but he had work to do. He cut weeds and cleaned out the orchard. Saturday, May 13, he cleaned the house inside and out.

When he did drive the car, he drove it to Elmira to the Johnson Garage for $20 in repairs but did not report the nature of the fix in writing. He went home to cut wood, likely by paid carfare. Could he have been disappointed with his first car? Could the car have coasted into a tree or down a slope into a ditch while Sam worked on wood chunks?

On Tuesday, Sam went to Father's, got Dewey, and brought the car back home.

Sam's own words...
Wednesday, May 17, 1922 – "Took Model 90 to trade it toward Model 4."
Thursday, May 18, 1922 – "Went up Johnson Hollow and saw Edward and Willa, learning to drive car."

As Sam and Edith expected, Edward was worse. Tuberculosis was not kind to Edward or his young family. Sam took Dewey home and went back to Wellsburg.

On Friday, Sam bought a gray mare for $85. He took it to Father's overnight where he had his cow. Uncle George helped him take the animals to his new farm on Saturday. He made a fence in the afternoon.

Sam needed to make the effort to sell his Shores line. He went out Tuesday and Wednesday and stayed at Father's two nights. He'd had trouble with the car. His Model 4 was from the Locomobile Motor Company as well.

On Friday, Sam harrowed, marked corn ground, and planted.

He went home with Grace and Dewey Sunday. Shores was sold on Monday, and he went back to his family in the evening.

Sam's own words...
Tuesday, May 30, 1922 – "Edward Walker died at 3 a.m. Planted beets, lettuce, etc."
Wednesday, May 31, 1922 – "Took Edith up to see Willa and came home in p.m. Done housework."
Thursday, June 1, 1922 – "We buried Edward. Edith stayed with Willa Girl all night and I at Father's."

Edward's parents, grandparents to two-year-old Louise (Lee), added information to their understanding about their 23-year-old son's illness and death. They believed he died from "a touch of gas" from the war. Supposedly, part of the training was to send men into gas-filled buildings to test masks and their endurance. It was thought to be a com- mon ailment from war involvement. It was said to mimic TB. The two together were a deadly combination. They passed the information down through the years as family lore.

Edith had related sadly to Sam of Willa's last day with Edward. She had held him towards the end. He requested that she play his favorite song, My Buddy, on his Edison phonograph. Willa stood against a door- way holding Louise on her hip and swayed to the sad refrain as Edward slipped away.

Could life get harder? Compassion for Willa Girl and little Louise (Lee) filled Sam and Edith's thoughts. They did need to go and take their children home.

Erick and his family were still in the area. Erick found small jobs but no steady work. He was not immune to hard times and experienced the worry that the rest of the population did. Relocating had not been easy on him and the family.

Sam had work to do no matter what life handed out. His responsibilities took no holiday. Saturday, June 3, he sprayed the chicken coop and set four hens.

Sam's own words...
Sunday, June 4, 1922 – "Came up to Father's. Carfare 31¢. Father not well."

Sam's Model 4 auto was unreliable. He took it for repairs at a cost of $5. The 36¢ worth of tobacco purchased was surely needed. Sam tried to sell Shores on Tuesday. The car needed $2 in repairs, and gas and oil of $1.21. He was thankful for Shores sales of $1.95. Wednesday's gas and oil were 77¢, and an inner tube was $2.05. Thursday's auto repairs were $3.15, gas and oil 81¢, and haircut 65¢. When would his perseverance cause better luck to appear?

Sam's own words...
Friday, June 9, 1922 – "Father very sick. Took care of him. Thunderstorms."

Saturday, June 10, 1922 – "Sold Shores goods. Took care of Father some and came home in p.m."
Sunday, June 11, 1922 – "Cut wood, cleaned spring out, worked on Shores books, etc. Willa came in p.m."
Monday, June 12, 1922 – "Pa went to heaven at 4 a.m. Paid Shores-Mueller $8.15. Am so lonely."
Tuesday, June 13, 1922 – "Cultivated corn in a.m. Went to Mothers p.m."
Wednesday, June 14, 1922 – "We took Pa's body to Galeton for burial and returned to Horseheads in evening."
Thursday, June 15, 1922 – "Came home in a.m. Sadie, Grace, and Roy came, too. Went back to Horseheads in p.m."
Friday, June 16, 1922 – "Stayed at Mother's all night."

On Saturday, Sam went to Elmira on business and home to his farm and family about noon. He planted corn and tomatoes. The rainy day reflected his gloom with Father gone. Work kept him going, or he kept work going. Rain continued Sunday. It washed over Sam relentlessly as he set out tomato and pepper plants. He cut wood and made fence. All the while he worked he considered how tough life could become for Willa Girl and Mother. They would all feel the effect of the losses.

Sam started out with big ambitions on Monday. He sent Shores-Mueller $4.85 and had a tire repaired. What could stand in the way of retail sales now? Not rain, although it stuck around as he made his stops for sales efforts. Erick was also making an effort to earn enough to keep his family.

Sam's own words...
Friday, June 23, 1922 – "Sold Shores, had trouble with car, had to leave it and goods overnight."
Saturday, June 24, 1922 – "Sold Shores and came home, spent three hours on car."

On Sunday, Sam set out 50 tomato plants, hoed, and planted cucumbers. He cut wood and repaired fence. It was no more a day of rest than Monday when corn was planted and beans cultivated before fence repair resumed. With those accomplishments behind, the Shores report was made out.

Sam caught up on garden work by planting more beans and hoeing on Tuesday. The car created an eyesore as it sat there with a flat tire. He shook his head, patched the rubber, and went to Elmira after groceries.

Sam went to his old Horseheads farm owned by Grace, Roy, and Dewey, to see Mother. Plans were made for her business to be taken care of. He sold his wares through Thursday while he stayed there. On Friday, he drove Mother to see the surrogate attorney, C. A. Phillips. His first chore on Saturday morning was to mend two tires before he went home to Edith in the afternoon. On Sunday, he picked huckleberries and cherries and cut wood. They went to see Mother and the others on the Fourth of July but not without tire trouble.

Wednesday brought a decision when Grace, Dewey, Mother, and Sam saw the lawyer again. Sam and Mother were appointed administrators over Father's affairs. They had had tire woes to get there. He sold Shores on the end of the day, had more tire trouble, and stayed the night at Straits'. Two tires wore out.

Sam's own words...
Wednesday, July 7, 1922 – "Came in with two wheels on rim. Went to Elmira after tires and tubes. Sold few Shores goods."

Sam drove to Montour Falls and signed a $160 note that he'd be obligated to pay in October. He left his Shores goods at Mothers and went home to family and garden work.

Willa-Billie and David went with him Monday to get his goods and go selling. He retailed all week and saw Mr. Collins about his late car payment. On both Friday and Saturday, his enterprise was worked on the Middle Road out of Horseheads. He and David, Willa and little Louise got home 9:30 p.m. Saturday, July 15.

Sunday involved garden work, wood, and a Shores report. His loan materialized on Monday, and he made his car payment in Elmira. He sold the Shores line six days straight.

His garden needed attention again on Sunday and Monday. He cleaned his cellar before he went to Mother's to stay Monday night. He stayed through Wednesday to peddle Shores and went home in the evening. He worked around home on his garden Thursday and went back to Mother's. He had more than a little car trouble. There went his plan to play salesman on Friday. It was necessary to pay carfare to get to Elmira for a tire and tube. He managed to get home by 7 a.m. Saturday morning. Later, he took Willa to Elmira.

At home on Sunday, he hoed in the garden and worked on his car. As Sam labored over it, he may have decided that a horse and buggy were a less troublesome conveyance. He wrestled with the thought that he hadn't even the money to buy gas. On Monday, he went up to Mother's to borrow $1.60 for gas and groceries. It put him in shape to sell Shores in Horseheads and Millport but allowed only Thursday night back home with Edith and the family when groceries were taken home.

On Friday, he saw Fred Hagar about taking the car. He stayed at Mother's to go out from there Saturday to sell retail, then went home to Wellsburg.

Erick had set himself a deadline to make good or relocate, but not back to Idaho. Sam couldn't advise him since they were in the same struggle to earn a livelihood.

Sam's own words...
Monday, August 7, 1922 – "Came to Mother's in a.m. Sold car to Frank Hagar in p.m. Stayed with him all night."
Tuesday, August 8, 1922 – "Taught Mr. Hagar how to start and stop car. Brought horse over to Mother's."
Thursday, August 10, 1922 – "Toby's heartless toward Willa. Went back to Elmira and Horseheads looking for wagon. Stayed at Mother's all night. Willa came home."
Friday, August 11, 1922 – "Bought wagon, came home, repaired it p.m."
Saturday, August 12, 1922 – "Rigged up single harness. Went to Wells-burg after groceries and to get horse shod."

Sam had put an end to the car breakdowns. There'd be no more flat tires for him.

Wood was cut on Sunday by demand of the cook stove. Gertrude and her family arrived from Oregon. They called her Maude like they had when she was a girl at home with her mother, Mary. Edith, no doubt, was ecstatic to see her niece. Sam was glad for her, but he could not let down on work. The women folk would enjoy each other's company and probably not miss him much as the routine of Shores sales continued. Sam stayed at Mother's.

By week's end, he sold in the Doty Hill area. At last a check of $39.58 was sent to Western Life Insurance Company.

On Sunday, wood was cut and the harness mended. Sam sold Shores three days. Plums were ripe. He picked a few bushels and took them to Elmira where they sold at $1.50 a bushel. It supplied the extra grocery money needed to feed relatives and provide his tobacco money.

On August 8, Sam had taken Erick and his family to Wellsburg for departure. They were bound for Cleveland, OH. Fond but sad goodbyes had been exchanged.

It came around to Sunday again and time to cut wood. But first, Sam went to Elmira to see John Howland regarding the Forrest affair. The man ought to pay for wood he cut and for which he owed Sam.

Sam went to sell Shores Tuesday and helped Dewey with chores because Roy was sick. He retailed wares and stayed at Mother's through Saturday. While there, he caught up on the news from the Elmira *Star-Gazette*. Radios were making more than noise. The Hawaiian station, KGU, had begun to broadcast, and President Harding had made his first radio speech. It seemed alarming that Germany had suffered hyperinflation since July and the value of the papiermark against the dollar rose to $1 thousand.

He had worked himself into the middle of September.

Sam's own words...
Saturday, September 16, 1922 – "Went to Toby's but didn't get Willa's goods."

He may have tried to convince the landlord to be reasonable with a young widow for the sake of her child. She had been faced with burial expense and had to pay $128 for Edward's plot in Elmira's Woodlawn Cemetery. Sam went back Tuesday and brought part of her belongings home. He may have had to come up with money, but never mentioned it. Sam stayed the rest of the week at his old farm at Mother's. It was a location from which to go out to peddle wares and help Dewey with chores four days since Roy could not. He bought groceries and went home Saturday.

On Sunday, corn was cut, tomato vines trimmed, and fence repaired.

Sam had gone home Wednesday evening. He had his troubles through the week with sale stock. On Thursday, he made a claim to the Erie Railroad for a lost order of Shores merchandise worth $7.56. The disappointment to customers was unpleasant for him.

Sam was in his most preferred element Saturday evening, which was home in the midst of his family. Corn was cut on Sunday. The work was about to increase, and he'd better enjoy a half day of downtime to finish the Sabbath.

Monday was the beginning of Sam's two weeks of work for Dewey as they made arrangements for an auction at the farm. He could not drop all of his own work. Sam hurried back home Wednesday night, took care of things, and was back to Horseheads to sell Shores. He helped Dewey in the evening and the next three days. Dewey went out two days to distribute sales bills to advertise. Sam harrowed, drilled wheat, and cut hay. On Saturday, he drew in alfalfa, shocked corn, and went home in the evening.

His one day at home was rainy and filled with many odd jobs. On Monday, Sam was back on the farm with Dewey to shock corn.

Sam had his own affairs to attend to on Tuesday. He hired a car to go to Elmira and Montour Falls at a cost of $1.01. Wednesday was a continuance with work for Dewey, which was for Grace and Roy, too. He shocked corn, cut weeds, and cleaned the blacksmith shop.

Columbus Day intervened on Thursday to give them a day off. On Friday, he husked corn, cleaned out the cow barn, and swept the shop. Sam and Dewey did all kinds of different jobs. They were as ready as they were going to be.

Sam's own words...
Saturday, October 14, 1922 – "Had our sale."

It required their attention to sale business. Cows had to be delivered to new owners. Sam went after groceries on Tuesday because he planned to bring Edith out to Mother's midweek. He was sick several days, but busy. They took Sunday to go home and rest. Dewey still needed his help. Sam was paid a top wage of $3 a day to work on crops. He was to bring potato and hay crops to completion so the family could move.

Sam sold Shores products Thursday through Saturday and went home. Sunday was a cold, windy day but corn was cut and the cellar banked with straw. More jobs on Monday secured the place for warmth even if he planned to leave there before the year was over. He'd have to make a start on that, but Shores goods had to be sold, too.

Wednesday, November 1, Sam went to Horseheads and sold merchandise for three days. He had to have the horse shod. While in Horseheads, he called a real estate company to start the process of finding a rental. Wellsburg was 15 miles away, and Sam had determined that the long distance kept him away from both of his families. When he was with one, he wasn't with the other. If Sam had needed a lesson on it, it had taught him that he was better off in Horseheads.

The news had it that 3,000 German marks were now required to buy one American dollar. What was Sam supposed to do with that? Was it affecting life here? Would it? He had enough to worry about without something for which he had no understanding. It was more interesting to learn that some archeologists, Carter and Carnarvon, had been the first people to enter the tomb of Pharaoh Tutankhamun in over three-thousand years. It was just a short piece of information as Saturday started. He paid off one bill at Montour Bank, renewed another, and went home to Edith. On Sunday, he cut wood, cleaned out the barn, and paid Mr. Smith $4.75 to settle up payment for roof work on the barn.

Monday saw Sam back in Horseheads to look for a house. He talked to a widow, Mrs. Gano, about renting a farm. One way or another, he'd get them a Horseheads address again. By Thursday, he was back home to cut wood in a cold wind. Options were talked over with Edith and back he went to sell Shores on Friday. He appreciated his well-established territory with repeat customers. Back on the Wellsburg farm Sunday, he cut wood and tore down a bedraggled grapevine.

He went after Willa and brought her to Wellsburg. He always paid her to help Edith. Dewey came to help him spruce up the farm he was leaving. He was to have the Gano farm in Horseheads. The realty company transacted the rentals of the Gano and Brown farms. Sam signed the contract. He still owned the Comfort Hill Farm but had rented it to La Verne Personius and Peter Brown. They were set to start a joint enterprise to raise fowl. The balance due of $87.65 on the contract down payment was due on February 4, 1923. After the initial amount, the two men would pay $6 per week. It was the same rental Sam would pay to Mrs. Gano. Sam could now rent and reside in Horseheads!

What a relief that it had been a quick, easy deal, almost like the gods were in his corner, and maybe it was true. Sam sold Shores four days straight. On Sunday, he predictably cut wood, took his cow to board at the Comfort's farm, and sorted potatoes. The Comfort hill road had been named after several related families who lived on the stretch.

Sam took 10 bushels of potatoes to Elmira and sold them at $1.50 a bushel. The $15 was needed. He stayed in Horseheads overnight and sold Shores products. Mr. Merrick was contacted to let him know he had hay to sell. Back home on Wednesday, he cut wood, sorted potatoes, and recorded the season's first snow fall.

Sam's own words...
Thursday, November 23, 1922 – "Swept upstairs, fixed up broken windows, packed books, etc."
Friday, November 24, 1922 – "Sorted and packed potatoes, packed Shores goods. Cold."

On a cold, windy Saturday, Sam went to sell five bushels of spuds. Seven dollars and 50 cents allowed him to bring groceries, and then some, home. On Sunday, he packed fruit and took it to the Gano farm. His Shores goods were transported to Grace's and left there where Sam stayed all night. He went home Monday and packed the rest of all they owned. The next day he moved almost all of it to the Gano farm. On Wednesday, he set up a cook stove and went to Elmira to pay $210 on his $435 note at Second National Bank.

Thursday was Thanksgiving Day. He and 8.5-year-old David went after their cow and the rest of their belongings. The horse balked, and they had to leave the items and bring only the milk animal. It was Saturday when they returned for the rest. On Sunday he set up another stove for the cold weather and did all kinds of odd jobs. Sam had to leave off getting settled

Monday long enough to go after coal. He paid $51 on his hardware bill of $96. His missing cow was hunted on Tuesday before he cleaned the barn. Finally he went to Grace's after his product line. On Wednesday he banked the house with straw to keep out cold air. Then he banked the water trough, the chicken coop, and the water barrel on higher ground above the barn. By Friday groceries were needed. He also did chores and other jobs. Shores was sold on Saturday in colder weather.

The next week he traveled four days to sell his list of items. It left him three days to patch up barn windows and go after coal and building paper. Sam finished banking up against winter's onslaught on Thursday when it snowed all day.

Sam's own words...
Sunday, December 17, 1922 – "Busy all day. Don't like to work all day Sunday."

He had a hope of less work for the Sabbath and may have decided it would be a nice try for a New Year's resolution. But that was a couple of weeks away.

The here and now had turned to Monday. Sam checked his Shores records and sent them $19 with the orders. While he was out, he got coal and groceries. Back again, he papered the exterior kitchen walls against the encroaching chill of the wind through cracks.

Tuesday was the day Sam picked to pay his obligations before the first of the year. He paid the balance of $215 on his Vet Moss bill and $225 to Marion Personius. Those outstanding bills were cleared the same as his pockets. But he'd fulfilled his aim to start the new year solvent. Didn't it go that the way a year ended was the way the next one would commence?

The next four days Sam concerned himself with housework, coal and groceries, and dry goods. While he was out on Shores business Thursday, his rig broke down. He made harness and thill repairs.

The annual letter was written to Lenore in Twin Falls. Sam and Edith looked forward to one from her, which was sure to come. On Saturday he went to see Mother and get corn. It was a snowy day as he applied for a job at the brick yard.

Sam's own words...
Sunday, December 24, 1922 – "Done housework and chores. David and I went after Xmas tree. Warm."

After the children had decorated the tree, the floor had to be cleaned up. Sam helped. He did chores Christmas morning, helped with kitchen work, and enjoyed his family. Their chicken dinner no doubt included mashed potatoes and gravy.

Sam spent the last days of the year selling Shores, husking corn, and hauling coal. He delivered coal for Mother and Grace, too.

It was time to catch up on the news. Germany's year-end inflation showed no sign of slowing down. It raged on with 7,000 marks now needed to buy one American dollar. In perspective, Sam was thankful he was in a much better situation than across the waters. On December 31 he helped around the house while it stormed outside.

19 – Hard Labor
Hard Times, 1923, Edith not well

Sam still intended to get a job. He found one at hard labor, which was nothing new to him. He cut wood for Vet Moss several hours every day. On shorter work days, he husked his own corn and cleaned his chicken coop, also repaired it. Anytime he went for coal and groceries; stops were made to sell Shores.

He and Edith were relieved to be back in Horseheads. They had both missed it, but she had also been isolated from friends and family. Sam was likely glad that she was happier again. Sadness hung on with him over the loss of Father. He started the new year lonesome and wrote a few lines taken from a book of poems into the front of his January 1923 diary.

Author: Henry W. Longfellow

There is no death,
What seems so is transition.
This life of mortal breath
Is but the suburb of life Elysian
Whose portal we call death.

Sam was eager to add work to husk corn a few hours a day for E. A. Treat. On alternate days, he continued to cut wood for Vet Moss. Short hours gave him time to get groceries and help in the house.

Sam's own words...
Sunday, January 14, 1923 – "Went up to Grace's, husked corn for horse, snowed all day, one and a half foot."

On January 24, Sam drew Dewey's corn into his barn for him and bought a couple of shocks of it for his own animals. Skies opened with an all-day snowstorm. Four days later six more inches fell. Sam had work with Moss and Treat but had enough time to help look after Mother and Grace along with his own family. He had not known just what the trouble was with Roy, an undetermined illness. The symptoms were out of control. He would not get better on his own. Grace came down to Mr. Treats on Wednesday to tell Sam they were completely out of wood and coal. He took leave from his job, an hour to rescue Grace on a cold day. It was worse than she had yet confided about Roy. Dewey could have gotten the heating materials for Grace but she needed Sam so she could let him know what things had come to. It gave her needed comfort to confide in Sam.

Sam's own words...
Thursday, February 1, 1923 – "Roy acting much worse. Obliged to send Roy to B., drew wood for self and Grace. Drew corn, warm."
Friday, February 2, 1923 – "Up at Mothers. Drew wood and husked corn. Roy giving us an awful time. Poor Fellow."
Saturday, February 3, 1923 – "They took Roy to hospital from Grace's in a.m. Went after coal and groceries, cold wind."

Poor fellow. It was how they all felt about Roy. The white confines of straight jacket sleeves had wrapped around him for the ambulance trip. The Binghamton Psychiatric Hospital, a state-run institution, was no vacation, but a serious step. It had to be done. Sam's support of his dear sister, Grace, was unquestioned as he took oil to her on Sunday.

Sam worked in the Elmira junkyard and listed small amounts earned over five days, a total of only $3.01. It amounted to pay equivalent to a nine hour work day. The meager earnings were all he had in front of him while he applied for steady work elsewhere. Sam filled out applications here and there and hoped to receive a positive response.

He went after coal and groceries at the end of work on Saturday. He

314

filled out papers again at the brick yard and inquired at the Eclipse in the Heights. On Sunday, he drew two loads of corn and caught up on the news. Hockey game broadcasts by radio had gained in popularity. Albert Einstein of Germany had been mentioned for his Theory of Relativity but was not understood fully. Sam was curious, but the local news was his interest.

He made 35¢ at the junkyard on Monday for one hour's work. He may have felt as if it was desperation pay, more desperately needed.

Sam's smile emerged, maybe for the first time in a long time. He was to start a full-time job at the Eclipse. He began on Tuesday, February 26, with a nine-hour day. He stopped at the scrap dealer each day to earn anywhere from 34¢ to $1.20, depending on how long he was needed to dismantle junk and stow it away.

The factory job at the Eclipse morphed into 10-hour days, but Sam's smile had gone. One-year-old Shirley was sick, so sick that she was watched every minute of the day and night. Sam worried and worked five hours Saturday. The afternoon held junkyard labor and a trip for coal and groceries. On Sunday he drew corn fodder for his animals and helped with his sick baby. Shirley was only a little better when Sam worked 10 hours on Monday.

Sam's own words...
Tuesday, March 6, 1923 – "Took care of sick baby and gave Edith chance to sleep a little, went after coal, storm."
Wednesday, March 7, 1923 – "Children all sick including Willa. John and Steele at Grace's. Helped Edith with children. Snow."
Thursday, March 8, 1923 – "Done chores and cared for the sick. Willa sick-a-bed."

Willa, Lee, David, Betty, and baby Shirley were all under care at home with exhausted parents. Sam had to go back to work to provide for them, but his mind was on his weakened family. He put in half a day Saturday and brought coal and groceries home. He hired out to milk cows for Mr. Treat. Sunday was catch up to haul corn fodder for his animals, enough for a whole week ahead. The next week was uneventful as Sam worked 10-hour days and five hours Saturday. A strong, cold wind blew through March. The last week caught Sam with a harsh cough. He lost two days of work. Edith was sick, and the children were coughing.

Sam's own words...
Thursday, March 29, 1923 – "At Eclipse 10 hours. Edith and Willa sick, not so cold."

Willa was out of sorts, besides ill. Sam supposed her reason would come to light, or not. Questioning her was out of the question. She would confide in her mother when she was ready, if she was ready.

Sam put in his five hours Saturday and got coal and groceries in a cold wind. His Eclipse job was stable, for which he was grateful. The company thrived on the production of the Morrow slotted sprocket bike brakes for coasting, a big seller for them. Their motorcycle and gasoline engine parts were also in demand.

Sam, Edith, and Willa had quite a few discussions about Willa going west. Until they settled it, the three of them would not sleep well. Willa was in the first stages of TB, perhaps caught from taking care of Edward. His parents and other relatives wanted to take Louise (Lee) for fear she, too, would be infected with the highly infectious disease. Willa was determined that her daughter go with her.

Her TB was mild at the onset, but it would develop to need treatment. Did she need more reasons to lose her naturally sweet disposition?

Willa relied on her parents for required help. Edith arranged for Willa and three-year-old Louise to go to Cleveland, OH, where her Uncle Erick lived.

Grace wrote a letter to Roy in care of the State Hospital in Binghamton, NY.

~**~

March 29, 1923

Dear Roy,
    ...Sam has a bad cold and has been off from his work two days. The kiddies are all better. Willa is going to Cleveland, Ohio in a few days for a month's vacation. Her Uncle Erick lives there.
    ...I haven't received a letter from you yet and can't see

why you don't write me just a line or two. I want to come and see you again as soon as I possibly can. And you must be nice to me and not act like you did before...

Will close with lots of love.   From Grace

~**~

Sam's own words...
Monday, April 2, 1923 – "Eclipse nine hours, warmer. Willa and Louise went to Cleveland."

Willa's Uncle Erick stood able to welcome the young widow with her little girl. Willa would ponder her situation in the midst of an extended family who loved her. She was desperately unhappy and needed a new start.

Sam worked his nine- and 10-hour days at the Eclipse through warm, rainy April days. He was able to pay his life insurance of $7.95 to C. D. Kipp. Willa's reoccurring life insurance of $2.25 fell to Sam to pay. She was in no position to keep it up herself. Sam and Edith both deemed it a necessary expense owing to her health circumstance.

Sam came to the conclusion that he would have no time to plant crops. His daylight hours were entirely taken up with his job, and it provided the security he wanted for his family. He spoke with Mrs. Gano about his idea to rent only the land to Osgood and Perry for crops. She agreed. He needed only a combination cow, horse, and chicken pasture by the barn. His red cow had a calf.

Mrs. Gano hired Sam to fix the roof and paint the house.

Sam's own words...
Saturday, April 14, 1923 – "At Eclipse five hours, went after coal and groceries. Sent Willa's trunk to Cleveland, Ohio."

Willa extended her stay and remained with Erick and his family for a few months.

Sam was content with his 10 hours per day work. It was predictable to get his coal and groceries after Saturday's half-day. Sunday was the only day he could spare to see Mother and get corn fodder for his animals. Fence repair fell on Sunday. As soon as he had materials assembled for Mrs. Gano's house renovation, Sunday's would be taken over with that work. At least he would be home with his active children and give Edith a hand when needed.

Before he got locked into a tight schedule, he took Sunday, April 22, to go down to his Comfort Hill Farm. He and Dewey rode along together.

Monday, after work, Sam bought butter, a magazine, and tobacco. He paid carfare to ride home. The next week, for some unknown reason, the Eclipse job was not ready to be worked until Thursday. Sam knew just how to fill the time. He was on the road three days with his Shores goods. Sam was well received and sold $27.82 worth of merchandise. Enough was collected to pay 60% on the orders. He would enjoy all profit when he delivered and received final payment at the same time.

Sam paid Mrs. Gano $6 rent.

His tight schedule allowed only quick trips to see Grace and Mother, but not every week. They had to rely on Dewey a little more. Sam started a small garden and would push himself to manage it. He got the seeder from Grace on Sunday and began with two rows of peas.

Sam's own words...
Wednesday, May 23, 1923 – "At Eclipse 10 hours...Sold calf, $10."

Sam's payment to the Federal Land Bank was $52.50. Forty-five dollars was interest, and $7.50 was principle. It was his remittance to cover the Comfort Hill Farm in Wellsburg.

Sam accomplished Sunday work as he took down a stove pipe to clean it, cleaned the cellar, and repaired the chicken fence.

Edith was quite sick Tuesday while he was at the Eclipse 10 hours. He stayed with her Wednesday, likely to watch three children too young for school. She was better by the end of the day. He did not feel too well himself on Sunday but went to work all week. He set out tomato plants, a few at a time.

Sunday, June 10, he planted potatoes and cucumbers. On the end of each 10 hour day, another vegetable was planted. Sweet corn and Bantam corn were sowed.

Sam's own words…
Sunday, June 17, 1923 – "Helped with housework. Read some in "God's World.""

The poem, *God's World*, was part of a collection. Edna St. Vincent Millay was one of the most prolific and respected poets in America. Millay won the Pulitzer Prize for Poetry in 1923 for *The Ballad of the Harp-Weaver*.

Sam packed starters for motors on Monday, the usual 10 hours.

Sam's own words…
Saturday, June 23, 1923 – "Eclipse five hours. Went to Elmira and listed Comfort Hill Farm with Mc Corkle for two months. Paid Mrs. Gano $6."
Monday, June 25, 1923 – "Eclipse nine hours. Raised to 45¢ per hour. Hot and dry."

Sam carried pleasant thoughts with him as his five days of vacation began the first week of July. He hoed in his garden, set cabbage plants in soil, and enjoyed "a dandy rain." He had to go to the Heights to get his pay and send $41.90 life insurance. Edith, Sam, and all of the children went to see Grace. It was quite an outing that they'd had no time for recently.

Sam delivered and sold Shores for three days. The gentle jingle of the harness and whippletree accompanied the clip clop of the gray mare's hooves. Old customers were glad to see him and rewarded his efforts with orders.

Sam's own words…
Sunday, July 8, 1923 – "Housework. Edith, Grace, Frank, Mary to Comfort Hill to pick cherries."

Sam stayed home to hoe the garden and repair chicken wire.

July was a month of nine-hour work days and five hours each Saturday. He helped in the house on Sundays after his garden work. No weeds were allowed to thrive.

Sam went to the depot for Willa's trunk Sunday, July 29. She was returning.

The standard work week changed on Wednesday when he arrived at work. He learned that United States President Warren G. Harding had died. Sam bought the *Elmira Advertiser* for 3¢, also a malted milk. The August 4 morning paper said, "Harding Death Brings Closer Berlin Crisis. Fatality Abruptly Terminates Discussion As to Policy Toward Germany and Europe."

Sam worked nine hours but read news that President Harding had died of a heart attack. The 3¢ evening *Star-Gazette* had consideration of the plight of Mrs. Harding. If precedents were followed, Mrs. Harding would receive $5 thousand per year life pension. Mrs. Grover Cleveland and Mrs. Theodore Roosevelt were given the annuities by a vote of the House and Senate. There was no doubt of similar action in the case of Mrs. Harding. Vice President Calvin Coolidge was sworn in as United States president.

Sam's work and responsibilities went right on. He paid Willa's insurance again, bought groceries, and fixed fence on Saturday, August 4. Edith had his help in the house Sunday, and he put boards on the barn and fixed the tobacco shed.

The week resumed and Sam paid 38¢ a day for two rides, which covered his trip to work and back. A shoe repair cost him $1.90. Groceries, garden, and laundry took up the weekend before another week at the Eclipse.

Sam's own words...
Saturday, August 18, 1923 – "Eclipse five hours. Paid Western States Life Insurance $38.56 and Mrs. Gano $6. Received letter from Edith."

Well, what? He hadn't written that Edith went anywhere. His diary for two months had been sparse, little more than a record of hours at the Eclipse, not of keen interest for journal material. It went on that way to start another week.

Grace wrote to Roy at the Binghamton Psych Hospital. Sam was never aware of it.

~**~

Horseheads, NY
Aug. 19, 1923

My Dear Roy,

...I was so surprised and glad to get those two letters from you. But I wish you had written them yourself. You could, couldn't you if you tried real hard?

We went to the reunion...

Willa is home again now but is going to Colorado to make her home. Her father is buying her a small farm for chickens and a garden. Edith is in Cleveland, Ohio on a visit, and Willa is keeping house. Different looking house and kids, too...

Now, Roy, behave good (sic), and we will surely come to see you next Sunday. Is there anything you want me to bring? Write and tell me, and I will be thinking of you all day and wishing I could have come to see you...

With all my love.   From Grace

~**~

Would Sam's brows have raised if he had read Grace's paragraph on Willa and Edith? He knew Grace was outspoken, but on this subject? Maybe not. If Roy's mind was back to some normalcy he likely found no surprise in Grace's opinion. It didn't mean much, just a protective attitude toward her much-loved brother. Sam understood Edith's frailty, and above all, her need to see her brother, Eric, one more time while the opportunity existed for Willa to do childcare.

Sam's own words...
Thursday, August 23, 1923 – "Eclipse 10 hours. Edith and Shirley came back from Cleveland. Cold."

Edith's three weeks with Erick and his family was her vacation before Willa went west. Erick was sure to have enjoyed the rare occurrence as much as Edith.

August meant no school in session, but taxes prevailed. Sam paid $26.25 to the town of Ashland. He stayed busy and kept to himself, only to see Grace or Mother on infrequent visits. Sam chased cows, fixed fence, and carried water for a wash. He went to work Monday through Saturday. Sam was a quiet man, a private man, but now he had disappeared inside himself. What was it? What were he and Edith keeping so close to the chest with no intention to talk about it to others?

Sam did go to Mother's for a brief visit on Sunday and helped Edith in the house.

Sam's own words...
Monday, September 3, 1923 – "Willa and Louise started west. Helped in the house."
Tuesday, September 4, 1923 – "Eclipse 10 hours. Terrible loss of life in Japan."

On September 1, the Saturday just past, the Star-Gazette reported that the Great Kanto earthquake devastated Tokyo and Yokohama, killing an estimated 142,807 people. Years later, a Japanese construction research center report confirmed only 105 thousand dead. It was still a horrific event for Japan.

Edith was sick, but Sam worked nine hour days. The wash was done at a cost of $2.50 on Tuesday. Willa's life insurance of $1.05 was paid. Pants, candy, and tobacco were bought for $2.70. Sam was short on money and renewed two notes at Elmira's Second National Bank, $30 and $65, for two more months. The Cleveland trips had set him back, but was not begrudged. The candy delighted the children, which he was sure they enjoyed as much as he did his tobacco.

The morning had brought the first frost and remained cold.

Sam's own words...
Thursday, September 20, 1923 – "Eclipse nine hours. Sent for oil-gas burner, sold peck potatoes 50¢."
Sunday, September 23, 1923 – "Cleaned bedrooms, went after horse that has been gone two days."
Friday, September 28, 1923 – "At Eclipse eight hours. Rainy. Received $23.30 from W. A. Osgood for hay."
Saturday, September 29, 1923 – "Eclipse five hours. Went for groceries and burner."
Sunday, September 30, 1923 – "Cleaned out kitchen stove and pipe, swept rooms, set up Oliver burner."

Sam elaborated on his oil stove, but otherwise, his entries were hours worked. The hay sale was a boon to his finances. Osgood bought more hay for $5.76. Sam spent $5.50 of it to buy oil for his burner and paid $2.25

again for Willa's insurance. He picked apples and put roofing on the water house. Sam paid to have the washing done each week. Edith was weak and needed help to cope with five children and household work. He did all he could and more on the weekends. On one of his long work days, Sam bought dinner and tobacco for himself at 50¢.

He puttied window panes in Mrs. Gano's house, a few each weekend. They had a letter written in agreement about it, and she was to pay for putty and labor when he finished the slow job.

Sam's own words...
Tuesday, October 30, 1923 – "At Eclipse nine hours. Dewey and Grace came in evening."

They didn't show up to admire the new oil burner but may have commiserated with Sam on the $6 for 50 gallons of oil he'd bought the day before. Love of Sam and his family prompted the call. He hadn't visited them for an extended time. Time was filled for Sam with his work, his private thoughts, and big family.

Roy was still at Binghamton Psyche Center, and it would have come up in conversation. Dewey, no doubt was helping Grace and Mother since Sam's time was filled. If they asked about Willa, it would have been a sad report about her TB and that she was now temporarily in Denver, Colorado, living near her Uncle Arthur Crow.

Sam and Edith held her in their hearts in quiet moments when they spoke of her in soft whispers in the depth of the night. Neither Willa nor Edith were avid letter writers. They preferred using the telephone.

Sam was home with a sore throat Wednesday, but he picked apples. Thursday, November 1, he recorded the first snow fall. Mrs. Gano, his landlady, came in person Saturday. He paid her the $6 for rent and showed her the windows to which he had applied putty.

Coal was bought each week since it was cheaper than oil.

Sam's own words...
Sunday, November 4, 1923 – "Went to see Mr. Thompson. Put in two window panes. Osgood paid $15 on hay and Thompson paid $1.75."
Tuesday, November 6, 1923 – "Five hours at Eclipse. Went out with Shores goods in afternoon, collected $2.70."

The shortened Eclipse hours were turned into an opportunity by Sam for his retail customers. November brought more snow and 10-hour work days. Saturday, after work, Sam got coal and groceries, then dug a deeper hole to sink the water barrel.

Sam's own words...
Sunday, November 11, 1923 – "Sorted potatoes. Roy came home. Stormy."
Monday, November 12, 1923 – "Groceries, coal, oil, $7.56. Roofing $2.50. Sold two-bushel potatoes $3."

Another peck of spuds went for 40¢.

Roy was home with a new sense of how good it was to be with his family. Love for him didn't keep apprehension at bay. Would his previous problems happen again? How well was he? What should they be on the lookout for as a sign of unstable behavior?

Sam bent into his work, even with the uneasiness about Willa and Louise's plight. Willa made it clear that her little girl would be called Lee from now on. Sam understood Willa's reasons. How was she really? It was the reason for him and Edith's late night worries that were only spoken after children were sleeping. They were thankful for Willa's Uncle Arthur, her safety net when needed. Edith talked to Arthur by phone to learn details of something no other would ever hear, except for Sam.

Sam's own words...
Sunday, November 18, 1923 – "Went to see Dewey. Picked a few apples. So lame I can hardly go. Oil $5.50."
Thursday, November 22, 1923 – "Saw Perry about repairing barn. Went after coal. Sick with back and leg ache."
Saturday, November 24, 1923 – "Went after coal, groceries, and to Elmira to see Mc Corkle about farm on Comfort Hill."

It had been days, and Perry made no move to do the repairs that were discussed.

Sam counted on Dewey to privately tell him how Roy and Grace were. He couldn't ask her in front of Roy. The truth was needed. He had thought about his brother-in-law and what he might do to help him. Dewey gave a favorable report. Sam could go ahead with what he had in mind. If a smile would crack from Sam's face, his next move did it.

Sam's own words...
Sunday, November 25, 1923 – "Saw Roy about repair work. Put straw around house. Read to children."
Monday, November 26, 1923 – "At Eclipse nine hours. Roy did repairs. Storm."
Thursday, November 29, 1923 –"Put roofing on kitchen floor. Helped in house. Went up to Grace's."

No doubt, when Sam went to Grace's, he paid Roy for his labor. He might have thought that it would help to restore Roy's self-opinion. Sam treated his brother-in-law as he ought to according to the Golden Rule.

Saturday, December 1, finished the same as those before it, same five hours, same errands. Sunday, Sam put more roofing paper on his kitchen floor. Monday started another week of nine-hour days on the job. On Thursday he paid $10 on his Rockwell loan of $69.91 and a week later he paid $2.88 for Willa's insurance. Friday's paycheck on December 14 was $21.15. The Wednesday after that, he spent 81¢ on Christmas gifts.

A small gray envelope arrived for Edith. Sam must have smiled to see her pleasure. Lora Nichol's hurried handwriting with her Encampment, Wyoming, address was postmarked December 18. The lyrical verse on the miniature card recalled the years of friendship that would now reach into the future to save a precious life.

~**~

Thinking of you at Christmas

No two ways about it,
This time of year I get
An overwhelming impulse
To show I don't forget
And that I wish you
A Very Merry Christmas!
Lora

~**~

Sam's own words...
Monday, December 24, 1923 – "Went to Elmira after shoes for family, $7. Cold, clear."
Tuesday, December 25, 1923 – "Put more banking around house and covered water barrels. Goose dinner and Merry Christmas."

Work resumed with nine-hour days. On Thursday, Sam attended Odd Fellows Lodge and paid $1 dues. It had snowed for two days, and he promised the children he would make sleds on the weekend.

Sam's own words...
Friday, December 28, 1923 – "Eclipse 10 hours. Brick plant destroyed by fire. Cold Wind."

He shook his head, not wishing the brickworks any bad luck. Sam couldn't help but think, "There went my job if I had been working there."

On Sunday, he made the promised sleds. They tested the waxed sliders on three new inches of white powder. The slope was soon packed down and slick enough for fast rides for noisy children. Sam worked around the house then in the barn to build a coal bin.

The news was varied on the last Sunday of the year. The German mark was at its height of inflation, and Gustav Stresemann's coalition government in Germany had collapsed. Roy and Walt Disney had founded Walt Disney company in late October. Sam wondered what would become of the December 29 first patent by Vladimir K. Zworykin in the United States for television systems. Would television amount to anything?

Nine hours at the Eclipse on Monday ended 1923 warm, all snow melted. How was Willa and where was she on New Year's?

20 – Tent
Sanitarium, 1924, 1925

Edith's unease surfaced every day about Willa. How was her daughter? Did she eat as she should? How was her attitude over her situation? Edith inquired by phone for answers from her brother, Arthur. Willa was still in Denver, not far from her Uncle Arthur. As near as could be determined, Willa planned to travel to Wyoming in late January or early February. Sam and Edith reported to the family that Willa's tuberculosis was in a flare up.

Willa needed a type of care that her father, Edward Haggarty, could have paid for. There is no record of what, if any, help he may have offered, but the belief is that he contributed what was needed for her. He was a Wyoming miner, not a pauper, and may have paid part or all of the expenses for the care required as outlined by Edith's friend, Lora Nichols. Several mines including Ed Haggarty's former copper mine were in the hills above Lora's ranch. He had sold it and married Edith. They immediately took a honeymoon voyage to visit his family in England. Edith knew the area well where his isolated cabin sat. Loneliness had driven her away after a year of marriage as he constantly sought his next big strike. He had divorced her for desertion even though he was out prospecting for extended periods of time and she had no close neighbors.

Edith's thoughts came back to the present. She could not help Willa herself since she and Sam had five younger children. Edith had been in touch with Lora Nichols about Willa.

The Nichols's sons were almost grown and as teenage cowboys were more often out of the house than in. Lora was busy with her photography service and a newspaper she owned. However; she offered to care for Willa and Lee until Willa recovered. Willa's move was approved and details were in the process of being worked out. Edith was grateful while she waited for word of the extensive preparations.

Sam came across another poem that "spoke" to him in a profound way to start the new year of 1924. He copied two poignant stanzas of it into his diary.

The Clock of Life

By Robert H. Smith

The clock of life is wound but once,
And no man has the power
To tell just when the hands will stop
At late or early hour.

The present only is our own,
So Live, Love, toil with a will.
Place no faith in 'Tomorrow'
For the clock may then be still.

His mind was set on worry. Mother, Sophia Crippen was sick on January 1. She was in Pennsylvania with Lynn, Iva, and family. Sam thought of her and Willa with more than passing concern when he copied the poem on the page. Losses already suffered informed him of the worst case that could happen.

The present brought him back to a better frame of mind.

The rocking seat frolics of the children required Sam to make repairs to the runner chair again. Edith was the gentle rocker who needed to lull baby Shirley into a nap. Their youngest girl was soon to become a two-year-old toddler on January 20. Sam rocked her at rare times for the enjoyment of it. New Years might be the perfect day for it and to let peace of mind rein in his wounded thoughts.

Edith knew how and why he had endured pain over his solemn responsibility. Only Edith, his Pal, knew and had suffered with him and loved him for it as he did her.

Tuesday, January 2, was the first nine-hour workday of the year and Sam was thankful to have it. He sent $5 to Shores-Mueller on his way home. His Friday paycheck was $14.40 and set him up for coal and groceries after his five hours at the Eclipse on Saturday. He was into the same familiar routine. He paid his $6 in rent to Mrs. Gano.

Sam and Dewey rode down to the Comfort Hill Farm with Mr. and Mrs. Personius, who rented it for a poultry business with the Browns. Sam was keen to sell it, but he would not sell too cheap. The potential buyers were non-committal.

Sam went to the Eclipse for his nine hours Monday, disappointed in no sale. The weather was warmer, a January thaw. He helped Edith in the house Tuesday, which was a shortened five-hour work day. He contacted Mr. Personius and tried to sell the farm again. No luck. On Wednesday, he had only four hours work. He went and borrowed $100 from the Second National Bank. He paid $41.90 for Edith's Western Life Insurance policy and $52.50 to the Federal Land Bank for the Comfort Hill Farm. After nine hours work Friday, he paid Willa's life insurance.

He would leave Personius alone on selling the farm. They knew where he was.

Sam's own words...

Sunday, January 13, 1924 – "Helped in house. Cleaned out stables. Went up to Grace's to see how Mother was."

Grace received word that Mother was improved at Lynn's in Pennsylvania.

Sam's work was constant again and the week uneventful. He visited Grace on Sunday, January 20. The warm spell ended and by the next Sunday. Sam had a hard time keeping the old house warm. Shirley was ill, had been for a week and was quite a worry.

"This drafty old house will keep us all chilled and sick," may have been the logical conversation between Sam and Edith.

Willa had remained a constant concern as well. They expected word from Lora Nichols on the readiness to manage her care. Edith and Lora's phone call may have taken place that same Sunday while Sam watched children. Edith used streetcar fare for 26¢ to travel to a phone.

Edith explained to Sam that Lora had had a stable platform erected several feet off the ground with steps leading up one side. It was built in expectation of Wyoming's normal snowfall, at times several feet and drifted. Heavy canvas had been stretched over a frame constructed for it and fastened down. It was Willa's private sanitarium of cold fresh air, her best chance at recovery. Nutritious food would be prepared by Lora and served by a person who was to be in charge of Willa's care. An accordion-type hoist was in place that would lift Willa in a sling while her bed linens were being changed. She would soon reside in a thick pile of quilts in the bed. It was better than a public sanitarium where other patients had TB. The only thing left to do was to send Willa and Lee to Wyoming. Edith immediately called Arthur in Denver to tell him that Willa must go at once. Edith and Sam could feel some relief, but it would take many months to know if their Billie would improve under the best care available.

Sam's own words...
Monday, February 4, 1924 – "Sold our farm in Ashland Township to La Verne Personius and Peter Brown. Paid taxes of $63.03."

The warmth of one success had arrived just as colder weather brought snow squalls that moved in swirls. Work hours remained steady. After Saturday's five hours of labor, Sam paid $6 to Mrs. Gano, $5 to Shores-Mueller Company, and $3 to the National Salesman Training Association. He went to see Grace on Sunday and helped Edith in the house. The snow hadn't stopped falling and mounted up to 12 inches. Coal and oil burned as the next week brought more cold crystals.

Sam's own words...
Friday, February 22, 1924 – "At Eclipse nine hours. Roads drifted badly. Had a hard time getting to and from work."
Saturday, February 23, 1924 – "At Eclipse five hours. Went through drifts after groceries..."
Sunday, February 24, 1924 – "Done chores. Helped in house, 17 degrees below zero."

A "warmer trend" started Sam's week with 14 below zero and only eight below on Wednesday. He took a 35¢ Shores order, likely at work.

Wednesday marked a milestone of one year on the Eclipse job. He wrote it down on the page with gratitude and looked toward heaven. "Thank you, God." Ten-hour days had already begun within the week.

It was still so cold that it was smart to stay inside. Sam could catch up on unread newspapers. He read that only two weeks ago a grizzly thing had taken place when the first state execution using gas took place in Nevada. They called it capital punishment. The Computing Tabulating Company (CTR) of New York state was renamed International Business Machines (IBM). Of more interest was the February 22 broadcast from the White House. Calvin Coolidge became the first United States president to deliver a speech on the radio. Sam likely was glad the message was in newsprint, too. Neither he nor anyone he knew had an expensive radio or had ever heard one.

March was melting into mush.

Sam's own words...
Sunday, March 9, 1924 – "Went to Millport, Midway, and Pine Valley looking for a house. Went to Grace's in evening."

Mush did not prevail. Snow, the wind, and cold held on through all of Sam's 10-hour work days. He paid Mrs. Gano $6 on Saturday to cover a week. The effort on Sunday to find a house in Horseheads went bust. A cheaper rental was needed to cut expenses. Mr. Treat paid in apples, worth $5 for one bushel, on what he owed to Sam. Sam tried again on Tuesday and Wednesday to find a place to move. A house was found near Horseheads Junction and they didn't object to five children. Sam paid $15 rent for a month.

On Saturday, the regular five hours had evaporated, unavailable. Sam went after coal and groceries, paid $10 to the Second National Bank on a note, and settled up with Mrs. Gano.

Sam's own words...
Sunday, March 23, 1924 – "Murray Bastain and Lama's paid us a visit. Packed up Shores goods and took them up to Mr. McDonald's. Sold oats and buckwheat straw to Mr. Charles. Warm, fair."

Monday and Tuesday were the last nine hour days of work for three weeks. He had foreseen the downturn in work hours. Mr. Treat paid him another bushel of apples worth $5. Saturday, March 29, gave Sam five hours on the job, after which a load of household items were moved to the Junction place. They had a doctor for Shirley, their youngest, on Sunday. Sam moved another load of belongings.

On Monday morning he took his horse up to Grace's and worked three hours at the Eclipse in the afternoon. Tuesday's eight-hour work day had snowfall all day. Grace came over and found them relieved that Shirley was better.

The news mentioned a jailed Adolf Hitler for participation in a Beer Hall Putsch. Sam thought of him as "that loud mouth over in Germany."

The roads were snow-filled when he went for his eight hours work on Wednesday.

Sam sent $5 to Shores on Saturday, $5 on the Rockwell Hardware note, and paid his Prudential Life Insurance. He got half of his chickens and the rest on Sunday when he went to Grace's. During the week of eight-hour work days, he had time to repair the chicken coop. The next Saturday he went after his horse and tried to sell him but had no luck.

Sam's jaw was set when he looked around the place again. He didn't plan on putting in much work here. They could make-do short term. He sold the horse to Leon Charles.

After work on Monday, he saw Lyle Hopkins about the Ward farm. Plenty of rain fell for the next few days.

Sam read that Metro-Goldwyn-Mayer (MGM) was founded on April 16 in Los Angeles, Calif. He shook his head as he dismissed the thought of seeing a movie. Wouldn't it be a treat to take Edith out? But he had five children and his priorities were as straight as hers.

Without work on Saturday, Sam went to the Ward farm again with Mr. Hopkins. The keys would be in Sam's hands by next Thursday. Meanwhile, he had nine hours of labor per day through Wednesday, then back to eight hours a day. He packed goods for the move to the Ward farm Saturday, April 27. Chickens were caught and transferred Sunday. Sam had no rest at all by the time the weekend was over.

Sam's own words...
Friday, May 2, 1924 – "At Eclipse eight hours. Lynn has pneumonia. We are all worried."

Anxiety over their 37-year-old brother was discussed among Sam, Grace, Dewey, and Mother. Bills that Sam owed had roiled his mind but not like Lynn's sudden illness. He sent $5 to Shores and put $5 on Dr. Leet's account and forgot about it. He would not forget about his dear brother. Uncle George arrived the same evening. He and Sam shook hands and assured each other that Lynn was strong and would pull through.

On Sunday, thoughts were partially on Lynn as Sam jiggled the reins and rode along down to Comfort Hill Farm. The other thought was that he shouldn't have to ride all the way down there to rustle up the farm payment from Personius and Brown. The chilled wind added to his grumpy mood to top off his two-way worry, but he'd not be out of sorts when he talked to them, not Sam. It became evident that they were as poor as the rest of the population. The payment remained unpaid.

Since it was Sunday, Sam watched children while Edith went to make a phone call to Lora. The fresh air and nutritious food had slowly strengthened Willa. Her health had a long pull ahead before it could be called recovery, but she was not worse. The warmer weather allowed little Lee (Louise) to climb the steps to the tent platform and see her mother's face. The toddler was not permitted past the threshold of the tent flap door into the contagious arena. Lora loved the dear sick widow and her child because they were Edith's own. She may have fondly sung Lee to sleep at night while supplying hugs. She photographed Willa in her sick-bed being lifted with the aid of the sling.

Sam's own words...
Monday, May 5, 1924 – "At Eclipse eight hours. Mr. J. Lamb's son, Bobby, seriously burned while trying to light a toy lantern candle."
Tuesday, May 6, 1924 – "At Eclipse five hours. Collected for Shores, cold wind."

Sam had said how sorry he was to hear about the boy's injury, and he inquired each day from Mr. Lamb at the Eclipse.

Shorter hours on Tuesday were not to be wasted. Sam made the most of them. He was less worried because his brother, Lynn, was better. Eight hours of work a day was the norm but none on Saturday. He went with Mr. Charles after their mutual need of coal and groceries, also because he had no horse himself. After he had cleaned his cellar and wood shed, he paid Lyle Hopkins $2.50 rent. Sunday, he helped around the house all day. The continuous rain kept on for three more days. Lowlands were covered with water. Every day he worked his eight.

Sam borrowed Mr. Treat's horse and went after coal on Wednesday. To return the favor, he helped him clean oats. Uncle George brought Sam's cow from Grace's the next day. Edith had wanted the milk for the children for days. Sam shook Uncle George's hand.

On the weekend he went to see Osgood and paid Lyle Hopkins $2.50 rent again for the week and helped with housework. He read that J. Edgar Hoover was appointed the head of the Federal Bureau of Investigation in Washington. It rained all day Sunday.

Sam's own words...
Monday, May 26, 1924 – "At Eclipse eight hours. Sent fire insurance to Land Bank on Comfort Hill Farm, $9.40."

Money had been saved so it could go out on bills, but now he needed more to come in. He was soon to be short a day of pay after a lack of work on Friday. He did housework and took 10-year-old David and eight-year-old Betty to Millport for a Memorial Day exercise with classmates.

Mr. Charles loaned his team to Sam to go after coal and groceries. Sam also plowed his garden after three days of rain ended and was about sick with a cold on Sunday. He did not let it keep him from work every day.

Keeping up with the news, Sam approved of President Calvin Coolidge's signed law, The Indian Citizenship Act, which granted citizenship to all Native Americans born within territorial limits of the United States. Maybe Sam thought of the help it might give descendants of Sitting Bull.

This shows Willa in the cold Wyoming tent that served as her TB Sanitarium. The sling had only to lift a slight of weight young woman.

~**~

The sturdy construction of the tent frame under a heavy canvas kept wind and snow out but not the cold. Quilts were piled on Willa's bed (below). She was only one month from her 22nd birthday coming in March 1924.

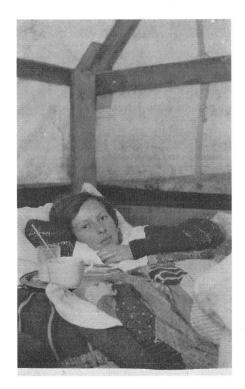

Sam's own words...
Thursday, June 5, 1924 – "Eclipse eight hours. Mr. Lamb's little boy died from his burns."

Sam shook his head at the terrible misfortune of his foreman over the loss of his son. He may have impressed upon his own children the danger of fire and candles.

Sam's good friend, Mr. Charles, loaned him a team for errands on Saturday. He also allowed Sam to renew the Rockwell note longer at Montour Bank. As the loan officer having many years of experience with Sam, there was no doubt in his mind that the loan would be repaid.

Sam helped in the house on Sunday with Edith's appreciation as his reward.

Sam's own words...
Monday, June 9, 1924 – "At Eclipse eight hours. Received $52.50 from L. Personius for payment to Land Bank."
Thursday, June 12, 1924 - "Two years ago today, Father died."

Sam's relief brought a smile when he saw the Personius name in the top left corner of the envelope. He wouldn't press his luck to try to collect a late charge. The Land Bank agency received a $52.98 check from him.

Uncle George came and helped Sam plant potatoes on Saturday. It was a good way to keep company with one another. He thought the world of his nephew and knew of Sam's loneliness after the loss of his father.

The June 23 headline spelled out news that amazed Sam as it captured the imagination of everyone. American airman, Russell Maughan, flew from New York to San Francisco in 28 hours and 48 minutes on a dawn-to-dusk flight in a Curtiss pursuit plane.

Work at the Eclipse ceased for two weeks from Sunday, June 29, through Sunday, July 13. Sam drew vacation pay for the first week. He hoed his garden day after day to prevent weeds from gaining a foothold. More spuds were planted. Buckwheat was threshed and cleaned.

Sunday, he gave John, age seven, and Steele, age five and a half, baths. He helped Edith with housework. She was struggling to keep her work up. They hadn't tried to celebrate the Fourth of July with her energy in short supply.

Sam's own words...
Monday, July 7, 1924 – "Weighed buckwheat. Sold 510# to B. Welch, 234# to L. Charles and to self, 60#. Set out cabbage plants."
Friday, July 11, 1924 – "Done housework. Edith not well."

Cabbage plants automatically brought on the thought of sauerkraut in the fall. But now was the time to hoe, pull weeds, and cultivate potatoes. He paid $5 to the Montour Bank on the note and bought groceries.

With Sam's garden work finished, he helped his much-loved wife. They talked of Willa whose health was in dire straits, but he had as much concern for his Edith. They missed Willa out of love but also because she had often taken over care of her younger siblings to allow her mother to rest. What was it that weakened Edith and made her take to her bed so often? Sam would continue to pick up the slack.

His Eclipse job opened up again Monday, July 14. The assembly of bike sprocket and motorcycle parts was repetitious, but he did not complain. The steady paycheck was his mainstay of money to support his family.

August and September copied of each other. Sam helped L. Hopkins with hay on a few weekends. On other Sunday's he did housework, picked cherries, and visited Grace. The renewal of the Second National Bank note took place when he paid $5 on it. Payment of Edith's life insurance of $38.56 was sent.

Sam's own words...
Sunday, August 24, 1924 – "Roy took us down to Comfort Hill Farm and around by Mansfield, Tioga, etc. Drove 100 miles."

It was quite the excitement for all of them to enjoy an extended excursion in good company with one another as summer scenery rolled by at a swift 20 miles-per-hour.

Sam helped get children ready for school on Monday, September 1. An Italian gardener, Charlie, made a visit. People talked about Sam's pristine garden. Charlie gazed on it as if before him lay the Paradise of Exiles: The Anglo-American Gardens of Florence. No weeds were in view as Sam and his visitor mopped their brows on a hot day.

Sam paid $5 to the Montour Bank and $10 on the Rockwell note. He wrote a letter to Personius. He had just been to the Comfort Hill Farm but was unable to collect money for the taxes.

Sam's own words...
Sunday, September 14, 1924 – "Helped around house, repaired table and chairs. Dewey has a Star car, brought Sadie up."

Dewey and Sadie were close just like Sam and Grace. The two sets of siblings got along well. Dewey's Star auto was from the Durant car com-pany, a former General Motors Company owner who was dissatisfied and broke away to manufacture his own brands.

Sam's own words...
Tuesday, September 16, 1924 – "At Eclipse nine hours. L. Personius paid county taxes $28.31...Moderate."

The arrival of the envelope with the Personius name in the corner brightened the day.

Family was arriving from Pennsylvania, and plans shaped up for Sunday, September 21. They all had an excellent dinner at Grace's. Frank and Mary were there.

New potatoes shone like pale yellowy pearls in the dark soil as Sam dug them out and filled a pail. What an enjoyment they would be.

Sam's own words...
Sunday, September 28, 1924 – "Edith not well. Helped around house. Lynn's folks paid us a visit."
Monday, September 29, 1924 – "At Eclipse nine hours. Army fliers land in Seattle after circling globe. Rainy."

Sam's jaw must have dropped as he read of the first-ever circumnavigation around the world. It had taken Army pilots Harding and Nelson 175 days and 74 stops to accomplish the feat. Sam had to believe now that airplanes would no more fade from view than automobiles.

His sister, Mary, took sudden illness and had an operation at the Blossburg, PA, hospital where she remained for care. It may have been appendicitis. Roy and Grace drove down to see her.

The Eclipse shut down at noon on Thursday, October 2, for the opening of the Chemung County fairgrounds. Sam used the time to clean a stovepipe and dig potatoes. He dug more on Saturday and Sunday. Nine-hour days resumed at work.

On Monday, October 13, Sam went to Elmira to take care of surrogate business and sent a certificate of indebtedness to Dairymen's League.

Cooler weather was the ideal time to clean out the hen house and the woodshed. He also repaired the railroad crossing to begin winter with best conditions. He never doubted of what to do next.

More spuds needed to see the light of day.

Sam's own words...
Saturday, November 1, 1924 – "Went to Elmira, paid state and county taxes on Lac Crippen estate. Went to see Osgood about money due me."
Sunday, November 2, 1924 – "Children and I gathered apples and pine knots. Helped around house. Colder and windy."
Tuesday, November 4, 1924 – "Paid $11.50 on Rockwell Hardware note and $5 on Dr. Leet account. We voted in evening. Helped in house."

The pine knots burned well once started and fueled larger chunks of wood while the fresh smell of pine sap sizzled in the fire.

Sam's own words...
Monday, November 10, 1924 – "At Eclipse eight hours. Mr. Thompson's car broke down. Henry Cabot Lodge dead."
Tuesday, November 11, 1924 – "Edith went to Elmira and had two teeth out. Looked after children."
Friday, November 14, 1924 – "At Eclipse nine hours. Edith still suffering from ulcerated tooth."
Saturday, November 15, 1924 – "At Eclipse five hours. Edith sick, done housework."

The broken down car made it difficult for Mr. Thompson and Sam to get to work. Sam didn't go to work the next day, but Edith went on the streetcar to the dentist in Elmira.

Senator Henry Cabot Lodge (1850-1924), a conservative Republican politician, had proved a long-term adversary of Democratic President Woodrow Wilson and, ultimately, his nemesis. Lodge was educated at

Harvard and acted as assistant editor of the North American Review, before lecturing on U.S. history at Harvard. Sam was partial to the man partly because Lodge wrote a series of historical works and biographies of Daniel Webster (1883) and George Washington (1889). Senator Lodge formed a close alliance with Theodore Roosevelt. Sam favored him most for that.

Sam was well aware of how much Edith suffered, but there was no quick solution. It took most of a week for the teeth situation to come to a pain-free conclusion. Sam did housework Sunday. He went down to Grace's and returned in a snow squall. The nine-hour days kept him busy and Saturday's five hours shortened his weekend. It ought to be worth a higher wage.

Sam's Own words...
Tuesday, November 18, 1924 – "At Eclipse nine hours. Cold, asked Mr. Lamb for increase in wages."

It would be awhile before Sam would hear if his request had success. Sam banked up Grace's house and started on his own. A snow storm on Monday caused him to start work on the chicken coop and barn to make them warmer. He contacted L. Hopkins to buy hay.

Sam's own words...
Monday, December 1, 1924 – "Eight hours at Eclipse. Edith received a letter from Arthur saying he might pay us a visit."

Edith whirled around with baby Shirley. Her oldest brother was coming. She settled into the rocker with her toddler and leaned her head back to smile. Sam was happy to watch her reaction. The only thing that would make her more content would be to hear that Willa's TB was cured. It reminded him to write to Willa because Christmas was not far off. He could get David to write to Billo, and Betty would not have to be coaxed either.

He bought coal and groceries, banked up the cellar, and helped clean house. Mother and Grace came for a visit and heard the great news of Arthur's impending visit. Eight-hour work days commenced again but did not dim the festive spirit as the house was cleaned and put at its best.

Children became unusually cooperative in preparation for their uncle's visit. None of them—except baby Shirley had ever met him.

Sam's own words...
Sunday, December 21, 1924 – "...Arthur Crow came this morning. Kids overjoyed."
Monday, December 22, 1924 – "At Eclipse eight hours. Roy and Grace came up in evening. Quite cold."
Wednesday, December 24, 1924 – "At Eclipse eight hours. Arthur made us all indebted to him by getting Xmas cheer. Moderate."
Thursday, December 25, 1924 – "Arthur went home: We shall miss him. Much colder. Roy and folks went to Frank and Mary's."

Sam favored his brother-in-law so well that they would keep their fond respect for each other over the years. Arthur had inquired about Willa's health and progress. The report from two months ago on her slow recovery had been uplifting. Arthur's help to Willa, while she was in Denver, would not be forgotten. They did not discuss any part of it in front of the children. The euphoric visit was over all too soon.

Sam was off work for a few days. He paid for coal and arranged with Mr. Rodabaugh for delivery on a cold, snowy day. It was eight degrees below zero. He worked on a frozen pump Sunday. The anthracite delivery came on Monday after work.

~**~
1925

Sam's own words...
Thursday, January 1, 1925 – "At home. Grace and Mary made us a visit. Quite busy but don't know what I done."

Edith knew what he did, no doubt, and appreciated his willingness to do housework and watch children. New Year's Day was the perfect time for her to call Lora Nichols to ask about Willa and Lee. One year had gone by since Willa's sequestration inside her private TB sanitarium tent. Had pristine, fresh air cooled her fevered lungs and teemed with nutritious food to heal her?

Edith was aglow when she came back to Sam. The prognosis was good. Willa was stronger and had been able to sit up and smile for a few weeks. Perhaps she would be cured in six months if treatment continued without impatience to cut it short. Edith and Lora were of one mind to make sure Willa would see it through. Lora was happy to adore and care for Lee until there would be no more danger of contamination.

Sam savored the gleam of Edith's radiance as she told her news. It was a dream scenario to end the year so well and the next one most promising. It hadn't a thing to do with lack of money, but everything to do with the happiness of shared love and good news between them.

On Sunday Dewey came to enjoy the evening meal at their table. Sam had bathed the youngest children. Their bright faces grinned up at their tall uncle.

Later in the week, Mr. Treat paid Sam $5 and still owed $11.75.

Sam's own words...
Saturday, January 24, 1925 – "Witnessed an awe-inspiring sight, the total eclipse of the sun. Cold, five hours at the Eclipse."
Sunday, January 25, 1925 – "Helped around house. Grace and Mother had dinner with us. Moderate."

The mild weather did not linger as lower temperatures and snow storms proved relentless. It was 12 below zero on Thursday while Sam continued nine-hour work days. By Friday, roads were impassable and a ride to work, impossible. Sam bundled up on Saturday and walked four miles to go after his paycheck and bring a few grocery items home. The roads remained in bad shape even by Sunday. He caught a ride to work Monday for his nine hours.

Changes were in store along with 10-hour days instated. Snow, rain, and wind teamed up in mild enough temperatures to cause widespread melt off and floods. Water and ice were everywhere. On Sunday, Sam got a weeks' worth of hay down from the mow for the cow. This habit was to make the week ahead easier.

Sam's own words...
Tuesday, February 10, 1925 – "At Eclipse 10 hours. Could not get home in evening on account of water. Stayed at Grace's all night."
Wednesday, February 11, 1925 – "Eclipse 10 hours. At Grace's again, more water than ever."

Thursday, February 12, 1925 – "Eclipse 10 hours. Still away from my dear family. It is so much colder, and I hope water goes down tomorrow."

But water did not recede even after his 10 hours on the job. His bridge had washed out enough that it was not crossable.

Sam's own words...
Saturday, February 14, 1925 – "At Eclipse five hours. Reached home by crossing at Mr. Van Doren's and very glad to get there."
Sunday, February 15, 1925 – "Repaired bridge...to walk across it, got hay out of mow for cow and helped around the house. Stormy."

No doubt the family was glad to have Sam home. A week of nine-hour days at the Eclipse went by uneventful but cold.

Sam's own words...
Sunday, February 22, 1925 – "Did odd jobs. Went down to Grace's, tried to get Roy and Dewey to agree about renting farm and settling estate."

The two men did not yet agree on details, and Sam would have to wait longer to finalize Father's NY estate. Lac had sold when Sam did but took his profits and bought back in. As executor, Sam needed to bring it to a solution for Mother's part. Dewey would have liked to be in charge. Sam supposed it would sit awhile longer while they stewed over it. He'd done what he could. Now let them discuss it among themselves.

The cow had gotten out and disappeared Thursday morning. Friday weather was so cold and windy that children could not go to school. After Sam's short hours Saturday, he found the cow and brought her home. Rain and snow alternated.

Saturday held an unprecedented event. An earthquake was felt throughout the eastern United States. A vast area of the northeastern U. S. and eastern Canada was shaken by a magnitude seven earthquake. A significant portion of New York state experienced 4.0 Richter scale intensity; lower concentrations were noted south of Albany.

Sam's own words...
Tuesday, March 3, 1925 – "At Eclipse nine hours. Cold and fair. Edith and children surprised me with a birthday cake."

It was a better day than he would face again for awhile. He struggled to work Wednesday, hardly able to move. How could his 42 years bring him such pain in his back? He worked his nine hours with compressed lips, determined not to make a sound when sharp stabs of agony made him flinch. Back at home, he could not perform his chores and remained motionless on his bed, except for muffled groans, right through Friday. Edith and the children did chores. She most likely fed the cow and pitched manure out while David sat astride a three-corner stool and milked. Betty may have fed chickens and gathered eggs. Roy brought groceries out on Friday.

Sam's own words...
Saturday, March 7, 1925 – "Received a valuable enlarged picture of Father from Willa. Managed to help a little."

Willa no doubt asked Lora Nichols to enlarge and develop the picture for Sam's surprise birthday gift. Willa was still in the tent bed but had gained in health. She wrote of her hope to come out soon, in a mere few months. The letter had been typed on a small typewriter on her lap. Fingertips were cut out of the gloves she wore. The glove trick was learned from Edith and Lora who both used the method to hang clothes on the line in winter.

Sam had Dewey take him to Osgood's who paid him $6 on his account. He accomplished chores regardless of a sore back. It saved Edith extra work. Monday, he was the same and Tuesday, he went to Dr. Jones. He asked Carl Withune to deliver coal.

Sam's unnatural stiffness stuck through nine hours Wednesday at the Eclipse. He was pain beleaguered while he worked Thursday and Friday. Saturday's five hours of work were a relief when he finished. On the way home, he paid fire insurance. The $7.50 covered Comfort Hill farm through February 1926.

Sam's own words...
Sunday, March 15, 1925 – "At home all day; John, Steele, and Shirley sick with a cold. Edith not very well. Mother, Grace, and Dewey came in evening."
Monday, March 16, 1925 – "At home with sick wife, sick baby, and sick self. John and Steele home with colds. Windy."

Tuesday, March 17, 1925 – "At Eclipse nine hours. Snowed all a.m. I wish I had a new back. Children and Edith better."

Eight-year-old John and six-year-old Steele knew little of their father's neuralgia pain. Children are absorbed in a play world at such an age and immune to small signs. Sam kept it to himself except for a hand pressed in against his back on occasion. But his Pal knew just as he knew when she was not well. The smell of liniment rubbed in, and a gentle touch of a hand on either shoulder was not missed by them as subtle signs of care for each other.

Sam's own words...
Friday, March 23, 1925 – "At Eclipse nine hours. Quite cold. Can hardly work on account of lame hip."

He worked, helped at home, and suffered without a lot of fanfare. But Edith and his diary knew all of his troubles. He just needed another problem to take his mind off the original one.

Sam's own words...
Sunday, April 5, 1925 – "Done chores and helped a little around home. My hip still bothering and have had the piles for a month."
Sunday, April 12, 1925 – "A fair spring day. My piles worry me."
Monday, April 13, 1925 – "Went to see Dr. Jones for medicine."
Tuesday, April 14, 1925 – "At Eclipse nine hours. Found Erick home when I came in evening."

Edith had been in better shape than Sam for awhile. Sam enjoyed her light-hearted nature because her youngest brother had arrived. Sam extended a handshake. They talked until late but if Sam were to get up for work, he'd have to turn in.

Sam's own words...
Thursday, April 16, 1925 – "Eclipse nine hours. Edith and Erick went to Elmira and saw Life of A. Lincoln portrayed."
Friday, April 17, 1925 – "At Eclipse nine hours. Edith, Erick, and children had dinner with Grace. Erick went home in evening."
Saturday, April 25, 1925 – "At Eclipse five hours. David and I saw Life of A. Lincoln on screen."

Edith enjoyed the rare chance to see a movie, something hard to do with five children and little money. She saw the value of making sure that 11-year-old David could learn the important history of Abe Lincoln through entertainment. Sam paid 40¢ for the theater and 10¢ each for street car fare.

On Sunday, Sam had Dewey take him over to E. Broughtons. He sold his plow.

Thunderstorms boomed; after all, it was April.

Peter Brown advanced $10 on Comfort Hill. Osgood paid $4 on his debt and owed Sam $5.75 yet. Sam's back improved.

Sam's own words...
Friday, May 1, 1925 – "Eclipse nine hours. Rainy and cold. Piles still giving me misery."
Saturday, May 2, 1925 – "Eclipse five hours. Saw Carl W. about plowing garden. Cold."
Sunday, May 3, 1925 – "Dewey took me up to Mr. Mc Donald's, and I brought remainder of Shores goods home. Mother and Grace ate dinner with us."

Sam doctored raw hemorrhoids that had caused him discomfort for weeks. Newsprint bloodied in the outhouse didn't exactly feel too good on his tender butt.

Work went right along at nine hours a day until Monday, May 25, when 10-hour days commenced. During the three weeks, Sam had recorded sleet, rain, and hail. There was snow on the ground as late as May 25. Sam looked ahead with plans for his garden on the last two days of May. When he had finished a few rows on Sunday, his folks came from Pennsylvania. "Folks" was his term for any of his relatives.

He was glad to accept a $52.50 postal money order from P. Brown for the Comfort Hill note. He sent it straight off to the land bank the next day, June 6.

After 10 hours work Monday, Roy and Grace took Sam and the whole family on an automobile ride. During that hour it was a life of leisure.

Sam's own words...
Friday, June 10, 1925 – "At Eclipse 10 hours. Warmer, no rain for days and everything drying up."

Sam worried about his garden.

Dewey took Sam to Osgood's Sunday to collect what was owed him. Two dollars was all Sam got, and he was still owed $3.75. In the evening of Monday, June 15, it rained. Sam was thankful. The straight line of his mouth turned up at the corners as he stood in the barn door smoking his pipe.

Sam's own words...
Friday, June 19, 1925 – "Eclipse 10 hours. School out today. Our twelfth wedding anniversary."

School had let out for summer vacation. Edith would have her hands full with children to tend along with her regular work.

On Sunday, Edith called Lora Nichols to get the latest news about Willa's health. When the carfare auto brought her back home, Sam was waiting to hear the news. Edith's face was flushed and wide-eyed as she hurried to relate the latest information. Willa would emerge from her cocoon on the last day of June. This was when Lora had captured a photo of Willa in the sling. After 18 months of Willa's confinement, she and her five-year-old daughter would finally hug and reunite. She was one of the lucky ones cured of TB.

Ed Haggarty would move Willa and Lee up to his cabin. Lora had made plans to help Willa by teaching her photography and photo developing. She would leave it to Willa to write home about that after she settled into her father's cabin.

Sam' own words...
Monday, June 22, 1925 – "At Eclipse 10 hours, a dandy rain."

Sam appreciated rain on his garden again Wednesday night and a rainy day Saturday. He helped Edith do work in the house Sunday. Her glow over Willa's renewed health had faded.

Sam's own words...
Monday, June 29, 1925 – "Helped at home. Edith not well. Rainy."

The first week of July was Sam's vacation. Sam worked in his home garden Monday and then down at Grace's to plant potatoes. The children helped. It gave Edith a break and a chance to rest. On Wednesday he worked around the house, planted more spuds, and took David and Betty to buy fireworks. They went to Eldridge Park in Elmira, NY.

Sam's own work...
Thursday, July 2, 1925 – "Set out cabbage and tomato plants. Edith went to the doctor and has dangerous blood pressure: an uncertain world."

Sam's reaction to her high blood pressure was a strong statement that reflected his alarm. She had put off seeing the doctor until Sam was home on a weekday and could watch the children.

All day Friday he worked in his garden and helped Mr. Moss in the hay field. He freshened up and went to Horseheads for groceries. They put up hay in the mow on Saturday.

The children had a big time on the Fourth of July.

On Sunday, Roy drove Sam and the family up to Comfort Hill. Work resumed with 10-hour days and nine on Saturday.

Uncle George arrived for a stay. He and Sam welcomed each other's company and leaned into a relaxed handshake.

Sam's own words...
Monday. July 13, 1925 – "At Eclipse 10 hours. Edith went to see doctor, her blood pressure 20 lower."

Uncle George helped here and there and made it a little easier on Sam and Edith. Sam talked with him about Pennsylvania folks, his garden, and anything else that came to mind. Sam saw that Edith might be better, but it was brief. There may have been more hope than actual evidence.

Sam's own words...
Tuesday, July 21, 1925 – "At Eclipse nine hours, Edith went to get a tooth pulled, but dentist would not pull it because of her bad health."

She must continue to suffer. Sam shook his head as Edith took aspirin to dull the pain. He watched the children while she lay down.

Sam's own words...
Friday, July 31, 1925 – "At Eclipse nine hours. Edith feeling sick. Lynn's folks at Grace's."
Saturday, August 1, 1925 – "Eclipse five hours. Edith no better..."

Lynn and his family visited them for a few minutes Sunday. Edith was much too ill to have company. Sam had his hands full and his worried mind occupied. His company of relatives were kind enough to cut their visits short so he could concentrate on his important care-giving.

Sam's own words...
Monday, August 3, 1925 – "Edith so ill I cannot go to work: Doctor came in p.m. and said go to hospital Monday."
Tuesday, August 4, 1925 – "Went to Elmira and drew my Christmas club early. Paid Edith's insurance. Did housework."
Wednesday, August 5, 1925 – "Done housework and big washing. Mr. and Mrs. Lamb and Buster came out in evening."
Thursday, August 6, 1925 – "Dr. Jones came out. Edith will go to hospital Monday. Went to Horseheads after groceries."

Summer vacation for children and a sick wife gave Sam plenty to do. Worry hadn't taken a holiday. He would not be earning a paycheck. Mr. Lamb, his boss, valued him so much that he had assured Sam he would have a job on hold for him when he could return.

Dr. Jones had set up the admission at the hospital, and Edith was expected there. Sam would be the keeper of the house. His grocery list written in his small Eclipse tablet included sugar, bread, bacon, butter, pancake flour, potatoes, tobacco, and matches. He was a master of pancakes and spuds. The children wouldn't suffer for food and their appetites were in force even when wondering about their mother.

Friday he worked around the house before going after items for Edith's imminent hospital visit. He listed them: a gown, toothpaste, comb and brush, slip, talc, and face cream, all for $5.10. Uncle George must have watched the children.

Sam's own words...
Monday, August 10, 1925 – "They took my Edith to the hospital today; alone with the children and Uncle George."

21 – No Cake Appeal
One continuous round of pleasure: 1925, 1926, 1927

What could Sam possibly care about the Ku Klux Klan march on Washington, DC, of two days ago on August 8? Their popularity of five-million members was lost on him as his mind was squarely on his wife and children. He had sent a payment of $45 to the hospital for Edith's admission. He'd give all he had to make her well again. His full heart, prayers, and hope went with her. Sam remained home to care for their five children.

Sam's own words...
Tuesday, August 11, 1925 – "Took care of children and washed socks. Very lonesome."
Friday, August 14, 1925 – "Done washing. Grace and Mother came up and helped me get dinner and arranged the washing."
Saturday, August 15, 1925 – "Don't know how Edith is although had a letter from her."
Wednesday, August 19, 1925 – "Washed and done housework. Another letter from Edith and she don't know how she is."
Thursday, August 20, 1925 – "...Edith came home in evening. We are very happy again."

Seven-and-a-half-year-old Steele had been sick a few days during his mamma's 10-days in the hospital. He was well when she returned.

Uncle George had gone to Spencer but was back on Friday. He gave Sam $10 and stayed with Edith and the children while Sam hired carfare to Horseheads for groceries and school supplies that cost $7.91.

Sam was almost as excited to once again work in his garden Saturday as he was to have Edith home. She was by no means well. Sam worked in the house Sunday and made sure she rested. He must go back to work, but there was another week of vacation from school for the children. Sam and Edith had difficulty getting through the week.

Sam's own words...
Monday, August 24, 1925 – "Back at the Eclipse again nine hours, have lost eight pounds and seem all tired out."
Monday, September 7, 1925 – "Labor Day. Alice and I did washing. Edith and Grace went to Ithaca in afternoon. David went to Watkins Fair."

Edith was better but not strong enough to do a wash for their large family. Grace's 19-year-old daughter, Alice, was hired for $1.50 to help Uncle Sam do the laundry. Edith rode with Grace to visit her oldest daughter, Ruth, in Ithaca. David had his ride with them to the fair and 65¢ he had saved. They picked him up on the return trip. What a glorious day of freedom for an 11-year-old boy before the start of school the next day. The same relief would come to Sam and Edith to have four children back in school. Sam had less worry if Edith had time to rest. He bought 15¢ crayons for three-and-a-half-year-old Shirley to keep her busy at home.

Uncle George had gone.

Rain had been sufficient for Sam's garden, a sign that God was in his heaven. Sam put in nine-hour days at the Eclipse for another week before a switch to shorter hours.

Sam's own words...
Tuesday, October 6, 1925 – "At the Eclipse eight hours. Shirley taken sick in night."
Thursday, October 8, 1925 – "At Eclipse eight hours. Shirley some better. David sick and Edith about sick."
Friday, October 9, 1925 – "Eclipse eight hours. Shirley better. Snow in evening. Sold our cow as she would not breed."

Saturday, October 10, 1925 – "Betty's birthday. At Eclipse five hours. Only 30 degrees and wind howling. Helped Mr. Hulzier put up stove. Betty not well."

Betty was ten years old, but it was hard for her to care about her birthday when she was ill. Cake held no appeal for most of the family right now. Sam picked apples on Sunday and paid Lyle Hopkins $3 for rent.

Sam's own words...
Tuesday, October 13, 1925 – "At Eclipse eight hours. Sent for underwear for family."
Wednesday, October 14, 1925 – "At Eclipse nine hours."

The thick catalog had been studied, shared, and ordered from by Sam and Edith. Sam's purchase from Montgomery Ward Company amounted to $20.63 plus 36¢ for the money order. His shoe repair was $1.50. All shoes were repaired to get a longer life out of them before replacements must be bought.

Sam's Friday paycheck was $22.50. After his five hours of work on Saturday, he brought groceries home. Soup and candy cost an added 20¢ and a mouse trap 10¢. He had dug potatoes before it was too dark. He used Sunday to help around the house.

The nine-hour work days continued. On Saturday, Sam bought Betty a tablet and pencils for 30¢. Tobacco, candy, butter, Lux soap, milk, and bread added $1.85 for typical family products. After the cow had been sold, the grocery list always had milk written at the top of it.

Sam's own words...
Tuesday, October 27, 1925 – "At Eclipse nine hours. Cold and fair. $1.25 to Edith for doctor and carfare."

The routine doctor care was to try to ward off another emergency but was no guarantee against it. On Wednesday Sam worked 10 hours. The day produced a snow storm. On Saturday, Sam worked his five hours and went to buy size 1½ shoes for Betty ($3). He bought groceries and came home to dig a half bushel of potatoes. In spite of frozen topsoil on Sunday, more potatoes were dug. The cellar was the best place for them out of danger of a deeper freeze.

Election day on Tuesday, November 3, had the Eclipse closed after the first five hours. Sam voted, dug spuds, and cleaned a stovepipe in the afternoon.

Saturday, he dug more tubers. Sunday included housework, andSam gave the youngest of the children a bath and made sure the oldest ones bathed, too. Another week of nine hour days finished.

Sam's own words...
Saturday, November 14, 1925 – "At Eclipse five hours...Mr. Thompson's wife sick."
Sunday, November 15, 1925 – "Finished digging potatoes, about tired out."
Monday, November 16, 1925 – "Eclipse nine hours. Having a hard time to get to and from work."

Mr. Thompson did not work while being needed at home. Sam had to find alternative transportation. Street cars were not convenient. First of all, he had to walk to the stop for pickup and then it did not run at the time he needed. He had the same problem after his nine or 10 hours were done. He managed the week.

Edith was not at all well on Saturday.

Roy took Sam to Comfort Hill on Sunday. Personius and Brown needed a nudge to make their payment.

Uncle George came Tuesday, December 1, in the evening. Every member of the family welcomed him. When Sam got his pay Friday, he joined Christmas club for $2 per week.

Sam's own words...
Saturday, December 19, 1925 – "Eclipse five hours. Done what Xmas shopping I could." (quantity six gifts - 10¢ each for 60¢)
Monday, December 21, 1925 – "Eclipse nine hours. Rainy p.m. Edith went to Elmira."
Friday, December 25, 1925 – "Enjoyed Christmas with the children. We ate dinner with Grace and Roy. Snowed."
Saturday, December 26, 1925 – "Helped around house, went to town in

afternoon. Christmas box from Erick Crippen. Cold, four below zero, two inches of snow."

Sam sent Shores-Mueller $3 and paid L. Hopkins $2 on rent. The year 1925 ended with nine-hour work days on tap.

~**~
1926

New Years Day, Friday, January 1, was spent at home with Edith and the children. Imagine the fun for children to play games like Chinese checkers and work on a jigsaw puzzle. Grace and Mother came for a visit. In the evening, all of them called on their neighbors, the Hulziers.

Sam went after groceries on Saturday. He purchased bread, yeast, butter, four cans of milk, bran, and flour. A number two lamp chimney was 10¢. It would be foolish to go home without the 35¢ jar of Vicks Vaporub. He came out of the Grand Union loaded down and paid 21¢ carfare to take the goods home.

Saturday evening, he and Betty went to the city with Roy and Grace to see a movie. They may have viewed a comedic 67-minute silent film, The Gold Rush, written by its star, Charlie Chaplin. It was about a prospector who goes to the Klondike in search of gold and finds that and more. It was a tremendous excitement and privilege for 10-year-old Betty. She was sure to have worn her best school jumper and blouse. It cost Sam 40¢ for the show tickets.

On Sunday, January 3, Sam helped around the house. It was back to nine-hour days at the Eclipse, on Monday. He paid $1 transport to have a ton of coal brought out on Wednesday. The fuel cost $4. His short five hours work on Saturday gave him time to buy Steele's shoes and rubbers for $3. The 10 inches of snow that fell dictated the usefulness of them. Steele would be sure to prance around in the yard to see how the brand-new tread on the bottom of his over-shoes imprinted his tracks in the snow.

Sam's own words...
Sunday, January 10, 1926 – "Helped around home. Edith not well."

Edith was ill the whole week. She had a toothache and earache. Sam had his hands full at home and the factory. On January 20, they gathered around the table on which Shirley's birthday cake and candles sat. After they had sung the celebration song to her, she blew out all of the candles. She told no one what her wish was, for then it would not come true, she believed. All four-year-olds understood that. Were the 15¢ crayons and a new tablet what the budding artist had dreamed of receiving?

Uncle George had been in residence almost two months by this time. Sam would surely miss him as he went away to Pennsylvania.

Snow storms took over for the first week of February. Fourteen inches of white flakes kept children out of school. Sam got his eight hours a day at work, but he worried about Edith. She'd have no chance to rest as she would if four children were in school.

Sam's own words...
Saturday, February 6, 1926 – "Edith not well. At Eclipse five hours, saw lawyer Bentley about settling Father's estate."
Sunday, February 7, 1926 – "Helped around house. Wrote to heirs regarding Father's estate."

More snow, cold, and wind kept children from school on Wednesday. Lincoln's birthday meant Friday off for the children and Sam. He helped accomplish an overdue wash and went after groceries. Butter and oleo were both on Edith's list.

In the United States, laws passed as early as 1877 to put restrictions on the sale and labeling of oleomargarine. States required labeling and color bans in New York and New Jersey, both dairy states. At the start of the 20th century, 80% of Americans could not buy colored margarine, and a hefty tax was levied on it at the point of sale. Colored margarine was bootlegged. Also, manufacturers began to supply colored capsules so consumers could knead the yellow color into the packet. Restrictions in 1902 on colored margarine reduced consumption in the U.S. from 120 million pounds to 48 million. A dozen years later it became more popular than ever.

World War I resulted in an increase in margarine consumption, as dairy products became scarce. Margarine and dairy lobbies went on. The depression in the U.S. brought more pro-butter regulations. The definition of margarine came from the legal definition of butter as both contained water and a minimum fat content of 80%. It was adopted by all the primary producers and became the industry standard. Beef fat was the principle raw material for margarine. When the beef fat became harder to obtain, vegetable hydrogenation developed. Between 1900 and 1920 oleo was produced from a combination of animal fat and vegetable oils.

Sam's own words...
Sunday, February 14, 1926 – "Helped Edith, went down to see Dewey and Roy. Snow and rain in p.m."
Monday, February 15, 1926 – "At Eclipse eight hours. We signed quit claim deed to Roy and Grace, so they could transfer farm to buyer and settle Father's estate."

Sam was gratified to have Father's New York state business finalized with all parties in close enough agreement.

David came walking in with a grin. The two rabbits he shot would make a meal. The fatter bunnies in the barn cage consumed food that cost 50¢ every time they purchased it. They would be good eating, too, because they were sedentary and bigger.

After five hours at the factory Saturday, Sam went after shoes for John and paid $2. He bought the Literary Digest and Castor oil for 10¢ each.

Snow, ice, and thawing ushered in Sam's 43rd birthday during the week of March 3. He didn't give it special notice as he was too busy working long days. After his short day, Saturday, he went to the junction for a box of dishes Erick had sent them. Erick made a generous gesture and had enclosed $4 in the box.

Sam helped around home on Sunday. He was aware that the next three weeks required longer days at the Eclipse.

Sam's own words...
Thursday, March 11, 1926 – "At Eclipse 10 hours. A letter for me from Willa, which was deeply appreciated."

~**~

Dear Daddy,   March 3, 1926

This being your birthday and I having nothing to send you, I thot (sic) that I would at least tell you that I thot (sic) of you and hand you a few bouquets. Of course, it seems to be usual to wait until the other fellow is dead or otherwise out of reach or hearing before passing out any such remarks but in this case you are going to get "the dad-burned bloom" now. So bruce (sic) up and take it like a little man.

I'm sure I've never told you how much I appreciate how kind and good you always were to me when I was at home, how loving and patient when, I now realize, I was a trying proposition. Nor have I ever said that I love you very much; quite as much as an "own" and a good deal more than some "owns." I never thot (sic) much about it when I was home. I suppose one doesn't. But I've often thot (sic) since about it, and I've always felt your home to be as much mine as if I were your own child. Without your love and kindness this would not be so.

You have helped me much in many ways, often when you were far away. Things I have heard you say, paying little heed at the time, have come back to me at a time when they would help me most. And when one sees so many dishonest, spineless, smirking sheiks all around it is good to know that there are at least a few men like you, honorable, good and true. Without a few men of your caliber, men who have a little principle and rear their children with a few ideals, this country would soon follow ancient Rome.

I hope that isn't too much sugar for one helping, but I truly mean it every word. And by way of a flattering touch to top off, the man I hope someday to marry reminds me very much of you in many ways.

With much love from your eldest daughter,   Billie

~**~

Deep pride was sure to have stirred in Edith's breast when Sam shared Willa's typewritten letter with her. They had not seen her in two years and six months from the time she last left Horseheads.

Friday, March 11, marked an important expenditure for Willa and

Lee's birthday presents to send west. Sam did not name what they spent $3 on. Edith's rubbers were size six, envelopes 23¢, and five combs 50¢.

Eight-year-old Steele was sick a short while on Sunday.

Sam's own words...
Wednesday, March 17, 1926 – "...Clear, cold wind. Grace informed us that they sold the farm."

Warmer temperatures brought a lot of thawing. The water-covered flats kept the children out of school several days while it rained.

On Saturday, Sam listed the Comfort Hill Farm for sale. There would be no more rent from Personius and Brown. He took his three boys for haircuts (90¢). Edith's hat and milk were $3.

David turned 12 on Wednesday, March 31. Snow squalls, rain, and the wind escorted the last week of March on its way. April did as April does to bring a mix of weather, a lot of it wet.

Sam was sick-abed the first week of May and unable to work. He went back to the Eclipse, May 7, but not in the best of health.

Sam's own words...
Sunday, May 9, 1926 - "Busy around home all day. Don't feel well. Mother and Grace came out. Cold, windy."

The only diary entries for two weeks were his records of nine-hour work days.

Sam's own words...
Sunday, May 23, 1926 – "Helped around home. Lame again. Cold for this time of year."
Monday, May 24, 1926 – "At Eclipse nine hours, cold. Edith sick and I'm near it."
Tuesday, May 25, 1926 – "Edith sick and my back and legs so lame couldn't go to work. Windy."
Friday, May 28, 1926 – "I guess we are improving, but there is plenty of room yet."

What an awful time they had with aches and pains. Sam plowed his garden on Thursday, June 3, and was back to work on June 4. He recorded a frost Friday. After five hours worked Saturday, a trip was made to pack out his groceries, carrying them home. He planted a portion of his garden on Sunday.

There had been hope to show the Comfort Hill property, but it was as if no one knew about it. At the finish of 10 hours work on Monday, Sam stopped by Dix and Treat to cancel the listing. They'd found him no prospects. For a man usually possessed of an enormous amount of patience, he had none for them.

Sam's own words...
Friday, June 11, 1926- "Eclipse 10 hours. Cool and dry. Edith hurt her right hand."
Saturday, June 12, 1926 – "Eclipse five hours, done housework. Father died four years ago today."
Sunday, June 13, 1926 – "Planted corn and cucumbers. Done housework. Edith's hand quite bad."

Sam pushed himself to make up for lost time on a late garden. Now would have been the best time for eight-hour days but they amounted to 10 every day. The Eclipse tried to stay even on production even though a few employee's vacations had started. Sam's turn would come. Betty's stockings were 49¢, liver 17¢, while 14¢ bought tobacco and turnips on Monday.

The garden was hoed. On Sunday, July 4. Edith and Grace went to Comfort Hill. Carl Withune ate dinner with them. The Independence Day holiday celebration stretched out for a week when Sadie stayed at Grace's the whole time. Mother and Mary came out on Saturday, July 17. They all found Sam's garden well kept, no weeds in sight.

Sam's own words...
Sunday, July 18, 1926 – "Roy took us down to Comfort Hill after cherries; rain and hail did lots of damage. Set out plants."

Nine-and 10-hour days became sandwiched between weekends spent to plant and hoe in his garden. On the last day of July, Sam cashed in his Christmas club and paid Edith's life insurance. He sent for a mop at $1.25 from the Delphos Mop Company. The money order was 4¢.

Mr. and Mrs. Withune came for a visit. The Crippens received their neighbors as warmly as friends can. Coffee or tea was sure to have been served.

Edith had her hair bobbed in early August. It was a fresh, young look and if it gave her a lift, Sam was all for it. Sam tried something out of the ordinary, too; the cigarettes cost him 15¢.

His next five weeks contained 10-hour work days right into September. During that time, Edith went to see Stella Dallas for 70¢, about a small town girl who is devastated by her father's death and quickly marries the upper-class Stephen Dallas, with whom she has nothing in common. The 110 minute silent, black-and-white film had printed information interspersed to tell the story as it unfolded. The film short is now available on YouTube.

The children sold two pups at $5 each. Proceeds were used to buy school supplies, which amounted to quite an expense for five children. Sam helped Mr. Hulzier cut wood.

John's materials were needed at the start of school classes.

1. The Winston Third Reader
2. Human Geography by J. Russell Smith, book one
3. Pen, Ink, and Crayolas

The list totaled $1.63, and he still needed a tablet. The pup sales saved the day for school materials. Five tablets were 50¢, enough to go around for all of them.

David's shoes were $1.69, Steele's $1, and Edith's shoe repair 70¢.

Sam's own words...
Sunday, September 12, 1926 – "Trimmed squash vines. Killed bed bugs, one continuous round of pleasure."
Sunday, September 19, 1926 – "Helped around house. Went with Roy after peaches. Warm."

Sunday was spent debugging children's hair and bedding of bug interlopers. The next Sunday was Sam's preferred job. The $2 bushel of peaches was canned, and the reward was peach pie after the labor. The savory aroma created anticipation of the palette pleaser.

The weather was predictably cooler at the beginning of October. Sam fixed the wheel barrow, picked grapes, and cleaned house. He recorded a frost on October 10.

One of Sam's greater pleasures in life was to see one or all of his siblings. Lynn and Iva came for a visit on Sunday, October 17. Lynn was a mild-mannered man, closest in temperament to Sam. They understood each other better than either of them had ever been able to predict Dewey's responses to anything. Sam had discovered that long ago with Roy Whiting when it came to Pa's New York state affairs.

On Sam's half day of work, Saturday, October 23, he harvested beets and rutabagas and put them in the cellar. His potatoes had been planted at Grace's when he planted for both of them. He went after a few of them and had a good visit with her. On Sunday he carried water for the wash and helped Edith.

Eclipse work was back to eight-hour days.

Sam's own words...
Thursday, October 28, 1926 – "...Nineteen years ago today, I went west. Fair and cool."

He had fond memories of most aspects of his westward years. He'd followed a dream and had no regrets. He'd met Edith. He'd loved her then and loved her even more now.

Back to the present, Sam had apples and nuts to gather. His two littlest boys helped and received 10¢ each. David had regular work around the place and earned a quarter every week. It was time to bank up the house, and he'd help with that.

Sam visited Mother at Grace's once a week or so. Sunday was a good day for it this week.

Sam's own words...
Tuesday, November 16, 1926 – "At Eclipse eight hours, rain all day, water over our road."
Wednesday, November 17, 1926 – "At Eclipse? NO. Shut off from work and town by water. Bridge out. Fair."

Thursday, November 18, 1926 – "Managed to get to work. Rain again this evening. Steele broke his arm."

Sam neglected detail on how Steele's arm broke. Consider that Steele had big brothers who he regularly tried to copy. There were lots of trees that an eight-year-old boy could climb and from which to fall. It snow squalled a few times up through Sunday when Steele was still doing well. Edith took him to the doctor on Monday, November 22. Dr. Jones was paid $1 for his work. Edith bought Senna Laxative 10¢ and five more school tablets 50¢.

On Sam's way home from work, he bought tobacco, 15¢, and a pipe elbow for 35¢. He mainly recorded eight hours of work at the Eclipse weekdays.

Sam's own words...
Sunday, December 5, 1926 – "Cold wind and blizzard, one foot of snow. Worked around home."
Sunday, December 12, 1926 – "Went with Lewis Carroll & Sons to look at Comfort Hill Farm..."
Sunday, December 19, 1926 – "Helped around house. Cleaned outhouse. Two below zero for we have a thermometer."

Steele's arm healed well. Comfort Hill failed to sell. The Eclipse continued eight-hour days, and December grew colder. A Christmas package for the family arrived from Willa on December 22. It stirred up the children's excitement so close to the magic day. Sam spent 90¢ for Christmas presents and 10¢ for his next year's diary. Dot Dilmore brought toys on December 24. Her benevolent group of women bestowed generosity in different forms throughout the season.

The sitting room was a scene of fun on Christmas morning. Sounds of playing and pretend announced the children's delight in cars, trucks, and dolls. Sam enjoyed his 3¢ newspaper and smoked Prince Albert over their sounds.

He went down to Grace's on Sunday, the day after Christmas, for a visit. He got a stove pipe from her. The year finished as eight-hour work days continued cold and snowy.

~**~
1927

New Year's Day was as good a day for housework and laundry as any. Wind and snow freeze-dried the clothes on the line in no time.

David was 12¾ years old, going on 13 when he told it, and had gained favor from his parents to attend a movie alone in Elmira. He had saved the money for the streetcar and the theater. He might have enjoyed Underworld, a silent film approximately 81 minutes long. When Bull Weed, a gangster on the lam, joined up with Rolls Royce, a well-educated drifter. Royce quickly became the brains behind Bull's gang. But this development left Bull feeling insecure and mistrustful of his new comrade.

The housework and laundry carried over to January 2. All was spit and polish to start the new year. Sam went after groceries at the Victory store toward evening.

The Eclipse opened January 3 with eight-hour days. He increased his Christmas club deposits from $2 to $2.50 each paycheck. The carfare was $1 for two weeks. E. Miles gave him a ride in the morning, and Jess Rose returned him home in the evening. They stopped on the way home, and Sam got a haircut and tobacco for $1. His pipe habit cost him about 15¢ a week. He'd had a good start to the new year.

David went to Pine Valley to join Boy Scouts.

Sam's own words...
Saturday, January 8, 1927 – "Went to Elmira to see Mr. Salmon about Comfort Hill farm. Carl brought out coal. Cold."

Sam needed to sell the farm. He could not make the payment in addition to paying Lyle Hopkins for the rent. One or the other had to end. The coal was $4.

On Wednesday, January 12, the two little boys went to a Pine Valley Boy Scout meeting. Most likely, they rode with another boy's parent.

The weather turned cold and windy. David developed a cold first then passed it down to Betty and Edith. The temperature dipped to zero for the two days that David and Betty were out of school.

Sam's own words...
Sunday, January 16, 1927 – "Worked around house all day. Edith sick with cold. Balance due Hopkins $37."

He must have shaken his head as he made the payment for Comfort Hill and none to Hopkins. It would help on a small level that nine-hour work days were needed again. Tuesday, after work, he bought garters for Shirley's cotton stockings and a 10¢ tablet for Betty.

A week of worry over Edith wore Sam down, too. She did not improve until the next Sunday. Sam did housework and the wash. Soft snow fell, and the creek rose higher. Ten-hour days commenced on Wednesday as a blizzard whipped.

Sam's own words...
Thursday, January 27, 1927 – "At Eclipse 10 hours, 14 below zero a.m. John has chicken pox. Children can't go to school now."

Just as Edith was well, Sam worried that more work was at hand for her with sick children. By Saturday, it turned warmer. After five hours work, Sam went to get Betty's black and white oxfords for $2.20

On Thursday, February 3, Steele was sick and broke out in chickenpox. The telltale rash broke out in raised red bumps all over his body for several days. He had a fever, and his appetite was gone. By Sunday, Betty broke out, too. David was all right on Monday when he went to a show with Edith in the evening. On Tuesday he and Shirley had rashes. Little sister took it mildly, but David had them hard and long. His headache and tiredness hung on. It was February 12 when Sam conceded that they were all better. Mother Crippen came out to see them.

Sam appreciated poems of bravery that spoke to him in a personal way. He found one now and copied two of the four stanzas into his diary.

Invictus
by William Ernest Henley

In the fell clutch of circumstance
I have not winced nor cried aloud.
Under the bludgeoning of chance
My head is bloody but unbowed.

Beyond this place of wrath and tears
Looms but the Horror of the shade,
And yet the menace of the years
Finds, and shall find me, unafraid.

Sam's own words...
Sunday, February 13, 1927 - "Worked around house. Went to see Harold Dillmore about buying Comfort Hill farm. Snow in a.m."

Mr. Dillmore wanted to purchase the farm but had no money to start a transaction. He planned to work on it.

The weather started to thaw and resulted in six days of snow melt off, rain, and sleet. Thunder and lightning and the wind finished the trend.

Sam's own words...
Sunday, February 20, 1927 – "Helped around home. Erick came in a.m. Two feet of snow fell."

They had a fine afternoon to get caught up in time gone by since they had last seen Edith's brother. It was to be a short visit. Sam worked his 10-hour shifts, and Erick went home to Ohio Tuesday night.

The two feet of snow began to melt, and the children were home because of high water danger. It was an opportunity for them to enjoy a box that had arrived from Uncle Arthur. Most likely, he sent fruit and toys.

The children were home-bound six days because of the flooded land. They all had colds but were back in school March 2.

Mother and Grace came for dinner Sunday. They had read about the U.S. Radio Commission that had begun to regulate the use of radio frequencies. Not one of them had heard a radio yet but they hoped they would soon.

Sam's own words...
Thursday, March 10, 1927 –"At Eclipse nine hours. Edith not very well."
Wednesday, March 16, 1927 – "Eclipse nine hours. Moderate, fair. Edith's birthday. Betty made a cake."

It was Edith's 48th year. Eleven-year-old Betty tied one of her mother's bib aprons over her dress. She smiled as she stirred, baked, and iced the special cake for her mother. Grace and Mother came out Thursday. Wednesday, March 21, brought the sorry story again of water over the road. The children were kept from school for a few days yet again.

Ten-hour work days started at the Eclipse.

On Sunday, April 3, David and Edith went down to Grace's for an evening visit.

Sam's own words...
Saturday, April 9, 1927 – "At Eclipse five hours. Went to Elmira to see Mr. Salmon about farm. Fair and moderate."
Sunday, April 10, 1927 – "Went to see Harold Dillmore regarding our farm. Helped around home. Cold wind."
Monday, April 18, 1927 – "At Eclipse nine hours. Warm and fair. Grace, Mother, Mrs. Gould, Edith and children had picnic in the woods."

It had been a light-hearted day as carefree as they come. But the weather was fickle. It turned cold to spew out snow as often as rain for the following three weeks.

On May 7, after short Saturday work hours, Sam went to Elmira and paid $9.50 on a note at the Second National Bank. It was cold and cloudy on Sunday when he planted peas and lettuce. The next Sunday he planted beets and chard on a sunny day, which was the first one in a week without rain.

Sam's own words...
Saturday, May 21, 1927 – "At Eclipse six and one-half hours. Fair and sunshine. Captain Charles Lindbergh flies from NY to Paris in a single-engine monoplane, The Spirit of St. Louis."
Sunday, May 22, 1927 – "Fixed garage for chickens, cleaned out stovepipe. Grace and Mother ate dinner with us. Warm."

The Lindbergh solo flight, which won a $25,000 prize, was no doubt a topic of conversation in their gathering. But it had not escaped notice that Bell Telephone had transmitted an image of Herbert Hoover, then Secretary of Commerce, which a month ago had become the first long-distance demonstration of television. They may all have agreed that there was something in the air, signals and flying machines.

The next day they would read that about 600 members of the American Institute of Electrical Engineers and the Institute of Radio Engineers viewed a live demonstration of television at the Bell Telephone building in New York City.

A couple of days later, Sam had unwanted signals of his own. His road and the flats were covered with water. Rain fell off and on for three days. He worked his nine-hour day.

Sam's own words...
Saturday, May 28, 1927 – "Went after groceries and garden seeds, shoes, etc. for children. Worked in garden. Edith not feeling well."

Sam worked just as hard Sunday as the day before. On Monday, he stayed at home to watch over his Edith. After housework, he planted lima beans, carrots, and corn. Lynn arrived and ate dinner with them but stayed at Grace's. Bill Tuck and his family arrived at Grace's. After nine hours of work Monday, Sam went over to visit with all of the Pennsylvania folks.

Sam's own words...
Friday, June 3, 1927 – "At Eclipse nine hours. Cool and fair. Dewey's birthday (29 years old). David and Betty went to a weenie roast at Everetts."
Sunday, June 5, 1927 – "Grace, Mother, Frank, and Mary were out. They want me to take Galeton farm. Rain nearly all day. Busy inside and out."

Before consideration of it, a visit was needed. A week later, on Saturday, June 11, Sam went over to Galeton to see it and to talk to Mr. Duboise in Coudersport regarding Pa's Pennsylvania farm. He got home at 11:20 p.m.

Life settled back into nine-hour work days and garden planting. There was a school picnic, and the children began summer vacation, on Friday, June 17. Sam's mind was full. He ruminated on the Galeton farm but not on his diary pages. In reality, he had to be aware that he had too much debt already and that it would be hard to leave the Eclipse job. Wasn't it too far to commute?

Sam's own words...
Friday, July 1, 1927 – "Went to Comfort Hill farm with Henry Hartman."

Saturday, July 2, 1927 – "Edith and Grace went to Comfort Hill after strawberries…"

Sam's own vacation was here. He hired a man to plow down at Grace's where both of them would grow potatoes. He planted a few rows and finished several more rows before the next Sunday was over. His garden was hoed, and he was ready to resume nine-hour work days.

Sam's own words…
Saturday, July 23, 1927 – "Went to Elmira and drew out Christmas Club and paid Edith's life insurance. Edith, Betty, David, and Grace spending night at Comfort Hill."
Sunday, July 24, 1927 – "Looked after three younger children and kept house. Edith and children came home in evening. Showers all day."
Friday, July 29, 1927 – "Hoed potatoes, helped around home. A young man, crippled, staying in our barn tonight. Rain."
Tuesday, August 2, 1927 – "At Eclipse eight hours. Cold, partly cloudy. Peter Vanos, the cripple, still with us, don't know what to do with him."
Wednesday, August 3, 1927 – "Eclipse eight hours. Peter expects someone to send him money, but it doesn't come."
Thursday, August 4, 1927 – "At Eclipse eight hours. Peter still here."

Suddenly, Peter vanished. Sam was glad he'd had a dry place to sleep while he was there, but it was time he moved on, and it had been made easier for Sam without the need of a discussion to suggest that he go on his way.

Sam started nine hour-work days again.

On Saturday, August 6, he went to Elmira to see Mr. Salmon and Mr. Swisher about the Comfort Hill farm. He hoed potatoes in the warm afternoon, often wiping his perspiring brow with his handkerchief.

Grace and Mother came for dinner on Sunday. Sam worked in the garden. He did his deepest thinking while he hoed.

Later he read that the Peace Bridge had opened between Fort Erie, Ontario, and Buffalo, New York.

Sam's own words…
Monday, August 8, 1927 – "John hit by automobile and taken to hospital: Oh! We are worried. God knows best. Rain."

They must wait to know how or if John would survive. Sam's only comfort was to turn it over to the God he trusted. He remembered when John was born in Idaho and given up by the doctor but held by Sam and his God, who did not let go. Had he brought him along 10½ years only to claim him now?

Sam's own words...
Tuesday, August 9, 1927 – "John seems to be coming alright (sic). Bless his heart and all that is good. At Eclipse eight hours. Cool."
Thursday, August 11, 1927 – "John coming fine. Mr. Chapman brought him a box of candy. Eclipse eight hours."
Friday, August 12, 1927 – "All went to hospital to see John in evening. Eclipse eight hours."
Saturday, August 13, 1927 – "Went to Elmira to see Mr. Salmon and Mr. Swisher about Comfort Hill farm. Hoed potatoes."

It had been a week since the car had hit John. Frank and Mary came Sunday and took the whole family to the hospital to see him; he was doing well. Sam went again Monday after work to see his son. It was cool like fall. John reported that he would be able to go home Wednesday. They were all thankful they'd have him back.

Sam's own words...
Saturday, August 20, 1927 – "Worked in garden. Edith, Grace and Roy went to show in evening. Cool and cloudy."

Wings, the only silent film to win an Oscar for best picture starring Clara Bow, Charles Buddy Rogers, Richard Arlen, and Gary Cooper, opened August 12 and was said to be excellent. It was an American silent war film set during the First World War, produced by Lucien Hubbard.

Sam's own words...
Sunday, August 28, 1927 – "Busy around home. Edith, Grace and children went to Eldridge Park. Rain in evening."

The amusement park outing was the children's last fling of summer freedom before school started. A picnic basket had been packed for the occasion. The magical music of the merry-go-round played as the horses revolved in a circle, up and down, up and down. The carousel would soon close for the winter with last rides remembered until the next summer season. Sam remembered when it was installed at Eldridge Park in 1924. The history was that a pharmacist, Dr. Edwin Eldridge, purchased the park land and built a sculpture garden. The city of Elmira later bought the land in 1889, after Eldridge died.

New socks and stockings were purchased for all of the children. Betty and Shirley admired their black stockings. Shirley may have been happiest of all of the children to wear them like the big kids, for she was going to start school. New pencils and tablets were furnished all around, highly approved by their little artist.

The five children were in school on Tuesday, September 6.

It seemed like forever that Sam sent between $1 and $3 every week to Shores-Mueller for orders duly noted in his book. This week it was $2. It added a bit to his bottom line, a small bit.

Sam's own words...
Saturday, September 10, 1927 – "Went to Horseheads for groceries. Warm, partly cloudy. Opened airport at Elmira."

The airport was big news. Sam and Grace had anticipated it since the construction had started. They were sure to have mentioned it among themselves when she stopped in for a visit on Sunday.

Sam worked at the Eclipse eight-hour days. Saturday, September 17, he went after groceries, did housework, and helped Mr. Hulzier on his well. Edith, Grace, and Roy went after peaches. Sam helped to can them Sunday afternoon.

Sunday was the same day they read that the Columbia Phonographic Broadcasting System (better known as CBS) went on the air with 47 radio stations. A radio was still out of reach for the Crippens. They might have longed to have one.

Thursday, September 22, was partly cloudy after the early frost.

On October 1, Sam went after dry goods, $2.47, also a Scholar's Companion, 25¢, and 39¢ for Laxative Links and tobacco.

Sam's own words...
Tuesday, October 4, 1927 "At Eclipse nine hours. Mr. Judson brought out 2,815# of coal."

Thursday, October 6, 1927 – "Eclipse nine hours. Edith sick: Betty stayed out of school..."
Monday, October 10, 1927 – "At Eclipse eight hours. Cool and frost. Can hardly believe Betty is 12 years old today."

Sam read that the actual carving had started last Tuesday on Mt. Rushmore in South Dakota's Black Hills National Forest, the site of a proposed massive four-head sculpture. Back in August, President Calvin Coolidge had allocated national funds for the presidential figures depicting the faces of U.S. presidents George Washington, Thomas Jefferson, Abraham Lincoln, and Theodore Roosevelt. Work was led by the sculptor Gutzon Borglum. Sam nor anyone else yet knew that the work on the project would take 14 years to its completion in 1941.

Sam might have called it to Edith's attention that the movie, The Jazz Singer, had opened in the United States to an enormous success. It had the actual music as sound! Silent films continued to be made for a long time.

Sam's own words...
Friday, October 14, 1927 – "At Eclipse nine hours. Cool and partly cloudy. David and Betty went to Pine Valley to a pie social and meeting."
Saturday, October 15, 1927 – "Went after groceries. Made apple bin. Helped in house. David went to church meeting. Cool and fair."

David was 13½ years of age. Sam may have recalled taking part in the same church activity from that age. He smoked his pipe and reminisced about how he had enjoyed friends at church and socials. But nostalgia gave way. A new line of goods arrived for Sam to try to sell, and he needed to plan a strategy.

Sam's own words...
Sunday, October 16, 1927 – "Payed (sic) J.J. Spargo a visit in regards to selling wall batts. Cool and cloudy."

J.J. Spargo did not buy the wall batts from Sam. Sam sold him a cloth coat, product #2217 for $14.95. His commission was $4, a sum he was pleased to report to Edith when he returned.

In the earlier part of the twentieth century, some insulation materials utilized on the inside of ice houses were horse hair and cork. Owens Corning developed the first fiber glass batt insulation no earlier than 1938.

The children stayed home from school on Monday since rain fell all night and the water level was up. Sam worked nine hours while it rained all day. He managed to get home, but water covered the road for several days. It canceled his ability to get to work and for children's school.

Sam's own words...
Tuesday, October 25, 1927 – "At Eclipse eight hours. Fair and moderate. Edith feeling bad."
Wednesday, October 26, 1927 – "Tried to sell Kleen Kwick table clothes. Sold two."
Thursday, October 27, 1927 – "Eclipse eight hours. Warm. Edith not feeling well yet."

His commission was $1.10 each on the wipe off table clothes. Sam hoped they would be a quick seller. On Saturday, Sam went after groceries and talked to Roy and Dewey about the Galeton farm. He was neither in a position to buy it nor to move to Pennsylvania. It would have to be sold elsewhere to settle Father's Pennsy estate. Sam may have been relieved to tell them.

Sam's own words...
Sunday, October 30, 1927 – "...David and Betty were baptized. Bless their hearts."
Friday, November 4, 1927 – "At Eclipse eight hours. First snow. Rain water over our road again. Children out of school."
Friday, November 11, 1927 - "...Went to Elmira after dry goods and saw "Ben Hur" played. Edith went with Grace and Roy in evening."

The tickets for him and Edith were $1.35. Sam and Edith often economized by eating liver. The tab for milk, newspaper, liver, and chicken feed was 45¢. Hamburger was 45¢, the reason they didn't have it much. The struggle to stretch a dollar was a way of life. Betty disliked liver.

Sam paid $3 to Lyle Hopkins for rent.

Sam's Own words...
Sunday, November 13, 1927 – "Busy around home. Sent farm ad to advertise – ask $1,850 - $150 down. Cool."

Thursday, November 17, 1927 – "At Eclipse eight hours. Rain all day. Children out of school again."

The water was over the road. Sam could pull his hair out. What he called a lake lay between their house and the main road to Horseheads. It lasted through Friday. He paid his $3 for rent on Saturday and talked to Lyle Hopkins about the water. He most likely said they would move when it was possible. His dissatisfaction had been registered.

Sam saw action from the ad he placed. He went twice to Comfort Hill Farm. He showed it to W. Gould and Mr. Monroe.

Sam's own words...
Thursday, November 24, 1927 – "Ate dinner with Grace, went to city to see Mr. Monroe about buying farm. Rainy."
Saturday, November 26, 1927 – "Saw Mr. Monroe, made appointment to close deal on Friday, December 2."

On his way home, Sam took a deep breath. What a relief. The sale of the farm was almost in sight. Eclipse work continued at eight hours a day. Two boxes arrived from Arthur as November ended. The packages were as joyous an event for the children as the pending farm sale for Sam. All of the children caught colds. School was missed and absence extended with torrents of water flow that isolated them at home.

On Tuesday, December 6, David caught his first muskrat. If he skinned it right, he'd have top money for the pelt.

When snow fell, the children were in the mood to go shopping with allowance money they had saved. Betty, Steele, and John went after Christmas presents.

Sam's own words...
Saturday, December 10, 1927 – "Eclipse five hours. Went to Elmira after boys caps and sold a slicker. Cold. Betty has an earache."

The three caps cost $1.18. Sam took in $1 commission on the slicker sale. He gave $3 to Lyle Hopkins for the rent. Two pounds of sausage cost him 45¢ and tobacco 12¢. Oysters were a costly 75¢ and cold medicine 50¢.

Water over the road again put children out of school two days. It had Sam unsettled along with another problem.

Sam's own words...
Saturday, December 17, 1927 – "Went to Elmira to see lawyer C. A. Phillips and Burge Monroe. Cold. Water over road, got a load of coal."

Burge Monroe expected to have the money any day now for the Comfort Hill farm. Hadn't Sam heard the same thing before?

He started nine-hour days at the Eclipse on Monday, December 19. The children were back in school, and Grace and Edith shopped in Elmira.

David and Betty went to Pine Valley to a prayer meeting Thursday evening. On Saturday, December 24, Sam went and spent 90¢ on Christmas presents, tobacco for 15¢, shoestrings 15¢, and safety pins 10¢. He stopped to talk with Mr. Monroe. There was no money yet.

Grace ate Christmas dinner with Sam and his family.

Sam's own words...
Tuesday, December 27, 1927 –"At Eclipse eight hours. Took Mr. C.P. Rennells measure for a pair of pants."
Saturday, December 31, 1927 – "Went to see Burge Monroe about farm sale; had not sold his hogs yet. Warm, rainy."

The outlook for the New Year was a letdown. Sam had to doubt the sale by now. Was it about to happen or not?

22 – Dewey
Disbelief, 1928, 1929, 1930

Sam was busy around home New Year's Day. He did take the time to go down to Mr. Treats after a half bushel of potatoes. The children made fudge and popcorn and enjoyed their time at home.

Sam's own words...
Monday, January 2, 1928 – "Killed and helped dress 18 chickens. Mother and Grace came out. Quite cold."
Tuesday, January 3, 1928 – "At Eclipse eight hours. Children received Xmas package from Willa."

Sam and Edith were a team while they dressed chickens. The Victory Store was poised to purchase the dressed poultry meat at $2 per bird for resale to their customers. The money would not be extra for Sam. The $36 was designated to help pay the Comfort Hill Farm payment. Sam needed the sale and would soon give up on Burge Monroe to raise the purchase money.

Sam's own words...
Thursday, January 12, 1928 – "Eclipse nine hours...Willa's baby, Edith Christine Jensen born."

Sam had failed to say Willa Girl was married again, but he was terribly busy. She had written to Sam and Edith from New Mexico where her little girl, named Christine Jensen, was born at the home of James Jensen's sister.

Sam's own words...
Thursday, January 19, 1928 – "At Eclipse 10 hours. Snow and rain in p.m. Edith had a letter from Rollo."

Rollo, of Nebraska, who was 47 years old, was younger brother to Edith by three years. He had written to inform her that their brother, Erick, was gravely ill. Sam was helpless as he watched sudden distress cloud Edith's expression.

Work days were 10 hours long for Sam right on through February. On Thursday, February 9, he made a sale of a suit to Philip Denunzio. He measured his customer and took a down payment to send the order. His commission was $3.50.

Sam went each week to see Mother and Grace while the spring season came closer. On his way home, he checked once again with Mr. Monroe about the purchase of the Comfort Hill farm.

Sam's own words...
Wednesday, February 29, 1928 – "At home in a.m. Went to see C. A. Phillips about transfer of farm to Federal Land Bank."
Friday, March 16, 1928 – "At Eclipse 10 hours. Letter saying Erick can live few days."

It had been only two months since Rollo had informed them of Erick's irreversible illness. Sam and Edith had written together of how sorry they were. It was hopeless to try to express the real sadness that he Edith had toward Erick's certain death.

Sam paid Mother a visit before she left for Pennsylvania on Sunday, March 18, to stay with Mary awhile. Ten inches of snow fell.

Bad news came to everyone who lived in or near Horseheads or Millport.

Sam's own words...
Monday, March 19, 1928 – "At Eclipse 10 hours. Moderate. Keeping children out of school because of scarlet fever at Millport."

Tuesday. March 20, 1928 – "Eclipse 10 hours. Windy. Three dead in Laura Danks Crandall's home, scarlet fever."
Wednesday, March 21, 1928 – "At Eclipse 10 hours. Warmer. Grace and Roy moved to Elmira."

The children were out of school eight days because of the scarlet fever scare, but Sam continued his 10-hour work days.

Edith was sick again at the end of March. Sam had his problems to juggle between his job, his children, and his ill wife. The children had fewer concerns and were busy hiding eggs before Easter, a few days away. Eggs were 50¢ a dozen.

Sam's own words...
Thursday, April 5, 1928 – "At Eclipse 10 hours. Fair, Warm. Grace came out to visit. Dewey marriage today."

Dewey, who would be 30 years old in another month, had married Emma Mildred Smith, about 14 years older than he was. Could that have raised eyebrows? He was to become stepfather to her daughter, Marcella, and her son, Elsworth Smith. Would Dewey's stern side surface?

The estate affairs of Lac Crippen needed to be handled in Pennsylvania since Sam had shown no interest to own it. Dewey was anxious to have Sam sign executorship over to him. He would take on the farm sale and dispensation to heirs. The Galeton land had been Dewey's stomping grounds, although he and his bride would reside in Elmira.

Sam's family and job remained his priorities. Horseheads was the place for him.

Sam's own words...
Tuesday, April 10, 1928 – "Eclipse 10 hours. Cool. Erick died 1:15 a.m. Edith sick."
Wednesday, April 11, 1928 – "Eclipse 10 hours. Edith quite sick. I have my heart and hands full."
Thursday, April 12, 1928 – "At Eclipse 10 hours...Edith about the same."

Erick's death brought Sam's memories back to his brother Ralph's death. Edith was likely as sick at heart as in body. She received all the tenderness Sam possessed when he was not at work.

Deaths will always occur, but the saying is that birth is God's opinion that the world should continue. Sam's sister, Sadie birthed a girl, Marie Alta, on Monday, April 16.

Sam's own words...
Sunday, April 22, 1928 "Did housework. Edith not well. Rainy."
Tuesday, April 24, 1928 – "At Eclipse nine hours. Dewey and Mildred came out in evening."
Saturday, April 28, 1928 – "Eclipse five hours. Went to the city, drew out Edith's Xmas club, bought 100 baby chicks. Snowed all day."

It was Monday when he read that southern central Pennsylvania had received 28 inches of snow. They had enough of their own. Warmer weather soon sent the melt-off water over the road for a whole day. No school, no work, no pay. Sam used the time to dig a hole and move the toilet shack. He resumed 10-hour work days.

They enjoyed a visit from Grace and Roy accompanied by their daughter, Alice, on Wednesday. There would never be a time when they failed to enjoy a visit from the Whitings.

On the weekend, Sam repaired a stovepipe and the outhouse shed.

Mild May shaped up for garden work. Sam planted peas and Swiss chard. David and Edith prepared a place in the corner of the coop for the expected baby chicks.

Sam likely glossed right over a big news report about the first regular schedule of television programs. General Electric TV was not part of his world, but he read just enough about it to inform himself.

Sam's own words...
Wednesday, May 23, 1928 – "Eclipse 10 hours. Mother, Dewey, and Mildred came out in evening. Cold and windy."
Thursday, May 24, 1928 – "Eclipse nine hours. Edith's 100 baby chicks arrived today."

The chick enclosure was small to serve short term and could expand later as fluffy yellow became feathered hens.

Sam had planted most of the garden by the time school was out on June 14 for the summer. He had only tomatoes and cabbage plants yet to set in the soil.

Sam's own words...
Tuesday, June 19, 1928 – "At Eclipse nine hours. Edith and I were married 15 years ago today. Rainy."
Friday, June 22, 1928 – "Eclipse nine hours. Dewey and I went to see Grace and Roy in regards to farm."

A sense of well-being warmed Sam. He and Edith had each other in sickness and in health. He was glad his younger brother was able to take over the sale of the Pennsylvania farm on behalf of all heirs of Lac Crippen. Sam asked Grace to notify all of the siblings that Dewey would handle the estate sale and distribution.

Sam was content to hoe in his garden and work nine- or 10-hour days, right through July without his usual vacation. In August, he took orders for Kwick Klean table clothes and made $2.67 commission. It was picnic time.

Grace and Alice were faithful visitors through the dog-day month. Mother had moved in at Dewey's, and Sam went there to visit her.

David highlighted his summer when he sold peanuts at the circus. Sam considered it a good experience for his 'big boy' at fourteen years old.

All of the children started school again on Tuesday, September 4.

Sam helped Mr. Hulzier set up a stove in October.

Edith's squinting and trying to read became more difficult for her. Grace was a good friend and sister-in-law and went with Edith to Elmira, November 2, to have her eyes fitted for new glasses. The old ones no longer served as they ought to.

Sam read a back page news article that Alexander Fleming had accidentally discovered penicillin. Fleming had noticed that mold germs were killed by penicillin in a petri dish. Sam gave it no further due and ignored it the same as the scientists had. He didn't know that it would be 1945 by the time it had been taken seriously and put into wartime use.

Sam's own words...
Tuesday, November 6, 1928 – "Went to Horseheads after groceries and to Millport to vote for Herbert Hoover. Fair, Windy."

Republican Hoover won by a landslide over the Democrat, Coolidge.

The harvest of Sam's garden was behind him, except for the cabbage he was putting in the cellar. Sauerkraut was his next project.

Grace and Roy came to dinner the first Sunday in November.

Sam worked 10-hour weekdays and nine hours Saturdays at the vital Eclipse factory. He was low on pipe tobacco and spent 24¢ on a two-week supply November 24.

Sam's own words...
Friday, December 14, 1928 – "Eclipse 10 hours. Moderate. Little boys caught their first skunk, received $3."

Happy grins glowed on John's and Steele's faces. They'd have $1.50 each for the pelt with Christmas shopping on their near horizon. Betty was the first one to go to Elmira with Sam for that purpose on December 15. Sam smiled down at her for the grand bit of fun she relished.

Sam's own words...
Wednesday, December 19, 1928 – "At Eclipse 10 hours. Cold. We mailed package to Willa."

Sam shopped after his five hours work on Saturday, December 22. Drugs and candy were 57¢. The Victory Store groceries were $7.04, and his new diary was 30¢.

On Sunday, he laid Congoleum vinyl on the floors. Edith's appreciation of the shiny surface was all he needed. A trip to visit Mother finished Sam's day.

Happy children and adults enjoyed a big Christmas dinner of chicken, side dishes, and mince pie.

Twelve-year-old John's sore throat kept him sick for a week. He recovered in time to end December healthy.

Sam received his 1928 earnings statement. He had earned a respectable $1,309.42 for the year.

~**~

1929

Good intentions started the year. He would try to see Mother more often. Sam went to visit her Sunday afternoon and saw her again Wednesday evening, January 9 when she and Mildred came for a visit.

Sam was always up early to start the day with a good breakfast of pancakes for the family. Edith had her job to feed chickens, gather eggs, and sell them at 45¢ a dozen. She started her year buying $2.55 worth of chicken feed and gave Sam $2.50 to help where it was most needed.

Sam's own words...
Sunday, January 13, 1929 – "Cold, windy, snow. Busy around home. Dewey and Mildred had all of us down to dinner."
Monday, January 14, 1929 – "At Eclipse 10 hours. Four degrees below zero. Snowy evening."

While Sam worked every day, Edith and all of the children were sick for a week.

Sam's own words...
Monday, January 21, 1929 – "At Eclipse 10 hours. Edith about the same, Shirley better: David and Betty went to Horseheads for exams."
Tuesday, January 22, 1929 – "At Eclipse 10 hours. Edith's brother, Phil, died January 7. Snow in p.m. Sick are some better."
Wednesday, January 23, 1929 – "At Eclipse 10 hours. Edith improves slowly. Sold Ernie Sopher a suit of clothes. Moderate."

Sam's commission on the suit was $3.50. It would buy shoes and pants for David. Worry plagued him right through Friday until Edith was better. His work never wavered.

The moderate weather ended as February descended into cold and colder. Rain and snow fell while the wind howled. The only visitors, once in three weeks, were Grace and Alice. February 19 dropped six inches of snow but was just the beginning.

Sam's own words...
Thursday, February 21, 1929 – "At Eclipse 10 hours. About 10 inches of snow. Children at home today."
Friday, February 22, 1929 – "Eclipse 10 hours. Nine below zero."

Tuesday and Wednesday it turned moderately melty. The children were home because water covered the road. It was an old story growing older. They missed eight days of school. When water receded enough to allow it, Grace came out to see them.

Sam's birthday on Sunday, March 3, made him 46 years old. A letter arrived from Willa on March 15. She did not forget him.

Sam's own words...
Sunday, March 29, 1929 – "Busy as usual. Cool, damp air. Edith not very well."

Sam's concern over Edith never stopped. Neither did rain nor wind in the last week of March. On Sunday, March 31, they visited Mr. and Mrs. Hulzier.

Sam's own words...
Friday, April 19, 1929 – "At Eclipse 10 hours. Warm, rainy evening. Have to move, place has been sold."

For two more days, deep water shut them in. It seemed more like a good idea to move, but it would be a challenge to find a place they could afford. When Grace and Mother came for a visit on Saturday, they heard all about it.

Sam's own words...
Sunday, April 21, 1929 – "Uncle Ed Crippen, Carl Crippen, Aunt Lue, and Cretia visited us a few hours. Mother, Grace, and Alice were out. Mr. and Mrs. Palmer and children here in evening."
Monday, April 22, 1929 – "At Eclipse 10 hours. Edith went to Horseheads to find house, no success."

They'd had enough company all on one day to count for a month of Sundays.

Children were kept from school again on Friday as rain fell non-stop. Sam was at work 12.5 hours.

Their ever faithful Grace and Roy visited often, and Mother came along when she could. On Saturday, May 11, Uncle George entered to a warm welcome.

Sam's own words...
Friday, May 17, 1929 – "At Eclipse nine hours. Dewey and Mildred were out in evening. Cold."

Dewey hadn't been over for quite a time but, like Sam was working a lot. Dewey worked for the Ransom-Biggs Oil Company. Both men had enough to keep them busy on the weekends. Dewey had shown the Galeton farm again and had a line on what was supposed to be a serious buyer in about six weeks. He said that anyone of them who wanted to see the old place once more should do so.

Grace and Roy were set to drive Sam and Edith and the children down to Galeton on Sunday, but it rained all day and dampened the excursion idea. They came to Sam and Edith's for the evening on Tuesday, May 21. The coveted time spent together by the four adults hadn't been missed after all.

A heavy frost dropped in on Thursday, May 23.

Mary came up from Pennsylvania on Sunday, May 26. Grace and Roy brought her out to Sam and Edith's for a visit. They all discussed the pending farm sale and the price at which Dewey had listed it. Mary could confirm all of it since she lived near there.

Sam's own words...
Tuesday, May 28, 1929 – "At Eclipse 10 hours. Warm, rainy p.m. Lindbergh and Ann Morrow wed yesterday."

Sam followed the story of the newsmaker aviator, Charles Lindbergh. He enjoyed the knowledge of the wider world and the extraordinary events called news. He was too poor to be a newsmaker himself, but for only 3¢ a day, he could read about it.

Willa sent word that she had been unable to get $360 together to send fare for the whole family to visit her in New Mexico. She had wanted it to happen so badly that they would have gone if it had been possible. James Jensen had not arrived yet to be with her.

Sam's own words...
Sunday, June 2, 1929 – "Done housework, cleaned oil stove..."
Monday, June 3, 1929 –"Eclipse nine hours. Cold. David went to work on road at 40¢ per hour, worked 10 hours."

David was sent home on Tuesday to get a work permit. He got it on Wednesday and went to the job on Thursday. The employer, Mr. E. Breese, decided he could not be responsible for David, and he could not work.

What was a boy to do? He and his second cousin, Edward Wheeler, went to the lake to fish. Edward's mother was Annabelle, the oldest of Sadie's children.

Sam's own words...
Wednesday, June 12, 1929 – "At Eclipse nine hours. Father died seven years ago today. Had garden plowed at last."

Friday, June 14, marked the final day of classes, and all of the children attended the picnic at Pine Valley.

After Sam's five hours of work on Saturday, he planted squash. The children helped plant beans and cucumbers on Sunday in a garden where perfectly straight rows had been marked out.

Betty went to Horseheads on Monday to take her Regents tests, which cost $1.

Sam's own words...
Thursday, June 20, 1929 – "At Eclipse nine hours. Grace and Roy out in evening; reported Dewey sold farm."
Saturday, June 22, 192 – "Eclipse five hours. Went to Elmira after Betty's shoes. Grace and Ruth were out. Warm. "

Betty's shoes cost $3. She was conscious of their worth and would try to keep them looking new as long as she could.

Dewey had sold the farm to McCorkle Company. Meanwhile, Betty and Shirley spent three days with Aunt Grace, who doted on them.

Sam read about the first public demonstration of color TV held at Bell Laboratories in New York City. It was separate from his everyday world, a marvel in which he had interest.

Sam's own words...
Saturday, June 29, 1929 – "Taking inventory at work, no job for me. Dewey paid me $174.44 as heir to Father's estate."
Sunday, June 30, 1929 –"Cleaned upstairs, part cloudy, some rain, tired, no good..."

Sam mulled over a subject in his mind, a deep thought that would not let go and may have been what made him tired. While John, Betty, and Steel went to town after Fourth of July fun stuff, Sam shook his head over the burden of thoughts and what to do. He knew but dreaded it.

Sam's own words...
Wednesday, July 3, 1929 – "At Eclipse nine hours. Roy and Grace, Frank and Mary here in evening. Very Cool."
Thursday, July 4, 1929 – "Went down to see Dewey about farm settlement. Grace and Roy out in p.m. Cool."

Sam had not been the only one to have second thoughts and questions about how Dewey had dispersed the money from the farm settlement. Had he taken an enormous fee to handle it? What was his reasoning? Sam's other siblings had given him due respect as the oldest and expectation that he would talk to Dewey for all of them. Sam had shouldered the distasteful duty and followed through.

Roy and Grace's next visit was predictable to find out how Sam had bargained on behalf of them all. He had only a bleak outlook that they could relay to Pennsylvania siblings who waited for information. Dewey was stubborn and also adamant that he was within his rights.

Sam's own words...
Saturday, July 6, 1929 – "At Eclipse five hours. Dewey does not offer to make fair settlement. I can't understand."
Sunday, July 7, 1929 – "Helped around house. Dewey does not come near."
Monday, July 8, 1929 – "Eclipse nine hours. It seems that Dewey can be crooked, within the law and is going to do it for a few hundred dollars."

Sam's own impeccable honesty had him shake his head in disbelief. He had hoped each day that Dewey would rethink his actions and make amends. He told Roy and Grace on their next visit that he had to put the subject aside. It wasn't the money, although it seemed like a small fortune, as much as the fact that Dewey would treat them all in such a manner. He turned his attention to Edith, who was sick again.

Sam's own words...
Tuesday, July 16, 1929 – "At Eclipse nine hours. Grace and Roy out in the evening. Children helping greatly."

Sam was gratified that the children had been a big help. They seemed to sense how ill their mother was. She improved after a few days.

Saturday, July 21, dropped frost in a few areas.

Mother and Grace dropped in on Sunday. Anything could and did drop when least expected.

Sam's own words...
Monday, July 22, 1929 – "At Eclipse nine hours. Dewey paid me $75.46 for a total of $249.90 as heir to Father's estate."

No doubt all of the siblings were as surprised as Sam that Dewey had relented and paid out the balance due each of them. The few hundred dollars that Sam spoke of as crooked but lawful amounted to $377.30 kept from them. It was now dispersed in a right manner, equal among siblings.

Sam was busy in the house Sunday. Edith was not well. Grace and Roy took her for a ride. Sam was home alone. After housework, he had his garden to hoe. The younger children were picking berries for Mr. Van Doren. David had gone to the lake with Edward and his mother, Annabell Wheeler.

"David should have a job," Sam mused. But the lure of the lake had claimed him.

John and Steele helped Mr. Withune make hay on Friday. The little boys were like best friends to each other and kept busy.

Edith's health did not improve.

Sam went to the dentist three times to have casts made of his jaw. New teeth were what he needed. He paid $10 for the visits to Dr. A.L. Epstein.

Sam's own words...
Monday, August 5, 1929 – "...Telegram from Willa."

Telegrams brought news of serious subjects. This one likely was the dreadful notification of the death of James Jensen. Sam wrote no more about it. Edith went down to Grace's to stay all night. She must have felt very low over what had befallen Willa again.

Grace and Roy had a good idea meant to cheer up all of the adults. They took Sam and Edith on an overdue trip to Galeton. Betty and Shirley rode along, but the little boys went to the park and David stayed home. They shared expenses of $5.05 in gas and oil for Roy's car.

Sam's own words...
Friday, August 16, 1929 – "At Eclipse nine hours. It looks as though Eclipse business would be slack. Cool."
Saturday, August 17, 1929 – "Eclipse five hours. Went to Elmira after my teeth. Warm."

Doctor Epstein's denture price was $25. Later, Sam had one more appointment to have a spot filed down on the denture material where it had rubbed a spot raw and sore on his inside jaw.

Sam's own words...
Monday, August 19, 1929 – "At Eclipse nine hours. Graf Zeppelin circumnavigating globe."

The rigid airship was German-built, operated commercially, passenger-carrying, and hydrogen-filled.

A letter came from Willa and managed to make them feel better about how she continued to cope with James Jensen's death.

Sam reiterated, "Have got to find a house." Edith went out looking for one Saturday and Sunday but found none they could afford. Since their current rental was sold, they would be forced to leave the garden behind and come back for produce later. Grace and Roy visited and commiserated the situation that must be solved. Sam and Edith needed to know where the children would start school.

Saturday work hours halted at the Eclipse. It would not help the rent situation.

Sam's own words...
Tuesday, August 27, 1929 – "Hunted for house. Paid $20 for one in Horseheads. Cool."

Wednesday, August 28, 1929 – "At Eclipse nine hours...Betty went down to Grace's to make dresses."

Mr. A. R. Newton had rented a house to Sam.

Sam bought Edith a higher strength reading glass for $1.75.

Edith was also at Grace's to sew. School dresses and boys shirts were needed right away. The children must start school as nicely dressed as most other kids.

Sam's own words...

Friday, August 30, 1929 – "Eclipse nine hours. Yesterday, Zepplin completed trip around world in about 22 days. Warm"

Saturday, August 31, 1929 – "Packed and moved one load of goods to Horseheads."

Sunday, September 1, 1929 – "Busy from morning to night packing. Hot and dry. School tomorrow."

Tuesday, September 3, 1929 – "Eclipse nine hours...Goods are still packed. Edith worn out."

On the way home from work September 2, Sam paid $1.25 for a dog license and 18¢ for a newspaper and tobacco. He wanted Edith to rest, and she was unable to do otherwise. The children liked the new school and adjusted well. Sam was pleased. School books were $11.51 for all of the children. Tablets and pencils added another $1.

By Saturday, Sam had household things in place when Grace stopped in. Sam spent $8.75 at the Victory Grocery chain. On other days at different stores, he paid 80¢ for tomatoes, bread 32¢, newspaper and Prince Albert 29¢, liver, paper, and tablet 43¢, coffee and eggs 58¢.

Sam's own words...

Saturday, September 14, 1929 – "Canvassed for Modern Kitchen-ware, no sale..."

Roy and Grace came to visit both Sunday and Wednesday. The factory shut down a half day on behalf of the Chemung County Fair on Friday, September 20. More school books and supplies cost $4.15. Sam ordered a ton of coal. It was put in the cellar Friday morning after a hard freeze.

Sam's own words...
Sunday, September 22, 1929 – "Brought vegetables from the farm."
Wednesday, September 25, 1929 – "At Eclipse. Factory work cut down to eight hours. Cool..."

On September 28, Sam paid Mr. Newton his $20 in rent. His canvass effort on Monday, September 30, to sell kitchenware resulted in no sale. Saturday he made 85¢ on the sale of one pot.

Edith washed clothes using Freeland's electric washer. She was quite taken by the convenience. Betty turned 14 years old on October 10.

Sam's own word...
Tuesday, October 15, 1929 – "Eclipse eight hours. David hunting when he ought to be in school. Cool and fair."

Shorter hours, shorter pay, and David's delinquency were enough concerns. His 'big boy' had a mind of his own.

The first snow fell, and coal was needed again.

Sam's 40-hour week kept his paycheck down on $20, leaving him in need of more money. He figured if he could make sales, he could supplement the shortfall. His Saturday, October 19, canvass trip for kitchenware produced none. He cut Christmas Club from $2 down to $1.50 per week. It was being saved to pay life insurance later.

On Monday he took a coat order that would bring him $3 commission.

Grace and Roy moved back to Horseheads. It was the place for them, too. Roy must have brought good luck when he accompanied Sam to canvass on Saturday. Sam sold a suit that would pay him $3.50 commission.

October held bad news for the economy of the whole world. Sam's brows knitted together in wrinkles. He read of the October 24 through 29 stock market crash of the New York Stock Exchange. The $30-billion loss was ten times greater than the federal government's budget. What else did he or anyone need to cause worry?

Sam's own words...
Wednesday, November 13, 1929 – "At Eclipse eight hours. Warm rain evening. Went out with suit samples."

Thursday, November 15, 1929 – "...Will work only 32 hours per week at factory until further notice."
Saturday, November 16, 1929 – "Canvassed for Jim Foster clothes. Rain."
Sunday, November 17, 1929 –"Roy took me over beyond Corning to see prospects."

Sam sold a drip coffee pot, which carried $1.50 commission. He was not alone in efforts to add income. Grace and Edith had baked bread to sell for several weeks. Betty watched Dr. Brook's baby at times. Sam sold a shirt to bring $1 profit, but it was not enough to allay worry, which lurked for Sam as the primary breadwinner of his family.

Sam's own words...
Monday, November 25, 1929 – "At Eclipse eight hours. Work very slack, laying men off. Mr. Good laid off."
Tuesday, December 10, 1929 – "Eclipse eight hours. Edith received $25 from Arthur."

The generous gift was a windfall, and careful consideration was given on how it would be spent. Christmas was near, and Edith spent a portion on a phonograph player they could all enjoy. A waterfront was bought for the cook stove. The ready-to-use hot water was a convenience to have to add to cold water in the wash pan for hands and faces or Sam's shave. The improvements felt like luxuries to them.

Sam's own words...
Sunday, December 15, 1929 – "Busy at home. Windy. Children ran talking machine all day. Grace here awhile."
Thursday, December 19, 1929 – "At Eclipse eight hours. Rain, sleet, and ice. Edith caring for Brooks baby in evening."
Sunday, December 22, 1929 – "Busy at home. Edith not well."

Snow and sleet squalled. One foot of snow added to the children's Christmas as excitement built to set up the tree. Edith and Grace visited Hulziers. Neighborly gestures between adults made the season brighter. Grace was well named as her friendship braced up her weaker sister-in-law.

Sam's own words...

Friday, December 27, 1929 "Eclipse nine hours. Edith not well."

Grace and Roy visited on Sunday. The factory closed down for inventory on the last two days of the year. Sam contemplated on his situation and had to wonder if the depression would deepen. How long could he count on his job?

~**~

1930

The start of the year saw thirteen-year-old John sick for a week before he could return to school. Steele was out longer, and Sam worried. His eleven-year-old boy was ill for two weeks.

Sam canvassed daily and had no luck with sales. No one had money to buy his wares. Still, the 32 hours at the Eclipse did not earn him enough income for a large family.

Sam's own words...

Wednesday, January 15, 1930 – "At Eclipse eight hours. Don't know what I am going to do unless I get more money."

All of the children had colds. Sam ordered a load of coal and a cord of wood. The wood was $3. He could not pay the electric bill, and the lights were out. He paid the $2.50 water bill and 60¢ for drugs and cough drops. He was grateful to sell pants and a shirt in the third week of January for $2.90 commission. A kitchenware sale added $1.80 to his share. Tobacco was 30¢, school supplies $1.11, and Victory groceries, $10.61.

Grace and Roy made regular visits.

Edith, Betty, and the little boys would pool their saved money and buy an electric washer. Sam agreed that it was needed and ordered it. He was glad for anything to make work easier for Edith. But the electric bill had to be paid. Sam worried about how bad her eyesight was. Another worry was on the way.

Sam's own words...

Thursday, February 6, 1930- "At Eclipse nine hours. Cold. Doctor doesn't know but what John has scarlet fever."

Sunday, February 9, 1930 – "Quarantined in with Scarlet Fever. Am at a loss to know what to do."
Monday, February 10, 1930 – "Just the same as being in jail. No one really sick but Edith, blood pressure."

Sam could not leave home to go to work. Their food was supposed to be provided under quarantine rules. It arrived on Wednesday. Sam was disinfected by the doctor, and he had to leave home and stay at Grace's. At last, he went to work. He shook his head and lamented to Grace and Roy how tough it was to be separated and worried about Edith. The children were not even sick and had to be shut in. John's rash had disappeared in two days, probably only hives, they surmised. The weekend brought no doctor, no attention, and no groceries. They were let down.

The doctor may have decided that extreme caution was needed more than the release of the sequestered family. He was not sure it was scarlet fever. But sure he was of his authority to quarantine the Crippen family.

Not one of them had the red rash that would look like a sunburn and feel like sandpaper. Scarlet fever typically appeared on the face or neck first then spread to the trunk, arms, and legs. The folds of skin around the groin, armpits, elbows, knees and neck usually became a deeper red than the surrounding rash. The face could appear flushed. The tongue generally would look red and bumpy, and might be covered with a white coating at the onset of the disease. The children had no symptoms.

Sam's own words...
Wednesday, February 19, 1930 – "Edith had a row with Dr. Bowman. They got groceries. All are well."
Friday, February 21, 1930 – "All well. At Eclipse eight hours. I miss my family."

Two more weeks of quarantine followed while no one was sick. Groceries did not automatically materialize, and they had to push to get them. It had been the sticking point of Edith's robust conversation with Dr. Bowman. She and the children needed Sam home, but his paycheck was needed just as badly.

Two weeks later, on Friday, March 7, the family could come out, and

Sam could return home. They rejoiced, but Sam hadn't been able to make up for the week of work lost at the start. He was broke. Grace came over on Sunday.

Sam's own words...
Monday, March 10, 1930 – "Eclipse eight hours. Fellows will not let me ride anymore, afraid of Scarlet Fever. Walked home."

The men with whom he had ridden for a long time were afraid that a germ lurked around his home and would infect them. Roy took Sam to work for a few days, and he walked back. On Saturday, he went to buy shoes for David but lacked enough money. Sam's shoulders slumped.

Sam's own words...
Monday, March 24, 1930 – "At Eclipse eight hours. Not earning enough to hardly live. Edith not well."
Thursday, April 3, 1930 – "Eclipse eight hours. David worked on road, am afraid it's too hard for him. Betty and Shirley home, sick."

David worked three days. Sam sold shirts and made $1.50 commission. Steele and John were sick with colds and home from school.

Sam's own words...
Wednesday, April 9, 1930 – "Eclipse nine hours. Betty and Shirley out of school. Steele not well. What's the matter?"
Friday, April 11, 1930 – "Eclipse nine hours. Our first real spring day. Children all in school again."
Saturday, April 12, 1930 –"Canvassed for clothing but not much sale in 'These Hard Times.' Boys visited rummage sale. "

On April 18, David received his first pay for road work, which he continued for three weeks until he was laid off. Sam canvassed without luck.

Sam's own words...
Wednesday, April 30, 1930 – "Eclipse nine hours. Had first greens for supper..."
Sunday, May 4, 1930 "Busy at home. Edith not well...What can a poor fellow do?"
Monday, May 5, 1930 – "At Eclipse. David has no work, and I'm back to eight hours."

Edith was "all in again." Steele had gotten a nail in his foot and limped around. David went to the lake but returned in a few days to look for a job. He found none. Sam hadn't enough money to pay expenses. He canvassed. No sale. Sam kept busy at home.

Steele had a turn at the lake with Edward. The next week it was John's turn. What fun he had while he learned to swim.

Sam's own words...
Wednesday, June 18, 1930 – "Don't know how I am to live on 32 hours a week. More rain and water doing damage."
Saturday, June 21, 1930 – "No Eclipse. Canvassed all day. Made one sale."
Thursday, June 26, 1930 – "Eclipse eight hours. Laid off until July 8. No work. No money."

Sam and Edith took a loan of $264.95 on her Western States Life Insurance. David had his road work money and went with his father to buy a car. He took David back to lake country where he took a job to pick cherries for a week. Sam used the trip as a chance to teach David to drive. Back home, Sam canvassed. Success eluded him.

Sam kept up on the news at home and out west. The dedication of the sculpted George Washington head at Mt. Rushmore in South Dakota was held July 4. The construction of Boulder Dam had started on the Colorado River in the United States. The Elmira *Star-Gazette* reported on July 14 that two Elmira aviators burned to death in a by-plane mishap.

Sam's own words...
Tuesday, July 15, 1930 – "Eclipse eight hours. Started to lake to see David but car went on bum."

More sputter from the car forced a trip to the Breesport garage to have a generator put in.

Sam's own words...
Sunday, July 20, 1930 – "Tinkered with automobile all day. Sold again on a second-hand car I guess."

Lora Babbett Crippen at age 14½. She is holding her favorite early spring pussy willows. She may have picked them for her mother, Edith Crippen for Easter on April 20, 1930.

Edith Crow Haggarty Crippen: age 52 - photo taken the summer of 1930.

Sam canvassed, drove to Hulziers, and went to the lake to get David. David got a small job to wash Dr. Brooks' house. Betty watched the little Brooks boy when she was needed.

Sam had not seen Mother in quite a while when she came to dinner on Tuesday, July 29. Sophia came again when Mary arrived on Sunday, August 3. Possibly, Dewey was mentioned over his switch to another job, this one with the Swartz Oil Company. He had chosen not to be around any of them since a year ago after he tried the shady deal over Lac's estate. Sadie always kept in touch with him and likely dropped information now and then to Grace. Dewey's estrangement was his own decision. He'd never once said to Sam that he thought all of them were wrong. Was it guilt he felt?

Sam's own words...
Thursday, August 7, 1930 – "Busy at home. Canvassed in afternoon. John fell from bicycle, broke his right. arm."
Tuesday, August 12, 1930 – "Eclipse eight hours, no work tomorrow, don't earn enough to buy food and rent."

John's arm was mending all right in a sling, but Shirley was sick for a week.

Worry drove Sam to canvass hard. By Saturday, August 23, he'd sold kitchenware, an overcoat, a suit, and blankets. The commission was $9.65. He had cut Christmas club savings to 25¢ per week. Shoe repairs and school books were needed, and Sam was short of money even before new demands. David intended to delay school to work on a hay press.

Sam visited Mother at Wheeler's before she went down to Mary's. Later, Roy borrowed Sam's car to take Sophia to Sadie's in Hazelhurst, Pennsylvania.

Sam's own words...
Wednesday, September 3, 1930 – "Eclipse eight hours. David started school, am thankful."
Thursday, September 4, 1930 – "Nine hours at Eclipse. Betty back at Mrs. Brooks again."
Wednesday, September 17, 1930 – "Eclipse eight hours, can't make money enough for bare necessities."

Sunday, September 21, 1930 – "…No money, no fuel, behind on rent, Cool."
Tuesday, September 23, 1930 "Eclipse eight hours. Could not get books, David quit school."

His big boy went duck hunting. Sam canvassed. He made a raincoat sale, which brought $1 for his part. Steele worked a newspaper delivery route again.

Sam applied for a loan from his paid up Prudential Life Insurance policy. He received $97.11 and paid his coal bill of $50.60. The first heavy frost came Sunday, October 5.

David helped Mr. Etenberger pull beans.

Sam's own word…
Thursday, October 9, 1930 – "At Eclipse eight hours, children interested in play at school, Betty one of the principals."

Edith and Grace took the little boys on a visit to Hulziers. On another Sunday, they all gathered hickory nuts. Sam had only 16 hours work at the Eclipse for the week and continued to canvass. He made a sale now and again. Grace was a loyal visitor.

On October 21, Edith took in a baby to care for full time. Mother arrived back from Sadie's on December 2 and came to Sam's for a day. The baby had remained entirely in Edith's care for 39 days when the mother came to get her on December 5. On December 12, a box arrived from Arthur. Sam was gladdened for the generosity of his brother-in-law to the children.

Sam's own words…
Monday, December 15, 1930 – "At Eclipse nine hours. Edith not well. Cold."

Sophia came to stay for two days to help Edith since Sam had Eclipse work. He went to the home of a neighbor, L. Evans, and got seven-and-a-half pounds of pork, which he accepted on what they owed him. Sam had relied on 15¢ worth of liver so often for the family that this was a king's ransom for their Christmas season.

It was December 23 and John turned 14 years old. Snow was falling when Sam went for groceries after work. He had cashed his check and also bought small presents.

Sam's own words...
Wednesday, December 24, 1930 - "Eclipse eight hours. Company gave everyone a $10 check. Mrs. Perry did us all a great kindness."

When Sam arrived home, his happy face and eyes signaled Edith that he had good news to share. The bonus had lifted the spirits of all who worked at the Eclipse.
Steele turned 12 on December 29.

Sam's own words...
Wednesday, December 30, 1930 – "Eclipse eight hours. At the end of another year, have a lot to be thankful for, but hope the new year will bring us more abundance of good."

When the Wall Street crash of 1929 had struck less than eight months after Hoover took office, he tried to combat the ensuing Great Depression with moderate government public works projects such as the Hoover Dam. The record tariffs embedded in the Smoot-Hawley Tariff and aggressive increases in the top tax bracket from 25% to 63%, coupled with increases in corporate taxes, yielded a "balanced budget" in 1933, but the economy plummeted. Unemployment rates rose to afflict one in four American workers.
Sam allowed himself to have hope. His optimism held no harm. He read that in December, just past, President Herbert Hoover had gone before the United States Congress and asked for $150 million to run his public works program.
Would this action make 1931 better?

23 – Depression Years
Owls, 1931, 1932, 1933

The depression deepened. Dark, hollow-eyed gazes of fear looked back from neighbors, friends, and relatives. Worry dogged Sam. He had so little to care for his own family that he had nothing to share with others when he wanted. Unemployment already affected many citizens and stalked the soon-to-be jobless.

Sam may have thought it interesting that the German, Albert Einstein, had begun a job as a research scientist at the California Institute of Technology. Einstein had gained favor because he was no admirer of the Nazis and was on a path to naturalization in the United States.

Sam's own words...
Thursday, January 8, 1931 – "At Eclipse eight hours, don't know how long before I cannot make a living."

He had worked 24 hours during the week, but it did not cover expenses for the poor conditions under which he, Edith, and the five children lived. A birthday could be remembered but not celebrated with a gift. Grace turned 46 on January 10, and Shirley was nine years old on January 20.

Sam was all too often disheartened after a day or evening when he had canvassed. Day after day there was no sale. The occasional 70¢ or more earned was hard fought. The sale of a suit, which brought him $4 commission, was a strong win.

In midweek, March 4, he sold two dresses. Even so, success was so elusive that mention of them on his diary pages occurred far less than his mention of housework or Edith's downward ebb of fragile health.

In late March, a note of encouragement came when Mother received her old age pension, a Robin sang, and David helped at Mr. Etenberger's sale. The news may also have been welcome, in Sam's opinion, that *The Star-Spangled Banner* by Frances Scott Key was named as the United States national anthem. Weren't they all bright spots to offset discouragement?

Sam's own words...
Tuesday, March 21, 1931 – "At Eclipse eight hours. David is 17 today and about as large as me. Cool and windy."

A 40-hour work week in May was enough to create Sam's smile. The hours were a one-time occurrence and hurried back to fewer hours.

In late May, he helped Grace and Roy move up to Johnson Hollow, a hilly northwestern area road in the town of Catlin near Midway. Other days he canvassed and made 45¢. He had the garden plowed June 15 and put in tomatoes. Charlie Scott visited during a down day from the Eclipse and watched Sam set cabbage plants.

Since school was out, Steele and John went to scout camp. Shirley went to stay with her Aunt Grace for a week. Sam was sure it was a charmed time for them, but he missed Shirley.

He had no more factory work for two weeks. His garden benefitted from the expert motion of his hoe. A partial day's work to load hay onto a box car was almost too much for him. He was better off back in his garden or canvassing.

Sam's own words...
Monday, June 29, 1931 – "Canvassed. David took Navy exam."
Tuesday, June 30, 1931 – "Canvassed. David took intelligence test. Warm."
Thursday, July 2, 1931 – "Went before notary, signed papers for David's Navy entry."

They all spent Sunday, July 5, at Grace's for a big dinner, since it was a farewell for Sam's big boy. He would be on his way to Buffalo on Tuesday. David faced his final Navy exam. Sam missed him as soon as he was out of sight. On Wednesday, Sam had word that out of 63, David was the only one who passed it and he was on his way to a Great Lakes training camp. Every day, the family wondered what David was doing and when they would hear from him, but none more than Sam.

David's first letter arrived Monday, July 13, to say he liked the Navy so far. Sam had hoped for the best and added glad to his thoughts.

Sam's own words...
Monday, July 20, 1931 – "At Eclipse eight hours. Sold dress in evening. Had a dandy letter from David. Gentle rain."

Sam's spirits soared. Another letter from his tall boy filled his heart and mind as his garden absorbed moisture. Both David and Willa wrote letters, which served to sweeten July.

Eclipse work stalled. Sam hoed and then he made an effort to sell goods to jobless people. They were all broke, but his persistence created the opportunity where he made $3.40 in one week.

Shirley, Steele, and John spent much of the second half of July at Grace's. Edith and Betty took turns to watch Doctor Brooks' little boy. Dr. Brooks had a dental office.

A letter from David elevated Sam's mood, which had sunk over his lack of work. He was lucky to secure a job as window washer for 27½ hours at the Eclipse the first week of August. Sam expected no more work for a while. The heat stayed on for August.

Only thirteen hours of regular work was offered and taken for the month. He canvassed day after day. Just once, he made a sale that included a commission of $1.90. As usual, Sam kept his hoe busy.

Sam's own words...
Saturday, August 29, 1931 – "Canvassed at Pine Valley. Mr. Newton says we may have to move, way behind in rent."
Monday, August 31, 1931 – "At Eclipse nine hours."
Tuesday, September 1, 1931 – "Eclipse eight hours. Letter from David."

Sam made $2 on sales but no more factory hours materialized. Grace and Roy brought them potatoes and fruit. They canned plums and peaches.

Sam's own words...
Friday, September 18, 1931 – "Canvassed all day, no success. Hard circumstances."
Thursday, September 24, 1931 – "Canvassed. Edith staying with a sick woman."

Edith was 53 years old and not well herself but was better in a week. Sam had 13 hours of Eclipse work to finish the month and no more suggested until late October. He got a job working for the State Highway Department for five and a half hours on Friday, September's last day. It was hard work that he hoped his 48-year-old body could stand when he took on 27 more hours. A portion of the time was spent drilling holes in the Chemung River bed. The state officials advised them to drill holes in the river bottom so the water could run out. Sam didn't argue about paid labor whether or not he understood the whole concept. Edith was sick again. He'd had no sales and few promises. It was a good omen on Friday, October 8, when he made 50¢ on a sale. It whet his appetite to push ahead or was it desperation's bid?

Sam's own words...
Saturday, October 10, 1931 – "Canvassed; sold overcoat, suit, and raincoat, commission $8.60."
Tuesday, October 13, 1931 – "Picked pears and brought in heat stove. Canvassed in p.m. Hard frost."

Betty was 16 years old on her birthday, October 10.

The family waited for days in anticipation of David's arrival. He walked in the door on October 18. If a house could vibrate from happiness of the people inside, it was today.

David easily upstaged the newspaper report of the conviction of American gangster Al Capone for tax evasion. Capone was put away for 11 years, and David was home for two weeks. Sam's lungs expanded to their fullest as he took deep, satisfied breaths on seeing that David looked so well, so fine, so confident. Grace and Mother came straight over to see him.

Sam's own words...
Tuesday, October 20, 1931 – "At Eclipse eight hours. Thomas A. Edison died October 17 at 84 years of age."

Inventor Edison created such great innovations like the electric light bulb and the phonograph. The savvy businessman held more than 1,000 patents for his inventions. Sam took notice with the rest of the world on his passing.

Sam was elated to finish 29 hours of work at the Eclipse for the week. He was aware that it would taper off again.

Monday, October 26, was David's last night at home for a long time. He left them on Tuesday at 4:30 p.m. for the Great Lakes Camp from where they would send him to San Pedro, CA.

On October 20, Betty quit school. A letter arrived from Willa, who had closed her small photography business in New Mexico and gone back to Encampment, WY.

Sam made $3.75 commission on his sales in Pine Valley on November 3.

Sam's own words...
Monday, November 9, 1931 – "Canvassed all day. Had letter from David. He is on the USS Colorado, says he likes it."
Tuesday, November 10, 1931 – "Canvassed. Letter from David telling of explosion on USS Colorado, five lives lost, 12 injured."

What parent would fail to be glad that their son had not stepped into harm's way when it struck so close? David's family always remembered him, but it was Sam who answered his letters. He had an interest in each one of his children. This was the same week that he first spoke to Al Herforth, a friend Betty had made.

Edith occupied herself on Friday to take care of neighbor children to earn what money she could. Sam took the rare and welcome opportunity to eat dinner at Hulzier's. They also wanted to hear how and where was Sam's big Navy boy.

Sam's own words...
Wednesday, November 18, 1931 – "Eclipse eight hours. Received washing machine from Montgomery Ward Company. Warm."
Thursday, November 19, 1931 – "At Eclipse eight and one-half hours. Discouraged with new gasoline washer, will not run."

It took patience to wait until Monday afternoon when Ward's appliance repairman came out to start the washer. Finally, the man flipped the lid shut on his tool chest and stood up. His frown and the mute motor would dictate what he wrote in his report on the attempted but unsuccessful repair. Sam mailed a pointed letter to Montgomery Ward the next day.

Thanksgiving was two days later, and Sam had much for which he was thankful. A letter arrived from David, who was now at Puget Sound, the region in the coastal area of the Pacific Northwest by the state of Washington.

A neighbor gave Sam five bushels of small potatoes. They would not go to waste in Sam's family.

It was Thursday, December 1, when Sam crated the defunct washer for shipment back to the department store. He mailed a letter to David and sold an overcoat.

Sam's own words...
Thursday, December 3, 1931 – "At Eclipse four hours. We all went to church to hear Dr. Rees and it did us good."

Betty was not in attendance since she stayed at Mr. Barney's to watch children all week. Edith watched Donnie Brooks now and then. Betty came home on Sunday to be with the family.

Sam went to Elmira on Tuesday, December 8, to try and get the electric turned back on. It had been off for several weeks and would remain so until Sam paid the bill in full.

Mother and Grace kept up their visits to Edith and Sam.

Edith and the children attended evening church services often. Sam and Edith also read one or two chapters at a time of The Covered Wagon by Emerson Hough to the children.

John turned 15 years old on December 23, the same day a Christmas box arrived from Willa. Rollo sent Edith $20 and David's letter came. It was the first Christmas without him home, and they missed him. Roy, Grace, and Mother came for a visit December 27. Sam sent a few New Year's cards. One was sure to have gone to Lenore Crow and another to Willa.

The electric was turned on December 29 but was in no way a pre-sent for Steele's 13th birthday. Rollo's $20 likely supplied the means for a paid-up account.

~**~
1932

In early January, David wrote that someone had stolen his pea jacket. The double-breasted wool blazer was Navy issue for every shipboard sailor to ward off the raw wind and rain on the bridge. Sam's eyebrows lowered in a pinch toward his nose. He shook his head over the theft, amazed at what a fellow Navy man to David had been capable of. David sent the family a box of glazed fruit. A few days later, Sam received a wallet and a silver dollar. Big brother sent sailor's jack knives for both of his brothers. Most likely John and Steele could hardly keep their feet on the ground and their glee quiet while they showed off their prizes.

Sam's own words...
Saturday, January 16, 1932 – "At home in a.m. Edith and me went to theater in afternoon. Colder."

The drama they may have seen starred actress Helen Hayes and actor Ronald Colman in Arrowsmith, to depict his bright future. His trajectory is waylaid after he marries and settles down in a quiet Minnesota town. A beautiful stranger, played by Myrna Loy, complicates his life. The getaway, the excitement of a film, and the closeness inside of the theater was a short reprieve from the worry of the headlines in the news and other displeasures.

Sam read the report that Germany had six-million citizens unemployed.

He was discouraged over failure to get Betty to do what he thought was reasonable. She still had a companion over which Sam had voiced his disapproval.

Sam's own words...
Tuesday, January 19, 1932 – "Work does not improve. 'These are times that try men's souls.' Colder."

Sam referred to the 1776 statement by Thomas Paine published in The American Crisis written before the American Revolution. Paine also wrote: "What we obtain too cheap, we esteem too lightly: it is dearness only that gives everything its value. Heaven knows how to put a proper price upon its goods, and it would be strange indeed if so celestial an article as freedom should not be highly rated."

David wrote that he would soon be on a Hawaiian island. Sam answered right away. The whole family added their own pages to send along to him. They were transmitted by air mail to San Diego. Hawaii was a foreign destination, and they wanted to connect before David was gone.

Hawaiian monarch, King Kamehameha I, ruled the eight islands southwest of the United States in the Pacific Ocean. (Sam would not know until 1959 that Hawaii became a U.S. state.)

Shirley turned 10 years old on January 20 and had a little party. The boys went to the Veteran Grange near Pine Valley with their scout troop on January 22.

Work slackened. Worry increased.

Sam's own words...
Friday, January 29, 1932 – "Canvassed. Mother and Grace here a while in p.m. "Pay rent or move," says landlord."
Saturday, January 30, 1932 – "Home most of day. Just don't know what we are going to do."
Tuesday, February 2, 1932 – "At home, four inches of snow. Must have work or be forced to ask for help."
Wednesday, February 3, 1932 – "One more humiliation; asked for help. Canvassed, no sales."

In the next two weeks, Sam's Eclipse hours added up to 30 hours, and his sales commissions equaled only $2.20. It did not pay their expenses. He called on creditors Saturday, February 13. Sam was not the only one whose finances had taken a downturn. He may not have considered that it would get worse. By the end of February, the Eclipse cut all wages by 10 percent. Sam's cousin, Cretia, came from Pennsylvania and brought them two chickens on the last day of February. She most likely knew how much it was needed.

The day's news had little meaning for Sam. The blowhard—Hitler of Germany—had become a naturalized German citizen so he could run for the 1932 election of Reichspräsident. It meant nothing to the average American like Sam. What were they to make of it in the middle of their own more pressing problems?

Sam's own words...
Wednesday, March 2, 1932 – "At Eclipse eight hours. Betty taking care of children for a Mrs. Gilligan. Lindbergh baby kidnapped."
Thursday, March 3, 1932 – "Whole country indignant. Canvassed nearly all day, no sale. I am 49 years old today."

The world and Sam waited for news of the stolen baby. The Lindberghs lived near Hopewell, New Jersey. Charles Augustus Lindbergh, Jr., 20-month-old son of the famous aviator and Anne Morrow Lindbergh, was kidnapped about 9 p.m. on March 1, from the nursery on the second floor of the Lindbergh home.

Sam had word that David was to come back from the islands to the U.S. mainland. Betty was still watching the Gilligan kids, and Sam made a sale to net a $5.50 commission. As hard as it was to make a deal, Sam kept at it.

Willa and David wrote every few weeks.

Sam's own words...
Saturday, March 26, 1932 – "Busy at home. Edith not very well. Stormy."
Friday, April 1, 1932 – "Eclipse nine hours. Must sell tomorrow, am up against it."
Saturday, April 2, 1932 – "Went to Pine Valley, canvassed; sold two suits. Mother with us tonight. Warmer."

A few days later, Sam earned two-dozen eggs and was given a hat. The case of the Lindbergh baby exasperated him by affecting his own heart as a parent and also as one of the many people who sincerely cared for the aviator.

Sam's own words...
Sunday, April 10, 1932 – "Lone Eagle will pay anything for return of his son. Why don't the heartless fiends do so? Boys busy with their rabbits."
Monday, April 11, 1932 – "Canvassed, no luck. Lindbergh paid $50 thousand ransom, and they do not return baby."

Edith remained in bed for two days. Sam was glad when she improved and was better after a week. He worked for the Eclipse nearly 10 hours on Monday, April 18. What would he do with so much money?

In early May, Sam had the garden plowed. He made no mention if he'd read the notice about the Jack Benny radio show that had begun broadcast on May 2.

Sam's own words...
Wednesday, May 11, 1932 – "At home in a.m. At factory three and a half hours in p.m., Navy Department will send allotment May 31."
Thursday, May 12, 1932 – "Eclipse eight hours. Report over radio saying Lindbergh baby found dead."

The news hit the airwaves before newspapers. The child was found not far from the Lindbergh home. Sam worked out his jarred senses in his early garden. He started a plot for his neighbor, Mr. Philips. Roy and Grace visited. Sam's landlord, Mr. Frank McQueen, was ill. A few days later he died. Sam continued work on the garden. The boys and Betty attended the funeral.

Sam's own words...
Wednesday, June 1, 1932 – "Eclipse eight hours. Edith received $10 allotment from David."
Friday, June 3, 1932 – "Eclipse eight hours, earned $14.63 this week at factory. Warm."

He'd had 32 hours work to bring him a larger paycheck. The next week gave him 21 hours and the third week, eight hours. With the spare hours, he tended his garden as if a preacher to his flock.

Sam sold a suit on June 17. It added $4 commission to his pocket for critical needs. Edith was busy mornings and evenings for a neighbor who needed childcare.

Sam's own words...
Saturday, June 18, 1932 – "Worked in garden. Edith, Steele, and Shirley went to Elmira clinic for TB test."
Tuesday, June 21, 1932 – "Worked in garden all day. Edith, Steele, and Shirley took final TB test today. Will know on 22nd."
Wednesday, June 22, 1932 – "At Eclipse nine hours. Steele and Shirley reacted to TB test. Warm."

The tightness in Sam's chest made him realize he was overthinking. It was no help, and he needed to keep his usual calm. "Just wait and see," he self-counseled.

Factory work had given him 16 hours for the week. Shirley developed mumps. More people joined the ranks of the unemployed. They had no money to buy Sam's products although he canvassed often. He found himself euphoric to make $1 on dress fabric, June 26.

Weeds needed Sam's attention. Half the year was over, yet plenty of time remained in 1932 for trouble. The Dow Jones stock report dived to 41.22 points as the depression dashed expectations.

Sam's own words...
Monday, July 11, 1932 – "Worked in garden, delivered dress goods. Shirley went to hospital for observation."

Sam missed his Shirley Girl and wondered if she was lonesome. He hoped she was not homesick. Edith went to see her on Friday, July 15.

Sam worked 24¼ hours at the Eclipse, stretched over two weeks. He rubbed his forehead but took no time for shoulders to slump since he kept a hoe in his hands or went out to see prospects and sell. The next two weeks added up 31½ hours of factory work. He made $1.40 commission on fabric and ordered it hither. The yard goods were received in the typical four days wait.

A letter arrived from David at the end of July. Sam wrote to him and Shirley.

August held the same lack of sales results and less factory work even though his efforts remained active. He received $3.69 in groceries from the town. Sam dismissed the idea of a trip with Grace and Roy to Gould, PA, for the Crippen reunion. He hung his head at the thought of having to explain his job situation to anyone. Betty stayed with her cousin, Ruth, while Grace and Roy were away overnight in Galeton for the reunion.

Sam's own words...
Friday, August 12, 1932 – "Canvassed, no sale. People have no money. Had to get $3.88 from town (food)."
Tuesday, August 16, 1932 – "Walked to Heights but no work. Canvassed, made $1.60 commission, found three prospects for suits. Warm."

Sam worried about money and David, Shirley, and Betty. He tried to be a steady rock and have a positive influence on Betty. She was a mixed up young woman after her marriage to Albert Herforth. Her unhappiness had brought her back home off and on while trouble brewed, stewed, and simmered. Sam's concern would last just as long as Betty's agony.

Sam's own words...
Wednesday, August 31, 1932 – "94% Eclipse of sun, hot day. Edith went down to see Shirley."
Tuesday, September 6, 1932 – "Canvassed most of day, sold boys four piece suit, made $2.50, which I sure can use."
Wednesday, September 7, 1932 – "Canvassed, received Tanner shoe outfit. Grace and Mother here few minutes."

The fancy, black, lace-up oxford pump in ladies size three had a two-inch stacked heel. It was close to the style that his sister, Grace, wore. Maybe he asked her if they really were a joy to walk in since those were the words printed on the soul inside the heel. It was a new product sample for Sam and renewed hope to sell.

Edith suddenly took ill.

Sam's own word...
Thursday, September 15, 1932 – "Edith had operation for strangulated hernia. We pray for her."

Saturday, September 17, 1932 – "Saw Edith and Shirley. Edith seems to be doing OK."

Mother and daughter were in the same hospital. Sam sent cards to Willa, Arthur, and David to let them know. Shirley remained under observation for tuberculosis and was a candidate to reside at Federation Farm when a bed became available. It was a federal government welfare hospital for children.

The Federal Children's Bureau brought together social workers, educators, juvenile court judges, labor leaders, and other men and women concerned with children's well-being. It was as early as 1903 when work supported by the then-sitting President Theodore Roosevelt began to look into the welfare and health of children. "There are few things more vital to the welfare of the Nation than accurate and dependable knowledge of the best methods of dealing with children," asserted Roosevelt. He was out of office by the time Taft signed a Child Welfare Act into law in 1912.

Sam helped Mr. Davis saw wood on Monday and mailed his fabric order. He worked 16 hours for the Eclipse during the week. Another week went by. Grace and Roy took him for another hospital visit. They all missed Edith and Shirley but not as much as Sam did. Edith improved. They brought her home on Tuesday, October 4, in a weak condition.

Sam's two younger boys worked to pick up potatoes for Waite Gould.

Roy was hospitalized. His old problem troubled him again.

Sam's own words...
Friday, October 14, 1932 – "Busy around home. Roy not well. His nerves are bad."

Sam's friendship and kindness led him to frame Roy's mental health breakdown in such a way. The hospital stay was short and was only for regulation of his medicine. Roy was soon home.

Edith tired quickly. Grace and Mother helped Betty can peaches. Sam worked for the water board on and off until his bill was paid through January 1.

Sam's own words...
Thursday, October 20, 1932 – "Walked to the Heights and back after $2.80 paycheck. Finished reading *The Covered Wagon* to the family. We need such courage."

The Covered Wagon by Emerson Hough had been made into a film back in 1923. It was months in the making for its 119 minutes and was the biggest thing since Griffith made *The Birth of a Nation*. Hough based his book on his historical articles written for *The Saturday Evening Post*. His subject was pioneers who left their farms and safeguarded homes in the territory east of the Ohio and started in prairie schooners for the Pacific Coast in 1847, before the Gold Rush of 1849. This particular wagon train, which had 300 vehicles, started for Oregon. A simple love tale runs through it.

Mother was ill, and Sam went to Grace's often to see her.

Sam's own words...
Sunday, October 23, 1932 – "Went to Heights to Free Methodist Church and confessed God before man. John and Steele went forward."
Thursday, November 3, 1932 – "Canvassed most of day. Went to Grace's to see Mother..."

There sat Dewey in Grace's living room.

There had come Sam to Grace's living room.

There resided inside Grace's living room, a charged silence with discomfited stiff human forms.

Neither he nor Dewey spoke to each other. Maybe it was best. But today concern over Mother was their priority. The last time they had spoken was June of 1929, more than three years ago. Did either of them have a hope of reconciliation? If they did, this day did not develop into the time or place.

Mother Sophia was slow to improve.

Sam's own words...
Saturday, November 5, 1932 – "At home most of day half sick. Roy took Edith and John to Federal Farm to see Shirley."

Sam was well on Sunday and went down to Grace's to see Mother.

He was glad to see his sister, Mary, a few minutes. It was time he wrote to Shirley again since he hadn't been able to see her.

Sam's own words...
Monday, November 7, 1932 – "At Eclipse nine hours. Edith and I (sic) heard President Hoover's final campaign address over Van Dines radio."

Horsehead's first radio station, WESG (now WENY), carried the broadcast.

Sam and Edith both voted for Republican Hoover on Tuesday. They visited Mother on the way home. Democrat Franklin D. Roosevelt won by a vast majority.

Grace came on Wednesday to tell Sam that Roy had a job. She would have wanted to enjoy the fact that Sam would be as glad as she was.

Roy was an excellent mechanic and may have gotten on a railroad line to make runs. Grace reported that Mother was the same.

On Friday, Sam walked to the Heights after his $3.60 pay for the week. He canvassed. The couples watched Mother in turns while each of them could attend church services. Sam stopped to see Mr. Lawrence on Thursday and got two sacks of Red Cross flour.

Sam sold fabric on Tuesday at $1.40 commission and sent the order. Whitings and Mother came to Thanksgiving dinner, a tremendous enjoyment for all of them.

On the following day Sam helped Pastor Crandall with his rummage sale. The boys were happy to play a few records Sam received. He measured Mr. Crandall for a suit and sent the order.

Edith traveled to visit Shirley on Saturday, December 3. Sam went to see Mother Sunday evening before he and Roy went to church. Sam cleaned the house Monday and helped Edith and Grace do laundry. Car rides and washing machine loads seemed like a fair trade and in good company. Sam sold a suit Tuesday. What a great day! The Eclipse worked him three-and-a-half hours on Wednesday after which he mailed the Mutual Fabric and Foster Clothes order.

Sam's own words...
Thursday, December 8, 1932 – "Canvassed in afternoon. Betty making Xmas (sic) owls and boys trying to sell them."

Sam went to the city Friday after shoes for Shirley. The gift would make her so happy on the next visit. Betty and the boys got along well crafting the crepe paper owls in red, royal blue and green. The cotton stuffed breasts of the owls were streaked with either gold or silver paint, the same as the twigs they sat on. Betty had stitched them onto their perches, and the boys were proud to market them door to door successfully.

Sam's own words...
Monday, December 12, 1932 – "My dear sister was taken to the hospital for observation and probable operation."
Wednesday, December 14, 1932 – "Edith had another strangulated hernia. Doctor says she may have to have another operation; our strength is surely tried."

Mother was taken to Mary's in Pennsylvania. Grace had an unnamed surgery. Edith was in better condition at home after a truss had been applied to contain further damage. Grace was coming along fine. She would be home in about ten days. Sam and Edith did their wash and Grace's, too. Roy took the three of them to the hospital to see Grace on Monday, December 19.

On Christmas Day, they all went to Federation Farm to see Shirley and to the hospital to see Grace, who would come home December 31.

John was 16 and Steele age 14 in the last week of 1932.

Unemployment in the United States left 14 million people jobless, and Germany suffered similarly. By December 31, 1932, there was a total of 100,959 persons receiving old age benefits in 13 states, more than half of them in New York state.

~**~

1933

Sunday, January 1, was a good day for the boys to go up to Waite Gould's and fill mattress ticks with straw.

Edith's letters from Arthur and Rollo arrived January 3. Sam canvassed on January 5 and sold enough for $1.20, his part. He had eight hours of work at the Eclipse this first week of the year.

Republican President Calvin Coolidge died of a heart attack on January 5, less than a year after he was out of office. Coolidge was known for his quiet demeanor, which earned him the nickname "Silent Cal." Frugality was another attribute of the popular former leader. He was president of the United States from 1923 to 1929. The country mourned.

Sam took Betty with him on Sunday to call on Grace and see how well she had recuperated. She would be 48 years old on Tuesday. Grace had a letter from Cretia. She wanted Whitings to move to Galeton and join them in farm work. Roy mulled it over and thought they had better go. Grace was not so sure. Sam and Roy went to Sunday evening church service.

Sam received a new item to sell, a spring dress outfit from the Foster line.

Sam's own words...
Thursday, January 19, 1933 – "At factory eight hours. Edith not well. Windy but moderate."

Sam missed Shirley as she turned 11 years old on January 20. He had not seen her since Christmas and considered it his shame.

Edith and Betty went to the Elmira clinic on Saturday. Neither of them was well enough to do much. Sam read to the family on Sunday.

Sam's own words...
Monday, January 23, 1933 – "Went to Elmira to get prescription filled for Betty and make arrangements so she can go to hospital. Busy washing, housework in p.m."
Tuesday, January 24, 1933 - "Busy around home in a.m., canvassed in p.m. Edith is surely in awful condition."
Friday, January 27, 1933 – "Home all day to do what I could. Edith miserable, called Dr. Gridley but it doesn't look like he intends to come. Betty went to clinic."

As it turned out, the doctor was in the hospital, sick, when Sam went again to get him. Grace and Ruth came for a visit, concerned over Edith.

Sam had weak sales and few Eclipse hours. It was mostly fabrics that sold as women saved money by making their own dresses. Edith was not well enough to do so.

Sam's own words...
Thursday, February 2, 1933 – "Delivered Mutual Fabrics and canvassed most of day. Grace here awhile in p.m. Windy, colder, and the groundhog saw his shadow."
Tuesday, February 7, 1933 - "At home in a.m. Canvassed in afternoon. Received letter from Shirley, bless her. Warm, rainy evening."

Sam worked at the Eclipse eight hours Wednesday. He had braved the snow and the wind to walk there. He read of deep snow in Chicago and 11,000 homeless. Exposure made him susceptible to a severe cold. Grace came for another visit.

Sam's own words...
Saturday, February 11, 1933 - "Cold. Walked to Elmira Heights after my small pay. Betty went to the hospital tonight to have her baby. God knows she needs his help."

Worry prevailed until Betty gave birth to her 8-lb. baby boy on Monday, February 13 at 2 o'clock. She and baby Teddy came through the ordeal well.

Grace walked up the hill to do her wash at Sam and Edith's. She could hardly make it because of the snow. They waited for word from Betty and prepared a room for her. The new mother had named her little boy after the 26th president of the United States, aware of her father's propensity toward an appreciation of all things Teddy Roosevelt. In her growing-up years, Betty likely had read from the navy blue hardcover; TR embossed volumes in her parent's bookcase.

Sam's own words...
Thursday, February 23, 1933 – "At Eclipse five hours. Canvassed in evening, made $5 for which I am thankful. Edith caring for Donny B. tonight. Windy."

Saturday, February 25, 1933 – "...Grace here awhile, about three inches of snow. Boys think Betty's baby just it."

Betty had come home on Friday after 12 days in the hospital. The boys were proud, first-time uncles. John and Steele had the same good-natured temperament as Sam. They came by it naturally.

Edith was in trouble of a painful sort again in March as her hernia bulged. It had popped out, and Sam had to have the doctor. She was in bed several days.

Sam spent part of his 50th birthday, March 3, on a walk to the Heights to collect his small paycheck. He continued his jaunt into Elmira to pay the electric bill.

The boys attended their evening scout meeting.

Grace came and sat by Edith Sunday night while Sam and Roy went to church.

Sam's own words...
Monday, March 6, 1933 – "Did wash and housework. President F. D. Roosevelt has declared a week's bank holiday to relieve financial difficulties. Edith in bed most of day."
Tuesday, March 7, 1933 – "At home in a.m., canvassed p.m. People all excited over bank financial condition. These are serious times, and men need faith. Rain."

Sam leaned on his faith when he was advised that he would not be called back to the factory until the bank situation became settled. Newspapers reported that the financial climate would be cleared up and it was only a one-week duration. The Eclipse factory remained idle.

Edith was better and went to take care of Dr. Brooks's little boy. Sam canvassed and hoped for manufacturing work to be available again. Roy took them to see Shirley at Federation Farm. Congress enacted the legality of beer on March 21. Willa wrote.

Although devoid of a job, Sam had begun to believe that F. D. Roosevelt was a great president. President Roosevelt boosted the morale of citizens who had the memory of his statement when he ran for office: The only thing we have to fear is fear itself.

Near the end of the month, Grace and Roy planned to move to Galeton.

Sam's own words...
Sunday, March 26, 1933 – "Busy around home. Mother here while Grace and Roy at church. Three-inch snowfall. Edith feeling pretty rough."

Edith was glad to have a letter from her brother, Arthur Crow. He alerted her that he had sent a 25-volume set of Funk and Wagnall's new standard encyclopedias. What a treasure to all of them.

Sam sent a fabric order. Any amount helped. As he sought another rental, he kept his need for a garden spot in mind. A new glimpse of spring was just ahead. David had not written in weeks. Grace, Roy, and Mother ate dinner at Dewey's. Could the strained relationship normalize?

Grace almost always brought her clothes and did her wash at Sam and Edith's, whose generosity was obvious. They'd have it no other way.

The newspaper explained in depth, President Roosevelt's establishment of the Civilian Conservation Corps as a mission to relieve rampant unemployment in the United States. Sam studied it thoroughly.

Sam's own words...
Tuesday, April 4, 1933 – "U.S. dirigible, Akron, falls in sea, 72 lost. Did work around home and canvassed with little success. Received a sample copy of The Aquarian Ministry magazine; will make the most of it."
Wednesday, April 5, 1933 – "At Eclipse five and a half hours. Had a precious letter from Shirley, God bless her. Grace, Roy, and Ruth here a few minutes."

Sam kept abreast of the news near and far. He noted that beer now legally flowed in 19 states. His factory hiatus ended but only to begin shorter hours.

Sam's own words...
Saturday, April 8, 1933 – "Did housework, canvassed. Grace and Roy went to Galeton to live with Uncle Ed and Cretia. I shall miss them. Windy, snow."
Sunday, April 9, 1933 – "...These are terrible times, and men need faith in God and man. Edith took care of Donny Brooks tonight."

Grace sent a post card from her address at the Crippen homestead. Edith looked for another house to rent and found one on Eleanor Street.

Sam's own words...
Saturday, April 15, 1933 – "At Eclipse eight and one-half hours. Sewage backing up into sink; expect to move before May, most any place more desirable than this."

Saturday night found Sam carrying out pails of sewage on into the early morning hours. It had to be done all day Sunday; "an awful condition to say the least," according to Sam. They called the doctor for baby Teddy on Monday. All members of the family were concerned for the two-month-old little boy. On Tuesday, Edith called the board of health about the sewer. Sam had started to pack for the move to 203 Eleanor Street, and he worked four hours for the town. Teddy was better. The proud uncle boys packed their stuff. They pushed a wheelbarrow and a cart to the new place.

Sam had a letter from both Shirley and Grace. Grace was not happy at Uncle Ed's in Pennsylvania.

Sam's own words...
Sunday, April 23, 1933 – "Busy at home all day. Edith had another attack, a strangulated hernia at 5 p.m. Was taken to St. Joseph's about 6:45 p.m."

Mary came Monday from Pennsylvania and took Mother home with her since Edith could no longer care for Sophia. It had taken a week of rest at St. Joseph Hospital before Edith had an operation. Sam, meanwhile, canvassed, put in a few hours at the Eclipse, and took care of his children. Through the years, he had become more than a suitable cook out of need and could rely on his ability now. There had also been the half accomplished move. Sam packed dishes and bought a kitchen stove to which he connected a hot water front. He was tired.

Sam's own words...
Sunday, April 30, 1933 – "Busy all day trying to get things in some semblance of order. I know I have neglected Edith and Shirley Girl, but I cannot help it. Steele cut his head and sprained his thumb."

Edith's operation day was May 1. Grace and Roy moved back to Horseheads May 5. Grace and Betty went to the hospital to see Edith. Whitings found a farm in Pine Valley on which to live and work.

An interested public read the same material that Sam discovered in the newspaper. A Loch Ness Monster was alleged to have been sighted in Loch Ness, a lake in the Scottish highlands. Another monster of evil deeds staged a massive public book burning in Germany by students and leading Nazi party members. Enthusiastic crowds witnessed the burning of books written by Brecht, Einstein, Freud, Mann, and Remarque, among many well-known intellectuals, scientists, and cultural figures, many of whom were Jewish. Which one was to become the most feared? Nessie or Hitler? The question had not been posed nor answered in 1933.

Sam's own words...
Sunday, May 14, 1933 – "We brought Edith home today after three weeks absence, and we are thankful for the consciousness, God is with us."

Edith was tired and sore but perked up a bit when she had a letter from Willa. Sam was busy in the house and with the preparation of a garden spot up the hill. He wondered again why no letter had come from David in a long time. Sam worked the sod harder.

Sam's own words...
Thursday, May 18, 1933 – "At Eclipse nine hours. Was allotted a welfare garden and worked on it in evening."

Sam wasted no time to put row after row of seeds and plants in his vegetable plot. He put in 44 tomato plants. The uncle boys planted three rows of corn.

Sam sold fabric more than any other items but not fast. On May 27, the Eclipse gave him nine hours work, and he sold a suit in the evening. He had his early garden and the welfare plot. His hoe was kept busy, perhaps more active than most. And there was the housework. Grace and Roy brought Mother back to Sam and Edith.

Sam set out cabbage plants on June 6. When he had no factory hours, he worked in one garden or the other hours on end.

Sam's own words...
Monday, June 12, 1933 – "Planted potatoes in a.m., canvassed in p.m. Sold a pair of shoes."
Friday, June 16, 1933 –"Eclipse nearly nine hours. We had a good letter from David. He's been to Alaska and back and is on his return trip to that country. Cool and fair."

It was a pair of ladies' laced oxfords he had sold. The thin blue chambray cloth cover kept his Tanner shoe sample in perfect presentation condition. He delivered Mutual fabrics.

The long overdue postal delivery from David was a euphoric moment for Sam and Edith. They were anxious to share the news when Grace and Roy visited. Alaska was a foreign country. (Sam did not yet know that it would become a state in 1959, the largest state in the United States in land area, more than twice the size of Texas, California, and Montana combined.)

Good news came that Shirley would be home soon. She had been away about a year. Another message the next day slowed down the plans. Shirley Girl must have her tonsils out. She was quite miserable as reported to Edith when she phoned the Federation Farm.

Newspapers reported that all non-Nazi political parties were forbidden in Germany.

Sam's own words...
Thursday, July 6, 1933 – "At Eclipse 10½ hours. They brought Shirley home in evening. My, she is a tall girl for 11 years old."
Tuesday, July 11, 1933 – "Worked in garden. Went to Elmira and got Mother's $85 from the bank. Not sure it was proper thing to do but she wanted it."

Sam wondered if Dewey would disapprove. But Mother was not in Dewey's care, and she had asked Sam. In another week, Mary came and took Mother for a stay in her home. Reverend Skinner took Edith, Betty, and Shirley to Sunday school. Grace and Roy brought them back.

Sam's own words...
Sunday, August 6, 1933 – "Helped at home. Went up to garden and got cucumber, found four ripe tomatoes. The book, *Abundant Life*, is a great inspiration to me."

The *Abundant Life Day Book* devotions contained a year's worth of daily reminders of what it meant to live in the abundance of God's blessing through Christ.

Sam's own words...
Monday, August 14, 1933 – "Canvassed all day, sold two suits."
Tuesday, August 15, 1933 – "...Mary brought Mother back. Betty and Shirley took baby Teddy to Elmira clinic. He has German measles. Cool and fair."

Teddy was all of six months old and well loved by every member of the family. His Aunt Shirley adored him, and the uncle boys still thought he was just it.

Winston Churchill's first public speech made the news. He warned of the danger of German rearmament. Could they not be trusted this long after WWI?

Edith was sick again as a harsh headache pounded.

Sam's own words...
Thursday, August 24, 1933 – "At factory nine hours. Newtown Creek overflowed its banks and both my gardens under water."
Friday, August 25, 1933 – "Eclipse eight hours, earned $16 there this week, biggest weeks pay in over a year. Flood water receding, sunshine again."

On Sunday, Sam could get into the garden to assess damage, which was plenty. It would take time and effort to see what would survive. He delivered fabric and canvassed.

The uncle boys were exhilarated on Wednesday, August 30, when they saw Wiley Post and his plane, Willie Mae, at Sing-Sing Road airport. He was known as the Magellan of the Air, the first man to circumnavigate the globe alone. Here he was almost in their back yard.

Steele developed measles.

Sam's own words...
Saturday, September 2, 1933 – "Looked for another house. Dewey here awhile in evening. Was glad to see him."
Saturday, September 16, 1933 – "We moved to 404 Center Street today. All are tired but think we will like our new location."

Sunday, September 17, 1933 – "Sadie, Bob, and their children, Uncle George, Dewey, and Grace were all here today. Mighty glad to see all of them."

Tuesday, September 19, 1933 – "At factory eight hours. Dewey delivered the old family bible to us this evening."

Sam's eyes softened and filled with an inner glow as he accepted the Bible from Dewey. All tension was gone. Unasked for and unspoken forgiveness had evolved.

Life went along, as usual, a day of factory work, garden work, and sales. The National Industrial Act, enacted by Roosevelt, required a markup of the fabric line. Sam set the prices higher; he had no choice. He had to wonder if it would curtail sales.

The boys dug potatoes again for Waite Gould and got their pay. Sam kept track of the World Series that had begun October 3 when the New York Giants won over Washington. The Giants went on to win three games out of four.

Sam's own words...
Thursday, October 5, 1933 – "At factory eight hours. Eugene Frost ate supper with us and says he is going to a Federal Forest Camp the 16th. Cool, cloudy, rain."

Gene Frost had been an intermittent friend who appeared on the scene when he was back in the area. Hulziers also visited the Crippens at times. Gene spent all day with Sam and the family on Sunday.

Betty was 18 years old on Tuesday, October 10. Sam couldn't understand why David didn't write. Gene went to the Conservation Camp, and Shirley was on the honor roll. Sam walked after his pay, delivered fabric, and canvassed. He used the trip to look for a heat stove.

Current news had it that the refugee from Nazis, scientist Einstein, had come over from California to a new position. He settled in at the Institute for Advanced Study in Princeton, New Jersey.

Sam's own words...
Sunday, October 23, 1933 – "Rainy. Canvassed and made out Mutual fabric order; sold a suit. Teddy drank kerosene oil and had to have doctor. Mr. and Mrs. May here in evening."

Curiosity landed Teddy in trouble when he sampled the foul tasting fluid. The danger was that a child could develop chemical pneumonia if they choked and inhaled the substance into the lungs. Teddy hadn't suffered that consequence.

Sam sold an overcoat on Tuesday. His sister, Mary, came to see Mother on Wednesday and ordered a pair of Tanner shoes. Sam had several reasons to smile if he still knew how. Teddy had been watched carefully and showed no further signs of harm from kerosene ingestion. Sam most likely sighed, "Thank you, Lord."

The industrious boys Steele and John stayed all night at Gould's and picked up potatoes all the next day. Sam worked eight hours at the Eclipse on October 31. He recorded, "Halloween spirits are abroad tonight." The children had a great time.

Sam's own words...
Friday, November 3, 1933 – "Factory again eight hours. The best week I have had in two years, $17.64. Mr. Manley Parks notified me that my community garden won a prize."

It was a great way to cap off a week along with a visit from Grace and Roy, plus a letter from Willa. Mother went home with Whitings for a few days.

Sam's own words...
Monday, November 6, 1933 – "Betty and I went to the city; brought home a speed hoe, the garden prize given me. At factory four hours in p.m., three inches of snow."

Speed hoe may not have been the best description for Sam's prize. This implement depended upon how fast the gardener walked behind it. An iron roller with teeth was the front wheel, which was meant to disturb the soil surface with its modest width. Behind the beefed-up cylinder, cultivator prongs broke dirt to discourage weeds. The power thrust was from the operator's effective push performance.

Sam voted on the morning of November 7 and finished the day at the Eclipse. Reverend Skinner took Sam, Edith, and Betty to church in the

Heights. Betty had a week or more of work for another family. She and Teddy were missed.

Sam's own words...
Sunday, November 19, 1933 – "Busy around home most of day. More snow seems more like December. Boys at Bud Kerns to hear Eddie Cantor tonight."

Comedian Cantor clowned and sang for coins on street corners in New York City before he made it big. He became a superstar of early 20th-century radio, stage, and film, notably on NBC radio's the Chase and Sanborn Hour. The boys were set to laugh.

Sam's own words...
Thursday, November 23, 1933 – "At factory eight hours. Mother not feeling very well. I can't understand why David has not written in three months. Teddy is beginning to take a few steps. Colder."

At the early age of nine months, Teddy had begun the effort to walk. Sam sighed in relief and nodded his head when Mother said she felt better on Friday. He had more reason to be in good spirits when he paid his rent up through December 16. Dewey made a friendly visit to Sam on Sunday.

Sam's own words...
Tuesday, December 5, 1933 – "Canvassed in afternoon. Shirley and Betty went to church in evening, and they both went forward."

Sam's heart was blessed that both of his girls had knelt at the altar and accepted Christ as their Savior. Maybe it would allow him to worry less about Betty as he'd had recent occasion to do. He would try to leave it in God's care. Sam had another concern.

Sam's own words...
Friday, December 8, 1933 – "Eclipse nine hours. Received postcard from David. He is in a hospital in San Pedro, California, no explanation."

Sam could think of nothing else. What was David's condition and why didn't he write more than a line that kept them wondering? At least Edith had a letter from Arthur. Willa's letter was not far behind.

Sam had a 35-hour week at the factory, the most in any week for two years.

Reverend Skinner drove them all to church on Christmas Eve. Roy and Grace brought them home. Mother spent Christmas in Dewey and Mid's home. Mildred may have had a warm side, evident to many since she earned a nickname.

Sam's own words...
Monday, December 25, 1933 – "Grace and Roy ate dinner with us. My children all home except David and not even a card from him."
Friday, December 29, 1933 – "Freezing tonight. Report 50 below zero at Malone in Adirondack region; some say 18 degrees below in Horseheads. At Eclipse eight hours."
Saturday, December 30, 1933 – "Factory, four hours. I find this month gave me better returns than a year ago. Still cold but moderating tonight. David does not write."

24 – What Was Wrong
David, Edith, Economy, 1934, 1935

Sam carried his worry in the back of his mind whether he worked on a large wash for the family, worked at the Eclipse, or canvassed. He made time to read to the family. The children were quiet as they enjoyed every word. Edith's magnification glass, which she required, was used less when Sam read to the family. It was as much for her benefit as for the younger set.

Betty and Teddy spent over a week in Pine Valley at Grace and Roy's, and the family missed them.

Sam's own words...
Monday, January 8, 1934 – "Received a letter from David at last; says he is in a hospital with a slight hernia."
Wednesday, January 10, 1934 – "At factory eight hours, am thinking of David this evening and hope he is coming alright (sic)."

Sam had let out a long sigh when he knew David's situation, for the unknown had been worrisome.

The children's ages ranged from Shirley's (12), attained on January 20, to David's 20 years, soon to be reached on March 31. Sam's children grew and changed, but other things remained the same. Edith was not well. Grace, Roy, and Mother continued to visit. Dewey and their sister, Mary, did as well.

Sam's own words...
Thursday, February 1, 1934 – "At factory eight hours. We received a letter from David today, and he says he is OK again and will go on duty tomorrow, good news."

The world was right again now that Sam understood that David was fit for duty, and hours at the Eclipse had increased. Five inches of snow were taken in stride, especially underfoot on the way to work.

Their February 9 issue of *The Saturday Evening Post* arrived. The cover, this time, had Rockwell's rendition of a boy who was seated on a scaffold, painting a picture on a wall. The issue held a story that every family member enjoyed, titled *Death in the Air* by mystery writer Agatha Christy. The publication came each week, and the six-part story continued. It was sure to be the reason that the subscription of $2 per year kept people interested. It cost more at the newsstand at 5¢ per issue.

Sam had a friendship with another salesman, Mr. Brewer, the Rawleigh man. Mr. Brewer stopped in and ate dinner at their table on Monday. No doubt their discussion centered around the climate of the few buyers they were forced to try to reach.

The world news held Sam's attention after the day at the Eclipse on Tuesday. The socialist revolt in Austria had led to deaths as the government shelled buildings.

Sam's own words...
Wednesday, February 14, 1934 – "At factory eight hours, five below zero again this morning. Men, women, and children, fifteen-hundred killed in Austrian rebellion. What a world man makes."

It was 23 below zero on February 15, the coldest since 1904. Improvement two days later brought it to minus 10 degrees. Sam suffered while he canvassed and was in hope of moderation just ahead. Wiggle his toes in his boots as he might, it was too cold to fool himself into thinking he was warm enough. Severity lasted until the end of the month.

Sam's own words...
Wednesday, February 21, 1934 – "We shall not mention "old fashioned winters" for awhile: 25 people lose lives in worst blizzard since 1888. Mother went home with Mary today."

Ten inches of snow fell in Horseheads on the 26th, but 28 below zero on February 28 trumped that. It was dangerous and worrisome when coupled with the fact that 100 people had already lost their lives because of extreme weather in the United States this winter.

Sam was at the factory eight and a half hours on Friday, March 2, while the weather was moderate and snow melted fast. Everyone was in a better state of mind to celebrate Sam's 51st birthday, one day late on Sunday, March 4, when Grace and Roy came to dinner after church.

Sam's own words...
Wednesday, March 7, 1934 – "Factory eight hours. Moderate is good after so much cold. Betty and Teddy are away overnight, and we miss the little tike (sic)."

Sam sold Mutual fabrics often. An $8 order was the catalyst for thankfulness. He had a full week at the Eclipse just before Edith's 56th birthday on Friday, March 16. She had letters from Willa and David. Sam had sent fabric for Willa's 32nd birthday so that she could sew dresses for herself and daughters. Lee was 14 and Christy was 7.

Sam's own words...
Saturday, March 24, 1934 – "Marked Mutual fabric line updates, canvassed in afternoon. Had marvelous success; sold $14 worth in three hours. The Lord helps me."

His own success contrasted against the hard time Grace and Roy faced. Roy had no job and was broke. Sam and Edith extended more invitations for supper to them. Grace could not remain downcast when Shirley went home with them.

Sam considered his circumstances to be better than a year ago in a mental, spiritual, and material sense. Eclipse hours were expected to increase. Brother Skinner continued to help the Crippen family get to church. Sam most surely conferred with Edith about the April 6 newspaper. It was announced that the Gothenburg Prize for poetry went to William B. Yeats and also to a favorite of Sam and Edith's, Rudyard Kipling.

Sam's own words...
Monday, April 30, 1934 – "At factory six hours. We have not heard from David in a long time."

Sam had Carl Withune plow the garden on May 2. He looked out on dark furrows of plowed earth and made out a fabric order. After seven-and-a-half hours at the Eclipse on Friday, May 4, his spirits soared to receive 4¢ per-hour pay raise.

Sam's own words...
Sunday, May 27, 1934 – "Edith not well. Went to Heights Church. Grace and Roy brought us back and were here for dinner."

Betty and Teddy went home with Whitings to stay the week. They were missed at home, but Grace and Roy also enjoyed them wholeheartedly.

Sam's newspaper of Monday, May 28, extolled the unusual headline, DIONNE QUINTUPLETS, Born, and Survived. The five Canadian girls were identical and the first set of quintuplets ever to live past infancy. The Dionnes would be newsworthy their whole lives.

Edith had been ill five days before she went to the doctor Thursday evening, May 31. With that help she improved slightly and was glad to hear from Lenore Crow. Lenore planned to arrive from Twin Falls, ID, in three weeks.

Sam's own words...
Wednesday, June 6, 1934 – "At factory nine hours. Nice rain. Edith and Betty went before the grand jury to have Betty's marriage annulled and see if Al H. could be required to pay support for the baby. Boys set out cabbage and tomato plants."

The uncle boys were quite the garden team. Sam had set his example and expectations. Edith languished in weakness, unable to get better. She went to the doctor again Saturday evening, June 9. Sam worked 45 hours, the most in any week of the past two years. The satisfaction translated into glad tidings of welcome when Lenore came on Saturday evening, June 19. Her four-day visit was much too short but was embraced by every family member.

Sam's own words...
Thursday, June 21, 1934 – "Factory nine hours. Lenore left on the 6:19 pm Greyhound bus to Buffalo. We miss her. Had not seen her since December 1917."

Both boys covered soil over corn kernels and buried potatoes. They took planting directions as well as Sam hoed. Sam had begun his exercise already, intent to prevent weeds. He never failed to notice how sick Edith was. He'd change that if he could and wished the doctor had real answers. What was wrong?

Sam's own words...
Tuesday, June 26, 1934 – "Eclipse eight hours. Rain in p.m. and cooler. Richard Dupont breaks glider record of the world – Elmira to Somerset, New Jersey."

Du Pont established a new world distance record for a motor less airplane flight. He covered 155 miles to float on air like a feather, climbing over the Alleghany Mountains at 3,000 feet altitude. His time was four hours 50 minutes while three other entrants were forced down. Silent flight over the Chemung Valley became one of the most scenic and historic soaring sites in America. Harris Hill, adjoined with the National Soaring Museum, and Harris Hill Park developed into a pleasant day trip for tourists amid the beauty of the Finger Lakes.

Sam's own words...
Monday, July 2, 1934 – "At factory eight hours. Eighteen high government men and of German Army put to death by Hitler."

The headlines were an affront to Sam. What kind of monster was this Hitler? Pastor Skinner took Edith, Shirley, Betty, and Teddy to the Free Methodist revival camp meeting. Brother Skinner needed a tire and Sam was glad to pay the $1 for it. The meetings lasted three days.

Sam's own words...
Monday, July 9, 1934 – "Went to see Dr. Empert in a.m. At shop four hours in p.m., am convinced I should quit factory."
Tuesday, July 10, 1934 – "At Eclipse nine hours. Told James Lamb, my foreman, that this week would be my last."

The repetitive work at the factory was known to wear workers down over time. Resignation had entered Sam's mind before but the courage to do so caught on now that sales had picked up. Friday, July 13, was his final day. He told himself and his diary page, "I must make a success of selling. I do not want to go back, but forward. God help me." Sam's sales needed to be built up full time as fast as possible.

Sam's own words...
Monday, July 16, 1934 – "Canvassed all day, made $3. Am lifted up because I broke loose from the factory. Betty came home."

Sam intended to fight it out. Sell, sell, sell. Fabric sold.

On Sunday, July 22, he and Edith had a summer picnic on their lawn. The pleased relatives present were Dewey, Grace and Roy, Sadie, Bob and Annabelle, Edward Dimon, Alice, Ruth, Frances McCann, Mother, and Sam's children.

Sam's own words...
Thursday, July 26, 1934 – "Canvassed. Chancellor Englebert slain by Nazis in Vienna. Heat caused deaths, over twelve-hundred in U.S. Whither are we going?"

Sam took notice of the August 2 news. Adolf Hitler became Führer of Germany.

Betty got a job at Mrs. Herbert Mays, which took her and 18-month-old Teddy away from home and missed by everyone. Sam mailed fabric orders and Johnstonian shirt orders on Tuesday, August 7. His sales were still short of goals he had in mind

Gene Frost stopped in for supper with them on Friday.

Mr. Brewer, the Rawleigh man, ate supper at the Crippen table on Friday, August 17. They may have exchanged reports to each other about poor sales. The slump continued right through September, long after school had started. Sam worked hard every day to canvass without success. He also kept his hoe busy, no neglect allowed.

Sam wished David would write. There'd been no letter from him since May.

Sam's own words...
Wednesday, September 12, 1934 – "Tried to sell but no luck. One Million textile workers on strike more than a week. Largest United walk-out in U.S. history."

The next day's news reported a textile labor strike riot in Rhode Island, one killed and several injured. Sam's fabrics did not arrive, and no delivery meant no collections. On Monday, September 19, he had to see a welfare officer to assist in buying wood. He was broke. The work stoppage went on awhile but gave in after 22 days. Textile mills opened, and strikers went back to work.

Sunday, September 23, was a pleasant day, made so by visitors Dewey, Grace and Roy, and Betty with Teddy. The Mays, who also liked to visit, had brought Betty home to see them and return on the same trip. She worked for them in their farm house.

Sam's own words...
Tuesday, September 25, 1934 – "Canvassed all day. Bruno Hauptmann, a German, was arrested in the Lindberg baby kidnapping and murder case."
Friday, September 28, 1934 - "Delivered and canvassed. Don't succeed no matter how hard I work, but I shall continue to try."

October chill required a heat stove. Sam saw Mr. Lawrence at the welfare office about wood. He dug potatoes for five days straight. Roy needed help and Sam went home with him for three days. They put buckwheat in Roy's barn, dug potatoes, and cleaned up the garden.

As weak as sales had been, Sam saved out $15 for rent, which he paid to William Myers on Monday, October 22. That afternoon Dewey came from 1114 College Avenue, his home in Elmira, NY, for a visit that no doubt was good for both he and Sam.

Sam's own words...
Wednesday, October 31, 1934 – "Canvassed all day. Found our toilet badly broken and rolled over in garden. Our (community-wide) boys and girls are out tonight."

It was perpetrated pranks night, Halloween.
Edith was sick, and Shirley broke out in measles.

Sam's own words...
Friday, November 16, 1934 – "Dewey stopped with his meat truck a few minutes. Mother still at Mary's."

Dewey was pleased to drive in at Sam's to present his company-owned vehicle that had the Armour & Company logo to announce his product throughout the area he traveled. His meat delivery took him on routes all over Elmira, Horseheads, and outlier points. Oil company employment was behind him.

Edith was still not well. She went to the doctor again on Saturday, November 17. Her elevated blood pressure was confirmed once more. She had to take to her bed.

Sam walked to Elmira to apply for a temporary job to take traffic census. He mailed his fabric order and sold an order for three shirts while he was on his walkabout.

Sam's own words...
Wednesday, November 21, 1934 – "Walked up to Middle Road in p.m. and again at night to commence traffic census at midnight. Cold wind."

Sam conducted traffic count for eight hours at another location on Thursday. He would see the Middle Road again for a new tally at a different time of day than the first tally. Sunday was different. After Grace, Roy, and Dewey's visits, Sam took an unprecedented nap. He readied himself for another midnight moving vehicle count. Sam recorded his earnings for the three nights of the census at $7.20.

Thanksgiving on Thursday, November 29, was a blessed event according to Sam. He listed 13 relatives at Grace and Roy's for dinner. Edith was happy with a letter from Willa.

Sam canvassed but had limited success. Snowflakes licked at his heels as December announced itself. Edith went to the city to see the welfare officer. Quite likely she needed vouchers for medication and wood, extras they lacked the means to buy. So many people in the depression faced the same or worse circumstances. These hard times challenged them all. In mid-December Sam reluctantly received a grocery order.

Zero degree weather kept the usual visitors home, but Sam canvassed during the sub-zero days. He made 32¢ for his efforts. Steele went to collect for a bottle of vanilla sold but had no success. People were broke.

Sam's friend, Carl Withune, faced the same hard times and struggles. He had entered the sales field to peddle the Janol line. The beauty and body care products were no apparent threat to Sam. Sam would not discourage him and was glad to offer a meal to his former neighbor.

Sam's own words...
Saturday, December 22, 1934 – "Paid William Myers $12 rent."

Undoubtedly, Sam was relentless in how he saved to keep a roof over their heads.

Betty and Teddy were home during the days before Christmas, and the happiness to have them back shone brightly on the family's faces. On Sunday, December 23, they all went to church. A Christmas card arrived from David. Gene Frost and Dewey visited on Christmas Eve.

A blizzard raged the day after Christmas. There were deaths across the U.S. due to cold temperatures and storms. Edith was unwell. Sam hoped for her improvement in the new year.

~**~
1935

Mr. Brewer, the Rawleigh salesman, ordered a suit from Sam on Wednesday, January 2. The $4 commission was all Sam earned for the week.

Sam's own words...
Wednesday, January 9, 1935 – "All day rain and homebound. Newtown Creek about to overflow its banks. Have been reading "Ben Hur," a tale of the Christ by General Lew Wallace, an infidel who became a Christian before he finished the book."

Sam's time for thought made him consider a change of his product lines. But would he get around to it?

On Friday, January 11, Betty and the boys went to the young people's missionary society meeting. Sam had a letter from David and was pleased with all of his children. David informed them of his departure for the Philippines. Sam prayed for his safety.

The news of Amelia Earhart's first solo flight from Hawaii to California held particular significance now.

The trial of Bruno Hauptmann, the Lindberg baby kidnapper, had begun. Sam followed the story along with the masses in hope for justice. Desperate times brought out the worst in a few unexpected places and people. The Barker Gang's sprees of kidnappings, murderers, and bank robberies needed to stop. It included Ma Barker and family members killed in an FBI shootout at her Ocklawaha home in Florida. People shook their heads, and Sam was no exception.

Sam's own words...
Friday, January 18, 1935 – "Canvassed all day, sold $1.52 worth of goods. Made out Mutual fabric order and mailed it one week late because I could not make necessary collections. Quite cold."

Was the first month of the year to be the pattern for the remainder of 1935, a fight for survival. Shirley turned 13 years old on January 20.

Sam finished reading Ben Hur during another all-day rain.

The weather deteriorated to minus temperatures as much as 14 below zero right into February. Mr. Brewer came to talk awhile on Monday, February 7, and warm himself by Sam's fire. Sam no doubt would have been glad to say that he'd recently sold three pairs of Tanner shoes. Sam told him, "I would like to live where it does not get so cold." Edith was down at the Heights Church and had little Donny Brooks with her.

Sam read of Bruno Hauptmann, who was sentenced to die in the electric chair, for the murder of the Lindberg child.

Betty and Teddy were home on the weekends. She worked in the Harrington household all week. On February 22, Sam read that planes were banned from flying over the White House and supposed it was the right idea. Eight inches of snow greeted them on Tuesday, February 23. Sam's 52nd birthday fell on March 3. Another eight inches of snow was ahead.

In Nazi Germany, Hitler ordered the reinstatement of the air force, the Luftwaffe, in violation of the 1919 Treaty of Versailles. On March 16, he announced rearmament, another move counter to the treaty agreement.

Sam's own words...
Tuesday, March 19, 1935 – "Sold $1 worth goods. War clouds hang darkly over Europe and many people think war is inevitable."
Thursday, March 21, 1935 – "Canvassed, sold $5 worth. Europe doesn't look so good. Teddy quite sick. Dust from dry region of west carried by strong winds surrounds mountains around Elmira."
Friday, March 29, 1935 – "Canvassed, made $1. Letter from Willa. She moved to Denver, Colorado."

Two weeks later the dust bowl storm in the United States hit eastern New Mexico, Colorado, and western Oklahoma the hardest. The Dust Bowl chronicles the worst man-made, ecological disaster in American history, in which the frenzied wheat boom of the "Great Plow-Up," of the 1930s nearly swept away the breadbasket of the nation. A decade-long drought followed. The Woodie Guthrie ballad about it became famous.

Sam supposed David's Navy enlistment ended March 31. He was expected home in a few days. Mother Sophia was not well. Dewey came to Sam's to see her Sunday, April 7. The doctor was called on Tuesday. She could retain no food or medicine. Day by day Sam recorded dismay over his mother's health. Many family visitors came to see how she was. Dewey was as attentive as all the others. Dr. Empert thought she ought to recover, but Sam was not so sure since she refused food and medicine. Grace spent a few overnights to take care of her. The county nurse stopped in.

Sam's own words...
Tuesday, April 16, 1935 – "...Betty in Elmira today sewing for welfare board."
Monday, April 22, 935 – "...David not home yet, nor does he send any message."

Roy and Grace had been notified to move as the Pine Valley farm had been sold.

The nurse who visited on Tuesday, April 30, informed them that Mother's pulse was not strong. Sam considered Mother to be a skeleton, compared to earlier. The new pastor, Brother Frances Pond, visited them all. Sam had to take the time to deliver and collect on Mutual fabrics.

There was someone with Mother night and day, either Sam, Edith, Grace, or Betty. They were all worn out with worry over her refusal to eat or take medicine. Grace's daughter, Alice Jeffrey, came to lend a few hours assistance.

The newspaper was a brief escape for Sam on Monday, May 6. He learned that under President Roosevelt's New Deal, an executive order was signed to create the WPA (Works Progress Administration) for the United States. He would know more later.

Bad news took no holiday. Sam read the May 21st Hitler announcement of intent to reinstate conscription to build a new army. It further disregarded the Versailles Treaty. Thursday, May 30, Sam gave no attention to the last game of Babe Ruth, who played for the Boston Braves. The eventual Hall of Famer went unacclaimed by Sam, because of preoccupation over his mother's failing health.

Sam's own words...
Saturday, May 11, 1935 - "Collected for fabrics in a.m. Mother weaker. Dr. Empert says she can't stay much longer. He thinks she has cancer of the stomach. I hope for her sake, it will not be long. Mary came today and will stay up part of the night with Mother."

Grace came the next morning just as Mother's spirit departed at 10:30 a.m. In three days the body of Sophia Dimon Crippen was laid in the family plot in Galeton. Sam wrote, "Her precious soul is with her maker."

Sam's own words...
Sunday, May 19, 1935 – "Grace and Roy were here, glad to see them. I can't understand why we don't hear from David. We have heard no word from him in several months."
Friday, May 24, 1935 – "Worked in garden. Tried to collect some bills. People do not pay me, and I cannot meet my obligations."
Tuesday, May 28, 1935 – "Edith went to city to have her eyes fitted with glasses."
Thursday, May 31, 1935 – "Edith to city and returned with her spectacles. She feels she will see and read much better. It is a godsend to her and almost too good to be true."

Not only did Sam plant cucumbers and squash, but also a variety of zinnias. It would satisfy his and Edith's finer senses evidenced by the love of poetry.

Sam's own words...
Wednesday, June 5, 1935 – "Worked in garden. Navy Department informed us David joined service two more years and is on the USS Ramapo. It is a great relief to know."

Sam planted late sweet corn, set out 42 pepper plants, and 52 tomato plants.

Sam's own words...
Sunday, June 9, 1935 - "An outstanding day to me; a reunion with all my brothers and sisters and their children and grandchildren. It did us all good, and I hope we will all meet this way once a year. Am glad I am learning to have faith in good rather than evil."

Sam and Edith had been married 22 years on June 19. On Sunday evening, June 23, John, who was 19 years old, was on his way to C.C.C. Camp with Gene Frost. He had a new car, at least new to him. The Civilian Conservation Corps was part of Roosevelt's New Deal. Fifty-million dollars had been allocated to finance school and job training for boys and girls between 16 and 25 years of age.

Sam tended his garden and canvassed most days. Everyone in the family had fun planned for Independence Day and dispersed to various activities. Edith and Shirley went to stay at Grace and Roy's until Sunday. Sam contented himself to stay home and cultivate a friendly relationship with his hoe.

Sam's own words...
Tuesday, July 4, 1935 – "Teddy and I are here alone. He is a darling. We lighted a box of sparklers, and he thought it was great fun. Worked in garden. Warm."

Grandpa Sam delighted in his 2½-year-old sidekick. He'd have no problem cooking for himself and the little guy who followed him around the garden.

Sam's own words...
Monday, July 8, 1935 – "Rain all day. Betty went to Watkins Glen, NY, yesterday and could not get back because of cloudbursts and floods. Steuben County nearly all under water and many lives lost along the line from Watkins. Ithaca and as far as Binghamton are reported to have all bridges gone."
Thursday, July 11, 1935 – "Newspaper said, Burdett (above Watkins) is isolated from other towns. I fear Betty may not get home very soon. Am thankful she is safe."

It was eight days before Betty was able to go home. She was with her friend, Gladys Voorheis but had the consolation of knowing how well Teddy would fare without her in the midst of her family. She had no reason to worry about him.

Edith had canned 28 quarts of cherries by July 18. Sam hoed his oversized garden. Canvass efforts brought only fabric sales. The electric was turned off for failure to pay. Grace and Roy moved to town.

On Friday, August 2, Betty and Teddy went to spend the weekend with her friend, Gladys Voorheis at her family home in rural Hector.

John had continued at C.C.C. Camp and drew a check for $19 on August 5. He was proud to help his family.

Sam's newspaper held information that was (and remains) relevant to every person. President Franklin D. Roosevelt signed the Social Security Act into law on Thursday, August 14. The act was to provide for the general welfare by establishing a system of federal old-age benefits. It enabled the states to make more adequate provision for aged persons, blind persons, dependent and crippled children, maternal and child welfare, public health, and the administration of their unemployment compensation laws. He also established a Social Security Board and revenue for the administration and other purposes.

In the Crippen household, the social security news overshadowed a report in the next days news. Sam saved the entire tabloid for John and Steele to pour over. The boys had a grand claim to having seen and idolized the famous and dearly departed.

Sam's own words...
Friday, August 1, 1935 – "Will Rogers, Wiley Post killed in airplane crash 15 miles from Point Barrow, Alaska. Our nation suffers a real loss in the death of two great men."

The Elmira *Star-Gazette* extolled Will Rogers as a cowboy, humorist, writer, lecturer, polo player, and world traveler. Wiley Post was a world-class pilot who flew around the world in just under 10 days.

Uncle George Dimon arrived August 20 for a few days stay. He and Sam caught up with all the world and local news of Horseheads and Galeton before Uncle George returned to Pennsylvania on August 25.

Betty and Teddy often stayed at the home of Gladys Voorheis Landon, who had married and now lived in Reynoldsville, NY. It was not far from the Voorheis family home. Betty had found an attraction there in the form of Gladys's brother, Edwin.

School was in session again for Steele and Shirley on September 3.

Sam's own words...
Tuesday, September 17, 1935 – "Canvassed all day, little success. Edith had a faint spell this morning, and we called Dr. Empert. She seems better this rainy evening."

All too often Sam had written, "Edith not well." She rested in her bed while Sam and Grace canned chili sauce and discussed the worrisome world on the verge of war. European warfare seemed inevitable. They canned peaches and did the wash. The two siblings would always be best friends. Edith did not improve fast as September ended.

Sam's own words...
Friday, October 4, 1935 – "Busy at home a.m. Canvassed p.m. Edith's eyes very bad but doctor says they may improve if she does nothing but rest..."
Sunday, October 6, 1935 – "Heavy frost this morning. Edith went to Heights Church with Grace and Roy."

Monday again. Sam made out a fabric order, cut corn, and pulled beans. They received a long-awaited and welcome letter from David. He was on his way to Manila in the Philippines.

Garden work on Tuesday meant the start of digging potatoes. John came home from C.C.C. Camp to have a tooth pulled. He also dug potatoes. Betty turned 20 years old on October 10.

Sam's own words...
Sunday, October 13, 1935 – "Edith, Shirley and I went with Betty and her Edwin Voorheis to take John back to C.C.C. Camp in p.m."

Sam harvested carrots, turnips, and beets. He dug a hole and buried the root vegetables in the garden. Dewey visited for a few minutes on Wednesday.

Sam's own words...
Friday, October 25, 1935 – "Delivered and collected Mutual fabrics. Grace went to city with Edith to see occultist about her eyes, and he says they are no better."
Sunday, October 27, 1935 – "Edith feeling quite miserable and doctor doesn't seem to help her much."

Sam and Edith were at a loss for her relief when not even the doctor could come up with an answer to help. What were they to do?

The news concerned the Nuremberg laws that went into effect two months earlier. The reason for them became evident now. The German Jews became deprived of citizenship. Sam may have pondered on the unfair situation and wondered what the Jews were to do. What could happen to them because of the deprivation?

Steele must have been a happy young man as he started to sell books on Saturday, November 16. He did well on orders for " The Life of Will Rogers." Steele may have used Rogers' quote as a selling point. He could smile as he repeated a quip by the famous man. Live in such a way that you would not be ashamed to sell your parrot to the town gossip.

Sam pulled turnips, canvassed, and mailed a box of dried corn to Willa. She was working on a Works Progress Administration (WPA) job as a clerk.

Sam's own words...
Wednesday, November 20, 1935 – "Am worried about Edith's eyes. I pray she does not go blind."

Saturday, November 23, 1935 – "Delivered, canvassed, worked around house. Big plane, China Clipper, arrived in Honolulu after fighting headwinds. Mussolini of Italy warns France against oil ban. Colder."

The China Clipper had flown from Alameda, CA, to carry the first airmail cargo across the Pacific Ocean. On November 29, the aircraft reached its final destination, Manila, to deliver 110,000 pieces of mail.

The Crippens had a quiet but blessed Thanksgiving, Thursday, November 28.

Sam's own words...
Wednesday, December 4, 1935 – "Went with bunch of WPA workers up to Terry Hill for road work. It was too cold and windy, and we came back. Saw Mr. Lawrence and was transferred to surveyors gang in Horseheads. Received letter from David, still in Manila at time of writing."
Friday, December 6, 1935 – "Worked on sewer survey. Edith saw Dr. Glover today, and he says she is in precarious condition and must go to hospital. Nothing can be done for her eyes until her physical condition is better. John came home this evening but must return to C.C.C. Camp tonight. We can only trust in God's love."

John's quick trip to see his mother came at the expense of his needed rest. His soft heart was as welcome as Sam's own along with his faith. Sam continued on the sewer survey with only Sunday off. His forehead was creased with wrinkles when Dr. Empert said he could not help Edith.

Sam's own words...
Monday, December 9, 1935 – "God is always the last resort of the helpless."
Wednesday, December 11, 1935 "Saw Mr. Lawrence and Dr. Empert on arrangements for Edith to go to St. Joseph's Hospital Saturday. We hope they may do much for her."

Sam watched over Edith on Thursday and Friday. A foot of snow fell while he managed the housework, rechecked his fabric line, and canvassed close to home. A company man delivered Steele's books to him and helped him distribute them while also collecting from his customers on Saturday. All of the children went to the hospital Sunday to see their mother.

Sam's own words...
Monday, December 16, 1935 – "Sewer survey work. Am thinking of Edith and hope she feels better and is not too lonesome. It's a shame none of us can see her every day."
Wednesday, December 18, 1935 – "Helped men clean town hall. Betty and Steele saw Edith this evening. She is cheerful and better but thinks she will be hospitalized a long time."
Thursday, December 19, 1935 – "Helped at town hall...Received first WPA check for $ 11.55."

While Sam worked Friday, Brother Frances Pond took Shirley and Steele to the hospital. Edith seemed improved. Willa had written with concern over her mother. Sam wrote to her again. She still had work with WPA but was a production hand now, possibly assembly work.

Sam's own words...
Friday, December 20, 1935 – "They say Edith has diabetes in a mild form. Am encouraged because they know her trouble and can devise help for her. Alliances are sought by British against Italian attack. Colder."
Saturday, December 21, 1935 – "At town hall work. Children to hospital to see Edith and she improves. Mr. and Mrs. William Voorheis stopped here a few minutes on their way home from Christmas shopping in the city. John came home in a.m."
Sunday, December 22, 1935 – "Edwin Voorheis took John, Steele, and I (sic) down to hospital to see Edith. Edwin took his brother back to job in NY City, and Steele went along. Betty went to church and John back to camp. Grace visited and is not well."

John turned 19 on December 23. The whole family went to the hospital December 24. Edith said she felt quite good, but Sam thought she was too thin. Christmas Day was a bit subdued without her at home. Betty, Edwin, John, and Steele went to see her in the evening while Teddy stayed home with Grandpa. Shirley stayed to play with her adored nephew.

Six inches of snow fell on Thursday, December 26. Steele got to see his mother. Edith had a card from Lenore that Sam sent along with Steele to her. John went back to C.C.C. Camp in the evening. Betty received her second WPA check for sewing. The children all gave a portion of their money for home support where it was needed most.

Sam got a ride over to see Edith, Friday. He thought she was better and hoped she could come out soon. They all missed her. Edwin had taken Betty, Grace, and Mary to see Edith on Saturday. He came back on Sunday, December 29, to take Betty, Teddy, Shirley, and Sam to see her. She sat up in bed for the first time during her hospital stay.

Sam's own words...
Tuesday, December 31, 1935 – "Only a few more hours in the old year. I am not complaining, but I hope the New Year deals more kindly with us than the one just closing."

But would it?

25 – Help Her Now?
1936, 1937, 1938

Sam and Betty continued their WPA jobs at town hall and the clothing bureau. As the only parent in the house, Sam cooked, washed, and cleaned. His children contributed money and helped with housework. They would all be glad when Edith came home.

It was in the evening, January 17, when she returned after 35 days absence from home. Sam and Edith took note of and commiserated with each other on the death of one of their favorite authors, Rudyard Kipling, on January 18.

The worst snow storm in Horseheads and the Southern Tier hit on Sunday, January 19. Betty, Teddy, and Steele took Edwin home to North Road (now Voorheis Road) in the afternoon, which was in Trumansburg in Hector Township. They returned in the early morning hours of the next morning.

Sam shoveled snow eight hours on Tuesday, half of it for the town hall. Snow shovels, which included his, were busy in the city for two more days. Big drifts blocked New York state roads while 8,000 cars stalled in it. The eastern United States was in the grip of sub-zero weather.

Sam went back to sewer surveying eight hours a day for most of February. Sales success was elusive but just once he sold $2 worth of goods for the month.

Sam's own words...
Thursday, February 13, 1936 – "Went over Mutual fabric line and worked around home. Teddy, my little grandson, is three years old today. Warmer and snowing."

Sam was Grandpa-Daddy to Teddy. While Grandpa cooked for the family, Teddy sat in his high chair to watch. No doubt he put food on Teddy's plate first and put it down onto his tray. Grandma was so often sick and lying down that she was unable to fulfill the role of housewife.

Sam's own words...
Saturday, February 28, 1936 – "Edith went to Dr. Glover, and he says there is slight eye improvement. Did cooking and canvassed."
Wednesday, March 4, 1936 – "On sewer survey eight hours. President Roosevelt's tax plan arouses congress. New Dealers hail program as recovery."
Saturday, March 21, 1936 – "Snowstorm prevented my work. Floods spread death and destruction—168 deaths and 260-thousand homeless in 13 states. These are terrible times. Canvassed in p.m."

The weather had been a fierce, wintery situation through several weeks of hardship.

Dewey visited Sam for a while on Sunday, March 22. Dewey had his appointment as a guard at Woodbourne Reformatory in Woodbourne, NY. Sam may naturally have thought that his self-assured brother was a laudable fit for the task. No inmate was likely to intimidate an individual as shrewd as Claude Dewey Crippen.

John had come home as he always did on Sunday. He expected to go west with his C.C.C. unit but was not crazy about it. One week later John quit. Sam hoped he could find another job.

Sam's own words...
Friday, April 3, 1936 – "On survey one day. News came that Hauptman was executed shortly after eight o'clock in evening. Cold and windy."

Hauptman died silent and unmoved, no confession to kidnapping and killing the Lindberg baby. Fifty-five people witnessed the execution.

Grace, Alice, and Sadie's mother-in-law, Mrs. Madison visited the Crippens.

April 6 news reported 1,000 people injured and 130 dead by tornadoes from Arkansas to North Carolina. Damage was estimated in the millions of dollars. It got worse with 2,000 injured and 380 more bodies discovered. The weather took an awful toll in 1936.

European news hit bottom. Italian forces had used gas on Ethiopian troops. Sam mulled over the newsprint as he worked on the survey and learned that appropriation had to be made to pay him and other workers before more work would be assigned.

He cleaned his cellar and canvassed without luck. Sam had been without work for two weeks when he was forced to call on Mr. Lawrence once again. He delivered fabric and canvassed. Near the end of April, Teddy had mumps. The uncomfortable little boy stayed with Grandpa while Edith, Betty, and Grace went to a sale. The two uncle boys went to a dance.

Sam's own words...
Sunday, May 10, 1936 – "Edith, Shirley, Betty, Teddy and I went with Edwin Voorheis to see about a farm he might rent and spent the p.m. with his people."
Wednesday, May 13, 1936 – "Planted beans, canvassed and helped at home. Showers."
Thursday, May 21, 1936 – "Worked in garden all day. Saw Dewey a few minutes. He likes his guard position and will go back to Woodbourne, NY, Sunday."

Appropriations had not materialized and left Sam and others jobless. After he canvassed, cooked, and cleaned, he could be found in the garden.

Edwin rented the Terry farm near Montour Falls. Sam, Edith, and everyone but the two boys spent all day Sunday there with him. Edwin had found a job with WPA, but John remained without a position. Edwin was in search of a used tractor. Edith, Betty, Teddy, and Grace went to stay three days on the farm and provided a civilized touch with thorough cleaning and hanging of curtains.

Sam had stayed home for the express purpose of planting his garden. He set out 80 tomato plants and 12 pepper plants. A downpour fell on June 11 and did a little damage. In his solitude, he may have read a notice about the issue of Margaret Mitchell's new book, *Gone With The Wind*, just published in the U.S.

Sam's own words...
Saturday, June 13, 1936 – "Canvassed a.m., worked in garden p.m. Betty, Teddy, and the boys are up to the Terry farm again; boys expect to run the Fordson Tractor Edwin bought. Edith caring for Donny Brooks."

Edwin left for Rochester on Monday, June 15, with the tractor motor to have it overhauled. In four days, he returned with an engine that ought to have been like new. Steele went straight back up to the farm to plow for him. Edwin and John both went to work for WPA.

Sam usually worked all day in his garden and just as often did the cooking.

The Democrats nominated Franklin D. Roosevelt for president and Garner as vice president. Gene Frost, Sam's friend, paid a visit and said he intended to bring his sweetheart from Mississippi and marry her. John and the whole crew got laid off the road work they were on. He was forced to hunt for a new job.

Sam's own words...
Thursday, July 9, 1936 – "Worked in garden in a.m. Did little in p.m.; the hottest I think we ever experienced—114 degrees."

Sam set out cabbage plants for Grace. Every member of the family went up to Edwin's Terry Hill farm and worked two whole days, July 4 and 5, to make a garden. Edwin's job and farm work had left him no time to establish one.

It was not a one-day affair, this heat. The newspaper reported 138 deaths in the United States and the next day another 300 succumbed.

Crops failed. Sam's garden suffered as he hoped for rain.

Dewey and Mildred visited Monday evening, July 13.

John remained jobless.

Heat and drowning took 1,400 more people to their deaths.

Sam's own words...
Wednesday, July 15, 1936 – "Canvassed in a.m. Edwin, Betty, Shirley and I went to Elmira in the evening and saw *Mutiny on the Bounty*, which we enjoyed. Cooler but still no rain."
Thursday, July 16, 1936 – "Busy at home. Edith not very well. John found two or three days work. Had to see Mr. Lawrence again."

The movie showed that HMS Bounty left England in 1787 on a two-year voyage over the Pacific Ocean. The ship's captain, William Bligh (Charles Laughton), was a brutal tyrant who routinely administered harsh punishment to officers and crew alike who lacked discipline or who defied his authority. Fletcher Christian (Clark Gable), the ship's lieutenant, was a formidable yet compassionate man who disapproved of Bligh's treatment of the crew.

Edith was sick.

The national drought wore on, and the death toll rose to 4,000. It was time to put up hay on the Terry farm. On Saturday, July 18, Betty, Teddy, Shirley, and Steele pitched in to help Edwin.

Sam's own words...
Tuesday, July 21, 1936 – "Busy at home all day. Canvassed in evening. Edwin and boys put up more hay. Teddy has a dog he calls Ginger, and he is a happy boy. Cool and dry."

The prize pooch probably was the color of the spicy name.

Thursday brought a most welcome shower. It was a blessing repeated again on Friday. Sam delivered fabric, collected, and canvassed.

On Saturday, Edith took a fall, which left her badly shaken. Two days later, Sam saw that she was still not well. The boys picked up junk iron and did pretty well to sell it. John found temporary work on a hay press. Saturday, August 1, Sam paid $5 to Mr. Myers on July's past due rent. Now Edwin had no job. He loaned his car to Gene Frost to go to Tennessee and bring back his intended bride, a Mississippi girl.

Sam concentrated on his garden and prepared three meals a day. He canvassed and made 12¢ commission.

Sam's own words...
Tuesday, August 11, 1936 – "If I lose my faith I lose all. I will myself not to lose my faith."
Saturday, August 15, 1936 – "Canvassed, collected for fabrics, cooked. Gene and Lucille returned from Tennessee. They had a collision in Virginia, both hurt, Lucille quite badly. Car damage considerable."

John started his WPA job, and Edwin started a truck driver job. He made two trips to New York City, which earned him $9. On August 24 he found a job in a sawmill. Edwin got a new car.

Edith received Willa's letter that told her about the death of Minnie, Arthur's wife. Sam and Edith no doubt wrote to Arthur right away.

September required canning of peaches, drying of corn, and more harvesting. Sam helped Edith as much as possible. The wash needed doing first then they canned corn and beans.

Pastor and Mrs. Pond came to a goodbye dinner at the Crippen's before going to their new appointment in Binghamton. Tomatoes, peaches, and pears were canned. Sam dried more corn every week. He checked his fabric lines and mopped floors.

Betty, Teddy, and Edwin went to the Voorheis Reunion.

Sam's own words...
Tuesday, September 22, 1936 – "Edith had a letter from David, the only one in months. He has a job in the Bellevue Hotel in San Francisco. Not in Navy since June 7."
Tuesday, October 6, 1936 – "Busy in house and garden. Teddy's second day in Kindergarten and he likes it fine. Ruth McCann took Shirley to see Shirley Temple in *Poor Little Rich Girl*. Edith caring for Donny Brooks tonight."
Thursday, October 8, 1936 – "Did cooking, which is no small task when you have eight to feed. John and Edwin went to Industrial school this evening."

Gene and Lucille Frost often stopped in. Sam started to dig his potatoes. Dewey and Mildred visited.

Sam's own words...
Saturday, October 17, 1936 – "Cooked, canvassed. Grace, Roy, Edith and I (sic) went to Elmira in evening to hear the great Argyle Salvation Army Band from Hamilton, Ontario."

It was an evening of entertainment presented by the Army's Metro Toronto Reservist Band, one of many member bands. The evening together for both couples was half of the enjoyment.

Sam had dug all of his spuds by October 21. The European situation made for tense news again.

Sam's own words...
Thursday, October 29, 1936 – "Edwin and Betty will be married soon and are going to take over a gas station at Watkins Glen."
Wednesday, November 4, 1936 – "Roosevelt and Garner win in 46 of the 48 states to set a new record."
Friday, November 6, 1936 – "Betty and Edwin Voorheis were married at noon today by the Reverend Mr. Travis of Burdett, NY. God grant they may be blessed."

Sam recorded the many visits that Betty, Edwin, and Teddy made to them. Gene and Lucille took Edith and Shirley with them up to the farm for dinner on Sunday, November 22. Betty put on a big meal.

Sam set up their cook stove in the dining room on Tuesday since Edith agreed to abandon the cold kitchen for the winter. The cool draft could be shut out with the closed door and rags stuffed tight under the bottom of it.

Sam's own words...
Thursday, November 26, 1936 – "Taken with chill last night and have been ill all day. The boys and Shirley ate Thanksgiving dinner with Edwin and Betty. Edith stayed home with me, the only Thanksgiving we have been entirely alone."

Steele remained on the farm to help Edwin cut wood, and Betty brought him home Saturday. Sunday became a treat for Sam when his sisters, Sadie and Mary, came with their children. Both Dewey and Grace enjoyed them in their homes, too.

Betty had no washer and came down to wash with Edith on Monday, November 30. Edwin came after Sam and Edith December 3 to take them to Watkins and show them the gas station he managed. His big grin was about pride in his work.

Sam had sold Foster extract deals and delivered those as well as fabric.

Sam's own words...
Friday, December 25, 1936 – "Saw all of my children but David. Grace ate dinner with us. Betty, Edwin, and little Teddy had to go to up to Edwin's folks to spend time. Gene and his Lucille were here a few hours, a wonderful day."
Saturday, December 26, 1936 – "Bill Tuck (old friend, Penn.) arrived in afternoon, and we were glad to see him. He insisted he wanted to take us to a show. Grace, Shirley, Mary McCann (Ruth's girl), Roy, and I all went with him, but Roy wouldn't go in the theater, against his religion."

Tuck remained overnight to talk at length with Sam as old friends will. Teddy was brought back to stay the night for his and his grandparents' enjoyment. John and several others were laid off. It was no way to face the new year.

Sam's own words...
Thursday, December 31, 1936 – "Tried to sell and collect but failed. 1937 to be first year of prosperity since 1929, says Roger W. Bobson, famed economist. Edith and Shirley looking after neighbor's children tonight. Boys went to city, I guess. I am all alone."

New Year's Eve was the reason the others were out on the town. While Sam was alone, no doubt he reflected on his hope that the economist was right and the economy would improve. Would the new year be better?

~**~

1937

It was the everyday stuff that made life worthwhile. Sam, Edith, Shirley, and Steele had dinner with Grace and Roy, who took them to Watkins to see Betty, Edwin, and Teddy. It was a fine way to start the first day of the new year.

Sam's own words...
Tuesday, January 5, 1937 – "Home all day. Fifteen General Motors Corporation plants are affected by strike. President Roosevelt may intervene."

Wednesday, January 6, 1937 – "Busy at home. Edith not so well. She went to doctor in p.m. John had no job since December 28. William R. Hearst earns $500-thousand and Mae West $480,833 per year."

Hearst was a larger-than-life figure who, for a time, controlled much of the U.S. news media. West was an American actress, singer, playwright, screenwriter, and sex symbol. Sam may have thought there was a glaring inequity from zero to riches. He was well read and picked out the earnings of the famous figures to make his point.

John went to the city each day to look for work. Edith was finally better by January 15. It was Friday, and Teddy stayed with them while Betty and Edwin went to a show. It was raining and cold, sure to turn to snow, which it did. John found short-term work January 26 in a pocketbook factory.

Sam's own words...
Tuesday, February 2, 1937 – "Did housework, helped wash. Troops bar food from sit-down strikers in General Motors plants in Flint, Michigan. Cold, windy."

The strike was over as soon as General Motors recognized the validity of the union. The factories were put back into production on Friday, February 12. It did nothing for prosperity in Horseheads that Sam could tell. He sold fabric and a few other items as time went on. Life's good times came along when Sam and Edith shared a meal with Grace and Roy or Betty, Teddy, and Edwin.

War rumors persisted.

Sam's own words...
Saturday, March 6, 1937 – "Canvassed, helped at home. Six governors protest cut in federal relief rolls."
Tuesday, March 9, 1937 – "Cooked, canvassed. Nine Chrysler plants closed by strikes – 100-thousand idle in U.S."

The newspaper reported on President Franklin D. Roosevelt's first fireside chat over the radio. Even better was Teddy's two-day stay with Sam and Edith. Edith turned 59 years old on Tuesday, March 16. Grace and Roy furnished a dinner and ate with them to celebrate.

Sam's own words...
Thursday, March 18, 1937 – "Busy at home, too stormy to canvass. Amelia Earhart and her crew of three from Oakland, California, to Honolulu, Hawaii, in less than 16 hours on what was named their Sunset Trail around the world."

As usual, the newspaper contained the background of the principle player. Amelia started her career during WWI as a nurse's aid in Toronto, Canada, looking after wounded soldiers. In 1920, after savings from multiple jobs, including photographer, truck driver, and stenographer, she saved the $1,000 needed to take flying lessons. In 1923, she had become the 16th woman to be issued a pilot's license. It was interesting to Sam and Edith and all who read it. Soon the everyday realities brought them back to the ordinary versus the celebrated.

Sam's own words...
Sunday, March 21, 1937 –"Cooked. Betty, Teddy, and Edwin came down, and we went to Corning to see Mrs. Charles Barney whose husband was killed by a hit and run driver three weeks ago. She has five children, the oldest only ten years old."

It is not hard to imagine that they all had a contribution for Mrs. Barney. Sam could have given fabric and maybe vegetables from his cellar. Edwin, perhaps meat from butchering, and Betty, possibly homemade loaves of bread. They would not have made the visit empty-handed.

Sam learned of progress in the Chrysler strike.

Sam's own words...
Wednesday, March 24, 1937 – "Canvassed, no sales. Chrysler strike settlement near. This world of ours is full of trouble, or is it me? Edith at Dr. Brooks to watch Donny again tonight."

On the last day of March, an Easter card arrived from David. Sam likely smiled to see Edith clasp the long-awaited missive over her heart for a moment. His own heart understood. He was just as glad for Roy's good news on April Fool's Day when he announced his promotion to foreman on a WPA road job.

Sam's Shirley Girl was with Lucille Frost for the weekend, an often repeated stay-over. Edwin, Betty, and Teddy came just as often to see Sam and Edith.

The strike of 462,000 miners of soft coal was in force on April 2. One of the Ford auto plants was off production by sit-down strikers, Saturday, April 3.

Sam's own words...
Wednesday, April 7, 1937 – "Cooked, canvassed in p.m. Edith and Shirley caring for neighbor's children tonight, boys both out. I am the woman of the family."

Sam could use more sales and a change of scenery to alleviate his self-doubts. He and Shirley went over to Grace's Sunday and listened to radio in the evening.

Sam's own words...
Friday, April 16, 1937 – "Delivered fabrics, cooked, cleaned bedroom. Mildred, Dewey's wife, died today. God help him. Edith at Betty's."

Dewey was at Grace's for a few minutes the next day. She told Sam that Dewey took the loss very bravely. Lynn, their brother, arrived on Sunday. Edwin, Betty, and Teddy came down from the farm. Everyone attended the funeral on Monday, April 19. Grace and Edith went to stay a few days with Dewey to help him dispose of a few things and arrange others. It had been a sad week, and Dewey would feel the loss. (Surely they all knew the reason for the death, but it was not recorded in Sam's diary.)

Sam's own words...
Thursday, April 22, 1937 – "Did housework, an all-day rain. Shoe strike, rioting in Lewiston, Maine area brings out militia; three C.I.O, organizers arrested."
Friday, April 23, 1937 - "Cooked, canvassed. A.F.L. ends hopes of reunion with J. L. Lewises C.I.O."

In its statement of purpose, the CIO said it had formed to encourage the AFL to organize workers in mass production industries along industrial union lines. The CIO failed to change AFL policy from within. On September 10, 1936, the AFL suspended all 10 CIO unions since they were not able to agree on policy. The Congress of Industrial Organizations as a rival labor federation became estranged from the American Federation of Labor until 1955.

The union strikes were serious facts to Sam as he followed news in the United States and the world as much as local happenings.

Sam and Edith enjoyed a visit from elderly Mrs. Playfoot on a Friday evening. It did them as much good as their visitor. It was a way of life to benefit from the comfort of neighbors. Betty and Teddy drove Sam and Edith up to Comfort Hill for a pleasurable time with the Smiths.

Uncle George visited Grace and ate his dandelion greens. He prepared them as well as Grace. A few of the seven million unemployed in the U.S. benefitted from dandelions when they used bacon, grease, and boiled eggs to get past the bitterness.

Sam's own words...
Saturday, May 7, 1937 – "Giant German dirigible, Hindenburg, exploded at Lakehurst, NJ. Thirty known dead and many near death. Canvassed and helped at home."

Uncle George's next stop was at Mary's in Addison, NY. Grace, Roy, Sam, Edith, and Shirley took him over and enjoyed the countryside and the visit. Lynn and Mary would take him to Galeton when he was ready.

Word came over Roy's radio that John D. Rockefeller was dead. He had died two years and two months short of 100 years old. Rockefeller was an American industrialist and philanthropist. He was a co-founder of the Standard Oil Company, which dominated the oil industry and was the first great U.S. business trust. His wealth soared, and he became the world's richest man and the first American worth more than a billion dollars, controlling 90 percent of all oil in the United States at his peak.

Sam's own words...
Monday, May 24, 1937 – "Supreme Court upholds Social Security Act, old age pensions, and job insurance. Had garden plowed."

It was agreeable to hear from Willa and know that she had work as a seamstress for WPA. No doubt she had learned to sew from her mother.

Three Supreme Court decisions settled the constitutionality of Social Security.

The last day of May brought a labor strike at U.S. Steel in Chicago. Workers were striking all over the nation. Sam shook his head.

It had cost $3 to have the garden plot plowed. The plants and seeds were set in or sowed methodically, day after day. Sam was in his element. Edith went home with Betty on Sunday, June 6. Sam worked his hoe but missed her until Ed returned her four days later.

Sam's own words...
Saturday, June 19, 1937 – "Tried to collect, cooked, and mowed lawn. Johnstown, Pennsylvania under Marshall law. State police ordered to close steel plant."
Tuesday, June 22, 1937 – "Steele graduated from Horseheads High School tonight."

Settling picket line disputes might go as high as the Supreme Court. To prevent an explosion of violence–and to pressure Bethlehem Steel President Eugene Grace to the bargaining table–Pennsylvania Governor George Earle declared martial law in Johnstown on June 20. George Earle soon revoked his declaration, after which the strike quickly collapsed.

Sam was thankful when Steele immediately got a job driving a truck to haul dirt to the school's new athletic field.

Sam's own words...
Saturday, July 3, 1937 – "Amelia Earhart and Fred Noonan, her navigator, adrift in a metal land plane in trackless Pacific sent out S.O.S. for aid by land and sea."
Wednesday, July 7, 1937 – "Cooked, scrubbed, and helped wash. Faint signals revive hope for Earhart and Noonan. Betty, Edwin, and Teddy here for dinner."

A cheap, canned, precooked meat product, Spam, was introduced to the market by the Hormel Company on Monday, July 5. Would it be a welcome change from liver now?

By Tuesday, July 13, the failure to find the lost Earhart plane seemed hopeless.

Sam's own words...
Monday, July 27, 1937 – "Did housework, wash, and garden. Jap and Chinese have had several clashes. War may be unavoidable."
Sunday, August 1, 1937 – "Edwin and Betty quit gas station today and went to Wellsville, NY where Ed expects to have a job (for one month). Teddy with us."

It was considered a fine day by all parties when Teddy kept Grandpa and Grandma company. Shirley had gone to Ithaca to stay with her cousin, Ruth McCann

Sam's own words...
Tuesday, August 10, 1937 – "Cooked. Staked up a few tomato plants. I miss Shirley. Edith at Playfoot's tonight."
Thursday, September 2, 1937 – "Edwin, Betty, and Steele fixing up the house on the farm they expect to buy near Watkins. Boys and Gene Frost at Chemung fair tonight."

A few days later, Ed and Betty brought their household goods back from Wellsville. Ed finished his job there. On Sunday, Roy and Grace took Sam and Edith up to see the farm, and they all enjoyed the round-trip ride.

School started for Shirley without siblings since she was the youngest of them at 15½ years old. Sam helped Edith and Grace can corn, beans, and tomatoes for several days.

War news continued in the headlines. The Chinese and Japanese were slaughtering one another.

Edwin had purchased bushels of peaches and was selling them in the city. Naturally, he stopped to see Sam and Edith. At times, Sam or Edith went up to the farm to stay for a day or two when the opportunity arose to get there and back. In mid-September, Edwin and Sam both bought peaches and went out together to sell them. Betty had a corn roast at the farm for all of her siblings on September 25. They all repeated the peach sales again because it had gone so well. No doubt they bought by the bushel and sold pecks and quarts to individuals.

Sam's own words...
Thursday, October 8, 1937 – "John took an examination today for entry into the U.S. Army, and all that remains to make him happy is his mother's and my signature."

They signed the papers. It would be a short while before John's departure. Sam prayed that he would prosper and return to them safe and well. Steele went to help Edwin harvest his buckwheat. Sam had potatoes to dig. He and John got started and unearthed all but two rows when an October 14 snow storm stopped them.

C.C.C. Camp boys, 300 in number, were ahead of John to register for the army. He did not leave until a week later. He was age 23. Steele was the only boy left at home, and Sam lamented the loss.

Sam's own word...
Tuesday, October 26, 1937 – "Had a letter from John to say he arrived at the Plattsburgh, NY barracks. Japanese push into Shanghai City; a terrible butcher. Colder."
Wednesday, November 10, 1937 – "Cooked, went to city. Italy's adherence to the German-Japanese anti-communist alliance stirs democratic nations in Europe."

Domestic demands did not dull Sam's need to keep up with the war news. Betty brought her family laundry down home and did her wash in the electric wringer washer with Edith. Steele had a job with Edwin, cutting wood. Edith took care of Donny Brooks many evenings and watched the Playfoot children other times.

No communication from John in three weeks caused Sam to wonder and to miss him. Willa kept in touch from Denver and had been working at indexing, filing, and working on compiling records in a hospital and the motor vehicle department. Thanksgiving's approach was a sentimental time for Sam's soft heart. He had a card from David and his Frances. The big feast day on Thursday, November 25, was a well-attended affair by Sam and his many siblings. They gathered at Sadie's daughter's home, Annabelle Wheeler, of Horseheads, NY.

Sam's own words...
Tuesday, November 30, 1937 – "Betty and Edith did their wash. Ed and Steele cut wood. Last night, Grace, Roy, Edith, and I heard an address by the author of *The Old Rugged Cross* on the radio."
Wednesday, December 1, 1937 – "Am busy at home, broke, and needy; what to do is more than I know. This, too, will pass."

The author of *The Old Rugged Cross*, George Bernard, was an old country preacher from Michigan, unknown until he wrote the enduring hymn. They relished the shared listening experience from the old-time minister.

Teddy had been with Sam and Edith several days. Edwin's father, William Voorheis, stopped in to return him to the farm where he was missed.

Steele was jobless and discouraged again. Edith and Shirley earned 50¢ apiece taking care of the neighbor's children on December 23.

Sam's own words...
Friday, December 24, 1937 – "Busy at home. We received a Western Union message from John, Bless him. Gene and Lucille here a few minutes in evening."
Thursday, December 30, 1937 – "I feel I have grown at least a little this year 1937 and shall seek higher ground in 1938. Am thankful as I count my blessings."

~**~

1938

The year dawned without the promise of economic improvement. Ordinary men who struggled to feed their families and pay rent felt it acutely. Sam sought higher ground in the spiritual sense, but everyday needs came in meager amounts determined by weak sales.

Sam's own words...
Friday, January 7, 1938 – "Edith had her eyes examined by Dr. Glover. One eye may be improved. We pray it may be so."
Sunday, January 23, 1938 – "Edith went home with Edwin and Betty to stay until Tuesday."

Sam stayed behind and received a shipment of Foster goods. He continued to work hard for a small income. Steele gave it a try to sell the Foster line but returned home. Betty brought Edith home on Friday and stayed all night, Teddy with her.

In three days' time, Sam, Steele, and Edwin sold a few Foster sherbet deals. Ed took a supply of them to Reynoldsville to sell. Too many people were without jobs and on relief. They did not buy.

Sam's own words...
Thursday, February 10, 1938 – "Ed and Betty saw Mr. Piper about renting his farm near Watkins. F.D.R. asks $250 million for relief."
Tuesday, February 15, 1938 – "Report German and Italian troops on Austrian border. In city to see about Edith's blind pension."
Wednesday, February 16, 1938 – "Busy at home. Betty did our washing at Grace's. Austria bows to Nazi ultimatum. Cold."

Terror swept across Austria with the Nazi uprising. It had sparse coverage in the United States, but the European nations were too close to let it fall on deaf ears even though it went without action to prevent the takeover of Austria by Nazis. Following the ultimatum from Berlin, the Schuschnigg government in Austria retired and was succeeded and head-ed by the Nazi leader, Arthur Seyss-Inquart, as chancellor. He immediately asked Germany to send troops to preserve order. Fifty-thousand armed and mechanized forces marched to the border. Nazi mobs took possession of Vienna and raided the Jewish quarter. The swastika flew over public buildings, and Fatherland Front forces disarmed. There were similar demonstrations in other cities. Europe was aghast at the coup of Hitler.

Ed, Betty, Teddy, and Steele moved to the Piper farm on County Route 16 just east of what is now Watkins Glen International Race Track. Edwin looked for a deal to swap their car for a truck and managed a trade on February 25.

Edith was not at all well, but she watched Donny Brooks for an evening when she was needed. The small pay counted.

They had not heard from John in more than a month and only the Christmas card from David. On Saturday, February 26, Sam wrote, "It seems the young folks can get along without the old folks much better than the old folks can without them."

A storm interrupted Edwin's plan to pick up Sam and Edith on Sunday to go up to the farm. Sam did housework, enjoyed his books, and read an old Unity magazine.

Sam's own words...
Wednesday, March 2, 1938 – "Saw Mr. Lawrence as hundreds are compelled to do in these hard times for survival."
Thursday, March 3, 1938 - "Fifty-five years on earth today—don't feel aged but cannot kid myself. I sense I am not a kid and my generation is looked upon as the old folks. I am reminded that I am the oldest of my parent's family."

Grace had expected Dewey on Saturday, but he arrived late in the evening. Sunday brought Sam and Edith the best company. Gene and Lucille Frost came, then Edwin, Betty, Teddy, and Steele. Edith wrote to John, who had sent no word in two months. David had neglected them twice as long. Sam confided to Edith and his diary that he did not consider it a compliment to them as parents.

Edith could not do much that was strenuous, but she baked two loaves of gluten-free bread, the kind her diet required. Sam cooked, did housework, and washed windows to keep himself busy in early March.

Ed and Steele stopped in to tell them that Edwin had bought a team of horses. They came down again with the truck on Friday, March 11, to load the mares and take them to the farm. Betty came in the car and took Grace, Sam, Edith, and Shirley home with her for supper. It was their first visit to see the farm. Sam believed they had a workable place and wanted them to do well.

Sam's own words...
Monday, March 14, 1938 – "Adolf Hitler entered Vienna like a conquering Caesar. Austrian Army took Hitler oath."

Sam wondered if the world was going back to medieval chaos.

Finally, a short letter came from John on Friday, March 18. Sam missed him even more than before. Two robins caught Sam's attention when they appeared on the lawn and sang. He accepted good omens whether they appeared or he found them.

Sam's own words...
Monday, March 21, 1938 – "Did housework and went with Edith to Dr. Emperts. He has decided that she will have to take insulin. She has tried to keep from it, but if she must, I pray she may receive the help she needs so much. Billion dollar Navy expansion bill passed by the House and now goes to the Senate. Grace came."
Tuesday, March 22, 1938 – "Edith took her first insulin today. I am delegated to administer it to her as she can't do so herself. She and Shirley are watching children tonight. She can do that, but I am sorry she has too."

Edith went to Dr. Empert again on Thursday, March 24, and he increased the units of insulin for her. The metal part of the insulin mechanism clamped onto a glass syringe, labeled as part TY1-40, which had marked increments from 20 to 40 units. The automatic injector, designed by Dr. Busher, was manufactured in 1932 by the Becton, Dickinson & Company of Rutherford, NJ. Sam had an extra supply of the steel needles. He fit one onto the glass tube for each use and pushed the solid glass plunger to inject the insulin.

A letter from Willa brought joy to Edith.

Edwin, Betty, and Teddy came to visit them on Friday evening, and they also had high hopes for the medicine to help Edith. Teddy had come prepared to stay awhile but had to be disappointed because the presence of scarlet fever and measles around the neighborhood prevented him.

Sam, whom Teddy had begun to call Grandpa Daddy, thought of Teddy as a five-year-old strong little man. He no doubt smiled as he recorded the names of his grandson's pups, Leader and Trailer. He was glad to see how much Teddy liked living on the farm.

Dr. Empert says Edith is responding well to insulin treatment. She had a letter from Arthur, which did her good."

Sam continued to canvass but sold nothing. He hoped for success on another day and found it hard to realize that the government fed millions who'd starve otherwise.

On March 31 Sam reminisced about David's 24th birthday. He was sentimental about his being gone from home from the time he was just a boy of 17. Now, seven years later, he was married and lived in San Francisco, California. His thoughts on former days and his children did not stop there.

Sam's own words...
Thursday, March 31, 1938 – "Willa lives in Denver with her girls, Lee and Christy. I believe she has been away 13 years. Life does strange things to us and for us. May we have faith in its ultimate good."

Sam went to see Jim Lawrence and waited behind a significant number of people who all sought relief at that office. He sold a $1 dress that afternoon.

It was April 1 when Dr. Empert said Edith was sugar-free and he reduced the insulin dose. They were grateful and felt rewarded for their faith in His good. Gene and Lucille visited for the first time in three weeks and heard the encouraging news.

Sam and Edith went on a visit to Grace and Roy's to listen to the radio, which they often did together. They heard Anton Lang Jr. tell about the Passion Play held every 10 years in Oberammergau, Bavaria. The four of them listened in awe. Sam and Edith had been without electric quite awhile.

The play was first performed in 1634 and is the result of a vow made by the inhabitants of the village that if God spared them from the effects of the bubonic plague then sweeping the region, they would perform a passion play every 10 years. A man traveling back to the town for Christmas had accidentally brought the disease with him. The man died from the illness, and it began spreading throughout Oberammergau. After the vow, not another inhabitant of the town died from the bubonic plague and all of the town members that were still stricken with the dreaded germ recovered.

Steele had gone to work for Ed at the farm. They cut wood and sold it by the cord in Elmira and Horseheads. They would keep up the belabored enterprise until late spring when only cook stoves required wood.

Sam's own words…
Wednesday, April 27, 1938 – "President confers with Henry Ford on business conditions. British pay new taxes on tea, gasoline, and incomes to cover the cost of Empire's armament."
Thursday, April 28, 1938 – "Scrubbed floors, cooked, and canvassed in afternoon."

They enjoyed lights and their own radio for the first time in three months. A good Samaritan had the electric turned on. Sam suspected it was Grace's son-in-law, Francis McCann of Ithaca, NY.

Dr. Empert ordered more insulin for Edith and said she had progressed well.

Betty came to use the electric washer, and Teddy stayed all night. It would have been hard to tell who enjoyed it more between him and his grandparents.

Sam had the garden plowed May 16. His sister, Mary, and husband, Frank Hess, came over from Addison, NY, for a visit. Frank ordered a suit from Sam, which was sent for at the same time as a fabric order. Sam recorded a heavy frost on May 25. He continued to plant his garden day in and day out.

Dewey took Grace, Alice, and Edith up to the farm to see Betty. He was due back at work in a couple of days. They learned that Betty needed to find a person to help her soon because her confinement would not be too far away. Word traveled, and it was but a week when Sadie's girl, Eloise, went to work in the farmhouse, which was on a hill above Watkins Glen. A day later, June 9, a baby boy was born to Ed and Betty. While Betty gave birth in the front bedroom of the farmhouse, five-year-old Teddy was banished to the other end of the house into an empty back room to ride his tricycle. He made figure eights on the dusty floor. Red Turkey brand flour sacks, which hung on the walls, had most likely been placed there for insulation in colder months.

Sam's own words…
Friday, June 10, 1938 – "Edith went home with Edwin and just arrived back. God is in his heaven, and all is well."
Saturday, June 18, 1938 – "Berlin Jews flee homes in fear of Nazi raid."
Sunday, June 19, 1938 – "Today, Edith and I (sic) have been married 25

years and need each other more than ever. May God help us to help each other as I know he will if we take him in partnership. We hope to see Betty soon and that wonderful baby of hers."

Sunday, June 26, 1938 – "Betty, Ed, Teddy, and 17-day-old Edwin William, my second grandson, were here awhile. Steele went up to the farm to help Ed for a few days."

It was also early in the life of the newborn, that Edwin's father, William Voorheis, upon seeing his grandson, pronounced that he was Buck. The nickname stuck. John surprised Edith and Sam when he woke them at 3:30 a.m. on Sunday, July 3. He and seven other boys had hitch-hiked all the way from Plattsburg. They all went to their homes but had to be back on base Friday by 6 p.m.

Steele could find no job. Sam thought it a darn shame when so many young and old men could find no employment.

At the end of July on Henry Ford's 75th birthday, he announced his belief that there would be a business boom in the fall. Sam thought he was a grand old man and hoped the prediction was right. Millions needed jobs. Sam hoped it meant a living wage like Ford advocated and paid.

Steele found work on a crew of traveling magazine salesmen. Sam figured he'd at least gain experience that would contribute to his life. The group moved north to Watertown, and Sam missed Steele already. Shirley was the only child at home, and she was often at Gene and Lucille Frost's. She also liked to go up to the farm and stay with Betty and Ed.

Dewey came and took Grace, Sam, and Edith on a trip down to Galeton. Their nostalgic journey took them to all the old places, and each reminisced as they rolled by familiar country on the way. However, troubles spared hardly anyone. Sam canvassed without sales, Ed's tractor wore out, and Europe was on the verge of war.

Sam's own words...

Monday, August 22, 1938 – "Humanities pot seems to be boiling over again in Europe."

The Czech-Nazi issue neared a crisis. Either a break or settlement on the Sudeten crisis was believed imminent. Britain warned and in earnest implored Chancellor Adolf Hitler of Germany to go slow in Czechoslovakia.

The reluctant British government prepared for a crisis of the first rank by the order of 42 warships to the North Sea. Sam pondered if the world must be plunged into another world war, God forbid.

In a few days, Hitler backed down and pledged no hasty steps.

Sam was glad to hear from Steele, who was with his magazine crew in New Hampshire. He reported he was not setting the world on fire yet with his sales. His next location was slated for Connecticut then New Jersey. They heard from John and then Willa. She stated that she and the girls were well, but she had to manage finances closely. Sam likely wished he and Edith had even a bit extra and could send help.

The mildest information that Sam read in September was, at least, interesting. It was the debut of the Haggar "new pant" concept, slacks, as the appropriate pant to wear during a man's "slack time." He might have smiled.

Betty came to do her wash on Saturday, September 17. Edwin insisted Sam take in a movie with him. Other times Ed brought wood along to sell while Betty laundered clothes.

Sam's own words...
Monday, September 19, 1938 – "I may be wrong, but to me, it seems a great shame to give Czechoslovakia's Sudeten area to Germany as the price for peace."

Sam was fed up with Hitler's aggression tactics. President Roosevelt made an appeal on Tuesday, September 24, that peace be sought before rather than after war.

Through autumn, Sam harvested, canned, and took care of Edith. She'd been better the whole summer as long as she did no real labor. Sam sheltered his wife to preserve her strength and avoid a challenge to her health.

Sam's own words...
Sunday, October 2, 1938 – "Busy around home. After absence of four weeks enjoyed visit from Gene and Lucille Frost and glad to see them. Yes, Jack Frost (no relation to Gene) came as I predicted last night and got in a pretty good (or bad) lick to most green things."

Steele had traveled to Washington, DC, and on to Richmond, VA, with the magazine peddlers. His sales held no bragging rights yet.

The colder weather meant people needed wood. Ed brought Betty and their two boys to Sam and Edith's at noon on Thursday, October 13. He went door to door and sold eight cords of wood so he could make his truck payment.

On Sunday, October 16, the newspaper reported on a broadcast made by Winston Churchill to address the United States. He condemned the Munich agreement as a defeat and called upon America and Western Europe to prepare for armed resistance against Adolf Hitler.

Sam's own words...
Monday, October 24, 1938 – "Fair Labor Act, better known as the wage-hour law goes into effect today; pay no less than 25¢ an hour—work no more than 44 hours a week."
Saturday, October 29, 1938 – "Prepared meals, delivered fabric."

On November 2 they received letters from John and Steele. Steele was in Knoxville, TN, hardly able to make expenses. Soon, it would be Nashville, then Chattanooga. John was in better shape, paid by Uncle Sam. No word from David in months caused anguish to his father. Sam wondered why, why, why?

Sam bought a tube for the radio. Edith needed it since she had to rely on her ears more than her fading eye sight. He noticed the hard work it took for her to read each bit of print using the magnification glass.

The first snow squall of the season came to Horseheads on November 14 with six inches, and it continued to fall. Thanksgiving saw 10 more inches but was no bother at all to the exuberant mood that the arrival of David's card created. The snow was welcome for deer season. Sam didn't hunt, but he heard about it from his Pennsylvania relatives. Bradford, Tioga, and Potter counties reported 3,000 doe taken on day one.

On November's last day, Sam did housework, canvassed, and went to Dr. Empert's office for insulin. They enjoyed Grace's visit when she came to dinner on Friday, November 2.

Sam's own words...
Sunday, December 4, 1938 – "Berlin maps ghettos, prohibits Jews from driving autos, cycles."
Mondays, December 5, 1938 – "Did housework and canvassed. Edith not so well lately. She saw Dr. Empert today, and he advised she cut down on starches and sweets. He gave her medicine for high blood pressure."

Sam didn't like the German news, but he had Edith's health on his mind. It helped them all to have supper with Grace and Roy. Shirley enjoyed it, too. On December 14, they enjoyed the annual letter from Lenore Crow. Lenore counted on their letter just as much, and they would not disappoint her.

Steele wrote that the crew was leaving Memphis, TN, and he'd be in Birmingham, AL. Sam decided that Steele certainly was seeing a lot of the country and was thankful that he was making his own way.

Sam's own words...
Saturday, December 17, 1938 – "Did housework and helped wash clothes. Ed and Betty and their two boys came in the evening. They were overjoyed to know that Ed's bid on 800 cord of wood on government land was accepted. They have a chance to make money, which they badly need. Ed was so elated; he insisted on taking me to a movie."

Sam and Edith made and sent fruitcakes to David, Willa, Steele, and John. Snow fell, and so did Edith. Her knee was hurt. Sam expressed a wish he had uttered aloud several times before, that he wanted to live where it did not get so cold. That would eliminate the slippery snow situation. Edith was all right before long.

Dewey mailed $2 each to Sam and Grace, which they received with pleasure.

John had turned 22 years old on December 23 and arrived home on Christmas Eve to surprise them. Their Army boy was home a few days.

Sam's own words...
Saturday, December 31, 1938 –"Soon 1938 will be only a memory. Though it has been very hard for many of us, I feel it has given us blessings. I am thinking of my three boys tonight, especially David as he doesn't write. Is he having a hard time?"

26 – High Hope
1939, 1940

David had sent a book, *Our Money System*, but no letter. Sam started to read it. He certainly may have wished he had at least a note from his oldest son. It would make a grand bookmark.

In the evening, he and his Shirley Girl went to Grace and Roy's to listen to the radio. They were all entertained by The Seth Parker program and also Edgar Bergen with Charlie McCarthy.

Cruise of the Seth Parker was followed around the world by shortwave radio listeners to the traveling Phillips Lord—an adventure that took on a harrowing real-life flavor when Lord's schooner became wrecked by a tropical storm.

Entertainer Edgar Bergen was born in Chicago to Swedish immigrant parents who grew up on a dairy farm. After 15 years of vaudeville and nightclubs, Bergen became an 'overnight' sensation on the radio as a ventriloquist. Charlie McCarthy, his puppet, was supposed to be a boy.

Sam was disappointed at the end of the day. He had hoped that Ed and Betty would make a visit to them for New Year's Day. On day two, he found out why they hadn't when Ed and Harry Landon stopped in. They dropped Betty off and went to Elmira to get an axle replacement for the broken one on Edwin's truck. Sam was glad to hear that Ed's wood job was coming along well.

Sam's own words...
Wednesday, January 4, 1939 – "President Roosevelt delivered to Congress, the nation, and the world, a solemn warning that forces making for general war are rising to unprecedented heights."

Sam read the news January 5. Critics rapped Roosevelt's argument for his huge defense spending.

Sam performed housework as usual, prepared meals, washed windows, and delivered fabric. A busy day ended with a visit from Ed, Betty, and their boys, Teddy and Eddie. Sam was elated to receive a letter from David, the first in a year. He was gratified to know that David had become best friends with a religious magazine publisher and minister, Judge Gardner. He and Frances were involved with him in the Lord's work. Sam thanked God.

Sam's own words...
Tuesday, January 10, 1939 – "Prepared meals, wrote letter to David. Edwin and his brother-in-law, Harry Landon, stopped a few minutes after Ed delivered wood he'd sold. British Premier, Nevil Chamberlin, left today to talk with Italian dictator, Mussolini to discover the 1939 aims of Rome/Berlin/Tokyo tangle; 48 giant U.S. bomber planes left San Diego, California in a mass flight to Canal Zone three thousand miles away."
Tuesday, January 17, 1939 – "Canvassed, prepared meals. We received a delayed package from Willa and the girls with the most wonderful gift in the lot to us, a record of their dear voices. We can play it on our talking machine."

Roosevelt urged pilot training with the use of gliders.

A letter arrived from Willa to say she had lost her job but hoped to find another one soon. Ed and Betty visited, and Sam relayed the need to ask God to bless Willa and the girls.

Good news arrived on January 20, Shirley's 17th birthday. The letter with a Los Angeles, CA, postmark was from Steele. He had quit sales, left the magazine crew behind, and had found David. Sam produced smiles all around when he pronounced to Ed and Betty that Steele had courage.

Sam's own words...
Thursday, January 26, 1939 – "Earthquake toll may exceed 22 thousand hurt or missing, disease and famine to follow."
Monday, January 20, 1939 – "Found a foot of snow on the ground this morning. Shoveled paths and did housework. Had a letter from Steele, who is making magazine sales in L.A."
Saturday, February 4, 1939 – "We are anxious to hear or see Ed and Betty as we have done neither since the heavy snowfall."
Friday, February 10, 1939 – "Canvassed one hour and took my lame aching leg home. Pope Pius XI died Thursday. His last message to a troubled world was, "Peace.""

The earthquake recorded in Sam's diary was 400 miles of Chili's coast, which killed thousands and wounded many more, on January 25.

Edwin and Betty visited Saturday evening, and Shirley went home with them. The next day Gene and Lucille took Sam and Edith up to the farm. They all enjoyed the celebration of Teddy's sixth birthday as much as he did. Sam pronounced him "a fine little man who helps his mother."

It's likely that Willa told them that she was working as a typist now. She had cultivated that skill on a small typewriter on her lap while she had TB years earlier and was whiling away time in a cold tent, her own private TB sanitarium. The black gloves with the fingertips cut out for added dexterity had helped keep her fingers busy pounding the keys while she practiced.

In a letter from Steele he remarked on his enthusiasm for Los Angeles where he was able to meet expenses. The joyful sentiment caught on with Shirley, who went with her class to Ithaca to attend Mrs. Franklin D. Roosevelt's speech.

Sam's own words...
Thursday, February 16, 1939 – "Helped Betty do the wash. Thomas J. and William F. Halloran, brothers and contractors, were swept to their deaths by a wall of ice and water in the Chemung River about 8:45 pm Wednesday."
Saturday, February 18, 1939 – "Went to Grace and Roy's, had a good visit with them and Dewey. Grace insisted I (sic) stay to supper, which I enjoyed very much. Edith at Brook's tonight."

Ed, Betty, Teddy, and baby, Buck, came to celebrate Sam's 56th birthday on Friday, March 3. Edwin said they had to move and were anxious to find another farm. A letter from Steele reported less than desirable work and his intention to start for home when better weather and work helped him manage it. The distance loomed long from Los Angeles, CA, to 404 Center Street, Horseheads, NY.

In three days' time, Ed and Betty stopped in to say they had found another place to which they would move during the week.

Sam likely shook his head when he read that Harvard University students had demonstrated to reporters, the new tradition of swallowing live goldfish.

On Wednesday, March 8, Sam, Edith, and Grace went to the funeral of 89-year-old John Hulzier. His elderly wife was alone now.

Elmira's trolley cars bowed out of existence on Saturday, March 11, 1939. The first car ran in 1891 and trollies had continued the city's public transportation for 48 years. Motor buses replaced them.

Betty and the boys were dropped off at Sam and Edith's on Tuesday, March 14. Ed's truck broke, and he went to find a junkyard repair part. Sam felt at least he could feed them when they stopped in with troubles.

Sam's own words...
Wednesday, March 15, 1939 – "Usual housework, canvassed. German troops entered Prague and moved to positions of control in the once proud Czechoslovakia."

Sam considered that a European war was inevitable.

Edith received a birthday telegram from Willa and a letter from John. Another day brought Sadie and Mary. Sam enjoyed them as much as Edith for her 51st birthday.

Sam's own words...
Tuesday, March 21, 1939 – "Cooked, canvassed. Our lights went off because I could not pay electric bill. Ed, Betty, and boys, Mr. and Mrs. Voorheis (his parents), were here. Ed and his father went to Sayre to get a rear end to put in Ed's truck. Last Saturday, Teddy nearly killed himself when his sled ran into a fence post. Now his eyes are swollen almost shut, and he has a deep cut in his head. The doctor says he is coming fine. We have much to be thankful for."

Ed and Betty had been only partly moved to a different place when the truck's rear end broke again. Sam shook his head over hard times that made their life tough. No one was immune, it seemed. Edith had nose bleeds, three of them, and worried Sam through the end of March.

Sam's own words...
Saturday, April 1, 1939 – "Delivered fabrics. Gene and Lucille visited. Ed's father and mother stopped for a few minutes and told us Ed and Betty are moved and will spend their first night in their own home tonight. I am glad and may God Bless them."

April Fool's Day marked the date of the 16th United States census.

John made a surprise appearance home on Sunday. He'd be able to stay until Wednesday. Steele's letter arrived with a small snapshot of himself. Sam saw that he was developing into a grown man. The newspaper announced that the United States Army had launched the build of 3,000 planes.

Ed was forced to secure yet another rear end for his truck. Sam disliked hearing such bad luck afoot for the young people.

Dewey was at Grace's Saturday, and Sam spent a full two-hour visit with him to do them both good. Sam learned from Grace on Monday that Dewey had left $5 with her to give to Sam. It was to finance sample products to sell extract deals, which enabled the new sales line for Sam.

Sam's own words...
Saturday, April 15, 1939 –"President asks Hitler and Mussolini to give 10-year pledge of peace and offers to act as intermediary for 31 nations. What a wonderful power for good if they will only do it."
Sunday, April 16, 1939 – "At home until 4 p.m., then Gene and Lucille came and took Grace, Shirley, Edith, and I (sic) up to see Betty and Ed's farm. It is real pleasant there but will require a lot of work. They are well and happy and deserve to prosper."
Thursday, April 20, 1939 – "Hitler displayed massive artillery, new anti-aircraft guns as part of Germany's celebration of his 50th birthday. Mussolini rejects peace plea of President Roosevelt."

On April 26, Sam planted zinnia seed and a bed of lettuce, prepared meals and canvassed. He kept busy and prayed to make more money.

The newspaper covered the opening of the April 30 New York World's Fair. It was reported to have 350,000 people counted as they passed through the gate at 75¢ each for general admission. On the same day, reports told that Hitler's speech rapped the United States, his 'special' greeting for May Day.

A letter from Willa on May 1 caused them to worry. She said she and the girls were all right but were having a tough time. Steele's letter on May 2 notified them that he was about to leave Los Angeles on sparse money for Denver. He'd see his Uncle Arthur Crow, Willa, and the girls. Sam must have smiled as he wrote on the diary page, "He is not afraid, God bless him." He felt gladdened for Willa that her brother was en route. Sam used a saying straight from his father, Lac, who more than once said, "I am not afraid."

Ed and Betty came by on Thursday, May 4, and helped fumigate the house and took Sam and Edith to the farm until Sunday.

Sam's own words...
Friday, May 5, 1939 – "Busy raking lawn and cleaning up outside of their house and enjoyed myself a lot. Betty went to the Montour Falls Hospital about midnight, child expected soon."
Saturday, May 6, 1939 – "Betty gave birth to a seven and one-half pound girl about 2 a.m. Both well, Thank God. I planted a bed of radishes and lettuce. Am chief cook, glad we are here to help out."

When Sam and Edith returned home to 404 Center Street in Horseheads, Teddy went, too. How they enjoyed him. Another pleasure accompanied Steele's letter. Inside were pictures of him, Willa, and her girls.

Sam's extract deals by Foster Brother's arrived. He was eager to peddle them and see if homemakers would purchase the dual flavor kits.

Ed and his mother, Theresa, came down to get Sam and Edith to go back home with them. Sam couldn't, but he showed Edwin how to give Edith her insulin shot. She could go. Betty was home with her new baby named Jean Lucille and would be in bed a few more days.

Down in Horseheads, Sam and Shirley received a letter from Steele.

He had a job on a cleanup truck for $8 per week. It had to work until he found a better rate of pay.

Sam's own words...
Monday, May 15, 1939 – "Did housework, canvassed. Three thousand coal miners bent on picketing, turned back by national guardsmen with machine guns today as men return to Harlen County, Kentucky, coal pits under troop protection. Most miners have been idle since April 1."
Tuesday, May 16, 1939 – "Lucille sold over $10 worth of Mutual Fabrics at the factory where she works, certainly swell of her."

Sam was probably not aware of the first McDonald's restaurant to open in San Bernardino, California. The news of five million pairs of women's nylon stockings, which sold on their first day of market across the U.S., got everyone's attention.

Arthur Crow sent a message. "Our brother, Rollo, is near the end of his trail on earth." Mr. and Mrs. Voorheis brought Edith home to Sam after her absence of two weeks to help Betty. Sam and Shirley were glad to have her back, but the news of her brother made her sad.

Sam's own words...
Wednesday, May 24, 1939 – "Prepared meals, canvassed. The U.S. submarine, Squalus, sinks off coast of N.H. near Portsmouth; 30 thought dead, diving bell rescues seven on first trip."
Thursday, May 25, 1939 – "Letter from Steele. He has a job in a car parking lot. Willa and girls would like to keep him. I don't blame them. Survivors are 33 at rest in the hospital from ill-fated submarine."

Sam had his garden plowed May 26. Edith received the sad letter that her brother, Rollo, had passed away Monday, May 22. Only she and Arthur remained from the family of nine Crow siblings. Sam's neighbor, Mr. Rex Playfoot, gave him enough onion sets to fill a row. He planted carrots, peas, and cucumbers.

Sam's own words...
Thursday, June 1, 1939 – "Canvassed. Planted limas and corn. We have a large garden, and I am slow but will get it done eventually. I find joy in doing it. Teddy ought to be here to help me, bless him; how he used to like to help Grandpa Daddy."

Sam desired to see Ed and Betty. He learned that they were in hard times because the truck was still out of order. All he could do was pray for them. It was another week when on Friday, June 9, Grace and Roy took Sam and Edith up to the farm. Ed was not home. They had come on a mission and carried it out. They planted potatoes in the garden to support Edwin in his work. The next day, Ed and Betty visited them in Horseheads. Ed went after parts for his truck again.

School was out June 19, and Shirley took a housekeeping job. She stayed with Gene and Lucille. Sam missed her. President Roosevelt signed the Naval Expansion Act into law on June 14.

Sam's own words...
Thursday, July 13, 1939 – "Canvassed. Letter from Steele and Willa. They moved recently and Steele has a low pay job. Willa expects to get back on WPA, and conditions will be better for them."

Sam surely hoped Willa's job would materialize but the day's news had just informed him that WPA dismissed thousands of workers. How would she get her job back?

Roy and Grace enjoyed a roundabout ride down to Breesport, taking Sam and Edith with them. Edith carried out her plan when she bought nine baby chicks and a hen from an elderly farm lady. She was altogether pleased with them.

Cooking, gardening, and salesmanship occupied Sam. Dewey made it known that he planned to marry again in October. Roy Whiting was laid off his WPA job for at least 30 days. Sam delivered fabrics. No one had heard from John or David in several weeks.

Sam's own words...
Monday, July 31, 1939 – "We received a card from David and Frances announcing the arrival of a boy on June 16, at 12:10 a.m., weight seven and one-half pounds, named David Arthur. He is my fourth grandchild. How I would like to see him and his daddy and mother."

The astounding news in print was that Albert Einstein wrote to President Roosevelt about the development of the atomic bomb using uranium. Einstein's penmanship urged the development of a nuclear research program later that year. Roosevelt saw neither the necessity nor the utility for such a project but agreed to proceed slowly. It would be later (1941) when the American effort to design and build an atomic bomb received its code name — the Manhattan Project.

A letter was received from Willa on Thursday, July 3, to tell the family that Steele had left for home on Monday. Sam felt sorry for how Willa and the girls would miss him but thrilled at the expectation of his arrival home.

Steele came up the walk about 7 p.m. Friday night with no attempt to wipe the grin off his face. Ed and Betty and the children had already arrived, and it was quite a reunion of full hearts. Likely, they were all in awe of Steele's courage and his great adventure that had come full circle. Steele was determined to find a job at once.

Bob Crippen, age 68, set up his stove, bed, and belongings in a room allowed to him by Sam and Edith. He probably paid reasonable room and board. He was widowed and independent.

Willa's earlier experience as clerk typist led to reinstatement in the job she had held. The program was now called the Real Property Project.

Sam's own words...
Sunday, August 27, 1939 – "Teddy went back home. He had been with us since Thursday, and we enjoyed him. Betty has to make clothes for him to start his first year of school."
Monday, August 28, 1939 – "Prepared meals, put in a strenuous day of sales; sold a pair of shoes and one dress. Steele helped Edith wash. Roy W. has had no job for quite awhile, and I hope he may find one soon."
Friday, September 1, 1939 – "Nazis invade Poland, bomb cities. Italy stays out; allies mobilize. Europe on brink of war as Britain and France move to fulfill assistance pledges."
Sunday, September 3, 1939 – "Great Britain and France declared war against Germany this morning and hell will again be turned loose. God grant it will soon be over."

September had its predetermined workload of harvest from the extensive garden. Sam canned tomatoes, did laundry, and canvassed. Many days were copies of the ones before.

Sam read news reports from Europe on Monday that the great

Krupps munition plant in Germany had been set afire. He thought it a much better way of crippling an enemy than to drop bombs on defenseless women and children.

Sam's own words...
Saturday, September 9, 1939 – "Did housework, canvassed. Steele helped fill a silo. He and his mother are both caring for neighbor's children tonight. Ocean liner's bring 2,900 Americans home from France today."
Monday, September 11, 1939 - "Edwin and Bucky (Eddie) were here for supper. Bob C. went home with them to pick peaches to sell."

Bucky's nickname had been bestowed on sight at two weeks old by Grandfather Voorheis, but now he was old enough to have earned the handle at one year and three months. Maybe he was a little boy with a mind of his own already, bucking directions given by parents.

Sam may have mentioned to Edwin how it seemed wrong that the electric company insisted on $2 deposit and $5-meter deposit before they'd turn the power back on. Sam guessed he'd have to pay it. The lights had been out for almost six months. Sam mailed a fabric order.

Steele got paid for several days of silo work and had the electric turned on. They were all glad. Steele and Bob Crippen went to lake country (Hector, north of Watkins) and picked up four bushels of drop peaches at 30¢ a bushel. Sam and Edith canned for two days, resulting in 85 quarts. They were thankful to have it and also for the finish of the work.

Edith babysat many evenings in neighbors' homes while Sam and Bob Crippen kept each other company. Steele was discouraged for lack of a job and looked in many directions, maybe a traveling sales job again or C.C.C. camp work.

Sam learned from Grace that Dewey had married a few days ago on September 23. His bride was Amy Morrissey of Woodbourne, NY.

Shirley was back in school but spent weekends at Gene and Lucille's. Sam and Edith took an enjoyable evening with Grace and Roy to listen to Edgar Bergen with Charlie McCarthy on the radio.

Sam's own words...
Friday, October 6, 1939 – "Adolf Hitler's speech this morning dashes peace hopes; allied powers see only repetition of broken pledges."

Tuesday, October 10, 1939 – "Steele has a job two days a week clerking in an A & P store in Elmira. He had no call from WPA."

Betty turned 24 years old.

Dewey and Amy were back from a Canadian honeymoon. Dewey presented Sam with a new pipe, which was given and received with pure pleasure.

Albert Einstein influenced the news again because of his expert knowledge that caused worry over Nazi activity in Europe. He addressed F.D.R. again with urgency regarding the Manhattan Project. He advocated for the rapid development of the atomic bomb. Sam never missed the news. October 15 brought a killer frost. It was time to dig potatoes.

Sam sold twenty-four 50¢ Foster deals. He believed that the two-bottle deals of extract flavors would be a bigger seller if he could find enough people with jobs and money. If.

Steele had work with the Works Progress Administration (WPA) to start the morning of Thursday, October 19. He continued the part-time clerking job at A & P and bought a used car.

Sam's own words...
Monday, October 23, 1939 – "War activity lulls as French dig in for the winter. Zane Grey, writer, dies at 64."
Wednesday, November 8, 1939 – "Report that Hitler narrowly escaped death in an explosion, which killed several of his followers."

Pearl Zane Grey (January 1872 – October 1939) was an American dentist and author best known for his popular Western adventure novels and stories, with his most famous being Riders of the Purple Sage. Lackawaxen, PA, is the location of the Zane Grey Museum, which is administered by the National Park Service.

Many wished Hitler could be stopped in his tracks. The blast killed seven of his men and wounded 63, many gravely.

An earthquake that jarred the coast south of New York City on November 15 captured the front-page news and people's imagination. It was the same day that Uncle Sam's first expedition in 100 years sailed from Boston, MA, for the bottom of the world under the command of Rear Admiral Richard E. Byrd.

On November 16, former gang chief Al Capone was released by G-men at Lewisburg, PA, after seven years in prison. Sam wrote that the whereabouts of the prohibition era gangland czar remained secret.

Steele's work hours were sparse and had him discouraged.

Sam's own words...
Tuesday, November 21, 1939 – "Steele insisted I go with him to Elmira and see *The Wonderful Wizard of Oz* showing at the Capitol Theater. I did so and enjoyed him and the movie."

It was MGM's (Metro Goldwyn Mayer) classic musical film based on L. Frank Baum's famous novel. It starred Judy Garland as Dorothy with the red shoes.

On Thanksgiving, a group of 13 relatives gathered at Sam and Edith's. In addition to themselves, Ed, Betty, and three children, Steele, Shirley, Bob Crippen, Gene, Lucille, and Gene's mother attended. Sam missed David in L.A. and John in the army in Georgia but was grateful for those present at his table.

Willa had moved to 1258 Grant Street in Denver and had a raise as senior typist. She also had duties as a library clerk. Billie was self-sufficient and apparently had the same spunk that Steele possessed.

Steele started work at a gas station in Rose Valley. Sam recognized Steele's courage and resourcefulness again because the Rose Valley Inn and gas station was 244 miles away near Philadelphia, PA. Did Sam smile and remember being young once himself and setting out to go west with no fear? And Steele had done that, too.

Sam followed the British news. King George VI had signed an order for seizure of Nazi exports. Britain had lost numerous ships because of mines and torpedoes.

Sam's own words...
Thursday, November 30, 1939 – "More hell broke out in Europe. Russia invaded Finland by land, sea, and air. Helsinki, other cities bombed. U.S. Congress may consider break with Soviet Russia."
Friday, December 1, 1939 – "Helsinki bombed again; women and children among slain. President Roosevelt condemns invasion of Finland in name of American people."

Saturday, December 2, 1939 – "Enjoyed Grace at lunch with us. President F.D.R.'s appeal against bombing of civilian centers was answered today in a note from Russia terming his appeal as pointless."

Sunday, December 10, 1939 – "Ed, Betty, the children, and Steele were here this evening. We were surely glad to have them. "Love fulfills the law of life." I realize its truth more and more. An oft-repeated prayer should be, "Father, teach me to love."

Sam did what he called his usual stunt, housekeeping, which came before canvassing. It was Tuesday, December 12, and winter had dumped snow on upstate New York to snarl traffic. The League of Nations had expelled the Soviet Union for its assault on Finland. Ousted Russia cared, Nyet!

Ed and Betty left the children with Sam and Edith and went Christmas shopping on Wednesday, December 20. Later, Sam would learn that they had bought him a 1940 diary as his present.

Sam enjoyed a letter John wrote from Fort Benning, GA. He did not like it there. The seasonal greeting from Lenore Crow pleased Sam and Edith.

Sam's own words...
Tuesday, December 26, 1939 – "We were glad to get a letter from Frances, David's wife. David is assistant manager on a ranch in the Bel Air Hills. David Jr is six months old and weighs 19 pounds. I sure would like to see all of them."

A sub-zero wave of temperatures hit New York state on December 27. Two days later in a fireside chat President Roosevelt declared: The United States must become the great arsenal of democracy.

Ed and Steele worked all night Friday into Saturday on Steele's car. Sam closed the last day of 1939 in the hope that more of humanity would lift up the Christ in their souls.

~**~

1940

Sam had one resolution for Monday, January 1. He would try to be tolerant of others. He, Edith, Bob Crippen, and Shirley spent New Year's

Day at home. Grace did not visit since she was in Ithaca with her daughter Ruth's children for a week.

Sam's own words...
Tuesday, January 2, 1940 – "Britain calls two million more men to the colors."

President Roosevelt addressed Congress. He told them the nation must maintain its own peace. He urged new taxes to prepare for defense. Sam was concerned about the war news but also for Bob Crippen.

Sam's own words...
Friday, January 5, 1940 – "Bob departed this morning for a visit among his relations and friends down in Pennsylvania. He's a lonely old man; has lost three wives and hasn't a chick or a child in his declining years."

Grace returned. Ruth and her girls had sent Sam a box of cigars. "Bless them," he said. They were worth a try, and try he would. If preferred, they could be cut into rounds and smoked in his pipe. Who but himself would ever know?

Sam's own words...
Tuesday, January 9, 1940 – "Did housework and helped wash. Charlie Barret whom I knew since I was 16 but have not seen since 1907 was Cretia's divorced husband. He was found hanged from a hot water tank yesterday p.m. at the house of Mrs. Grace Williams, 214 W. Miller St., by her two children. Poor Charlie. Only God knows what brought him to this. If I had known how desperate he was, I might have helped him."

A letter from John grabbed Sam's attention until he read the conclusion. Hospitalized in Fort Benning, GA, since before Christmas, John evidently hadn't wanted to worry his mother during the holidays. The problem had been a twisted knee. He was out. He was well. He was on duty.

A card arrived from Cretia on January 13. Sam was sorry to read that she was still full of resentment toward Charlie and had no mercy for his soul. "God help her to a greater understanding," Sam penned. He was soothed on Sunday when he read poetry to Edith and Shirley and listened to radio sermons.

Monday brought another day of no sales. He and Steele were discouraged for want of a better income. Sam missed Ed and Betty and was aware that it had been 11 days without sight or sound of them.

Sam's own words...
Friday, January 19, 1940 – "Marian Anderson, Negro contralto, whose magnificent voice has brought her fame on three continents, held her audience spellbound last night at the Keeney theater in Elmira, with tones ranging from high C to low B."

No doubt Sam would have enjoyed hearing the superior voice. On reading and copying the account from his newspaper, he certainly was impressed that she had appeared in Elmira.

He and Edith were delighted when finally Ed, Betty, and the children came to visit on Sunday, two weeks since their last visit.

Bob Crippen returned on Monday, glad to be back.

The cold snap had not let up and threatened citrus crops as it dipped further south. Heavy snow was not new to Sam or New York. Dewey and Amy came to visit.

The year had started out to be no different than the hard way of the previous one. Sam cooked, did housework, and canvassed. The war news was about the same Nazi rhetoric from across the ocean.

Sam's own words...
Tuesday, January 30, 1940 – "Adolf Hitler made a speech today to denounce all democracies and France in particular."

Edith had gone to Ed and Betty's for a few days. Shirley was staying with a school friend, Ruth Lanterman. It meant that Sam and Bob were the only ones home on Wednesday, February 7. Bob had slipped on ice the night before, and the hard fall had left him sore.

Dear, old Mrs. Hulzier sent a card to Sam and Edith. The bereaved widow was alone all the time and said she missed her husband. She wanted to see the Crippens. Sam planned to ask if Roy might take them up to Pine Valley to visit her when Edith returned.

Sam's own words...
Saturday, February 10, 1940 – "Delivered a few fabrics. Grace came and read a letter from Maud, who lives in Dillon, Montana. We enjoyed it. About 32 years ago I went up that way to register for a homestead on the Flathead Indian Reservation."

He supposed he'd neither forget that time in his life nor its association with the legendary warrior, Sitting Bull. In his mind's eye, he envisioned the unforgettable rolling hills in the area.

Teddy's seventh birthday on Tuesday, February 13 was certain to be remembered. Sam would also recollect if he'd heard from Steele, but he hadn't for two weeks. It started to bear down on him like a memory that begged for action to make it right.

In spite of a traffic-snarling snowstorm Thursday, Sam made it uptown and sold two pairs of Tanner shoes. Sunday brought relief when Steele appeared. His hospitalized employer had left him responsible for more than gas at the Rose Valley Inn.

Edith was not well.

Uncle George Dimon answered Shirley's letter and assured her that he was well.

Sam's own words...
Friday, March 1, 1940 – "For seven years Adolf Hitler has presented the world with a brand new crisis almost every March—and the Ides are approaching again."

Sunday, March 3, 1940 - was Sam's birthday, and the house was filled with family all day. They each made the start of his 57th year a happy occasion.

Sam's own words...
Friday, March 8, 1940 – "My sister, Mary was here. Edwin Markam, one of the world's greatest poets and author of *The Man With the Hoe*, died last night. To me, he was a great man. I was blessed by knowing him only through his writing."
Thursday, March 14, 1940 – "Grace came over, and we got started in tying off a quilt. Snow and rain all afternoon."

During December 1898, Markham completed a poem that changed his career overnight. *The Man with the Hoe* poem, inspired by Jean-Francois Millet's painting (1862), owned the same name. The painting depicts a stooping peasant with a brutish expression on his face, who in Markham's poem becomes the embodiment of the suffering of oppressed labor throughout world history. Markham read the poem to an editor of William Randolph Hearst's San Francisco Examiner at a New Years' Eve party, and that newspaper published the work two weeks later. The Man with the Hoe attracted wide public notice and was reprinted in news- papers across the United States. Its appeal for better treatment of the working class became the subject of national debate and launched Mark- ham's career as a poet, transforming him into a national celebrity. Markham, more than any other poet in the English language, can claim the honor of being the Bard of Labor—Markham enjoyed the immense public prestige.

The Thursday snow threat was a prelude to six inches for Friday morning. Winter weather was worse around Watkins and Burdett. Ed was unable to drive the school bus to Watkins. Betty came to do her wash, and Ed took Sam and Bob to a movie.

Gene and Lucille brought Easter presents for Teddy, Bucky, and Jeanie. "They never forget the children, God bless them," Sam wrote. An Easter card from David and Frances had two small pictures of David and his baby son. Sam thought he looked like a healthy little fellow. On April 1st, Sam made out fabric orders to mail and smiled as he looked out at a cheery robin on the lawn.

Sam's own words...
Saturday, April 6, 1940 – "Roy and Grace took Edith and I (sic) in their car for a ride up the Middle Road then over to Pine Valley. We stopped at Mrs. Hulzier's and visited with the dear old lady awhile."

The news told of Nazi advances into Denmark and Norway.

Sam went to the drug store after insulin (99¢) and needles (25¢). Edith had gone to the doctor. John wrote that he had six more months in the army and felt glad about the prospect of being out soon.

Roy Whiting took a job on a farm. Grace had to remain alone unless they moved but it was too early for such a decision.

A letter from Willa told of 20-year-old Lee's marriage to Roy Harris. Sam's brows knitted together as he fretted and hoped they would see Willa and her girls again in the changing world. Lee was three years old when they'd last seen her. And Christy, they never had seen, except for pictures. It couldn't make up for the longing to have them near. He knew how much it would mean for Edith.

Sam's own words...
Wednesday, May 1, 1940 – "Did housework, called on Jim Lawrence, and visited surplus food office in Elmira. Will be glad when this sort of thing is not necessary."

Sam included housework in his triad. It was one thing that never ended. The surplus food was needed but the fact that they needed to get itwas distasteful to them.

On Saturday, May 4, Dewey paid Sam a visit. He told about a ride he took to Bath, NY, in the company of Grace and her daughter, Alice, also Eloise Madison, Sadie's daughter. They'd gone to see Bob Crippen, who was in Soldiers Hospital, but had improved. Dewey went back to Monticello.

Steele quit the Rose Valley job and came home.

Sam's own words...
Friday, May 10, 1940 – "The expected happened. Nazi Germany has loosed its immense forces. German bombs are falling on Holland, Belgium, France, and Switzerland. Is half of Europe to be laid waste and its people enslaved as in Poland? How many more ages will men act like beasts?"

Sam kept his balance of mind by relying on God. Otherwise, the war news had the capacity to overwhelm.

Roy was working his job on a farm near Ed and Betty. He put in crops, cultivated them, and would harvest them in the fall. He and Grace kept their Horseheads house. Sam and Edith benefitted by Grace's nearby presence.

Roosevelt asked Congress for one billion dollars for arms. He said,

"We need 50 thousand warplanes for security." Americans were urged to leave Italy.

Sam's own words...
Saturday, May 8, 1940 – "Around home all day. A neighbor gave me a hen house, which he wanted moved from his lot. I have it partly taken down."

Steele helped him finish the demolition and he was glad to be home. Betty, Bucky, and Jeanie were with Sam and Edith while Edwin went to Elmira. Sam and Edith were always glad to have them.

The garden was plowed, planted, and enjoyed by Sam. June was half over. Roy came down to see Grace and brought Teddy with him. They were delighted to eat at Sam and Edith's table.

Steele didn't smile much while he was discouraged and without a job. John wrote from Louisiana, expecting to be in Camp Devens, MA.

Betty came to try to persuade her parents to go home with her for a few days.

Sam's own words...
Friday, June 7, 1940 – "Edith went with Betty but I couldn't as I must do collections that I may pay the Mfg. Co. Edith isn't very well, to say the least, and doesn't see much. God knows I want to help her."

Edith was in attendance for Bucky's second birthday. Sam described him as a husky, livewire boy, and thirteen-month-old Jeanie as a sweet little thing.

Sam's own words...
Tuesday, June 11, 1940 – "Henry Ford says one-thousand high-speed pursuit planes for the U.S. Army, in production every day for six months, will be an easy task."

Americans had no problem of disbelief because Henry Ford had an assembly line capable of being tooled for more airplanes than cars. He had their backs and the president's ear. Lonely Bob Crippen was back at Sam's.

Sam's own words...
Thursday, June 20, 1940 – "Prepared meals, cultivated garden. Contacted the Associates of the Blind for aid to Edith if it is possible."

Shirley was out of school for the summer and had a job staying with and helping an elderly lady for $2 per week. The pay was not much but better than nothing. Sam hoped the experience would be useful for her.

Sam's own words...
Tuesday, July 2, 1940 – "Prepared meals. Saw Jim Lawrence about having Edith's eyes examined. Put considerable time in the garden."
Wednesday, July 10, 1940 – "Betty took Edith to the city for her eye exam. I kept the children. If they cannot help her eyes, they may grant her a pension. She is unable to do much, and a small pension would be a God send (sic)."

Betty and Ed left the children with Sam and Edith long enough to go buy a wringer washing machine for the farmhouse. Sam was glad for them as it would make life easier. Sam sold two pairs of shoes, gardened, and prepared food.

Sam's own words...
Monday, July 15, 1940 - "Robert Wadlow, the 22-year-old Giant of Alton, Illinois, who was eight foot, nine and one-half inches tall, died today. He was believed the world's tallest man and died from complications of a foot infection. His weight was 491 pounds, shoes size 39, and cost $86 a pair."

Sam was as interested in the rare statistics of the unfortunate young man as anyone else. Most likely, he felt compassion for the youthful and gentle giant.

Sam's own words...
Monday, August 5, 1940 – "We had Grace and Roy over for dinner. Edith's right hand bothers her, and she drops things."
Tuesday, August 6, 1940 – "Edith's hand worried us, and we called Dr. Empert. He says she has suffered a slight shock. God's will be done."

The hand continued to fail her as she staggered around the house like she had for years, but now with a more unsteady gate. Sam would do anything to help her, but her needs were many. Only God's will could help her. Appeal to the higher power helped Sam to do the best he knew how.

Edith remained the same as summer waned.

Sam's own words...
Tuesday, August 13, 1940 – "Much of my time is required at home since Edith is unable to do things. Dr. Empert saw her again this evening and says she is better but blood pressure still high."
Monday, August 26, 1940 – "Received Willa's letter and they are getting along well now. She enclosed pictures of herself, Christy, Lee and her husband, Roy Harris. Various crops, especially tobacco, were damaged by frost Saturday night. Frost is unusual in this vicinity in August."
Monday, September 2, 1940 – "Did housework and the wash. Betty gave birth to a baby girl at 10 a.m. Keith Voorheis, Ed's brother, came to tell us. Ed named her Gail."

Sam paid his two-month light bill of $2.50.

John wrote to say he'd had an appendicitis operation and remained in the hospital but was recovering well. Steele did not fare so well. He had lost the end of his second finger on his right hand in a machine he was operating at the factory. But perhaps worse, he lost his job. Dr. Hamilton in Elmira dressed his wound.

Sam's own words...
Friday, September 13, 1940 – "Nazis drop five bombs on Buckingham Palace. King and Queen safe in air raid shelter."
Sunday, September 17, 1940 – "Bob Crippen was here awhile in the evening. He seems interested in a lady at Millport whom he thinks wants a husband."

Sam might have smiled. Maybe Bob could find constant companionship and leave his loneliness behind.

Sam's own words...
Tuesday, September 17, 1940 – "President Roosevelt, today, signed the Selective Service Draft Bill Act calling for the first peacetime conscription in history. On October 16, all men 21 to 35 years of age will register at locations established in each neighborhood."

Sam's awareness was the inclusion of his three boys falling within the service category. David age 25, John 24, and Steele 22, would comply like all others compelled to do so. He had tomatoes to can, and worry while he worked was nothing new. Peaches were next.

Sam's own words...
Saturday, September 28, 1940 – "Ed and Betty came for an evening visit. Me, Ed, and Teddy went to the city for groceries and a movie. We saw Gene Autry in Old Monterey, which Teddy especially enjoyed."

It was a Western about an army sergeant and former ranchman who runs into opposition from local ranchers when the United States Army sends him to purchase their land needed for a strategic air base.

Steele brought 81-year-old Mrs. Hulzier down for a visit in the afternoon Tuesday, October 1. She was happy to stay the night to appease her loneliness. Sam felt that a feeble, old lady should not live out in the country alone. It just wasn't right.

Sam was always busy but never caught up with his work. He kept moving toward that goal as he canvassed, made out fabric orders, and mailed them. Garden work, housekeeping, and laundry waited for his attention. Robert Brown ordered a suit and Sam measured him for size. The commission was needed.

John came home on October 21. The drawing for the draft lottery began a week later on October 29. One after the other names came from the hopper for 17½ hours. Twelve-month terms in the military were the objective for everyone picked. It ended October 30. They all wondered how soon notifications would arrive. Who would go? Who would stay?

John got a job at American Bridge Works in Elmira.

Sam's own words...
Monday, November 4, 1940 – "Feelings are running high in regards to presidential election. The fact that F.D.R. is running for a third term and breaking all precedence is said to be sure proof he will establish a dictatorship in the USA. I don't believe it and judging by his deeds, shall vote for him tomorrow."

Sam made up his mind and could not be swayed. Roosevelt's win was a landslide.

Ed and Betty came Sunday afternoon, November 10, and took Sam and Edith to the farm for an overnight. Edwin worked on his chicken coop. Sam knew a thing or two about it to be of help. Ed had purchased 100 pullets that he had to be ready to receive. It was about to bring his total number of chickens to 300.

Back home in Horseheads again, Sam resumed housework and canvassed on Wednesday. It was what he called a glowing day as John brought home his first paycheck and paid room and board of $7.50. Steele was to give a similar amount weekly.

"Praise God," we shall be independent of relief assistance. Sam thought it incredible how they were all lifted up and filled with courage.

Sam's own words...
Friday, November 15, 1940 – "Ed butchered one of his nice hogs and brought us a big piece of pork."

The generous gesture glowed with good will and Sam's pleasure at receiving it. John knew how to provide when a few days later he bought three hens from Grace on November 19, to provide for Thanksgiving coming up.

Sam's own words...
Thursday, November 21, 1940 – "This has been a day with which we are blessed. We in America have much to be thankful for and may we continue to appreciate our heritage and be a blessing to all the world."
Tuesday, November 26, 1940 – "Did housework, delivered fabric. It is snowing to beat the band this evening."

Snow amounted to only three inches by morning.

Sam's own words...
Wednesday, December 4, 1940 – "Each day for me seems to be filled with about the same physical activities. I shall strive to live every day that each tomorrow will find me thinking higher thoughts. I want to live a thankful life and never grow bitter..."

Sam's pre-Christmas musings were New Year's resolution

statements. John came home Friday, December 6, glad to tell about his pay raise of 10¢ per hour. Steele was laid off indefinitely on December 9. Just as discouragement closed in, they called him back in. Steele's work went on with a day on then a day off.

Gene and Lucille Frost shared a letter with Sam and Edith that came from David. He had been in the hospital for three weeks with the flu. Now driving a truck, a temporary job, he vowed that as soon as he could save enough for bus fare, he was coming home.

"God bless him and Frances and little Davey and bring them safely home," Sam prayed.

There were enjoyable visits with Grace and Roy, also Betty and Ed's family. On December 21, they thought Teddy was coming down with whooping cough.

John, Steele, and Gene all wrote to David on December 21 and sent it by airmail in hopes that he would receive it by Christmas. Sam and Edith spent Christmas up on the farm with Betty, Ed, and the children. The day after, Willa's package arrived. They missed her.

Shirley quit school and went to work at Precision Tool. She stayed nights with a lady whose husband worked nights and earned her keep.

Arthur Crow sent a letter received on December 30, a gift in itself. Edith's 69-year-old sibling was well. All of Ed and Betty's children had whooping cough. Betty's days, full already in her farm kitchen, were made harder.

David answered the letter from his brothers and Gene. He and Frances felt overjoyed that the boys had jointly committed to raising the money to arrange their trip home.

Would John, Steele, and Gene be able to do it?

27 – Peace Time Draft
Pearl Harbor, 1941, 1942

It was January 10 when John and Steele gave their father a diary to start 1941. Sam backtracked one day to record a happy occurrence. It was contingent on the boys still being employed, and they were.

Sam's own words...
Thursday, January 9, 1941 – "We mailed a letter to David to tell him he can expect enough money to bring his family home. Won't he be gladdened?"

Now they were all on the same thought path. David wanted to get home, and his brothers had promised the means to do so sooner than if it was him alone on the plan. The loveable uncle boys, John and Steele, had brought their big hearts into manhood with them. Sam had a right to be proud, another reason to thank God.

Steele was laid off but hustled to get a job at the Eclipse. His enthusiasm served him well. Grace was 56 on her birthday, January 10. Sam went to visit her. He did housework and canvassed. Sam had been writing in his diaries for 33 years up to this point, an ingrained habit, he reasoned.

Sam's own words...
Sunday, January 19, 1941 – "Steele wired David the promised money. I bet he was excited, and there will be the same on David's end."

Tuesday, January 21, 1941 – "Edith is sick with a cold, and we called Dr. Empert."

Edith had grippe, influenza with bowel troubles, which hung on for most of a week. Finally on Sunday, January 26, she was able to ride along with Grace, Roy, and Sam to watch skiers on Harris Hill slopes. David's letter came several days later on Monday to tell them that he and his family had made plans to arrive in about a month. It was celebrated news in the Crippen household.

Sam packed lunches and also served meals at all hours. Steele ate earlier so he could be at work by 5 a.m. John slept longer, ate later, and arrived at work by 7:30 a.m. Sam and Edith ate later still. Shirley came to join the family when she could and especially enjoyed it when Ed and Betty were there, too.

Sam's own words...
Tuesday, February 4, 1941 – "Did housework. Set up stove in bedroom David and family may occupy."
Friday, February 7, 1941 – "More housework, washed. Sold a pair of shoes in the evening, made 75¢ for which I am thankful."
Thursday, February 13, 1941 – "David, Frances, and Little David (Punky) arrived 4 p.m. Gene, Lucille, Shirley, Betty, Ed, and children, Grace and others came to welcome them."

What a great time it was to embrace the boy who had gone away more than eight years ago when he was 17 years old. Frances was eager to help Sam when she saw how true it was that Edith was ill and nearly blind. Sam thought of Frances as a sweet, fine girl. And Punky grabbed them all by their heart strings. It was grand to have them close and no longer 3,000 miles away in California.

Sam's own words...
Friday, February 29, 1941 – (leap year) "Cold windy day. Ed and Betty expect to drive to New Jersey tonight to see a lady who owns the farm where they live. David and Frances staying with the children. Did housework, canvassed. Ed and Betty arrived from N.J. at 8:45 pm and stayed here all night. They made arrangements to buy the farm and are quite happy."

Edith went home with the happy farm owners and returned when they brought David and Frances back to Sam's. Sam managed to turn 58 years old. He never said a word but worried about finding enough to feed so many well-wishers on his special day. Snow accumulated 10 inches on the ground. More fell March 10.

Dewey visited early on March 15. He was going to Galeton the next day for a visit with relatives and take Grace with him. Sam was surprised three days later to learn that they returned early, visit denied. Heavy snow had kept them away from Galeton.

Sam's own words...
Monday, March 31, 1941 – "Busy at home and collected a little. David turned 27 years old today. I was 27 when I came back home from Idaho on a visit. He and Frances are at Gene and Lucille's tonight."
Monday, April 7, 1941 – "David is still without employment, and it is hard to make ends meet. Had a card from Gene and Lucille posted at Dunnville, Ontario, Canada, on their trip to a job in Flint, Michigan."
Wednesday, April 9, 1941 – "David to have a job at the Precision Tool Company, which will be a godsend to him and us."

When David came home from work he announced that he liked the job. Steele was the only one who had to go to work Saturday night.

Sam's own words...
Saturday, April 12, 1941 – "Everyone else but me, Edith, and Punky are out looking for pleasure. Ed and Betty just came, and we are glad to have them."
Friday, April 18, 1941 – "Did usual housework, trimmed hedge. My days are much alike, busy from early morning until late evening; the boys pay their board, and I spend it all on rent, fuel, and food."

Shirley came home to stay again. Sam's head nodded in appreciation as he ushered her in with his heart glad like hers. As she came, they all learned that one must leave.

Sam's own words...
Monday, April 21, 1941 – "Steele received notice to appear before selective draft board in Elmira Heights at 8 a.m. April 28. Prepared meals and put up usual four lunches. Colder."

The lunches were for David, John, Steele, and Shirley. The board they all paid kept the household going for all of them under Sam's management.

Steele was inducted into the army on April 28 in Syracuse for one year. An official letter was sent from the military to say that Fort Niagara, NY, was his destination. Bob Crippen came for an evening visit on May 1. He and Sam leaned in closer to enjoy their conversation. Steele wrote that he had a cold, received his shots, and played baseball. He missed home and said so in John's letter. He transferred to Fort Bragg, SC, on May 5.

Sam paid $3 to have his garden plowed on May 14.

Sam's own words...
Friday, May 16, 1941 – "Edith so ill we had the doctor for her this morning. She may have had another slight stroke; she hasn't been well for years. May God Bless her."

Shirley wrote a letter to Steele to tell him how ill their mother was.

As two days went by, Edith had moderate improvement. Sam cooked and planted garden and Frances helped him. Together they did the wash for the whole household. Edith was upright only to sit at the table to eat. She was weak and unsteady. Sam took care of Punky while Frances went out again to seek a job. Steel's girlfriend, Ruthie Coles, came for a visit.

Steele was fit to be tied when he received Shirley's worrisome letter about Edith. His return letter to his mother postmarked May 22, was straightforward and frantic because he could not obtain leave until June 8 unless it became an emergency. He wanted to be better informed, but it was what Shirley intended when she wrote to him. They understood Steele's worry and disadvantage. He dearly loved his mother like all of them.

Sam set plants, sowed seeds, and established his garden day by day. The May 27 news on WWII was President Roosevelt's proclamation of an "unlimited national emergency."

Sam's own words...
Thursday, June 5, 1941 – "Did my usual duties. I have found no time to

canvass in weeks. Edith isn't strong and is about blind and so discouraged. May God bless her."
Saturday, June 7, 1941 – "Prepared meals and canvassed the shoe line, for the first time in weeks."

More gardening occupied Sam as he put in six rows of corn. The beans were still in a small paper sack. As long as he was close by, he could check on Edith often. Little David (Jr) was two years old June 16.

The news reported that all German and Italian assets were frozen in the United States. U.S. consulates for those countries were ordered closed and their staffs to leave by July 10.

Steele arrived June 19 on three days leave. A jubilant group consisting of Edith, Ruthie, Frances, and Punky went with him up to Betty and Ed's farm and back.

Sam's own words...
Thursday, June 19, 1941 – "Prepared meals. Married in Twin Falls, Idaho, 28 years ago today."
Tuesday, June 24, 1941 – "John likes his new job and transfer to the night shift. Edith's feet are quite sore, and she seems more unsteady than usual, perhaps because of her feet."

Doctors Empert and Gridley were out of town, unavailable to offer wisdom, cure, or comfort. Sam looked higher as he uttered, "God help her." Edith was about the same for days on end until a week later when she started to improve.

Sam's own words...
Tuesday, July 1, 1941 – "I don't record much about the war, but it is terrible."

He informed himself at all times about WWII news. In response to the Japanese occupation of Indonesia, President Roosevelt ordered the seizure of all Japanese assets in the United States. F.D.R. also may have kept in mind the faint rumor from January. The public was not aware that U.S. Ambassador Joseph Grew passed along a whisper overheard at a diplomatic meeting about a planned surprise attack on Pearl Harbor, HI.

David got a car and a license plate for it. The Fourth of July brought suspension of factory work. All of Sam's young people had a great time.

Sam's own words...
Monday, July 7, 1941 – "Busy in house and garden. Everyone is back at work again after three days vacation. In my role as cook, vacation days are the hardest. Edith seems improved. Thank God."

Sam took a deep, satisfied breath. A letter from Steele spoke of resignation to the fact of his draft. In the beginning, he had disliked his forced situation. An office job now, which he was good at, had allowed him access to a typewriter to type the letter announcing that he and Ruthie planned to marry.

John announced that he and Mary Polovick would wed on labor day. Dewey was around for visits again the last of July. He took Sam and Grace to Galeton with him to see Sadie, Lynn, Mary, and Uncle George. It was a glorious day for Sam and the others.

Time had advanced toward a wedding day for John and Mary. Shirley and John pooled money to buy Edith a coat, hat, dress, and accessories for the big day. Edith's practical side and her failed sight may have prompted her and Shirley to select a stand-out navy and white polka dot dress that could be worn later for every day. They would not know that the now stylish polka dots would remain so popular that Elizabeth Taylor wore them on a ruffled dress in 1944 and Marilyn Monroe in the equally famous yellow polka dot bikini of 1951.

Sam's own words...
Tuesday, August 12, 1941 – "Congress authorized the bill to keep boys 18 months longer in the army. We are living in perilous time and must prepare for anything."

The House of Representatives passed the legislation by only one vote, 203–202, to extend the draft to 30 months total. It had followed F.D.R.'s order of August 1 to ban export of U.S. aviation fuel from the western hemisphere except to Britain and the allies.

David traded his red car for a 1934 Ford.

Steele came home and married Ruth Coles on Saturday, August 6, in the Catholic church of her faith. John and Mary were wed in the rectory of St. Cecelia Church by Father Smith.

Sam had harvesting and canning to do after the stressful week, and he sighed relief to get back to normal. The newlywed couples ate dinner at Betty and Ed's on Monday, September 1. It was Betty's gift to them.

Sam's own words...
Tuesday, September 2, 1941 – "Kept busy. Thirty-seven-year-old Albert Herforth, Teddy's father died Saturday, August 30, from injuries received in an automobile accident near Wellsville, NY. He caused Betty and others to suffer—poor misguided—May God have mercy."

Sam meant it, the mercy part, as he canned 11 quarts of tomatoes September 5, just the start.

Sam's own words...
Sunday, September 6, 1941 – "Edith had a bad spell today, and we called Dr. Empert. She has slept several hours, 9 p.m., and still she sleeps."

Steele was back at Fort Bragg, but all of his siblings and their spouses came on Monday to see Edith. They showed up every evening and knew when she began to improve and talked for the first time on the following Saturday, September 11. Sam did not leave her for fear she could not be trusted to stay still. Within days, she began to push a chair ahead of her for support from the bedroom to the table. Her appetite was intact.

Grace and Roy went to the lake country for peaches and brought back two bushels for Sam. He canned 21 quarts on Monday and 17½ on Tuesday. Sam wiped his brow and sat down at the table to rest when his last batch processed. He was exhausted from being on his feet considerably long and worrying over Edith.

It wasn't just tiredness. Sam's plight and Edith's were tied together. When had he first known in his heart that she never would be well enough? Well enough for him to have the freedom to go out every day and make a living, well enough that he didn't fear leaving her alone for hours.

Sam's own words...
Thursday, September 18, 1941 – "Didn't awake in time this morning to call Shirley and David for breakfast and they had to hurry, hungry to work. I hope this doesn't happen again."

David, Frances, and Punky went to Ed and Betty's Friday evening. Only David returned to Horseheads. Frances left on Sunday morning to go to New York City to see her sister. Punky stayed behind at Aunt Betty's and fit right in with his cousins, contented it seemed.

Edith had regained her strength and helped Sam do the wash Monday morning. A letter from Steele mentioned his expectation for a transfer closer to home.

Sam missed the time to canvass and wanted to do so again, which he did on Friday, September 26, for the first time since March. He went out again Saturday morning. On Sam's return, Edwin was there and had come after him and Edith. Ed needed help to shock beans all afternoon. Edith would be with Betty while Sam earned a few dollars.

Sam could see that Punky was getting along quite well as if he was part of the family on the farm, which he was. It bothered Sam that little David hadn't seen either of his parents in over a week. After work Monday, David went to the farm to see his son and took clothes to Betty for him.

A frost the morning of September 30 reminded Sam of how glad he was to have picked all of the green tomatoes the night before. The spuds were next.

Anna White, ordered a pair of shoes from Sam while he had been at Betty's. She came to Horseheads to pay him $5 for them.

Frances had not returned, and David made himself scarce and tight-lipped. Little David remained as part of the family at Aunt Betty's. Steele came home on furlough for a few days. David loaned him his car, and Steele drove Ruthie, Sam, and Edith up to the farm for dinner on Tuesday, October 14. Betty gave her father a rooster to take home and dress out for supper or the next day's dinner.

Steele had visited the army's Watertown Pine Camp and favored transfer there as it was closer to home. Sam had fabric orders to be mailed, and the satisfaction of it turned up the corners of his mouth. Edith was better, and Sam took advantage to go out and canvass. His smile spread as the corners of his eyes crinkled.

Sam's own words...
Tuesday, November 11, 1941 – "Did washing, scrubbing, cooking. Armistice Day. President Roosevelt said, 'America has duty to defend freedom, to make the world a place where freedom can live and grow into the ages.' First snow squall."
Saturday, November 15, 1941 – "Edith not feeling as well as usual."
Sunday, November 16, 1941 – "Edith must have had a shock last evening. Her speech is affected, and she is less steady in her walk. We are worried."

Of course, they called the doctor. Could Dr. Empert have called it a shock instead of a stroke, or was he vague and therefore Sam expressed it that way?

Punky, who had been in residence with his grandparents for a week, would go home with Uncle Ed, Aunt Betty, and his cousins. Little David took his dog with him, which his father had gotten for him days earlier. A week later, Edith was better but still unable to speak well.

John brought a 10-pound turkey to Sam for Thanksgiving. Grace helped to prepare it. Steele had a five-day leave from Pine Camp. He was a welcome sight to all of them around the table. War news was not on their minds. It had been quiet lately, but it was about to change.

Sam's own words...
Monday. December 8, 1941 – "Congress voted a declaration of war against Japan today as an answer to Japan's unprovoked and dastardly attack on Pearl Harbor, Hawaii yesterday. American forces lost two warships and three thousand dead or wounded."

When the smoke cleared in days to come, the numbers settled out at 1,247 wounded and 2,402 dead in the America military. The surprise aerial attack on December 7, 1941, on the U.S. naval base at Pearl Harbor on Oahu Island, Hawaii, drew the United States into World War II. Within one hour of the Pearl Harbor onslaught, President Roosevelt gave his Infamy Speech. He read his speech to Congress to ask for a declaration of war. America, the sleeping giant, had awakened. Freedom would be defended.

War news heated up as Germany's Hitler, and Italy's Mussolini declared war on the U.S. to support Japan. Hungary and Romania piled on against America, too. The U.S. conscription was changed from ages 21 to 35 and became ages 18 to 45.

Steele's army job had him making out furlough and payroll for soldier's Christmas leaves. He sent notice that he also expected to get home. His postcard had a scene of Pine Camp barracks and provided more information in which the family pictured him while he was absent.

Sam's own words...
Saturday, December 13, 1941 – "Dewey and Amy were here a few minutes today. Also, Bob Crippen in p.m. We have four inches of snow."
Tuesday, December 16, 1941 – "Did housework and large wash. John came 9 p.m., told us Mary was badly hurt last night on a return visit from Gene and Lucille. John drove."

Shirley went to the hospital to see Mary.

A neighbor, Mrs. Judson Thomas, had the *Christian Herald* sent to Edith for a year as a Christmas present. Sam thought it was 'sure fine' of her. It wouldn't hurt a bit if he enjoyed it, too, since he would be reading it to his Edith.

The Christian Herald mission spread the good news of the gospel of Jesus Christ. One of the most remarkable characters in the history of the *Christian Herald* was Dr. Thomas Wilkinson Riddle, who edited it from the Second World War until 1982. He had been the Baptist minister in Plymouth, and thanks to the high society company he kept, was referred to by some as a "Baptist Pope." Crippens would never know when in 1979 Colin Reeves acquired the business. Dr. Riddle was listed in the *Guinness Book of Records* as the world's oldest working editor at age 94.

Sam delivered fabric and did a little shopping. He prepared food every day. Dewey sent a picture of himself in his guard uniform and $1 each for Sam and Grace in a Christmas card. Dewey stood tall and proud in that photograph.

Sam moved the stove to the dining room and closed off the cold, drafty kitchen.

Claude Dewey Crippen — Reformatory Guard, age 43. This was a picture given to his family members at Christmas 1941.

Dewey was proud of his profession and had the confidence to be successful.

CLAUDE D. CRIPPEN

He died in 1973 at age 75 in a North Tampa, Florida Veteran's Hospital.

Sam's own words...
Wednesday, December 31, 1941 – "The last day of eventful 1941 and most of the world involved in war: America and her allies are fighting to maintain freedom in the world. My New Year wish is that they may soon triumph over those powers that would enslave all mankind."

~**~

1942

The world was full of hope and fear with humankind lined up in two separate camps: Totalitarians believe the state is master of the people, and the people are servants or slaves. Democracies believe as Americans do that the state serves the individuals and promotes freedom.

Sam's own words...
Thursday, January 1, 1942 – "It will be a fight to the finish. Freedom wins or freedom dies. If we fail to win, life will not be worth living. We will trust in the Lord and know that we are battling for what's right."
Sunday, January 4, 1942 – "Sunday is always busy for me. Steele and Ruthie, Ed, Betty, and the children were here in the evening. Six inches of snow fell last night. We are to have a practice blackout tonight."
Monday, January 5, 1942 – "Busy with housework. They say our blackout was a success. Let us hope we never need one because of an honest to goodness air raid."

Willa had sent a Christmas card and was still a clerk typist in Denver. Sales of new cars were banned to save steel. William Hitler, the nephew of Adolf Hitler, came to the United States and joined the Navy to fight against his uncle. President Roosevelt revealed that U.S. armed forces would go to join Britain. His war budget ballooned.

Snow fell while temperatures dipped to 20 degrees below zero. David's car froze solid. He and Shirley missed half a day of work but were not the only ones.

Little David stayed at his grandparents' home. He saw more of his father but cried if he went out evenings and was absent on the weekend. David was a hunter and often went to the gun club. He also had a private life since he and Frances were apart. Sam was busy from morning to night with the household and taking care of Punky and Edith.

Shirley had turned 20 years old in January. On February 2,

when his new little step-daughter went by Willa Haggerty Crippen at school. Sam felt blessed by the frequent visits home that Steele was able to take away from Pine Camp.

President Roosevelt signed the executive order to direct the internment of Japanese Americans. It included seizure of their property. Daylight saving time went into effect on February 8 in the United States.

February brought Teddy to nine years old. Sam wrote his name as Teddy Herforth Voorheis. He may have reminded himself of way back

Grace watched Edith and Punky for Sam a couple of hours on February 19. While she was there, she wrote a letter to Willa for Edith.

A blizzard raged on Sam's 59th birthday, March 3, while Grace baked him a cake.

Sam's own words...
Friday, March 6, 1942 – "Ed and Betty came for a visit. Teddy came in with his left hand in a sling, having lost part of his middle finger. The family had been to Ed's folks. Teddy and Russell, Ed's little 12-year-old brother, decided to split wood. Russell was wielding the ax when his stick fell, and Teddy quickly grabbed it and replaced it on the block. He was not fast enough to avoid the blade already poised for the blow. Russell felt terrible, although he wasn't to blame. We are sorry but are thankful it was not his whole hand or several fingers. Teddy is brave through it all."

Insulin, which had been 99¢ for a one-month supply, went up to $1.

When Dewey came for a visit from Woodbourne, NY, on March 22, Sam believed he missed his family.

Sam's excited face reflected how he felt when he'd sold a pair of Tanner's shoes in late March. From the end of February, Little David had lived at Aunt Betty's. Now he was back with his grandparents again. Before long, he broke out with German Measles.

Sam's own words...
Tuesday, March 31, 1942 – "Our firstborn, David, is 28 this birthday. Busy housekeeping, care of Punky and Edith. I despair of Edith ever getting much better. When weather warms and she can get outdoors, I hope fresh air and sun may do her much good."

He looked back over the years and remembered how long ago it had been when she was young and well in the early days of their marriage. He saw that she had gradually faded and never had gotten better, other than temporarily. She seemed never to have health that allowed her the strength to enjoy life. He, in turn, had no freedom from worry, no freedom from today's despair over her health. David went fishing on Saturday, April 4, with his second cousin, Edward Wheeler. Easter brought company to visit Sam and Edith. They learned that Betty had been ill, and all of the children except Teddy had had German Measles. He'd had them when he was younger. His finger was healing well after a lot of pain and setbacks until now.

Steele said he was not sure he would get home much going forward. He returned to Pine Camp. Sam thought of other American boys fighting on foreign soil, many never to return home. It was another worry.

Sam's own words…
Sunday, April 5, 1942 – "The whole world is suffering from this terrible war and praying for God's Kingdom on Earth. God can do for man only what he can do through man."

Willa's welcome letter arrived Monday. She was working as a photographer in Denver now and still lived at the Pearl Street address. She, Lee, and Christy were getting along well.

Monday, April 20, was as good a day as any to have his and Edith's shoes repaired. Did the cobbler shop count as part of the outside world that he seldom saw these days? Sam had been glad to talk to the man at the work bench, which doubled as an intake area. But Sam had not tried to sell him a pair of Tanners. That evening, David walked in to announce that he'd received 8¢ an hour raise. Sam was glad, too.

John put the new wringer roles on the washer. John and Shirley's generosity came into play when they bought them for $5.60. It was another extra added like times when Sam's youngest daughter spent the $1 to pay Dr. Empert when needed for her mother. Sam recorded from whom and where the money came and what the expenses were.

Sam's own words...
Monday, May 4, 1942 – "John and Mary took me to see Dr. Jones this evening. After examination, he said I should have an operation for my piles. They are too bad to be cured with the electric needle and would cost $110. The folks (family) are anxious that I have it done as soon as they can raise the money, bless them."

Sam had to plant his garden. Grace came to paper a bedroom that Shirley would soon occupy. She was so glad to move back home and contribute room and board there.

Edith received lovely flowers sent from Willa and the girls on May 10. Steele no doubt did not want to be absent for the occasion. He had sent a letter that arrived after Mother's Day. He and hundreds of other soldiers were required to attend a two-hour lecture on that Sunday.

Sam's own words...
Friday, May 15, 1942 – "Did housework, planted two rows of peas. Grace just told me that Dewey was accepted in the Navy-Marine Reserves at Albany yesterday. He is somewhere on his way to SC for training."
Saturday, May 16, 1942 – "Delivered fabrics, did housework, received a much-needed rain."
Saturday, May 23, 1942 – "Looked after Edith and Punky, did housework. Canvassed one-half-hour. David took Punky to Elmira to stay with Frances tonight."

Dewey's enlistment might have had a possible prediction to where and how long he would serve. He had avoided the certain 30-month term if he waited to see if they drafted him. Then it would be too late to enlist and have the shorter choice of 18 months.

On Monday, June 1, Sam planted 71 tomato plants that had cost him $2. It was a whole day of work added on beside his cooking. There was no time to rest his tired back, but satisfaction filled his thoughts.

The light bill was $3.25 for the two-month charge. Frugality allowed Sam to save the $15 Mr. Myers had coming for one month's rent. The balance was used to run the household, buy groceries, and purchase fuel for cooking. Between David's $52.25 and Shirley's $37.41 paid on May's room and board, it added up to $90.06.

John and Mary took Sam to see Gone with the Wind by Margaret Mitchell, staring Clark Gable and Vivian Leigh. The historical coming-of-age story was set in Clayton County and Atlanta, both in Georgia, during the American Civil War and reconstruction era. It depicts the struggles of young Scarlett O'Hara, the spoiled daughter of a well-to-do plantation owner, who must use every means at her disposal to claw her way out of the poverty she finds herself in after Sherman's March to the Sea. They thoroughly enjoyed the almost four-hour movie.

Little David was on an overnight with Frances on June 6. It gave Sam time to deliver fabric and also to canvass. He was gratified to work awhile in his garden on this and other snatches of afternoons.

Sam's own words...
Tuesday, June 16, 1942 – "Another day engaged in house and garden. David's little son, David Jr. is three years old today and a fine little man he is."

Sam went over to the school house Wednesday afternoon to register for extra sugar for canning. John and Mary stopped on Thursday to inform Sam of the arrangements for him to enter the hospital Monday night, June 22 at 6 p.m. to be ready for his hemorrhoid repair. Edith was taken up to Betty's the day before Sam's ordeal was to begin. They all appreciated another one of Betty's generous farm-style meals. Sam worried about leaving Edith there while he recuperated enough to care for her again.

Sam's own words...
Sunday, June 21, 1942 – "I don't like to leave her for I know she needs me more than any other one but feel quite sure she will be alright (sic)."

Sam came home nine days later, the evening of July 1. Shirley had sprung her father out with $55 paid to the hospital. John divvied up $50 to Dr. Jones and owed him $60 more.

Sam's face lengthened with gravity as he considered himself too frail and sore to have Edith brought home yet. He must regain strength and healing. Betty surprised him by bringing her mother for a short visit that same evening. No doubt, both of her parents faces widened with smiles as they set eyes on each other.

Edith came home to stay on Sunday, July 5. Sam was strong enough to look after her, but Punky stayed at the farm. Sam wasn't fit for gardening just yet. Shirley bought two linoleum rugs, one for the sitting room and the other for Sam and Edith's bedroom. She and her Aunt Grace installed them to make surroundings pleasant and set senses soaring. Willa and Christy sent a letter that arrived Friday, July 10. Sam prepared a new batch of beets, chard, and endive greens for supper.

Sam's own words...
Sunday, July 12, 1942 – "David went up to Betty's this a.m. to see David Jr. Edith and I (sic) were alone until 6 p.m. when John and Mary arrived. They were returning from the farm and informed us that the farmhouse had burned to the ground Friday morning. The family has had to go to Ed's folks until they can do differently. Certainly too bad but thank God that all are safe."

On Tuesday, Sam's renewal to strength may have been visible to Edith when he cleared his throat, and she waited to hear what came next. His sense of well-being came through to her as he said, "I guess I've let the garden alone long enough." She knew it would take him over when the smooth handle of the hoe became his old friend again.

Steele and Ruthie's daughter, Sandra Marie Crippen, had been born two days earlier on July 13 at 1:30 p.m. Their cherished baby girl weighed seven-and-one-half pounds. On the same day, Edwin had found another house for his family. Sam had the good grace to know that both points were of equal glad weight when he shared the news with Edith. They agreed on how good it would be to see Steele's new baby and see Ed and Betty settled again.

David took Frances up to Ed's folks on Sunday to see Punky. In another week, the little guy would be back in Horseheads with grandparents.

Sam borrowed Grace's canner to put up seven quarts of beans. It was just the start of harvest and preservation.

Sam's own words...
Sunday, July 26, 1942 – "Shirley went to Lucille Frost's, David went soon after. John and Mary visited a few minutes, same for Grace. Outside of that,

Edith and I (sic) have been alone all day. That does not bother me much, but Edith takes on so about it, especially since her radio does not work."

Monday, July 27, 1942 - "Pulled weeds, cooked. Ed and Betty moved into a small house on a farm not too far from the one they are working."

Sunday, August 2, 1942 – "David went to help Ed and Betty this morning. The house they moved into needs lots of repairs."

Sam sold a pair of Tanner's shoes on Thursday, August 6. He bought rubbing alcohol for 38¢ at Brown's Drugstore in Horseheads. He used it when he administered Edith's insulin shot.

Lucille Frost entered Arnot Ogden Hospital on August 6 and gave birth to Eugene Raymond Frost at 5:30 am. Shirley planned to become Lucille's helper when she and her son came home. Steele appeared out of the blue, ate supper, and went to Ruthie's. He was anxious to see his new baby, Sandra, for the next eight days of his furlough.

Sam canvassed on Wednesday.

Sam's own words...
Monday, August 17, 1942 – "Teddy stayed here Sunday and expects to remain for a week. We enjoy him, bless his heart. Shirley had his hair cut, bought him a pair of shoes and a whole outfit. She thinks there is no one like Teddy, and she is right."

Shirley took her next paycheck and Teddy shopping again and got him another whole outfit. When they came home, Teddy bounced on his toes as the school supplies spilled out of the bag. His shining eyes followed his aunt as she handed him tablets and pencils to touch and admire. Her dark-haired nephew liked school and his Aunt Shirley.

On Sunday, Sam lamented to himself, "I guess a cook has to work every day unless they can manage better than I do."

Sam's own words...
Monday, August 24, 1942 – "Davie left us this morning, poor little fellow. His father took him to the city to stay with his mother for awhile. A lady will take care of him days while Frances works. I love him and will miss him. It doesn't seem right to pass him from pillar to post, but I have my hands full. Ruthie and Steele arrived back at Pine Camp."

Teddy had been to the Chemung County Fair with his aunt and would have lots to tell when he got home to the farm. Ed and Betty came and left Bucky while they went to the fair. Sam patted the small blonde head and pronounced Bucky an active little man.

Davie was back at his grandparents' at the end of August. Teddy was in school August 31. Sam canned tomatoes and peaches for several days. The third Crippen reunion was held in Dennison Park, Corning, NY, on Sunday, September 6. There were only 14 relatives present, but they enjoyed themselves, according to Sam. He, Edith, and Shirley rode there with John and Mary.

Little David was again back with his mother.

Sam had his work to can tomatoes and take care of Edith. It was a full-time job to keep up with the work and her care.

Sam's own words...
Wednesday, September 9, 1942 – "Betty, Ed, and children, except Teddy, who was in school, were here awhile. We received news from Willa today that was so wonderful that it was hard to realize for an instant that it was true. Roy, Lee, and Christy left Denver on Monday, September 7 for our place. Willa will follow in a few days. They may remain east indefinitely. Willa expects to get a government job and may go to Washington, DC. This certainly is a godsend for we had just about given up hope of ever seeing them again. It has been 19 years since Willa and Lee went west, and we have never seen Christy."

Sam looked at Edith when he heard a great sigh escape from her lips. She had long suppressed her longing to see Willa; her hand was an open palm over her heart. He reached out to touch Edith's arm. "I'll read Willa's news again," he said. Sam was also eager to see Willa and her children who would soon arrive in Horseheads.

Sam cooked, scrubbed, and washed windows in preparation for the visitors they could hardly wait to see. There was excitement in the telling of it to everyone. Sam wore himself out, but when his head hit the pillow at day's end, he slept well from exhaustion.

The young people drove in the driveway Sunday at 6 a.m. stuffed in a Ford Model B Coupe with a rumble seat. The seat was a lid for the luggage storage space underneath it.

Lee, age 22, was pregnant, and had a little girl, Babbette, and her younger sister, Christy, under her responsibility. Lee's husband, Roy Harris, had his friend Butch along. They had traveled on emergency gas coupons and scrap rubber tires, which had 27 blowouts in seven days from Denver to Horseheads.

Roy was a drummer and harmonica player, but he and Lee would not be doing their singing and musical act while she was with child. Roy and Butch went job hunting right away.

Willa arrived in Horseheads two days later. Her entire group of siblings clamored to see her. It was a shorter reunion than planned since Willa's transfer notice had arrived. The photographic job from Denver translated to photo static work for the government. She left Horseheads on the 10 a.m. outbound bus to Washington, DC, a day later. Sam wished that she'd had time to stay longer and relax. He commented to the others, "Bless her. She has courage."

Willa's youngest daughter, Christy Jensen, went home with her Uncle John and Aunt Mary. She expected to attend Elmira Free Academy. She stayed at Sam and Edith's on the weekends. Her mother would send Sam $7.50 every two weeks for her keep.

Sam's household was busy as everyone came, ate, and went here and there. Baby Babbette often stayed with him and Edith. Roy and Lee were looking for rooms to rent in Elmira. Roy Harris and his friend, Butch, were not fond of their government construction jobs. The two of them were laid off and drew their wages. The duo snuck off while Lee was sick in bed and did not return until 4 a.m. Lee had words with Roy when he came back. She told him to stay away unless he could do better.

Sunday, Grace and Roy took Sam along on their trip to Galeton, Pennsylvania. Sam's eyes were soft, filled with an inner glow while they visited friends and relatives. The all-day drizzle did not dampen spirits or conversation as they drove along together. Sam took deep breaths, savoring the moments. Non-stop housework and food preparation for the busy household would resume soon enough. Butch and Roy were still out.

Sam's own words...
Monday, October 5, 1942 – "I can't understand how a young husband can

do what Roy has done when he has a wife and sweet baby that love him, and another baby on the way. I hope he decides to mend the error of his ways and returns and faces his responsibilities as a man. Lee is very brave, and I feel so sorry for her."

The wayward males came back Monday evening. Roy told a story about being in jail 72 hours. He said the police found a loaded firearm in the car. Lee exclaimed, "It was my rifle. I wonder who loaded it?
Sam's pained expression caused him to turn his back on them. Wasn't it best if he stayed out of it? He didn't know the whole truth, but he was ashamed of the delinquents and hoped they'd feel embarrassed.

Lee, Roy, and Butch went job hunting. Shirley was their guide since they were new to the area. The girl's presence may have ensured the objective did not go off track. Roy had success and expected to go to work immediately for Harding Machine Company on Tuesday, October 13. It fell into line beautifully. Sam may have thought the same when Butch received a card from the draft board and an automatic schedule for a physical in Dr. Empert's office.

Sam harvested a bushel of carrots and buried them in the outside cellar. It was a wood box buried part way in the ground, and a cover laid on top. Later, soil or straw would be thrown on it for more insulation to the cold storage of these vegetables near the house for the winter. He'd dug the harvest with gusto and thought about how it might be inconsiderate for so many people to come and go with neither rhyme, reason, or notification. He had expected them back for supper, but they were still out at 10 p.m. It would be no use for him to turn in until they arrived. He wouldn't sleep, and if he did, it would mean disruption when they came. They are young people he reminded himself. He started to wonder if they 'd had car trouble, but they turned up soon after.

Ivory soap made suds as flakes poured into the agitating water in the round tub beneath the rollers of the wringer washer. The clean scent of the white particles was as mild for baby Babbette's soft skin as it was for Great-Grandmother Edith's delicate wrinkles. Lee was humming, and Sam's eyes sparkled while they worked together on a big wash. It was Tuesday and Roy Harris was at work.

Sam's own words...
Saturday, October 17, 1942 – "Busy with household duties. Ed, Betty, and children came down in p.m. Ed, Teddy, Bucky, and I went to a movie, the first one for me in two or three months. I certainly enjoyed it."

The excited boys looked up at the star, Gene Autry, in his cowboy hat on the theater marquee, most likely the thrill of their lives. The 70-minute movie, Heart of the Rio Grande, was playing in many theaters since March and finally had come to Horseheads. What boy or man could resist opening lines, action, and music of *Deep in the Heart of Texas*? The film was about a singing cowboy and dude ranch foreman who helped a spoiled teenager and her business tycoon father discover what was most important in life.

Sam and Edith went home with Ed and Betty for an overnight on Saturday, October 24. John and Mary, also Lee and Roy, went to the farm Sunday where they all had a sumptuous dinner prepared by Betty.

Monday required the continued work of several meals a day for the household of people who came in and out at all hours. Sam rewarded his weary self with a visit to Grace. He felt whole and appreciated when he talked quietly with her.

Sam's own words...
Tuesday, November 10, 1942 – "Dewey was here awhile this a.m., and we enjoyed him. He is looking well and likes his Navy work. It may be a long time before we see him again."
Sunday, November 15, 1942 – "Grace and Roy drove up to Ed and Betty's this afternoon and insisted I go with them. I was reluctant to go because Edith's feet are so sore that she thought she ought to stay home. But she also urged me to go, so I did. We enjoyed the trip and our visit very much."

Dewey was a guard at the naval prison at Portsmouth, NH.

On Saturday, November 14, Lee and Roy picked up Christy from Sam's. They had Lee's grandmother, Mrs. Joe Roberts, who was the mother of Edward Walker (Willa's first husband, deceased). They were on their way to Syracuse to see Mrs. Robert's daughter, an aunt to Lee. Her Aunt Louise was anxious to see her after all the years gone by since Lee was three years old in Horseheads.

Sam bought salve at a cost of 50¢ for Edith's feet. David had kept Punky at Sam and Edith's for a few days. When the small boy arrived he had bounced happily in the door in anticipation of seeing his grandfather. Now he was back at his mother's Friday evening.

Sam's own words...
Sunday, November 22, 1942 – "John and Mary stopped on their way to Ed and Betty's and took Shirley with them. Steele, Ruthie, and little Sandra came in the p.m., also Grace for awhile. Steele left for Pine Camp 7:30 p.m. and will hitch-hike back, hopes to reach there 4 a.m. in time to get breakfast as he is first cook now."
Thursday, November 26, 1942 – "Prepared Thanksgiving dinner (chicken, pumpkin pie). Edith, Shirley, David, Christy, and I were the only ones here as everyone worked today turning out war materials for our boys and allies fighting for freedom of mankind all over the world. David and Shirley worked also, and it was Thanksgiving supper. We have much to be thankful for here in America. I think most of us have realized today more than any other how kind Providence has been to us."

Gasoline rationing began in the United States on Tuesday, December 1. It was 15¢ per gallon. Sam made fruit cake so it would have time to age and enhance the flavor by the time Christmas rolled around.

Grace looked glum, an almost forlorn look on her face, when she came to see Sam and Edith on Sunday, December 6. "Roy seems to be losing his sense of proportion and is causing me worry," she said. Grace wrung her hands as she spoke. "I hope he comes to his normal senses and won't have to go to the sanitarium as he did 20 years ago."

Sam prayed that it would turn out all right. He went to talk to Roy Whiting for quite awhile on Wednesday, in hope that he might help his brother-in-law find himself again. He came away shaking his head, afraid he'd had no success at all. Unless Roy could change his thoughts to a more constructive channel, Sam feared they would have to send him to Binghamton. Grace was heavy on his mind as he told Edith what a brave soul his sister was. "Action must be taken for her sake," he said.

By Friday, December 11, Grace came for another visit to let them know that she needed to carry out her conclusion that Roy get help. "Poor fellow," Sam said but with no blame on his dear sister.

Sam's own words...
Tuesday, December 15, 1942 – "Good visit from Ed and Betty. The annual letter arrived from Lenore Crow. Dr. Empert and Dr. Erway examined Roy W. today, and he may be removed to Binghamton soon. I wrote letters to Steele and Willa, wonder of wonders."
Thursday, December 17, 1942 – "Roy was taken to Binghamton, the state hospital this afternoon. May God bless him and straighten out his muddled mind. His body is strong but his brain registers in the negative. I feel so sorry for Grace. She is a kind soul and will carry bravely on, but we must not neglect her."

Betty and Ed stopped in to visit while on their way to shop for Christmas, December 19.

Shirley and Christy went to the Old Barn dance for awhile. Sam always gave Christy 50¢ allowance for the week, taken from Willa's support for her. The girls also liked to go roller skating and other times, take in a movie.

Grace came to dinner Sunday, December 20. Sam went to visit her Monday, one on one. She felt her aloneness and thought of Roy often.

"Will he ever return to his normal self again?" she stated.

Sam tried to pull her out of her sadness. He turned the subject to David's car. It had frozen solid that morning, and he'd had to take the bus to work at an expense of 25¢. It registered with Grace because she had already placed herself on frugal rations for lack of money being earned by Roy.

On Wednesday, Grace came over with a quart of canned venison that her daughter, Alice, brought to her. The mid-day meal was worth much more to Grace when shared. She remembered that John had celebrated his 26th birthday. They all smiled and complimented Christy and a neighbor boy, Billie Cook, who set up the tree and decorated it.

Sam's own words...
Thursday, December 24, 1942 – "Grace came over with John, and they informed us that Willa had arrived at Lee and Roy's. She would be over late or maybe Christmas Day. Cretia arrived at Grace's tonight and may stay the winter. I hope she does as it would be a fine thing for both of them."

Nearly every family member appeared at Sam and Edith's in the span of Christmas Day. Ed and Betty had Frances and Punky with them. Sam's heart warmed.

Willa's short vacation was over on Sunday, December 27, when she returned to Washington, DC. Sam was blessed to keep David Jr. for a few days. Steele and Ruthie brought baby Sandra in the afternoon. Sam wrote, "She is the cutest little thing." Sam received a photograph of her as a gift.

Sam's own words...
Monday, December 28, 1942 – "I hope Willa is back in DC and not too tired as she has to work at 11 p.m. tonight through 7 a.m. Punky, Grandma and I got along fine today. Grace and Cretia were here awhile. Grace, Alice, and Annabelle went to Binghamton today to see Roy. As yet, there is no improvement in his condition. Of course, he has not been there long."
Thursday, December 29, 1942 – "Steele, my youngest son, is 24 years old today. He is a fine fellow, and I miss him as he only occasionally gets leave of the army. Betty, Ed, and the children were here for awhile. Edwin is cutting wood to sell when the weather permits. Rained for two days, snow about gone, creeks and rivers high."

By Wednesday, the downpour turned to snow.

The old year was about to disappear as Sam wrote, "God grant it may have taught mankind many needed lessons." He ended the year by copying a meaningful poem on the last diary page of 1942.

To be something is more than to get something;
To make a life is more than to make a living;
The demands of love and honor are the highest
interest of practical men.

By Edwin Markam

28 – Washington, DC
1943

David worked on Sunday, January 3, and told his father he had found a place to board in Painted Post, NY, near Remington Rand where he worked. He did it because of gas rations that made it difficult to get enough fuel for his car. It was his last night in his parent's home.

Steele was on an eight-day furlough, and Ruthie's parents supplied the ride over to Sam and Edith's more than once. John came for a visit when he could snag a ride. On Wednesday, January 6, Mary gave birth at Arnot Ogden Hospital to baby girl Mickelene Crippen. John could hardly sit still with his pride over the big event.

Willa's letter reported that she was getting along well in Washington, DC. She wrote her feelings on how wondrous it had been to spend time talking to them and storing up the love that she felt directed at her. She said to tell her little sister, Shirley, that she was collecting information on several jobs that might interest her. She asked about Mary and the expected birth. Sam had the news about Mickelene's birth, which he could write and tell her.

Grace quietly turned 58 years old on January 10.

Lee was not very well, perhaps because of her pregnancy. She and Roy were having a hard time. Christy went over on Tuesday evening to help big sister.

Sam continued his regular house work and hurried to the drugstore after insulin for Edith. The first two weeks of the year had passed calmly for each in their own way.

Franklin D. Roosevelt became the first president of the United States to travel by airplane while in office. On January 14, he flew from Miami, FL, to Morocco for the Casablanca Convention. He and Winston Churchill of the United Kingdom talked about World War II.

Sam's Shirley Girl turned 21 years old on January 20, and Sam marveled that she was the youngest. How had so much time passed?

Sam's own words...

Saturday, January 23, 1943 – "Wondering if any of our boys will come. They should for their mother's sake...John and Gene Frost came in late evening. John said he could not contribute anything toward our maintenance and suggested I get a job in a factory. Edith cannot be left alone as she is too infirm and nearly blind."

Sam was unsteady as he took a step backward. The lack of understanding was a sudden propelling punch. Undoubtedly it was hard for his children to share any part of their paychecks when they no longer received room and board at home. There was no one else but Sam to give Edith the care she needed. Her hair was as gray as her health was poor. Sam thought back through the years to when their lives had first entwined, and she'd had a crowning glory of voluminous dark hair. The two of them had stood smiling into each other's faces, barely seeing the minister who performed their nuptials. If only Sam could go back to the time of the suspenders, suit, and bow tie. The vision of Edith in a full-length dress was that time of perfect health for her.

She couldn't see his moist eyes, but she had and always would feel his love through the devotion of his care. Edith was sick in bed more often now. She had more bad days than good days, which were almost non-existent. Her debility discouraged Sam. She was incapable at times even to lift her head and feed herself. A few sips of soup wore her out. She got more of it when Sam leaned her forward and spooned the nourishment to her lips. He believed she might benefit and improve again if he didn't let her care slip. Sam watched her dear, pale face as her eyelids fluttered open again from the draw of his gaze. She uttered one word before she sunk back into exhausted sleep, "Pal."

Sam's heart bled. The gravity of her illness weighed so heavy on both their lives. He couldn't allow himself to be overcome with the difficulty. He closed his moist eyes as he held her feeble hand and prayed, "God help us both." When he looked at her closed eyes and lined face again, he whispered, "Pal."

He was glad to get the usual $7.50 every other week from Willa. Shirley Girl still paid for her keep at $8 per week. David had not appeared in two weeks. John was over on Monday after work, worried because his baby girl was sick.

Sam's own words...
Monday, January 25, 1943 – "No one knows more than I what anxiety sick children can cause. I do hope she will be alright (sic)."

Sam talked with John, encouraging him about little Mickey.

Sam shoveled snow off the walk regularly. He could worry standing on his feet while he figured every way to become more frugal. Steele, Ruthie, and Sandra visited on Sunday, January 31. Steel had been promoted to technical sergeant and displayed three stripes on his sleeve. John and Mary came with 3½-week-old Mickelene, who was already well. The couples rode back to the Heights together. Grace came for a short visit, but there was no sign of David. Sam missed him and David Jr.

Betty got a ride with a neighbor, Floyd Doan, to drop her off at her parents. She brought Gail, her youngest, along for the visit and spent the whole evening with them until 11 p.m. when Floyd finished at the Eclipse.

Ed and his brothers, Fred and Keith, all rode together to their job at the Rand in Corning. The necessity of sharing gas affected most Americans.

Grace and Cretia came to dinner on February 7 and brought a pumpkin pie. Sam mentioned the newspaper article that informed the population about shoe rationing. They may all have checked the condition of their foot attire and discussed shoe repairs.

Shirley paid $22 into the household for the week because she could, and her heart was right. She had no husband or child obligations yet, as her siblings did.

Sam's own words...
Tuesday, February 9, 1943 – "Shirley is anxious to go to Washington DC and get a government job and Willa glad to have her. We would certainly miss her and hardly know how to get along without her. But it might be a good thing for Shirley."
Wednesday, February 10, 1943 – "Grace had a letter from Roy today, written by one of the nurses but dictated by him. He wants Grace to bring him a shirt and his glasses. That sure is encouraging."

It was Sam's habit to talk with Edith about everything, his concerns, his hopes, and his newspapers. On February 11, he discussed with her that General Dwight D. Eisenhower was selected to command the allied armies in Europe.

Bob Crippen came in the door Friday afternoon. What a pleasant visit it was. Sam's hand clasp and the warmth in Bob's face were sensed by Edith, who was pleased to have his company, too.

Monday morning, February 15, greeted them with 16 below zero.

Sam's own words...
Thursday, February 18, 1943 – "Busy with household duties. John Cullen, our Scotch bachelor neighbor, brought over a book on Russia by Maurice Hindus and I shall read it out loud so Edith can enjoy it, too."
Monday, February 22, 1943 – "Americans learned today that rationing of canned foods is going to be tough on their pocketbooks as well as food habits."

Sam was spared the additional hardship since he had grown much of their diet and even now the vegetable stores he had in his cellar sustained them. People would need to plan ahead and start victory gardens in May. There was need to start a learning curve for those not familiar with a hoe and seeds.

The headlines extolled patriotic American movie studio executives who all agreed to allow the Office of War Information to censor movies. No American wanted to jeopardize soldiers.

Sam's own words...
Thursday, February 23, 1943 – "I went over to the schoolhouse in the afternoon and registered for war ration book number two."

Before the outbreak of war, Britain imported around 55 million tons of food per year from other countries: tea, sugar, fruit, oil (used for gas), wood, and rubber. Large cargo vessels floated the shipments across the Atlantic. Once war broke out, Germany did everything to cut off these much-needed supplies, by hunting down and destroying the convoys that carried them with their battleships and U-boats. In America, all families (including children) would save anything metal or rubber and turn it in for processing, wasting nothing.

With imports of food declining, the British government set up a committee of nutritional experts to advise the War Cabinet on a food policy. The board issued limits: 12 oz. of bread, 6 oz. of vegetables, 1 lb. of potatoes, 2 oz. of oatmeal, oz. of fat, and six-tenths of a pint of milk per day. Supplements were small amounts of cheese, meat, fish, sugar, eggs, and dried fruit. Everyone was allowed 16 points per month (later increased to 20) to use on whatever food items they wished. Of course, these items had to be paid for. All adults were issued colored ration books, except for seamen and travelers who could not register with a particular shop. Ration books required renewal and new ones issued every summer.

The ration books had to be handed in at hotels or boarding houses if a person was staying there. Citizens were required to register with their local shops. The shopkeeper was then provided with enough food for his/her registered customers. Once items were purchased the shopkeeper would then cross off and subtract the relevant points used for that product for that particular month. Sam was aware of Britain's even greater hardships than the U.S.A.

Shirley was sick with a cold and home from work. Her presence had given Sam the time he needed for his trip after the ration book because she was there with her mother. Shirley's shift was from 3 to 11 p.m.

Sam had ordered a half ton of coal for $5.59 and hoped that the known shortage didn't keep them from getting it in two days, which was how long he figured his current supply would last. He sighed deep when delivery came the next day.

Four inches of snow covered the ground on his birthday, March 3.

He rubbed his jaw and decided he didn't feel like 60 yet. His sisters, sent cards. Willa sent S. V. Benét's best known book-length narrative poem of the American Civil War, *John Brown's Body* from 1928, maybe a rummage sale find. It had won the Pulitzer prize for Benét in 1929. Sam would read it to Edith and thought it was sweet of Willa. A letter from Betty told him why they hadn't been around lately. The children all had chicken pox and were just getting over it now. They'd be down soon.

Sam's own words...
Wednesday, March 10, 1943 – "Shirley has decided and is making preparations to go to Washington DC in two or three weeks. She wants to become skilled at a government job. We shall miss her sadly, but I think it is her opportunity."
Thursday. March 11, 1943 – "We have not seen David in two months and longer yet since we saw Little Punky and his mother. I understand David and Frances are divorced. What a shame it ended this way, and my heart aches for Punky."

Grace's neighbor, Mrs. Thomas, took her and Cretia to Binghamton to see Roy on Sunday, March 14. Grace's opinion was that the poor fellow wasn't improved much. March 16 was Edith's birthday, number 65.

Sam's own words...
Wednesday, March 17, 1943 – "I went to see James Lawrence in the a.m. regarding application for Edith's old age pension. In the p.m. I went to Elmira on the same mission, and it looks like I will have to make still more trips."
Monday, March 22, 1943 – "Busy with household duties and finally succeeded in filling out the application for Edith's old age pension and mailed it. I do hope she gets it soon. She is in need. Shirley and Christy are excited over their trip to Washington DC and don't know whether they are coming or going. They are scheduled to leave this Friday evening."

Sam crossed his arms and clasped his hands on his shoulders. "This old house will be mighty empty," he said to Edith.

Shirley gave her father $25.

Lee expected her baby most any time.

David turned 29 years old. He and John kept wondering if they would be called into the service soon.

Sam used instructions from a newspaper clipping he had saved with dimensions listed on how to make a cold frame. He tucked the directions away in his ledger for the future and planted lettuce and tomato seeds in the weather-protected frame space. Coal ashes were wheeled to the garden and spread for fertilizer. Edith was left alone in the house longer than he wanted. She was all right when he checked on her, and he went back to work longer. What was he to do? They had to have a garden and were quickly running out of money.

Shirley sent a card saying she was taking a civil service exam for junior clerk. Sam hoped it turned out well for her. He wrote her a letter of encouragement and missing her.

A lady from H. Hillman's office visited Sam and Edith to check on the application for old age pension, or service for the blind. The need was dire for either one that could be granted.

Sam went to the welfare office to see about a job. Maybe he could leave Edith a few hours each day out of desperation to support them. The job offered to him required 10 to 11 hours of labor a day. He swallowed hard and shook his head. He just couldn't leave his wife that long and was quite sure there would be no one found to watch her. It was a dead end for now.

Sam's own words...
Tuesday, April 19, 1943 – "Mrs. Blampeed came from the welfare office again regarding Edith's old age assistance. Betty, Ed and Bucky were here in p.m."
Wednesday, April 20, 1943 – "Ed brought us a cord of wood this afternoon, Bless him. Grace invited us to supper, and we all enjoyed it and each other very much. Grace misses Roy."

Edwin gave Sam money each week, what he could manage. It was $2 or $5, the most he could spare from the support of his own family of six people. Shirley sent $5. She had cashed a war bond ($18.75) to live on and shared it. She had passed the civil service exam but had no job yet. From all these sources Sam had received $44.37 for the month of April, and they existed on it by withholding payment of $15 rent.

Ed was having tractor and truck troubles. Betty and all of the children spent an afternoon with her parents while Edwin went to Elmira for parts. John gave up $4 for Sam and Edith's cause and brought them slices of cooked ham.

On April 26, a letter arrived from Shirley. She had gone to work at last. Her 10-page report from Washington, DC, gushed and glowed.

Suddenly Sam's little girl was aware of black and white, which had not been part of the Horseheads scene. The big wide world was out there for her to make her way as she learned.

~**~

May 1, 1943
Washington, DC

Dear Mom and Daddy,

I really like my job now, altho' (sic) at first, I didn't. I'm getting so I can just overlook the fact that the girls I work with are colored, and they aren't so bad as girls go. In fact, I think they are OK. Last night three of them helped me do my work so I could go home when they did. I thot (sic) that was swell of ém (sic). I didn't think I'd get along with them but guess I'm doing OK, huh?

I have a little booth all to myself. It's fun. I staple, inspect, and collate mimeograph sheets of gov. stuff, etc. It's rather interesting but monotonous. You can get up and run around whenever you want to (only I don't think it pays to run too much). I have fallen asleep because we don't have enough work to keep us busy.

I might get into camera work later. You see, there is an opening, and I hope I might get it. I don't think I'll go for Photostat (like Willa). I don't like the guy who has charge of it on our shift. He's white, but he goes with a colored girl. It's really disgusting. No one likes him, don't know how he ever holds his job.

Now it is Saturday afternoon, and I'm supposed to be ironing clothes. Excuse me while I do.

Hello again. I've been trying to get a bath all day. We share the facility with other people in the apartment house. Every time I get my water heated, somebody hooks it. I've hooked theirs too, but Judist, (sic) it's a dirty trick...

I'll get my first paycheck next week and send half of it home. It will be $14 or $15 (half of it) the first time. It's good earning my own way.

Hello again, dear people. I just went and took a bath (A COLD ONE) Brrrr.

Our new address is 905 E. Capitol, Wash. DC. It's a grand location. Willa, Christy, and I have an innerspring mattress bed. We sleep in it in shifts. Also, have a gas stove, refrig., dressing table, bureau, cupboard space, and a large closet. $30 a month just for one room.

I don't guess my letters are very interesting to you because I'm just putting down what I think when I think it.

The Congressional and Shakespearian Libraries are just around the corner from us. I wish you could see the Congressional Library. It's so wonderful. And now I'll be able to go and see it all. Oh boy! More fun and sights to see!...

No one ever writes. I wish maybe someone makes believe I am a soldier and start a letter where everyone adds their 2¢ to it. I've heard of soldiers and sailors who get letters 10 to 15 foot long. Not that I want that big-a-one, but don't I wish someone would write just a teeny weeny bit of news. I was and am always glad to hear from you, Daddy. You tell me everything in a little space. How do you do it? But how about the rest of the family, John for instance?

Sunday — Billie, Christy, and I (sic) went to the zoo. Imagine, the Zoo on Easter. Wow! What a mob of people. More fun. They have an air-raid shelter in the basement of the reptile house. Look what would happen if a bomb lit on it. Judist! Snakes in the bomb shelter. Ugg. (sic)

Willa is going to see about talking records.

How is Aunt Grace? Tell her hello for me and will she write? (I hope) Is she still doing washings, etc.?

I must write to Betty, Ed, and kids. Billie owes her a letter, too. I wish you didn't have to go up there. Can Mom get her pension if she is out of the county?...

Love, your baby, Shirley

~***~

Sam felled an old locust tree to use for firewood and worked on it for several days in snatches whenever he could.

In May John kept his head down along with slumped shoulders. He and Mary had not been getting along well, often in disagreement. Other news was that Lee was ill but was home from the hospital with her new baby. Willa had come from Washington, DC. John went after Betty to bring her to see her sister while she could.

Roy Harris was working in Binghamton.

Shirley and Christy sent a letter from DC. to Sam in which he found $15 enclosed. Shirley had earmarked it to pay her parents rent. She didn't forget them, and Sam blessed her.

Willa was on her way back to Washington on Saturday, May 15, now that Lee was on her feet again. Grace made a meatloaf and brown bread, which she brought to dinner Sunday.

Sam had a problem, helped only temporarily by aspirin. He had to wait for inflamed, infected teeth to heal somewhat before Dr. Brooks could pull them. It seemed like the last few original teeth in his jaw were anxious to jab him again before extraction. The situation was worrisome as he pondered how he would pay $3 to have his garden plowed and $3 to Dr. Brooks. His brow furrowed as he rubbed his sore cheek bone. He couldn't afford to have teeth pulled.

Mrs. Blampeed came on Monday, May 24, and let them know that Edith's first check would arrive June 4 or 5. Sam's brow smoothed as the relief of the great news washed over him and Edith.

Sam sold a pair of Tanner shoes and had $2 commission, which was sorely needed. On Wednesday, May 26, his extracted teeth meant soreness would end soon.

A vengeance of garden activity ensued. Grace brought Spanish rice to share for dinner and had 12 tomato plants for Sam. "Bless her," he mused.

Sam's own words...
Tuesday, June 5, 1943 – "Edith received her first old age assistance check today. Did my shopping, baking, and mowed lawn."

The check was $25.90. Shirley sent $20. Sam's energy soared, and he may have felt like running a victory lap, but it was his garden that would be the victor. He studied his book on the subject. All of the diagrams on how to plant and the suggestions on what would grow well were meant for novice gardeners. But he could always keep abreast of current methods and pick up the newest information.

Sam's own words...
Wednesday, June 9, 1943 – "Ed and little girl, Jeanie, stopped here a few minutes on the way to deliver a horse to Sullivanville. He brought the good news of their new 9 lb. 1 oz. baby boy born June 5, named James Earl. Betty is home doing fine."
Sunday, June 13, 1943 – "Grace had Edith and me over for a good dinner. John, Mary, and Mickey came before supper time and brought ice cream, cold meat, and coke-a-cola to eat with us. We fared pretty well today, and it amounted to quite a vacation for me, besides the pleasure of having them. John said...David and Hilda Drake are married and seemed happy. They are to come to see us soon. God knows we want to see him."

Withholding taxes from people's paychecks began June 9, 1943. Congress passed the emergency measure to obtain money to fight Hitler. The idea came from Beardsley Ruml, treasurer of Macy's and chairman of New York's Federal Reserve Bank. He called it the "pay-as-you-go" tax. So much money came in with so few complaints that it continued after the war.

On Wednesday, they received a letter from Shirley. She complained of the heat in Washington and sounded homesick in Sam's opinion. Steele and Ruthie's letter of June 24 said their weather was sultry.

Sam spent $1.35 for radio repair on June 25, an absolute necessity for Edith. With that, she could find enjoyment in spite of her inability to see well. Imagine his smile as he bent over and plugged it in for her. Now he'd feel less guilt while he left her alone and tended his garden. He spent time near her when he did housework, cooked, and wrote letters.

Sam's sisters, Sadie and Mary, were at Grace's, and they came over for a visit. They planned a meal together for the four of them at Grace's, which was equally enjoyed by all of them on Sunday. When Grace hadn't had house guests, she'd established a habit in weeks past, to visit Sam and Edith every evening. They had missed her for the few days but understood the importance of sisterly chats.

Sam's own words...
Wednesday, July 7, 1943 – "Received a letter from Frances and Punky and she says they are getting along well, and he is just fine. He is so entertaining, becoming a real person and learns many things. I would like to see them. God bless them."

Sam saw his great niece, Margie McCann, when she accompanied her grandmother, Grace, on a visit. Due to gas restrictions on family members, Sam and Edith were alone a lot except for Grace close by. John came to get Sam and Edith on Sunday, July 11, about noon. They all went to Gene and Lucille's and then John and Mary's to be surprised when Dave and Hilda arrived. The warm embraces were not over when Steele and Ruthie came, brought by her parents, the Coles. The happiness of the reunited gatherers lit up all of their faces. The glow would last Sam and Edith for days.

On Tuesday, July 13, Sam took Edith over to Annabelle's beauty shop for a haircut. She needed it for her sense of well-being even though Sam practiced frugality. It often included liver at 15¢ for half a pound. Shirley sent $10, and Sam was able to pay $15 rent for a month. No doubt Edith experienced his elation when he sold a pair of Tanner shoes on the 16th. His mental preparedness had come through for him. He hadn't let negativity stop him from his sense of purpose. Well now, his commission would buy insulin and then some. He could go back to the hoe with a lilt in his step.

Sam's own words...
Friday, July 23, 1943 – "Grace received a card from Roy today, the first he has written himself since he was taken away. He wants her to come to see him Sunday, says he is working in the rug factory, and he is much better. We do hope so."

Grace was never alone in her wish for her husband to be well. It carried with it the hope he would come home with a whole mind again. She and Sam understood each others problems, wishes, and enduring love for both of their spouses.

Groceries, jar lids, and can rubbers had cost $1.02 and were as necessary as a loaf of bread or a carton of eggs. Canning began when Sam hot bathed six quarts of beans.

Grace visited Roy in Binghamton. Elation was theirs when she returned and said he was much improved. Her news included Roy's planned parole to come home in a few days. Sam felt great love for Grace as he watched her face brighten while she told her exciting news. Her words were as welcome as a generous shower on Sam's Victory Garden.

Mr. Myers was showing the house that Sam rented, which they had lived in for 10 years. If it sold, they would face the task of moving, again. Fresh beets and chard greeted Grace when she came to supper, Saturday, July 31. She said Roy would arrive home the next day and he did.

Their brother, Lynn, his wife, Iva, and sister, Mary came to support Grace and visit Sam and Edith. The much thinner Roy was acting reasonable again. Sam followed his diary report with "Thank God" and meant it.

Sam's own words...
Wednesday, August 4, 1943 – "Shirley will visit home about the 25th. We miss her a lot and shall be very glad to have her. More showers today and all living things are taking on new life. Edith and I went to see Grace and Roy this evening. Had our first mess of sweet corn."

Wasn't life grand? If Sam could make the money stretch and last, yes. Edith's third assistance check of $25.90 arrived. Shirley sent $15 to cover another month's rent. Sam's garden would ensure a certain amount of food. The sale of a pair of shoes to a neighbor meant Sam could pay his $1.53 electric bill. Without power, the Crippens couldn't operate the radio.

Edwin often stopped by in his truck. He delivered horses for Joe Miller of Odessa and took them to Corning and all places where the horse trader needed them delivered. They enjoyed having Ed stay for supper and tell them all about Betty and the children. Betty came with him on the evening of Saturday, August 14, to arrange to pick Sam up after they delivered one horse to Breesport. Sam hurried around to make sure he left no household chore undone. His bright outlook helped him prepare happily for the unexpected outing. Grace stayed with Edith while Sam went to a movie with Edwin and Betty.

The next day, Sam made brown bread and canned jars of applesauce. A letter received from Shirley was all aglow about her interest in a sailor, Mr. Thomas Broadhead, of Hattiesburg, MS.

The U.S. Seventh Army under General George S. Patton arrived in Messina, Sicily, followed several hours later by the British Eighth Army under Field Marshall Bernard L. Montgomery. That news gave Sam impetus to pull out a full-page clipping with information on Patton. He had saved it from October 20, the year before. It was a different slant on the general, a softer side known by his wife. She had provided it to a magazine, the Women's Home Companion. It was her treasure from the time her husband wrote it.

God of Battles

George S. Patton
Lieutenant General, United States Army

From pride and foolish confidence
From every weakening creed
From the dread of fearing
Protect us, Lord, and lead.
Again we seek Thy counsel,
But not in cringing guise.
We whine not for Thy mercy—
To slay: God make us wise.
Great God, who through the ages,
Hast braced the blood stained hand,
As Saturn, Jove, or Woden
Hast led our warrior band,
For slaves who shun the issue
Who do not ask Thy aid.
To thee we trust our spirits,
Our bodies unafraid.
From doubt and fearsome 'boding,'
Still Thou our spirits guard,
Make strong our souls to conquer,
Give us the Victory, Lord.

Sam's own words...
Tuesday, August 17, 1943 – "Wrote to Shirley and Steele. Grace was over towards evening and said Roy will go to work tomorrow at Ward La France. Am glad he has found work for things will be better for them. Owing to circumstances, I couldn't go to work but how I wish I could."

The Ward LaFrance Truck Corporation was an American manufacturer of trucks and fire apparatus founded by Addison Ward LaFrance in 1916 in Elmira Heights, NY. The company ceased operations in 1979. Sam was not about to waste time with envy. He excelled at what he could do and cared for his wife and garden. His acts of love were performed without begrudging Edith because of her impaired health. Men of supposed greater valor could fail at this but not Sam.

He sold $1 worth of sweet corn and canned eight pints of cucumber and onion sweet pickles. John and Mary picked Shirley up at the bus station and brought her home. She had one week of basking in the love she received at home. John drove them all up to Betty's. After a good visit, they brought Teddy, Punky, and Bucky back with them. Shirley took Teddy everywhere she went. The two younger boys had their fun with Grandpa and a dog named Jack that belonged to Christy. Lee, her babies, and Christy came up from Binghamton to see Shirley and all of them. Little Babbette called her baby brother Burr.

On Sunday, September 5, John and David came and took Sam for a ride in John's "new-used" Plymouth. Edith was not well enough to go to the Crippen reunion.

Steele's change of location became Camp Ellis, Illinois. Ruthie stayed with her parents in Elmira.

Sam started canning tomatoes. He certainly knew how and the job would last several days, if not a week. A light frost dropped in on Sunday night, September 12, to serve as a warning of the season to come.

Shirley was back in Washington and wrote long letters about Tommy Broadhead, who wanted to marry her. She was not convinced yet.

Ed came after Sam and Edith to go home with him and stay overnight. Sam's work was at a cut-off point, and they rode along in a happy mood. Sam and Ed buzzed poles into two cords of wood. The next day Ed delivered all of it to Horseheads along with Sam and Edith. The satisfaction to have their wood supply built up shone like a light on Sam's face.

Sam picked all of the green tomatoes ahead of a freeze sure to come. His next job was the making of grape jelly. His work was in good shape, and they could go back to the farm for a week. Ed planned to pay Sam for help with more wood, and they would all enjoy one another. Sam's diary was forgotten for now.

Back home again, a three-page letter was received from Steele. He described basic training at Camp Ellis. The usual infiltration course was a belly crawl for 50 yards through barbed wire and mud holes under simulated battle conditions. It meant live machine gun fire 26 inches overhead and charges of dynamite going off all around. Steele said he appreciated letters from Father, Shirley, and Aunt Grace.

Sam prepared a chicken that Ed and Betty had given them for a good meal or two. They felt rather alone now after being amidst the children and adults on the farm. Sam made green tomato mincemeat and canned 7½ quarts. He worked outside, dug potatoes, and picked lima beans.

Sam's own words...
Sunday, October 10, 1943 – "Mr. and Mrs. Coles, Ruthie, and Sandra were here, and we enjoyed them. Sandra is walking now and is she a sweet one. We sure missed Steele, and I thought how he would like to see his wife and baby. Ed, Betty, and baby James were here in late evening, stopped on their way as they delivered horses."

Edwin liked to have Betty along for a ride when they could manage it. It was her 28th birthday and maybe they could get an ice-cream cone. Sam canned tomatoes again. On rainy Friday, October15, he baked a pie, a cake, and bran muffins.

Sam's own words...
Monday, October 18, 1943 – "Ed, Betty, and Bucky were here a few minutes in the afternoon. They want Edith and me to move to their farm and live in a part of their home. We may do so."
Tuesday, October 19, 1943 – "Received a nice long letter from Shirley and must answer it soon. Sold Mr. Thomas, our neighbor, a heating stove and Mrs. Thomas a pair of Tanner shoes. I sure can use the money."

Finances had been tight, not enough to stretch and cover all needs. Sam's complaint of his sore leg had added to his woes. Ed and Betty knew about Sam's worries and had taken responsibility onto themselves. The purpose of their invitation was to relieve Betty's father from part of the burden.

A large private room to themselves at the farm seemed almost too good to be true. He wrote a letter owed to Shirley and may have told her that he couldn't see any other answer in front of them. He preferred independence, but help with Edith's care was welcome. It could give him some freedom to help Ed and earn their living. Was it more plus than minus? Sam started packing.

Bob Crippen and his Elizabeth visited them on Thursday evening, October 21. Sam sold them the electric washer. He felt decisive and packed more belongings.

Steele wrote again. He'd been on a rifle range for several days and then was transferred to the 369th Q.M. Bkry. Co., 3rd Platoon, Camp Ellis, Illinois. They carried him as a casual, which meant attached, unassigned. He was only there for rations and quarters while he awaited another transfer. Shirley had written, but Steele wanted his father to nudge Betty to write. Before he closed, he asked his dad to write a nice long letter. He had enough time on his hands to read letters if he could get them.

Sam planned to write at length once he had time and a clear mind to do so. He had the decision to make, and he seemed pushed to move to the farm. Mr. Myers was selling, and they had to go somewhere. Edith had to have care around the clock. He wanted to make a living, but Edith was first. His thoughts went to the fact that Shirley was jobless. She hadn't had extra to send money yet in October. Wouldn't it be nice if she were free of it? All of Sam's thoughts circulated to look at all his reasons why this might be the best answer. He'd gladly help Ed with wood and Betty with cooking. Sam likely believed it would allow him to earn their keep. He finished garden harvest, and they could go for a trial stay at the farm.

Sam's own words...
Friday, October 22, 1943 – "Betty came in p.m. Edith and I went home with her."
Saturday, October 30, 1943 – "Edith and I arrived home about noon today after a week on the farm near Bennettsburg, NY. I was busy making the

rooms ready for us to move into besides helping Ed. It rained most of the time."

Letters from Steele and Shirley were waiting, and Sam must answer them. Shirley had sent $10. It was for postage to send the belongings she listed: shoes, flat iron, roller skates, and clock.

Sam packed more of his belongings each day. Grace would miss them but thought it was the right solution for Sam and Edith. She knew firsthand how infirm her sister-in-law was.

On Wednesday, Sam registered for ration book number four, cooked, and boxed up more items.

Sam hadn't improved on what he thought was an infected leg. John took him to see Dr. Empert Saturday. The diagnosis named it an ulcer, and he received a prescription. John drove him into the city to fill it. It cost him $2.83, and the money may have been hard to part from, but he needed it as much as Edith needed insulin.

Sam packed canned vegetables and went uptown after insulin and groceries. He sold a pair of Tanners while he was gone. The chance to do so was irresistible when the opportunity presented itself. He prepared supper and packed preserved fruit and empty jars. He'd laid his diary aside, too busy and preoccupied with moving duties. The change could be good, but he'd have to get used to it before it became comfortable.

Sam's own words...

Tuesday, November 16, 1943 – "Ed and I (sic) moved the third load and last load today. We ate dinner at Grace's. Saw Dr. Empert and he said my leg is about healed. He gave me medicine for my lameness. Ed and I drove to Elmira and ordered windows for the rooms we are to occupy."

Quite a few of their things were unpacked and arranged. Sam left much of it in boxes because of the need for a new chimney. Windows were yet to arrive and plastering planned.

Ed needed to cut poles, buzz them up, and sell the wood by the cord. He and Sam did it in two days. On the third day, they drove to Horseheads and sold seven cords at $5 each. They stopped to see Grace. Sam quickened his step a little when he went up her front walk. She and Edwin invested just as much enjoyment in the short visit as Sam.

Ed moved Harry and Gladys Landon (his sister) to a Pine Valley farm. Sam was busy enough with chores. Grandpa and Teddy, who was going on 11, made a new road into the wood lot in the afternoon. Teddy was so glad to help his Grandpa that Sam never had to prod him to keep up.

Steele had been home but was on his way back to Camp Ellis, uncertain of his next transfer, maybe overseas. Ed and Sam cut wood into five cords and took it to Horseheads and sold it. Another day, Sam helped Betty and did a few chores. As expected, it turned quite cold at the end of November.

They skidded logs on Monday and Tuesday. On Wednesday they buzzed and delivered six cords to a buyer. They bought cinder blocks in Watkins and built the chimney on December 2.

Sam couldn't hold back a smile when he sold two pairs of shoes to neighbors who stopped in. Maybe they were bought for Christmas or the necessity of replacement for those already repaired too many times to count. He knew how that was.

The news of December 4 announced that the Great Depression had officially ended in the United States. With unemployment figures falling fast due to World War II–related employment, U.S. President Roosevelt closed WPA. The Works Progress Administration had helped Sam and all of his family in past years. He was helping Betty today as they rode in the truck to Elmira to pick up the new windows that had finally come in.

Ed took his truck and Joe Miller to Buffalo after horses on Monday, December 6. Sam did chores and helped Betty. No doubt, his sidekick, Teddy, helped do the chores before and after school. The next day, Ed hauled hay for Joe. The horses had to eat. Ed went again to Buffalo, same mission, another group of equine.

Sam sold a pair of Tanner shoes to Mrs. Arney Morgan, Betty's friend. He didn't mind a bit. He did chores and husked some dry corn. Betty made a delicious chicken dinner for Sunday, December 12. Meat in her farm kitchen was plentiful. It was grain-fed and raised by Edwin. It was a treat to all of them and Grace and Roy. No wonder Sam considered them a happy, healthy bunch.

Ed and Arney Morgan butchered two large hogs on December 13, one for each of them. Sam helped Betty, who was so sick that Sam got supper ready for them.

The next day he helped Ed buzz wood. By now everyone was sick or half sick with a cold. In a couple of days, Ed managed to cut up the pork. John came on the 15th to cut a tree to take home to Elmira for Christmas. All were well by December 18, except for Edith, who was miserable. Ed and Sam plastered the small bedroom. It was progress. Edwin took him to Burdett to cash Edith's check.

Dewey, Grace, and Roy came up. Dewey had been a U.S. marine for 19 months and was on his way back to his guard job at the state institution in Monticello, NY. Sam helped Ed cut wood as a natural part of each day. On December 22 they had bad luck and broke the wagon. The bobsled was a hard pull on ground that hardly had any snow on it, but it was their only alternative.

Sam's own words...
Thursday, December 23, 1943 – "Ed got two of his neighbors, Mr. White and Mr. Kellogg, to help us buzz wood. We loaded seven cord on the truck. They left the five children with Mrs. Morgan and went to Horseheads to sell firewood. Betty intended to Christmas shop. I stayed home to do chores and look after Edith. It is 9:30 p.m. and they have not returned yet."
Friday, December 24, 1943 – "Betty and Mrs. Doan went to Watkins to Christmas shop a little. Edith gave Teddy a $1, and he went with them to do his shopping. You can't get much for a $1 this year, but I bet he did very well, bless him."

On Christmas Ed, Betty, and the children went to Reynoldsville to have dinner with his folks. Sam looked after Edith and did the chores. John, and also Gene Frost, came about 4 p.m. and brought Frances and Punky. Sam opined that he hadn't seen them in a year and what a gratification it was to see how David Jr. had grown. They stayed overnight.

Grace and Roy came on Sunday. Later, Ed went to Binghamton on a paid job to transport furniture there for a young couple. The truck rolled in home by 10 p.m. after the children were in bed. Edwin and Betty took

Frances and Punky to Painted Post. Sam tried not to think of the worst that could happen, but he fretted about the rain freezing on. He shifted in his chair and looked at the clock. Surely it would be late when they got back. He rolled his shoulders to alleviate a stiff neck as he waited. There would be no relaxation, let alone sleep, until he saw the sweep of the headlights in the driveway again. His eyes were drooping by the time the light beams flashed their return.

Sam's own words...
Monday, December 27, 1943 – "Having tooth trouble. Did chores and work around the house. Ed delivered horses for Joe Miller. Received a nightshirt and Edith a nightgown from Dave and Hilda."
Wednesday, December 29, 1943 – "Betty drove the truck to Watkins, and I went and had a tooth out. We were surprised this afternoon when my three sisters, Grace, Mary, and Sadie arrived."

Betty and Mrs. Morgan did a large washing. Sam managed to get midday dinner and help Ed buzz up three cords of wood. Sam's jaw and throat gave him trouble, but his sisters' visit had taken his mind off it temporarily. By Thursday, he felt relief and then it was history, just like 1943 would soon be. Ed and Sam cut wood on December 31.

29 – Edith
Soldier's Letters, 1944

There had been a flu epidemic in Burdett and surrounding areas lasting more than two weeks. Betty, Teddy, and Jeanie went to the Bennettsburg school entertainment Sunday evening, January 2. It was supposed to have been put on for Christmas Eve, but had to be postponed due to so many illnesses. Sam sat at his desk, deep in thought about Shirley, whom he missed a lot. He was sure to feel better if he found the strength to write her a letter. That day he and Ed had been industrious and had accumulated quite a pile of wood.

Sam's own words...
Monday, January 3, 1944 – "Received a Christmas package from Shirley, Willa, and Christy and it contained presents for most everyone in our large family including Gene, Lucille, and baby Raymond."
Tuesday, January 4, 1944 – "Helped buzz 30 cords of wood today. Am quite tired this evening."

The next day was easier after the initial loading of the truck with seven cords of firewood. Ed and Sam rested as they rode along to Horseheads and to sell it. They ate supper with Grace and Roy. They went back and took six lots to sell on Thursday. Friday repeated; seven cords were sold and afforded another visit with Roy and Grace Whiting, which was a bonus for Sam to see his sister. Ed knew it. His sociability made him just as pleased to visit them as Sam.

Betty received a letter from Lenore Crow telling that she finally had a letter from her son, Donald, after months without any word. The communication was a relief to Lenore even though Don, his wife, their daughter, Marjorie, with her husband and four children were prisoners of the Japs in an internment camp in the Philippines. They were all concerned for Lenore because of the mysterious silence of her families but none were more worried than Lenore. They were all right and received proper treatment, which included plenty of rice and vegetables. Lenore was grateful that they were alive and well.

Sam did chores and split posts while Ed helped his brother, Fred, cut wood for two days. The 250 chestnut posts sold January 12. Sam received his share of $10. He, Teddy, Ed, and Arnie Morgen went to a movie that night and saw *Pistol Packing Mamma*. It depicted Westerner Sally Benson cheated out of her bankroll by Nick Winner, a gambler passing through town. In New York, Nick opened up a combination nightclub/gambling joint. While he was away, Sally used the name of Vicki Norris and got a job singing there. Getting to the end of the situation held suspense for the movie-goers to the 64-minute film that had come out in December 1943.

Old Mr. Bob Bennett lived across the road from Ed and Betty. Sam bought an Aladdin-style lamp from him and spent another 40¢ for a glass chimney and tobacco. He assembled it and smiled at the light that fell across Edith's page as she struggled with her magnifier to make out a few words. She had no success and fumed with frustrated.

Sam's pleasant frame of mind was unhindered because he remembered that Shirley would arrive and be able to spend six days with them and away from Washington, DC. She came the next day and was brought up to the farm by John and Mary. Sam thought his youngest daughter was too thin, but he was delighted to see her.

Sam's own words...
Monday, January 17, 1944 – "Betty drove the old truck to Watkins; took me with her, and I had another tooth pulled...I do hope when my jaw heals that I won't have any more trouble from that quarter for awhile."

Sam helped inside for a couple of days instead of out in the cold to be sure he did not thwart healing. Sam was smiling with the assurance that his opportunity to bask in Shirley's attention would benefit him well.

Lyle and Fred, Ed's brothers, needed extra hands to buzz 40 cord of wood. They knew who to call. After Ed and Sam had helped them, Sam was paid $5 for his 10 hours of labor. Edwin had more of his wood that needed buzzing. Neighbors Frank White and Theodore Kellogg came for a late start, but 25 cords were finished off.

Shirley didn't get back to the farm for a visit on her 22nd birthday on Wednesday. Later, Sam found out that they had started out, but John's car broke down. At the same time, Sam heard that Steele was to have a 10-day furlough. It was nice to look forward to his visit. Meanwhile, Frank White and Theodore Kellogg needed turnabout work to buzz logs into chunks.

Four inches of snow was on the ground Sunday morning. Monday, Ed and Sam loaded several cords of wood and went to sell it. It brought $10.50 at $1.50 per cord. Just as important as the sale was the trip to see Grace, then John and Mary. It was quite a disappointment that Shirley had left on the train to DC the night before. Sam was more disheartened than anyone.

On return to the farm, they had missed a visit from Steele and Ruthie. Sam likely shook his head and figured that it was just one of those days for missed connections. Betty told them about precious baby Sandra in the hospital recovering from an operation for mastoiditis. The fever and pain from her bone infection behind the ear was under aggressive treatment with antibiotics.

As if that were not bad enough, later Steele's furlough was canceled, and he had to return to Camp Ellis at once. Without warning he was stationed at Kessler Field, Mississippi.

Shirley wrote about her unhappiness of not seeing her parents more when she was at John's. She was worried about paying her income tax and thought about quitting and coming home. Sam was sure he did not know what was best for her.

Sam and Ed worked on wood. They were all glad to see John, Mary, and little Mickey, who came up on Sunday. Edwin repaired his truck tire because part of a double pair had blown out. By Thursday, February 10, he and Sam went to Elmira and sold eight cord of firewood. It was the perfect opportunity to visit again with Grace and Roy in Horseheads.

Sam had not played it up too big about how good it felt to earn his and Edith's keep with a few dollars here and there to put aside. His satisfaction, freedom, and sentiments were not shared by Edith. While his self-worth soared, hers dipped. At times he felt she was angry. He understood that she was ill. But had he spoiled her too much? Didn't she understand his opportunity and responsibility? He wanted her to be happier.

Sam's own words...
Friday, February 11, 1944 – "Busy around house and barn. Ed and I went to Odessa in the afternoon. I bought a battery radio (cost $15) for Edith...She can do nothing, not even read and the radio will give her more pleasure than anything I know of. Received letter from Shirley. If she and T. Broadhead marry, she may come home, otherwise probably won't. This terrible war makes it hard for those who would marry."

Several inches of snow slowed down Saturday's world until a plow opened roads on Sunday. The family went to visit Ed's folks in Reynoldsville, NY. It was Teddy's 11th birthday. Sam and Edith had a few hours alone, and he gave her plenty of attention.

It was time to sell more wood on Monday. Sam spent 40¢ on tobacco while they were out. The weather turned colder. Bad luck showed its mean edge when the tongue of the bobsleigh broke in the woods. Work halted.

Sam was glad to have a letter to read to Edith from Steele in Mississippi. He wrote about a few exams he and other soldiers took to determine placement. His eligibility for combat crew had him killing time to wait and wonder what came next. Mainly, he wanted to receive letters.

Snow piled up steadily. Ed repaired the bobsled to haul the logs out of the woods and down to the buzzing station between the house and the barn. His sister needed wood. Gladys's husband, Harry, drank alcohol to excess and was not dependable. Sam helped throw two cords of wood in the truck, and Teddy rode with his father to deliver it. Ed wouldn't receive his cord rate that fluctuated from $1.25, $1.34, or even $1.50. Harry drank up the money, and Gladys had hardly enough to buy food, forget fuel. She and her many children needed help, and Ed provided it.

The wood business required hard labor, but when they had 18 to 20 cords accumulated, they were ready to sell it. It was a welcome break to ride along and deliver the goods to city-folk in Horseheads. The low temperatures and snow insured sales to regular customers and a few new ones. They sold three cords to Grace and Roy and ate supper with them.

Sam grinned at Edwin's good-natured banter during the meal. He ate faster than anyone, a habit to inhale his food instead of chewing and swallowing. While they ate, he had time to talk. Sam might have wished that Edith took his sort of harmless humor for the friendliness that was intended. She saw no fun in it when he teased her as he did everyone else. It was sad that she was so ill that life stopped being enjoyable for her even with Betty's good care.

Sam's own words...
Friday, March 3, 1944 – "My sixty-first birthday. Was surprised and gladdened when John and Grace arrived 10:30 a.m. They ate dinner with us to everyone's enjoyment. John brought me a dandy pipe and a can of tobacco. I shall get a lot of enjoyment."
Friday, March 10, 1944 – "...Lucille Frost gave birth to twin boys."

Cold and snow meant they would stay busy on timber work.

When they went to sell firewood, a stop was made especially to see the twins. Later, at home, they told how cute they were.

Edith's 66th birthday was the occasion for both she and Sam to receive a card, letter, and presents from Willa and Christy. Steele had been home but the furlough ended, and he went back to Camp Lee, Virginia.

Sam's own words...
Friday, March 31, 1944 – "It was great to have Steele but tough to see him go again. Hearts break all over the world, and still this terrible war goes on. Man persists in marking the earth with ruin. God helping us, some day we shall see the light."

Throughout the months they had cut chestnut posts. Ed and Sam sold and delivered 200 of them, which brought 6.25¢ each for a total of $12.50. Sam realized a few dollars from the sale for his labor.

Grace and Roy came for Sunday dinner on April 2. Betty put on one of her big meals to fill the big wooden table in the farmhouse kitchen. Edith received as much attention as her strength allowed. It was not a bad thing if Edith grew tired as long as she did not get cross. Sam watched for the balance to tip to know when it was time to retire to the quiet restfulness of their private quarters in the north end of the farmhouse.

Sam's own words...
Thursday, April 6, 1944 – "Ed, Betty, and the children went up to his brother, Lyle's until 2:30 p.m. We took Edith's radio to Odessa to have it checked as it refused to operate about a week ago..."

Sam sold four Foster deals on Friday. The success and the warmer weather had him in good spirits. Ed's big family, neighbors, and friends were customers. The children were having an exciting afternoon coloring eggs. After they were put to bed in the evening, Ed and Betty went to Watkins Glen after groceries and also candy for five Easter baskets.

Sunday became a banner day for children who had not been disappointed by the Easter bunny. Company came calling. They were glad to receive John, Mary, and Mickey, and also David, Hilda, and Bonnie.

Snow fell on Tuesday, April 11. Betty had an over-sized washing to finish. Sam did housework and prepared supper. The next day, Ed and Sam cleaned out the brooder coop and moved it up near the barn.

Gladys needed wood again. The two men delivered two cords to her. They built a new fence around Ed's barnyard. There was always manure to draw out and spread on a field. Sunday came around again. Ed delivered a horse for Joe Miller. Bob Bennett needed a couple of days labor across the road on an adjacent farm. Sam received $8.50 for his effort.

Sam almost got an adrenalin rush when he deemed it the right time to make a hot bed on Friday, April 21. He sowed seeds for tomato, cabbage, and lettuce in it Saturday.

Edwin and Sam went riding together to deliver horses Tuesday evening. Ed had more of such work coming up for Joe Miller. A few days later, he went to Buffalo after six equines.

Sam's own words...
Saturday, April 29, 1944 – "Baby James (Jimmie) has been sick for some time. This evening they took him to the doctor. He has or had pneumonia. He was given sulfa drugs, and it was thought he would get along alright (sic). God knows we hope so. Drew out manure."
Monday, May 1, 1944 – "They took Jimmie to the doctor again, and his lungs were cleared up, but there's need to be extra careful he doesn't get it again. Received letter from Shirley. Drew stone, put them in the driveway, dug toilet hole, and finished hauling out manure. A nice spring day."
Wednesday, May 3, 1944 – "Helped Ed sheer his sheep."

Ed's immediate work was caught up. Sam hired himself out to a neighbor, Mr. Sebring Cox, for two half days. It turned out that Mr. Cox paid only $2 for a whole day.

Sam's own words...
Sunday, May 7, 1944 – "John, Mary, and Mickey, Ruthie, Sandra, and Grace came in the p.m. I went home with John to look for a job. John, Gene Frost, and I went to a movie and had an enjoyable time. Shirley telephoned that she would arrive in Elmira at 4:20 a.m. Gene and I (sic) met her at the train."

Gene slept all day Monday to be ready to work at night. John worked days but didn't get off early enough to take his father to apply for a job. Sam enjoyed Shirley for the day, but a job hunt hadn't worked out. John took him back to the farm Wednesday evening. Shirley's girlfriend brought her to the farm Friday, and she went back to Washington, DC, Saturday.

Betty took the sheep wool to Interlaken and when she returned, she felt quite ill. Sam looked after the house, children, and Edith. Ed ate the supper Sam prepared before he and Joe Miller left in his truck for Buffalo after a load of horses. Sam kept up his housebound job for several days until Betty recovered.

Mrs. Floyd Doan came half-a-mile down the hill to visit on Monday. She was a close friend of Betty's and came to buy a pair of Tanner Kushiontread shoes from Sam. He enjoyed Mrs. Doan, a Christian woman, and conducted the sale and paperwork in an unhurried fashion.

Sam had ordered his replacement for a lost social security number card while he was at John's last. Ed took him to John's on Tuesday, May 16, to see if it came. No one was home, but he was dropped off at Grace and Roy's. He became sick the next day, and Grace called Dr. Empert. He received medicine and paid $3. Sam nodded his approval when John came after work with the social security card.

Betty and her friend, Eva Morgan, stopped at Grace's Friday, and Sam rode back to the farm with them. He was mindful of the good care Grace had given him and told Betty how he appreciated it. Ed and Joe Miller left early on Saturday for Buffalo to get a load of horses.

Edith received a letter that Sam read aloud to her. She clasped it to her chest when she learned that Willa would arrive on Thursday. Betty did the wash while Sam did housework Tuesday. Ed worked all day long Wednesday on his truck. He put it through a lot and depended on it for their livelihood. Sam stayed inside, still not back to his best health and strength.

Willa's train came into Horseheads on Thursday, and she took a bus to Bennettsburg where Betty picked her up at 2:30 p.m.

Sam's own words...
Friday, May 26, 1944 – "Planted some garden. A severe electrical storm about 7 p.m. Lightning struck a big willow tree near the house and set it on fire. Still burning at 10 p.m. We are mighty thankful it was not the house."

Six-year-old Jeanie held on tight to Gail all afternoon as the two of them huddled together on the front steps. Craning their necks around grownups pacing on the lawn, they peered across the driveway at the burning willow. Gail was a few months short of her fourth birthday, but she consoled her big sister as they worried about their dolls at the base of the huge tree. The crack of lightning that ignited the lace-leafed gnarled tree had frightened Jeanie to shaking in her skin. Gail couldn't let on that she had been startled, too, because she liked the superior role of shielding her big sister anytime the vast open sky lit up from such a storm.

"It's OK, honey," Gail said as they hugged close together.

The tire swing hung lopsided from a branch until the rope burned through and set the smoldering black tire rolling down a slight slope into the roiling, formerly shallow stream.

Edwin and Sam worked all Saturday to clean up debris from the burnt willow. Betty and Willa made a picnic dinner for Sunday. All of their siblings, except Shirley and Steele, were there. John, Mary, and Mickey brought Grace and Roy for a big gettogether.

Sam went to Horseheads to stay with the Whitings and also John and Mary on different days. He applied for jobs and had physicals at various plants, some of which he could not pass because he had varicose veins. It prevented work that would have him standing on concrete floors.

He was turned down at Thatcher Glass but Dr. Turner approved him for janitor work at Ward La France

Sam started treatment for his veins with Dr. Empert, and he scheduled more for every Tuesday. It took only a few days before he missed Edith and everyone at the farm.

Sam's own words...
Tuesday, June 6, 1944 – "Invasion of France—D-Day."

U.S. and British paratrooper divisions jumped over Normandy while 155,000 Allied forces landed on the beaches below. The U.S. parachute and glider troops were the 82nd and 101st Airborne. "Operation Overlord" was the largest amphibious undertaking in history. It helped liberate France from Germany and weakened the Nazi hold on Europe.

Sam's own words...
Wednesday, June 7, 1944 – "Worked my first day for Ward La France cleaning windows. My legs are sore where the doctor stuck needles in them, but the veins seem smaller. John and Mary have gone to a movie this evening. Wonder how everyone is up at Betty's. I miss them very much."

Sam's usual workday was eight hours. John took him up to the farm on Saturday to stay overnight. The time seemed so short late Sunday afternoon when he returned as far as the Eclipse. Ed and Betty's neighbor, Mr. Berry, worked there and gave him a ride. Sam walked to John and Mary's.

Sam's own words...
Sunday, June 11, 1944 – "...I don't like leaving Edith a week at a time, but I must earn money while I can..."
Monday, June 12, 1944 – "Hope Edith isn't too lonesome tonight. May God bless her."

Edith may have had thoughts on loneliness that she shared with Sam. Most likely it was necessary to spend more time in the midst of the family in the evenings to lessen time she spent alone. Without Sam there, Betty needed to keep an eye on her at the same time she washed supper dishes and then put children to bed. Edwin would not have been of much help inside on summer evenings as he had any number of jobs to do on the farm.

It was Tuesday night again and time for more needles in Sam's veins. He ached afterward but supposed he'd feel better in the morning. He'd get through it every Tuesday for the sake of improved health.

Steele called from New York City and was on his way overseas in a couple of days. Sam wondered if Steele would ever return. Would he see his son again after the danger the military faced? Edith sunk lower, weaker, and more sickly again.

Sam's own words...
Friday, June 16, 1944 – "...We took Edith to Dr. Empert. Grace and Roy will take her home to the farm tomorrow."
Saturday, June 17, 1944 – "Steele has been on my mind all day. Wherever he is, may God bless him. I hope to see Edith tomorrow and hope the doctor's medicine will help her..."

John took his father up to Betty's for awhile Sunday evening. Edith seemed the same.

Sam's own words...
Tuesday, June 20, 1944 – "Worked from 1 to 9 p.m. and then John took me to Dr. Empert for shots in my legs...The doctor said Edith is in awful condition and can't see how she lives. I wish I could help her. I place her in God's care. His will be done."
Wednesday, June 21, 1944 – "Am wondering where Steele is tonight and how he is faring. He may be in England. God grant that peace may come

soon to this war-ravaged world. Hope to get up to the farm Sunday and see Edith and all the others. John is to be inducted into the army June 30. We shall miss him."

Sunday morning John and Mary left for a three-day vacation to Niagara Falls, NY. Sam was left alone and had no ride up to the farm. He shook his head and ran a hand through his hair as he thought of his ill wife who needed to see him. The garden could do with a hoe put to work, and he'd feel better if he didn't sit around. It was Wednesday when John returned and took him up to the farm and back. Edith was stronger but unhappy. She may have felt deserted and a bit miffed at Sam. She didn't understand like Ed and Betty did that Sam needed to make money while he was still young enough to do so. Ed could not pay him wages because he had a large family in need of his resources. Sam's help was in less demand since wood cutting had ended when warm weather started. It left him with time on his hands, time that could be filled earning wages.

Sam's own words...
Friday, June 30, 1944 – "John and his friend left for Fort Dix, New Jersey, about noon. My heart feels his absence but then I think of the millions of other homes where boys and girls, too, have gone. I place mine in God's care and trust him to help me carry on. (8 hrs. Ward La France)."

Sam went to Horseheads after work to see Grace and Roy about staying with them. They were his first choice, but they were not home. Since John was gone, Mary was renovating the house and planned to rent it out quite soon. Gene and Lucille were home, and he ate dinner and supper with them. They said he could board with them, so he moved his baggage over.

Sam had no ride to the farm and was disappointed not to see Edith and also Betty's family. By Tuesday he was even more concerned that he hadn't gotten up there. He wondered about John and Steele. Was Steele overseas?

July 4 came and went, and still he had no ride to go to the farm. On Friday, July 7, Grace and Roy took him to see Dr. Empert for more shots in his leg. He stayed at their home all night and went to work eight hours Saturday.

Sam's own words...
Sunday, July 9, 1944 – "Roy and I went up to Betty's and came back in the evening. Edith seemed about the same. Ed's crops look good. He just got back from Buffalo with a load of horses for Joe Miller. Bucky may be coming down with the mumps."

Monday, Sam was back at work. John made a quick trip home and reported he liked army life.

The Democrats nominated F.D. Roosevelt for a fourth term as President.

Sam worked every day but Sunday. He went to a movie with Gene and Lucille Saturday night. Sam's agreeability to attend *Home in Indiana* with them had Gene bouncing on his toes. It was about a boy having just been sent away to live with his uncle and aunt in Indiana. Teenager Sparke Thornton had a penchant for trouble. At first, he was not satisfied with the arrangement and continued to express his rebellion. On his first day he already planned on running away, but after he crossed a harness racing track he was convinced to stay.

Grace and Roy took Sam up to the farm on Sunday and Sam was satisfied that they were all getting along all right. Edith's health hadn't changed.

Lucille saw Mary on Monday and learned that John was at Camp Croft, SC. Sam had a letter from Steele on July 2. He wrote that he was in "merry old England," which looked like New York state to him except all the buildings were brick. During his first meal there, he met an Elmira soldier related to Charlie Danks, a family friend back home. Steele was glad to have work to do in the kitchen and remarked on the great food. "I am too busy to be homesick. I'll be waiting anxiously to hear from all of you," he wrote.

Sam's own words...
Wednesday, July 26, 1944 – "People are alarmed over infantile paralysis epidemic; 120 cases reported to the Elmira health department since June 20. At factory eight hours. Had a letter from Shirley. Gene had one from John."

Friday, July 28, 1944 – "Gene took me to Dr. Empert to have more needles stuck in my legs. I'll be glad when I get the last treatment. Have to go again August 12. At factory eight hours."

After work on Saturday, Sam had a chance for a ride with Grace and Roy, who were driving to Ithaca to see their daughter, Ruth. He was dropped off at the farm and picked up on the way back. He stayed all night with the Whitings again and enjoyed their mutual friendship. They planned a similar trip the next weekend. The idea pleased Sam, and he walked over town to the Horseheads theater to take in a movie. Life was going along well for Sam.

Sam's own words...
Sunday, August 13, 1944 – "Grace, Roy and I (sic) went up to Betty's in the afternoon. Edith is very thin and unhappy and seems quite a burden to others. God knows I would do more for her and others if I knew how. Stayed with Grace and Roy all night."

Edith was a burden to herself in her misery. She could not be well. She could not feel happy. But lash out, she could, and it was no secret except to Sam who was now mostly absent from the premises.

Betty stood in the kitchen turning the handle to knead the bread dough in the 10-quart cast-aluminum pail-like vessel clamped to the kitchen countertop.

Six-year-old Bucky with blonde hair as unruly as some of his actions studied his grandmother from a safe distance. She sat on alert near the opening between the living room and kitchen with a spyglass in her hand. What Bucky called a spyglass was a magnifier, but it was useless to Edith now for that purpose. She could pretend to read and look busy with it while she grasped her cane, ready for another use.

Bucky was determined to go through the area at full speed. If he was fast enough, he could slide lickety-split in his socks on the waxed linoleum to end up beside his mother and get a small lump of raw yeast dough to eat. The challenge was too good to pass up.

Grandma Edith's hearing had sharpened as her sight dimmed. She could hear a feather float, a spider weaving its web, or a marshmallow toasting. But Bucky had no idea of that. He ran his fastest. The cane lashed out, but he caught it in both fists and slid to a stop beside his mother's bread operation. Betty had a fine line to maneuver.

"Give the cane back, Bucky. She needs it to go to her room," Betty reprimanded. His heart leapt in his chest as he placed the cane on the table reasonably close to Grandma, whom he considered a mean old woman. He hurried out of strike range.

Sam's own words...
Sunday, August 20, 1944 – "Stayed with Grace and Roy last night. They took me up to the farm today. Everyone seems fine but Edith. She is very thin and so unhappy. Came back and stayed at Grace's."
Monday, August 21, 1944 – "Arrived at Gene's 10 a.m. Received a letter from Betty that had been at John and Mary's. She wants me to relieve her of Edith and says she is going to have a baby in December and just can't have her mother any longer. At La France eight hours."

Edwin and Betty did not speak about it in front of Edith. It would not improve her disposition and could certainly have made her feel bad. It was a problem for Sam. He answered Betty's letter.

He wished he'd hear from Shirley since no one had heard from her recently. He, Gene, and Lucille planned on attending the Chemung County Fair.

Sam's own words...
Sunday, August 26, 1944 – "At factory eight hours. Quite cool and feels like fall. Still no word from Shirley. We went to the fair and had a grand time."

The day did not include a visit up to the farm. The next Sunday was no different, save Sam's disappointment in having no ride to travel there. Gene and Lucille took him to a movie in the evening.

Grace and Roy went to the farm Monday. They brought back news that Ed and Betty's neighbors, the Doan's little girl, Mary Ann, had mild polio. It was a scare for all of their children and to Ed and Betty for their kids, too. Gail had turned four years old on September 2.

Sam's own words...
Sunday, September 3, 1944 – "Grace and Roy took me to Betty and Ed's. Hate to think it had to come to this, but Edith has consented to go to Breesport County Home. I can't see any other solution. Shirley is in Washington, DC, Steele in France, and John in S.C. I can't get their opinions, but I can see David."
Tuesday, September 5, 1944 – "Went to Elmira to see Mr. Hillman regarding Edith's entry into the county home. He was out, but I saw Mrs. Bampeed, and she will take the matter up with him and let me know."

Sam wrote to Betty to tell her about it. He was worried about her children because they'd learned of numerous cases of polio around Bennettsburg.

David and Hilda took Sam up to Betty's on Sunday. Edith wore a stony expression and slumped in her chair. Her disappointment over Sam's inability to secure a position in the Breesport location showed impatience all over her person. She may have quietly grasped onto the idea that if she were in Breesport she would be closer to Sam and see more of him.

Sam raised his hands up and let them fall to his sides when he told them all that he hadn't heard back from Mr. Hillman yet. They all felt sympathy for Edith as she rocked slowly back and forth. There was no question that her old-age pension would furnish funds for her placement and care.

Sam's own words...
Monday, September 11, 1944 – "Saw Mrs. Bampeed. She said they couldn't take paid inmates at the county home, and she is going to find someone who will take care of Edith in a private home. Perhaps that will be even better. At factory eight hours."

Mrs. Bampeed sent a letter dated September 14 that she had found no person but "would assist as needed" if Sam found a place. He was at a loss. A quiet place without children and a caretaker for Edith's needs was elusive.

"God knows I hope to find someone," he wrote.

He, Gene, and Lucille went to a movie Saturday night. On their way to Ithaca on Sunday, Grace and Roy dropped Sam off at Betty's. He found Edith in the same poor health and unhappiness. It may have been hard to tell her that there was no new placement for her yet.

Sam's own words...
Wednesday, September 20, 1944 – "Received a letter from Shirley requesting me to mail her war bonds as she needs money badly. As those are all at the farm, I can't get them before Sunday. Sent her $10. At factory eight hours."
Friday, September 22, 1944 – "Dewey and Amy stopped a few minutes on their way back to Monticello. They had been to Galeton and saw most everyone. Received a letter from Steele, still in Normandy; must write him."

Saturday was reason enough for the trio of Sam, Gene, and Lucille to see a movie. Cretia was visiting at Grace's and Sam saw them both. Mary, John's wife, took Sam up to Betty's while on her way to get peaches at a location up along Seneca Lake just north of Watkins Glen.

Sam's own words...
Sunday, September 24, 1944 – "...Mrs. Steve Kellogg says she will take Edith and care for her in mid-October or a little later if we agree on the price."
Monday, September 25, 1944 – "Back at factory again. Mailed Shirley four $25 war bonds."

Other than work for the next few days, Sam wrote to Steele. He kept up on the war news and was aware of Normandy, France, and the landing of forces on land by sea or air. Steele had made it safely across the beach with his unit, but not all of them did.

Sam had enough on his mind, and more was on the way.

Sam's own words...
Saturday, September 30, 1944 "My foreman, Mr. Pautz came and told me a fellow wanted to see me. It was Ed come after me. Edith took very ill, and I went from the factory about 10:30 a.m. Ed thought I better go to her. We stopped in Montour and saw Dr. Schmidt, who said he could not get there until late p.m. She seems in a serious condition. May God bless her...Dr. C.W. Schmidt came about 6 p.m., left vitamin pills and said to get regular insulin to give three times a day. Her blood pressure is 210. Ed and Betty

have gone to Watkins after insulin. We gave her 20 units of U40 insulin."

Edith was better the next day, Sunday, and Sam was as thankful as anyone of the others. Roy, Grace, and Cretia came for two hours. Edith wanted pie, so Grace made her some, but she ate little of it.

On Monday, October 2, in the evening, Betty went to see Dr. Schmidt. He told her that Edith still had as much sugar as she did Saturday. The insulin order was increased from 20 units to 35. Sam thought Edith had become more rational. Dr. Schmidt said people sometimes recover even when doctors believe they can't. That hope alone was worth the $4 Sam paid.

"May God's will be done," Sam sighed.

He was busy looking after his frail wife. He gently wiped her hands and face, the small comfort he could think to bring her. Edith put in a painful night. Her left arm and leg became paralyzed.

Sam's own words...
Thursday, October 5, 1944 – "The ambulance came, and we took Edith to the hospital this morning. She was glad to go. Nearly all last night she suffered terrible pain, particularly in her right leg and neck. I hope they can and will give her something to allay the pain if it starts again...9:30 p.m. Am in need of rest and will go to bed. God's will be done."

Friday morning Betty took her little girls, Gail and Jeanie, with her and Sam in the truck to Elmira. They went to see Mary. John had arrived from Camp Croft, SC, and he spent $1.50 to phone Shirley and Willa in Washington, DC. Shirley was to come into Elmira that evening and Willa to Bennettsburg Saturday morning. Lucille received a message about Edith. Sam went with Betty to Grace's where she gave them lunch. She agreed with them that the $26.98 for the ambulance had been necessary.

On the way home, Sam and Betty stopped at the Montour hospital to see Edith. She knew them, and the nurse said she had improved.

V-mail (Victory Mail) from Steele came from overseas. He wrote his communication on October 2 when he was aware only about the mention of hope for his mother's placement at Breesport County Home. Betty mailed David a gas coupon, and they expected to see him the next day.

Edith lingered in and out of coherence, not wholly aware of visitors or who they were. In a few days, they all had to return to work. Only Sam, Edwin, and the children remained at Bennettsburg on Betty's 29th birth- day, October 10. Edith's condition remained unchanged, but her mind cleared. Sam sent a letter to Steele about the hospitalization of his mother.

Sam and Edwin worked to fork beans in the field and got a load of gravel for the foundation of Edwin's new barn. The next day they mixed the gravel with cement and poured a portion of it.

At 3 p.m. on Thursday, Ed and Joe Miller left to go after a load of horses. Sam had to see his boss and make arrangements to take a guard job at the La France plant in Elmira Heights on Monday morning. Betty had driven him there, and they ate dinner with Gene and Lucille. They did not neglect a visit to Grace and needed her warmest brand of comfort.

They stopped in Montour to see Dr. Schmidt at his office. He said Edith's condition was such that it was only a matter of time before she leaves this earth. He did not know how long or short a time she had left.

Sam placed her in God's care. It would be their great loss, but she was so ill, so blind, so helpless, that no one wished her to continue to suffer.

A letter from Steele came for Edith, and Sam read it to her on Friday, October 10. He was glad it brought her comfort and she was more rational that evening. He and Ed had finished pouring the foundation for his barn this day, and also buzzed up some wood.

Betty took Sam to visit Edith on Sunday afternoon. She was comfortable, quiet, and weak. He hated to leave her, but he needed to stay at Gene and Lucille's so he could go to work in the morning after two weeks absence.

Sam put in 12 hours as a watchman. He wanted to hear from someone about Edith. The job was demanding as he worked 11 hours Tuesday and 14 more on Wednesday.

Sam's own words...
Thursday, October 19, 1944 – "Betty woke me about 1 p.m. and informed me that Mom died at 10:45 a.m. I went home with her. I can't help but feel

thankful that her dear soul is set free from the poor tenement in which it strived to live for so long. God knows we shall miss her, but he will give us strength and courage to carry on. Some time, His time, we shall meet again. We called Willa, and she will tell Shirley."

The girls would be there Saturday morning. Sam paid $1.50 for a telegram to Arthur Crow in Denver, Colorado. On Friday, Betty and Sam went to Horseheads and made arrangements for Edith's burial at Maple Grove Cemetery. Sam purchased three grave plots for $75, knowing that he would need one beside Edith some day in the future. It cost $17 to have her grave dug. John was on his way from camp. They laid Edith to rest Saturday with the extended family present, except Steele.

Sam returned to work Wednesday. After the girls had left Thursday for Washington and John for Camp Croft, SC, Sam felt his aloneness. He worked 11-hour nights the rest of the week.

Arthur Crow's letter was in Sam's shaky hand as he sat in his chair with a bowed head. His brother-in-law had typed the full heartfelt page the same day he had received Sam's telegram about Edith's passing. It was a letter Sam read now and would again later. Arthur felt the loss of his sister heavily on his nearly 73 years. He was the last one above ground of six boys and three girls. He listed them all by name as he wrote. It was the last part that Arthur wrote that affected Sam so much.

~**~

October 20, 1944

Dear Sam,

I have just received your telegram advising of Edith's death yesterday. Anticipating it because of Willa's letter, but as always, the final news brings with it a shock....

In this great social and business atmosphere of America, I have not solved the problem of why we are here. I have, however, arrived at a point in my thinking, where to me, passing is as natural a phenomenon as coming in. It must all be part of that universal order that extends far beyond our powers of comprehension. Omar Kyaam wrote centuries ago:

> The moving finger writes, and having writ
> Moves on. Nor all your piety or wit
> Suffice to alter half a line,
> Nor all your tears wash out a word of it.

We live for a little while, and most of us do our best even though we stumble and fall and rarely rise to great heights of achievement. But I think that most of us are entitled to feel at the end that "It is well with my Soul."

You and all the children have my love and sympathy at this time. I will always be sending to all of you, my good thoughts.

Your devoted brother, A.H. Crow

~**~

Sam wiped his moist eyes and blew his nose.

Sam's own words...

Monday, October 30, 1944 – "Slept in a.m., go on duty again Wednesday night at 7 p.m., November 1. Gene, Lucille, and I saw the movie Waterloo Bridge in the evening."

The film *Waterloo Bridge*, made by Metro-Goldwyn-Mayer, recounts the story of a dancer and an army captain who meet by chance on Waterloo Bridge. After Britain's declaration of World War II, Roy Cronin (Robert Taylor), an army colonel, is being driven to London's Waterloo Station en route to France and briefly alights on Waterloo Bridge. He reminisces about events that occurred during the First World War when he met Myra Lester (Vivien Leigh) whom he had planned to marry. While Roy gazes at a good luck charm, a billycan that she had given him, the story unfolded.

Another V-Mail arrived from Steele. He wrote it November 2 in answer to one he'd received with bad news about his mother's poor health. He felt terrible that he could not get home to see her. The form letter had the top left circle with the inspector's signature inside. It was approved as it passed censorship. This kind of mail came across the ocean on microfilm, miniaturized. It was printed normal size before delivery in the U.S. to the addressee. It saved tons of letters being sent by ocean liner at a significant cost of space and weight. V-Mail was tiny in comparison and transported with thousands of other communications.

Sam's new foreman, Mr. Van Devee, came to see him. He wanted Sam to come in early, in fact, the same evening, Tuesday at 7 p.m. in Plant 2. It became more convenient to go to Grace's for dinner and then to work later. Sam continued working the night shift. On November 3, he sent insurance papers to Dr. Schmidt at Montour Falls.

Sam stayed at Grace's for a week. He was there Tuesday, November 7, when Franklin D. Roosevelt was elected to his fourth term as president.

On Wednesday Sam went back to Gene and Lucille's. He answered a knock on the door. When he opened it, he nodded his head as a smile lit up his face. Betty was just as happy to see him. She and Mrs. Arnie Morgan had been to Elmira Christmas shopping and were on the way home.

Sam's own words...
Friday, November 10, 1944 – "When one works nights, he doesn't know much of anything else."
Monday, November 16, 1944 – "Received a letter from Steele saying he had one from Ruthie about his mother's death and how he feels his loss so keenly. God help him. Am going to Grace's in the morning."

Steele's feelings laid bare as he wrote his words of anguish that pulled on Sam's heartstrings. His request for everyone back home to write was a plea to fill his loneliness in knowing he would never see his dear mother again. Steele promised to write more, and Sam nodded as he read it, hoping he could live up to that, too.

Shirley wrote that she was staying in Washington, DC, to finish an art course. It brought Sam a smile of gladness for her enthusiasm and his pleasure that she was able to pursue her heart's desire. She'd had art talent since she was a little girl.

When Sam stayed at Grace and Roy's, he appreciated a good bed. He could close his eyes, slip into a deep sleep, and wake up without a backache. Roy had no such luck and was laid up with lumbago. His painful rheumatism of the lumbar region between the lower ribs and pelvis had his tendons and muscles screaming at him not to move and stir the situation. He was out of work for a week in the midst of a big storm. Sam remained with the Whitings. He stacked wood in the shed out of the weather and commiserated with Grace about her pain of having four teeth pulled. Sam helped them both by taking over important jobs and by being there.

Sam's own words...
Wednesday, November 22, 1944 – "...The storm has ceased, and it has turned much colder. Grace and Roy are good to me but at times I feel very much alone."

A holiday ensures that a loved one is missed, perhaps more poignantly. Thanksgiving was low key as Sam and Roy both had to work. Grace accommodated the work requirements and prepared the traditional dinner for supper. She recognized Sam's faraway look and his self-hug with slow rocking, as preoccupation with his thoughts. Grace was in front of him, but he didn't see her at the moment.

On Monday, November 27, Sam stopped at Gene and Lucille's to see if he had mail waiting for him. There was none, but Lucille's mother, Mrs. Frost, told him they had news from John that he would be home soon on his last furlough. A chill seized Sam. Did that mean John was to be shipped overseas, too? Sam stayed with Grace and Roy from then on.

Betty wrote to her father. She let him know she missed him and would like to see him more but was glad he was with Grace and Roy. December 10 dipped the temperature to six below zero. Sam and Grace went to a movie, but could not entice Roy to come along.

The next weekend, Saturday, November 9, John walked in. His army uniform was a reminder that Uncle Sam had plans for his time; and his visit was temporary. They'd all embrace him while they could. Sam's dread was confirmed. When John returned to Camp Croft, SC, on December 20, he was scheduled to ship overseas. John's whereabouts would be unknown to the family for Christmas.

Sam woke to a foot of snow that fell Tuesday, December 12. The shovel was put to good use and he was glad he had cleared the walk and driveway when Ed showed up with two cords of wood. They had a good visit and a few laughs. Sam doubted that Edwin could drive further than

Bennettsburg on his way home. But he could walk the mile uphill around two sharp bends in the road to make it back to Betty and the children. It snowed and blew all day. Sam wrote to Steele and made a package with new house slippers to send to Shirley for Christmas. He worked his 11-hour night shift. Sam received an envelope from Betty containing school pictures of Teddy and Bucky, a pleasing interval in a grandfather's day.

Grace, her granddaughter Margie McCann, and Sam each spent 70¢ to see the movie Show Business with Eddie Cantor and others. It was about a song-and-dance man and his comedic partner undergoing romantic ups and downs when they team up with a female duo and transition from burlesque to vaudeville.

He'd seen John again before his furlough ended. David made a holiday effort and took Sam to his home for a visit and dinner. A Christmas card arrived from Steele. Even that greeting had been censored, stamped, and signed.

Sam's own words...
Thursday, December 21, 1944 – "Grace received a letter from Betty, who is in Montour hospital with a new baby girl born December 16: Carol Loretta, nine pounds, both are fine. This makes them three boys and three girls."
Wednesday, December 27, 1944 – "What a winter, more snow and wind piles it in the road and on sidewalks. Sure a tough walk from the bus line to grass hop hill this morning. At Ward La France 11 hours."
Sunday, December 31, 1944 – "An all-night rain. I shall always remember 1944 as the year that brought me joys – but much sorrow. Good by old year."

30 – War
1945

Early in Sam's new year, he received V-Mail from Steele. It had been censored and stamped on January 7. Even so he did not have confirmation that John was overseas. Sam could not give acknowledgement or evidence of it in a return letter as none of them knew anything for sure, certainly not his whereabouts, yet.

~**~

27 Dec/44

Dear Dad,

I don't remember how long ago I wrote. I'm just getting out of the hospital.

Do you like your new job any better than the old one? Just as soon as you get John's new address, I'd like you to send it. I don't understand why he hasn't written at least once in awhile. I've lost his address and Shirley's, too. I am so glad Shirley has the art course opportunity to do. She has always wanted it. Am glad she can continue it long enough to do her some good. I miss you and think of you a lot. This is even so during the holidays. I'll try to write a little more often from now on.

Lots of Love, Steele

~**~

Sam's own words...
Wednesday, January 3, 1945 – "Was so glad to get a Christmas card

571

from Steele, who is in Paris, France. It is good to know he is still alive and well. At factory 11 hours. "

Sam shook his head. Why had Steele been hospitalized?

Betty wrote to tell her father that they were snowed in most of the time, and it was so deep that it prevented Ed from cutting wood. It created a hardship for them with the lack of income and for those who needed the wood.

Sam slept days and did watchman work at night. The snow continued, too. Several more inches fell on top of what they already figured was too much. It made it tough for Sam to get to work, but he always managed.

Worry about where they would get fuel ended January 8 when Ed brought Grace and Roy two cords of wood. Betty and the four youngest children were with him. The healthy bodies and rosy cheeks of the children were a wholesome sight to Sam. He proclaimed what a happy, healthy group they were.

A letter from Lenore restated her angst that there was still no word from her son, Donald, and family in the Philippines. They were feared dead, caught up in the war with the Japanese. Sam wrote to her and Steele. She needed encouragement as much as Steele needed to hear from his father.

On Sunday, January 14, Sam, Grace, and Roy took a ride to see Ruthie, Sandra, and the Coles. Ruth gave Sam three pipes and a scarf that Steele had sent to him from France. She remarked that Steele had had a sinus operation. Sam nodded, glad to know why Steele had been in the hospital.

Sam's own words...
Monday, January 15, 1945 – "Slept until noon. Grace and I walked to Horseheads movie theater in the evening and saw Gary Cooper in *Casanova Brown*."

Cass Brown is about to marry for the second time; his first marriage, to Isabel, was annulled. But when he finds out that Isabel just had their baby, Cass kidnaps the infant to keep her from being adopted. Isabel's parents hunt for the child and discover that Cass and Isabel are still hopelessly in love. It was snowing hard when they emerged from the theater. Sam and Grace were glad to get a ride with neighborhood friends who had attended the show. Surely they'd had enough winter, but seven more inches of fluffy white stuff fell easily out of the sky during the night. Shoveling was an everyday affair for walks and paths. They had to get to the back shed for firewood.

Shirley's 23rd birthday, January 20, shared the inauguration date of Franklin D. Roosevelt to his fourth term as president. He was thinner and grayer but reported to be in good health.

Steele's newest letter came in which he wrote that the mail was slow. Sam believed him when he saw the January 18 date, and it was now the 29th. He mentioned a letter from John who said he might go across the ocean soon. It was old news for Sam, but they both wondered where John was and how soon they'd hear from him. Gene and Lucille had no word either. Meanwhile, Grace's hearing aid had been fitted. Sam was hopeful that it might open up a new world for her.

Cold prevailed in the below zero range with snow for icing. A letter from Dewey to Grace proclaimed the same conditions in his locale and kept him from travel. All he did was work. Sam nodded his head as it rang true for himself as well.

A letter arrived from John. Sam closed his eyes and held it momentarily over his heart. "Thank God," he muttered, glad to know his son was alive.

~**~

Pvt. John R. Crippen 6906739
Hg & Hg Co. 3rd Bn. 325 Glider INF.
HPD. 469. New York, NY

February 10, 1945
Germany

Hi Dad,

It's been quite some time since I've had a chance to write. I wrote to Mary and Gene yesterday, but then I ran out of paper. How do you like this? It is some that I found.

How is everybody? How is Aunt Grace and Uncle Roy? Tell Aunt Grace she will have to make me some doughnuts when I get back home. How are Betty and the new baby? I sure would like to see her family now.

    I can't come right out and tell you just where I am. All I can say is someplace in Germany. This would be a nice country in peace time. I don't see what makes the German people as they are. The country is great, and I don't see any sense in trying to hog other countries.

    Dad: I might send money to you from time to time. If I do, put it in the bank for me.

Write soon, Love, John

~**~

Sam supposed it was no surprise that it was Germany. Between Steele and John, Steele was the safest in France since Paris had been liberated from Germany many months ago in late August 1944. He didn't know anything about the 82nd Airborne when they were at La Fiere where they fought off four days of attacks from German troops trying to retake the strategic bridge. Maybe it was better not to know since John was part of that unit of thousands of soldiers now. Maybe he would find a hint of the location in Germany if he studied every detail in the newspaper but probably not, he reasoned.

    After 12 straight nights of work, it was a gift to Sam to have two nights off. How he did enjoy it. Sam could catch up on rest and a few important things. He sent Teddy a belated 12th birthday card.

    A knock on the door announced a visitor. The stooped figure of Bob Crippen appeared. The visit and catching up was an enjoyable one for Sam, Grace, and Roy, not to mention for Bob, who looked noticeably older. Maybe they wondered if they, in turn, seemed more aged to him.

    In the evening after Bob departed, Sam and the Whitings went to a production of Fiber Magee and Molly with Edgar Bergen and Charlie McCarthy. They were home before Saturday night snow dropped six inches. Mid-February brought Sam a Valentine from Shirley and a coveted letter from Private John Crippen.

~**~

Germany
February 14, 1945

Hi Dad,

    How is the world treating you? Are you still on the

same job or have you got a better one? I wish I were back there so we could stop in and have a beer together. Wouldn't it be fun for you and Gene and myself to go to a show and get a few beers afterward? I know I sure used to enjoy the times we did. Remember the night you and Gene stayed up a full night? I guess times like that are gone for a while. Maybe it won't be long before I get back. Remember the last time I was out with you and lost the keys to Gene's car? I am kind of ashamed of how drunk I was. I thought that was the last trip home for quite a while. I was lucky though and got home once more before I came over here.

It is pretty rough here. I guess some of us have to have it that way. It might as well be me as anyone else. I seem to make it OK, so far.

By the way, what is the news back there? How do people figure this war? Do they think it is about over? It should be, but you can't ever tell. I don't see how they can hold out much longer.

I saw a movie last night that was pretty good. The name of it was "Nothing But Trouble" with Laurel and Hardy. I thought of you because I know you enjoy a picture like that. What shows are playing back there? How is that Horseheads theater?

Tell Annabelle to write. I will drop her a line if I ever get time. Tell everybody I know to write. Letters really help over here.

I don't know whether you can read this. It is getting awful dark, and I can hardly see what I'm writing

Love, John

~**~

Sam could not know at this time that John was right in the thick of the battles. What he knew was that a short letter from John, written February 11, expressed that food quality was poor and not enough of it.

Stores were closed in Horseheads on Monday, February 19, because there was a fuel shortage. It required consolidation of trips. If Ed and Betty had not been snow bound, lack of fuel would have kept them home. When they finally came on Tuesday, Sam thought it was grand to see them. They would be back Saturday with wood for Grace and Roy.

Sam gave considerable worry to the fact that John was in Germany, the enemy's country. A letter from Steele confirmed the same line of thought.

~**~

Paris
24 February 1945

Dear Dad,

Am sorry I didn't write more often but just don't manage to get to it somehow. I do think of all of you a great deal though and keep thinking of the day when we can all be together again. The news these days is very encouraging, but it is difficult to know just what to expect or what lies ahead of us. We're all hoping that this new push in the west is it, combined with the drive of the Red armies.

I had a letter from John today dated the 11th. He is somewhere in Germany with the Glider Infantry. His address is: Hq & Hq Co. 3rd Bu. 325th Glider Infantry, A.P.O. # H69, % Postmaster N.Y.C. Leave it to him to get right in the midst of things. I'm looking forward to seeing him in Paris before long. That will really be great. It seems like years since I've seen anyone of you. I've got a bottle of champagne that I've written his name on and am saving for that little reunion. I also got a letter from Walter Dykens today, still in England and healthy if not too happy, but who is happy over here?

Perhaps I shouldn't speak for Walt for maybe it's my own feelings cropping out. A lot of things I would like to write will have to wait until I can say them. I guess I'm not in a very appropriate mood to write tonight, at least not the type of letter I prefer to write.

Sometimes I get so disgusted and fed up with the type of civilians I have to work with that I'm not even good company for myself. Don't get me wrong though for these moods aren't too often or too long. Hope you'll excuse the sour note in this letter, but it's been so long since I've written and hope you'll consider it better than no letter at all.

I do think of all of you plenty even if I don't write often. I'll try hard to do better, though.

I love you all. Steele

~**~

Sam shook his head. What could he say in the letter he was just writing to John when Steele's letter came? He wrote about his work, Grace and Roy, Gene and Lucille and their babies. Now the weather, all the snow they'd had, but most important was the mention of Ed and Betty and the children. That was it. His soldier boys needed to hear about all the ones they loved. He would write about the same to Steele. He hoped they really could get together in Paris but could not imagine it. But he didn't have to imagine that there was no picnic even in Paris after Steele had laid it out, "Who is happy over here?"

Bob Crippen visited. Grace, Roy, and Sam took in a movie. Sam's 11-hour nights as watchman remained steady.

Sam's own words...
Saturday, March 3, 1945 – "My 62nd birthday, received cards from John and Mary Long, Cretia, Christy, and Willa. At factory 11 hours."

Sam nodded and smiled over each card, but reminisced over John Long. He was a boyhood friend, the man who went west with him. They valued each other and would as long as they had breath.

Another letter arrived from his son, John. As often as Sam had sent a letter to him, John hadn't received one yet. He was in the thick of battles but not letters. Sam could do nothing but keep writing and hope the correspondence caught up to him soon, especially in a foxhole. He supposed a letter from Mary could make a cold hole in the ground cozier.

~**~

France
February 27, 1945

Dear Dad,
How is everything back there? I wish I would get a letter from somebody back home. I've been here quite some time. It seems longer because I haven't received any mail. I ought to start getting some pretty soon.

How are Aunt Grace and Uncle Roy? These letters that I write are for everybody. You know how I hate to write. Have you seen Betty and family lately? I sure miss going up there. I would like to have one of her meals. They don't feed too bad in this army mess kit, full of hot oatmeal, grapefruit, and coffee. It really was good. It is not like eating at home, though.

Have you and Gene been to any good movies lately or don't you see him much anymore? How is his house coming? What do people think about the war back there? Do they believe it is about over? My idea is that it is getting pretty well started. I hope I am wrong.

Dad, if you can find a pipe, not too big of one, how about sending it? Cigarettes are kind of hard to keep track of over here. I can get all the pipe tobacco I want, but no pipe. I sure would appreciate it.

How is your job making out? OK, I hope. Still on nights? I wish I were back working the night shift. I think I was nuts to join this army. One way I do and another, I don't. It might as well be me over here as anyone else.

I'll write again in a few days.

Love and Stuff, John

~**~

It seemed to Sam that two different opinions on the war left him wondering which way it was. Steele thought it was winding down, and John said it was starting up. Could John's words have meant the immediate action only? Sam knew for sure they were both missed and he placed them in God's hands. He could tell them that again along with all the details of families about which they asked. The movie seen with Grace and Roy, *Frenchmen's Creek*, was something to mention. He'd tell them it lasted one hour and fifty-three minutes about a 17th-century English noblewoman (Joan Fontaine) who hides with a French pirate (Arturo de Córdova) from her husband and his henchman (Basil Rathbone).

Sam surveyed his finished letters with a satisfied expression. He was pleased to mail them on a walk to the post office. It was more important than the haircut gotten over town. His reflection in the mirror while he was in the barber chair hardly registered to him as thoughts circulated again that John said it was tough over there. Sam wondered, how tough?

Sam's own words...
Thursday, March 8, 1945 – "A letter came to Grace from Mrs. Smith, the lady who takes care of Uncle George and other old age pensioners at Har-

rison Valley, PA, informed her that he had suffered a stroke and been in bed for eight weeks. Am so sorry for him and hope he may recover soon if it be God's will. At La France 11 hours."

Sam's fond memories of Uncle George replayed during watchman duty when he had an unlimited time to think and remember. John wrote aletter on a War and Navy Department V-Mail form on March 4, which arrived in record time, March 10. Victory mail was a good name for it.

~**~

V-Mail-
Pvt. John R. Crippen H.P.O. /
469 % Co. M 325 Glider Inf./
Postmaster New York, NY

Mr. S.P. Crippen
Broad Street
Horseheads, NY

March 4, 1945
France

Dear Dad,

I have had a letter from Steele. Now when I get one from you, I will be satisfied. Steele is only about five hours ride from where I am. If I am lucky, I might get a pass and get to see him. I think I know where to locate him. It sure would be great. I bet we could have a good time. What is new and how is everybody? I miss coming up to see you. How would you like to have me drop in for dinner? I would like it. I will someday. How are Betty and family? How about Gene and Lucille?...Why don't somebody let me know? Well, I haven't had many letters from home. That must be the reason.   Write soon and often.

Love, John

~**~

Sam wished his and others' letters would get through to John somewhere in that awful war. He shook his head in acknowledgment that John was discouraged for lack of mail. His heart fluttered for a second when he read that John expected to get a pass and see Steele. He was sure that Steele could not go to a battlefield in Germany, so it stood to reason that John would head over the border to France.

Sam's own words...
Sunday, March 11, 1945 – "Grace received a phone call from Mrs. Smith saying Uncle George passed away at 11 p.m. last night. The funeral will be 3 p.m. Wednesday. Haven't seen him very often these last few years but miss him now that I know he is gone. He must have been 85 or 86. God's will be done."

He went to Elmira on Monday to file his income tax. He returned to unexpected visitors. Ed, Betty, and most of the children had come to visit, except the school boys, Teddy and Bucky. He leaned forward and touched each little arm and looked into the eager young faces of his grandchildren. Little Carol with red cheeks was a soft bundle in her mother's arms.

The ladies aid society sent a member to get John and Steele's addresses so that the women's committee for Horseheads veterans could send cards and letters to them from time to time.

On Tuesday, March 13, Sam received a letter from John. He sighed his relief as he always did when one of the boys wrote, and it reaffirmed that they were still alive.

~**~

Germany
March 8, 1945

Dear Dad,

I'm beginning to get damn mad. I've had a few letters from most everybody but you. I probably have one or two on the way, but I'm getting impatient. Do you blame me?

How are you anyway? Why don't you stop over and see Mary sometime then you can let me know how things seem to be running at my home. Mary said in her last letter that she was kind of hurt that you hadn't. For some reason, she kind of likes my dad. Maybe because I do and think he is one swell guy. I don't know of a better fellow, do you?

I finally got letters from Steele. It doesn't take very long. He is only about five hours ride from me. Maybe I told you that. I am pretty sure of getting to see him. It sure will be swell. He and I write back and forth quite regular. That is one way of being sure to get mail every week. He sent me some pictures of himself that were very good.

Our gaslight is about out of gas, so I will have to quit

this. We have to see to get up the first thing in the morning.

There will be more at a later time.

Love, John

~**~

If John was angry, Sam was a little miffed himself, as to why his letters hadn't gotten through yet. The whole idea was to support his boys and make sure they knew how much he cared, the only thing he could do for them. His writing would continue while a higher power was consulted to give a little help.

Sam, Grace, and Roy went to Uncle George's funeral Wednesday. Sam paid $2 for his share of the gas for Roy's car. They ate with Sadie and saw many others in Pennsylvania. Sam came back to the factory, which required the same 11 hours watchman work. Another letter from Germany greeted Sam. His heart leapt with gratitude as he read the first line.

~**~

Germany
March 19, 1945

Dear Dad,

I got your letter today and was I glad. I don't know of any letter anyone has written that has done me more good. I think I got more news in your letter than a half dozen of anybody else's.

I apologize for the last two I wrote. I was feeling blue and not getting much mail kind of makes one that way. I know how Steele feels now. I can remember when I didn't write to him very often. I do better now, both to Steele and to all of you people over there. By the time you get this one, you will already have my new address.

I am glad you turned down that guard job. It is too long of hours. It would not be any better than the job you have.

This is the first news I have had about Betty and family. I am sure glad they are alright (sic). This snow that the papers talk about had me worried. I think I have seen enough snow to last me the rest of my life. We hiked in it all day, drank it for three days, and slept in it for about ten days. I really mean I've done these things. I have also laid in it for half to three-quarters of an hour pinned down by machine gun fire. So, I think I have had all of it I want.

I don't have much time left and want to write to Mary and Mickey. So this is it for now.

Lots of Love, John

~**~

It was a sobering letter for Sam, more so than any before. The part about being pinned down by machine gun fire did it. Sam's dry lips were in a severe straight line as he read it over again. It hit home why letters were so desperately wanted from home by soldiers to mitigate at least temporarily, the danger and loneliness of a fox hole.

Sam's own words...

Tuesday, March 27, 1945 – "Received a letter from John, also Willa. John evidently is in the thick of the fighting as he tells of lying in the snow pinned down by machine gun fire. May God bless him and keep him. Willa expects to pay us a visit about April 10. She has asked for a transfer from Washington back to Denver. If she gets it, will go back to stay as Lee and Roy Harris and children are there. She will be happier and healthier."

Sam wrote to John and Shirley but expected he'd see Willa soon. Shirley sent an Easter card. Sunday brought a welcome change for Sam to get his mind off Steele and John. Gene and Lucille came for a short visit. They had not been gone long when David and Hilda came with their children, Bonnie and Douglas. They all visited Grace and Roy awhile before Sam went to their home at 540 Gains Street, Elmira, with them. After a filling meal and visit, David drove him to Ward La France.

Grace, Roy, and Sam took in a movie on Monday. Sam mailed the Burdett undertaker a final payment of $25, paid in full, for attending to matters pertaining to Edith's death.

The house that Grace and Roy rented on Broad Street was up for sale, and people were interested. Sam supposed they'd have to move. He mailed letters to John, Shirley, and Steele. Every letter that came to him, he answered.

He smiled to see Ruthie on the bus, both of them going to work. Another letter arrived from John.

~**~

Germany
March 19, 1945

Dear Dad,

You asked me if I heard from Steele. Just after I received your letter, I got a phone call from him. If everything works out alright (sic), I will see him tomorrow. I sure hope it does. I don't think that we would hardly know what to say to each other for the first few minutes. It would be enough just to look at him. Boy, was I surprised when they told me at the orderly room that someone wanted me on the phone. I knew that it couldn't be anyone except Steele. It took him nearly all afternoon to get in contact with me. Then we could hardly talk we were so glad to hear one another's voice. I'll write and let you know if we get together Tuesday. I am sure we shall.

I'm glad to know that you are answering all my letters. I'll write more often because that will mean that I will get more letters from you, and I sure do enjoy them. They make me feel as though I were back there.

I don't know what we kids done or will do to deserve such a good Dad. You don't have to take my word for it. Ask any of the rest of us. Ask Aunt Grace. I bet she will say the same thing.

I wonder if Betty has received the letter I wrote to her. I got one from Shirley. She ought to have one from me by now. I would like to have Willa's address. I asked Shirley for it and probably will have it before long.

It seems to me that about all I do is write letters. Maybe someday I'll get some answers. I haven't been drunk since I left the states. Maybe I quit. At least when I'm writing, I can't get into trouble. I don't know yet. I don't like the stuff that they sell over here. I hope and think I have quit for good.

I guess I had better call this good enough for now. I have three more letters to write tonight.

Love, John

~**~

The next post Sam received was written by Steele and John on American Red Cross paper.

~**~

                                                        France
Dear Dad,   March 22, 1945

John and I have at last managed to get together over here, and this is the beginning of a letter from both of us. It's the greatest thrill I've had in a long time just to be with one of my own family. We've done plenty of talking and thinking of all of you back home. I only wish we were stationed a little closer together and might see each other more often. Now I'll let John take over for awhile.

As you can see, it has happened at last. I was just standing guard duty when a soldier walked up to me, and it was Steele.

We have some pretty good guys in my outfit. So, I was relieved from guard duty. Steele and I had so many things to talk about; we just didn't know where to start. I'm still so thrilled and excited, too. I guess I can't hardly believe it is true. I would be satisfied just to stand and look at him. He really looks well. I guess I had better let him take over.

Hello again. There' so darned many things to say and I just sit here at a loss for words. I want you to know that we both think you are the best Dad in the world, and I am ashamed that I don't write more often than I do. I can't wait for the day when the three of us will be going out for some good American beer. There will be plenty to talk about then, too. Until then, I'll try to do better and tell you more about my visit with my Big Brother.   Next:

Back again: What to write has got me beat. Tell everybody hello for us. We wish we had time to write to everybody. If we did, we would not know what to say. I'm glad we got the chance to write to you. This might give you some idea how glad we are to be together at this time. We hope we will have plenty more of them.

Love and Stuff, John - Me too, Steele

~**~

Sam's body shook halfway through the letter. He wiped his eyes and then his nose as he finished the page of flamboyant writing from two happy brothers. Sam was so glad for them that he could hug himself since they were nowhere close enough to embrace. He wore his broadest smile as he handed the letter over to Grace. He couldn't have imagined a better or happier message.

While Grace read, Sam supposed John would be assigned back to foxholes and snow drifts. He didn't know how long or why he had been on duty in France, just that it was short-lived.

Grace and Roy had gone to Ed and Betty's on Sunday, April 1, while Sam slept to be ready to go to work on his night shift. He was awake and happy to hear about Betty's family when they returned. Ed would be coming after him on Monday evening so he and the family could enjoy each other.

Ed didn't arrive until 9 o'clock the next night after his busy day. When he and Sam arrived, Jeanie and Gail got out of bed to sit on Grandpa's lap for a minute. Sam didn't mind. "Bless them," he wrote.

On Tuesday afternoon, April 3, Betty took her father to Montour Falls in the truck. He saw Dr. Schmidt, paid his $32 bill, and asked him to fill out the insurance form about Edith's care. Sam had written to the doctor about it without success. On Wednesday Edwin drove Sam to Watkins in time to catch the bus to Horseheads. He arrived there at 11:40 a.m. The rest of Sam's week consisted of sleeping days and working nights. The postman delivered a letter from John and also one from Steele on Wednesday, April 11.

~**~

3 April 1945
Paris, France

Dear Dad and all,

I received your letter today written March 21, also got one from Aunt Grace last week but seem to have misplaced it. I hope you will consider this an answer to both of them. I never seem to get around to writing like I should. About the only time I get to myself is when I get clear away from the installation. There seems always to be something or someone to interrupt me whenever I do start a letter. I just threw one away that I started to you last week. Also, when I write too often, it tends to bring on the blues. Maybe you can understand just what I mean. I think my worst spell of said color was right after coming back from seeing John. It was really wonderful to be with him though it was such a short time. You have by now, no doubt, received our letter of combined efforts. I am afraid we were too taken up with the present that we didn't say much, but it must have given you some idea how we felt. For further tangible evidence of our meeting, I'm sending a few pictures that we took. Right now I'm waiting and hoping that John will have an opportunity to visit Paris soon. Then there will be another bunch of pictures headed your way. To say nothing of the enjoyment we'll have together.

John, too, has surprised me about writing quite frequently. I think he had written only two letters since I've been in the army, that is before he got over here. Now I get one or two a week from him. He is exactly the same John, and I did most of the listening while we were together. (You get what I mean I think.) There really isn't a sweller (sic) brother in the world, though, and I do plenty of worrying about him.

The way things are shaping up over here, this part of the war could be over by the time this letter reaches you, that is unless they've improved the mail service considerably. I guess it can't end soon enough to please any of us. I think that this time the job will last more than 20 years.

We had typical April showers with the sun shining in. It reminds me very much of home. (I mean the weather.)

I think I've rather outdone myself. (and only one interruption, so far). My conversation is about to lag for lack of a new subject. If I could see you, though, I could think of plenty.

Lots of Love, Keep writing.   Steele

~**~

Sam sat up straighter and shifted his feet. The letter was full of hope and got his attention. Could it be that the war in Germany would soon be over? He wondered what John's opinion was on it. He had fought at full force when he was in Germany, but he was well aware that both boys would know more than anyone in Horseheads. John went one place and then another, never able to say where in Germany, unlike Steele in Paris.

Sam wrote to Steele. He never kept a letter long without answering it. He had terrible news to tell the boys, but it did not affect action in the war. It was such big news that they would hear it even without his letter, probably before it arrived.

Sam's own words...

Thursday, April 12, 1945 – "The nation and the world, the Allied world at least, was shocked by the sudden death of President Franklin Roosevelt. One of the greatest evidence I can find that he was a great man is the fact that those who didn't always believe in his principles or policies, but when they knew he was gone, felt like crying. He gave his life for his country just as surely as those who die on the battlefield. As Stanton said of Lincoln, "Now he belongs to the ages." I for one feel as though I had lost a great friend."

The mourning Capitol Hill community, received the body of FDR for his last farewell to the White House where he had lived longer than any other president. On Sunday, 400,000 citizens paid him silent homage. Simple rites took place at the White House, and burial was at Hyde Park, NY.

Sam went to the Ward La France office and got the insurance check covering Edith's bill at Shepherd's Hospital in Montour Falls. He, Grace, and Roy went to a movie.

The great front-line correspondent, Ernie Pyles, made headlines again, but this time, it was the account of his death. A Jap machine gunner felled him on Okinawa. It could make Sam shudder if he thought too much about it. Steele or John could meet with the same fate. He couldn't allow himself to dwell on the worst scenario.

On Thursday, April 19, John's letter, written nearly three weeks earlier, arrived.

~**~

April 1, 1945
France

Dear Dad,

By this time or by the time you get this, you will know that Steele and I have seen each other. I still can't believe it is true. I think I will wake up and find it is all a dream. I only hope I can get another pass and go to see him. Maybe some-day this damn war will be over, and the world can go back to normal.

Aunt Grace, I received your letter, at the right time, too. A guy gets awfully lonesome over here, and a letter from home really helps. I don't see how you can get so much on a V-Mail. Keep them coming. I get more news from you than anybody else.

I'm very sorry to hear that Uncle George passed away. I suppose it is for the best. He was pretty well lamed up and old. I'm sure he is better off.

How do you get the idea that I may be back before long? The newspapers must read very good but don't believe all you read. Things are beginning to shape up, though. I hope.

I am going to close this and write to Billie. I received a letter from her, so I have her address now.

Love and Stuff,   One of the Little Boys, John

~**~

The message was a matter of confusion, being so out of date, old news, of when the boys had met in Paris. John had been scheduled to go back to Germany. Wasn't he there now? France would be better because Sam would rather John was lonely instead of dodging bullets. "Which was it?" he pondered.

Old friends, the Dykens, came by on Sunday, April 22. They all talked about the war and their sons in France and Germany. The Dykens's son, Walter, was a captain somewhere in Germany. Sam was able to visit with them longer as they dropped him off at work on their way home.

Sam had a couple of days off. He walked uptown and also enjoyed quite a bit of time to read. An all-day rain was good reason to stay inside for the day with his studious self if he needed an excuse.

His sister, Mary Hess, and Lynn's wife, Iva Crippen, drove over from Addison, NY, and naturally took Grace with them to shop in Elmira.

Sam's own words…
Thursday, April 26, 1945 – "Grace was alone in the back seat and as they were crossing Grand Central Avenue at Broad Street, Horseheads. A car coming very fast rammed into the rear of Mary's car. Grace was hurt. She is quite lame and sore in her right shoulder and neck. We are thankful it was not worse."

Friday, April 27, 1945 – "Was positively surprised when I arrived home this morning and found Shirley waiting for me in Grace's kitchen. She looked thin to me, and I will miss her when she has to go back to Washington, DC. Wednesday. Willa came with her but was going to Binghamton on business preparatory to going back to Denver."

Sam had to go to work later, but Shirley had many others to visit. By Saturday, Willa was up at Betty's, and Sam hoped to get up there to see her and everyone else. Roy took Shirley to the farm while once again, Sam was at work.

Shirley had a call on Monday and made haste back to DC because her sailor, Tommy came ashore.

Ed came for Sam about 10:30 a.m. on Tuesday, May 1, and Sam, at last, could join the get-together at the farm. How he enjoyed them all along with Willa.

Sam's own words...
Tuesday, May 1, 1945 – "Rumor persists that Adolf Hitler is dead."
Wednesday, May 2, 1945 – "Ed went on Wednesday a.m. after a part for his tractor and brought me home...Found a letter from John on my arrival. God bless him. Wrote him one."

~**~

April 9, 1945

Dear Dad,

I received a letter from you yesterday. I sure was glad to get it. Your letters are beginning to come through pretty regular. I'm sure proud and glad that I have a Dad who writes real often.

I am back in Germany again, and so far we have had it pretty decent. These are the nicest quarters that we have been stationed in since I've been over here. We are in a nice house. We have hot and cold water, bath and showers, and all kinds of furniture. This place is really the mints. I only wish I could spend the rest of the war right here.

What is the news back there? I imagine that they have the battle won. Take it from me, it is a long way off. Why don't you have Betty write? I've written two letters to her and haven't received an answer. I probably will get a letter from her one of these days.

I haven't said much in this letter, but you know that I'm well and thinking of you all. If you don't hear from me

for a few weeks, don't worry. I may be too busy to write.
Dad, keep writing.

Love and Stuff, John

~**~

Don't worry? Tough not to, Sam thought. He would not learn until months later that John was on a path with his regiment in a sweep across Germany. But the letter in his hand was more than three weeks old, arriving weeks after the action, as usual, action that John could not mention by post regardless.

America and the other Allies, French, Canadian, British, and Russian were on a sweep from all directions, fighting the Germans bent on stopping them. The 82nd Airborne's 505th and 325th regiments had dispersed from Soissons, France, in three directions. That was why John had been in France, the jumping-in point again. John's unit was on a cautious 600-mile march straight toward the Elbe River, which they reached. It would account for the few weeks mentioned by John when he said that he may be too busy to write. Busy wasn't the half of it as learned much later from John.

On April 5, they came upon a gated camp north of Berlin. The troops were innocent of what unimaginable horrors they would find behind the barriers of Wöbbelin Prison Camp. It was only one of dozens upon dozens big and small to be discovered in all directions out from Berlin. The 325th was not yet aware that one day before, on April 4, another part of the 82nd guys had opened and liberated Camp Ohrdruf in Germany as the American's first discovery of a concentration prison.

At Wöbbelin the guards knew the Americans were a short distance off but approaching, and they shot prisoners until they ran out of bullets. Then the murderers fled. The inmates still alive were little more than walking skeletons. It was not a concentration camp with an incinerator. The method here was starvation. Dumped bodies of victims piled up in the still-open pits in the yard. One pit contained 300 corpses.

Shock and horror wore off as desperation set in on how to feed the barely alive, liberated prisoners. It was an emergency in need of solving with so many on the verge of death. The town of Ludwigslust four miles away was enlisted and compelled to see what they denied knowing, the atrocity almost on their doorstep. Adequate personnel of the 82nd Airborne troop stayed to enforce and handle the situation.

The rest of the unit moved on, intent on their mission of more fighting. After the 82nd had crossed the Elbe River, at Bleckede, paratroopers and glider men rapidly stormed over heavily mined roads and fields. They swept all opposition before them and captured hundreds of prisoners until it became thousands due to capitulation, who were disarmed and herded to the rear. Intelligence officers estimated that 150,000 prisoners passed through the division area. John was there in the thick of it, soldiering on.

The German units were badly battered and without hope, caught between overwhelming Russian forces enroute from the east and in the face of American, Britsh, French, and Canadian assault on the north, south, and west. German Lieutenant General Von Tippelskirch surrendered his 21st Army to the 82nd Airborne at Ludwigslust, Germany. Stalin's army arrived at the area two days later. The 82nd Airborne and the Allies had delivered a final coup to the crumbling Third Reich with the capture on April 30 of an entire German army.

Adolf Hitler had committed suicide on April 30, 1945, according to the next day rumor of May 1.

American 82nd Airborne General Gavin called the surrender of an entire army to a single division "without precedent" in American military history. On May 5, a larger concentration camp, Mauthausen, was liberated by the U.S. 11th Armored Division. More horrors were revealed and the world was notified. President Roosevelt hadn't lived to see it.

Sam's own words...
Monday, May 7, 1945 – "A note from Shirley at last. She and Tommy had three days together in Washington and then he went to his folks in Mississippi. They may marry when he returns, and she wants me to announce the engagement. At Ward La France 11 hours."
Tuesday, May 8, 1945 – "Slept until noon. Was routed out of bed when a prospective buyer wanted to look at the rooms...V.E. Day; Germany quits. Thank God."

On May 7, the German capitulation had been signed at Reims, France.

Snow, heavy and wet, fell all day May 10. Damage to trees would affect the year's crop of fruit. Grace and Roy stopped at the farm on their way back from Ithaca. They told Sam that Ed had the cinderblock addition for his barn started. Sam started a garden with Swiss chard and a row of flowers.

Sam's own words...
Wednesday, May 23, 1945 – "...Now that the fighting is over in Germany, I wonder if both or at least one of my boys can come home."
Thursday, May 24, 1945 – "At factory 11 hours. Since I work nights and sleep days, I don't know much even though I read the paper."
Saturday, May 26, 1945 – "It has been some amount of time since I heard from John or Steele."

Sam, Grace, and Roy put flowers on Edith's grave. The May 28 mail brought Sam a packet from Willa. She had taken his pictures of John and Steele back to Washington with her and enlarged them on the Photostat machine. He was gladdened as he pulled his smiling soldier boys out of the cardboard reinforcement to prevent bending.

Willa expected to leave Washington, DC, on June 1, for Denver. Bless her, Sam thought.

On Memorial Day Sam set out tomato plants. There was a frost on the 31st and the next morning plants laid limp on the soil with no life left in them. Dewey came on June 4. Sam was glad to see him looking so good and was doubly satisfied to have a letter from John the same day.

~**~

Germany - May 22, 1945

Hi Dad,

How is everything going? Things over here are better than ever. The only trouble is, I'm sweating out the South Pacific. I'm pretty sure of going there with no furlough home first. I guess I can take it. I'll have to.

All we are doing over here is guard duty, guarding ammo dump and things like that. It's a tough racket but beats combat. I'm sending one of the 82nd Airborne patches, I mean windshield stickers. I don't think Uncle Roy will want to clutter up his windshield, but I'm sending it anyway. The two letters, AA, stand for All-American.

I received Aunt Grace's letter last night and was very glad to get it. Thanks. I still have to write to Gene and Steele. I have fallen way behind in my letter writing. I think I'll call this good and write to one of the others.

Love and Stuff, John

~**~

Sam shook his head. It did not seem right that John should be going to the South Pacific before a visit home.

Sam's sisters, Sadie and Mary, came to Elmira to shop. While they were there, word came that Mary's husband, Frank Hess, had suffered a heart attack in the doctor's office. Mary hurried home to Addison. Frank was in pain but was kept sedated.

Sam's own words...
Friday, June 8, 1945 – "Found letter from John who was still in Germany when he wrote it. It seems he saw one of the German prison camps, and he says it is beyond belief that human beings could do such atrocious things..."
Monday, June 11, 1945 – "Received a letter from Steele. He doesn't say where he is, but I suppose he is still in Paris. He had appendix removed and is hospitalized. Not a word whether he will be kept in Europe, sent to the South Pacific, or can come home. Cultivated garden and replaced tomato plants, which had been killed by frost and too much rain."

~**~

June 1, 1945

Dear Dad and Folks,

I've just acquired myself a new scar. My appendix got acting up on me, and they took the nasty thing out. I'm not out of bed yet but will be in a few days. Am feeling fine and would like to get up but they keep me tied down. They took the stitches out today, and it is a great relief to get rid of the adhesive plaster they had me taped up with. The hospital here is a beautiful place. As a matter of fact, too beautiful to be a hospital.

I haven't had any mail since I have been here, which is over a week now. It gets a little lonesome, and I miss all of you just a little bit more. I guess that's because I have more time to think about you.

Do you have a garden this year? I can't imagine you

without one, and I'd sure like to see it.

Have you seen Ruthie and Sandy recently? She has an apartment at 668 Park Place. It's not far from the shopping district. I'd like to have you stop and see her once in awhile when you are in Elmira.

As soon as I get out of bed, I intend to catch up on a lot of people I should write to. Looks like I'll have lots of time for I am scheduled here for a full 30 days.

I'm sorry I don't write more often, but that's just me I guess. When I'm at the company, I have plenty of other things to do. I do think of you all a lot, though.

Lots of Love, Steele

~**~

V -Mail

S/Sgt. Steele D. Crippen
/q. & Hq. Co. 63rd L.M.B.D/467
A.P.O. 1887 - % Postmaster
New York, NY

S.P. Crippen
Broad Street, Horseheads, NY   June 12, 1945
Dear Steele,

I was so glad to get your letter yesterday. It found us all well as usual. Am thankful you are recovering from your operation so nicely. You didn't say whether you would be kept in Europe, sent to the South Pacific, or could come home. We hope it is the latter. Had a letter from John dated May 22, and he expected to go to the S. Pacific and no furlough home first. That's pretty hard to take. Do you hear from him?

Willa has been transferred to Denver where I think she will be happier and healthier. Shall miss her being so far away. Christy is still in Washington and will follow later. Shirley was here three days the later part of April. ... Yes, Steele, I shall try to see Ruthie and Sandra. Since I work nights (11 hours), it is hard for me to see anyone.

Haven't been to Betty's but once since Mom went away. I am getting along very well, and Aunt Grace takes good care of me, but miss all of you and pray for the day when the war is done and can see all of you again. Uncle Dewey was here a few days on his vacation...Frank suffered a heart attack and is seriously ill.

This isn't much of a letter I'm afraid.

Take care of yourself, Steele. God Bless you.

All my Love, Dad

~**~

Back in France, John wrote to Steele on Red Cross stationery.

~**~

France
June 8, 1945

Hi brother,

I bet you can't guess where I am, back in Soissons. We had some trip. It was about 600 miles. I was one of the assistant drummers. Did we have fun!

I am trying my damnedest to get a pass to Paris. I don't know how long I will be here. The rumor is that we move out soon. Where to, nobody knows. I just hope it isn't the S. Pacific or C.B.2. I imagine we will get one of them, though.

What is new on your end of things? Do you have any hopes of getting to the States?

I didn't get any guns or anything like that. All I was able to get was a 120 camera. I don't know much about them, so I don't know how good.

I am going to have to call this note good. Write soon.

Love and Stuff, John

~**~

Most likely this trip coming back to Soissons, France, was by train. Rail tracks were immediately repaired throughout war time. Resistance and fighting at an end in Germany allowed return to more normalized travel for a regiment of soldiers. John traveled light since he had neither guns nor burdensome souvenirs taken from German soldiers as many others did.

Sam's own words...
Thursday, June 12, 1945 – "Cultivated garden in a.m. Rain in p.m. Received Father's Day card from Betty. Okinawa fallen after 82 days of terrible slaughter. At Ward La France 11 hours."
Monday, June 25, 1945 – "Roy had vacation this week and is repairing his car."

Wednesday, June 27, 1945 – "Roy finally got car repaired at a garage. He and Grace expect to go to Galeton this evening. I shall be alone for a few days. Watchman 12 hours."

It was just Sam and his newspaper. No one to make eye contact with, to give a nod and a smile to, or talk to. He wasn't given to talking to himself. His only companion was the routine he adhered to at home and work. The letter from Shirley on Saturday was quite welcome. She had considered coming back for a visit but then Tommy was stationed in Washington for two months.

Grace and Roy were a welcome sight when they returned. Sam was disappointed that not many flags flew on the Fourth of July. He used the holiday time to write to Shirley.

One of Cretia's neighbors telephoned Grace to say that Cretia was sick and wanted to have Grace and Roy come after her. Sam supposed he couldn't fault their older first cousin for wanting to be with Grace. She lived alone and didn't feel good about it right now at nearly 69 years old. She got her wish when they went after her the next day.

Sam's own words...
Sunday, July 8, 1945 – "...Had one of the greatest surprises of my life when Steele, Ruthie, and Sandra came about 7 a.m. Steele is looking fine. Will be home 30 days then sent to Camp Lee, Virginia, for further training. I thank God for everything."

It was only natural for Sam to wonder about John and want to hear from him, too. Sam started guard duty on the day shift, and it seemed hard to get used to it. Cretia's arthritis had her lamed up and in pain. They all hoped the doctor's medicine would help.

Sam hadn't even gotten used to days when they wanted him back on nights. At least he was home the day Mary and Frank came. Frank had recovered well from his heart attack, another reason for which to be thankful. A letter arrived from John, written two weeks prior.

~**~

France
July 1, 1945

Hi Dad,

One of us is slipping. It has been quite some time since I have heard from you. I don't think I am writing as often as I used to. I still believe that you are a swell Dad, the best Dad a guy could ever have.

I don't suppose you have seen anyone down at my house. I wish I knew for sure how my wife and daughter are. Mary's letters say they are OK. But if they weren't, Mary wouldn't say anything. And I'm the guy who never worried about anything before. I guess a guy has a right to concern for his family. I still can't believe I have a family. I never intended to be married. Love is a funny thing.

How is everybody? You know who all I mean. I miss people.

I just returned from Paris. I went to see Steele, but his outfit had shipped out to the states. He ought to be home by the time you get this. I hope so. I wish I could have seen him before he went back. But I am really glad he is in the states By the time you get this, I hope I'm in Berlin. The quicker we get there, the sooner we get back home. I hate to think of spending another winter in Germany.

I'm going to go and eat. It's chow time, so until next time.   Love and Stuff, John

~**~

Berlin? What were they doing there? Did he mean that — the quicker he could get home? Probably just an off-hand remark, a way to finish a sentence. But Sam was free to hope.

Sam's own words...
Friday, July 13, 1945 – "Received a Western Union telegram that Shirley and Tommy are to be married this evening. God bless them and guide them."
Sunday, July 15, 1945 – "Slept until 3 p.m. Just got downstairs when Steele, Ruthie, Sandra, Mary, and Mickey came. They were on their way to Betty's and wanted me to go along, but I have to work tonight as much as I would like to have done so. Had not seen Mary and Mickey in a long time. Don't know if Mickey remembered me. She was so shy but is fine and healthy. It would do John's heart good to see her."

Shirley sent a letter, the first one as Mrs. Thomas Broadhead. Sam leaned back at ease with a deep sigh, glad for her. He'd try to find time to write to her and also John. He could say he had seen Mary and Mickey. It was hard to write when Sam had worked for a month straight, no time off from 12-hour nightly shifts. He hardly got enough rest to form good responses to their letters. He closed his eyes momentarily and mentally vowed to do better.

On Sunday, Steele picked his father up to go with him to visit his mother's grave. Sam felt blessed. The accompaniment was an effort to comfort his son. Sam cherished how kind Steele had always been to his mother. After the solemn venture to Maple Grove Cemetery in Horseheads, Sam was dropped off at work.

Friday, July 27, was not too bad of a day, the day Sam received 8¢ an hour raise. He supposed he must have done something right. He smiled at his good fortune. It was also welcome news when he learned that Cretia was feeling much better. Grace could have taken credit, and Cretia was certain to assign it to her.

Sunday again, July 29, and Sam went with Steele and Ruthie to David and Hilda's to have a meal. They all spoke of missing John, who was far away in Berlin, Germany. Sam was enjoying his long-awaited two nights off.

Sam's own word...
Wednesday, August 1, 1945 – "Received a 'newspaper' diary of the 325th Airborne Division serving in World War II. John wants me to keep it until his return home. At factory 12 hours." (The legendary newspaper, "All-Americans" Paraglide, remained in Sam's trunk always.)
Saturday, August 4, 1945 – "Steele and Ruthie came and took me to work. Ruthie has to have an operation, and Betty is caring for Sandra. Steele has to return to Camp Dix tomorrow and probably then to Camp Lee, Virginia. We shall miss each other so. May God help us, especially Ruthie, Steele, and sweet little Sandra."

"God help us" was Sam's sentiment when he learned that President Harry Truman announced the successful bombing of Hiroshima with the atomic bomb. Otherwise, the Japanese would continue to fight on. Their orders were never to give up and the continuing loss of lives was assured. Grace had a letter from Dewey who hoped to get transferred to Elmira Reformatory for guard duty in the fall. Steele was back briefly for Ruthie's operation. His beaming face told how he felt that he'd had the opportunity to take a route through Washington, DC, and had stopped to see Shirley and Tommy.

Sam's own words...
Wednesday, August 15, 1945 – "President Harry Truman answered to the nation that Japan had accepted the unconditional surrender terms of the U.S. and her allies. The terrible war is over...Oh! We have so much to thank God for. Steele came along about 2 p.m. and picked me up to go to Betty's. Sandra is there and will remain until Ruthie can take over again. First sweet corn from our garden."
Saturday, August 25, 1945 –"At factory 12 hours. We are supposed to be moved by September 17 as the new owner wants the place."

Grace and Roy would need to get serious about looking for a place to live. They seemed not the least bit worried. Why not go to a movie? And the three of them did. Steele's seven-day pass extension was expired. He went back to camp.

Sam's own words...
Sunday, September 2, 1945 – "...President Truman proclaimed today as V-J Day: After the signing, General Douglas Mac-Arthur reported to America that a great tragedy has ended, a great victory won, that we must go forward and preserve in peace what we won in war. That the world has had its last chance, that we must go the way of the spirit if we are to save the flesh..."

It was September 5 when Sam and others read about Japanese-American Iva Toguri D'Aquino, suspected of being the wartime propagandist, Tokyo Rose. Her arrest came in Yokohama, Japan. Iva was convicted of treason and sentenced to 10 years in jail though her release took place after only six years for good behavior. (In the 1970s, President Ford pardoned her, clearing her name.)

The factory hours were cut to eight hours a day, six days per week. It would mean a considerable reduction in pay.

Sam, Grace, and Roy went to the movie, Call of the Wild, by Jack London, starring Clark Gable. It held them spellbound watching the story of a young boy who heads off to the Yukon after hearing tales about the Gold Rush, and he forms an unwavering friendship with a heroic Alsatian dog called Buck.

Sam had time for family visits and went up to the farm with Grace and Roy. They found Betty, Ed, and the children doing as well as ever. Gail had turned five years old a few days earlier.

Another day, Sam rode with Mary and Grace to Seneca Lake country where they picked peaches at $3 per bushel. Now he had time to write Shirley a post card and a letter to John.

Steele was home again briefly and was animated, rushing his words to tell them all that he would muster out of the service in about two weeks.

It was September 18 and they'd not yet found a different place to move. The new owner reiterated that he needed them out so he could perform repairs and live there himself. There had been no frost yet for late September, but Sam started digging potatoes.

The three house dwellers went to a Horseheads movie on Sam's night off. It was titled *The Picture of Dorian Gray*, from the only book ever written by Oscar Wilde, a familiar story of greed, sin, and arrogance. A young man, infatuated with his own handsomeness and youth as depicted in a perfect portrait, makes a bargain he will come to regret. No one can save him from his appetite for pleasure and his awful fate.

There was frost on pumpkins and anything else left in gardens on September 30.

Sam's own words...
Wednesday, October 3, 1945 – "...Roy and I took canned fruit to the farmhouse cellar they expect to occupy this winter."

The move proved to be slow because the Andrews were still on the premises while they prepared the place to which they were moving. Grace was steadily packing. Sam noted on October 10 that Betty had turned 30. The move to the Andrew farm, which was about two miles north of Horseheads on the Ithaca Road, was accomplished on October 13. It had been a long time since Sam milked a cow, but he did so that night.

Sam recorded that October 19 was when "Edith left this place of wrath and tears one year ago today. God bless her soul."

Sam's own words...
Sunday, October 21, 1945 – "Was glad to see Steele and family when I went down with them to Park Place in Elmira until time to go to work at 10:30 p.m. Sandra is so cute and sweet. She must be three now. Steele is learning to be a meat cutter at the Market Basket store."
Tuesday, October 23, 1945 – "...I have a letter from John. He is in Berlin and doesn't know when he can come home. His picture looks good but a little older I think. How we would like to have him and pray it may not be too long."

~**~

Berlin
Hi Dad,   September 29, 1945
It has been a long time since I have written. Now I can't think of much to say except I am OK and longing to get home. I don't know when that will be. We have a lot of rumors, but none of them seem to come true. Well, all I can do is wait. I'll get there someday.

How is everybody? OK, I hope. I bet Betty's kids have grown so much I wouldn't know them. Has Teddy still got the 22 rifle I gave him? The last letter I wrote to Betty came back, wrong address it seemed. I'm sending you a couple of pictures, and one is for Betty, OK.

I am working 15 or 16 hours a day just so I can stay out of trouble. I work in a beer joint for our battalion. I haul beer during the day and sell it at night.

I don't get much sleep, but I guess it is alright (sic). I have to go to work in 15 minutes, so this is all for now.

I'll write again soon. This will let you know that I haven't forgotten you. You are still the best Dad in the world.

Love and Stuff, John

~**~

The letter had been written more than three weeks before.

Sam likely did not wonder but knew why John looked older even though he was to be only 29 years old come December. He'd been through so much in the war, and now his unit was on guard duty in Berlin. Even if he pulled duty on beer work the whole time, he was still in that dangerous environment. Sam had no idea how it was, thinking it was benign because John characterized it as nothing to worry over. There would be a disclosure of how it really was when he came home, and the men folk could talk among themselves.

The nature of the situation was not apparent to the battalion until they arrived in Berlin. It didn't take long to surmise the situation once the 325th G.I.R. Glider and Paratrooper Divisions landed or jumped into the Tempelhoph Airdrome. They hurled down into the American's sector of Berlin.

The captured city had been divided into four areas. East Berlin was occupied by Russia, and the western three sections by American, British, and French, each under separate control. A suggestion was made by an unknown Soviet lieutenant to a mother superior of a convent upon leaving the Russian sector to Stalin's regular and lower rank men. "I must tell you; however, the men who follow us are pigs," he said. It was hard to take seriously since the frontline Red Army veterans were not of that description.

John was in the middle of a roiling, boiling site that was so dangerous at night that soldiers were under orders to never patrol alone. And that was the American sector where the Nazi killer youth did not accept capitulation. They were dangerous pockets of resistance groups. The orientation to John and all Americans and allied soldiers cautioned about Russian trespassers into the American sector. Each patrolman armed themselves with an M1 Garand rifle and a knife. Sergeants and officers also carried a Colt 45 caliber pistol.

Sam knew nothing of this and John didn't want him to. The Soviet soldiers, Stalin's pigs, were untrained, poorly disciplined rear echelon troops. They'd been unpaid slaves for years, desperate men prone to loot, beat, rape, and murder. They could not be trusted under any circumstances.

Defeated post-war Berlin, Germany was demoralized. The aggressive military Russian guard dogs were somehow programmed to attack American soldiers. The only solution was to shoot them. Armed Soviet incursions were halted into the American section. The Americans and Allies had also been free to go into the Russian side before this but were now forbidden, permis sion withheld by their own superiors. No lines formed to gain a pass for the trip as soldiers preferred to live and go home to the states.

Many of them could go home a little richer. The Americans could send their Marks home converted into dollars for relatives to keep safe for them. The remainder not sent home was used for entertainment and alcohol in Berlin nightclubs like the one in which John worked.

An average U.S. soldier received a base pay of $17 per month. Paratroopers' bonus "jump pay" was $55 per month (as of 1942) for the inherent hazards of parachuting behind enemy lines. Many had been encouraged and signed payment to home before they arrived in Berlin.

By the time the 82nd Airborne arrived in Berlin for sector occupation, the black market was a thriving, inflated industry. Customers included German civilians and Russian soldiers.

Many of the troops had collections of wrist and pocket watches, which they had liberated from German soldiers. Watches sold for 100 to 250 Marks, depending on quality. Mickey Mouse watches were in highest demand, selling for as much as one-thousand Marks.

To acquire additional goods to sell, the men would visit the Army PX (Post Exchange) where they obtained their rations of cigarettes, cigars, tobacco, candy bars, peanuts, and chewing gum for trade. A ten-pack carton of cigarettes cost 50¢ at the PX. They sold for an inflated 200 to 300 Marks. One chocolate bar went for 25 Marks. It made Marks sweeter than candy.

John had the right idea. Stay busy and keep out of trouble. At the end of October, Americans, including Sam, learned of a brand-new piece of merchandise available at Gimble's Department Store in New York City. Newspapers and magazines carried advertisements for the first-ever ballpoint pen on sale at $12.50.

Sam's own words...
Friday, October 26, 1945 – "When I arrived from work this a.m., Sadie was at Grace's. She isn't as well as usual. Her doctor says it's her heart. She needs more rest than she gets at home."

Sadie stayed at Grace's two nights then Cretia came for a few days. Steele had been sent to Wellsborough, PA, to manage a Market Basket Store. Sam praised him as Grace listened.

November 16 was the beginning of the Cold War with Stalin's Russia. The defeat of Germany had been accomplished, and Russia's needs met to help them as a strong allie. Their oil production had dropped by half with industrial economic disruption, but America imported chemicals to upgrade Soviet fuel to high-grade aviation fuel. Even so, the Russians turned their back on the U.S. and seemed to forget the mighty big hand of help for them to defeat their enemy.

The United States imported 88 German scientists to help in the production of rocket technology. This controversy was in the news, although not to its full extent and understanding for the American people. There was no better answer for the men who had a ravished homeland and certainly would not choose Russia. They came willingly because of circumstances.

Steele bought a Ford car to get to his job in Pennsylvania. Shirley wrote that Tommy was in New Orleans about to muster out of the Navy on December 1.

Winter took its name seriously and dumped a foot of snow November 29. Sam nodded as he thought of how thankful he was that military boys would not be fighting and dying in it this winter. It was Thursday, and Sam went with Steele and Ruthie to her parents, the Coles, before they dropped him off at work.

Dewey came on December 1 to stay at Grace's for a few days. Brother to brother time was savored as Dewey drove Sam to work each night. He left for Addison to see Mary and then to Galeton to visit Sadie and Lynn. In a few days, he was back to make a final visit before leaving for Monticello where he lived. They'd all been glad to have him for awhile.

Sam's own words...
Monday, December 10, 1945 – "At factory 8 hours. Was glad to get a Christmas card from John today saying he expects to get home about the middle of January."

Steele received a letter from John.

~**~

France
December 12, 1945

Hi Brother,
    This is just going to be a little quickie, one of those little old beat up notes. If I had a V—Mail form, it would be one of those.
    Today, I finally received a letter from you. It was written on October 4. You might think I am being nasty but all I am slamming is our mail service.
    I am glad you are out and working. Save me a good pork roast for the middle of January. I ought to be out by then.
    As you probably already know the 82nd is supposed to be in the states and pull a parade in N.Y.C. It looks as if we might make it, too. We are being issued a lot of new crap.
    This is just to let you know that maybe I'll get home sometime and to wish you a Happy Christmas and a Merry New Year.

Love and Stuff, John

~**~

The events of last December 16 repeated this year: a baby girl was born to Ed and Betty. Her name was Linda Kay. she was Ed and Betty's seventh child. One day later, David and Hilda Crippen's new baby girl arrived at six pounds and 15 ounces. They named her Velma.

Sam's own words...

Friday, December 12, 1945 – "General George Patton Jr., famed leader of the 3rd Army, died of complications resulting from automobile crash injuries."

It was all too sad that it happened at all, Sam thought, for such a hero to leave the stage with no further input for the success of the U.S. military.

Sam wondered about Betty and hoped she would get home from the hospital before Christmas even if she needed a few more days in bed. He was also aware that Roy was suffering from lumbago again. Sam grimaced as he remembered his past experience with varicose veins. He sympathized with his brother-in-law.

Sam felt disgust when Steele's car was stolen and wrecked. It had been parked in front of the store Steele managed. Gene Frost loaned his car so Steele could come home for Christmas.

Shirley had sent presents for all of Betty's family, but they were in the same package for Lucille Frost. It shouldn't be a problem because Gene and Lucille would make a holiday visit up to the farm. The weather intervened and prevented the timely trip. The children would have their gifts late, but there was no chance they'd refuse them.

Sam tipped his head back and closed his eyes for a peaceful moment. He might have imagined the enjoyment he was to have reading So Well Remembered by James Hilton, which Shirley had sent him. Grace had given him the treasured *Sermon on the Mount* by Emmet Fox. Now if he could just get a night off to read to his heart's content. He had worked every night for seven weeks in a row.

Sam's holiday mail had included a much happier letter from Lenore Crow, telling that her son, Don, and all of his family had survived Japanese prison camp and were back in America. Sam was pleased to hear it. How he longed for his son John to come home. His old friend, John Long, and his wife sent a greeting card.

Sam's own words...
Monday, December 31, 1945 – "The letter from Shirley makes me feel pretty bad, for her and Tommy Broadhead, husband of five months, are having a serious time. She has not seen him since November 12. He wrote December 15 that he wants to be free, his only reason. He said if she comes to Mississippi, he won't see her. She is all broken up, says she loves him and always will. God help us all."

Sam's eyes closed before he rocked forward and back for a moment. How could he help her? He couldn't. There would be no upbeat spin to start the New Year as long as his Shirley Girl remained in misery. He hoped his plea to a higher power would be heard and ease her suffering.

31 – A Letter to Burn
1946, 1947

Sam wrote to Shirley right away to buoy her up if it were possible. He tried to choose his words carefully, and most of all, lovingly. There was no advice to be given on what to do. But he could speak of patience and to welcome her home if she needed to come.

It is said that you can't read a person's mind, but Sam's thoughts may have been pretty close to a parody he had copied into the last page of 1945.

By Thomas Hood

Lives of great men all remind us
As their pages o'er we turn,
That we'r apt to leave behind us
Letters that we should burn.

Perhaps Sam wished Tommy Broadhead had sent his letter up in flames before the postman took up its delivery. Work went along for eight hours per day at Ward La France. He had not forgotten his Shirley Girl, who was always on his mind.

Sam's own words...
Wednesday, January 9, 1946 – "Received a letter from Shirley and she intends to go to Hattiesburg, Mississippi, to see Tommy, although he wrote he wouldn't see her. I'm sure I don't know what I can do about it, but am sorry their marriage has come to such a pass. I pray for them and pray they find the right way."

Grace had heard that the Dykens' two sons would soon be home from Germany. Sam understood that the Longs in Pennsylvania also had two young men returning. He couldn't help but wonder how soon John would arrive.

Sam's own words...
Saturday, January 12, 1946 – "...82nd Airborne Division; All-American fighters in N.Y.C. January 3rd - 15 from vicinity among veterans of most decorated outfit and John is among the five from Elmira — Thank God."

Word of this event had come through Steele a few weeks ago by way of John's letter, and now here it was in the Elmira *Star-Gazette*. He and Grace were quite pleased to share the reading of it and see John Ralph Crippen listed in the honors. They didn't have to imagine the new uniform for marching because John's Christmas card bore a picture of it, right down to the white gloves.

Sam's neck cracked as he rolled it. He'd been lost in thought and had stayed too long in one position while he wondered when John would walk in and if Shirley had, in fact, gone to Mississippi. Or would she return home? He wanted happiness on this, her 24th birthday, January 20.

John answered the question of his return when he stopped into Ward La France but did not find Sam there. He'd thought his father worked nights. Word traveled, and Sam called over to Mary's just to confirm it for himself and hear his son's voice. The furlough allowed only three days, and he was to report to Fort Dix, NJ,to muster out of the service. John, Mary, and Mickey came for two hours with Sam before John's departure. It was below zero outside but warm in their hearts.

Shirley left for Hattiesburg, outcome uncertain. Sam prayed.

Willa sent a letter sure to bring a smile to Sam as he looked at the pictures of Lee, Babbette, and Burr. Burr was Babette's name for her baby brother. Sam would have news for her that John was home. He started letters to her, to Lenore in Albany, Oregon, and to John Long in Pennsylvania. As he wrote a birthday card for his old pal's 64th birthday, he reminisced to himself about 1908 when the two of them had set out by railroad to go west all the way to Oregon.

Sam's own words...

Thursday, January 31, 1946 – "...Shirley wrote to say that she and Tommy now know that everything will be alright (sic) but have a lot to learn. She would be back in Washington the 4th and planned to write from there. I am so thankful. Steele and family are on their way to Wellsborough, PA, this evening to an apartment they found. He is still employed in the meat department."

Sam transitioned back to the 11 p.m. to 7 a.m. shift.

In mid-February, Sam, Grace, and Roy took in a movie, *Our Vines Have Tender Grapes*, with Margaret O'Brian, Edward G. Robinson, and Butch Jenkins. The one-hour forty-five-minute movie was about a Norwegian farmer lovingly raising his daughter in rural World War II-era Benson Junction, WI.

John worked at the Eclipse. He and Sam did not try to contain their happy smiles as they both rode the night bus line to work February 19. A few days later, Ed and Betty visited Sam and took him to work.

Shirley steadily payed back the money she had borrowed from Sam.

Sam's own words...

Thursday, March 21, 1946 – "John informed me that Steele will have to quit his store job in Wellsborough to go to the Bath, NY, government hospital for treatment of a heart condition. I only pray it isn't too serious and that he will recover his health. Poor fellow. He certainly has his share of trouble."

Sam did have good news to be thankful for as he was able to go back on a five-night work shift. Two nights a week off naturally offered more rest for him. He was in need of a little more relaxation, not that he felt any older after his 64th birthday two weeks ago. David was half Sam's age when he turned 32 years old on the last day of March. Willa was the oldest sibling when she became 44 earlier in the month.

Shirley arrived Saturday, April 6, embraced by all members of her family before departing for Mississippi a week later to live with Tommy. Sam had high hopes that they would now have a chance to get to know each other and build on their relationship and marriage.

Grace had begun to have pain for several days from a bad back. Sam went to town and got some Porus Plaster for her to apply in hopes it would help her. The thin sheets of plaster contained the active ingredient capsaicin, which provided a warming sensation to the skin. Besides helping to relieve the pain from a sore back, it may also have promoted better blood circulation and relieved sore muscles, strains, sprains, and arthritis pain. The user would peel it away from the paper backing and apply directly to the affected area. If needed, the plaster could be cut into small pieces and applied to a spot. The plaster was more efficient if used after a bath.

The people who owned the farm were threatening to move in before Grace and Roy moved out. "Of all things," Sam thought. The Whitings were actively looking for a place. Sam mainly worked, paid his room and board, and was now helping Grace pack. Finally, Roy rented a house on the outskirts of Horseheads on the Corning Road. Grace became very ill, and Roy went to get the doctor. She remained in bed while Roy, their daughter, Alice Jeffries, and Sam did the moving.

Shirley wrote about her displeasure with hot Hattiesburg weather but was happy with Tommy. She was gaining the weight that her thin frame needed. Tommy was an excellent cook. His specialty was southern fried food.

Two days off meant freedom for Sam to enjoy himself and rest a little more. Thursday included hoeing. May 9 was not too early to spade ground for the start of the garden. He felt as alive as the seeds of lettuce, beets, Swiss chard, and carrots he planned to sow. On Friday, Sam surveyed his earthworks project with pride. That evening he spent a spontaneous night at the movies with John, Mary, and Mickey. Before the start of the 93-minute film, *Breakfast in Hollywood*, the screen was bright with previews while he and John leaned forward in their seats to talk. John said, "I'll be taking Steele to the Bath hospital on Saturday." The family awaited this news as they all worried about him. The musical was based on the popular 1940's radio show by the same name. The romantic comedy involved a lover's quarrel that Tom Breneman attempted to resolve via his radio program. Spike Jones, Nat King Cole, and others performed various musical numbers.

Sam's own words...
Thursday, May 16, 1946 – "Slept until noon. Planted four rows of potatoes in p.m. Dewey has been transferred to the Elmira Reformatory and goes to work in the morning. He was here awhile this evening."

Time again for Sam's two days off to further his planting with potatoes and flowers. Grace and Roy were glad to have Sam along for a ride up to Ed and Betty's farm. They easily saw that Betty had her hands full. All of the children except Teddy were in various stages of measles. She put on a big meal for them, taking it all in stride.

Sam's own words...
Sunday, May 19, 1946 – "...John brought Steele home from the Bath hospital Friday, and I talked to him on the telephone. They say his only trouble is nerves."

A week later heavy rain had caused devastation for 50 miles. Roy took Grace and Sam for a ride to Big Flats and up Harris Hill to look over the damage. It curtailed bus service, and Roy took Sam to work Tuesday, May 28.

It was late in May and safe enough from a threat of frost to set out cucumbers and put in 33 tomato plants. Within the week, Sam saw Steele, Betty and Ed, and also Dewey. Between severe storms, Sam managed to plant a garden for the landlord, Mr. Sayre Wells.

Sam's own words...
Saturday, June 15, 1946 – "...About 10 minutes before I had to leave for work, Ed and Betty came with butter for Grace. Teddy has broken his wrist playing softball."

Sam cared about details about each one of them while he waited on what had not yet happened: a job for Steele. Dewey and his friend, fellow guard Mr. Beattie, had not found a house to suit their needs.

Ah...June! The three, Roy, Grace, and Sam drove to Eldridge Park to watch a free show before dropping Sam off at Ward La France.

June, the month of vacations for many, saw the six—John, Mary, Mickey, and Gene, Lucille, and Ray-take a trip to Mississippi. They would see Lucille's father, Mr. Pitts and intended to try to convince Shirley and Tommy to come home with them. They could hope for it and were on their way. But as they did, Sam received Shirley's letter saying she had secured a job working in the commercial art department of the *Hattiesburg American* newspaper. Sam's grin widened. He was sure that with this opportunity, something she had always wanted, there was no chance Shirley would leave there now.

Grace and Roy visited the farm and brought back news to Sam that Frances and Punkie had arrived at Ed and Betty's. Fran was on her way to New York City and left a thin little David behind.

July had some items of note, depending on who cared about them. Sam kept himself informed. Housewives and mothers were paying attention to Dr. Benjamin Spock because of his new book *The Commonsense Book of Baby and Childcare*. A general subject of notoriety was a screaming headline about a lynching in Georgia. A mob of white men shot and killed two African-American couples near Moore's Ford Bridge in Walton County. Only hindsite knows July 25, 1946, to be the last mass lynching in the USA.

It was a sweeter July in New York state, which had its sweet cherries. Grace and Roy picked 40 quarts at 14¢ each in Brockport. There would be pie, cobbler, and canning. The visitors returning from Mississippi gave a sweet report that Shirley was happy and thriving.

Sweet notes were nowhere in sight August 11, when Mr. Wells's hogs raided, rooted, and raised heck with the gardens. Sam swallowed hard with lips pressed tight. But in the next instant, he may have uttered, "Thunder and lightning and seven hands around!" It was not the first rip up and may not be the last memory of all his hard work that had him throw his hands in the air.

The episode was left behind while Sam went with Grace and Roy for a weekend trip to Galeton. They visited many family members, and Sam stayed at John and Mary Long's. He and John stayed up talking until midnight about old times and the present. Sam was on vacation and remained in Pennsylvania after Whitings had departed. Later, he took the Erie train to Addison, NY, and had a good talk with his brother, Lynn. He was home Friday and John took him to stay at Ed and Betty's until Sunday. All of the children were delighted to have him. Eight-year-old Jeanie sat still beside her grandpa in the sunshine and released a satisfied sigh. She loved the scent of Prince Albert tobacco he was smoking in his pipe. For her, it was synonymous with Grandpa Sam.

They all came to the Crippen reunion at Eldridge Park on Sunday.

Back at the Wells farm, hogs raised havoc in the garden once again. To try to appease them, Sam and Grace had fed them corn husks from the corn as they canned it. More activities were in progress as they picked blackberries, preserved them, and took in the Chemung County fair. Sam's vacation was full but finished when he returned to night watchman work, Wednesday, August 21.

A letter from Shirley said that she and Tommy were both out of work for over a week now. Sam had not cashed the $100 check repayment she'd sent him awhile back. He had to smile as he sealed and mailed it in an envelope back to her on August 31. Little did she know she still had money in the bank.

In September, Steele was selling fruit from his panel truck and doing better than he had in the grocery store before he became sick.

Sam started to dig potatoes, which was secondary to the sleep he must have before his night shift. His mind became wholly occupied with another idea. A property on Holsec Avenue in the Fair Fax tract on Elmira's south side looked attractive to him for its possibilities. Sam purchased four lots on which a small bungalow sat and concluded the sale on September 29. Sam's plans to expand the small abode took shape. Roy was already digging the cellar.

Sam saw Dewey often. His younger brother was in a blue mood and had too much time on his hands. The divorce from Amy had become final. Dewey had hired Grace to provide supper and his work lunch, which she packed for him.

The three, Sam, Grace, and Roy went to see the movie, *The Green Years*. The black-and-white movie, which was about two hours long, told the story of an orphaned Irish boy who was taken in by his mother's Scottish relations.

Sam bought building materials, which included 363 cinder blocks, and had them delivered to his Holsec Avenue lots. Betty's 31st year was not forgotten by her father as Sam sent off a birthday card. Steele had switched to huckster of vegetables from his truck. They were grown by his brother-in-law, Jimmy Coles, in Montour Falls. By October 5, Roy was laying blocks for Sam's cellar.

Sam may have held his breath as he wished for his luck to hold since there had been no killing frost yet by November 1. The leaves had become ripened and fell off but not from freezing.

Dewey's idle hands meant that Sam might hire him to start renovations at the Holsec Avenue property. With Dewey's help, the shell of the building had been erected and enclosed. David and Hilda moved into the sparse structure on November 6. David would pay rent by his labor to install the windows, sink, and doors while they lived in two rooms of the original bungalow.

Shirley arrived to be on hand when Lucille was ready to have her baby in December. Shirley hoped Tommy would follow.

November 16 finally produced a real freeze. Dewey hung around a lot out of loneliness and was welcome by all of them the same as was Shirley.

Sam sighed with relief when he was not one of four watchmen laid off at Ward La France. When Steele went to work on November 27 at the Eclipse, Sam was as pleased as Steele. Steele believed Sandra had chicken pox.

Sam bought his Christmas cards and his 1947 diary before the supply at the stationers dwindled. He had the pleasure of receiving letters from Arthur Crow of Denver and Lenore Crow in Albany, OR. Sam answered with newsy letters and cards. Correspondence also came and went between Willa and Sam.

David had steadily worked on the Holsec house, and finished it, at least enough for use by December 20. John reached age 30 on December 24. Sam ate Christmas dinner with Steele and Ruthie. Grandpa's face radiated delight as Sandra played with two new dolls.

Steele was now 28 years old as of December 29. Sam received pictures to smile over when Willa sent photos of Lee's children, Babbette and Burr.

~**~
1947

The new year started with Sam's hope that, as the world healed, it would lead in the direction of universal brotherhood. He was at Ward La France eight hours. The snow and ice were not surprises for January.

Life carried on in a familiar pattern. An old friend in Galeton, Bill Tuck, was hospitalized after weeks of poor health. Sam hoped he would recover. He thought of him as he put in a 12-hour stint as a watchman from 7 p.m. to 7 a.m.

A surprising card arrived from Frances thanking Sam for his kindness to David Jr. God knows Sam would be kind and not because he had to, but because he loved his grandson. Bob and Elizabeth Crippen visited now and then as they had all along.

A letter from granddaughter, Christy, said that she and her new husband, Jack Lowall, lived in Denver.

Lucille Frost's new baby, Johnny, was born January 15. Shirley was right there to help when they came home from the hospital. The winter gave more ice than snow and was seven above zero on Shirley's 25th birthday, January 20.

Sam's time off usually included more rest. On January 31, Grace and Roy invited him to see a movie with them titled *Jesse James*. Sam had no desire to go. He refused to see the outlaw made into a hero when he was anything but.

Neuralgia flared up and caused Sam to grimace. February 5 had dipped to minus four degrees. The next day it warmed up to zero but didn't help his ailment.

Bill Tuck died. "Another good one gone," Sam opined to himself.

Shirley often came over to visit and floated the idea that she might go to Mississippi.

The news held a great deal about the Cold War with Russia. Stalin had not one ounce of ally blood left if he'd ever had in the beginning. He had gotten the defeat of Germany with the Americans and the other allies and had no further use for any of them. Total control of the east section of Berlin was under his oppressive thumb. On February 17, the Voice of America had begun transmission of radio broadcasts into Eastern Europe and the

Soviet Union. Such things worried Sam but also gave him hope for America's positive influence for good.

Roy's car froze up on February 19, requiring that he and Sam ride the bus to work.

Shirley left for Mississippi on February 25. She may not have met with a warm reception there because she was back in a few days. Sam's face was long and unsmiling when she returned because he had no idea how to help her or change a thing.

Newspapers carried news of Edwin Land in N.Y.C., who demonstrated the first instant camera to a meeting of the Optical Society of America. It was the Polaroid Land camera.

Seven inches of snow fell on March 2, the most for any single snowfall of the winter. Sam had been sick for several days and was unable to work. His boss came to see him on March 3 and brought his paycheck. It was his 64th birthday.

David and Hilda's little son, Douglas, had been hospitalized on March 15, for what was to be his first kidney operation, followed by another one if he did well.

Sam sent Willa a card for her 45th birthday. Betty and Ed's eighth child was born March 26. Little Roland Lee Voorheis was the fourth son to bring their total to four boys and four girls.

The April 1 headline touted Jackie Robinson, who signed with the Brooklyn Dodgers, as the first professional African-American baseball player to sign a contract since the 1880s. Sam supposed he'd enjoy that but hadn't a chance unless by a radio somewhere.

Frances sent Sam an Easter card in early April from N.Y.C. where she was a hospital nurse. Betty's recuperation was slower than from any other pregnancy. Sam wrote, "God bless her," as he felt concern. Shirley received a letter from Tommy who said he would come north after he got a job and saved money. It sounded as if it would take time and only time would tell when it happened or not.

Sam gave no opinion but thought, "God bless them." He left it perfectly in the only place that made sense to him, in God's hands.

Eighty-three-year-old Henry Ford suddenly died of cerebral hemorrhage on April 8. The pioneer of the automobile industry, who developed a horseless carriage into a billion-dollar empire, died in his suburban Dearborn, MI, home. Sam copied it from the headlines into his diary.

Grace and Roy visited Ed and Betty and came back to Sam with a worrisome report. Betty still had not gained strength nearly fast enough after the last birth. Dr. Schmidt had expressed his opinion that she should have no more children. She had lost too much blood and he had a difficult time stopping it. Her recovery would continue to be slow.

Sam worried about Steele, too. He had a bout of pleurisy. The pain of inhaling was hard to witness. The doctor prescribed antibiotics for an infection in addition to anti-inflammatory drugs for pain. He was also ordered to bed rest for two weeks when he tested positive for TB.

Sam's own words...
Friday, April 25, 1947 – "Put in 12 hours watching 32 new trucks in a large parking lot. An all-day rain turned to snow in evening."
Monday, April 28, 1947 – "David and Hilda were at Steele's Sunday night, and they said the doctor told them that their three-year-old little boy, Douglas, who has been in the hospital several weeks cannot get well. They are to bring him home. I hope the doctor may be mistaken. Hilda says she is not going to believe him."

Sam listened to Hilda, and in his heart he wanted the truth to be different than the doctor had laid out, just like she did. Every single one of Sam's children had problems about which he could do nothing. John and Mary were not on good terms and seemed ready to quit. Steele was ordered to stay in bed for another 10 days. Shirley was ill and scheduled for an operation unspecified.

Sam's own words...
Monday, May 16, 1947 – "I went down to the Heights in the afternoon for my pay (and then to John's). I was never more surprised in my life than when Mr. Wilson handed me my check and told me that I was laid off, maybe for good. John and I went to the hospital in the evening to see Shirley. She seems improved and looks much better..."

Sam brought Shirley to Grace's in a car, thanks to Dewey's help. He wanted to oversee her care. The unemployment office was a priority as well. He had to apply and start receiving compensation. He had another quest to go to the farm to see little David. Sam thought his thin grandson may have a lack of appetite because he missed his parents. He saw no fault in Betty for that. She loved Punky along with her own eight children. His Uncle Ed had agreed with Betty to keep him right on through her confinement. "What was one more mouth to feed?" he said. Now that Betty was well, Sam believed Shirley needed fresh milk, vegetables, and meat, which was in abundance at the farm. Ed and Betty wanted to have her for the month that Sam thought was necessary for her recovery.

Sam and Shirley saw a movie, *The Razor's Edge*, a Twentieth-Century Fox film that shows how a man who has studied in India uses an ancient coin to cure another man's headaches. The film was based on W. Somerset Maugham's 1944 novel of the same title, familiar to Sam. John took Shirley up to the farm.

John had not lived with Mary for a week. It had nothing to do with his sudden gall bladder operation, and it took time to recuperate. Sam weathered these things well because he could do nothing about them but care. Circumstances were not under his control but he could control how he spent his time. He went to a movie at Grace and Roy's urging. The Yearling was worthwhile, as he told them later, and he was glad they pushed him to go. The two-hour and 24-minute film was about a Florida boy's pet deer that threatens the family farm.

Grace and Roy had waited on Alice and Roy Jeffrey to move to another place. Now the Whitings could renovate their house at 125 East Mill Street in Horseheads. Dewey helped Sam move a few items. Sam worked on a garden, and Dewey did a little painting.

Strange news was in print. Sam didn't know what to make of it. On June 21, seamen claimed to have seen six UFOs near Maury Island in Puget Sound. On the heels of that report, June 24, another man made the first widely reported UFO sighting near Mount Ranier, WA. On July 7, there came a report of a supposedly downed extraterrestrial aircraft found in the Roswell, UFO incident, near Roswell, NM. Sam couldn't make anything of it, as strange as it was. He'd leave it to history or let it die a slow death if it was a hoax.

Real news was welcome on July 18. President Harry S. Truman

signed the Presidential Succession Act into law, which for all time places the Speaker of the House and the President Tempore of the Senate next in line of succession after the Vice President, in the event of the president's death. Heaven forbid it ever happens, Sam thought, but it needed to be stated.

Snatches of work were carried out at the Mill Street house by Sam and Dewey, who were more able-bodied than Roy, at present. They all moved in on July 16. There was new linoleum in the dining room, but more paint was needed other places. As residents on the premises, they could accomplish more. Sam went with Grace and Roy up to the Odessa, NY, Cotton-Hanlon store for paint and wire screen for the doors.

The garden was Sam's domain as well. A new address brought old friends to visit them. Bob and Elizabeth Crippen were just ahead of Walter and Blanche Dykens on the evening of July 24.

Sam's own words...
Sunday, July 27, 1947 – "Grace, Roy, and I drove up to Ed's and Betty's, arriving about noon. They served a pancake and sausage dinner and how we enjoyed it. The children just about mobbed me, but I like it. Grace and Roy returned home at 4 p.m."
Monday, July 28, 1947 – "At Betty's all day enjoying my visit and the children. Ed and Teddy drawing gravel for a concrete foundation under their house. Ed and Betty brought me home in the evening. Grace had bought ten quarts of red raspberries on their way home yesterday for 40¢ a quart. She said Steele hoped to see me on his way to work."

Teddy was 14 years old and worked alongside his father. Ed valued his help. Sam had nothing but pride in his first-born grandson.

On Tuesday, Sam reported to the unemployment office and wondered when he would get his first check. He could use it.

Dewey was with them for now but still reserved himself a bit separate. Quite likely, Sam and Dewey paid the same amount for room and board. Sam had recorded spending between $5 and $7 each week since February. He always paid between 42¢ and 50¢ for tobacco per week; a shoe repair was 85¢, and an occasional $1 went for gas in Roy's car. Union dues of $5.40 per quarter had ended, but Sam had to contact Ward La France for $8 taken from his last paycheck toward a savings bond he would not get now.

These details needed attention. He had made a typical $168 for April from La France. When the unemployment kicked in, it would be $21 per week. He needed to spend 65¢ for a haircut and wished his check would arrive.

Sam, Grace, and Roy went to Eldridge Park in the evening now and then. Sam helped Grace wash windows and carry canned fruit and empty jars to the cellar.

Steele had pressing bills to pay and wanted to borrow $300 from Sam. The U.S. government was to pay $300 bond on September 1, and Steele could repay it then. Sam let him borrow it.

Sam hoed cabbage and picked beans in mid-August. A little rain would have been nice to alleviate the dry spell. John bought a trailer to live in at Gene and Lucille's mobile park, and Shirley was going to live with him and do the cooking when she was off duty from her new drill press job at the Remington Rand plant.

Sunday, August 17, was the date of the Crippen reunion held at Stewart Park in Corning, NY. Of Sam's family, he was pleased for the attendance of Ed, Betty, and all of the children, including little David. Steele, Ruthie, and Sandra were there, too. Even without his other families there, whom he missed, Sam took in the joy in front of him and spread good cheer to others.

Sam's own words...
Monday, August 18, 1947 – "...Picked two dozen ears of corn and took them along with Grace and Roy up to Betty and Ed's and ate supper with them. Betty drove David Jr. down to David and Hilda's last night and both he and his son feel blessed. I am so thankful the poor child has his father, and they are together where they belong at long last. Hoed cabbage plants and a few beans."

They all wanted David Jr. to get acquainted with new surroundings in the family before the start of school for him there.

Steele paid the $300 back to his father on September 1, exactly as promised. September 2 was the day Ed and Betty came down to shop for school clothes. They left five-month-old Roland with his great Aunt Grace while they went to outfit the school-goers, Teddy, Bucky, Jeanie, and Gail.

Pears and peaches were in season. Of course, Sam helped Grace preserve them. He never doubted her appreciation of him for making her work easier.

A trip down to Holsec Avenue on September 11 to see David and Hilda, did Sam good. Warmth radiated through his whole body when he heard that David Jr. was happy and doing well in school. Sam no doubt beamed as much as his grandson who was happy because he was with his father. Since Sam was still unemployed, David agreed to pay $18 a month for rent, starting on October 1. Sam finished picking sweet corn on September 12 and sold two dozen ears to a neighbor. A few days later on Monday, he road down to the Holsec house with Dewey who had a repair job across the street. He was glad to see them all, and little David was especially happy to see him. His grandson wanted him to walk with him back to school when he finished lunch, and Sam did just that.

For one who had no gainful employment, Sam was busy with a project whether he got a ride or took the bus to Holsec Avenue. More cellar would materialize if he kept digging it out and removing dirt. There were days when he dug eight hours. His bus tokens and tobacco were $1.12 for the week.

September 23 through 27 Sam worked for Ed at the farm to pull the bean crop. The throng of grandchildren delighted with his presence was as sweet as the syrup on Betty's pancakes.

Sam was back to cellar digging until Reverend Snyder of the Walnut Street Free Methodist Church of Horseheads hired him for renovation help. The job ended his unemployment pay for two months while he was to make $135 each for October and November. Dewey was quiet, sad, and free. The end of September had brought with it the finish of divorce proceedings.

Sam sent a card with $1 enclosed for Betty's 32nd birthday, October 10. He, Grace, and Roy had driven to the farm a few days earlier and left a bushel of carrots from Sam's garden for Betty to can. Right then, she, Edwin, and Teddy had gone to the Owego auto races while Ed's sister, Pearl, stayed with the younger children. Sam imagined the enjoyment for the trio out on a Sunday for a well-deserved break from farm work. His serene face held a peaceful countenance as he thanked God for this large, happy family.

Margie McCann, Grace's granddaughter, and her friend arrived for a big parade and the special exhibit of the American Freedom Train that celebrated the United States Bicentennial. The train had its own itinerary and route around the 48 contiguous states, stopping to display Americana and related historical artifacts. The 1947 exhibit was integrated—black and white viewers were allowed to mingle together freely. When town officials in Birmingham, AL, and Memphis, TN, refused to allow blacks and whites to see the exhibits at the same time, the Freedom Train skipped the planned visits, amid significant controversy. Snow fell Saturday morning and threatened the procession but only shortened it. Sam heard through other eyes and exuberant utterances, of the distinctive red, white, and blue paint scheme on the sleek bullet-like train.

A second daughter, Kathleen, was born to John and Mary on November 16. John and Mary had never gotten back together since June and never did again.

Sam indulged himself on November 26, buying a necessary new pair of footwear at a cost of $6.45. Tobacco and bus tokens added $1, and he paid $7 to Grace for the week.

Sam's own words...
Tuesday, November 25, 1947 – "Was bothered by a stiff neck all day. Canvassed a little and sold one pressure cooker. Cold wind."

Snow flurries flecked on the ground but left no accumulation. It was a white surface at the farm for Thanksgiving where Sam, Grace, and Roy enjoyed a wholesome day of food and visiting.

Sam's own words...
Sunday, November 30, 1947 – "Mary went home to Addison in the evening. Dewey and Millie, his lady friend, and Grace accompanied her in Dewey's car."
Friday, December 5, 1947 – "We were surprised when Betty, Frances, David Jr., and Betty's Jimmy came about noon today. Betty met Frances at the Delaware, Lackawanna & Western Railroad Depot and then at Gene Frost's trailer camp where his father left him. They were here only a few

minutes and on their way again up to Ed and Betty's Benettsburg farm. Frances expects to return to N.Y.C. tomorrow for her nurse job. She is looking very well..."

The next day, Saturday, Sam canvassed and sold another pressure cooker. He had organized his merchandise and knew all about his products when he went door to door. It paid off more than a commission to include the jubilant joy of success for his effort.

Sam fastened cardboard to the chicken coop walls to make it warmer. Grace was sick with a cold, and he relieved her by helping with housework. The next day Sam went uptown to the employment office and to buy meat Grace wanted. For himself, he bought postage stamps, shaving supplies, and suspenders, all for $2.10. A haircut and tobacco cost 90¢.

Sam's own words...
Thursday, December 11, 1947 – "Wrote a note on a Christmas card and mailed to Lenore Crow...Cold. Roy and I set up an oil burning stove. Shirley, Steele, and Sandra were here awhile this evening. They say Frances took David Jr to N.Y.C. when she went back instead of returning him to his father where he has been really happy with his half brothers and sisters. I wonder what is in store for him now."

~**~

December 20, 1947

Dear Sam,

I'm late with letters this year, and it seems but a few weeks since I wrote 1946 greetings. We have been so plagued with colds all the fall and winter that we haven't had pep enough to keep up. But we all keep going...

...At home, this winter and it seems wonderful. This method isn't very remunerative but the Lord sends us a little "manna" from heaven, and we manage. We keep goats, which are profitable as well as pleasurable, the very nicest farm animal we've ever handled.

...I so enjoy hearing from Betty. She's one grand girl and certainly has her hands full. I've seen only one of her brood. Heard from Willa last year...

Uncle Arthur is well and lives happily and busily in Denver. His son, Arthur, is quite a fox breeder.

Nothing I'd like better than going tripping again, but for my responsibilities, which are pretty heavy...

Remember me to all of the young folks.

Best wishes to you, Lenore

~**~

32 – Appendicitis
1948

Aside from the usual busy December and getting ready for holidays, John had turned 32 years old and right after Christmas, Steele was 30. In all the preparations and chaos of a big family, neither Betty or anyone else heard from Frances and David Jr. Betty's girls, Jeanie at eight-and-a-half years old, the same as David Jr, and seven-year-old Gail, imagined how grand and glorious their cousin's enchanted city life was compared to life on the farm. They may have read one of Aesop's Fables about a country mouse and a town mouse. The illustration of an artistically rendered gas light post on a street cast a warm glow down on snow-specked holly and jingle bells wrapped around the pole, which romanticized their child's eye view.

New Year's Day at the farm with Ed and Betty where he enjoyed an overnight. The children's contagious glee over having their grandfather near was pleasing to him. Sam played no favorites as he gave each of them attention. He was like a celebrity among them and sought no higher fame.

New Year's was just past, and with the four oldest children installed in school, it made Betty's work easier. Sam went back to Horseheads. He visited the watch repair shop operated by Mr. Titus. Sam had deposited Mary's watch there for repairs before Christmas.

Sam's own words...
Wednesday, January 7, 1948 – "Did the few chores, swept two inches snow off the walks. Went uptown and subscribed to *Boys Life* for Bucky. Roy went to the unemployment office."

Bucky was 10½ years old, and his grandfather thought he was quite a little man who would get full use out of the $2 magazine subscription for the year.

Sam's own words...
Friday, January 9, 1948 – "...I suppose Dewey will not be with us after tonight as he is getting married tomorrow. We shall miss him."
Saturday, January 10, 1948 – "My eldest sister, Grace's 63rd birthday. Dewey married Mildred Sadler at 11 a.m. I surely wish them all the happiness in this world and may God bless them. Sadie, Mary, and Iva (Lynn's wife) came, and we had a good four or five-hour visit."

All company was gone, and it left time for Sam, Grace, and Roy to go to a movie Monday evening. The newlyweds visited them the next day. Sam surmised that their happiness was added to because they both had a little money and good jobs.

Steele was working at the Eclipse and Shirley at Artistic Card Company in Elmira. On January 17, they and Sam were shocked to learn that Dewey's new wife had fallen on ice and had broken her left leg below the knee in two places. She was at Arnot Ogden Hospital. Their sympathies included supper for Dewey.

Grace served pie and hot Postum when Steele and Shirley visited Sunday evening.

Early Monday morning it was a frigid 17 degrees below zero. An emergency was ready to strike.

Sam's own words...
Wednesday, January 12, 1948 – "Ed came about 11:30 a.m. with the two little girls, Carol and Linda. He informed us that Betty had an emergency appendicitis operation at Shepherd Hospital in Montour Falls. Her appendix broke before the operation. I came home with them and will try to help what I can. We stopped and saw Betty a few minutes. She seemed cheerful and

doing as well or better than expected."

Ed saw her again the next day and also the head nurse who said she was doing very well considering the condition of the burst appendix. Sam had become Betty's temporary replacement.

Sam's own words...
Friday, January 23, 1948 – "Gladys and Harry Landon (Ed's sister) came and so did Eva Morgan (neighbor). Harry helped buzz wood, and the girls did a big washing, which was mighty fine of them. Jimmy has been over to Ed's brother, Lyle, ever since Tuesday night when Betty went to the hospital. The little fellow got so homesick that Lyle had to bring him home this evening. Ed just returned from the hospital with good news that Betty is still improving. God knows we pray she will recover soon. Seven children and five adults for dinner and supper."

Sam was the great cook who served it all up on plates warmed on the stove shelf for the throng of workers. He appreciated each one of them as they did him. No doubt he could use a slackened pace.

Jimmie had been sick for an extended illness of pneumonia during Christmas holidays not all that long ago. The dear little guy, only 4½ years old, had to be back with his family for the love that had pulled him through once already.

Sam's own words...
Saturday, January 24, 1948 – "It sure keeps me busy cooking, etc., and looking after children. I don't see how Betty ever stands it. It looks like we may get a heavy snowfall. It has come down steadily since noon. Below zero this morning."

Ed managed to get Sam to his appointment time at the unemployment office Tuesday while Eva and Arnie Morgan watched the children. Traveling back from Elmira they stopped at Montour Hospital to see Betty. She was well enough that she wanted to go home.

The day wore on as Ed and Teddy buzzed wood. Harry Landon helped at times. He needed wood, too. Gladys came and baked. She had three young children with her and four in school.

Neighbors Mrs. Cox and Mrs. Doan sent food. Sam withstood it all and kept on cooking for the "crowds" that came to the table.

Betty came home Friday night, January 30, after her 10 days forced hiatus. She was weak but feeling well enough considering her ordeal. Ed had nose bleeds that lasted much too long and worried Betty and Sam.

Sam likely read that the Soviet Union had begun to jam Voice of America broadcasts. Truth told, Stalin was at least as bad as Hitler or worse, considering the thousands upon thousands he had ordered killed. They were in an evil class of their own making.

Below zero weather kept the school bus away to add to the commotion of all of the children home for two days. Sam took it in stride and fed them all.

This week when Ed took Sam to the unemployment office, they also stopped to see Grace. An answer to Sam's letter sent a week ago to Idaho friends, the Southworths, had arrived in Grace's box. Southworths were retired and lived in Florida and thought Sam might like it there, too. Only one frost had hit so far this winter at the southern couple's home near Tampa. Sam smiled. He could dream, couldn't he?

Ed and Mr. Cox butchered a steer that Ed had fattened for just that purpose. Sam appreciated the provisions Edwin made for Betty and the children. It was a pleasure to serve Ed first with a warm plate piled with food. How Ed smiled with his stomach full.

Sam spent a few days at Grace's. He reported to the unemployment office and then got tax forms. While he was in town, he bought a Wee Wisdom book to take to Betty's with him. The 9" x 12" green hardcover book of rhymes was all about animals. Little blonde Carol was just past three years and enjoyed the poems as she heard them so often read by older siblings. The book became well used for years, so much that Baby-Hon, as Carol was affectionately nicknamed, remembered it into adulthood.

Ed took Betty to Dr. Schmidt, and he changed her bandages. She was healing well but would have to come back again. She was not ready for farmhouse work but sat at the table and helped Gail and Jeanie make valentines for school. They used colored construction paper, magazine cut-outs, and imagination.

Sam's own words...

Friday, February 13, 1948 – "Teddy Herforth Voorheis's 15th birthday, my eldest grandson and I am proud of him. He is always on the honor roll at Odessa High School and a little man around home and on the farm. This has been an awful day: Wind and rain and freezing on as it fell on everything, especially trees. Ed's brother, Harold and his wife, Gladys, were here a few minutes this evening and delivered Betty's washing, which Gladys did for her."

Ed, Betty, Carol, Linda, and baby Rolly accompanied Sam to Horseheads on Monday. Grace made a dinner for all of them. Sam stayed overnight to file his taxes and report to unemployment on Tuesday. Grace and Roy took him back that afternoon. Ed and Teddy were splitting posts. Ed called his buyer to come after them because he needed the money badly to buy groceries for his large family. His next job was radiator repair on his truck.

Sam took the time to write to Willa on March 1. She had not written since her Christmas card and then only her signature.

Sam made out his state tax and sent $15.21 with it on March 3. It was also his 65th birthday. Cards arriving from everyone pleased him. He went back to Horseheads since he needed to go to the Social Security office to apply for old age benefits. It was a bit disparaging that the young lady who took up his case seemed to think he lacked enough work hours of coverage to qualify. He thought otherwise. The written report would flesh it out when it arrived in two weeks.

Grace made him a birthday cake. Dewey stopped over, also Bob and Elizabeth Crippen. Bob was not well. While Sam was at Grace's, he learned that John moved out of Gene Frost's trailer camp.

Eight inches of snow fell. Combine that to the coldest of temperatures to discourage spring thoughts just around the corner.

Sam went back to the farm to stay with Teddy, Bucky, and Jimmy while Ed and Betty went to Long Island with their friends, the Hubbses, who were originally from the city of Long Island. The other children stayed with the Doan and Morgan families.

Teddy went to Reynoldsville to help spread manure with Ed's youngest brother, Russell. Russell brought him back in time for chores, but was back again to get him to stay all night in Reynoldsville.

Sam's own words...
Sunday, March 14, 1948 – "Everything is quiet on the Wabash. Russell brought Teddy home around 3 p.m. The only complaint I have is that Teddy and Bucky didn't get their chores done until 7 p.m. On the whole, all of them have been very good boys. Warmer and snow going."

Ed returned Sam to Grace's about noon March 16. David's son, Douglas, had another operation and remained in the hospital. The doctor made it clear that it was a miracle that he was alive, and it would be years before he was normal. A stomach tube remained in place.

Sam's and Grace's Burpee seeds arrived. He spaded a row in the garden on March 20 for early peas.

Steele came for a quick visit on Sunday to tell his father that he had taken the civil service exam on Saturday for correctional officer. Sam worked in the chicken yard or park, as he called it. He spaded more ground, and the hoe felt right in his hands. Sam planted additional peas, lettuce, and cabbage seeds. Tomato seeds were punched into the soil in a window box upstairs. Back to spading, and soon he put in onions, parsnips, carrots, beets, and radishes.

John and Lucille were together and stopped by to invite Sam to supper Saturday night. As it turned out, the meal was late because Gene purposely did not return the boys on time. He was not finished treating Lucile badly for leaving when he had another woman.

On Tuesday, Gene came to Sam to ask his advice. Sam said he could not undertake that and thought those concerned most were the only ones to know what to do about it. Sam held privately that one could not escape the law of "sowing and reaping."

Dewey and Mildred visited. She had another month to wear the leg cast. Thirty-four-year-old David went to work for the Corning Glass Works, and they were moving to the city of Corning, NY. Roy hired Sam to dig a cesspool. He put in eight hours on the job on March 31. That was long enough for one day because Sam had garden work waiting.

Lucille was forced to go back to Gene or lose her children. Maybe he would treat her better now. Steele had his troubles, too. His double hernia operation scheduled for April 16, was also the month when Sam planted sunflowers and swiss chard.

Dewey picked up the laundry that Grace washed for him and bought eggs from her, too.

Lucille found out that Gene still had a girlfriend. Lucille and John rented Sam's Holsec Avenue house on Monday, April 26.

Sam went home with Betty for three days. Ed had hired him to put in 14 acres of grass seed. All of the children were ecstatic to see him. Steele was laid off from the Eclipse while he was still bent over in a painstaking walk trying to affect a cautious recuperation from his hospitalization.

Grace had a scrappy rooster killed. He had attacked her and Sam on several occasions. The adversarial cock made a delicious Sunday dinner on May 1.

The half cord of wood Grace bought cost $2.50. While Sam split it, he remembered that he had a birthday card to mail to Jeanie for her ninth birthday.

The verdict on his eligibility for compensation was not ready at the social security office when Sam went there on Monday, May 10. He shook his head; went back to his garden work.

Dewey and Mildred stopped in as they did from time to time. They had news that they were buying a house on First Street in Horseheads. John helped wash and wax Steele's car, which he hoped to sell for $500. He made the sale and intended to make a down payment on a dry cleaning business.

Walter Dykens ordered a pair of Tanner shoes from Sam when he and his wife, Blanche, came to supper in the middle of May. Sam imparted the news of the day that the United States had now recognized Israel as a country.

Gene Frost, with his new woman, and John and Lucille, all went to lawyer Hoover together to arrange for divorce proceedings. Gene concluded that he was not a family man and had no desire to continue with it. John was glad to have Lucille and her four boys.

On May 1, Sam received $126.70 back from over payment on federal taxes.

Between Ruthie's jitter and Steel's excessive planning for the opening "bell," their enthusiasm was enough to propel them ahead with the dry cleaning business. One drawback was the lack of start-up money. Sam loaned Steele $100 of the tax money he had just obtained.

Sam walked over town and mowed Bob Crippen's lawn. Bob was not well and expected to enter Arnot Ogden Hospital on Friday, May 25.

Sam put up a clothes lines for Grace and emptied the tubs of water when she had finished the laundry. Meanwhile, he had set out 75 heads of lettuce. He did so with the hope that May 22 meant no more frost was due. He hoed established garden sections. He dug up Hollyhocks from the southern property edge along the railroad tracks and set them along the border of the garden.

Unfortunately, Steele hit a little dog with his car. He stopped and took the dog and its owners, four children and their mother, to the veterinarian's office. The vet did what he could and said the dog would improve in two days or die. Steele drove the family home.

It was time for the annual pilgrimage to the Crippen cemetery in Galeton. Roy, Grace, and Sam drove down, picked Cretia up, and made the respectful visit to their parents' graves for trimming and mowing. So many willing hands made a quick job of a loving task. They were ready for visits to friends and relatives throughout the area.

Dewey's 50th birthday was Wednesday, June 2. He was Sam's youngest (living) brother by 15 years.

Sam registered at the unemployment office. He had a three-hour job to put hot caps on melons for Leo Walker. The work earned him $4.50. By the end of June, he would pay Sam $28.50. It included pay for the labor of asparagus cutting and his expertise with the hoe.

Grace ordered a pair of Tanner shoes and paid $5 up front. The balance remained $3.81 for arrival, which was to be July 1.

Shirley wrote from Washington where she was visiting a friend. All was well.

Sam and all of them were hit hard by the death of Bob Crippen on June 14. He would have been 78 years old in a few months. Many attended the Maple Grove Cemetery service in Horseheads.

Sam's previous landlord, Mr. Walker, hired him for garden work. He may have smiled at the thought that he didn't need to show up without his hoe. As he worked, his thoughts were on Bob's elderly widow and Cretia all alone. He believed that too many elderly were lonely without a spouse and some so feeble that it was not right for them. It took only a few days to build up 19.50 hours of labor for Mr. Walker.

While it rained all afternoon on Wednesday, June 23, Sam cleaned out the hen house. When Roy went to his job at Langwell Hotel the next day, Sam went with him. Roy had told him of a position that had just opened. Sam secured the employment as houseman and got along well his first day when they put him right to work. He continued with eight-hour days and kept up his garden, too. It could be worked in since it was light outside until 9 p.m. On July 8, Dewey surprised Sam with a pound of Prince Albert. Dewey said it was for the many fresh vegetables he and Mildred had enjoyed from Sam's garden. Sam accepted it graciously.

Shirley wrote that Tommy had previously agreed to the divorce she asked for but had now changed his mind. All Sam could do was pray for her and also for rain for his garden. He continued his Langwell Hotel job. Steele enjoyed success with the dry cleaning business.

Grace and Roy visited Ed, Betty, and children. Ed had just butchered and gave them a piece of beef. It hit the spot for supper with new potatoes Sam had dug.

It was time for a walk to the barber shop for Sam's 75¢ haircut, the hardware for 35¢ insecticide, also bus tokens and tobacco at 50¢. He continued to pay Grace $7 per week for room and board. His Langwell pay was $24.50 to $30 per week. The first summer squash harvested made an appetizing hit on Grace's table July 20.

Sam's own words...

Wednesday, July 21, 1948 – "Received a letter from Frances B. Crippen. She is having a hard time supporting herself and David Jr. in N.Y. City. David isn't paying anything towards his son's support, and she wants me to talk to him. I think he should do something for his boy and shall speak to him if I have the chance. On the other hand, David and Hilda had him, and he and they were getting along fine until Frances practically kidnapped him and took him to NYC. A dandy rain much needed. At Langwell eight hours."

~**~

The news concerned a Berlin blockade, which had begun June 24. Friendly allied relations and Cold War hostilities had become a crisis. Profound privations were already faced and shutting East Berlin's Russian sector off from the other three sectors meant starvation for its people. It was the Russians intention for the German citizens to starve. In response, the United States ordered the launch of Operation Vittles, the Berlin Airlift. At the height of the campaign, one plane landed every 45 seconds at Tempelhof Airport. John followed the news of its progress as close as Sam did. He had been stationed there with his 325th Glider regiment.

They could only imagine the plight of German families there. A 10-year-old German refugee boy named Adolf Busse received one of the airplane distribution drops, a food box for his family, two parents and a brother. It contained non-perishable items including powdered milk. Young Adolf believed forever after that the Americans had saved his life. He felt that way because his family had escaped by subway from East Berlin to West Berlin and depended on American benevolence for food. The family made the getaway just before the final closing of the underground rail between the eastern Russian and western American sectors of Berlin. The elder Herr Albert Busse, Adolf's father, had put himself in danger to secretly and illegally listen to Radio Free Europe where he had heard clues about the imminent blockade and closing of the subway. Their family left a German location to make their way out of a homeland that was now hostile to them. They never owned or saw their home again. (Adolf is the author's husband, a naturalized American citizen.)

~**~

Sam sold a pair of Tanner's shoes on June 27 and felt lighthearted as he worked at the Langwell Hotel. In the evening, harvesting ripe tomatoes and cucumbers from his garden extended his good mood.

Sam had answered Frances's letter awhile back. Now she wrote that she had not received help from David. What was Sam to do? He couldn't make promises that were not his to make.

Shirley's letter didn't exactly say so but seemed to hint that she and

Tommy were back together. The firemen's convention of August 14 convened in Horseheads with 20,000 men. A block dance and a big shebang parade pranced down the center of town. Sam, Grace, and Roy watched until they were tired and walked home.

Sam's own words...
Tuesday, August 17, 1948 – "Usually my day off, but 'Old Bill Sterling' is having his vacation and I had to help out. The famous ballplayer, Babe Ruth, died today of cancer. He was 53."

Sweet corn was fresh and abundant. Sam enjoyed the compliments dished out with the variety of vegetables Grace served to her daughter and grandchildren visiting from Ithaca. He sat tall with his grin and watched reactions while he took a deep breath.

Sam and Grace sold a dozen ears of corn each to several neighbors. Willa sent Sam an announcement about Lee's August 28 marriage to George Robertson in Idaho Springs, CO.

Sam sent Gail a birthday card and a funny book for her eighth birthday. He imagined the happiness on her face as soon as she would receive it but thought she was about seven and called her a little dearie. Ed and Betty had so many children that it was hard to keep track of their exact ages.

Roy was building a front porch and called on Edwin for help. The Crippen Reunion went on while Sam worked at the Langwell. Steele picked him up at 3:30 p.m. and he went late just to visit and how he did enjoy it.

The pull back and forth between Gene and Carrie, his-on again off-again lady friend, continued to stall John and Lucille, too. Initially, Carrie left her husband for Gene and pushed Lucille out.

Sam's own words...
Monday, September 6, 1948 – "Of course, John wants a divorce from Mary so he could marry Lucille, but he is broke. Mary sold their home for $7,000, and he didn't get a dollar, besides he has to pay her $15 each week for support of the children. I do hope they get this knotted skein unraveled. At Langwell eight hours."
Tuesday, September 7, 1948 – "Raked lawn, went uptown and got a postal money order to the I.B. Vry, Co. for an aluminum nine-piece kitchen set. Rested."

Only a week went by when John and Lucille came with exciting news. John was about to get his divorce and Gene his, too. John and Lucille planned to marry and also Gene and Carrie. Sam wished only happiness to them.

Grace, Sam, John, and Lucille went to a movie Wednesday night and saw *Green Grass of Wyoming* on Lucille's birthday. "Thunderhead," a roving, big white stallion, causes problems for the Wyoming ranchers when he leads their blue-blooded racing mares off to join his wild horse herd in the mountains.

Dewey and Mildred had bought a home on Liberty Street in Horseheads and were waiting for tenants to move out. Patience was new to Dewey, but he needed it now. Gene Frost sold his trailer camp property to friends, Jud and Marguerite Moffitt. Clocks got turned back to Eastern Standard time.

Sam's own words...
Monday, September 27, 1948 – "...Lyle Austen came again, and I decided to rent my house on Holsec Avenue to him and his young wife..."

Sam charged $30 per month for rent. Gene Frost helped move some of Sam's stuff out to store it in Grace's barn. John painted the kitchen. Mr. Austen expected to move in right away. Sam got a copy of a blank tenant lease form uptown for his new renter's signature.

Sam's own words...
Thursday, September 30, 1948 – "Dewey and Mildred here awhile this evening. Mrs. Theodore (Teddy) Roosevelt died today, age 87. At Langwell eight hours."

Warmth radiated from Sam's countenance, his face, and body, his whole being as he read Shirley's letter of October 1. She and Tommy were happy, and she had a good job doing mechanical and free-hand drawing. She expected to learn lithograph work later. Sam was as glad as she was that she was engaged in what was to her a pleasurable occupation.

The first fall frost carpeted the landscape on October 1. It was a sign for Sam to dig potatoes. He answered Shirley's letter and sent Betty a birthday card with $5 tucked inside. There wasn't anyone who could make much better use of money than Betty. She and Ed, with Jeanie, Gail, and Jimmy stopped in to see Sam, Grace, and Roy in the evening.

Gene Frost and Carrie left for St. Petersburg, FL, to see if they could make a go of it there. A quick letter from Shirley spoke of Tommy having malaria and a possibility of his having to go to the vet's hospital. She was still ecstatic about her job.

Sam harvested sunflower seed. For the next two weeks, he gleaned cabbage and root vegetables and cleaned off the garden to a fare-thee-well. Stacking wood in the shed went slowly because he worked eight hours a day at the Langwell Hotel.

Sam's own words...
Thursday, October 28, 1948 – "Forty-one years ago this morning, John Long and I left Galeton on our way to Roseburg, Oregon..."Of all the written materials that Sam had access to his eyes brightened the most at recalled memories of yore. He would always retain his memories of those times as he wrote them down again when they popped into fond thoughts and took him back to the way he had come. His faraway gaze ended in a smile as he returned to the present with his hand over his heart."

Roy's car engine stopped, refused to turn over at all. He and Sam used the bus to get to and from their Langwell Hotel jobs.

Democrat incumbent Harry S. Truman was elected president for a second term. The ongoing Cold War threat was the reason his peacetime draft had been carried on since July. Instability brought on by Stalin's threats brought the need for readiness.

A postcard from Shirley reported that she and Tommy were well. John expected to start for Florida in three weeks. Steele moved his dry cleaning business to Fifth Street in Elmira.

David was on a quick trip to sign for the sale of his lot on Mount Zoar Street and saw Steele. He said Hilda had an operation, and Little Douglas would soon have another one. They were having a tough time. Lucille told Sam that she had a letter from Shirley, which said she was laid off her job for awhile.

On November 18, Sam, Grace, and Roy saw *The Rose of Washington Square* starring Al Jolson, Alice Faye, and Tyrone Power. The

American musical drama film was set in 1920s New York City. The film focused on singer Rose Sargent and her turbulent relationship with con artist Barton DeWitt Clinton, whose criminal activities threaten her professional success in the Ziegfeld Follies.

The Elmira *Star-Gazette* carried a November 20 story about a rabies epidemic in Schuyler County near Watkins Glen. Mrs. Berry of Burdett was bitten on her leg when she defended her children, Nancy 12 and Eddie 13, from a rabid red fox. The broomstick she used had broken and her husband, Seward, killed the ferocious animal with a stick. The head of the mammal was sent to Cornell University for testing. Sam knew the Berry family who lived less than a mile from Ed and Betty. He may have had a concern about their close proximity while he clipped out the article and saved it.

Sam's own words...

Tuesday, November 23, 1948 - "Ed, Betty, and Teddy stopped here awhile on their way to Elmira for shopping. I was sure glad to see them. Teddy is getting to be a good size boy and can do as much as most men. Steele ate lunch with Grace and I (sic) and then was on his way in his truck for his dry cleaning. Received a postcard from Shirley. She hasn't had a paying job in about two weeks."

On Thanksgiving, Sam, Roy, and Grace had dinner in the blue room of the Langwell Hotel. After work, they all rode up to the farm where Sam stayed while Grace and Roy went on over to Ithaca to see their daughter, Ruth. John and Lucille were at Betty's. The children's hurried words and dancing feet delighted Sam. He did not have to wonder how they felt about their grandpa, and he felt the same about them. Grace and Roy benefitted from the children's good graces, too. Betty and Lucille prepared an excellent supper that everyone enjoyed.

A new card from Shirley said she was working again, but on a different job that she liked less than the previous one. Sam sighed. A job was important to have but also important to like the job you had. She was making more money, and no question, she liked that part of it.

John brought his daughter, Mickey, to visit. Sam could see that she was a pretty girl and was afraid she wouldn't see her father much after he and Lucille married and moved to Florida, which would be soon.

Sam's own words...
Monday, December 6, 1948 – "Fair morning, much colder evening. John was here. He will see Dr. Empert as he wants to get a leave of absence from work and needs the doctor to OK it. They want to leave for Florida in 10 days and me with them. I may do so."
Thursday, December 9, 1948 – "John and Lucille intend to marry next Monday and leave for Florida Friday. I have decided to go with them. Mr. McCartley, the hotel manager, and my boss, Ethel (don't know her last name) say they are sorry to lose me and if I ever want a job and they have an opening, I am sure to get it. At hotel eight hours..."

Sam pondered, "If he didn't take this opportunity to go south, when would another chance happen?" Besides, John could use his help with gas, oil, and tires. John had looming responsibilities, and Sam wanted him to succeed. It was John's and his chance together, and they'd see what they could make of it.

On December 13, Sam rode on Steele's dry cleaning pick-up and delivery route all day. They ate dinner with Ruthie and Sandra. Sam turned his efforts to the busy job of packing his belongings to move to Florida. Steele planned to take him up to Ed and Betty's mid-week for a goodbye.

It was quite a bit colder on Wednesday when snow arrived. The grand reception by the children at the farm was bittersweet for Sam. They were all aglow with excitement over the approach of Christmas. He would miss them.

Sam's own words...
Wednesday, December 15, 1948 – "...I wonder if sunshine and flowers will partly compensate for being away from so many of my dear ones."
Friday, December 17, 1948 – "We left Horseheads at 2:45 p.m., arrived in Wellsburg, Pennsylvania 4 p.m. where John and Lucille were united in marriage by the Baptist minister...Found lodging at a tourist home, paid $5.50 for it and $2.75 for supper at Bebee's Diner."

Lucille's four young boys coped well as the travelers moved on the next morning. A bad knock developed in the auto engine as they approached Keysville, VA, near cabins where they stopped for the night. They got the car to a garage Monday morning. It had a broken rod and worse. John and Sam figured they would be lucky to leave there by the next morning. Four days were gone, and it boosted the cost of $15 to $20 a day for food, gas, and lodging.

Sam busied himself with a newspaper that reported 20 inches of snow in NYC. Sam figured Horseheads had their share, too. They would soon put more distance between themselves and snow country.

The road stretched out ahead of them as Keysville was finally in the rearview mirror on Tuesday at 2 p.m. The soil had become sand and red clay as they neared Aiken, SC, on Tuesday evening. They'd been on the road seven days by the time they reached the camp where Gene and Carrie were 30 miles north of Tampa, FL. It was Christmas Eve. People were in shorts and shirt sleeves. Sam noticed the palm trees.

It was all strange to Sam, and he'd take awhile to decide if he liked it. Part of it was beautiful, but the swamps were not. A foray into Hattiesburg, MS, was a bonus because loved ones were there. Shirley was happy to introduce her father to her husband, Tommy, and his mother, Mrs. Broadhead, whose southern fried chicken tasted delicious.

Meanwhile, John, Lucille, and her four boys had ventured to Laurel, MS, to see her father, Mr. Pitts, whom she had not seen in years. Sam felt satisfied when he located Fred and Millie Southworth, whom he had known 40 years ago in the Idaho of 1909. Sam appreciated the locations close together, but he did not like the area.

They returned to Indian Rock Camp near Gene and Carrie. John was broke, and there seemed to be no prospect of a job in the vicinity. He and Sam worried what direction, what to do? Would they find their niche in this warmer climate?

33 – Florida Quest
1949, 1950

Sam wrote to Grace. She would be anxious to hear from him, and he was anxious, period. He reported to the unemployment office in Tampa while Gene and Carrie looked for work there. Sam gave Gene $3 for gas. The trip across the narrow, four-mile land strip, which was called the causeway between Clearwater and Tampa, was a new and enjoyable experience for Sam. He also liked the beautiful backdrop of the sunset over the Gulf behind the palm trees and flowers. In Tampa, they saw a banana boat from the Yucatan unloading and bought a whole stem of bananas for $1. Sam made a note of it to write to Grace about this part of his adventure.

John and Lucille would go out next to job hunt. One couple or the other had to watch the four little boys: Ray, Rex, Roy, and Johnnie. Lucille and Carrie found jobs. Gene was not looking for anything but a new place to go crabbing with his long pole net. He had paid zero support for the boys and surprise—no camp rent. John looked the hardest for employment but without success. Sam bided his time between boredom and occasional rides. Worry? Maybe.

Sam's social security check that kicked in on January 1, which was forwarded by Grace, caught up with him. It was $39.10 per month, which he was pleased to count on into the future. Lenore Crow's newsy letter also arrived, but neither his unemployment check nor his Holsec house rent came. It all contributed to unrest. The plan to stay in the south until warmer weather arrived up north meant they must find a house here in which to live. They went on the hunt for an affordable place.

Sam's own words...

Wednesday, January 19, 1949 – "At last we are going to have a home. John, Lucille, and I drove to Tampa today and finally located two and one-half acres about six miles west of the city center but within city limits. It is all cleared land with a small new house, unfinished but livable in this warm climate. It has city water and a small shed but no lights. It isn't grand now, but it has possibilities. We can at least be independent and by ourselves. The payments are such that I should have no trouble paying them, especially if I can get rent from my Elmira place as I should. Gene talks as though he is going to get a job right away. Suppose we will have the children, which will be alright (sic) if he will start to pay for their support. Expect to conclude the home deal tomorrow. Warm, fair."

Sam purchased the Jones Avenue, Tampa, FL, property from Mrs. Essie Hearsey. They drove to Saint Petersburg and bought four cots and four mattresses for $20. Another day Sam purchased a three-burner Perfection oil range with an oven, also a Savage electric washing machine for a total of $35.45. Mrs. Hearsey sold him three hens for $6. More essentials were needed, and Sam was the only one with any money. He and John went after gas for the car, oil for the cooking range, groceries, light switch, and fuses. Sam was not complaining and had enjoyed it all. He wanted John and Lucille to have a chance to succeed, and he was not likely to have been able to establish himself in Tampa without the help they all offered each other. It was not just money that was important. Still, it cost plenty, and there was no unemployment check or Holsec rent coming through.

Holsec had to have another renter because the young couple had moved out without paying and had taken a few of Sam's furnishings.

On Sunday, January 23, John and Sam went after an ax, shovel, hoe, and wire to connect to the meter box. These supplies cost $2.50. When they returned from Indian Rock to get Lucille and the boys, the hens and wire had been stolen. It discouraged all of them, but they would buy more wire. They must have electric. John needed to concentrate on finding a job, but there was work to do.

Sam went to see Mrs. Hearsey, who had sold him the place, to ask what he might plant that would be sure to grow. She confessed that she had taken the hens because her daughter insisted that the $2 she had sold them to Sam for was not enough. She returned his money. Sam shook his head. The hole in his bank account had grown, and that did not fill it.

Sam kept busy around the place, hoeing garden while John wired for electric. They had an elderly neighbor lady from whom Sam learned plenty about what to plant. Sam admired her healthy garden of tomatoes and corn, which she said could be seeded in now. She ought to know since she had been a resident for a long time. Sam saw only sand and no stones, so he was sure it was not New York state.

He felt like he'd had a big break January 28 as he spent not one dime that day.

The lights and water were turned on in Sam's name on January 29. Without a job, John was broke, blue, and discouraged. The employment service had no job to offer. His bad luck continued, but Sam got a boost. On February 7, Sam received word from Grace that Steele had rented the Holsec property for $30 per month.

John borrowed $75 and on Saturday, February 12, Sam and Lucille drove him to Seaboard depot where he departed for Elmira. John had to go back to his job. As soon as he could pay Mary up to date for child support and then send gas money to Lucille for the car, he would. Sam would support her and the three younger boys. The oldest son, Ray, was with Gene and Carrie and in school.

Sam remembered that it was Teddy's 16th birthday on February 13. He concentrated on his pleasant thought and worked in his garden with a hoe, rake, and labor.

Thick grass roots were dug to clean off the land, and a pit hollowed out to burn them up. He decided that he preferred New York rocks instead of those roots. It was 90 degrees in the sun.

It took John five days to get to Steele's in Elmira. He borrowed $100 from his insurance for sick benefits. Steele had John send the Holsec rent money along with his letter. The $30 was Sam's first intake of money except for the $39.10 per month for social security. It was as good to receive as the rain shower in his garden. The moisture was only one-half inch for the year, so far. The watermelon seeds' sparse sprouting made an unlikely location to make produce profit. It was a warm place to visit for a few months of winter.

Gene gave no child support. He, his wife Carrie, and his son, Ray, left for Elmira. The couple had asked to leave Ray but were turned down by John and Lucille. Sam had enough to support Lucille and the three boys, but he thought well of her and them.

Grace wrote that everyone in Horseheads had Florida fever now. Several of them wanted to come down right now but could not. She said maybe they would next fall.

Sam answered letters from Jeanie and Gail and blessed them for their loyalty and missing him. March 3 brought his 66th birthday around.

Sam visited his neighbor, Mr. Courtney, a 73-year-old carpenter. He talked to the old gentleman about installing wallboard on the walls and ceilings and also about installing a door. He felt the need for the more insulated walls because it was only 34degrees at 6:30 a.m. It warmed up to 80 by 1 p.m., but it didn't help the morning temperature. Mr. Courtney prepared a list of supplies needed to complete the job and would do it for 80¢ an hour. They rode in his truck to buy the items he had totaled up to cost $23.53.

John sent Lucille $100, which arrived on March 13. She set about mending, planning, and packing for her trip north. Sam worried about her with three children alone on the highways. The car needed to be greased and checked over.

Sam watered his overly ambitious garden and exclaimed, "It doesn't rain. It doesn't rain."

They bought one new tire and lubricated the car. Lucille and her children were on their way Wednesday, March 16. Sam, and no doubt John, would be nervous until she reached New York state safely. Her box and trunk had been sent on ahead when Mr. Courtney delivered them to the depot in his truck. Lucille had left the radio to Sam to keep him company, and he needed it.

Sam and Mr. Courtney had part of the renovation finished when Grace wrote that Lucille made it to New York in four days. It was quite a feat in light of several car repairs and her son, Rex, car-sick all the way. Sam made a slow, disbelieving shake of his head over her courage. He sighed deeply with the episode ending well.

Here he was in Florida as he had always wanted; a warm place without ice, snow, and cold. "It didn't rain. It didn't rain."

The days were 90 to 95 degrees and Sam's large garden required much water that did not fall from the sky. If not for the constant breeze it would be unbearable.

Sam rode with Mr. Courtney each week to get groceries. They got along fine.

Sam's own words...
Wednesday, March 30, 1949 – "Was certainly surprised today when the mailman delivered a box from home. Grace and Roy and no doubt others contributed. A book, magazines, a jack knife (lost mine), apples, Grace's brown bread, jam, candy, tobacco, a pipe, etc. and a note from Lucille telling about her trip and experience on the way to Elmira. It was mighty fine of all of them and did me a lot of good."

In April, Easter cards arrived from Frances Crippen and David Jr. Sam was glad to receive it except for no mention of how David was doing.

Sam's own words...
Thursday, April 28, 1949 – "...Grace says everyone is anxious for word from me...Was shocked to learn that Russell Voorheis, Ed's youngest brother (he was only 17) died last week. He had measles and caught cold. Also, was about a year older than Teddy, and they were great pals. It seems such a tragedy when young people die, and he was so full of life, healthy, and strong. My heart goes out to his people..."

Painting the new wall board in his little house kept him busy. He hoped to rent the place when he went north. Standing on his feet so long made them hurt more than they had back home. There was no certainty in his mind yet when he would return. His mind worked on a garden with stones, but here he had melon, rutabaga, and tomatoes in sand. It was May 7, not yet the time to plant in Horseheads. Black-eyed peas had done well, and a neighbor bought some for 70¢.

He was keeping two hens for Mrs. Hearsey and had one egg every other day.

His watermelon patch was beset with Hessian flies, aphids, and lack of rain. He had sprayed 65¢ worth of insecticide on it, had watered it faithfully. Even so, he had not competed well against the assault on his efforts. He vowed not to continue watering the plot but did not keep his own council.

The real estate men said he might get $20 a month and also have a tenant pay their utilities. He hoped they'd find a renter soon, and he would return to Horseheads.

Sam's own words...

Monday, May 30, 1949 – "Memorial Day in most of the nation but not in many southern states and Florida is one of them. They consider another day more significant: Confederate Memorial Day, April 26."

Sam placed an ad for rental of his house in the *Tampa Morning Tribune.* On Friday, June 3, a Mr. Tom Underhill rented it for $26.60 a month, to be handled by the realtor for $1.40 commission each month.

Mr. Courtney took Sam to pay his utility bills and arrange for transportation to New York state. Back in his Jones Avenue home, he sold a few melons to neighbors.

On Monday, June 6, Sam's tenant took him and his baggage to the bus station.

Arrival back in Elmira on Wednesday at 7 p.m. gladdened Sam as he hired a taxi for a $2 ride to Horseheads. He tipped his head back as he rode and thought he'd had quite an extended adventure. Now he was ready for a comfortable bed and good food at Grace's table.

He could not rest yet when there were so many on hand to welcome him home. Even Betty was there, also John and Steele. The next morning, Mildred and Mrs. Lodar came in Dewey's brand new Chevrolet car and took Sam for a ride.

Life picked up the same in Horseheads when Sam took up his hoe. It wasn't long before he went to the farm for a couple of days to be cheered by children and start fattening up on Betty's healthy food. He had lost 20 pounds working in the Florida sun. Grace would surely try to put it back on him, too.

Back row: Teddy Herforth Voorheis age 17, father — Edwin Voorheis age 33.

~**~

Middle row: Gail 8 ½, Edwin (Bucky) age 11, Jean 10 ½.

~**~

Front row: James 5 ½, Carol 4 ½, Linda 3 ½, Roland 1 ½, Mother —

Betty Voorheis age 33

Steele and Ruthie were having trouble. Nerves that had plagued Steele in the past flared again. Sam wondered how such things happened more these days and worried about the outcome for sweet little Sandra, too.

Sam went to his Holsec house to clean up around it and sweep it out. It was badly in need of weed removal and grass mowing, which he did. Steele took the physical exam for Reformatory guard. Sam hoped he would pass and get an appointment. Father's Day cards in mid-June brought greetings from all of Sam's children, including Willa.

Roy Whiting turned 70 years old on June 21, and Grace served strawberry shortcake. The three of them drove to Eldridge Park in Elmira and stayed until 10 p.m. when they were rained out. It would be good for Sam's dry garden.

Betty and Mrs. Arney Morgan visited at Grace's on June 24. They learned that Ed was having much of his hay baled right in the field from windrows, entirely different from the old way of hard work and long days.

~**~

In October of 1949, Steele got his guard job, which was an appointment at Green Haven Prison in Stormville, NY, 215 miles and 3½ hours away, near Poughkeepsie. His friend had the same appointment, and they would drive there together.

Steele and Ruthie were not living together.

The Moore Realty Company rented out Sam's Holsec Avenue house with an option to buy. It seemed like good news to Sam even if it was only rented. It eased the price of his payment.

November spelled cold weather, and Sam checked at the Greyhound bus terminal for the cost of the fare to Tampa. Buffalo had a 16-inch snowfall on November 16, but didn't purchase his ticket yet since he was unsure of when he wanted to leave for Florida. Sam had not even once missed the snow and cold while he was in Tampa.

Ed, Betty, and the children visited. They were soon to have electric on the Burdett farm. They wanted him to visit for Thanksgiving and came back after him on November 23. Sam went to Hornby, NY, for Christmas with David and Hilda. Poor little Douglas was in need of another worrisome kidney operation.

Sam wrote his 1949 closing memoranda.

"My idea of religion is one that banishes fear. Hell-fire and Eternal torture could never embody a just religion backed by a kind, ever-forgiving, and ever-loving God." He copied a poem onto the last diary page to end the year.

By Blair Rich

I thought I knew humility;
I didn't, not until
I heard a man speak well of me
Of whom I've spoken ill.

34 – Lenore from Idaho
1950

Betty had fantastic news, which arrived on a card from Lenore Crow. Lenore's son, Donald, lived in Virginia and she was coming to visit him. But first, she would arrive at Ed and Betty's farm for a stop-over visit on Tuesday, January 15. For Sam, it held disappointment due to his disappearing act—with departure to Florida. He would miss her visit. The ride to Florida with Frank and Mary Hess was planned for Friday, January 11. His eyebrows arched inward along with the slow back and forth of his head. What a shame to miss seeing Lenore: the chance to keep company with his sister, Mary, didn't come often enough and he did not wish to lose his ride.

The usual flurry of visits for family farewells ensued before the departure. January's below-zero temperatures allowed Sam, Frank, and Mary happy thoughts to take their leave to points south. The shared expenses gave savings to the three of them. Sam's $5 for gas and $2.50 lodging helped his smile as much as the warm sunshine did. Gas was 18¢ per gallon.

Later, Betty wrote to her father about her Aunt Lenore's visit as a pleasant day of getting acquainted. Everyone from adults to children had their favored impressions.

Lenore wrote to Sam: I am amazed at how well Betty and Ed care for their large family. Betty certainly has her hands full.

Nine and one-half-year-old Gail sat side by side with Great Aunt Lenore, nearly mesmerized. Her aunt had a black and white purse made from calf hide, which Gail was invited to touch. She liked the big over-shadowing flower adorned hat that her slim aunt wore. She wished her own pretty mama had one, too.

En route on the travel down south, the trio certainly heard, like everyone everywhere, about the Great Brinks Robbery. Eleven thieves stole more than $2 million from an armored car in Boston, MA.

Sam's Jones Avenue home in Tampa was a jungle outside with an overgrown weed situation he needed to conquer. First, he dug a hole in which to burn garbage and weeds, then the second one for his outhouse that had been blown over. It was important to accomplish the muscle work before the afternoon reached 80 degrees. Sam figured they may have had quite a wind because his mailbox, also battered, needed replacement. The new postal depository, groceries, and oil added up to $2.70. Two days later, it took another $1.05 for groceries and tobacco.

Sam's own words...
Friday, January 27, 1950 – "...Mary states they may start home to Addison, NY, Monday but will see me before they go. Cut and burned more weeds and went to the hardware, bought a toaster cord for 95¢ plus 3¢ tax."

Sam appreciated Grace's letters. She often included the *Elmira Telegram* and the Horseheads newspapers. Grace missed him, and he wrote bac k that he missed her, too. He read in those newspapers about Albert Einstein's warning that nuclear war could lead to destruction turning back on the United States from enemies.

Betty, Jeanie, and Gail wrote to Sam to express the same sentiments as Grace. They missed him.

Every couple of days, he took a 20¢ bus ride to Sulphur Springs where he bought groceries and Prince Albert tobacco, generally at a total cost of 70¢. On such a trip on February 9, Sam spent $3.17 on a gallon of paint and $3.65 for two brushes. He intended to paint the outside of his house.

Each month, as now, he sent $25 to Mrs. Essie Hearsey on his land contract for his small Florida abode. Shirley and Tommy Broadhead lived in New Orleans, LA, and wanted to visit him but could not get time off their jobs at the same time.

Sam's own words...
Saturday, February 18, 1950 – "I walked over to the grocery store located on the corner of Water and North Rome Avenue after a gallon of stove oil and 48¢ tobacco this morning. On my return about 9:30 a.m., I was struck by a car driven by a near neighbor of mine, a young man by the name of Hubert Waters. It broke the glass oil jug and lamed and shook me up considerable. The police came and wrote the particulars and Mr. Waters took me to the Tampa Municipal Hospital where they examined me. He took me back home. No bones were broken but I can 'just' manage to get around the house tonight. (I was facing the traffic, and he came up behind and struck me as he passed a parked car on his side of the road, although I was entirely off the macadam.) Mr. Roy Hammond, one of my best neighbors, came at 6:30 p.m. with my mail, which included Grace's letter and a postcard from Shirley that I was sure glad to get. He also got a pail of water for me and offered food, bless him, but I managed to prepare my own. (7 a.m. 30 degrees - 5:30 p.m. 57 degrees - Frost killed many things.)"

Independence was hard to let go of even when accepting help was reasonable and probably necessary. Hubert came to see him Sunday and felt bad about injuring Sam. His auto accident insurance did not cover hospital care as understood by the nurse at the hospital. The policy cost him $16 per year to cover his car. As sorry as the young man was, it left Sam shaking his head over his developing bruises and painful hobble.

Neighbors came over, Mr. Courtney with five pullet eggs, and Mr. Hammond with Sam's mail containing more letters from Shirley and Grace. The gestures from friends were helpful and appreciated.

Sam hobbled to the outhouse and back and managed to prepare supper. He got off his wounded limbs that felt worse after he put weight on them. All that was possible was to sit and answer letters, and did he ever have news to tell Grace and Shirley. Sam explained that he'd been well off the street on the side facing traffic, yet a car veered over from the opposite side of the road and hit him. What more could he say?

Mr. Courtney brought him a chair because all Sam had was a stool. Mr. Hammond brought the mail again and also carried in a pail of water. The only place Sam could go was to the little outback shed, which sat over a hole in the ground. His swollen legs and feet, until healed, would dictate his limits.

On Wednesday, February 22, the fifth day following the accident, Mrs. Hammond came over with slippers she had carved out of an older pair of her husband's shoes. She carried two pails of water. Her compassion was such, upon seeing the condition of Sam's legs and feet, that she phoned the Huberts and insisted that their son visit Sam. It was difficult for Sam to get around, and the slippers were a great help to him.

Two days later, a Christian friend, Mrs. Wagner, walked all the way from Kirby Street to bring homemade vegetable beef soup to Sam. "And was that soup good," Sam wrote.

Sam's own words...
Saturday, February 25, 1950 - "Shirley arrived about 2 p.m. after 21 hours on the bus. She expects Tommy tomorrow. Mrs. Hammond came over this p.m. and met Shirley. I am feeling better today. Perhaps Shirley being here helps."

Shirley had felt nauseated when she read her father's letter about the accident. She agonized over it being eight days since the mishap and she was just now able to be with him. Shirley carefully placed a hug as he sat with his swollen feet pointing out. She struggled to keep her tears under control.

She and Tommy had taken emergency leave to come to her father. Tommy arrived Sunday at 3 p.m. He and Shirley walked after groceries and eggs. Sam had real difficulty getting around and was sure that it would be a slow healing process.

On Monday, the two of them had done the washing for Sam. Tommy walked to Sulphur Springs and bought a chicken and more groceries. He fried up the bird, southern style. Mrs. Hammond heard all about it when she came over.

Shirley made up a warm foot soak for Sam, and afterward, Tommy rubbed his legs with alcohol. Tommy made him comfortable and ready for bed.

The Greyhound bus left at 5:30 a.m. Tuesday with Tommy on board, returning to his guard job. Shirley stayed to continue administering tender loving care to her father until her Sunday departure. They both enjoyed the numerous letters arriving from families in New York state.

After Shirley was gone, Sam could get around better than he had, but his legs throbbed at night from use and interfered with sleep. Mr. Hammond got his list of groceries, and Mr. Courtney brought the mail and water.

Sam's own words...
Wednesday, March 8, 1950 – "The Moore Realty Company of Elmira, NY mailed me an agreement by clients to purchase my Holsec Avenue property if I take nothing down and accept $40 per month at 6% interest. If I decide to do so, I will have to go before a notary and sign. I seem much improved today for which I am thankful."

On Saturday, Sam hired Mr. Courtney to take him to a notary. The out-of-state notary signature cost $1.50 before mailing to Moore Realty. It was Sam's opportunity to buy stamps as well. Groceries, writing paper, and gas for Mr. Courtney's car cost an additional $2.37. It was Sam's first trip away from his home in three weeks.

He was improving, but that night his leg was throbbing worse than ever and spoiled his sleep. By Tuesday, March 14, Sam walked to his mailbox and had the pleasure of seeing his tulips in bloom. He was able to plant three hills of muskmelons and was glad to be recovering. The next day he walked to the postal box again but when he hoed and planted two rows of collards and carrots, one leg ached. His face brightened when Mrs. Wagner came with oranges and eggs.

The Moore Realty company of Elmira sent a $30 check for the Holsec Avenue house payment. It would be $40 a month only after the sales commission became fully paid with a portion of each client payment. Sam was glad to receive his part.

Shirley was back on March 23 to spend time with her father. It was rather cold sleeping on a cot in the shed, so she brought the mattress in the house and slept on the floor. She and Sam were smiling to hear from Steele that he had gained 20 pounds since the start of his guard job last October, and he was feeling fine. They walked after $4.85 in groceries and found a 50¢ cookbook. Shirley's time was soon gone, and she returned to Tommy in New Orleans.

Sam's radio provided comfort as he listened to Easter programs. Willa and her girls sent cards, among many others, to include Frances and David Jr. He couldn't help wondering how the little guy was, but she only signed their names.

Sam's own words...
Wednesday, April 19, 1950 – "Was glad to get a fine letter from Arthur Crow this afternoon...He says he does some writing for a magazine and a lot of correspondence, thus helping himself from entirely rusting out. Said he was not much good physically, but eyes are good, and his brain still functions. Bless him. Wishes he could come and bach with me, but I am too far away. I wish he could, too."
Thursday, April 20, 1950 – "Received a nice letter from Shirley. When she left Tampa, her skin eruptions, which have troubled her for some time, were much improved. She says it is getting worse since she returned to New Orleans and she may have to visit Florida again. Wrote to Arthur Crow, went to the store..."

Letters between them would have to satisfy the two elderly bachelors. They were both communicators. But did they take care of the detail to determine who would notify the last one standing about the other's demise? It may have been a nostalgic thought on Sam's part to remind himself that Arthur was almost 79 years old, and hinself only 67.

Sam bought groceries, oil, and tobacco for $2.40 and paid his 95¢ electric bill.

Sam's own words...
Monday, May 1, 1950 – "Received letter from Hilda and a card from Gail. The doctors tell David and Hilda that little Dougie isn't going to be with them very long now. Brave little tyke, he has put up a brave fight, but if he

must go, God bless him and help strengthen David and Hilda...God bless them all, Amen. I did my washing and wrote to John and Lucille."

Tuesday, May 2, 1950 – "...While waiting for a bus to take me to Sulfur Springs, I watched men and women voting under a tree, which surprised me. No voting machine there. Paid my water bill ($1.65) and mailed a letter to David and Hilda. 87 degrees." (dinner, bus, etc. 71¢)"

Much of Sam's water pipe was on top of the ground, and he began to dig a trench one foot deep next to it. If he lowered the pipes and buried them, he hoped to have cooler water. It was not a one-day job, but he kept at it.

A sweet card from Jeanie, who would be 11 years old in a few days, had Sam nodding as he smiled and visualized her enthusiasm over the baby lambs that she thought were so cute.

Sam's own words...
Saturday, May 6, 1950 – "...Mrs. Hammond gave me a tall glass of iced tea and some guava sauce, which sure hit the spot. I haven't an ice box, and my water is so warm it doesn't quench my thirst. 87 degrees (groceries, eggs, lunch, bus, $2.55)"

Monday, May 8, 1950 – "...I did not live the life of a hermit today for I walked down to Mrs. Wagner's this a.m. and we went to Tampa and saw the movie "Cheaper by the Dozen," which Grace wanted me to see. We visited stores, ate in a restaurant, and had a fine time. Am sure we both enjoyed every minute...A needed shower this evening."

The lack of an ice box and therefore no ice was also the reason Sam could not store perishables; therefore, he walked to the grocer often. A new electric refrigerator cost $325 and may have made a second-hand one pricier than he would consider to purchase.

Cheaper by the Dozen was a 1.5-hour comedy based on the real-life story of the Gilbreth family. It follows them from Providence, RI, to Montclair, NJ, and details the amusing anecdotes found in large families. Frank Gilbreth, Sr. was a pioneer in the field of motion study and often used his family as guinea pigs (with amusing and sometimes embarrassing results). He resisted popular culture, railing against his daughters' desires for bobbed hair and cosmetics. Sam's friend, Mrs. Wagner, had two prospects who wanted to rent a place and was trying to interest them in Sam's home so he could go north. He was eager to leave.

Tommy and Shirley had their tickets to leave for New York state on June 5. She had quit her job for health reasons, mainly a skin condition not yet identified. Tommy planned to find a job near Horseheads because Shirley's family lived there.

Sam's $30 (after commission $10 deducted) check from Moore Realty arrived regularly to pay for the purchase of his Holsec Avenue house in Elmira, NY. With the means to leave, he was anxious to end his self-imposed exile and go home. The temperature, which hovered between 88 and 92 degrees, was pushing him northward. Grace's letter beckoned him because she'd had her garden plowed and harrowed, and if it got planted, Sam would be the one to do it. He thought of Dewey and sent him a card for his June 2 birthday celebrating 52 years.

Sam heard over his radio that President Harry S. Truman, on June 27, ordered military forces to aid in the defense of South Korea. He shook his head at the thought of American boys and girls entering the Korean war.

He had hung on longer in Tampa, hoping to find a renter, but had no luck. Finally, at the cost of $30.73, the bus ticket was purchased. Sam thanked all of his friends and neighbors again for their kindness after his pedestrian and car accident. His departure was Monday, July 3, at 8:55 a.m. Horseheads was in his sights by Wednesday, July 5, at 12:50 p.m. The trip on the Greyhound involved little sleep. Sleep, sleep, sleep, in a comfortable bed, was Sam's biggest need. How he enjoyed sinking into the mattress.

The rounds of visits to his children's families began. The dinner at the farm was a wonderful welcome when he arrived to ovations from the children. He had a surprise for them. His trip to the store for a $1.40 dessert item and candy before he left Horseheads, was what he shared after the meal, and was a big hit.

Back in Horseheads, Sam tackled the garden for Grace. It needed cultivation and weeds burned. He had enough experience to proceed. He paid Grace $5 for room and board.

Little Douglas Crippen was not well, and then he had whooping cough. David and Hilda experienced angst over the added assault on his small, weakened body. Sam rubbed the back of his neck and beseeched God to help him, according to His will.

Sam wrote to the Social Security Administration in Baltimore, MD, to have his check for August come to Horseheads. He walked over town to mail it and spent $1 on a haircut and tobacco.

Sam was as glad to be back as was Shirley. Tommy had gotten a job at the Remington Rand right away. They stayed with John and Lucille temporarily.

There were 50 in attendance at the July 16 Crippen reunion, but Dave and Hilda were not among them. Douglas was too ill. Steele, too, was absent, unable to get time off from his guard job at Green Haven Prison in Stormville, NY.

Sam worked regularly in the garden hilling up potatoes and dallying his hoe around all those vegetables. Prince Albert attended as usual. Sam lit his pipe and leaned on his hoe when he needed a rest.

Shirley and Tommy Broadhead rented an apartment house across the street from Sam, Grace, and Roy. What could be better for them? They had cleaning and painting to do before they could occupy the rooms. Broadheads had a refrigerator and could store ice cream, which they were fond of sharing. Shirley had acquired a part-time telephone operator job in Horseheads.

Sam again worked as a janitor for the Village of Horseheads beginning on September 21. He was filling a vacancy for a person who was out on sick leave.

Sam's own words...
Wednesday, September 27, 1950 – "...Grace, Roy, and I listened to the fight between Joe Louis and Ezzard Charles. Louis lost the 15 rounds on decisions and was badly beaten. I was at town hall job."

Roy was on the edge of his seat "helping" with the blow-by-blow dance of the boxers, on behalf of the champ, the American, Louis, who was called the Brown Bomber. Grace and Sam exchanged amused glances over the spectacle.

Betty and her girls came to the city for shoe shopping on Saturday,

September 30. Gail and Jeanie showed off their new white shoes. Betty had red ones. Bucky had sold the buck lamb he'd raised and paid for his mother's new footwear. Ed, Teddy, age 17, and Bucky (12) were filling the silo.

Sam had a gleam in his eye as he told Grace and Roy about his paycheck. "I have worked 10 days," he explained, "but the check was for more. I brought it to the attention of the town clerk, and she says I have done 15 days' work in 10." It was quite a compliment, and the money was his, no mistake made.

Sam's own words...
Friday, October 6, 1950- "Today was a red letter day for me. I have received my social security check, $39.10 per month. It may not seem like so much, but I can depend on that amount regularly, and it is a God send (sic)..."

No doubt Sam thought his lot to be easier than his father's had been in his declining years. Sam appreciated the regularity of the check.

Dewey, Mildred, and Mitzy, their black-and-white bulldog, often came to Grace, Roy, and Sam's. They visited Ed and Betty at the farm as often. Most, but not all, of the children liked the rotund little canine who could snap or nip if you got too close to her portly "parents." The children were safe because they did not invade closer to their great uncle and aunt than Mitzy's comfort zone allowed.

Sam consistently paid Grace $7 per week.

In late November, he sold Mrs. Bowers a pair of shoes. A victory fist wasn't exactly thrust into the air, but Sam was quite happy to have the sale. He could buy Christmas cards and postage stamps for all of his holiday greetings from the commission. He wrote several of them each day and sent them piecemeal. Willa and Lee had posted theirs already. Frances wrote that David Jr. was growing fast and remained a good scholar. How Sam wished he could see him, even a picture.

But he did see several of Betty's children on December 29, when she, Ed, and Bucky came by to drop off Teddy, almost age 18, and Gail, 10 years old, to stay three days with Aunt Shirley and Uncle Tommy. Ed and

Betty went over to Big Flats, NY, where Ed bought two cows to add to his milk herd.

Three of Teddy's friends, neighbor boys, came in a car to pick him up for an evening. Gail and Aunt Shirley were content to draw pictures and cut out paper dolls on the last day of the year.

35 – Time Advances
1951, 1952

Things do change slowly as time advances, but in 1951 much was still the same. Sam was pleased to receive correspondence from his widow friend, Mrs. Wagner, from Tampa, FL.

Sam's own words...
Friday, January 1, 1951 – "...They are having cold weather for Florida, but she has a good supply of wood that an old black, John, keeps cut for her. She surely accepts good and ill with a fine spirit."

Even on Sunday, Sam walked to Horseheads town hall three times to tend the furnace and shovel sidewalks. Heavy snow was coming down, and he hoped to get ahead of it for Monday when it was his job to have it cleaned early. He considered it an old-fashioned winter when he faced another nine inches of fluff on Monday morning.

Sam's room and board increased to $8 per week.

Steele came to town for a few days and was downhearted at failed attempts to find his daughter with Ruth's parents in Elmira. She was being kept from him. What in the world had Ruth told them to make them act this way? He had to return to Stormville. No doubt he knew firsthand how his brother, David, felt about not knowing where David Jr. was. A post office box was not a place he could visit, just somewhere in a vague proximity of the vast city where his son was kept from him.

Sam's weekly paycheck from Horseheads Village increased from $50 to $55. Gail sent Grandpa a letter through Ed and Betty when they visited him.

Sam's own words...
Thursday, January 18, 1951 – "I was tickled when I received a dear little letter from Jeanie. I guess she doesn't intend to let Gail get all the laurels. Bless them both..."
Saturday, January 20, 1951 – "Shirley's 29th birthday. She and Tommy had Alice and Roy Jeffrey, Grace and me over for sandwiches, cake, and coffee in the evening. Twenty-nine years ago we were living in Johnson Hollow, and Edith never had good health after Shirley's birth."

Sam reminisced about Edith when memories stirred him. He dusted them off and thought lovingly of her. John Long's 69th year was remembered and acknowledge by a birthday card Sam sent to him.

Frank and Mary traveled down to Zephyrhills, FL, to buy a home. Iva and Lynn accompanied them. On February 8, they sent word to Sam that Florida was having its coldest winter in years. He had no plans to go down yet and was unsure of making it this year.

The current news made sense to Sam. On February 24, the 22nd amendment to the United States Constitution, which limited presidential election to two terms of office became ratified. A week later, the news lit up red, a red scare about Julius and Ethel Rosenberg, who were to stand trial on charges of conspiracy to commit espionage. The Cold War spies remained suspects in passing secrets about the atomic bomb to the Soviet Union. They upstaged the familiar news that American boys were still involved in the Korean War.

Sam's 68th birthday arrived along with many cards and well wishes for March 3 and all year. He planned to send the same lofty sentiments to Willa and Lee for their March 19 birthdays.

John was in need of a car and tried out a Pontiac and later a Kaiser 48. There was no decision yet.

Sam's own words...
Tuesday, March 20, 1951 – "...Lucille was here this evening with a Hudson Six, which I think she and John will buy..."

Wednesday, March 21, 1951 – "...Was glad to get an Easter card from Frances and David Jr. and especially a photograph of him. He is a fine looking boy, and I believe he is about 12 years old. I should like very much to see him again. Teddy's high school class is going to Washington, DC, and he is going with them."

Hudson introduced the Narrow Block Big Six engine line in 1948. The 2½-year-old car wasn't heavy duty but the price was right and would get John and Lucille to work and back.

Sam's own words...
Thursday, May 22, 1951 – "John came this evening and told us that David and Hilda's little Douglas died today. He was hospitalized this morning as he had been many times before but his physical life could not be prolonged this time. May God sustain David and Hilda and the children in their loss and know he has gone to the land where little children never die or suffer pain or disease."

Sam's heart bled for David and Hilda. David had steeled himself against the harsh blow; one son lost to death and his first born stolen from him at 8½ years of age. David had since heard only the small snatches of information about David Jr. that his father or his sister, Shirley, could gather. It was sparse and unsure. Frances strung them along on thin threads. Dave had no recourse available. He figured her actions punished Little David as much as himself.

Grace and Sam accompanied John up to Betty's on Friday evening to let them know of six-year-old Douglas's death. When they had brought Grace home, Sam went with John to Dave and Hilda's to find them feeling their loss deeply. David's sunken sockets held no tears in his somber silence. He seemed to have turned inward to suffer stoically. He could not speak of it. Hilda was an open wound.

Steele came the next day. John, ever a faithful brother, surprised him by bringing Sandra. She and her father became inseparable when they had the chance.

Sam's own words...
Friday, April 6, 1951 – "Shirley was refused employment at the Eclipse because of her skin problem, which has been troubling her off and on for a long time..."

As Sam planted early peas, he may have wondered if he had conveyed enough reassurance to Shirley. Her raised eyebrows and hurt look when she told him the reason given to her for the job refusal showed how terrible it had made her feel. Could either of them have yet known that this was psoriasis? So little was known that many thought it was contagious when it was not. This lack of medical understanding may have originated a term: The Heartbreak of Psoriasis. It would be 1960 before coal tar shampoo and creams were employed to help somewhat but limited.

Sam planted a few cabbage and tomato seeds.

Sam's own words...
Wednesday, April 11, 1951 – "President Truman removed General Douglas Mc Arthur (sic) from command of the Army in Japan and Korea. The U.S. Congress is in an uproar. We are living in dangerous times, and opinions are divided. We must decide on a course at least and stay with it. Tommy and his boss are fishing this evening..."
Thursday, April 12, 1951 – "President Truman talked to the nation on the radio last night explaining his reason for firing General Mc Arthur (sic). It seems the majority of public opinion is against his argument, upholding the General. It appears his decision was rather drastic and unfair to the average man in the street and some in high places. Received a sweet letter from David Jr. He wants me to tell him about my place in Florida. I must do so. Rainy."

Tommy fished off and on for a week and put his catches in the freezer until he had enough to serve a fish supper to include Grace, Roy, Sam, and a couple of neighbors.

Sam read the MacArthur news and smiled. General MacArthur left the flower scented hospitality of Hawaii on April 17, to embark on his stern mission to challenge Congress on the views of the president who had fired him over war policy. His plane, the Bataan, took off for San Francisco and Washington. San Francisco cheered; Congress listened.

Sam's own words...
Sunday, April 20, 1951 – "New York City went wild over Mc Arthur (sic) today. An estimated one and a half million people turned out to welcome him."

Steele entered the hospital in early May for another hernia operation, which took a few weeks for recovery. It was harder to face because his marriage was in shambles.

Sam's life consisted of janitor work, gardening, and enjoying his grown children and grandchildren. His job, social security old-age pension, and the Holsec house payment brought in a reliable income preserved by his frugality.

The house remuneration was $40, social security $39.10, and his janitor job $220 ($55 a week). The regularity of the $299.10 per month brought the same satisfaction as his garden and tobacco.

Sam's own words...
Monday, June 18, 1951 – "John and I drove over to David and Hilda's place near Hornby, NY, in the early evening. We had a grand visit, and they have a TV set, best I ever saw. The only one I saw before is one the firemen have at the town hall, and the pictures are unclear most of the time."

Sam realized there weren't many households with TV sets, at least not near him. A brand-new black-and-white console price of $339.95 added up to more than he made in a month. He would never fathom that television broadcasting stations and networks in most parts of the world would upgrade from black and white to color transmission in the 1960s and 1970s.

Sam received Father's Day cards galore. Willa did not forget him, ever. Roy Whiting's similar Father's Day tidings competed with his June 21st birthday as he turned 72 years old.

Mrs. Wagner in Florida had facilitated the rental of Sam's house in Tampa. It would help him pay the $25 payment on it to Mrs. Hearsey from whom he'd purchased the property. He was pleased.

Sam's own words...
Monday, June 25, 1951 – "Had our first peas out of the garden, cultivated. John, Shirley, and I drove up to Odessa in the evening and attended the Odessa Central School Commencement exercises and saw Teddy and about 40 other students receive their diplomas. Ed and Betty insisted we drive over to the farm for coffee and cake, which we did, also enjoyed the visit."

On Friday, June 29, after work, Teddy drove Tommy, and Shirley in his car as far as Washington, DC, where they parked it. The rest of the trip was by train to Hattiesburg, MS, where they arrived on July 2. They visited Tommy's family. Four days later they were back to attend the Crippen reunion at Ed and Betty's farm in Bennettsburg, NY.

Sam's own words...
Monday, July 9, 1951 – "Teddy is staying with Shirley and Tommy. He found a job at the National Homes plant today, goes to work tomorrow on the same shift. Tommy works from 3 to 11 p.m. I hope he does well and feel sure he will. Am afraid Ed, Betty, and children will miss him very much and no doubt he will miss them. He might be called into the Army soon if the world situation doesn't improve. God knows we hope to avoid a third world war. The U.S. already has 70 thousand casualties in what we call the Korean situation of only one-year-old. Very warm."
Thursday, July 12, 1951 – "Ed came to Horseheads to trade his Farmall Combine toward an Allis Chalmers. Betty and the children came with him and were here awhile. They all miss Teddy. Roland (age 4) says he has been gone long enough and will have to go home..."

Sandra had long since captured her father's heart. She turned nine years old on Friday, July 13.

Sam was shocked to learn of the passing of Mrs. Elsie Hearsey back on July 1. He received a letter from a Tampa lawyer informing him to make future house payments to her daughter, Mrs. Winifred H. Mc Gill, her only heir.

Sam bought tobacco at $1.44, along with postage and medications for $2.14, when he picked up his shoes with repairs costing 95¢.

Roy drove home a 1941 Chevrolet on Monday evening, August 20. He intended to trade his 1936 Oldsmobile for it and pay the difference. Sam thought it seemed like a good car.

Mrs. Wagner had been sending Sam his rent money of $20 per month for his Tampa house, at times piecemeal. But he received it.

Sam's own words...
Saturday, August 25, 1951 – "...Mrs. Wagner used poison to kill ants in her house, and she said it nearly killed her, but she is OK now. She was 73 years young August 14."

Just like Mrs. Wagner, Edith had been five years older than Sam. He may still have been contemplating his compatibility with Mrs. Wagner. Months earlier, the thought of asking her to marry him had been put in limbo without his mention of it before the return north. Perhaps the stay in Horseheads for the whole winter, instead of traveling south, served him to reconsider. Maybe he thought it would complicate coming back north every summer. Couldn't they remain friends without encumbrance? Weren't things fine the way they were?

The last day of August had been unusually hot. A switch seemed to have been pulled the next day when it was 30 degrees lower and required a coat.

Sam's own words...
Wednesday, September 5, 1951 – "Teddy came over this evening, and I knew there was something he wanted to ask me. Finally, after Grace and Roy went to bed, I made it easy for him by asking if he wanted to see me about anything. He told me about his chance to buy a Ford Coupe at less than it was worth because the young owner was enlisting in the Army. Teddy didn't have enough money, but another lad who did would buy it, but Teddy had a first chance until tomorrow. Of course, I loaned what he needed. He has a good job, works every day, and is trustworthy. Bless him."

Sam and Teddy cemented the $80 exchange and promise with a handshake. Sam wrote it in his ledger tablet under Teddy Herforth Voorheis in a calm manner, relishing the satisfaction of taking part in his oldest grandson's big step. Teddy showed off his first car to Grandpa when he drove in with it the next evening.

Sam received a letter on September 8 from Mrs. Wagner saying they were having a terribly hot summer in Tampa. She hoped to get away summers after this one. Was the lady hinting her amicable thoughts to going north like Sam, with Sam, because of Sam? Did she hope her words could help him think about a proposal?

His brain may have synced with her exciting company for a time. Had she reminded him of Edith or a younger self? Had he come to his understanding that there was no replacement? Mrs. Wagner may have become an intrusion on Sam's fondest memories. As time had passed, he was back to himself, comfortable. Sam felt the quiet, embraced the quiet, was the quiet. He connected deeply with the reverent man that he was inside. Was his labor in the rich dark earth enough for him?

Sweet corn from Sam's garden went well with fresh tomatoes and potatoes. Grace, Roy, and Sam took a selection of all of the produce up to the farm. Betty fried beef steak taken from the freezer and what a meal and visit they all had. The children were breathless with excitement as usual to see them.

Dewey and Mildred enjoyed the sweet corn Sam gave them the next day. Steele and Sandra came to visit before he returned to guard duty in Stormville.

On Thursday, September 25, it rained all morning and stopped Ed from silo work. All of the children except the youngest, 4½-year-old Roland, were in school when they came to visit Sam. He gave Rolly a treasure of several empty Prince Albert cans, perhaps with instructions to share half of them with his sister, Linda, who was almost 6 years old, for she liked the red containers, too. In a few minutes, the little guy tried to make a deal for his grandfather's pocket knife. Sam had to turn away for a moment to collect himself on that one. A wide grin was sufficient as he shook his head. Every wishful boy wants a pocketknife, but Rolly was much too young.

Sam dug potatoes. On September 27, Teddy returned $30 to Sam on the car loan. It had only been three weeks since the initial transaction, reason enough for both of them to feel uplifted. All spuds were dug and stored in the cellar by the time double frost hit on September 29 and 30.

Sam's own words...
Tuesday, October 9, 1951 – "Raked our lawn, did my janitor work..."
Wednesday, October 10, 1951 – "Betty, Ed and Roland came. Today is Betty's birthday and am sorry to say it completely slipped my mind. On this day 36 years ago we were putting up our third cutting of alfalfa near Buhl, Idaho. The years have gone by bringing both joy and sorrow, but I have so much to be thankful for. I have our three sons and two daughters and many fine grandchildren, but I miss Edith so much."

Sam rubbed his jaw as he thought of her. The pain he felt had gotten worse and reclaimed his attention. His last six teeth needed attention from Dr. Brooks. The dentist treated him, and Sam vowed to have them pulled when his mouth was not quite so sore. Two days later, Dr. Brooks lanced the jaw. The ulcerated teeth were on the path to less pain for Sam. It was a good thing because when he woke up Thursday, November 1, he had his neuralgia to groan over as he reached back to rub a sore muscle. He shook his head when he looked out on two inches of snow. It was too soon to suit him. Saturday added five more inches and several hours of shoveling sidewalks around city hall. Temperatures had dipped.

Dr. Brooks pulled three of Sam's teeth Monday. Sam paid $8.

Sam's own words...
Monday, November 5, 1951 – "Mrs. Sweeney, our neighbor who lives upstairs over Tommy and Shirley, is very ill. She needs a doctor, but they belong to some cult that doesn't believe in human physicians. They are praying, and I am praying. I believe in spiritual help but also that God uses his creation to help him, including doctors. God's will be done. Quite cold this evening."
Tuesday, November 6, 1951 – "It is ten degrees above zero this morning. Mrs. Sweeney is still very ill...Dewey and Mildred were here awhile in the evening."
Wednesday, November 7, 1951 – "Neighbor indignation finally insisted on calling the Red Cross nurse and Dr. Norman Gridley, public health physician."

Mrs. Sweeney was taken in the Barbers ambulance to the TB sanitarium. She has had several hemorrhages. God's will be done for her and Mr. Sweeney, too."

Sam's $40 from Moore Realty arrived, and he took it and his $55 from the janitor employment to the bank.

About 200 of the employees of National Homes plant in Horseheads walked out on strike. Tommy and Teddy's jobs were affected, and they had no work.

Sam's own words...
Friday, November 9, 1951 – "...The mystery of the disappearance of Shirley's kitten, Boots, about two weeks ago was solved today. It was found

dead on the railroad bank, perhaps killed by several dogs in our neighborhood..."

Tommy and Teddy drove up to Ed and Betty's. Sam supposed they would help Ed and do some hunting. National Homes settled the strike, and work resumed Monday.

Dewey, Mildred, and their wise little dog, Mitzy, came to visit. Many considered the dog spoiled.

Sam had a set of elderly neighbors, Rip and Helen Rackett. The colder weather caused a difficulty for Rip to get outside in his lamed up condition. It was painful to watch, and Sam could not just look on while he prayed for both of them. Wishing to alleviate the situation, he took it upon himself to go over and chop wood.

The firemen planned to have a December 15 Christmas party at town hall. The way the snow was coming down, Sam saw shoveling in his immediate future along with clean up after the seasonal celebration. He was already putting in more trips to walk over town and tend the furnace. The temperature was much lower, around zero he thought, but he could not be sure since a neighborhood boy had broken their thermometer.

Sam's Christmas spirit was in good shape as he sent out greeting cards. Many holiday wishes of good cheer were arriving in the mailbox for him. The notes and letters were a great pleasure to Sam, but one outspoken message was no pleasure at all.

Sam's own words...
Wednesday, December 19, 1951 – "...Cretia thinks I'm not being fair to Grace and Roy, especially to Grace; that they are getting old and should be able to enjoy their home by themselves, that Grace shouldn't have to get three meals a day, do my washing, ironing, and mending: Also, that I'm getting much more than I'm paying for and should go to my Florida home and stay during the winter at least. I don't feel it to be an honest judgment, and I don't believe Grace thinks I am imposing on her in any way. God knows I hope not."

Happy holidays from Cretia, who may have been jealous because she was not favored above Sam. Probably she went about it the wrong way to talk around the real reason, which may have been her fear of being a senior woman alone in Pennsylvania. Cretia wanted to be where Sam was and she needed him out of the way.

Technically, Sam didn't work Sunday, not janitor work, but he walked over town four times to add fuel to keep the furnace burning. Another fire for an elderly neighbor needed to keep its flame. Sam split wood for Rip Rachett on December 23.

Teddy and Tommy received plump turkeys from National Homes on December 24. Teddy gave his to the Mott family on their street. They had many children. Tommy went up to the farm with Teddy on Christmas Eve as they both delivered gifts. Aunt Shirley loved to shop and had a hand in helping Teddy with his.

They had a foot of snow for a white Christmas.

Sam showed Mr. Milton Barker how to do the town hall job to take his place when Sam looked forward to take his leave January 1. He had a good opinion of his replacement by the time he had familiarized him with janitor work and furnace care. Sam still needed to hear from his Tampa neighbors to know that his place was vacant so he could go south.

He bought Prince Albert and matches for $1.35 along with medicine, postage, and gifts for another $5.85. The keys to town hall were turned over to Milton Barker on December 31.

Sam's earnings for 1951 totaled $2,301.70. He may not have known that it was below the national average of $3,700 for the year.

~**~
1952

Sam's own words...
Wednesday, January 2, 1952 – "...Grace received a letter from Mary Hess saying they ate their Christmas dinner under a grapefruit tree at their place in Zephyrhills, Florida...Helped with washing and split wood for Rip Rachett. Poor old fellow. He can hardly get in and out of the house."
Thursday, January 3, 1952 – "Four or five inches of snow fell last night, and I had sidewalks to shovel off. Wrote to my Tampa neighbors, the Roy Hammonds, to find out if tenants have left my house yet. Spent $1.60 at the post office and barber shop. Split more wood for Rip Rachett. Dewey and Millie were here awhile last evening."

Sam wanted to cut the wood supply ahead for his elderly neighbor. He didn't know who would do it if he left for Florida.

Teddy paid $50 to his grandfather, the balance of his loan. It would have been hard to tell which of them had a more satisfied countenance. If there were a personal measuring stick, each for the other, it would have been pretty tall in either case.

Sam received the books, finally, that he had ordered for Betty's children for Christmas. He asked Teddy to deliver them since he was going up to the farm. Gail sent a little thank you note back with big brother.

A letter came from Mrs. Wagner January 8, saying his Tampa house had no tenants. Sam was still in town for Grace's 67th birthday. She and Roy went to Dewey and Mildred's to have supper and cake. Sam was half sick with a cold and declined the invitation.

Sam had a tentative plan to leave for Florida on January 15 but had not purchased a ticket yet. He was offered a ride down for the 24th with Dewey and Mildred. Theirs was the most compelling invitation, which he accepted. What were a few more days? He wrote to his Tampa neighbors to let them know of his impending arrival.

His cold, or maybe the flu, hung on to keep Sam from feeling his best. Shirley got him some Histoplus, and he felt a bit better by evening. He was well enough to enjoy her 30th birthday the following night. Rounds were made to all of his children's families because he wouldn't see them for a long while.

Dewey, Millie, and Sam rolled down the highway at 8 a.m., January 24, in Dewey's new Mercury. Frank and Mary greeted them two days later on Saturday at 3:30 p.m. in Zephyrhills, and all was well. It was Monday when Dewey took Sam 30 miles to Tampa. They stopped at the utility companies and Pasley grocery. The last stop was Mrs. Wagners for Sam's keys.

Sam awoke in his cabin Tuesday, January 28. His window shades were missing, and his stove was a mess. He wished he hadn't rented it to anyone. His distaste softened when Mrs. Hammond and her two children next door invited him for supper. Sam hastened to accept. Mrs. Hammond had walked to the mailboxes on her way over and handed him letters from Shirley and Lucille. Tiredness had taken its toll, but a friendly chat during an enjoyable supper had him relaxed.

Mr. Hammond had a discussion in mind. He wanted to fence off part of Sam's vacant lots and use the space to pasture two or more yearlings. Sam agreed because it would keep weeds down and save him considerable grub work. They'd both benefit.

On Wednesday, Sam walked to the hardware and bought a broom, light bulbs, and a screwdriver, all for $2.25. Incidentals added $4.88, probably screws and plenty of etcetera.

Thursday, January 31, was a busy day of cleaning up the shed. The tenants had turned it into a chicken coop. They'd punched out big holes in the side and made pens. What a mess it was.

Sam's spirits were lifted Friday after a one-hour visit from Dewey, Millie, and Mary. His sister brought grapefruit, which she had picked from her tree for him.

It was Sunday, February 3, by the time Sam walked down to Kirby Street to see Mrs. Wagner. He was not the only guest. Her cousin, Mrs. Warren and her husband, as well as Mrs. Warren's niece and her husband sat down to a good supper and lively chat. Sam returned home at 7:20 p.m.

He was immediately surprised by a horn heard out front. There came Mrs. Mabel Packard walking toward him. He had talked to her recently in Horseheads. She would be another friendly face in Florida for as long as she stayed.

As busy as he was getting his place in shape, the mail, when he had any, was a welcome sight. Monday's envelopes were from Shirley, Betty, and Gail, also sweet little notes from Carol, Linda, and Roland. Sam's eyes sparkled and lit up his face from the warmth enclosed in every I love you. Betty mentioned their cold New York weather at 15 below zero. Sam appreciated his current 70 degrees.

Sam's own words...
Wednesday, February 6, 1952 – "...Went to Sulphur Springs after groceries and a butcher knife...Did hardly any work around home. Bought vegetables from Hammonds and made a stew, also some fertilizer from the same place. King George VI died this morning."

King George VI was the great-grandson of Queen Victoria. In the mid-1920s, he had speech therapy for a stammer that he never fully overcame. Sam and most Americans knew the story of the 57-year-old British Commonwealth king. Sam took notice of the news about the USA's first use of a mechanical heart for the first instance of a patient survival of heart surgery. The heart pump kept the patient alive for 50 minutes while his own heart was repaired. Its success soon made open-heart surgery a common practice.

Sam's groceries, oil, tobacco, hardware, bus, and etcetera came to $3.69.

Dewey, Millie, Frank, and Mary stopped in for a 45-minute visit Thursday. It was Sam's last visit from Dewey before he and Millie's return to Horseheads, NY. They delivered Sam's four chairs that were worth the $4 he paid previously. His stool had been his only seat.

Sam's own words...
Friday, February 8, 1952 – "...Princess Elizabeth of England became Queen Elizabeth II today. Wrote to Grace."

After suffering from lung cancer for several years, King George VI died in his sleep on February 6, 1952, at age 56. Upon his death, his oldest daughter, Princess Elizabeth, became queen. She was 25 years old.

Sam tried unsuccessfully on Saturday to start the washer. With a grim face, he gave up in defeat. Sunday was enjoyable as he kept his invitation to dinner and supper with Mrs. Wagner and the relatives living under her roof. He arrived home in time to listen to The Big Show. A far-away longing spirited him away momentarily as he thought of Grace and Roy listening to the same program at home in their sitting room. The Big Show premiered on November 5, 1950, and played every Sunday night. It was a rousing success with MC, Tallulah Bankhead. The guest list varied but included such names as Ethel Merman, Danny Thomas, Fanny Brice, and Bob Hope. Sam's Sabbath had been engaging, warm, and pleasant.

He seemed to be in demand. Mr. Courtney had visited Sam, and the neighborly chat was due to be repaid. Hammonds invited him to dinner again. Mrs. Packard drove over to get him on Thursday, February 14, to have dinner with her and Mrs. Brinks, a cousin she was staying with in

Tampa. The three of them rode to the airport to watch in awe, Eastern Airlines planes land and depart. They were entertained with the great sight and counted 50 passengers get off a plane from New York. They hadn't even counted the crew.

Teddy had turned 19 years old. Sam remembered and thought fondly of him. Grace sent the Elmira *Star-Gazette* and *The Pathfinder* magazine.

The useless washing machine sat there. Sam's clenched jaw over his defunct machine turned to a smile when Mrs. Hammond insisted that he bring his load and run it through with her clothes. It was as if the young mother had passed a hand over his face and exchanged the old look for the new. While the wringer washer sloshed, they had a good chat and he bought a half-dozen eggs from her. He helped dispose of the wash water and hung his laundry on the line.

Grace sent *Newsweek* along with the newspapers. She reported that they had icy streets and six inches of snow. Sam was glad he was out of it even though he got a little lonely at odd moments. Trusting in the Lord allowed him to get along well and there he was, washing woodwork on a Wednesday. Other days, he had prepared the garden ground and proceeded to plant.

He listed all of his expenses together on the tablet at the end of the month, bunched up into one total price. February groceries, oil, Prince Albert, postage, hardware, bus, and etcetera added up to $38.98. His pair of beige shorts were included as dry goods.

Frank and Mary came along with a whole picnic to share on March 3 to celebrate Sam's 69th birthday. It came and went amidst a flurry of cards for sentiments expressed and appreciated.

Time went by as trips to town served for getaways from his bachelor quarters. On one of his grocery store jaunts, he paid his 48¢ electric bill. To pull him further out of his many ordinary days, the news of March 22 no doubt raised his eyebrows. The first in a series of articles from a German now in America were titled Man Will Conquer Space Soon! It included ideas for manned flights to Mars and the Moon designed by Werner Van Braun. Sam may have rightly supposed that it would not happen in his lifetime, if ever. But he did read and later had mere glimpses to see progress toward that end. He would never live to see that the United States human spaceflight program carried out by the National Aeronautics and Space Administration (NASA) accomplished landing the first humans on the Moon from 1969 to 1972.

Sam hired Mr. Packard to put asphalt siding on his cabin, a birch grey, which he liked. The exterior covering was $50 and the labor $35. His small abode had become a bit finer of a dwelling place.

Willa wrote that Arthur Crow had a heart condition and after a hospital stay, was home with oxygen. Sam was grateful to receive word about his esteemed friend. He shook his head and to his mind, proclaimed Arthur to be a fine specimen of a man.

Sam started the application of super Kem-Tone to interior walls. It cost the large price of $3.68 for the gallon. In his opinion, the Bermuda turquoise would brighten up the room.

Frank and Mary surprised Sam and brought him an icebox. He smiled as he agreed that he could get ice for it at the nearby grocer. John and Lucille sent him a food care box, and Packards brought a pumpkin pie and cookies. "I shan't starve right away," he wrote in his diary.

More paint was needed, this time costing $2.48 for the woodwork. Sam had eaten at the Mayfair Restaurant before and repeated it this time when he went after the paint.

Sam's own words...
Friday, March 28, 1952 – "Left my self-imposed exile long enough to mix with the multitude awhile. Walked (one mile) to Mrs. Wagner's and we went to Tampa where we partook of a good dinner at Morrison's famed restaurant. Afterward, took a bus ride through YBOR City, Tampa's Spanish quarter, and back. She knows Tampa like a book and is a good companion."
Monday, March 31, 1952 – "...Used up all of my paint but not entirely on the house. I had about a pint of it left, which was sitting on the step ladder and forgot to take it off before I moved the ladder. The first thing I knew, it was running down the back of my neck. I sure was a mess, and to say the least, plumb disgusted with myself. I used kerosene oil, wiped for an hour, but will have places that will be green for a month unless I have help. High 82 degrees."

It was no laughing matter and remained that way because no help was at hand and none other saw it.

March was over. Sam swung the whistle-billy on a few weeds and hoed his small garden. On Monday, April 11, he had the washing machine taken to the Springs for repairs. He got it back Thursday, ready to slosh his clothes clean.

Cain's electric shop had charged him $10.06.

Packards returned to Horseheads, NY, and Hesses to Addison, NY.

Sam's own words...
Saturday, April 19, 1952 – "Went to Sulphur Springs in forenoon after groceries and ate dinner at Dog Track Restaurant. Ordered a stew and had all I could eat for 50¢. Bought five sweet grapefruit for 10¢...81 degrees."

Grace had implored Sam to come home. He missed them, too, but was not ready to go back yet. He'd rather wait until it was warmer up north. Leary about renting out his place after last years' experience, he procrastinated on the decision to do so again or not. The not won.

He often visited with his neighbor, Mr. Courtney. Shirley wrote that dandelion greens were in season in Horseheads. Sam wrote back that he'd had tomatoes from his garden on May 2.

He was not unhappy but would be more contented if one or more of his relatives were near enough to pay him a visit now and then. It was 92 degrees, sufficiently hot to make him think about returning home. He shook his head as he was pulled further homeward by Grace's letter saying the garden was plowed and potatoes and peas planted.

John had traded his Hudson for a 1951 Ford.

Sam's own words...
Monday, May 19, 1952 – "Was glad to get a letter from Frances and David Jr. He sent me a picture of himself taken on the day of confirmation, which was April 16. He is getting to be a tall lad and how I should like to see him. God bless both he and his mother...90 degrees."

Sam saw Mrs. Wagner again but was alone for the most part. It explained why he went more often to the Dog Track restaurant where he could get an excellent dinner in the middle of the day and talk to strangers.

He also got a whole quart of milk for 27¢ to bring home to his ice box.

He heard an announcement on the radio May 30 that the temperature was 38 degrees in Elmira, NY. Shirley was right that it had not warmed up yet.

There he was on his lonesome plantation on June 1. He walked to the sundry at North Rose and Waters street after a ham sandwich and a glass of orange juice, all for 42¢. He had time on his hands and made up his mind to go north. He went to the Springs bank to close out most of his account. He had a pancake dinner with Mrs. Wagner and her friend. After-ward, he went after his $29 bus ticket to Elmira. He and Mrs. Wagner went to a movie, and he provided supper in Sulphur Springs.

Tuesday, June 10, it was 97 degrees and provided his chaser to go north on Thursday. He arrived in Elmira, NY, at 12:30 a.m. Saturday, June 14. He was worn out and grateful to go right to bed at Grace's.

The heartfelt visits from his families placed between his gardening that was in full swing. Steele came from Stormville and brought Sandra. She was interested in their two baby kittens and just as much so with Aunt Grace's Chinese Checker game.

Sam worried about the seeds that didn't sprout through the ground. The lawn was brown and dry. He was uneasy without much to do. John and Lucille went to Hattiesburg, Mississippi, and returned July 5 with her father, Mr. Pitts. The mountains were strange to him since he had always lived in the flat country. Finally, July 9, they were getting rain, and Ed's crops were in as much need as Sam's garden.

Sam was euphoric to attend a movie with Grace on July 18. They saw a rip-roaring comedy, Oklahoma Annie, starring Judy Canova. The 1½-hour western comedy was about a storekeeper who got involved in cleaning up corruption in her town and also hoped to attract the attention of the handsome new sheriff.

Everyone zeroed in on phenomena happening in Washington, DC, from July 19 through 26. Several UFOs tracked across multiple radars. The reported incidents caused jets to scramble on several occasions. The announcement stated that the objects took evasive actions, only to return after the planes left the area.

Sam's own words...
Friday, August 1, 1952 – "...Many people are excited over seeing flying saucers or whatever they were, and two jets have been chasing them in this vicinity today..."

Sam was as interested as any other resident, but probably not prone to speculating that they might capture an alien. Sam was not given to ridiculous imaginings.

Sam helped Mr. Walker next door in his garden and earned $3. Earlier he had received $13 from the same source for brush and weed labor. Sam voted in the Republican primary on August 19, on John Street in Horseheads. It was this summer that Sam loaned John and Lucille $1,130 on a land contract for the home they purchased at 752 Copley Street, Elmira.

September evenings cooled, and Sam elected to cut wood for Rip Rackett.

It was a first for Sam when he rode with Grace and her granddaughter, Margie, over to Big Flats to attend a drive-in movie. It was nearly midnight when they returned home.

Excitement mounted over the expectations for the Grand Prix auto races to be held September 20, 1952, in Watkins Glen, NY. The 6.6-mile circuit ran through the village streets, starting and ending in front of the Schuyler County Court House. It was necessary to have permits from six governmental entities: the state, county, village, Town of Reading, Town of Dix, the New York State Parks Commission, and the New York Central Railroad to close the public roads for the event. The trains had to stop during the race, as the course crossed the tracks. The circuit continued in use for races from 1948 through 1952. It may be toured today as public roads, unchanged. For those who were there in the early days, it is a sentimental journey. For those who have never been there, it is a lesson in motor racing history. American road racing was revived at Watkins Glen on October 2, 1948, the first road race since before World War II.

Sam's own words...
Saturday, September 20, 1952 – "A terrible thing happened when two racing cars side swiped and one of them out of control, went into the

crowd of bystanders and killed a seven-year-old boy, also injured 12 other people."

Sam did not attend and did not see the bales of straw that lined the main drag, as the only barriers between spectators and racing cars on the street in Watkins Glen. Edwin Voorheis and several of the children were there in the sunshine where street vendors were weaving in and out to hawk their cotton candy and popcorn. It was an exhilarating day for them. They only learned of the terrible mishap in the next day's news. No doubt Betty vowed that the kids would not go next year.

October held a moment of excitement for Sam when his social security check was raised $5 per month to $44.10. He received another $15 from their neighbor, Mr. Walker, for outdoor work. Sam dug dahlia and gladiola bulbs from his own garden and stored them in the cellar.

Winter proclaimed itself ahead of schedule when Sam woke to snow on the ground October 20. He cut more wood for Rip. Temperatures turned milder.

Betty wrote to her father that she was without a car. They had sold it and bought more cows. Ed had become employed as a carpenter.

On November 4, voters elected Republican Dwight D. Eisenhower as United States president. As supreme commander of allied forces in Western Europe during World War II, Eisenhower led the massive invasion of Nazi-occupied Europe that began on D-Day (June 6, 1944). In 1952, leading Republicans convinced Eisenhower (then in command of NATO forces in Europe) to run for president; he won a convincing victory against Democrat Adlai Stevenson and would serve two terms in the White House (1953-1961). During his presidency, Eisenhower managed Cold War-era tensions with the Soviet Union.

Frank and Mary planned to leave for Zephyrhills, FL, on Friday, November 7, and Sam decided to go with them. Visiting rounds were hurried by all who wanted to see him. Shirley gave him an early Christmas present of $10.

Sam was in his Tampa home by November 12. The same weed whack and lawn work commenced. A new purchase, a weed culler tool cost him $1.55. It took his concentrated effort to make the place civilized again.

Four new window shades set him back $3.67.

The neighbors seemed pleased to have him back again. A postal money order arrived from John and Lucille. It was the start of paying Sam back. He was glad.

It was an unusual Thanksgiving, but made enjoyable by spending a couple of days with Frank and Mary. They played a game called Sorry both days, trying to win at getting their own color pieces around the board the fastest. Neighbors came over, and Sam watched as the other four people played a double-deck card game called Canasta.

Sam's own words...
Monday, December 1, 1952 – "Received Horseheads and Elmira newspapers and defense bond I asked for from Grace. She's wonderful. I don't know how I could get along without her help..."

He felt his aloneness again and turned to his radio and reading materials. Drying weeds and brush burning needed advancement each day, along with preparation of three daily meals.

Sam's own words...
Friday, December 5, 1952 – "Glad to get a letter from Grace with all the news from home. Roy was laid off from the Langwell Hotel December 1...Teddy has been drafted and went to Syracuse, NY for his physical. What a shame we can't live in this world without war and its miseries. God grant that the whole world won't become involved again..."

The washer worked well now, and he hung his laundry on the line in no time. Sam wrote Grace a letter and mailed it when he walked to the post office, bank, and Dog Track restaurant. His last errands for the day in Sulphur Springs were to pay the 95¢ water bill and get groceries.

December 12 dawned with a frost in the sunshine state and only 25 degrees. The oil stove did not keep the inside temperature comfortable, and it remained that way four days.

It was time to write cards and letters for Christmas. Sam mailed them out December 19. A card from Frank and Mary was also an invitation to spend the Christian Holiday with them. He smiled as he wrote a card right back to accept.

Sam stayed over through December 26 and went with Mary to a lecture on Egypt and views of the ancient country, which they found enlightening.

Sam enjoyed the time with His sister and her husband. Back in Tampa again he felt alone. He had the grounds to keep up and neighbors to see. Lonely was no inducement to entertain spending the winter in the north.

36 – Korea
1953

Sam's own words...
Thursday, January 1, 1953 – "The dawning of a new year and the world's prospects don't look very bright. Our boys are still dying in Korea along with South Koreans against the menace of Communism and other North Koreans and hordes of Chinese who are for it. God grant us peace, show us the way, your way of light, love, and peace..."

Sam needed a change of pace from being alone and thinking so much that his worry increased. Mr. Courtney was doing carpenter work and wanted Sam to go along as a helper on the job for Mr. Lloyd. Sam agreed. When they returned, he finished his day grubbing weeds. Once again, he helped Mr. Courtney for eight hours.

Sam's own words...
Monday, January 5, 1953 – "The Christmas Box John said they would send me came today and what a box. It contained a great variety and must have cost plenty; canned meats, fruit, honey, mayonnaise, a box of candy, nuts, cigars, and tobacco, two pot holders, a dishcloth and towel, all with the joy of loving and being loved. How precious my boys and girls are to me..."

It had changed Sam's mindset all right. Just what he needed. He was in an upbeat mood when he walked to town Tuesday. In Sulphur

Springs he paid his $1.65 water bill, got a 75¢ haircut, and had an excellent dinner at the Dog Track for 50¢. When he arrived home, he had mail from Moore Realty with a check for $40 on his Holsec Avenue house. Sam took it to the bank Wednesday and also bought himself a watch. His former tenants had broken his electric clock.

Bill Courtney and Sam put in another day of carpenter work for Mr. Lloyd. When they finished, Mr. Courtney's car wouldn't start. They got four kids to help push it, but it was no-go. When the Spanish Mrs. Lloyd came home, she used her car to push them, and they were on their way.

A letter from Shirley and a home newspaper from Grace were appreciated, and so it went, as usual. If these items didn't show up once a week, something was wrong.

Sam's own words...
Tuesday, January 13, 1953 – "I found a letter from Arthur Crow's wife informing me that he passed away June 19, 1952. To say the least: I was shaken and surprised. Why Willa or anyone hadn't let us know is beyond me. I wrote to Arthur as usual at Christmas time, and only today his wife revealed the late sad news. God bless his soul. He is the last of nine children...70 degrees. I went to the Springs and mailed my letters and paid my Florida taxes of $37.75."

Sam read his Florida agriculture bulletin, and it said he could plant summer squash. He established four hills.

Grace's letter almost made his heart race. She said Roy was waiting on his unemployment and social security checks and when he got them they were ready to leave for Florida. He could not dwell on the swell of Grace's notification too long because he had rare mail from David. Sam's heart pumped fast, but David, Hilda, and the children were all just fine. And so was Sam just from reading his words. Another envelope that Betty sent contained sweet little notes from her youngest children. Sam blessed their hearts, grown-ups and children alike.

Sam's own words...
Tuesday, January 20, 1953 – "Dwight David Eisenhower, 62, a soldier battle tested in the service of peace and freedom took office today as the 34th president of the United States..."

The Hammonds next door had sold their place and were hastily proceeding to move in two weeks. Sam would buy eggs from them as long as he could. Mr. Courtney was ill and had been taken away in an ambulance. It turned out he had double pneumonia.

Sam's own words...
Wednesday, February 4, 1953 – "Did my washing. Helen (Mr. Courtney's girl) brought over a pair of Mr. Courtney's bib overalls and put them thru (sic) the wash with my clothes. They haven't a washer, and since one of her hands is disabled, it's rather hard for her. Went to the store. The sea has broken through the sea walls of Holland; two thousand drowned and thousands marooned on islands, hundreds drowned in Southern England. 72 degrees."

Sam wondered if Grace and Roy were on their way down. He could hardly keep his mind away from the happy thought and then learned it could be another week.

Sam's own words...
Monday, February 9, 1953 – "...A Chevrolet with a NY plate drove in at my place. I sure knew who it was and was I glad to see Grace and Roy. They seem to have stood the trip well. Mabel Packard came this evening to see if they were here."

Mrs. Packard was glad to see the Whitings but could not have been more tickled than Sam to enjoy their presence.

Roy tried to repair his car but in frustration, concluded he'd have to take it to a garage. Sam saw that they enjoyed Florida but needed more rest after their long trip. Mrs. Hammond and both children came over that afternoon with oranges and grapefruit. She happily met Grace and Roy.

Roy hired the car towed to Cantrell's Garage and stayed with the vehicle all day. Sam walked to the store for groceries to make sure he could prepare adequate meals. He and Grace had lots of catching up to do.

Not all meals would take place at Sam's. They drove to the Springs where Sam bought curtains for $2.20, and they ate at his favorite place, the Dog Track restaurant.

Back home, he hung the curtains to divide the big room by half and converted it into a bedroom. The shed was not where he wanted them because there was no heat out there. He had cots and mattresses to bring inside. Meanwhile, Grace had bought a quart of strawberries and hulled them for their enjoyment.

The three from Horseheads went out driving and sightseeing two days in a row. On one trip they ended up at Frank and Mary's. Mr. Courtney called on them Saturday evening, without a Valentine, although it was February 14. Sam and Grace visited Mrs. Packard and her mother, Mrs. Brinks. It pleased all of them.

The early morning frost promoted the need for Sam and Roy to get a sheet-iron stove in which to burn wood. The stove pipe and damper cost $2.67. It was 34 degrees the next morning but warmed up to 65 degrees.

The Hammonds moved, and a new family replaced them. Sam had his pasture empty.

Roy helped Sam pipe his water over to the back porch. It was so much handier than when it was six rods away from the house. The pipe had cost $1.97 but was well worth it for the convenience.

More sights were seen on a trip out to Piney Point to watch a ferry between there and Saint Pete load and unload cars and people. Sam enjoyed it all with them for the first time. He hadn't seen many places since he didn't drive or own a car.

A day at home was spent washing and drying clothes. A letter came from John and Lucille with $10, and Sam sure could use it. Early birthday cards started arriving for him.

The three went on a trip to Immokalee, FL, which took from 8:30 a.m. to 3 p.m. to reach their destination. They located their grandson, Roy Jeffrey, Alice's son. He had a small place there. Sam paid $2 at the Seminole Lodge for the overnight. They spent the next day traveling back a different route to see new scenery.

Back home, Sam found a card from Willa telling of Christy's marriage to Raymond P. Nelson. He thought she was a sweet girl and hoped she had made a better choice this time. Sam had arrived at three scores and ten years and thought he had much for which to be thankful.

Sam's own words...
Wednesday, March 4, 1953 – "Received card from Steele and he is still having marital trouble, poor fellow...The news today reports Joseph Stalin is near death. Grace and I wrote to Steele. L 60 degrees, H 80, windy."

Sam's social security check, $44.10, arrived to supply relief for dwindling funds. He didn't mind that he spent a lot more because of his company on hand and for his share in the cost of excursions. They companioned with Frank and

Mary on a day trip to see the famous drug store in Saint Pete's known as Webb City and also the Million Dollar Pier.

The mail was exciting when they heard from Shirley and Tommy, Ed and Betty, John and Lucille, and Dewey and Millie all at once. They always missed Sam.

Sam's own words...
Friday, March 6, 1953 – "...Joseph Stalin died last night behind the 12-foot walls of the Kremlin."

The arrival of the check from Moore Realty was a big help to Sam. A day later a belated birthday card from Shirley, Tommy, and Teddy arrived with $15 for Sam. Maybe they knew what a boost it would be for him. "Bless them," he wrote.

Grace and Roy started for Horseheads on February 9. Sam missed them and felt alone again.

Sam's own words...
Monday, March 16, 1953 – "...Alice Jeffrey, Grace and Roy's daughter, had a letter from Cretia condemning Grace and Roy's trip to Florida. Did my washing and usual chores indoors and out."

Sam was not amused as he shook his head over his cousin Cretia's negative attitude. It wasn't the first time they'd heard of her irregular ideas about people who loved her and had often gone out of their way for her. The problem Cretia had was no doubt ongoing jealousy that Grace's sibling, Sam, was also her best friend. There was no need for her to feel slighted, but evidently, she didn't see quite straight at the age of 77 any more than she had years earlier. The Packards left for Horseheads, NY, and a couple of weeks later, Frank and Mary headed back to Addison, NY. Sam had offers from both couples to return with them but decided to stay past March.

He saw Mrs. Wagner on the bus, and they greeted one another. Sam wore his slight smile, the one with politeness reserved for any stranger. Encouragement was likely withheld to ensure that he not suggest false hopes.

Sam's radio malfunctioned and left him feeling alone. It was as much a companion as a human when he had listened to programs.

Betty sent a quart jar of home canned beef, and he made a pot of stew with it. Sam smiled at how dear she was to send it. There was no better use for potatoes, carrots, and onions from his garden.

The distress in Grace's letter of April 3 was about Ruthie who had been under a psychiatrist's care. The doctor told Steele that Ruth was not fit to bring up Sandra, and he was afraid to leave Sandra alone with her. Grace mentioned that the Rip Racketts had removed to the county home in Breesport. She hoped they would not be allowed to return because they were unable to care for themselves properly.

Sam helped Mr. Courtney remove an oak tree from a man's yard and earned $2.

Grace wrote that Teddy was at Camp Gordon, Georgia, training for, military police. She opined that Sam had been wise to stay another month in the sunshine state. He involuntarily shivered as he read about snow squalls and chilly damp weather. His cleverness seized on a dandy idea. Maybe it was a long shot, but a card was written to Teddy mentioning what a welcome he'd have if he visited Tampa. A smile accompanied the mailed invitation.

Sam's own words...
Friday, May 1, 1953 – "...I got bitten up by chiggers yesterday when we went after logs. Got some Lysol today, which I hope will stop the itching. I don't know which is worse, the fleas in Oregon or chiggers in Florida, but think the chiggers have the edge. Low 74 degrees, High 92."

His longtime neighbor, Bill Courtney, had sold an adjacent second house and lot to an 84-year-old gentleman, George Minard, who had only one arm. Boredom was pushed away to go and talk to them awhile. Old Mr. Minard was well acquainted with Galeton, Pennsylvania, among other places, and knew men with whom Sam had worked.

The chigger bites had company called dew poisoning. Sam found out the hard way just what it was. There was no danger, just mighty uncomfortable for both legs below the knees. Dew poisoning or "ground itch" sores are lesions that form on the feet, legs, and arms caused by scratches becoming infected with bacteria. Maybe he had scratched the chigger bites too much. He didn't know how long the healing would take, but decided that he had been alone long enough.

Sam's checks arrived, and he went to the Union Bus Station for his Grey-hound ticket costing $30.90 for travel to Elmira. He wrote Grace that he would be home May 14, and he was. By the 15th, Sam had seen every member of his family. They had all come to Grace and Roy's eager to welcome him back. Sam embraced all the love imparted to him. He paid Grace $6 for room and board.

Sam and Tommy Broadhead went to see *The Big Sky*. It was a two-hour-20-minute western drama. In 1830, two sturdy Kentucky mountaineers joined a trading expedition from St. Louis up the Missouri River to trade whiskey for furs with the Blackfoot Indians. They soon discover that there is much more than the elements for contention. The success of the journey focuses on keeping an Indian girl alive as well as themselves to complete a trade with the Indians.

Sam wrote to request a new Tanner shoe catalog. Maybe he could sell a few pair. His haircut was $1 and had gone up 25¢. He thought it was steep, but he paid it.

He planted three rows of potatoes and rested. Leaning on his hoe, he looked over the plot to plan his next effort. It might have been time to sit in the shade with Prince Albert and his pipe.

Tommy and Shirley were having walls painted. They were glad to keep money in the family and hire Sam. He was pleased to earn the $29.95 that they paid him. The commission for selling a pair of Tanner shoes added to his bottom line.

Dewey turned 55 years old on June 3.

Teddy was on furlough and brought his bride to be, Hazel, for an introduction and visit with Tommy and Shirley.

The wedding was June 11.

Sam's own words...
Thursday, June 18, 1953 – "Elmira has a TV station now, and Tommy and Shirley got a television set. Grace and I went over this evening and be- came so interested in the show we didn't leave until 10:30 pm, which is late for us. TV is wonderful but cheats people out of the sleep they need..."
Friday, June 19, 1953 – "Julius and Ethel Rosenberg, the atomic spies, were electrocuted at 8 p.m. tonight. They betrayed their own country and gave secrets to communist Russia. I finished planting the garden today. We are getting a few strawberries from the sets I put in last spring..."

Sam's friend, Arthur Share, confessed he still had Florida fever, and he hoped to make it there this fall. Just the mention of the place prompted Sam to write to Mr. Courtney, his Tampa neighbor.

Roy went to work July 1 as a watchman on the new highway under construction through Horseheads. He worked 6 p.m. to midnight, a great shift to avoid the sun.

On the farm, Ed was in a bind for haying and harvesting help. Bucky was in the hospital healing from an appendix operation. Carol had a deep, barbed wire cut on her knee. Teddy had written that he'd gotten into miserable poison oak in Georgia. All of these things would take their time to resolve. Ed and Betty had work to do to get ready for company. Somehow they managed it all.

Sam went for a haircut and had another surprise when he was charged $1.25.

Sam's own words...
Sunday, July 19, 1953 – "The Crippen Reunion was held at Ed and Betty's today, and we had a grand time with 48 present..."
Tuesday, July 21, 1953 – "Steele and Ruthie came about 5:30 p.m. on their way to Ed and Betty's to get Sandra (age 11) who had been there since Sunday. Grace and I rode along and enjoyed our trip and visit very much."

Sam had a payday of $19.50 gained from various days of short hours worked for Mr. Wheater. On July 20, he had started mowing for Mr. Walker.

Dewey had been ill for a couple of months and was worse. Sam had thought he was gaining in health and on the mend.

Sam's own words...
Wednesday, July 29, 1953 – "Shirley telephoned Millie this evening. I was surprised to learn that Dewey isn't well enough to work yet. The doctor thinks it may be his eyes that cause his headaches..."

Sam continued mowing for Mr. Walker. He had also been summoned by 80-year-old Miss Weaver from the neighborhood to clean up her yard. His true character was well known. He received $5.

On Sunday, August 2, Hilda came from the Bulkhead area in Southport, NY, and picked Sam up to go and spend time with them and have supper with David and the family. David was still at work even on a Sunday. He had never been a communicator like his siblings, but lack of love was not part of his quietness turned inward. His moodiness was as single-minded as a broody hen with a one-track mind for setting on eggs. Sam suspected it was as Betty believed, that his grief over Douglas was held inside and that he felt the great loss of David Jr. as anger toward Frances. There was no law to protect either parent. Possession was the law. If you wanted a child back, then find them and steal them back.

Betty had done all she could to appease Frances and allow her to visit Little David at the farm. When Frances was expected from New York City to the Bennettsburg farm, Betty spoiled her like no other. She fried chicken and the gizzards, which were a delicacy to Frances, who ate them and picked at other food before dinner was on the table. Betty couldn't allow a large family of 10 the leniency to do that, but she made Frances the exception with a smile.

Looking back, Sam figured the absconding of David Jr. would have happened sooner if not for Betty. Frances had made her move as soon as she found out he was spending extended happy times at his father's home. No one could have guessed what that would set off in Frances's mind. It was starting to sink in with Betty and all of them when she said aloud to Edwin with a bit of sarcasm, "I wonder if I'll have the chance to pamper Frances again?" No answer was needed. From time to time, there were comments made, "Where could David be? When will we ever see Little David again?"

Dewey had a worrisome spell August 12 and was attended by Dr. Chamberlin. What a speculation Sam, Grace, and all of them had because of Dewey's dilemma. It had not been a stroke, as far as they knew, but he went by ambulance to Arnot Ogden Hospital. Steele had been taken to St. Joseph's Hospital with pleurisy. There was enough concern spread around. Sam fell back on the comfort of prayer and thanked God as they improved. August lived up to its reputation of "dog days." As it reached into September, 100 degree days continued. The heat wave simmered down to 95 on September 4 and 5.

Finally, September turned cooler. Sam put in several hours labor for Dewey who was healing but not back at Elmira Reformatory for work yet. Sam steadily dug out an oak tree root that had been Dewey's nemesis for quite awhile. It was serious grubbing to dig the long octopus-like tentacles out of the garden. The $20 paid Sam, in the end, was earned, and Dewey was glad to say so.

Dewey improved and began to walk. He surprised them all by walking all the way to Grace's on Mill Street. He had overdone it a little and had to rest two hours before he went back.

Sam and Grace continued to enjoy watching TV evenings at Shirley and Tommy's. Sharing the viewed entertainment was half the enjoyment for all of them. Despite the big hit of filmed programs such as I Love Lucy, both CBS and NBC kept most programming on its networks to the spontaneous nature of live television such as The Dave Garroway Show, which competed with Mama and Ozzie & Harriet. Roy still worked nights from 5 p.m. to midnight.

Sam's own words...
Tuesday, September 22, 1953 − "The last time I had my haircut it cost $1.25. Today I changed barbers and paid $1. I say it's still too much. I trimmed blackberries for Mr. Walker in the afternoon. Cool and fair."

Sam paid $2.98 for *Literary Digest*, and it was $2 last year. No doubt he had his opinion on the big increase. Dewey continued his walks and built up his strength. He appreciated Sam's essential repairs on his sewer system. September 27 woke them to Eastern Standard Time again.

Sam received his $5.50 on work finished for Mr. Walker. His next agenda was potatoes that needed digging.

Sam's own words...
Wednesday, September 30, 1953 – "Dewey has a new 21 inch TV set, and I was with him most of the afternoon during the first game of the world series between New York Yankees and The Brooklyn Dodgers...I dug all of the potatoes and put them in the cellar."

Sam watched all of the remaining games at Shirley's. The Yankees won the series on October 5 by beating the Dodgers, 4 - 3.

They all woke to a heavy frost October 8.

Sam's own words...
Saturday, October 12, 1953 – "...We received the good news today that Teddy and Hazel have a baby girl, born October 6, named Sharon Lee, weight nine pounds."

Betty's first grandchild had arrived two days after her 38th birthday. Little Sharon would be nicknamed Sherry.

Roy was laid off. The three from Mill Street took their time traveling to Galeton. Cretia was having a porch built. Sam saw her, too, but went to stay one night with John and Mary Long. Sam's full heart gave him to write that he'd had a grand visit. The trip home was equally pleasant as they visited their brother Lynn and his wife, Iva, also Frank Hess in Addison, NY. Mary was not home. Hesses planned to leave for Zephyrhills, FL, on October 28. Sam didn't like to go south so early.

Sam took a leaf raking job for Elmira College on October 20. He went to stay with John and Lucille who lived near there so he could walk to work. Ten days work went on through the 30th for his paycheck of $47.87. He resumed for the college on Monday, November 2. The week brought him $49.39 with the job completed.

Several inches of snow were on the ground Saturday, November 7, perhaps a nudge to think about Tampa. A bigger nudge came along when Arthur Share called on Sam on Monday. Arthur had a good car and wanted Sam's company to go south within a week. Sam supposed he'd better accept the opportunity. It meant carrots to harvest, people to see, and packing to do.

He went home with John for a supper Lucille was preparing to include David, Hilda, and the family. David's new job meant moving to Buffalo. They'd sold their Orchard Park home in Southport.

Betty came to spend a few hours with Sam and Grace on November 18. It was a rare and excellent visit for them.

Sam and Grace attended a Horseheads movie together, Little Boy Lost, played by actor Bing Crosby. The 1½ hour film was a drama about a war correspondent stationed in Paris during World War II and once married to a French girl who was murdered by the Nazis. Following the war, he returns to France trying to find his son, whom he lost during a bombing raid, but has been told is living in an orphanage in Paris.

Sam's own words...
Tuesday, November 24, 1953 – "Lucille came to Shirley's in the Jeep after she took John to work. The girls insisted on my going with them to Iszard's Studio in Elmira and have my picture taken, and they won out. I called at the social security office to have my check sent to my Florida address..."

Sam, Grace, and Roy enjoyed Thanksgiving at John and Lucille's.

Sam's own words...
Saturday, November 28, 1953 – "...We received the sad news that David is in a Buffalo hospital with double pneumonia. God grant that he recovers soon."
Sunday, November 29, 1953 – "...Steele helped Bill Drake, Hilda's brother, load David's household of goods on his truck to take them to Buffalo...Lucille said Steele drove her and John's Jeep to Buffalo to help on that end and also transport David's TV there safely."
Monday, November 30, 1953 – "Arthur Share and I left Horseheads at 8 a.m. for Tampa."

Sam and Arthur were tired and glad when they reached Tampa on December 3 at 1:30 p.m. The Courtney's came and visited a few minutes, but 84-year-old George Minard spent two hours with them. He had gotten married and wanted to sell his house and lot.

The Dog Track restaurant charged the two men 52¢ apiece for Sam's favorite supper there. Sam appreciated a 75¢ haircut.

Arthur knew a lot of people whom he proceeded to look up daily before he ate suppers in town. David wrote from the hospital that he was recovering. Sam wrote right back about his pleasure in hearing it.

Arthur helped around the place but was looking for employment. Sam went to town with him to mail his letter and several Christmas cards he had ready to send out. They both took supper out, away from Sam's place.

Frank and Mary came for a visit on December 21. They invited Sam and Arthur for Christmas dinner. The two were happy to accept.

Arthur's disappointment over having found no employment pushed his decision to leave for Horseheads on December 26. An avalanche of late holiday mail pleased Sam along with $10 from Steele. At last, he had word from Willa and Christy. Nothing was amiss. Sam summed up his expenses for the long trip traveling down to Florida with Arthur. His food, gas, and lodging were $33.50. Gas had been 22¢ per gallon.

Grace warmed Sam's heart and brightened his face as usual by sending hometown newspapers and a letter. A lasting glow set in when he read that she and Roy planned to come south around January 15. The year ended well, and their arrival would start the next one in pleasant company.

~**~

1954

It had become evident that old George Minard, judging from his talk, he and his new missus were not getting along as well as they might. Sam might have mused, "maybe Marilyn Monroe and Joe Dimaggio will do better." The famous couple's marriage of January 14 splashed across the last newspaper Grace sent.

Sam started a garden and added to it daily while letters arrived in his mailbox. As Sam hoed, he wondered if Grace had received the road maps mailed back to her. Arthur had borrowed them to use for the trip down. "When would Whitings arrive?" Sam wondered.

Sam went to pay his $1.82 water bill and ate at a different place.

Arthur Watkins, an acquaintance from the year before, was there. They picked up again with a good visit.

At home, Sam was becoming familiar with the Batemans who moved in when the Hammonds moved out. He likely thought he knew a little more than he wanted to about the snide stance between Old Minard and his wife. George had a habit to come over to Sam's two hours at a time and speak about it.

Grace and Roy drove in Thursday, January 21. It had been 10 below zero when they left Horseheads, and it was now 82 degrees in Tampa. Sam elected to sleep in the shed on a cot and let Grace and Roy have the house. It left no doubt how he felt about having their company.

Sam took his radio to the repair shop when the three of them set out on an excursion. Three days later the radio talked, and Sam paid $18.23 for the privilege. He splurged further on February 5 on linoleum for the floor of the cabin. Delivery was a day later, and the three of them installed it. Sam's room changed to positively pleasant.

Sam's own words...
Wednesday, February 10, 1954 – "Grace received a letter from Dewey. They are getting along well, but he says he gets tired on his guard job and has to lie down before he can eat supper..."

Sam slowly expanded his garden. To his surprise, Grace and Roy stopped in to see Mrs. Wagner. He was glad to know she was well.

The news was hopeful about the mass vaccination of children, which had begun in Pittsburg, PA, against polio. All citizens, no matter their ages, had high hope for its success, and that included Sam, Grace, and Roy.

Dewey wrote that he was not well even though he did his job, but was always tired. The doctor had advised that he lose 20 pounds.

Sam and the Whitings often went out driving and asked the Minards to go along. They were never turned down by the two elders.

Sam's birthday was memorable as he turned 71 years old. Grace packed food and a cake for a trip to Frank and Mary's in Zephyrhills. They all went to Hillsborough State Park to enjoy the picnic in each other's company. The river flowing by lent an idyllic setting for a lazy afternoon in the shade of the trees.

A slew of cards arrived for Sam from the north. Roy and Grace departed for that cold place on Saturday, March 6, at 7:30 a.m. Old Mr. Minard returned at once to his former habit of visiting Sam twice a day.

A birthday card arrived from Willa. Her 52nd birthday was coming up, and that was reason enough for Sam to make a trip to Sulphur Springs to get a card. He met up with Arthur Watkins again, and they enjoyed a meal and conversation.

Sam reluctantly took a ride with the one-armed and nearly deaf George Minard. The elder was positioned in the middle of the road most often and made turns on the wrong side of the road. There was no enjoyment in the ride, and Sam was glad to return in one piece.

Sam hired Mrs. Minard to do his load of wash. His machine had quit again.

April was warmer in a range of 70 to 86 degrees. Sam called it good chigger weather. He rode the bus all the way to Tampa. Mrs. Wagner got on at Kirby Street, saw him, and sat next to him. They ate dinner in a favorite restaurant and had a friendly visit.

Sam's own words...
Wednesday, April 21, 1954 – "...My flowers are certainly beautiful; the large red Calla blooms in particular. They are higher than my waist, and the red zinnias at the base fit right into the picture..."
Tuesday, April 27, 1954 – "Went to Sulphur Springs, mailed my letter to Grace and ate Dog Track dinner. I met Mrs. Wagner again as she boarded the bus near where she had purchased an armload of groceries and was on her way home. She asked me to come down, bless her, but I'm afraid I'm not interested in the way I was a year ago. George Minard and his pup came over this morning but didn't stay long. The puppy is full of fleas, and yesterday he ruined some of my flowers, and I didn't like it. He hasn't any control over him whatsoever. I'm sorry if I hurt his feelings, but I can't have it."
Wednesday, April 28, 1954 – "George called on me twice today without his pup. I guess his feelings aren't hurt..."

On Memorial Day Sam wondered if anyone had visited Edith's

grave. A Greyhound bus ticket home, purchased on June 7, cost him $27.17. Sam packed, made neighborly visits to say goodbye, and sent Grace notice of his June 9th departure. His taxi to Tampa was $2.07, and he was on his way at 11:20 a.m.

Sam's own words...
Friday, June 11, 1954 – "It sure is good to be home again with those who love me...I'm still weary from my long ride, but more sleep will set me right."

Sam no doubt approved 100 percent of the June 14 news that the words 'Under God' were added to the United States Pledge of Allegiance. He sent postcards to his Florida neighbors to let them all know he was safely in Horseheads, NY. Now he launched into gardening with flowers as part of his effort. Sam paid Grace $7 per week for room and board.

Dewey bought a brand-new Mercury. He came over to Grace's on July 2nd and took her and Sam for a ride to Odessa and back. They were both glad for Dewey and enjoyed the ride.

Steele took Sandra to her Aunt Betty's to stay again. He and Ruth could not make a go of it. The problems from the past had not disappear-ed. Ruth and Steele were at odds and further apart than ever.

Sam worked on lawns, gardens, and hedge trimming. It was for himself, Grace, and Roy, but also for the same few people who had hired him in the neighborhood the summer before. His time was well spent and the money, too. Weeds were easily visible, but reading had become difficult. He took a job to earn more money a little further afield at Artman's nursery and had plans to purchase new eyeglasses.

Sam's own words...
Thursday, September 16, 1954 – "Elmira honored the memory of Mark Twain with a grand parade, and many dressed as if back in the 1870s. He wrote many of his books here, married an Elmira girl, Libby Langdon, and was buried in Woodlawn Cemetery. Rained but managed to work four hours at the nursery."

The next day's eight hours of work were hard enough to make him tired and lame. Sam hoped he could continue. Teddy, Hazel, and new baby

Sherry had been home on his 16-day furlough and were on their way back to Georgia.

Old George Minard wrote to Sam to say he missed him. It surprised and touched Sam while he read the rest of the news about other Tampa neighbors that Old Minard reported. There was no flattery written about Bill Courtney's treatment of his common-law wife, Helen. Old George said he couldn't see Sam's place for the weeds.

Sam's total September pay from Artman Nursery was $83.75. He paid Grace a little more for room and board.

Sam's own words...
Monday, October 4, 1954 – "...Everyone received a raise in their social security checks today. Mine was only up $5, but it will help. Put in seven hours at nursery. Warm."

The social security check was $49.10, and he didn't mind the increase a bit. There was a killing frost early on October 7. It did away with flowers and crops. Sam could start the fall clean off of the garden.

Half of October 10 had passed before Sam remembered it was Betty's 39th birthday.

Sam's own words...
Saturday, October 16, 1954 – "Elmira area recovering from a hurricane. Trees, power lines felled; 491 foot TV tower toppled, 14 dead and scores injured in NY State. County airport reported winds up to 98 mph in what is believed to be the first tropical hurricane to reach this section of the state..."
Tuesday, October 19, 1954 – "Ten years ago Edith departed this earthly life. May God bless her soul. At nursery seven hours."

Grace, Roy, and Sam rode over to John and Lucille's on Sunday, October 24. John's daughters, Mickey and Kathy, were there and faces lit up just to see them.

Frank and Mary announced that they were leaving for Zephyrhills, FL, right after voting in November.

Sam's pay from Artman's Nursery was $213.15 for the month. He rewarded himself with a subscription to Pathfinder magazine for $3.25.

His $49.10 social security check arrived to add to his account.

Wednesday morning, November 3, they woke to six inches of snow, wet and cumbersome. Sam shoveled the walks. It ruined lilac bushes and worse yet, dogwood trees at the nursery. Sam shook his head.

Sam's own words...
Friday, November 20, 1954 – "Gail V. is visiting Shirley and will be with us until Sunday. They went to Elmira today, and both are happy in each others' company..."

Betty had eight children, and Shirley had none. She borrowed one or another of Betty's kids from time to time to indulge them with love, attention, and a few gifts. For Gail, it meant art supplies that her generous aunt provided.

Tuesday, November 30, was the day that Steele had time to hunt deer at Ed and Betty's farm. Sam went along for the day, his last chance to see all of them again before he went south for the winter. There was snow on the ground, the better to track deer, although Steele did not get one. Sam enjoyed all of the children and the big farm meal that Betty put on the table.

The November income that Sam tallied was $204.30 from all sources. John had returned $10. An early Christmas developed when Dewey and Millie came for a visit. Sam was pleased with a can of Prince Albert and a pipe. They were all aware that they would miss each other. But Sam would not miss the constant snow flurries. He, Grace, and Roy departed Horseheads at 8:30 a.m., Monday, December 6, glad to put distance between them and a temperature of 18 when they awoke that morning. Three days later they were in Tampa, Florida. Sam's trip expenses were $33.62.

On December 10, Old Minard came over three times. Sam smiled as his neighbor exclaimed that now he had someone to visit. All of the neighbors were happy that Sam and his kinfolks had returned. The three from Horseheads enjoyed the sunshine on their shoulders.

Sam began pulling, hacking, and hoeing at the brutish overgrowth that had benefitted from his seven-month absence. As Sam burned the dried weed pile, Grace and Roy took Old George to Sebring and De Soto

City, places he had once lived. They, too, appreciated their unique elderly friend. Grace was cheered up to be kind to Old Mr. Minard. Shirley had sent notice to her aunt that Grace's elderly cat had died one day after they left for Florida.

Sam decided to try mulching to keep moisture in and weeds down around his flowers. They drove over to Gunn Highway and bought six sacks of peat. His purchase of a washing machine costing $41.20 was a necessity.

Grace and Roy were going to Wauchula, FL, to stay with their grandson, Roy Jeffrey, Alice's son. Old Minard gave them a bed, springs, and mattress. Roy strapped it to the top of his 1941 Chevrolet car and drove away the day after Christmas.

The spent year of 1954 was about to turn in its records and depart forever.

Sam's own words...
Friday, December 31, 1954 – "...I believe we have made progress, although we have an uneasy peace. At least, the guns are silent. God grant that the world may learn that men must live in peace or we shall perish..."

37 - Addition
1955, 1956, 1957

Shirley and her friend, Ruth Lanterman Brown, and Ruth's brother, George, arrived at Sam's on January 10. They stayed two days, a pleasure for Sam, and left for Okeechobee. George Lanterman was well acquainted with the east coast area, and the girls were glad to have their own personal tour guide in him.

Grace and Roy moved back to town and took an apartment on Dexter Avenue in Sulphur Springs. Sam was delighted. They all went to see Frank and Mary in Zephyrhills for one big happy get-together.

Sam's own words...
Monday, February 7, 1955 – "Grace, Roy, Shirley, and I drove to the Tampa Town Hall where I spent $2 for my building permit. In the afternoon we went to Hunts and ordered lumber for an addition on my house..."

The used wood delivered on Tuesday cost $66.30. Sam was occupied pulling nails out of the materials. Five concrete bases and five pier blocks added $5.15. The hardware purchase was 15 pounds of nails at $1.86. Roofing and miscellaneous were $7.77. He was out $81.08 so far. Sam and Roy made a big start on the room. They constructed the roof the next day.

Sam was not the only one with an expansion. Shirley telephoned to say that Tommy had made a down-payment on a National Homes three-bedroom house in Windsor Gardens. Shirley was as supremely happy as Sam had ever known.

Sam's own words...
Friday, February 11, 1955 – "...Shirley received a letter from Gail saying Ed has been real sick with pneumonia..."

Gail added that Aunt June Voorheis, her father's sister-in-law who was a nurse, had been coming over to the farm and giving her dad prescribed penicillin shots. He was able to avoid going to the hospital. Edwin lay in his bed, and they were all worried. Bucky, Jeanie, and Gail were doing chores before and after school while Betty directed the whole show.

Bill Courtney was hired to finish up Sam's building, and it was nearing a completed state. He framed windows and put in a door casing. Meanwhile, Sam was hired by Bill to help him on a job. In the end, Sam earned $22.50 at Carpenter work and paid out $42.50 to Mr. Courtney.

Sam's own words...
Tuesday, February 15, 1955 – "...We were glad to get a letter from Teddy. He has 34 days left to serve in the army and is anxious to return to civilian life..."

Sam bought a screen door for $14.94 and hardware to hang it added $1.94. The project was a new kitchen almost ready to use. Sam had sore legs from too many bumps and fatigue from work. He soaked them in Epsom Salts in the evening while the others went to a drive-in movie. A letter from David was welcome news to Sam, who was glad he liked his work at Bell Aircraft in Buffalo, NY.

Alice Jeffries sent Sam $5 to buy a cake for Grace and Roy's 50th anniversary. Shirley bought ice cream and invited all the neighbors in for a grand celebration.

The news made a big deal about a Montgomery, AL, bus incident. A 15-year-old African-American girl, Claudette Colvin, refused to give up her seat to a white woman after the driver demanded it. She was kicked, handcuffed, and harassed while being pulled off the bus backward to be taken to the police station. Sam shook his head. He'd never seen anything like it and hoped he never would.

Sam's 72nd birthday was not lonely but the days to follow would be. Roy, Grace, and Shirley were heading north on Friday, March 4. Sam smiled as he read many cards that had arrived from Willa, Betty and others. His sisters never forgot him.

Old George Minard was constant at Sam's two or three times a day. Sam tried to stay off his game leg but offer a welcome when his friendly neighbor came over.

Sam's own words...
Thursday, March 8, 1955 – "Had to have some groceries, so I took the bus to the Springs, got them at the A & P and my dinner at a restaurant...I saw Arthur Watkins and a fine colored man in the Springs, and they both asked where I had been so long. L 51 degrees, H 70."

The next day Sam went to get a haircut and to the hardware store for paint and brushes. His leg felt harassed and let him know it. Another day he went to mail a card for Willa's 53rd birthday and to buy ice, groceries, and ointment. If the $1.49 for one ounce of salve was an indication of effectiveness, the ulcer ought to have healed up on one application. He planned to stay off his leg by postponement of the painting for a few days.

Sam's hot plate petered out on March 18.

After more than a week to rest his limb, he got around to filling cracks in the kitchen floor and painting it. The leg protested again, and Sam spent a lot of time applying hot and cold packs. He was sure it was slowly healing.

Teddy's first son, Russell, 9 pounds and 3 ounces, was born on Saint Patrick's Day. Ted gave him the name to honor the memory of his friend, Ed's young brother who had died. Shirley's letter bringing the news also said that she and Tommy would move into their new home by April 1.

The leg, the stubborn ulcer, and the time it took to doctor it, was a worry. Sam plastered a bread and milk poultice on it to try to draw the poison out. Later, he gently dabbed Gentian Violet on it again. The antiseptic dye was used to treat fungal infections of the skin like ringworm or athlete's foot. It also has weak antibacterial effects on minor cuts and scrapes to prevent infection. Old Minard got Sam's groceries and eggs for him. Mrs. Packard stopped in to check on Sam, and he told her that his leg was better.

New York state weather was harsh. Sam's radio reported that northern New York had 18 inches of snow. Old Minard had more static than the radio some days. He had many faults to find with his wife, Lillian, and Sam grew tired of hearing it.

When Sam used the oil stove to cook, it heated the kitchen too much. The electric hot plate needed replacing. He went to make the purchase and buy groceries. Sam was disappointed when he returned to find a note on the door. He shook his head because he'd missed Frank and Mary's visit. He was the complainer now instead of Old Minard but for a better reason. A huge sigh escaped as Sam's shoulders slumped.

Sam's own words...
Friday, April 8, 1955 – "...Easter. Received a card from Frances and David Jr. Frances says David wants his father's address. He might join the Navy, too."

David Jr. was 16, an age to begin thinking about what he might want to do with his life. Maybe it was Frances who wanted her former husband's address. And might the elder David have wanted more than the New York City post office box address for his son, which had been withheld by Frances. Where did David Jr. and Frances live? Sam didn't know either. Little David had been missing half his life from his cousins and aunts and uncles who all loved him. In Bennettsburg, NY, Betty had wondered aloud about their address. She had answered Jeanie and Gail's questions with the truth that she didn't know just where in the big city of New York they lived. They all wished they knew. P.O. Box 613 at Grand Central Station did not reveal a place anyone could visit to see David. It only deepened the mystery of the great city life imagined by his cousins on the farm.

Sam's own words...
Monday, April 11, 1955 – "Glad for Shirley's letter. Teddy is back working

at National Homes. Old George is talking divorce, whether he does anything about it or not..."

Spring had opened up in Horseheads. Robins were back, trees were budding out, and trout fishing was in full swing. A stream was where Shirley said her avid fisherman, Tommy, so often went. The Packards had gone north and moved to Waverly, PA, according to their postcard. Grace wrote and requested that he come back around May 1 when Frank and Mary returned. Sam had time to think about it. No reason to decide right now.

The radio and newspapers of April 12 reported the success of the Jonas Salk polio vaccine having passed large-scale trials earlier in the United States. It was now under full approval of the Food and Drug Administration (FDA).

Sam's own words...
Monday, April 18, 1955 – "...One of the greatest scientists of this century, Albert Einstein, 71, died today."

Sam and others thought it a sad loss for the brilliant scientist to leave humankind so soon. It was right up there in stature with Franklin D. Roosevelt, to his mind.

Old George said Lil was beyond the pale. Sam might have wondered what her side would be, but he wanted no involvement. He already knew more than he wished to. George went to a lawyer. It raised Sam's eyebrows, cornered listener that he was, to hear the recent revelation from the newly enlightened grumbler. Mr. Minard had decided to make the best of the situation and stay married, sighting loss of money if he proceeded. His free railroad pass as a retired employee would get him away to Niagara Falls, NY, to visit relatives as soon as his railroad pension check arrived.

Sam's garden was bountiful with carrots, onions, and snap beans that he was proud to share with neighbors.

An envelope had been returned back to Sam's mailbox. He followed the address with his index finger to check the accuracy of the destination address he had put on it. It was the same one Frances had given him on her last envelope. His finger tapped the writing as he wondered what the problem was. Naturally, the puzzlement was mentioned to Frank and Mary when they came for an hour's visit. Sam told them he was not ready to leave Florida yet since the produce from his garden was just now ripe for enjoyment.

Old Minard went on his railroad trip.

Sam repaired his outhouse and contracted Jim Gordon to paint the new siding. Sam wanted it done before his trip north. He didn't have time by himself to accomplish all that was needed before leaving. The new room kept Sam busy painting the outside window frames.

Sam's own words...
Wednesday, May 18, 1955 – "I took the bus to Florida Avenue and saw Dr. Elsin concerning the ulcer on my leg. He gave me some ointment and told me to get Tincture of Merthiolate, pills to take, sterile gauze pads, tape and also a shot in my hip. He wants me to come back next Wednesday and to stay off my feet as much as I could."

The pills were $1.80, and all of the other supplies came to $2.25. Sam made his best effort to follow the doctor's advice. He wouldn't ever know that the Food and Drug Administration (FDA) banned the use of Merthiolate in over-the-counter products in the late 1990s. The mercury found in Merthiolate and Mercurochrome was toxic to both people and the environment.

Old Minard was home Friday night, May 20, after his two-week escapement vacation. The next day his abundance of neighborly visits resumed.

Grace sent a plea for Sam to return home. He was already in that mindset and nodded a smile at her insistent words. Sam rode the bus to the Springs and treated himself to dinner at the Dog Track restaurant before the purchase of his Greyhound ticket costing $27.17. Returning on the local bus, he chatted with Mrs. Wagner.

Sam arrived in Horseheads on Saturday, June 11, at 9:30 a.m. Many came to see him immediately although he tried to rest from the trip. In a couple of days, Grace and Roy took Sam to see Shirley and Tommy's new house. It was a bonus to find Teddy there. On the way home, Roy made a stop to get materials for his bee hives.

Sam was back in the midst of everyone he loved. A letter from Willa capped it all off to heighten his feeling of well-being and blessedness. He got his hoe out. He would be busy in the garden. Dewey and Millie had a habit of stopping in. Dewey's health had recovered from two years of illness and slow recuperation. Sam paid Grace $8 for room and board.

Sam's own words...
Thursday, August 4, 1955 – "I received a letter from W. H. Sallas verifying that this August payment on my Florida land contract pays the mortgage in full. 90 degrees..."

Sam tucked the confirmation in the envelope, leaned back in his seat and clasped his hands behind his head. The last payment was to be $34.74, and he'd soon send it to Florida. He smiled, pleased about the double payment of $40 he had paid every month from the beginning.

Sam was called to work for Artman's Nursery and also a few hours for Mr. Wheater. It would be a satisfying summer if he could get his leg completely healed. Four-or five-hours of work in the mornings would have to do for now because afternoons got up to 85 to 95 degrees and made it hard on him. It bothered his leg to walk far.

At the beginning of September, before school started, Betty and several of the children were going door to door in Horseheads and Elmira selling sweet corn. The money would buy school clothes.

Roy had begun work for Mr. Wilcox in Odessa to care for his bee hives. He'd taught himself the talent many years back by having an apiary for harvesting honey. It came in handy now for a paycheck.

Steele appeared in late September, and Sam rode along with him up to Ed and Betty's farm. They were gratified with the reception everyone gave them. Betty's children would neither know how to withhold affection from their grandfather nor would they want to. Their warmth extended easily to Uncle Steele. Before Steele's visit finished, he repaid Sam for a loan from a while ago.

Back in Horseheads, Sam dug all of the potatoes and stored them in the cold cellar. It was a sure sign that September was at an end.

Sam's September hours for Artman's Nursery added up to earnings of $134.50.

The first frost came on October 22. Frank and Mary left for Zephyrhills the week before, too early for Sam to consider going south.

Helen Rackett, 81 years old, died, and Sam thought kindly of Old Rip, who was without her now in the Breesport County Home for the poor.

Everyone turned clocks back one hour and awoke Sunday, October 30, to Eastern Standard Time, which Sam was glad to welcome. He earned $90 from Artman's Nursery for October and gave Roy $50 toward the vehicle trade he was making. The older 1941 Chevy was replaced by a 1950 model that they'd all enjoy.

November 5 brought news of racial segregation forbidden on trains and buses in U.S. interstate commerce. No one yet knew how well it would hold. It made no problem to Sam's mind if he might sit next to a black person on a bus. Many southerners considered it unacceptable that blacks were refusing to be pushed to the back of the bus.

Strong north winds in mid-November made Sam think he belonged in Florida. Light snow fell all day November 15 to reinforce the message. But they needed him for more work at Artman's, and so he stayed on through November.

December, with its rough weather, drove the three Mill Street residents to make arrangements to go south. Visitors galore came to say goodbye. The trio left Horseheads at 8 a.m. on Wednesday, December 7. They arrived at Sam's Tampa place at 5 p.m. on December 9.

Old George Minard was predictable but welcome during three visits he made to them the next day. It was not predictable to hear the first news he had salivated over that early morning. He could hardly spit it out that Bill and Helen had married after many years of their common-law marriage. Sam thought they should feel much better about themselves and was glad to hear it.

On Sunday, December 18, Sam, Grace, and Roy attended church services at the Hillsborough drive-in theater at 8:30 a.m.

On Friday, December 23, they went to the Tower Theater and saw Clark Gable and Jane Russell in *The Tall Men*. In the two-hour western, two brothers join a cattle drive from Texas to Montana. While heading for Texas they save Nella from the Indians, and she decides to ride with them. Ben and Nella start to get romantic. Ben isn't ambitious enough for her, and she soon meets up with the boss of the cattle drive.

Sam was pleased with the thoughtfulness of David, Hilda, and the children when he received a December 26 parcel with the 1956 almanac and a box of cigars.

He had worked on weed eradication on his property every day since he arrived there. A rash had developed on his right hand and wrist. Now he needed Dr. Elsin's help for eradication. By December's end, the month of expenses had cost Sam $86.79. It included trip expenses, paint, oil, groceries, and sundries too small to be specified.

~**~

1956

Besides sightseeing excursions in Roy's car, the three of them visited Frank and Mary in Zephyrhills. Sam splurged and sent $2.30 to the Doubleday One Dollar Book Club. No gardening took place while they had frosts several mornings and temperatures down to 29 degrees.

Sam bought a cupboard for his new kitchen. Dewey and Millie arrived on Sunday, January 8. They upheld the opinions expressed in letters from Shirley and Betty that said it was too cold in upstate New York. They had ice and snow to keep it that way.

On January 17, the three inseparables drove to the Floriland Theater and saw Liberace in *Sincerely Yours*. The two-hour movie was about Tony Warrin who has it all. A popular pianist who plays any style, he has money, great clothes, a penthouse overlooking Central Park, a gorgeous blonde fiancée, a loyal brunette secretary secretly in love with him, and a date at Carnegie Hall. On concert night, disease deafens him.

The visits continued between Zephyrhills and Tampa. Dewey and Millie bought a building lot near Frank and Mary and planned to construct a house on it the next year.

Sam tried to convince Grace and Roy to stay another month, but they departed early on Sunday, February 5, bound for Horseheads, NY. He felt their absence. His 73rd birthday on March 3 came and went like any average day, except for receiving several cards.

Sam was glad the Packards came down from Pennsylvania and were in Tampa. His Doubleday Book Club would soon supply reading material.

Sam's own words...
Sunday, March 19, 1956 – "...Mabel Packard drove us up to a gas station where it was 21¢ a gallon and said, "Fill her up," but all the tank held was 58¢ worth, though the gauge showed near empty. We all had a good laugh including the attendant."

Old Minard was not laughing and in the heat of the moment, went to the lawyer again about a divorce. He came to the same conclusion that it was cheaper to forget it. Sam just shook his head. What was there to say?

Sam's leg gave considerable trouble again. Gauze bandages were bought and used with a refill of the same prescription from last May that had healed it. He tried to stay off his feet.

Shirley and Tommy arrived, and she stayed with her father while Tommy went to his mother's in Hattiesburg, MS.

Betty wrote that Jeanie had married Henry (Hank) Simmons back on March 9 in Burdett. She was just short of 18 years old. Sam hoped the same as Ed and Betty that they'd be happy. Hank was back at Fort Knox, KY, and Jeanie remained at home. Betty said Bucky wanted to join the service.

Tommy was back, and the Broadheads left for Horseheads on March 22, and Sam was alone again. The leg was a little better but still in need of doctoring.

Sam had to buy groceries and sundries and couldn't stay off his feet entirely. He took advantage of opportune visits with friends and passed winter days in sunshine the same as previous years.

April 2 brought news of Ted and Hazel's new baby, Steven Paul Herforth, born March 25. He was a healthy newborn at nine pounds 13 ounces. Sam noted with a smile that it made him a great-grandfather three times over. Shirley also wrote that Gail was staying with her through Easter vacation, and they were having a grand time. His Easter weather would be more pleasant than theirs from what Sam heard on the radio. The report said they were getting more snow in Pennsylvania and New York, as much as 16 inches in some sections. He would not be enticed home by Shirley's letter hoping he would return soon. The Packards and Hesses were going back in less than a week.

Gail wrote that Bucky had been inducted into the Air Force on April 16. She added that her mom and dad were having a farm auction on the 25th to sell livestock and tools. Ed would go back to carpenter work.

Old George and Lilian had another spat, and Sam had to hear about it, but he didn't have to comment. One-armed 87-year-old George Minard was waiting on a railroad pass, and he would be on his way to Niagara Falls, NY, again.

Sam was alone for sure when the Courtney's went on vacation for three weeks. He watered their flowers while they were away.

Sam's own words...
Sunday, May 20, 1956 – "One of Jehovah's Witnesses called on me and left without saying goodbye because we couldn't see eye to eye, although I said goodbye to him. He seems to believe their way is the one and only way there is to heaven. At home all day. L 64 degrees - H 89."
Saturday, June 2, 1956 – "I was gladdened and surprised when the mail carrier drove in about 1:30 p.m. with a package, found to contain a new radio sent me by my boys and girls and no doubt others...It sure gives perfect reception, and my old one had become poor. I am pleased and thankful. Home all day. Old George called twice. 78 to 88 degrees."

A brand new portable electric radio was $69.25, precisely why Sam hadn't had one so fine. There would be many who could purchase the General Electric Telechron's latest featured introduction, a snooze alarm.

Sam sent for a 78¢ gallon of milk when Old Minard went to the store.

Sam's own words...
Thursday, June 14, 1956 – "Jim Gordon came about 1:30 p.m. with a snoot full, and he was piloting a couple, a man, and wife, who are interested in buying a place. He had set the price of my place at $3,500. I told him in their presence that if I wanted to give it away, it wouldn't be to strangers but to my children. I was disgusted. After they left, two real estate men came. He had told them about my place. They wanted me to list it with them, but I did not."

The next day Bill Courtney told Sam that Jim Gordon had gone home so drunk and rowdy in the trailer park that he was ordered to get out at once. They were moving their trailer to another park, and Mrs. Gordon was worried in her old age. Sam was indignant all over again that an old man quaffed with alcohol had besotted himself into a staggering wretchedness.

John Crippen and Hank Simmons, who took turns driving, arrived Monday, June 24, to bring Sam home. They were on their way by 6:40 a.m. on Tuesday. They spent an overnight in Fayetteville, NC. The Elmira destination, John's home, was reached Wednesday at mid-night.

Sam did not miss the July 30 news that in two weeks on Flag Day, June 14, President Eisenhower would sign the authorization to make In God We Trust the United States national motto. In God We Trust first appeared on U.S. coins in 1864 and has appeared on paper currency since 1957. Sam smiled as he read it in his morning newspaper.

Sam's own words...
Wednesday, August 1, 1956 – "In the evening, Grace, Roy, and I (sic) drove from Horseheads to Elmira and back over the new road, which was opened today on Route 17. It certainly is a beautiful piece of road and makes Elmira seem nearer."

This summer was different in that Sam seldom worked for hire, earning only $1 or $2 for small, short duration jobs. He took care of his ulcerated leg.

It was the summer that 13-year-old Jimmy, Ed and Betty's son, was in an accident on a dirt road not far from the Bennettsburg farm. He was driving Ed's truck, and it went out of his control on the gravel road and rolled over twice. Jimmy was in the Montour Falls Hospital. Sam thought to himself, "Thank God" when he learned that his grandson was not seriously hurt. The truck did not fare so well, but Ed could replace it.

Sam's own words...
Sunday, September 9, 1956 – "...Steele came in the afternoon and asked me to go to his place on Walnut Street and have supper with Sandra and him. Sandra did the cooking, and she had a good meal, which I enjoyed and my visit very much. She is 14 years old, I believe..."

Sam went to stay at John and Lucille's for a few days because Grace and Roy were bringing Cretia from Galeton for her visit with Dr. Brooks for denture repair. She would stay awhile to enjoy herself as long as she was already there. The house had ample bedrooms for both of them, but Sam may have been kind to Grace to let the women have the time all to themselves. It was also a kindness to Cretia, too, whether or not she thought so or even gave Sam credit.

A few days later, he rode to Galeton with them when Cretia was taken home, which was on the corner of Clinton and Crippen streets. Sam, Grace, and Roy traveled back on a different route and enjoyed each other and the countryside.

When they returned, Shirley reported to the three of them that Ed and Betty's little girl, Carol, had fallen from a beam she was walking on in the barn and was in Montour Hospital. After well placed private stitches she healed in a few days and went back to school November 2. They were all thankful to hear when she was well.

Eisenhower was handily re-elected as United States president. Frank and Mary high-tailed it to Florida right after they voted.

Sam bought himself and Grace each a 1957 diary while they were in plentiful supply and easy to find. He spent $3.30 total.

The November 13 news reported that the United States Supreme Court had declared the Alabama state and Montgomery, AL, laws supporting segregated seating on buses to be illegal, thus ending the Montgomery bus boycott. Rosa Parks, a young African American woman, arrested for refusing to surrender her seat to a white person, led to this ruling that segregation on buses was unconstitutional. Many important figures in the Civil Rights Movement took part in the boycott, including Reverend Martin Luther King Jr. and Ralph Abernathy.

Sam went home for an overnight with Ed and Betty on Saturday, November 17. They had come in the truck to take lambs to sell at the stock yard. Sam may have enjoyed the visit as much as the children did.

Sam was greatly surprised when Charles Artman, nursery owner, came to see him December 3 and brought him half a pound of Prince Albert. He no doubt missed Sam and wanted to see how he was doing. It lifted Sam's spirits and Grace's, too, from the way she dabbed at her eyes and smiled. Cold weather had Sam's leg bothering, or was it just ready to ping him again because it could?

Sam's own words...
Saturday, December 8, 1956 – "Ruth McCann and family came over from Ithaca and were here about an hour in early evening. To top it off they brought Grace and Roy a fine portable TV set, a gift from Francis McCann, they said. It surely is wonderful of him. We stayed up until 10:30 p.m. watching programs. The neighbors will think someone is sick for we usually retire at 9:30 or before."
Sunday, December 9, 1956 – "Snowed off and on all day. We spent much of our time watching the new TV."
Monday, December 10, 1956 – "Roy and I drove over to Dr. Emperts in early p.m., and he gave me a cod-oil salve for my leg. I hope it does the work. If not, he gave me a prescription to fill at the drug store...I shoveled off the walks."

The three of them most likely enjoyed the Lawrence Welk show or the Huntley-Brinkley Report that had debuted back on October 29 on NBC-TV. The doctor call cost Sam $4 as he sought relief.

Steele stopped in on Friday, December 21, and told them that he and Ruthie were recently divorced.

The time had come shortly after Christmas, December 29, to leave for Tampa. Grace, Roy, and Sam arrived at Sam's place on Monday, December 31, at 5:20 p.m. Old Minard came right over and could hardly stand still with his delight. His eyes gleamed as he bounced from foot to foot.

~**~
1957

Sam's own words...
Tuesday, January 1, 1957 – "A new year dawns. God grant it may be a peaceful one, at least one without a major war. Grace, Roy, and I are thankful to have had a safe journey to Tampa. Today we are resting. My neighbor, Art Lapham, mowed weeds around my yard but as usual, I have a bumper crop to cut. L 40 degrees - H 70."

Their rest included a leisurely ride over to Zephyrhills to see Mary and Frank. On return, Sam put in a new stove pipe for his stove while Roy hung up a shelf for the radio. Old George made many faithful visits.

Sunday saw the three at the Hillsborough drive-in at 8:30 a.m. to attend church.

Mr. Daniel Harrell, who lived nearby on another street, stopped in to state his interest in buying several of Sam's lots of 65' x 60'. The real estate broker said they needed surveyance first. Mr. Harrell called a surveyor who said it would be $35 per parcel, which Sam thought was ridiculous. Mr. Harrell found one who would do the entirety for $75. Sam thought that was enough, too, but they settled for it. It would all take time to get to the sales transaction.

Sam's own words...

Saturday, January 12, 1957 – "Around home most of day. In afternoon we drove to the Springs after a few groceries. On our way home, we stopped in Lowery Park. Roy seems to be homesick, and Grace says he wants to return home."

Sam and Grace thought another trip to Frank and Mary's might help. It didn't. Roy felt even less contented. Grace decided Roy might like it if they lived in a Zephyrhills cabin or trailer. They looked at a cottage and would no doubt take it. Sam believed Grace might also be happier near their sister, Mary.

The next morning as soon as he awoke, Roy announced that he wasn't going to live in that coop and pay $35 a month plus oil, electric, and water. Nothing suited him as if he had no regard for what Grace might want. He acted like he was on a hot seat and had to get off. It wasn't like him to seem unreasonable.

The surveying took place and was completed January 14, but Sam had to get in hand what he called his plot of the lots. The three of them went out on rides. Sam and Grace wanted to appease Roy and keep his interest in anything but going home before Grace was in agreement. It took a search and more than one excursion to find the trailer park where Jim and Martha Gordon resided. Roy was all for it when they went to the drive-in church service again.

Sam planted watermelon, squash, and morning glories. He kept busy while he and Daniel Harrell were waiting for title insurance to come through before the lot sales completion. Sam planted flower seeds.

Dewey and Millie arrived in Zephyrhills, and Sam, Grace, and Roy made the trip over to see them on February 2. The sale of the five lots finished, and Mr. Harrell started the groundbreaking on the house he had planned. Sam had five lots remaining. On Sunday, February 10, Grace and Roy bought a bushel of oranges to take north with them. They embarked on the homeward trek Monday.

Another neighbor, Mr. Spivey was concerned about the ulcer on Sam's leg. He suggested that Sam use gallberry. They went in Spivey's car and picked a selection to bring back to Sam's place. Under directions his neighbor supplied, Sam steeped the leaves and darker-than-night berries.

Mr. Spivey said he believed Sam would be healed in two months if he took two tablespoons before meals until healed. Sam found the brew bitter but not more so than the boneset his father used years back.

Boneset was for a different purpose. It was supposed to reduce fever and serve as an expectorant. Sam remembered the green bush with creamy flowering tops steeped as a tea.

Old George Minard was a real friend in addition to his many visits. When he was out on an errand in his car, he often brought a gallon of oil for Sam's stove. It saved hand carrying it with groceries when Sam walked after them. Sam repaid the favor when George had presents to send to his daughters in Niagara Falls, NY. Sam wrapped the gifts and did up a big package for him. Grace's crossword puzzle dictionary was left behind, and Sam sent it along to her with a letter, which George would mail for him. Grace and Roy had arrived home on February 13.

Sam planted his onion sets that arrived from the Burpee Company. There were three rows, which he had planted to have enough for himself and neighbors.

Sam's own words...
Wednesday, February 20, 1957 – "Mary, Lynn, Iva, and daughter, Margarite drove in about 2 p.m., and I was shocked to hear that Roy Whiting passed away yesterday a.m. God bless his soul and be with Grace, Alice, and Ruth, and we who are left behind. I, too, shall miss him. I'm thankful it did not occur on the way home. The funeral is to be Friday, and I couldn't possibly get there in time. It is too bad so many of us are in Florida at a time like this when Grace needs us so much. She is like a

mother to John, Steele, and Shirley, and they will do all they can for they love her."

Dewey, Millie, and everyone from Zephyrhills visited Sam before Dewey's departure back north on February 25. They'd all learned that Grace's daughter, Ruth, and Ruth's daughter, Margie, were moving in with Grace in two weeks. Sam was glad for that and for Dewey's return home. Grace would not be so alone.

Sam had a prescription filled to doctor his leg. A slew of cards had been arriving. Even without them, there would be no forgetting about his turning 74 on March 3.

Mr. Harrell made his first $30 payment on the $2,000 mortgage for the lots. It was to take him about 5½ years to pay it off.

Sam was chief cook and bottle washer, but that was not all. It may not be what he wrote to Grace about, but he wrote the following episode in his diary.

Sam's own words...
Sunday, March 10, 1957 – "Old George came over this morning, said he had pain and hadn't had a bowel movement in three days and wanted me to give him an enema, which I did. It did little good, and in the evening George came again, so I went home with him and gave another one without results. He is going to the doctor in the morning, and I pray he can help him. L 32 degrees - H 74. Light frost."

Mr. Lapham took Old George to Dr. Elsin Monday, and George seemed better when Sam called on him twice.

Sam received a card from Christy who said all was well and that she had a job in Reno, Nevada, and Willa in Denver, CO. Sam wrote right back and sent Willa a note in a birthday card.

Sam ate dinner with Bill and Helen Courtney on Thursday, March 14. She had suffered terribly with an abscess in her nose but didn't ask Sam to lance it.

Sam's own words...
Friday, March 15, 1957 – "Received a card from Grace written the 11th, wondering if I was lonely, too bless her. I have been lonely many times in the last 12 years, although some of it has been my own making. Ruth will

move in with Grace tomorrow. Dewey comes nearly every morning for a few minutes she says."

Old Minard came twice daily for shorter visits since he was weak and trying to gain his strength back. A few days later, Sam took his whistle-billy over to George's yard and cut weeds around the house.

Sam's first issue of *Coronet* magazine subscription arrived. Coronet was a general-interest monthly magazine published in the United States from October 13, 1936, to March 1971. It produced 299 issues.

A letter from Steele told of his hopes to transfer to Attica, near Buffalo, for guard duty. He and Ruth Lanterman Brown intended to marry as soon as her divorce came through from Harlow, who lived with another woman in California.

Sam rode the bus to Sulphur Springs and had his dinner there before he bought his medicines and groceries. In the course of his day, there were people he ran across and enjoyed conversations.

Sam's own words...
Wednesday, March 27, 1957 – "Received letters from Grace and others. Ruth has her furniture and all of her things moved in and all topsy turvy. Grace says sometimes she wishes she and I had a place to ourselves for we are used to each other and think alike. Poor dear..."
Thursday, April 4, 1957 – "Was glad to get a letter from Shirley. Ted and wife have another girl, Lyn Marie. Trout fishing opened April 1, and Tommy is doing his share...(also) dear letters from David and Hilda's girls, Bonnie and Velma. The girls report Lester will be in fourth grade, Velma sixth, Bonnie high; Daddy getting bald and fat, Mommie a few gray hairs. Bonnie likes Tab Hunter better than Elvis Presley."

Sam might have wondered where he would fit in if Grace's house were overflowing with people and things. He did know that she wanted him there. He appreciated all the letters from home.

Old George seemed weaker and was using a cane. He had his 88th birthday on April 10.

Sam's own words...
Saturday, April 20, 1957 – "Received a card from Mary saying she and Frank are planning to come for a picnic in Lowery Park tomorrow. In the

evening, Mrs. Lucas gave me a fish, and I appreciated her kindness and thanked her. I am ashamed to admit that I don't much care for fish and never cleaned one in my life. Finally buried it under my Brazillian (sic) Pepper tree. Mowed part of lawn. L 65 degrees - H 85."

The Lowery Park picnic was an enjoyable four hours for Sam. He wouldn't see Frank and Mary for quite awhile since they were leaving soon for their Addison, NY, home. They would experience colder weather again, but the radio reported 52 degrees in Buffalo. Sam thought it was mild for New York state and was glad for them. Old Minard talked about making a trip to Buffalo for what he believed would be his last rail trip.

Sam's own words...
Friday, May 3, 1957 – "Was glad to get a letter from home. David Jr. has joined the Coast Guard for three years..."
Wednesday, May 8, 1957 – "Received letter from Grace with the shocking news that my old pal John Long died Saturday, May 4, of a heart attack. He was 75 years old on February 2. I miss him as much as I would a brother. John and I went west together 50 years ago, come October 28. Also word from Steele. Sandra is at Ruth Brown's...and seems happy. Ruth expects her divorce the 25th, and they can go ahead with their plans. May God bless them..."

Sam was deep in melancholy thought of long ago when he and John Long were young. His longing was not to wish him back but to cherish the memories and wish his dear old friend's soul to rest in God's blessings. He wrote, "We are going out of this world one by one, and one generation is but a jump behind the other. The Lord's time is my time."

His thought about the Lord's time was from his mother, Sophia Dimon Crippen, who said it often in her last year. It was a great comfort to hold in his heart, and he missed her still.

A special envelope arrived for Sam from his granddaughter, Mickey Crippen, John's daughter. She wanted to come south if her dad came after Grandpa Sam. He smiled as he wrote a note to put in with a vivid multi-scene folder of Tampa to mail to her.

Sam installed a new wick in a burner of his oil stove. It cost him 73¢, which he thought was too high of a price since the old one was 52¢.

He mowed lawn Saturday, May 18, and did not enjoy it one bit. Maybe his lot was too large. Maybe it was too hot at 92 degrees. There was no maybe that all of his chigger bites needed doctoring. It was their season, not his. They could drive him home to New York.

The stove was taken down and put in the shed.

Mickey wrote to thank Grandpa for the Tampa picture booklet, saying, "I love it." She reported that her sister, Kathy was doing well in school.

Sam listened to sermons on the radio every Sunday. They were a comfort to keep him grounded in Christ. He wrote his opinion for all who would remain after his passing. In later years, his Shirley copied one she deemed important for her keeping.

~**~

Life is a state of being, not a reason for being.
We all have life whether we know how or why.
Therefore, to me, it seems as reasonable to
Believe in a future life as in this one.

~**~

Sam's own words...
Monday, June 3, 1957 – "Was glad to get a letter from Betty, although the news wasn't all good. Jeanie was riding a horse, and the saddle turned under him, and she broke her leg above the ankle. No doubt it will mend for she is young and healthy. Did my washing, etc. and cut a little more lawn."

The big yard included the five empty lots. Of course, it was oversize. Old Minard came over three times Wednesday. He had decided that he was not well enough to make a trip to Niagara Falls.

John arrived Monday, June 24, to take Sam home, but first, they had to have the car repaired. In the end, it cost them about $60. They left for home four days later and arrived at John's on Sunday. Sam had all kinds of offers for where he could stay, but he was glad to go to Grace's, bag and baggage. It was where he wanted to be more than any other place. She needed him. He needed her.

Steele and Ruth had married a week earlier. He had his guard job at Attica now. They visited Sam and brought Ruth's five children and Sandra.

Millie called with information for Sam on Saturday, July 20, to tell him that Sandra, who was in Ruth's care, had an appendicitis operation and was doing all right. Steele was on his way from Attica to be with her.

Sam had been hoeing and finally cleaned off the garden. He considered it too late to have much of a garden. Grace needed a flower bed to plant poppy seeds and he'd see to that.

Sam's own words...
Thursday, August 1, 1957 – "...Shirley and Gail were with us in early evening. Gail is staying awhile, several days."
Monday, August 5, 1957 – "...I was glad to get a card from Willa and to know everyone is well...Babbette was married last spring. She was very young, but Willa says they are doing fine. She certainly was a sweet little kid."

It was a week before Sam wrote back to Willa.

He learned of the death of Charles Artman on September 17. He was a former boss and nursery owner, who had become a friend. Sam wrote, "We all have our entrance and exit." Could Sam have read a Shakespeare play and remembered that line?

September news heated up for the American Civil Rights Movement. Little Rock, AR, was in crisis. Governor Faubus called out the National Guard to prevent African-American students from enrolling in Central High School in his town. The Ford Motor Company may have unintentionally played second fiddle to that news as far as Sam was concerned, except he wasn't concerned at all. Ford introduced the Edsel on what the company proclaimed as E-Day.

On September 24 President Eisenhower sent federal troops to Arkansas to provide safe passage to school for "The Little Rock Nine."

Sam's own words...
Saturday, October 5, 1957 – "We were glad to have Sadie with us again today...The Russians have launched a satellite, which is circling the globe every 95 minutes."

It was surprising, unexpected news to hear about the successful satellite, Sputnik 1, by the Soviet Union. Many Americans were shocked and frightened as the small satellite orbited the earth. How had the

Russians gotten so far ahead of the supposedly technologically superior United States? That was the dismay, and Sam was not immune to wondering about its full meaning.

Betty's 42nd birthday was just ahead, and Sam wrote out a card ready to mail. He had only a few carrots to dig and store in the cellar for late October.

Sam's own words...
Saturday, November 2, 1957 – "Was glad to see Bucky when he stopped for a few minutes. He has another week at home before he returns to his Air Force duties..."

When Sam and Grace came from voting November 5, Buck called on them again in early evening. Dewey was ever faithful visiting them, too.

President Eisenhower suffered a stroke on November 25. It was serious news to Sam and any reasoning person. While speaking to his secretary on that date, Eisenhower found he could not complete his sentences. When examined, he had neither motor nor sensory impairment. The diagnosis was occlusion of the left middle cerebral artery. Eisenhower, who was 67 years old and had three years remaining in his second term of office, was already taking Coumadin. After three days of seclusion, Eisenhower returned to work, his speech not yet back to normal. He was able to finish out his term, three more years. Years later the world would experience Ike's death on March 28, 1969.

John took his family, Grace, and Sam up to Betty's for Thanksgiving dinner where they all enjoyed each other's company and her good food. It was partly a goodbye before Sam left for a warmer locale.

John took his father to Dr. Empert on December 6. Sam received free samples of pills to take to Florida with him. Family members made last visits to Sam while they could and called it an early Christmas. Millie brought Prince Albert tobacco to Sam. John and Shirley pooled their money and gave him a Stetson hat.

Snow fell four or five inches deep the night before they left. Edward Wheeler was driving them down on December 10. Sadie was on board and was as happy about it as her siblings. It was her first experience to see Florida and in the dead of winter. They arrived at Sam's place in Tampa on

Thursday, December 12, at 6 p.m.

Frank and Mabel Packard had the same idea and were down south already to winter in Tampa. Mabel picked up Grace and Sadie on December 21, to go to North Gate shopping center. Sam was dropped off at Dr. Elsin's office. They picked him up an hour or so later. His sisters asked how he had made out. He said he had high blood pressure, new pills, and had paid $7.

Daniel Harrell brought Sam and his sisters a homemade fruitcake on Christmas Day. "Mighty fine of him," agreed Sam and his siblings. Mr.

Harrell was introduced to them by Sam as the man who had bought five of Sam's lots.

Frank and Mabel came from Zephyrhills and took Sam, Grace, and Sadie to Lowery Park for a picnic, no snow in sight and smiles all around, shaded by a palm tree.

38 – Explorer
Old George, 1958, 1959, 1960, 1961

Sam rose first every morning to make a fire. By the time his sisters stirred it was a little warmer. They experienced frosts now and then right through February. Dewey and Mildred arrived on February 6, as did Frank and Mary. The women went shopping at South Gate. Grace bought Sam a pair of pants and a chambray shirt for an early 75th birthday present because she wouldn't be in Florida in March. Dewey accomplished what he came for when he bought another lot in Zephyrhills for future building plans. Sam was alone again when all of them departed for Horseheads on February 11.

Sam had his radio for company and short visits from Old George Minard who didn't feel well much of the time. Sam received a passel of birthday cards, and Grace wrote to him as often as he did her. She told about a recent call from Dewey. He said Millie had painful gallstones and a hernia. Dr. Empert declined to operate until she reduced her weight. Sam smiled at learning that Tommy Broadhead returned the plump Sears catalog he borrowed from Grace awhile ago. She told Sam that she had marked on her calendar that it was one year since Roy died, March 13. Lastly, the TV was acting up, and she was disgusted with it.

Sam had been aware of the first successful U.S. attempt into outer-space on January 31 when Explorer 1 launched. More likely hc was glad, like any other, American when the United States played catch-up to Russia again with the March 17 orbital path of the Vanguard 1 satellite. Again, Americans cheered, Sam with them, when the U.S. Army sent Explorer 3 into orbit on March 24. He heard it all on his radio and read details in the newspapers Grace sent.

Poor old George Minard was admitted to the county hospital on March 25, without much hope of recovery. He died that day. Sam felt alone.

Grace reported in her next letter that Gail was staying with Shirley and told them that her brother, Buck, was coming home and getting married. She didn't know which would happen first, but his bride to be, Jean, was from Maine. Grace wanted Sam to return home and filled the rest of her letter with reasons why he should do so. First of all, Ruth and Margie had moved out, and she was alone. Second, the poppies and tulips were out. Third, she missed him, and April was advancing already. She was cleaning Sam's bedroom and was ready for him.

Sam wrote back that Frank and Mary were coming over from Zephyrhills after him April 22, and they might start home. It was Sunday, April 27 when they arrived in Addison, NY. Dewey went to get Sam on Monday.

The year was not much different than the year before. Sam and Grace were a comfort to each other as summer slipped into November. It was the month when American radio debuted a new show, *Have Gun, Will Travel.*

~**~

1959

January 5 dipped down with frosted lips to kiss zero, and the wind blew in an icy blast. Sam thought about Florida sunshine and his place in Tampa. Maybe his mode of travel to go south would materialize soon. He had business to take care of before that avenue opened.

Sam's own words...
Wednesday, January 7, 1959 – "Dewey came about 10:30 a.m. and took me uptown to lawyer Shull's office to have my will made ($5). We will have to return tomorrow morning to conclude it..."
Thursday, January 10, 1959 – "Grace's 74th birthday..."

Teddy's wife, Hazel, and her friend, Onolea, had teamed up to transport Sam, Grace, and Sadie to Florida. They all drove out in Ted's car on Saturday. Tire trouble and dim lights plagued the trip, but they kept going after each repair was made. Then the car died. A good Samaritan driving a 7-Up truck pushed them to a garage. They were there four hours at the cost of $35. It was their fourth day of getting there the hard way. They reached Sam's place at 4 p.m., tired and glad to arrive. The trip cost Sam $72.51. His sister, Mary Hess came over to see them immediately.

Sam discussed with Daniel Harrell about building a new room and a bathroom. Harrell got started right away. Sam was impatient with himself since he couldn't do the work. His legs were a handicap, and he couldn't even help with the job.

Sam's own words…
Monday, February 2, 1959 – "I took the Rome and Waters bus to Florida Avenue to see Dr. Elsin…He tended my ulcers and gave prescriptions for them and high blood pressure. I am to come back Friday…"

His legs hurt him more than usual after the activity and gave no let up on Tuesday for good behavior. The plumber had been working on plumbing for the new bathroom and kitchen. Sam would have a sink and toilet now and a new kitchen with a $20 sink. The septic had been inspected and was not deep enough. Sam doctored his legs as prescribed, although they seemed better they gave him misery.

Sam's own words…
Sunday, February 15, 1959 – "Frank, Mary, Lynn, and Iva came about noon, and we all had a picnic in Lowery Park. They left for home 4 p.m. I made a settlement with Daniel Harrell on the material and labor for the building. Has cost me $911 to date."

Dewey and Millie were in Zephyrhills. Annabelle and her husband, Edward, came after Sadie, Sam and Grace. They left Florida on March 14. At least the three siblings had eight weeks in Tampa. Sam's cost for the return trip amounted to $46 for meals, lodging, and gas, which was 25¢ per gallon.

John took Sam to see yet another doctor over on Lake Street. Dr.

Harold F. Game charged $6 for two visits. High hopes were free.

John traded his Nash for a 1952 Chevy. He continued transporting Sam to the doctor once a week and to the drug store, at times.

Sam's own words…
Wednesday, April 1, 1959 – "Grace did her washing, but there's little I can do until my legs get better."
Wednesday, April 29, 1959 – "Lucille took Grace and I (sic) with her when she picked John up at 3:30 p.m. at the Eclipse. She and Shirley had been working on a painting job." Grace did her washing. I don't do much of anything. Harold Applebee is taking over most of the garden."

Sam could not do his usual amount of gardening but neither could he forfeit the complete enjoyment and only watch Harold. He managed to plant two short rows of potatoes. A whole day of rest let him plant four rows of peas. After another day, he seeded in Swiss chard and zinnias. He doggedly focused on the hoe he had put to work. Onion sets went in. Beets, carrots, and a few gladiola bulbs were last. Slowly it amounted to a real garden but smaller than ever before. Maybe the satisfaction was that much greater.

Sam's own words…
Saturday, May 9, 1959 – "Lucille came and took Grace to the A & P for groceries. Ed, Betty, and Roland came about 9 a.m. for one and a half hours. They had a mother's day gift for Grace. I planted lettuce and cabbage seed. A light frost."

Roland was 12 years old and always found his grandfather interesting. He had learned to play Chinese checkers as instructed by Grandpa years earlier. There was no one else in the world who had told him all about Sitting Bull's life and escapades on and off the Flathead Reservation. When Rolly was a little younger, he was even more spellbound listening to the tales of the renegade during Grandpa's stays at the farm. A few days later Steele and Sandra visited.

Sam sowed beans, sunflowers, and lovely zinnias. Within days, he put in corn and 12 tomato plants. It was May 22, and he leaned on his hoe to survey all he had accomplished. A sigh escaped him. Soon he would do more hoeing to maintain it.

Sam's own words...
Saturday, May 30, 1959 – "John and Lucille came, and we walked over to Lake Street to watch the Memorial Day parade at 2:15 p.m...Afterward, we drove over to Maple Grove Cemetery and put flowers on Edith and Roy's graves...I mowed most of the front lawn."

On Mother's Day, Sam mowed tall grass along the bank by the railroad tracks, which gave a better view of irises, peonies, and lilies. They were coming into bloom, and he wanted to show them off to best advantage. When Sam cultivated or hoed in the garden, his eyes landed on them every time. He supposed that any passersby would be drawn to gaze at them also.

Sam's own words...
Friday, June 5, 1959 – "...I walked up to the bank and drugstore in the morning, the farthest I have walked in a long time."

Dewey entered the Arnot Ogden Hospital on Thursday, June 11, to have varicose veins removed. Sam hoped the aftermath would not be as bothersome for Dewey as Sam's ulcers had been to him. It turned out that Dewey was hospitalized fewer than three days and was getting along well.

Sam and Grace expected a Sears & Roebuck technician to install a gas water heater on Wednesday, July 1, but he did not show up. It was the same day after day.

Alaska added the 49th star to the U.S. flag. Alaska had been admitted to the Union earlier in the year, on January 3, 1959. Sam would not be going further north. If he went any direction, it would be south to Galeton or Tampa.

But summer enjoyment was in front of him and Grace. They went to the Crippen reunion at Denison Park in Corning, NY. There were 60 in attendance at the Sunday, July 5, get-together. It was pleasing to all who went.

Grace's granddaughter, Margie, came over from Ithaca on Monday and took Grace and Sam for a ride to Elmira. She went into Sears and told them to install Grace's water heater or come and get it. They made the installation Tuesday. Sam and Grace held in subdued smiles when they exchanged glances.

Dewey's legs were better than they'd been in a long time. On July 22, he took Sam and Grace to Addison with him. They all enjoyed Mary's meal and a grand visit with Frank and Mary, and Lynn and Iva.

Ed and Betty stopped in now and then on their way back from the Horseheads auction where they sold lambs, pigs, or an occasional cow.

Sam's smile on July 31 marked the first time he harvested new potatoes and sweet corn from his garden.

Sam's own words...
Wednesday, August 5, 1959 – "...Edgar A. Guest, famed poet, died today. He would have been 78 on August 20. Millions have read his poems. He wrote, "I have this faith that when I make the turn, Somewhere I still shall live and love and learn."
Friday, August 14, 1959 – "...Jeanie, Linda, Roland, and Buck's Jean, also her brother from Maine stopped in a few minutes around 4 p.m. They had been selling sweet corn."

Betty came other times when the hardy group peddled corn door to door. Success was theirs. It was usually a good ending and reward for their afternoon sales to visit Sam and Grace.

The 50th state was in the news. Hawaii achieved admittance to the Union on August 21. The stars on the flag would need rearranging again. Sam supposed that it would be a couple of months before the new design appeared as a picture in the newspaper.

Sam's own words...
Thursday, August 27, 1959 – "Fierce electrical storms last night, which did much damage, burned down one house, set fire to others and struck the TV tower six times..."
Monday, September 14, 1959 – "Soviets landed a rocket on the moon."
Tuesday, September 15, 1959 – "Nakita Khrushchev's huge airliner landed today in Washington, given greeting by President Eisenhower. Four thousand guard Soviet chief. Ike bids Khrushchev to aid a just and universal and enduring peace."

The Luna 2 crashed into the moon's surface and was Khrushchev's big show as he arrived in the U.S. It was the first man-made object to land on the moon. The spacecraft carried Soviet pennants and several scientific instruments. There was a Geiger counter to measure radiation and a magnetometer to measure the magnetic field. It ceased operation after impact. Sam read the report in the newspaper.

On Friday night, Sam rode along with John and Lucille to Valent's meat and grocery market in Montour Falls. He went home with them up Snake Hill to have supper. When he got back to Horseheads, he dug potatoes.

In a few days, September 24, Sam and Grace were pleasantly surprised when their brother, Lynn, came about 1:30 p.m. He was staying three days. They didn't see him too often for neither he nor Sam or Grace drove a car.

Sam's own words...
Saturday, October 10, 1959 – "Betty's 44th birthday. John and Lucille and two of her boys came this morning, and we moved the old Bengal range out of the kitchen, which Grace has used for years. John installed a modern combination coal and gas range, bought some time ago. The junk man took the old one..."

John and Lucille stopped one day after work, in late October, and helped Sam get the storm panes on the downstairs windows. Grace ordered three tons of coal at $45 for the cellar. John stopped over several times in the days to come and brought a box of coal upstairs each time for their use.

Sam's own words...
Monday, November 9, 1959 – "Betty ate dinner with Grace and me. She was on her way to Elmira to begin a course in beauty culture and eventually have a beauty shop of her own..."
Wednesday, November 11, 1959 – "John works on the first shift nights. He stopped and got our TV set and took it to the repairman..."

Cold weather kept them inside, and they missed their television shows. They needed the television set working.

Steele's appearance was a surprise when he arrived from Batavia for a quick stop. He was on his way to Ed and Betty's for an overnight and to hunt deer the next day.

John took Shirley to Dr. Empert on November 19. She was having trouble with bunions. Sam was concerned that she might need to have an operation.

The TV was in the shop 10 days before John brought it back in working order. Entertainment was back, and together they watched popular programs.

Sam's own words...

Thursday, November 26, 1959 – "...Shirley entered the St. Joseph Hospital this afternoon to have an operation to modify the bunions on her feet. L 31 degrees - H 42."

Tommy got around to telling Sam and Grace that Shirley was doing well. Sam was finally able to let go of his apprehension as if it melted away like snow. Whatever affected him, was the same for Grace. She relaxed and let it all go, as thankful as Sam that Shirley's recovery was underway. Weeks passed.

Ed, Betty, Carol, and Linda stopped in to visit Sam and Grace, also to hear about Shirley's progress. They had been shopping in Elmira, and the girls had new coats and broad smiles. In a couple of days Linda would be 14 and Carol 15, born on the same day, December 16, but one year apart. Roland was the only one that wasn't a teen yet, but if you asked him, he'd say he was going on 13. He had a March birthday and wasn't far off from reaching the beginning of his teen years, and he was in a hurry to get there. Sam might well have wondered how all of Ed and Betty's eight children had grown up so fast.

Shirley faced wheelchair use for what was estimated to last seven or eight weeks. Sam thought she seemed to take in stride the original forecast of the time needed for healing.

Time rolled methodically forward with the support of Shirley's wheelchair. Christmas dinner was not her responsibility, but Tommy was more than efficient, and Lucille helped. John brought Sam and Grace to the holiday feast at the Broadheads' home in Windsor Gardens. Bowed heads and joined hands around the table honored Sam's simple prayer.

Sam's own words...
Thursday, December 31, 1959 – "...God help the world to find light and love and peace. Amen."

~**~

1960

Sam received Daniel Harrell's offer of $700 cash for one of the lots that Sam owned in Tampa. Sam replied to the letter and respectfully advised that he could purchase it for $1,000.

There had been a lot of family and acquaintances making last visits before Sam and Grace's departure for Florida. Packing took place here and there in the midst of all the excitement. Grace was also dealing with an ear problem of impacted cotton. When Ruth McCann and daughter, Margie, arrived to pick them up for the trip on Monday, February 1, Grace couldn't go. Sam didn't either. He was more concerned over Grace than for his warm weather prospect.

Dr. Empert had tried without success to withdraw the offending material. The next day he tried again and robustly removed it, but not without abrasion to the sensitive area. Grace needed an antibiotic injection. Her ear was in pain, and she was deaf because she could not wear the hearing aid. Needing comfort, she unpacked the new electric blanket that was intended for Florida. She could use it here most of all.

The headlines stood out as Sam read the newspaper. It was all about the sit-in at Woolworth's lunch counter in Greensboro, NC. Four black students from North Carolina Agriculture & Technical State University took seats at the segregated location. They were allowed to remain seated, although refused service. The event was about to trigger many similar non-violent protests throughout the southern United States. Six months later, the original spot,

Woolworth's, served the first four protesters. Sam may have wondered if the decades-old Civil Rights riots were to continue.

A card came from Ruth and Margie to exclaim their enjoyment of Sam's Tampa place in the sun. Serious winter arrived February 14; they had wished to escape the bad weather but hadn't. It was only 18 above zero, and 12 inches of snow had fallen. The wind drifted in white swirls and raised havoc with roads. They both wondered if there'd be any other ride heading south.

Sam's own words...
Friday, February 19, 1960 – "I was surprised to get a letter from Daniel Harrell today offering a check of $1 thousand for lot number six, my NE corner lot. It has snowed and blown all day, and I have no way to get to the bank and notary."

Lucille came Saturday and took Sam to the bank and Grace for groceries.

Sam and Grace received their fourth ton of coal for the winter. Their eye contact with knitted brows was because the price was $14.98 a ton.

Dewey and Millie were leaving for Zephyrhills, FL, on Sunday, February 25, and offered the two siblings a ride. Grace was ill with a fever on the 24th, unable to recover in time. Well then, Sam was not leaving her. Dewey and Millie went on their way. More snow began to fall.

Teddy considered the southern trek, but that fell through because his National Homes employer hadn't dispersed expected bonuses yet.

John came along at 4 p.m. on Sunday, February 28, and took Sam, Grace, Shirley, his Lucille and her son, Ray Frost, up to Ed and Betty's farm. It was a change away from any thought about Florida to family camaraderie and love. They created their own sunshine.

Sam was in Horseheads for his March 3 birthday to turn 77 years old. It snowed all day, but he considered that the Lord had been good to him all of his years.

Lynn and Iva were on their Greyhound journey back from Zephyrhills, FL, to Addison, NY.

Tommy and Shirley had visited Sam and Grace before they left by bus on March 25 for Hattiesburg, MS. Tommy had been transferred to a division of National Homes Company in Memphis, TN, and was to start work there April 1.

~~Dewey and Millie were back from Florida on March 26.~~

Sam and Grace depended on the radio and arranged for repair in mid-April. The unwelcome static would not do. Sam's leg ulcer, his nemesis, and poor circulation had him at Dr. Empert's every two weeks.

Sam's own words...
Tuesday, April 19, 1960 – "Grace did her wash and went over to Annabelle's and had her hair done. John took me to Elmira Drug Company where I got an elastic stocking for my leg."

Sam supposed that with the use of the reinforcement, he'd be able to stand longer, and tried it out with determination. Four rows of onion sets were put in. He rested awhile and hoed eight rhubarb plants. Two weeks later on May 8, they hired the garden plowed. Sam intended to prosper his garden and rest his limb when he needed to. He'd seen Dr. Empert again and had followed his instructions to wear the compression sleeve. The flowers, vegetables, and lawn mowing were Sam's priority. Grace helped him plant four rows of potatoes on May 17.

John and Lucille planned an outstanding outing as far as Sam and Grace believed. On Saturday, May 21, they picked up Sam and Grace, and Annabelle and Sadie, also Mary in Addison, on the way to Galeton, PA. The destination was the Old Crippen Homestead. They stopped at Cretia's and borrowed her power mower to use on the Crippen cemetery in the field behind the well-kept home and ramshackle barn. After the work-bee, they returned to Cretia with the mower and visited her an hour. They were back in Horseheads by 7 p.m. Sam and Grace thanked John and Lucille as they had many times for other things. John and Lucille's big hearts and minds realized the satisfaction of tending to parents' and grandparents' graves.

Sam's own words...
Wednesday, May 25, 1960, – "I did a lot of lawn mowing, maybe too much for my good. So much rain and the grass grew too high."

Pushing the mower over tall grass was not so good for a bum leg. Sam gave the sensitive limb a few days rest by having groceries delivered and hiring a young man to mow the yard the next time. Sam was in fair shape again and planted 12 tomato plants. It was timely to receive rain off and on the next day.

Sam's own words...
Friday, June 3, 1960 – "Dewey's 62nd birthday. I walked to the bank and barbershop and back. Was about all in. Warm."

On Saturday Dewey visited Sam and Grace first, then Steele and Sandra came. Sam thoroughly enjoyed them as much as his sister did. Steele's new wife, Ruth, was visiting her mother in Horseheads.

Sam decided to tackle the lawn trimming piece-meal. He mowed half on Monday and the remainder on Tuesday. The same method kept him up with the garden chores, a piece here, a piece there. At times he sat on a seat in the shade to watch the flowers grow. It was an added kind of peace. Smoke from his pipe gave off the rich aroma of Prince Albert.

Sam's own words...
Monday, June 13, 1960 – "I managed to walk over to Dr. Empert's and back. He says my blood pressure is improving. My legs give me a lot of trouble."

John came Saturday and took Sam and Grace to the A & P after their groceries. The walk around the store was no good for Sam's leg pain, but he had wanted to take part in the outing, and he did so. To rethink it, he supposed if he was going to put his leg through such a test, it had ought to be with garden work. The hoe didn't work by itself. But Grace did. She had painted the kitchen woodwork and had another job in mind. The two siblings might have been quite similar in attitude as they had both previously surmised.

Sam's own words...
Monday, June 20, 1960 – "John and Lucille stopped by after work and helped Grace finish papering the kitchen. I'm not much account anymore."

The walls were beautiful with the completion of the other job Grace had started. Not one of the three doing the work would have wanted Sam to berate himself. He relegated his efforts to the garden. A neighbor boy, Harry Mott, was hired to mow the lawn.

When Sam rode with John, Lucille, and Grace after groceries, he stayed in the car. His ride was for companionship and scenery.

Dewey took Sam to Dr. Erway on Tuesday, June 28. It wouldn't hurt to have a second opinion, would it? The secondary benefit was to satisfy those who worried about Sam, and it was a small relief to them. Millie had prepared a tasty supper to offer Sam and Grace who accepted and enjoyed it.

Sam's own words...
Sunday, July 3, 1960 – "Crippen Reunion held at Dennison Park, Corning, NY. Seventy or more in attendance. Took chaise lounge for me to lie on."

Sam hadn't wanted to miss what he had always considered to be a great occasion. He had proudly served as Crippen reunion president for several years, presiding over the short business meeting of the yearly family gathering.

He went back to Dr. Empert satisfied that what could be done was being done. The leg seemed improved.

Lucille came on Saturday, July 23, to take Grace for groceries. Her oldest son, Ray Frost, and his Navy pal, were with her. They were stationed at Newport, RI, and would be at Ray's home with John and Lucille for a few days. Lucille's pleasure was on display in her naturally sweet nature enhanced with smiles she had no inclination to contain or curtail.

Sam went on long rides; Grace was included when chances presented opportunity to do so. John and Steele took them out at different times. In early August, Steele and Ruth provided a long tour up over Harris Hill and down to Pine City and back to their Mill Street home.

Apparently, Sam felt useless at times because of the limits his leg caused him to observe. Lucille took him and Grace up to Ed and Betty's on a Sunday while John was clerking at the Red & White grocery store from 1 to 10 p.m. Sam and Grace agreed on how lucky they were to have the generous help so often from John and Lucille. No one else lived as close since Steele was in Batavia, NY, Shirley in Memphis, TN, Betty in Bennettsburg, NY, and David in Buffalo, NY.

Dewey took Sam to Dr. Empert for his appointment on Tuesday,

August 9, and Sam came home in a taxi since his brother had gone on to work.

Frank and Mary came over to the Chemung County Fair in Elmira on August 19. Sam's leg could no more allow him to take them up on their invitation than he could manage to stand on his head. He wanted Grace to go anyway, and she went along with them.

Sam's own words...
Monday, August 22, 1960 – "Received card from Shirley. She is going in the hospital for second operation on her bunions. Tommy is doing well selling insurance. Frank took Mary to the Sayre Hospital today for a physical checkup."
Saturday, August 27, 1960 – "...Frank Hess stopped here after he got Mary from the hospital...Doctor says the opening to her stomach is too small, and part of her trouble is nerves. They stretched the opening, and she was told to return in two months."

The outcome was a relief to everyone in the family. Maybe that same feeling would allow Mary to be less nervous and start to feel better. Her imagination of a worse illness had kept her up nights.

Sam's own words...
Thursday, September 8, 1960 – "We received a letter from Willa. She and Lee and her two boys expect to visit us the 18th. I haven't seen them in about 16 years and have never seen the boys."

Betty stopped in two days later. They all made sure that not one was left out of Willa's news and the chance to see her. Big sister was coming at last and no one intended to miss out.

Sam's own words...
Sunday, September 18, 1960 – "Annabelle, Sadie and her younger daughter, Mary Jane Outman, came at noon for Grace and me to accompany them to Ed and Betty's farm. Soon others arrived including Steele and Ruth with her children, Joni, Sonny, Jerry, and David, also Frank and Mary Hess. John and Lucille picked up Willa, Lee, and her two boys from the bus station. We enjoyed a wonderful reunion. It was a great joy to have them again after a long absence."

Tuesday, September 20, 1960 – "Betty brought Willa, Lee, and the boys, Glen and Tony, down about 12:30 p.m. for a visit. They departed Betty's at 4:30 p.m. They want to see David's family in Buffalo before they leave for Denver on Thursday. It's sad to see them leave but wonderful to have had them awhile."

A week later, Sam had an appointment with Dr. Empert, and John drove him there before he went on to work. Annabelle and Edward picked Sam up to go to Dewey and Millie's. Frank and Mary were there with their car and trailer. It was a last visit for all of them as Hesses were leaving for Florida in the morning.

Sam's own words...
Monday, October 10, 1960 – "Betty's 45th birthday. May God bless her and her family."

Betty came after Sam and Grace to take them to the farm for the day on Sunday, October 30. It was a breath of fresh air and excited teenage children glad to see them. Sadie remained behind at Grace's to sleep overnight. She would be there when they returned. Dewey and Millie were taking Sadie and Grace to Galeton in the morning. Sam was not going to Galeton but enjoyed her for the evening. He went back to the farm when Betty came after him the next morning.

Sam's own words...
Tuesday, November 8, 1960 – "Our neighbor took Grace and me to vote. My first vote was for Teddy Roosevelt. Hard frost."

He had thought back to when he was 21 years old in 1904, and Theodore Roosevelt was up for re-election for a second term and won. He enjoyed the memory and no doubt his attending thoughts of his grandson named Theodore, also called Teddy. Sam's influence just might have inspired Betty's name choice. Sam still had his 14-volume hardcover set of books written by Teddy Roosevelt before he became president. They were stored at Betty's on the farm along with Sam's full trunk.

Ed Voorheis had come to town to get a part for his chainsaw, and Betty was dropped off at Grace and Sam's for a quick visit. Grace was at Annabelle's beauty shop getting her hair washed.

Sam's own words...
Thursday, November 17, 1960 – "...Clark Gable is dead at 59."

Anyone who went to the movies was familiar with the famous star. Clark Gable appeared in 67 motion pictures, as himself in 17 "short subject" films, and he narrated and appeared in a World War II propaganda film titled *Combat America*, produced by the United States Army Air Forces. His fame would go on for years.

Grace got young Laura Mott to help her carry groceries home. Sam couldn't walk far. Neither could he put storm panes on the outside of the windows. John started the job by fastening four of them in place.

Sam's own words...
Saturday, December 3, 1960 – "John took Grace to the A & P and me for a ride over a new road just opened, Route 13 east of town."
Monday, December 5, 1960 – "Dewey took me to the bank to cash mine and Grace's checks, and we enjoyed having him with us for two hours. John took me to an appointment with Dr. Empert."

Sam and Grace were greatly surprised when Shirley unexpectedly arrived from Mississippi. There she was, on crutches due to her foot operation a few weeks back. Tommy's sister and family had come on their way to relatives in Buffalo. Shirley could not resist the opportunity, and it was wonderful for Sam and Grace to have her a few days. No doubt it was a Christmas gift to Sam. Shirley had other visits to make, one to see Betty and the children at the farm.

Lucille took Sam and Grace for a ride on Christmas Day to see the Christmas decorations and lights in Horseheads and Elmira. She rode with Ruth's daughter, Joni, to Batavia to share Christmas eve with Steele. The next day they went up to Ed and Betty's. Shirley's journey back south was right after Christmas day.

~**~

1961

Sam had forever enjoyed poetry. When he found stanzas that resonated with him, he copied them into his diary, perhaps to live on after he was gone.

By Robert Frost

The woods are lovely, dark and deep
But I have promises to keep
And miles to go before I sleep.

Sam's own words...
Sunday, January 1, 1961 – "Ruth (McCann) departed for Ithaca at 4 p.m. to prepare for her duties of being 'mother' to a school for underprivileged boys. I sure hope she makes out OK. Steele, his Ruth, Sandra, and Joni were here a few minutes this evening. One foot of snow."

The school was the George Junior Republic in Freeville, northeast of Ithaca, not far from where Ruth lived. Sam was in sync with Grace for high hopes on Ruth's new venture. She would live at the center.

John accompanied Sam to see Dr. Empert again on January 3. Sam had his ongoing discomforts in addition to his leg problem, but he was more concerned about Grace. Her one hearing ear was giving her problems again. Pain kept her from wearing the hearing aid. Dr. Empert gave Sam medication for her to use. She was to turn 76 years old in a week.

A letter from Mary in Zephyrhills, FL, spoke of a mild winter there while Sam recorded 13 inches of snow. He'd be sure to tell Mary or have Grace add it to her letter to their sister.

Sam's own words...
Sunday, January 8, 1961 – "Ed and Betty came about 5 p.m., ate supper with us and left for home 7 p.m. We enjoyed them so much. They brought us some meat."

No doubt Edwin had butchered. The meat was a prime food item in the grocery budget. Bacon was pricey at 67¢ a pound. Beef might have been what Ed brought them. A chuck roast was 49¢ a pound and hamburger almost 45¢ a pound. Fresh ham cost 39¢ per pound, but if it was hickory smoked, it was 49¢ per pound.

Dewey came by at three- or four-day intervals. He had taken their radio for repair and brought it back on January 1 and spent a couple of hours with Sam and Grace.

A few lines from Mr. Harrell, next door in Tampa, pleased Sam. He was glad to know that his neighbor had mowed his lawn when he did his own.

Sam's own words...
Friday, January 22, 1961 – "Shirley's 39th birthday. John H. Kennedy was sworn in as our 35th President of the United States. Sadie was with us over an hour."

Sam became lax about writing in his diary, not feeling like it a lot of the time. His small lined notebook continued to hold expense items. He paid Grace $10 per week. Prince Albert, matches, and the paper boy costs became grouped under one price between 38¢ to 61¢. The Mott children cleared the walk from snow for 25¢ when necessary.

The temperature dipped to zero most early mornings. Dr. Empert saw Sam often. John took him to the office Monday morning.

Sam was concerned about Grace for she could neither wear her hearing aid nor hear much at all. He'd be glad when Saturday came, and it was time for her to see Dr. Monahan, a specialist. She kept that appointment, thanks to John and Lucille, ever faithful to help both of them. The doctor gave Grace relief, and she had another office call set up for the next weekend.

Ed and Betty and Dewey and Millie were stopping in once a week to see Sam and Grace because they both had more problems than any time before. Sam was going downhill with his health faster than Grace. Grace's daughter, Ruth, came over once a week from Ithaca.

Sam's own words...
Tuesday, January 31, 1961 – "John and Lucille were here a few minutes after work. Mickey, John's daughter, stopped a few minutes in the evening, and we were so glad to see her. She intends to go to college and become a teacher."

Dewey took Sam to the bank with his and Grace's social security checks. Sam's $49.10 had become $53 per month. John came later and brought coal up from the cellar. It would have been a hardship if there was no one doing that particular task to make life easier.

Sam Crippen and Grace Whiting
1960 ~ Brother and Sister

Horseheads, NY

Sam's own words...
Saturday, February 4, 1961 – "Thirty-one inches of snow fell last night and today, on top of what we had. Most all traffic tied up."
Monday, February 6, 1961 – "John and Lucille took Grace to the A & P and me to the barber shop. Near zero or below for 16 days."

The shorn locks had cost Sam $1.25 as he shivered through what was a sedentary chore for him that he'd put off since the last hair cut back on November 29.

The deep freeze required more fuel, and they had to buy another ton of coal, which was sure to disappear in flames. Steele came down from Batavia for a quick visit on Sunday, February 11. He was on short shrift because he had to get back to his guard job at Attica prison.

Wednesday came around again, and John took Sam for a visit with Dr. Empert. The repeated office calls were as regular as church on Sunday for Christians.

The two best friend siblings enjoyed yet another call from Reverend Kent Lattimer, the Free Methodist minister.

Temperatures flaunted single digits below zero for the latter part of February until a thaw started. It was different from previous New York state winters, but Sam may have thought so because he hadn't experienced them for several years. Dewey and Millie were leaving for the sunshine state on the morning of Tuesday, February 28.

Sam's own words...
Friday, March 3, 1961 – "My 78th birthday and I am living in the consciousness of His love ever unfolding in me..."

Steele and Ruth and all of the children visited Sam and Grace. Ed and Betty came at the same time because it made it possible for Steele to see them. Otherwise, there would be disappointment. Sam and Grace never failed to embrace such visits. John and Lucille continued to faithfully take the two elderly siblings to doctor visits and the A & P grocery.

At the end of March, Steele and Ruth had put the Batavia house up for sale. He expected transfer to the Elmira Reformatory for guard duty. Sam took rides with Steele while he searched for a home in the southern-tier. Sam's bright eyes as a willing passenger told how pleased he would be to have them closer. Sam rode around with Steele more often than he wrote in his diary these days. It may have helped him forget that he was not feeling as well as he might. It was not unusual for a lapse of five or six days of blank pages. On March 29, Sam and Grace listened to the news with the rest of the country to learn that the 23rd constitutional amendment was ratified, allowing residents of Washington, DC, to vote in presidential elections.

Sam's own words...
Tuesday, April 4, 1961 – "Lucille took Grace to the bank to cash our checks and pay electric and gas bills. Dewey ate dinner with us. He and Millie arrived home from Florida last Sunday..."
Sunday, April 9, 1961 – "We were surprised and glad to have David and Hilda with us a half hour this afternoon. They had been to the hospital to see Hilda's brother. It has been two or three years since I have seen them."

Grace had the misery of a cold and Sam just felt miserable but did not specify why. Relief was not on the way if it depended on better health for him.

Sam's own words...
Wednesday, April 12, 1961 – "Steele and Ruth drove over from Batavia to look for a place to buy. Grace and I (sic) rode along. They haven't decided on anything. Russia has put a man in orbit around the earth and brought him back on Russian soil."
Thursday, April 13, 1961 – "About eight inches of snow fell today."

Sam wrote nothing more for a month.

Sam's own words...
Saturday, May 13, 1961 – "Lucille and her four boys came. She took Grace to the A & P for groceries, and I rode along...The boys mowed our lawn..."
Sunday, May 14, 1961 – "...Dewey and Millie were with us awhile in the evening..."
Monday, May 15, 1961 – "Lucille took me to the barber. John took me to Dr. Empert. I am to enter Arnot Ogden Hospital tomorrow for a throat checkup."

Sam never wrote again in his diary.

~**~

Grace's own words...
Wednesday, May 17, 1961 – Grace wrote: "Lucille and I (sic) took Sam to the hospital this afternoon. They found out that he has cancers of the throat and chest."

~**~

A sparse life of big responsibilities, as noble as many great men, carried a vice that killed him in the end. But tobacco may not have been considered a vice in his day. It had provided him lifelong comfort before it appeared that his last breath was near.

He languished in his hospital bed inside a transparent oxygen tent for three weeks and finally succumbed to throat cancer from years of smoking pipe tobacco. He heaved great sighs of resignation as he lingered in and out of his labored sleep. Sam rallied now and again to see anxious faces filled with concern, faces of love from his family gathered around.

Sam's children, up in their middle years, had accumulated in his hospital room. Grandchildren, from 13 to 20-plus years at that time, arrived and departed. At the sound of a soft voice, he opened his eyes and just as often not, but it was their final chance to say, "I love you, Grandpa."

Sam lay on his deathbed with no regrets. There was a lifetime of 78 years that took place before he left this sod below, elevated to a higher station. His mind wandered far back to earlier years and enduring love, then to the Light. There would be no more written in the diaries that had already spanned Sam's last 53 years. His imperfect time here had been spent to the best of his human ability. In finality, he rested in the knowledge of his faith and belief in his Savior, that heaven awaited. Samuel Paul Crippen passed into peaceful eternity on June 11, 1961.

1883 – 1961
Samuel Paul Crippen late in life
(Photo from 1976)

Sam with his
pipe in hand

Sam's trunk was bought in Twin Falls, Idaho in 1918, to make the trip back east by train. The trunk is about to turn 100 years old and counting.

Part III

39 – Unchanged

The immediate aftermath of Sam's death and funeral in Horseheads, NY, brought probate filing and carrying out his wishes as set down in the will. Since Dewey had a Florida residence, it had seemed right to Sam that he name his youngest brother as executor of his estate because he was the younger sibling most likely to outlast him. Dewey and Millie often went to the sunshine state to their vacation home in Zephyrhills, FL, and they planned to live there full time in declining years. Dewey could keep an eye on Sam's place and put it on the market. The Florida getaway that Sam had held for years in Tampa would go up for sale, and there was no reason for Dewey to waste time. It was his duty to finish Sam's affairs and execute the will. Sam's five grown children in New York state were the beneficiaries, and Dewey would see to it.

Dewey as executor filed the probate in Elmira and waited for court papers to proceed with Sam's estate. Several months went by, and winter arrived. Dewey and Millie traveled to Florida as usual, but with the proper paperwork to move forward with the sale of Sam's home and remaining residential lots. It all sold quickly enough, and Dewey concluded the sale for the new owner (s). He might not have been in a hurry to send out checks. Perhaps it was not incumbent on him to have written an in-depth explanation. What he wrote to David, John, Steele, and Shirley, if anything, other than sending a check, did not come to light. John owed quite a large sum to Sam's estate from when he borrowed from his father to buy his house. It may have been paid in full by the same method in which Dewey notified Betty. Her letter came minus one speck of remuneration enclosed. She and Edwin sat at the kitchen table of their farm house as Ed shook his head in disbelief. Dewey's terse letter told them that executor charges, loan interest, and what Ed still owed Dewey had taken all of Betty's inheritance. He'd charged them every possible cent that he could. Dewey kept Betty's share with a fare-thee-well write-off.

A daughter was there for a visit and overheard her father say to Betty, "I'm sorry Betty. I wish I had the money to pay you back now. Who could think that Dewey would take your money when I was sending him regular payments for that loan?" They discussed that there hadn't been a formal loan with interest, nor had any of the siblings known there would be executor fees charged. It was within the law if they thought about it now. They hadn't processed any idea like that, and there was no recourse. It left a bad feeling to Ed and Betty that all of a sudden they'd been treated this way by an uncle who had spent many years coming to the farm and receiving the same welcoming hospitality and big farm meals as Betty's other aunts and uncles. Who would have thought? Most likely the others received checks for their share but had been charged an executor fee as well. And what about John and Lucille who still owed Sam money for the loan on their house purchase? Did Dewey treat them the same? If so, Dewey made quite a haul, just inside the law. Sam would never know of Dewey unchanged.

40 – A Thief by Day and by Night

Surely a man of Samuel Paul Crippen's high caliber would meet his maker. Had he beseeched his one true God for the forgiveness of a deed he had willingly committed but could not, would not, and felt no hint of reason to repent? If discovered in the act, would it have been considered a crime with consequences or no crime at all? How did one regret the unselfish action taken that he believed had no other solution? Sam took that knowledge to his grave. It was over 41 years later before his east coast, now older grandchildren learned of the nefarious act. He recorded no details of it in his diaries of 1908 through half of 1961. Those pages contain hints, possibilities of it ferreted out later, only when learned about from a person who was there and had first-hand knowledge. And there was that person, Marilla Lee Walker, Willa's oldest daughter, a human source who talked all these added years later. Lee was proud to tell what her mother, Willa, told her about Sam. It confirms the pervasive statement used by all who knew him well that he had been the kindest man they ever knew.

~**~

It was 2002, 41 years after Sam died. Betty's daughter, Gail, who was one of eight, lived in a small hamlet in upstate New York. The phone rang. It was Steele's only daughter, cousin Sandy, who telephoned.

"Hi Gail, this is a long lost relative."

Gail laughed. "I would know your voice anywhere, Sandy. What makes you feel lost?"

They laughed for some reason, no reason, every reason!

"Did you know that our Grandpa Crippen, wrote diaries for many years of his life and I have them?"

As Gail smiled, she said, "Yes, Dad told me a long time ago that you had them. They are in good hands, and you have every right to them, the same as I would if they'd been in Mom's possession when Grandpa died."

It happened that Steele kept them, read them, and preserved them. When he died, his wife Ruth possessed them. Several years later, Sandy asked her step-mother for them and received the entire holding. As Sandy read them, she realized that her Aunt Betty's family should see them. No doubt they would value the diaries as much as Sandy did. Through the diary pages she understood that her eight cousins had played an integral part in Grandpa Crippen's life.

"Gail, I want to share the diaries by copying each one and sending it to you one at a time as each one becomes duplicated," Sandy said.

"I will be thrilled to receive them and share with all of my siblings," Gail replied. Thrilled didn't cover it.

The dedicated work began as Sandy painstakingly flattened two diary pages at a time against a platen and copied a quantity to fit a reasonable amount into a three ring binder. It was a banner day when the postman delivered the first installment of diaries, four years' worth starting with 1908, were delivered into Gail's rural mail box. Sandy repeated it many times over in the next 12 months until all diaries through 1961 had been reproduced, sent, and shared. All the while Sandy worked on copies, as Gail received each binder, she also duplicated them twice more and started the distribution to her siblings.

Gail's father, Edwin Voorheis, was first to read each production before it went to Ted a few miles away, oldest of the eight siblings. All of the New York state brothers and sisters had their turn to read, and if they wanted a copy, to make their own before it traveled to the next in line. The line ended with Jean, the oldest sister, who kept them and eventually collected the whole set. The second copy was mailed to Florida to siblings Carol and Linda to share. Gail kept the original copy supplied from Sandy. It took time and filled nine, three-ring binders to contain the diaries. It brought first cousins closer with a common bond, which was Samuel Paul Crippen, a much-loved grandfather. Sandy's dedication to the work month after month, followed by Gail's new mission to do so, culminated in a reading richness of legacy to everyone.

Another project was begun by Gail because the diary provided a name she needed. Finally, the last name of a male cousin materialized. Maybe she could trace where Willa's grown children, Lee and Christy were. Gail's mother, Betty, had always talked about them. But girls often change their last name when they marry. Betty and Willa had long since died, as had all of their siblings. Lee had a son, though, and the diary gave his name, which was Glen Harris. Could she find him?

Gail went online to White Pages Internet to find every Glen Harris in the United States. There were more than 250 of them. She typed up a half-page inquiry to Glen Harris and the information about who she was and why she wanted to find him and his Aunt Christy and his mother, Lee. Two-hundred fifty contacts were a lot. She determined to start with sending five at a time to see it through no matter how many it took until she found Cousin Glen. Strategically it made sense to send the first notifications to the most likely states, which she thought were Idaho, Iowa, Oregon, Colorado, and Wyoming in the west where Willa had relatives. Gail mailed out the first five envelopes. No others would be made ready until more than a week had passed, allowing time for the initial batch to reach their destination and be answered...if anyone answered.

A few days later the phone rang in Gail's country home in New York state. The missives had landed.

"Hello, Gail. This is your cousin, Glen Harris." He chuckled with delight. "Would you like my mother's phone number? She wants to talk to you and is thrilled you've found her!"

The long, warm conversations began as Lee told Gail that she was as glad to be found as Gail was to find her. Lee was in her early 80s. One of the first things she told Gail about was what her mother, Willa, said about Lee as a stolen child when she was only three years old in Horseheads, NY, in 1923. Willa Haggerty Walker was Lee's mother, a 21-year-old widow at that time. She was desperately unhappy because of her widowhood and illness. Mild TB, which likely was contracted from her late husband, Edward Walker, pushed Willa to get treatment before it became more serious, perhaps deadly. Her mother, Edith Crippen, and step-father, Sam Crippen, went all out to help her make plans to go west. Edith's longtime friend, Lora Nichols, would put up a tent in the cold mountain country of Wyoming as her private TB sanitarium. It was not far from where Willa's father, miner Ed Haggarty, lived. He would help.

But first Willa had to get there. They were making plans in Horseheads, NY, for her to board a train and follow her trunk that had been sent west ahead of her. There was another problem not yet spoken. She had a reason to stop in Ohio and get an uncle's significant help before continuance of the trip to Wyoming just over a month later.

The departure from Horseheads was set for Willa and three-year-old Louise (Lee) to leave for their journey west. An episode occurred as a huge problem for Willa. She had gone from Sam and Edith's a couple of days earlier to make a loving last visit to little Lee's other grandparents, the Walkers. They snatched their three-year-old grandchild, refusing to let Willa have her back. Their intention was to prevent Willa from taking her little girl west with her because they felt she might contract TB, too, and die. Either way, distance or illness, they thought they might never see her again.

Willa arrived home at Sam and Edith's without her daughter and sobbed out her heart to them. She told how Mr. Walker had spoken with flat indifference as he turned away from Willa to leave her no possibility of retrieving her daughter. Sam assured Willa that he would reason with the Walkers, and everything would be all right.

The Walkers would not answer the door. They neither discussed it with Sam nor relented on their refusal to give little Louise back to her mother. The Crippens contacted Louise, the Walker's daughter who lived in Horseheads, to implore her to reason with her parents. She was no help since she was on their side. They had lost Edward to TB illness and had no intention of letting go of his only child even though it meant stealing her, exactly as they had done.

Sam had a quandary tougher than any problem (save one) in recent memory. In fact, his mind became preoccupied with Willa's immediate problem, and nothing else as the train departure loomed for her, marking the impossibility of court action. Police officers do not get involved without a court order to move a child back and forth.

Hadn't Willa suffered enough? Wasn't losing Edward, becoming a widow, and having TB all the problems she needed (save one)? She could not solve it on her own as she coughed, suffered want of her child, and knew it was imperative that she board the late night train.

Sam Crippen, a mild-mannered man, thoughtful and careful, paced the floor after he had assured Willa and Edith both that he would rectify the situation. He turned his mind to what he might do, what he must do, what he was sure to do. If he were to be caught in the act, would he be able to have the Walkers arrested? Hadn't they stolen a baby? Was one crime worse than the other, depending on who did it? Would they remain quiet about it to avoid the trouble that could result from being accused of child stealing turned around on them? Would Sam get caught or could he successfully take strong action to prevent the eventual quagmire of court involvement? What affect would it have on Edith and their several children if he were found out and did not succeed? It couldn't be discussed in the house. There was no time for talk. Only his action would suffice.

Sam felt safe against arrest; after all, Willa was sure to grant permission to him if he brought little Louise to her arms. He was sure of it even without the discussion.

He paced as he planned that which could alter his life adversely but most especially Willa's. He was compelled to help Willa regain her child, her life, or end in his failure. He couldn't stand still with his restless mind and legs. Silence had set in while Sam wrestled details. He disengaged and stood apart. This problem was his to take on alone, this irritation with the Walkers and their creation of the situation. He was gambling that no retaliation would occur, for if it did, it could be turned back upon the first guilty party, the Walkers, who had started it all.

He may have wondered whether the toddler was kept in the Grandparents house or Aunt Louise's, therefore he'd have planned to surmount such an obstacle if needed. So much could go wrong. In 1923 no one locked their doors. Sam silently snuck into the Walker's house in the Heights and stole the sleeping little Louise out into the late night while all households slept. He took her home. Imagine how grateful Willa was when Sam saw to it that she and her child boarded the train bound for Uncle Eric's in Cleveland, OH, just hours later. Her journey would take her to Uncle Arthur in Colorado before last stop Wyoming for TB treatment.

Yes, Lee (Louise) had been stolen two times when she was three years of age, a twisted turn of events, now told of a thief by day and a thief in the night. Sam, who had firsthand knowledge, did not write it in his diary. Lee knew the details of it since her mother, Willa, told her all about it many times over the years. Neither Sam nor the Walkers drew accusations or charges. The stalemate held.

Willa subsequently dropped the namesake of Louise and called her daughter Lee. In the west, Willa told anyone within the family of Haggarty and also Lora Nichols, that Sam Crippen was the kindest person she had ever known. No one in the east learned of the episode from Sam, Edith or Willa. They took the knowledge with them to their graves.

~**~

Look back to June 19, 1935: Sam and Edith had been married 22 years. It is sure that Mrs. Roberts, who was also the former Mrs. Walker and Willa's deceased husband's mother, knew of the importance of that Wednesday evening in June when she came to visit the Crippens in Horseheads, NY. Indeed, she had never visited before. Sam wrote in his diary every day, and this was his first mention of her since Lee was a baby. Had she seen too many years gone by without contact and felt the need to try to see her granddaughter, Lee? It had been 12 years since 1923 when Willa and her small toddler, Louise left Horseheads, NY. Lee was 15 years old now and too old to be stolen away by anyone. Had 12 years removed or softened the situation and made it a moot point? Willa had bowed to allowing Lee's grandmother to contact her now.

Years after her mother's death in 1971, Lee wrote the story of what her mother told her years before. Yet, she never knew another piece of the story that unfolded and was kept secret in Denver, CO (i.e. save one).

~**~

Marilla Lee wrote:

Born Louise Marilla Walker in 1920, Elmira, NY, Mom changed my first name to Lee due to a falling out with the Aunt Louise whom I was named after. I was age two (almost three) when my young, 23-year-old father died of tuberculosis. My 21-year-old mother, Willa, very ill with the disease, fled with me to Encampment, WY, a mining town. Its creation was in the early days of mining by her father who found a rich vein of copper there, becoming wealthy and famous. The mine closed during the market crash of 1929.

On arrival in Wyoming, Willa was put to bed in an outdoor tent, which was on a platform. That was the way to cure TB, to fight for her life and win after 18 months. I was cared for by her loving and busy "Aunt" Lora Nichols who ran a large ranch, a passel of boys, and the only drug store and photographer's studio in this territory. My mother stayed on in Encampment and learned photography, also loved and lost a handsome forest ranger.

When I was seven, we moved to Tucumcari, NM, where my mother opened a photograph studio. My sister, Christy Jensen, was born there.

Mom expected her future husband, James Jensen, to become disentangled and arrive there near his sister's family.

Time went by, too much of it.

I knew something was terribly wrong when Mother walked into the bathroom and locked the door. At a young age, I had learned our rules of mutual courtesy. My mother was very firm about rules of courtesy. We directed our lives by them. If you needed the bathroom and it was occupied, you waited. If the need was urgent, you knocked gently, but we did not lock the bathroom door. It had something to do with trust and respect. There were no men in the household, just Mom, the baby, and me, so we didn't have to worry about anyone leaving the seat up.

Mom and I were sharing the worry. Every day I sat on the day bed, swinging my feet and playing with the baby. I swallowed the lump in my throat as I watched her pacing the floor, white-faced, her hands clenched at her sides or pulling at her hair. We both watched out the window for the mailman, praying this time that he would stop, then sinking into despair as he passed us by and moved on down the street. Now, with the clicking of that lock, I was alone with my fear. I tiptoed over to the door and gently tried the knob. Yes, it was surely locked. I tapped a little with my nails and scratched slightly on the door.

"Mom? — Let me in." There was no answer from the other side. "Mother? I have to go. I really do."

In the dead silence, I found myself filled with resentment of the baby sleeping innocently in her crib, oblivious to the danger. I became more insistent.

"Mother, please!"

Then I heard the familiar squeak of the medicine cabinet door and the whoosh of water filling a glass. As terror swept over me, I could feel my hair lifting on my head. My face went numb. My spine turned to ice. In an agony of fright, I flung myself against the door, crying, screaming, kicking, and beating at the locked door.

"Mother, please! Let me in. Please!"

The frantic noise woke the baby who began to cry. Sobbing, pleading, begging to be let in, my legs gave way, and I sank toward the floor, breaking my nails as they scraped down the paint. Kneeling against the door, I was unaware of wetting myself until I saw the widening puddle and felt all hope had drained away. Then, incredibly, I heard the lock click over. Slowly she opened the bathroom door, and I fell into the tiny room. Grabbing Mom tightly around the legs, I watched as she tipped the evil looking green pills, pouring them into the toilet. They hissed as they hit the water and she flushed them down. Then Mom pulled me up, gently unwinding my clinging hands. We walked out of the bathroom and to the crib where she picked up the screaming baby. We sat down on the flowered, chintz-covered day bed and she pulled me close to her side. We sat there with our arms around each other, our bodies trembling, as we rocked back and forth, soothing baby Christy. Her cries became soft shuddering sobs, and then hiccups as she fell asleep and evening darkened the room.

It was not long before we learned of Christy's father's death. James Jensen was married to a wealthy woman who refused his plea for divorce. Instead of gaining his freedom to marry Willa, he was dead of pneumonia in Wyoming. After losing two loves to death, my mother didn't try again but devoted the rest of her life to raising and caring for her two daughters. (She went under the name of Willa Jensen for the rest of her life.)

We made several sojourns to Wyoming where we kept house for my grandpa, an independent, dour, old Scotch prospector eternally looking for another strike and finally dying hot on the trail. He was Ed Haggarty, quite a historical figure in Wyoming. Many of his things are in the museums in Laramie and Encampment, including our old cook stove and his oversize granite coffee pot.

Encampment, WY, is a little mining town on the North Platte River near Snowy Ridge. The air is clear and cold. It was my mother's birthplace. We also lived from time to time in Denver, CO, and I had the latter part of my schooling there. I left school in the tenth grade to attend art school and ease the family finances by working. Through Franklin D. Roosevelt's WPA program, I was able to get a job at the Colorado State Museum. A group of artists were putting together miniature Indian scenes, the Buffalo Hunt, Breaking Camp, and On the Trail, etcetera. These are still in the museum—beautiful, intricate, culturally accurate even to blanket patterns. I was proud to be a part of such a project.

I was married a couple of years later to Roy Harris, a drummer and harmonica player. I was a singer, and we were more of an act than a marriage. With a little girl born, Babbette, we tried being old married folks, which was the thing to do in the 1940s.

When WWII started, my mother, Willa, then a Photostat operator for the government, transferred to Washington, DC. She decided to take some time in between to visit her relatives in New York state. Roy and I, bored to the eyeballs with our quiet, domestic existence, and expecting our second child, packed to go along. We traveled in a Model B coupe with a rumble seat. My mother, my sister Christy, then 13, my husband, two dogs, very pregnant me, and our luggage filled the car. We had emergency gas coupons and scrap rubber tires, and we had 27 blow-outs from Denver, CO, to Horseheads, NY, where my grandmother lived.

Mom went to Washington. We stayed in New York state for work but after a while returned to Denver and divorced. Babbette was four years old and Glen six.

~**~

Years later in 1971 at the age of 69, Willa passed away. She had been living with her daughter Christy Nelson and family. Christine's son, Steve Nelson revealed that Willa sat in a recliner with her feet up, chain-smoking Lucky Strike 100s until the day she died.

41 – Revelation
2007 - 2014

Marilla Lee was a treasured daughter, sister, wife, mother, grandmother, aunt, companion, and cousin. Lee's eyes failed and emails to her cousin, Gail, had stopped as her body prepared for the end of her physical life. She passed on to a brighter band of light on February 25, 2007, at age 87. Lee was missed by her daughter, Babbette, and other family members, but also by Gail. Gail and Lee had enjoyed only four years since their first communication. After months had elapsed, the emails started back and forth between second cousins, Gail and Babbette, who are close to the same age.

Maybe kind-hearted Lee was allowed a glimpse and tipped her halo. Could she have been sitting right there on a cloud beside Willa, her mother? Maybe Willa was ready to share another secret concerning Denver Colorado that she never spoke of in her earthly life, not a word to anyone, save Sam and Edith, not this side of heaven.

Willa, Sam, and Edith had all three taken "another secreted knowledge" to their graves. How could it matter to them now to protect it? None of them who had lived it could be affected.

But it surfaced. It mattered to all relatives learning of it in the next century.

Edith died in 1944, Sam in 1961, and Willa in 1971. Betty (Sam's daughter) passed in 1982. Her eight children had all grown up and raised large families as time marched along. Between Edwin and Betty's eight children, they gave her 38 grandchildren.

The news arrived all of a sudden in October 2014, first with contact to Babbette in Oregon and immediately from her to Gail in New York state. Those emails sizzled across the miles with the acceptance and excitement of the revelation.

Babbette: "Gail, we apparently have a new cousin! Do you know who Claude Crippen is or was? He and Margaret Haggarty had a son."

Gail: "Claude? No—never heard of him but I'll consult the big volume of Crippen genealogy and get back to you. Who is Margaret? Tell me about the new cousin!"

Within 10 minutes Gail found Claude in the thick tome. There in print resided Claude Dewey Crippen. Gail and her seven siblings had known their Great Uncle Dewey without ever having heard the first name attached or mentioned. Maybe he didn't like the name. The moniker, Claude, was foreign to them until now. She explained it to Babbette.

Gail: "I found Claude. We only knew him as Uncle Dewey Crippen. Who is Margaret Haggarty? Who is the new cousin? How do you know this?"

Babbette: "Holly Timm of Florida is our new cousin. Her father was Claude Dewey Crippen Jr., but she knew him only as John Stanton Adams. That was his new adoptive name. His mother was my grandmother, Willa. I'll let Holly fill you in."

Gail nor her many siblings had ever known that their Aunt Willa's name was also Margaret. Two new names were worth a chuckle along with the exciting revelation of a "Holly-come-lately" blood relative! That was not all. She has two sisters, Dory and Carol.

Gail called her brother, Ted, to tell him and get his reaction. He laughed, too, after he found out that Claude and Margaret were, in fact, Dewey and Willa. "There's no accounting for what young people might do," he said.

Babbette was altogether happy to ask cousin, Holly, to provide information. Holly was a thorough communicator, and the three-way emails went in a triangle among the three cousins. Holly related the whole story. Gail read about what amounted to gregarious genealogy work and a court order to obtain and open the birth certificate, which Holly shared.

Holly's father was born as Claude Dewey Crippen Jr. in Denver, CO, on November 13, 1923. His mother was Margaret Willa Haggarty. At one month of age, Claude Dewey Crippen Jr. became adopted in Denver, CO. His name change to John Stanton Adams was final. He had a family to love him and was brought up with privileges and education to become a lawyer. He died in Denver, CO, in 1974 at the age of 51, all too soon.

Holly was aware of her father's history of adoption. But she, like most people, had a family and a busy life. It was many years after his death that she, as a professional genealogist, took steps to discover his original birth family. The copy of the initial birth certificate came into her possession on March 20, 2014. She had names of his birth parents now. Further investigation began. Where would she find relatives?

It was October of the same year, 2014, when she contacted Babbette. She knew this was Willa's granddaughter and hoped it was a good place to start. It was. Babbette was as surprised as Gail because Willa never told a soul on either coast that she'd had a son. Willa had been gone 43 years before this information surfaced. The consensus within the family has it that Dewey never knew at all.

~**~

Back to 1923

Sam Crippen did not notify his diary about his mental turmoil or his clandestine and private cause for action on Willa's behalf. He wrote only of helping her leave for Cleveland, OH, to her Uncle Eric and from there she went to Uncle Arthur's in Denver, CO. It seemed reasonable that she was visiting for love of her uncles before going on to Wyoming for a TB cure. With no other agenda for Denver mentioned in Sam's diary, the assumption had no information on which to go astray. It was their intention that it remain that way. Sam and Edith knew full well of another reason, the desperate reason why Willa was in Denver just as we do now, and did not want it unearthed. The news of the birth seemed effectively buried because they neither spoke about it in Horseheads where they lived nor wrote about it for the ages.

Willa's uncles were the other persons who knew about it as part of the reason she left from her family and Horseheads.

The few times later in her lifetime when she came back east were not cause for disclosure. Time doing its job like an iceberg sliding in its glacial slackened pace seemed likely to serve as a thick eraser.

Willa's situation in 1923 left no doubt in Sam's mind that his step-daughter needed his help and his silence. Dewey never needed assistance. He'd help himself first and had done so in the recent past with his father's will. Sam had a sufficient memory to inform him of Dewey's reputation. It was believable that Dewey had been as crass and unforgivable as Willa had said. One thing had become as sure as the slow changing of the seasons with the ticking of the clock. She was never going to speak to Dewey again. The ticking and movement of the hands bought her time closer. Even without the exact details of the fallout between the two young people, Sam likely and intuitively believed Willa was wronged. The present call to action for Sam had everything to do with why he would help Willa and nothing to do with love of his brother. That would not be altered for the future and had no weight against his helping Willa Girl.

There was every reason in Sam's mind why Willa Girl needed his help. If he failed to rescue her, his inaction would aid another. Urgency pushed Willa, Edith, and Sam by extension. They were all too well aware of Willa's late-term pregnancy and by whom.

She had made a mistake out of the months of loneliness and pain in the aftermath of becoming a widow. Blind trust hadn't worked out so well. The man with whom she had involved herself was not the same temperament as Willa's stepfather, and she had learned it too late. She was never going to marry Dewey Crippen. He was never going to hear of this child's impending birth from her or anyone else if she had her way.

A mother having a baby out of wedlock faced instant ruination and an illegitimate label for the innocent child. It was the reason for her destination, Denver, and anonymity, except for Uncle Arthur whom she suddenly learned could help her. Before traveling on to Wyoming for her seclusion to recover from TB, Willa accomplished the adoption of her newborn son.

A long ago letter discovered only in 2016, found in Grace's belongings left behind, was unknown to Sam. It confirms what the family knew back in 1923, simply that Dewey and Willa had been dating each other.

~**~

(Letter to Roy Whiting at Binghamton, NY Psyche Center Hospital from his and Grace's daughter, Alice Jeffrey)

Sullivan Street
Elmira, NY
March 28, 1923

Dear Daddy,

I have my work all done so will write to you. The wind is blowing just terrible here. We had a blizzard this morning.

Jeff is working at the knitting mill for $9 a week now.

Grandma said that Dewey and Willa were mad at each other. Dewey hasn't been down to see her in two weeks.

...We took some pictures of the baby when Grandma held him Sunday. They won't be done until this Friday, but I will send you some next week...

With Love, Alice

~**~

Back to Sam - 1923: He shook his head. His stormy eyes were more than likely a reflection that he felt troubled over not disclosing the situation to Dewey. He naturally was pulled toward telling his younger brother about the child to be born. What decent man would turn his back on his child? He probably didn't believe that about Dewey, but he couldn't destroy Willa (and maybe Edith) by his telling it. It would not bring the two young people together. Hadn't Dewey been unpredictable in his own interest before and at the expense of his siblings? It didn't hold hope for Willa either. Sam remembered what it was like to call Dewey out in a situation. Sam more than likely had been sworn by Edith and Willa, never to disclose anything to Dewey.

Dewey victorious and Willa devastated was not a good image. The aftermath of that was unthinkable. Dewey was out of the loop on this permanently. There was no turning the decision around. However hard, Sam would hold firm in honor.

No. Dewey didn't need Sam's help. Willa did. A vein throbbed in Sam's temple to accompany his trouble beset human heart.

Another matter in Sam's troubled heart and mind concerning his grandson, David Crippen Jr. could be set at ease now in 2016. Besides keeping David Jr. from his father, there was another reason Frances had a post office box. She never told her family that she had a son. David Jr never knew how to contact his father or his grandfather, or his Aunt Betty.

Frances had sabotaged his memories and confused him. After his mother's death, he found information in her safety deposit box that she had a sister, his aunt, and he had more cousins. Frances Bowden Crippen invented the inadequate pretense of information about Little David that she wrote to his grandfather, Sam Crippen.

There is no proof that Frances was mentally ill, but it is suspected. How could anyone believe that it was just meanness done for her benefit and ignoring her son's needs for family?

David Jr. stated that never, at any time, had he ever lived with his mother in New York City. She vindictively stole Little David and placed him within a Catholic home for children. He was never allowed contact with any relatives on either side. Frances never informed her family that her son existed. His aunt and cousins had a surprise in store when Frances left this earth.

David left the Catholic home when he joined the Navy as a teen and made himself into an excellent man. An intelligent person was misled and confused by untrue and misleading information supplied by his mother about his father and extended family. David was in his retirement years when cousin Gail used the Internet and with cousin Sandy's input, found him. These days, all of the cousins are reunited. David has a supportive wife, Chrissy. He is a much-wanted man, a beloved cousin, and has an elderly 96-year-old Aunt Sue Joan Bowden Switzer in St. John's Creek assisted living in New Jersey who treasures his visits. David's Aunt Sue, in her older years, finds him to be a blessing, as do his many cousins in the Finger Lakes and elsewhere.

~**~

The culmination of the life of one man, an exemplary human being, Samuel Paul Crippen, leaves a legacy we might use as a roadmap. His life of actions as a son, brother, husband, father, stepfather, and grandfather speak of love, perseverance, forgiveness, and belief in a higher power. Sam's faith in God was his comfort and salvation. No doubt he had a purpose in writing the record of his life day by day in his diary. He wouldn't have viewed it as supplying wisdom, although it was. His faith in God is wisdom imparted. He wrote several times in journal pages that his father, Lac, said, "I am not afraid." Sam wasn't either and with good reason.

His words invite us to accept Christ so that we may not miss out, that we will not experience fear, that we do know in whom we have believed. Believers see in Jesus all that sinners can ever need for their present and eternal well-being. God has freely given all things to us in Him. Receive Him! To possess Him is to gain a full salvation.

"Grace to you, and peace, from God our Father, and the Lord Jesus Christ." Romans 1:7

~**~

Note From the Author

This half page is written in memory of Sam Crippen to honor his Love of God.

The bible tells the story of Paul and Silas when they were in prison. As they prayed behind bars, a great earthquake broke open the jail and also the wooden stocks around their ankles. The frightened jailor discovered that the men remained in their cell. He asked how he could gain such faith. Their answer was, "Believe in the Lord Jesus Christ." (Acts 16: 31)

It is never too late to seek salvation. What must be done to be saved? Searching for truth through reading the Bible, combined with a sincere and open heart, may lead to a decision for salvation. Start with these verses and you may hunger for more.

Ecclesiastes 3:14 - "And I know this, that whatever God does is final—nothing can be added or taken from it; God's purpose in this is that man should fear the all-powerful God." (Implied, The Author : Solomon of Jerusalem, King David's son, "The Preacher.")

Ephesians 2:8-10	Romans 3:24	James 2:19
John 16:7–11	Isaiah 64:6	John 1:29
John 6:44 and 65	Jonah 1:29	Revelation 7:10
Romans 12:1–3	John 3:16-21	

"To reject that dear Savior is the sin of all sins, which damns the soul." By J. Sidlow Baxter

1902 ~ 1971
Willa Haggerty Walker Jensen ~
This is a picture of her in her
Prime in Washington, D. C.

This is Willa at an
older age nearer the
end of her Lucky
Strike days.

42 - Finding the Natural
By Holly Timm - 2016

*(daughter of Claude Dewey Crippen Jr. whose
adoptive name was John Stanton Adams)*

O ur whole lives my two sisters and I have known our father was adopted. It was just something that was mentioned here and there, just part of life. My dad passed away in 1974 before I really got into chasing my family history, so I didn't think to ask him for details nor from my adopted grandfather who passed away in 1980. Sometime in the 1980s or so I did consider finding out about his natural roots. At that time it was made pretty clear that he could have tried to find out, but now, since he was deceased, I could not.

I focused instead on the adopted lines which go deep into New England and the Middle Atlantic for my mother's lines. But a couple of years ago I was talking with someone about his adoption and found that nowadays there was a process available to try to find out his natural parents. It took months and several hundred dollars in court fees (my sisters contributed some to that funding). I was finally rewarded with dribs and drabs of information and finally a copy of the original birth certificate!!

His original birth certificate gives his birth name as Claude Dewey Crippen Jr. and names his parents as Claude Dewey Crippen, age 25, and

Miss Margaret Haggarty, age 21. Claude's birthplace is difficult to read but appears to be Geltone, although it is definitely in Pennsylvania and later research showed it to be Galeton. His mother's birthplace is clear: Encampment, WY, which is in Carbon County, so I started in that direction.

A primary resource for genealogists is the federal census. I searched there. Margaret Haggarty was born about 1902, so I looked for the surname Haggarty in 1900 and 1910 Carbon County, WY. I quickly located an Edward Haggarty in 1900 when he was single and in 1910 when he was listed as divorced. Born in December 1866 in England, he was an excellent candidate to be Margaret's father. In 1910, I also found an Edith Haggarty listed as divorced, living with her brother Arthur Crow. Also in the household is Willa M. Haggarty, age 8, thus born about 1902.

Although not directly identified as Edith's daughter, it is a near certainty that Willa M. Haggarty is the Margaret Haggarty of the birth certificate. Certainly, there are no other Haggarty's in Carbon County by any spelling! Another resource had popped up during this search showing an Edward Haggarty, age 34, in the 1901 census of Cumberland County, England. Not expecting to find an actual connection, nevertheless I looked at the household, and the answer was exciting. The home of Thomas and Hannah Haggarty list a son, Edward, age 34, as a mining operator, and, more importantly, also in the family is Edith M. Haggarty, age 23, daughter-in-law, born in the United States of America. As they are the only members of the household listed as married besides Thomas and Hannah, they must be a couple, and the Wyoming results are tied together with a neat little bow!

Additional research reveals Edward Haggarty's line going back into the early 1800s in Cumberland County, England, and shows that he immigrated to the United States by the age of 18 or 19, possibly stopping first at his Uncle Daniel Haggarty's home in Ontario, Canada. Edward supported himself as a shepherd and prospector, and in 1898 he discovered copper, which was developed into a mine, as described in the Weekly Boomerang in 1909: "The old Ferris-Haggarty mine...was discovered in 1898 by Ed Haggarty, a sheep herder while he was trailing sheep through the fertile mountain valleys. He became enthusiastic over his find and interested George Ferris, who financed a superficial development of the prospect. The following year capitalists became interested in the project. After several discouraging delays in its development, Haggarty sold out his interest; it is believed he received only $40 thousand in a mine that afterward brought $1 million."

Bits and pieces from newspapers show that Edith Crow and Edward Haggarty married on New Year's Day at Edith's mother's home in Ord, NE.

They then went on an extended wedding trip through June that included a visit to Edward's family in England. Willa was born the following year on March 19, 1902. Edith soon took her infant daughter back to her family in Nebraska and in October of 1903, the *Grand Encampment Herald* announced that their divorce was one of three granted in the local district court.

After the divorce, Edith settled in for several years with her brother, Arthur Crow, and his family. By 1913 she met and married Samuel Paul Crippen in Twin Falls, ID, a discovery, which bringing in the Crippen name, made me sit up and take notice. I quickly determined that after a few years in Idaho, Sam and Edith settled in Chemung County, NY. In looking at Sam's family, I immediately discovered his younger brother, Claude Dewey Crippen, the man named as father on MY father's birth certificate.

Both the Crippen family and Edith's Crow family have deep roots in this country. The Crow's go back into Rockingham County, VA, where William Crow (c1757-1854) served in the Revolutionary War, including being at the Battle of Yorktown. His son William (1790-1853) was living in Ohio when he enlisted in the War of 1812. His son Jonathan (1840-1892) served from Illinois in the Civil War, and after a few years in Iowa, he homesteaded in Nebraska where his daughter, Edith, was born.

Homesteading was hard living, and the first home Jonathan built there for his wife and five children was 16' x 20' in size, only 320 square feet. It was a sod house with one door and two windows. His sister Jane did not fare as well. In the spring of 1873, Jane and her husband Dillon Haworth and their two little girls were living in their partly built log dugout with one door and one window when the Easter blizzard hit. They apparently tried to get to other family and all but the youngest child, Eva, died, just a mere half mile from their home. Eva's grandfather, Mathias, raised her where he also homesteaded there in Howard County, NE.

The Crippen family traces even further back to Edward Fuller (c1575-1621) who traveled with his wife, whose name is unknown, and his son Samuel (c1608-1683) on the Mayflower. William Bradford's 1651 recollection of the family states: "Edward Fuller and his wife died soon after they came ashore' but their son Samuel is living, and married, and hath four children or more." Samuel's brother, Matthew, came some 20 years later, and in the following generation, the two lines intermarried when John Fuller married Mehitabel Rowley. It is their daughter Thankful Fuller who married Jabez Crippen. Jabez and Thankful's son, Roswell Crippen, served in the Revolution.

Over the centuries there have been several instances of the various branches of my family being "ships that passed in the night." One of the most exciting and I suppose spookiest, is when my father's natural great-grandfather, Erastus Crippen, and his adopted great-grandfather Chalkley Sears were just a few yards from each other at the McPherson Farm on July 1, 1863, in Gettysburg. Erastus, in the 149th Pennsylvania, and Chalkley, in the 150th Pennsylvania, were both wounded that day. Erastus was hit by a piece of shrapnel from an exploding shell, and Chalkley when his hand was injured, probably by a bullet.

I have been doing genealogy research for more than 40 years. As every scrap of data appeared I chased the records, but it was the court-appointed intermediary that made the initial contact with the natural family, children of my father's half-sister. I thus met, by Internet, another grandchild of Willa Margaret Haggarty: Babbette in Oregon. She soon introduced me to Gail in New York state, who is both author of this book and a second cousin twice over.

DNA testing had already made some connections with some natural family members but before having the names and information from the original birth record, I did not know what these connections were. I soon made contact with others in the family, most especially my cousin, Steve

Nelson in Colorado, who immediately, upon getting to know him, felt a part of my family.

Thanks to DNA and historical research, there is no doubt whatsoever that my father was Willa's son. Genetically, it is possible that Dewey or any of his brothers are my father's father. Dewey had no children, and my deceased father had no sons, so further testing is not possible, but I see no reason to doubt his name on the birth certificate. With absolute certainty, Lac Pulaski Crippen and his wife Sophia Dimon are my great-grandparents and Edith Crow Haggarty Crippen is my great-grandmother.

There is no way of proving exactly what happened but I know what I feel in my heart. Willa, a lonely young widow, dallied with Dewey Crippen. Finding herself pregnant, she turned to her mother who arranged for her to go to Cleveland, OH, to her mother's brother, Eric Crow. It is likely that this is where it was intended for Willa to have her child and give it up for adoption, but another of her mother's brothers, Arthur, was living in Denver, CO. Arthur was involved in the oil and mining industries, and it is very likely that he became acquainted with Arthur Adams. Certainly, just the coincidence of their first names would be enough to start the conversation. It is likely that Arthur Crow learned that Arthur Adams and his wife Dorothy were unlikely to have children of their own probably due to a fireworks accident in Adams'es childhood. Knowing this and learning about Willa's pregnancy brought the two situations together. Willa went further west to Denver to have her son and give him to Arthur and Dorothy Adams.

~**~

The End

43 - Army and Air Force Service Records – WWII
By Gail Mazourek

The U.S. Government website (http://vetrecs.archives.gov) was used to search for every scrap of information available on two uncles, Steele and John Crippen. A form was available to print and fill out with information, which was completed with John Crippen's information. One soldier at a time would be sufficient. I had more than enough anecdotal details from Grandfather Sam Crippen's diaries, his trunk artifacts, and WWII correspondence supplied by Steele's daughter, Sandy. Official records remained the objective.

I included John's army number, enlistment date, muster out date, and that he was in the Battle of the Bulge. His social security number was provided as well. Then I sent the information off and went back to work on the biography. The address is:

> National Personnel Records Center
> 1 Archive Drive
> St. Louis, MO 63138-1002

Three months passed, but writing the nonfiction manuscript kept me busy. I had already written past the WWII time frame when a government addressed envelope arrived in my mailbox to surprise me. They spelled my name wrong consistently in three places. Having potential official information in my hands was exciting. I began to read.

~**~

Thank you for contacting the National Personnel Records Center.

The complete Official Military Personnel File for the veteran named above is not in our files. If the record were here on July 12, 1973, it would have been in the area that suffered the most damage in a fire on that date and may have been destroyed. The flames destroyed the major portion of records of Army Military personnel who separated from the service between 1912 through 1959, and records of Air Force personnel with surnames Hubbard through Z who separated between 1947 and 1963.

A partially reconstructed file for the veteran named in your request contains limited data from an alternate record source. Reconstructed files typically contain limited service data, some from request documents.

~**~

To retrieve a copy of a file that was empty until they received the information I supplied with my filled out request for official information, they require that I send $70. While I won't remit the dollars, I may send them more information.

The above letter is a condensed version with actual words from the longer message received.

I am aware that they send out prepared form letters and don't answer individuals with information until money is sent to them. Even then you probably get a copy of a file and no letter need be written.

The End

Gail Mazourek is the author of the Samantha Trilogy Series: *Samantha's Revolution, Samantha's Anguish,* and *Samantha's Perseverance.* She writes a weekly column for Finger Lakes Community Newspapers, paints on rocks and canvas (when cooking is under control). Gail lives in a country acres setting with her flowers and husband (the one who appreciates her culinary efforts) near Ithaca, NY. She contributes art earnings to supply the annual Rudolf Mazourek Memorial Scholarship in auto body studies at Alfred State College in Upstate, NY.

These books are available at *www.amazon.com* and through most book stores.

Contacts: gmazourek.com.ipage.com
Emails - gmazourekart@aol.com
gaymazourek@aol.com

BIBLIOGRAPHY

Books, magazines, and newspapers

Theodore Roosevelt - 14 volume set from 1899
Diaries of Samuel P. Crippen—1908 - 1961
The Century magazine - February 1888, Vol. XXV, no. 4
        Ranch Life in the Wild West, Scribner's monthly magazine
Some Luck by Jane Smiley
This Cold Country by Annabel Davis-Goff
Stalin's Daughter by Rosemary Sullivan
The Emotion Thesaurus by Angela Ackerman and Becca Puglist
Ithaca Journal - Rick Marsi column, April 2015
Elmira Star Gazzette - varied dates from 1918 forward, 1940-1945
        and 1961
American Heritage Dictionary of the English Language
        New College Edition – Houghton Mifflin
Preserving Family Legends by Carolyn Steele
The Living Bible – Paraphrased – Tyndale (Doubleday)
Complete Poetical Works of John Greenleaf Whittier 1880
Awake My Heart by J. Sidlow Baxter – Daily Devotions –
        Twenty-fifth printing, 1982
Samantha of Saratoga by Marietta Holley 1887
Why the Allies Won by Richard Overy 1996

Departmental Ditties of Rudyard Kipling 1899
Soldiers Three by Rudyard Kipling, New York book company
The Courting of Dina Shadd by Rudyard Kipling from Life's
        Handicap (1891). First published in Macmillan's Magazine
        and Harper's Weekly in March 1890.A Kipling Pageant by Rudyard
Kipling 1935
The Complete Works of Tennyson, 1880 Worthington Press
        https://en.wikipedia.org/wiki/Poet_Laureate_of_the
        _United_Kingdom
Anderson's Fairy Tales by Hans Christian Anderson, Grosset & Dunlap
        Publishers, NY, lived 1805 – 1875
The Achievements of Stanley and the Explorers by J.T. Headley, 1878
        published before 1923, https://www.amazon.com/Achievments-
        Stanley-J-T-HEADLEY/DP/B00AZVX3OO
The Poetical Works of Lord Byron, 1917

Book of Classic English Poetry 1926 – 1934: Wm Langland for the
      Common folk, no rhyme, Henry Howard poem, Charles Lamb
      riddle of destiny

Henry the Eighth by Henry Hackett, 1929
The Complete Works of O. Henry, Collier's, 1930
The Poetical Works of Sir Walter Scott, 1931
Prose & Poetry of America - by H. Ward McGraw, 1934
      https://www.amazon.com/Prose-poetry-America-Including-
      literature/dp/B00085BL5K
Best known works of Voltaire- Book League, 1940
Best Known Works of Oscar Wilde, Poems, Novels, Plays, Essays
      And Fairy Tales, Book League, 1940
Short Stories of De Maupassant – titles - The Necklace, The Price of
      String, Babbette, Book League, 1941
Best Known Stories of Robert Louis Stevenson – includes Treasure
      Island, Book League, 1941
Essays of Ralph Waldo Emerson, Reliance – one of many, Book
      League, 1941
The American Album of Poetry by Ted Malone, 1945
Rubaiyat of Omar Khayyam - https://www.amazon.com/dp/
      014005950b20&hvadid=3487970476&hvqmt=b&hvbmt=bb&hvdev
      =c&ref=pd_sl_6z9b1iaojb_b#reader_0140059547,
Persian Poetry into English by Fitzgerald, Edmund Dulac, T. Crowell
      Publisher (NY 1952)
http://classics.mit.edu/Homer/iliad.html (1890 Publisher T. Crowell, NY)
      Homer's Iliad books I – XXIV, rhyming
www.fas.harvard.edu/.../1907/docs/Kavoussi-Panic_of_1907.pdf
https://en.wikipedia.org/wiki/The_Town_Mouse_and_the_
      Country_Mouse
Great Spy Stories by Allen Dulles, 1996

      Internet Research

http://www.biography. com/people/theodore-roosevelt
      -9463424. (2015) The Biography.com website
http://www.amazon.com/Theodore-Roosevelt-Ranch-Hunting
      -Trail/dp/1596058358
http://USAtoday/30.usatoday.com/lifebooks/reviews/
      2007-12-16-america-1908 N.htm truncated
http://stlouisspeakersseries.org/spk2001/weathers.htm truncated

http://chronicleaugusta.com/news/metrol/2012-03-03/cons-sunday
    -alcohol-sales truncated

www.elmorecountypress.com/twinfallsconews.htm

www.wikipedia.org./wiki/Mark_Twain

www.farmcollector.com/steam-traction/steam-show-and-threshing-
    bee.aspx

www.moaf.org/exhibits/checkbalances/woodrow-wilson/liberty-
    bond en.wikipedia.org/wiki/Liberty-bond

www.hzn.com.au/stubble.php

www.lifeontherange.org/assets/doc/range-stories/frank-shirts-
    feature-story.pdf

www.wikipedia.com/Harness-a-Horse

www.minitack.com/mwbr.htm

http://en.wikipedia/Theodore_Roosevelt_National_Park

www.joycetice.com/theaters/1915entertainment.Atm

www.en.wikipedia.org/wiki/Chautaqua

www.historynet.com/red-baron-world-war-1-ace-fighter-pilot-
    manfred-von-richthofen.htm

http://en.wikipedia.org/wiki/Post_World_War_1_recession

www.midwiferytoday.com/articles/timeline.asp

www.circushistory.org/Routes/AGBarnes.htm#1917

https://libcom.org/library/us-green-corn-rebellion-us-1917

http://hubpages.com/games-hobbies/Oleomargarine, Revenue stamps

http://hubpages.com/games-hobbies/Oleomargarine-revenue
    -stamps-provide-an-interesting-glimpse-of-history

https://www.fbi.gov/about-us/history/famous-cases/the-lindbergh-
    kidnapping

http://www.empirestateroads.com/cr/crchemung.html, Johnson
    Hollow Road

www.smithsonianmag.com/history/National Anthem

https://www.ssa.gov/history/reports/ces/ces2witte2.html,
    Social Security Administration (US)

http://www.netstate.com/states/intro/hi_intro.htm,
    Hawaii a US State

https://cb100.acf.hhs.gov/CB_ebrochure the-story-behind-the-star
    -spangled-banner   1903 - Child Welfare -Theodore Roosevelt

http://www.chemunghistory.com/pages/timeline.html—1919 shoe
    repair

http://www.history.org/Foundation/journal/Winter04-05/smoke.cfm
    Colonial Williamsburg Journal

rmc.library.cornell.edu/EAD/pdf_guides/RMM02614B.pdf
    (Dairymen's League)

http://search.aol.com/aol/search?s_it=webmail-searchbox&q=where
    %20was%20T.Roosevelt%20buried%3F&s_chn=wm_t20
https://songbook1.wordpress.com/fx/1910-1919-selected-
    standards-and-hits/additional-popular-

http://www.aol.com/aol/search?s_it=webmail-searchbox&q=
    1918 child birth NYS&s_chn=wm_t20
Bill Federer at crosswalk.com – Thanksgiving, 2016
https://en.wikipedia.org/wiki/Catlin,_New_York
Thomas A. Edison - http://www.biography.com/
    people/thomas-edison-9284349
https://en.wikipedia.org/wiki/Puget_Sound_region
The Covered Wagon by Emerson Hough - Keep Rolling –
    Utah History to Go, www.historytogo.utah.gov
http://variety.com/1923/film/reviews/the-covered-wagon-1200409409/
    The Covered Wagon
http://www.listal.com/movie/arrowsmith, 1931 movie, December
www.goodreads.com/...these-are-the-times-that-try-men-s-souls
    summer Thomas Paine, THESE Are the Times That Try Men's Souls.
www.biography.com/people/calvin-coolidge-9256384
https://en.wikipedia.org/wiki/Loch_Ness_Monster-
http://www.ushmm.org/research/research-in-collections/search-the-
    collections/bibliography/1933-book-burnings-Hitler sanctioned
http://www.barnesandnoble.com/w/the-abundant-life-
    day-book-nancy-guthrie/   Abundant Life
https://en.wikipedia.org/wiki/Dionne_quintuplets
http://query.nytimes.com/gst/abstract.html?res=9E07E3DE103
    EE53ABC4E51DFB066838F629EDE
www.harrishillsoaring.org/HHSC/Passenger_Flights.html
https://en.wikipedia.org/wiki/Textile_workers_strike_%281934%29-
http://www.macraesbluebook.com/search/company.cfm?
    company=1068516- Janol
https://en.wikipedia.org/wiki/Ma_Barker
http://www.biography.com/people/ma-barker-14515515, Barker Gang
www.pbs.org/kenburns/dustbowl
https://www.ssa.gov/history/35act.html, Social Security Act of 1935
http://socialsecurityinfo.areavoices.com/2012/05/24/may-24-1937-
    supreme-court-declares-social-security-act-constitutional/

https://en.wikipedia.org/wiki/Mutiny_on_the_Bounty_%281935
_film%29

http://heritagebrass.ca/?s=Argyle (Salvation Army Band)

www.biography.com/people/william-randolph-hearst-9332973

https://en.wikipedia.org/wiki/Mae_West

https://en.wikipedia.org/wiki/Congress_of_Industrial_Organizations,
C.I.O.-

https://www.marxists.org/archive/foster/1937/01/x01.htm
American Federation of Labor A.F. of L.

https://en.wikipedia.org/wiki/John_D._Rockefeller born in
Richford, NY

http://explorepahistory.com/displayimage.php?imgId=1-2-1D70
Pennsylvania - 1937 steel strike and marshall law

http://search.aol.com/aol/search?s_it=webmailsearchbox&q=
author%20of%20the%20old%20rugged%20cross&s_qt=ac
Author -The Old Rugged Cross

http://www.freerepublic.com/focus/news/1984337/post
Nazi ultimatum to Austria

https://en.wikipedia.org/wiki/Oberammergau Passion Play

http://www.old-time.com/mcleod/top100.html, Seth Parker
Radio programs

https://www.otrcat.com/p/bergen-and-mcca-edgar-bergen-and-
charlie-mccarthy

http://www.ushistory.org/us/51f.asp, Manhatten Project

www.mapquest.com/us/pa/rose-valley-282023880

https://www.mapquest.com/directions/list/1/us/pa/
rose-valley282023880/to/us/ny/h Rose Valley

http://www.poetryfoundation.org/poems-and-poets/poets/detail
/edwin-markham, The Man With the Hoe, Road Not Taken

https://en.wikipedia.org/wiki/In_Old_Monterey Gene Autry

http://www.cameronbridgeworks.com/links

https://www.amazon.com/Prose-poetry-America-Including-
literature/dp/B00085BL5K

http://www.growingseasons.com/Growing_Seasons/
Threshing_Day.html

www.farmcollector.com/steam-traction/steam-show-and—
threshing-bee.aspx

www.moaf.org/exhibits/checlbalances/woodrow-wilson/liberty-bond

en.wikipedia.org/wiki/Liberty-bond

www.hzn.com.au/stubble.php

www.lifeontherange.org/assets/docs/range-stories/frank-shirts-
    feature-story.pdf
www.wikihow.com/Harness-a-Horse
www.ministack.com/mwbr.htm

http://USAtoday/30.usatoday.com/life/books/reviews/
    2007-12-26-America-1908- N.htm
http://stlouisspeakersseries.org/spk2001/weathers.htm
http://chronicleaugusta.com/news/metro/2012-03-03/cons-
    sunday-alcohol-sales truncated
www.elmorecountypress.com/twinfallsconews,htm
www.wikipedia.org/wiki/Mark_Twain

www.Jaycetice.com/theaters/1915entertainment.htm
www.circushistory.org/Routes/AGBarnes.htm#1917
https://libcom.org/library/us-green-corn-rebellion-us-1917
American Minute with Bill Federer - Withholding taxes from
    people's paychecks began JUNE 9, 1943
https://en.wikipedia.org/wiki/Ward_LaFrance_Truck_Corporation
http://www.genealogytoday.com/guide/ww2/book_two.html
    WWIIrationbookno.2
Tokyo Rose - https://www.otrcat.com/p/tokyo-rose-wwii-japanese-
    propaganda
http://www.imdb.com/title/tt0106506/   Call of the Wild by Jack
    London
http://goodwatch.co/item/dorian-gray/B0093AZKDU
    A Picture of Dorian Gray movie
http://www.brainyquote.com/quotes/quotes/t/thomashood
    389836.html   Thomas Hood quote
http://search.aol.com/aol/search?sit=webmailsearchbox&q=
    movie%201946%20%20Our%20Vines%20Have%20Tender%20
    Grapes 1945 Movie:
https://blackthen.com/july-25-1946-the-moores-ford-lynching
    -occured-the-1946-georgia-lynching-was/
http://www.tcm.com/tcmdb/title/76987/The-Green-Years/,
     1946 Movie
http://www.webmd.com/lung/understanding-pleurisy-treatment
http://www.tcm.com/tcmdb/title/2523/The-Yearling/   Film
https://en.wikipedia.org/wiki/Maury_Island_incident   UFO
https://en.wikipedia.org/wiki/Freedom_Train, 1947

https://en.wikipedia.org/wiki/Delaware,_Lackawanna_and_
    Western_Railroad

http://www.imdb.com/title/tt0040402/   Green Grass of Wyoming,
    1948 movie

https://en.wikipedia.org/wiki/Rose_of_Washington_Square, Film

http://www.distance-cities.com/distance-horseheads-ny-to-
    poughkeepsie-ny

http://www.imdb.com/title/tt0042327/plotsummary?ref_=tt_ov_pl,
    1950 Movie, Cheaper by the Dozen

https://en.wikipedia.org/wiki/Joe_Louis

http://www.history.com/this-day-in-history/julius-and-ethel-ros
    berg-executed, Soviet Spies

http://www.jalopyjournal.com/forum/threads/hudson
    232-262-308-engine-tech.539734/   Hudson 6

https://en.wikipedia.org/wiki/Color_television

https://en.wikipedia.org/wiki/George_VI   Stammering King

http://history1900s.about.com/od/1950s/qt/queenelizabeth.htm
    Princess to Queen

https://archive.org/details/OTRR_The_Big_Show_Singles

https://en.wikipedia.org/wiki/Apollo_program, first landing on
    the moon

http://www.solsticemed.com/Chilli-Brand-Porous-Capsicum-
    Plaster-Medium-50-Sh-p/cl1m.htm

https://www.rottentomatoes.com/m/breakfast_in_hollywood/,
    1946 Movie

https://en.wikipedia.org/wiki/Twenty-second_Amendment_to_the
    _United_States_Constitution_Presidental term limits Ratified

https://www.psoriasis.org/advance/history-psoriasis

http://www.tvhistory.tv/1951%20QF.htm

http://www.heart-valve-surgery.com/heart-surgery-blog/2008/02/
    24/first-mechanical-heart-valve-replacement/

http://history1900s.about.com/od/1950s/qt/queenelizabeth.htm

https://en.wikipedia.org/wiki/The_Big_Show_(NBC_Radio)

https://www.abebooks.com/book-search/author/pathfinder-
    magazine/

https://en.wikipedia.org/wiki/Wernher_von_Braun

https://en.wikipedia.org/wiki/Moon_landing

http://www.grandprixfestival.com/map.html

http://www.history.com/topics/us-presidents/dwight-d-eisenhower

https://en.wikipedia.org/wiki/Sorry!_(game)

https://en.wikipedia.org/wiki/USAF_units_and_aircraft_of_the
   Korean_War

http://www.biography.com/people/joseph-stalin-9491723

https://local.yahoo.com/info-14456053-tampa-greyhound-track-tampa

http://www.wildflorida.com/articles/Chiggers_in_Florida.php

https://www.arcadiapublishing.com/9781467120371/Elmira-
   Reformatory

http://www.tcm.com/tcmdb/title/81509/Little-Boy-Lost/
   Bing Crosby 1953 movie

https://en.wikipedia.org/wiki/Pledge_of_Allegiance,
   Under God added

http://www.americanswhotellthetruth.org/portraits/claudette-colvin
   bus segregation

https://en.wikipedia.org/wiki/Crystal_violet

http://www.history.com/this-day-in-history/polio-vaccine-trials-begin

https://secure.rrb.gov/ U.S. Railroad Retirement Board

https://en.wikipedia.org/wiki/Thiomersal Merthiolate Tincture

http://www.imdb.com/title/tt0048691/
   Movie 1955, The Tall Man - Clark Gable & Janc Russel

https://en.wikipedia.org/wiki/Sincerely_Yours_Liberace, Film

https://en.wikipedia.org/wiki/Doubleday_(publisher)

http://www.philcoradio.com/gallery/1956.htm#w

https://www.youtube.com/watch?v=bW59pRcW_yc   GE radio

http://www.famousdaily.com/history/phrase- in-god-we-trust-
adopted.html

http://www.history.com/topics/black-history/montgomery-
   bus-boycott

https://en.wikipedia.org/wiki/1956_in_television

http://www.classic-tv.com/features/schedules/1956-1957-tv-schedule

http://www.naturalmedicinalherbs.net/herbs/i/ilex-coriacea=large-
   gallberry.php

http://medicinalherbinfo.org/herbs/Boneset.html

http://www.burpee.com/

https://en.wikipedia.org/wiki/Coronet_(magazine)

https://en.wikipedia.org/wiki/Attica_Correctional_Facility

https://en.wikipedia.org/wiki/Little_Rock_Nine

https://en.wikipedia.org/wiki/Edsel

https://history.nasa.gov/sputnik/

Stroke - http://doctorzebra.com/prez/z_x34cva_g.htm

http://www.space.com/17825-explorer-1.html, U.S. Explorer Satellite
http://www.space.com/17825-explorer-1.html
    TV series - Have Gun Will Travel
http://www.history.com/topics/us-states/alaska
https://www.poets.org/poetsorg/poet/edgar-guest
http://www.americaslibrary.gov/jb/modern/jb_modern_
    hawaii_1.html
https://en.wikipedia.org/wiki/Luna_2

http://www.npr.org/templates/story/story.php?storyId=18615556
    Woolworth's lunch counter sit-in (Civil Rights Riots)
https://en.wikipedia.org/wiki/Clark_Gable; (death)
https://www.amazon.com/Combat-America-Clark- Gable
    /dp/B00005B1YG
https://www.flickr.com/photos/42444189@N04/3987101926/
Horseheads/NY_A & P (Atlantic & Pacific Tea Company)
    https://en.wikipedia.org/wiki/The_Great_Atlantic_%26_
    Pacific_Tea_Company
http://www.poemhunter.com/robert-frost/
https://en.wikipedia.org/wiki/George_Junior_Republic_

http://pix.cs.olemiss.edu/econ/1960s.html
    1960 prices, meat, foods, etc, cost of living
https://en.wikipedia.org/wiki/Twenty-third_Amendment
https://www.law.cornell.edu/constitution/amendmentxxii
    (23rd amendment)
https://en.wikipedia.org/wiki/Tucumcari,_New_Mexico
http://bible.org/seriespage/8-what-must-i-do-to-be-saved?
http://vetrecs.archives.gov (Request Service Records)